COMMENTARY ON THE DOCUMENTS OF VATICAN II

COMMENTARY
ON THE DOCUMENTS OF VATICAN II

GENERAL EDITOR:

Herbert Vorgrimler

EDITORIAL COMMITTEE:

Heinrich Suso Brechter
Bernhard Häring
Josef Höfer
Hubert Jedin
Josef Andreas Jungmann
Klaus Mörsdorf
Karl Rahner
Joseph Ratzinger
Karlheinz Schmidthüs
Johannes Wagner

COMMENTARY
ON THE DOCUMENTS
OF
VATICAN II

Volume III

DECLARATION ON THE RELATIONSHIP OF THE CHURCH TO
NON-CHRISTIAN RELIGIONS
DOGMATIC CONSTITUTION ON DIVINE REVELATION
DECREE ON THE APOSTOLATE OF THE LAITY

HERDER AND HERDER

1969

HERDER AND HERDER NEW YORK

232 Madison Avenue, New York, N. Y. 10016

BURNS & OATES LIMITED

25 Ashley Place, London S. W. 1

Original edition:
"Das Zweite Vatikanische Konzil, Dokumente und Kommentare",
Part II, Herder, Freiburg, 1967 (pp. 405–701)

Translated by
William Glen-Doepel, Hilda Graef, John Michael Jakubiak, and Simon and Erika Young

Library of Congress Catalog Card No. 67-22928
First published in West Germany, © 1968, Herder KG
Printed in West Germany by Herder

CONTENTS

PUBLISHER'S NOTE

The publishers have not given the text of the Council documents in this book, as separate text editions, both in Latin and English, are easily available. All quotations from the English translation of the Council texts in this volume have been taken from *The Documents of Vatican II* (Walter M. Abbott, S. J., General Editor; Joseph Gallagher, Translation Editor), © America Press, published in New York, 1966, by Guild Press, Herder and Herder, and Association Press, and in London, 1966, by Geoffrey Chapman Ltd. Grateful acknowledgment is made herewith for permission to quote from these texts.

The arrangement of the commentary in these volumes is based on the order in which the documents of the Council were promulgated (see Preface, vol. I, pp. VII–IX). However, the publishers regret to announce an exception: the commentary on the Declaration on Christian Education will, for technical reasons, appear in vol. IV instead of in this volume.

ABBREVIATIONS

AAS   *Acta Apostolicae Sedis*

BZ   *Biblische Zeitschrift*

CIC   *Codex Iuris Canonici*

D   H. Denzinger, *Enchiridion Symbolorum* (32nd edition, 1963); see also *DS*
DC   *Documentation Catholique*
DS   H. Denzinger and A. Schönmetzer, *Enchiridion Symbolorum* (33rd edition, 1965); see also *D*

EB   *Enchiridion Biblicum. Documenta ecclesiastica Sacram Scripturam spectantia* (3rd edition, 1956)

Gr   *Gregorianum*

HDG   M. Schmaus, J. Geiselmann and A. Grillmeier, eds., *Handbuch der Dogmengeschichte* (1951 ff.)
HK   *Herder-Korrespondenz*

LTK   J. Höfer and Karl Rahner, eds., *Lexikon für Theologie und Kirche,* 10 vols. and an index vol. (2nd rev. edition, 1957–67)

NRT   *Nouvelle Revue Théologique*

PG   J.-P. Migne, ed., *Patrologia Graeca,* 161 vols. (1857–66)
PL   J.-P. Migne, ed., *Patrologia Latina,* 217 vols. and 4 index vols. (1878–90)
PO   R. Graffin and F. Nau, eds., *Patrologia Orientalis* (1903 ff.)

RB   *Revue Biblique*
RSR   *Recherches des Sciences Religieuse*

ThRv   *Theologische Revue*
TLZ   *Theologische Literaturzeitung*
TTZ   *Trierer Theologische Zeitschrift*

ZKG   *Zeitschrift für Kirchengeschichte*
ZKT   *Zeitschrift für Katholische Theologie*

Declaration on the Relationship of the Church to Non-Christian Religions

Introduction and Commentary

by

*John M. Oesterreicher**

This Declaration holds a special place among the documents of Vatican II. It derives, at least in its original core, the declaration concerning the Jews, from an express wish of John XXIII. Its special character, however, is not limited to its origin. In it, a Council for the first time in history acknowledges the search for the absolute by other men and by whole races and peoples, and honours the truth and holiness in other religions as the work of the one living God. It is the first time also that the Church has publicly made her own the Pauline view of the mystery of Israel. To that extent the Declaration is an acknowledgment by the Church of the universal presence of grace and its activity in the many religions of mankind. Furthermore, in it the Church gives glory to God for his enduring faithfulness towards his chosen people, the Jews. It seems to me important to start with an account of the development of this aspect of the Council Declaration, in order to avoid certain false interpretations. Although born out of the experiences of the recent past, it is not a merely contemporary or even political document: it is deeply theological. Wide though it is in scope, it in no way obscures the uniqueness of God's dealings with Israel.

THE ORIGINS OF THE DECLARATION

It was on 18 September 1960 that Pope John personally commissioned Cardinal Bea, in his capacity as President of the Secretariat for Promoting Christian Unity, to prepare a draft declaration on the inner relations between the Church and the people of Israel. At the first session of the Secretariat, the Cardinal reported that various applications had reached the Pope from the Jewish side. The Pope had been asked what possibilities there would be for the Jews to be kept informed about the Council. Some Jews had even asked for a separate commission to be set up. Pope John had decided, however, to entrust problems to the Secretariat for Unity. The Cardinal said that there had been various reasons for this, but he did not give them. One may well suppose that the risk of setting up

* *Translated by Simon and Erika Young (pp. 1–85) and Hilda Graef (pp. 85–136)*

an excessive number of commissions counted in the Pope's mind against the establishment of a separate Commission *De rebus iudaicis* or *De Ecclesiae affinitate cum populo Iudaico*. It would probably also be right to assume that the Pope was moved to entrust the discussion of Judaeo-Christian relations to the Secretariat for Unity both by the role of the Jewish people in the history of salvation and by the personality of the Cardinal, a man of wide experience in whom he had great confidence.

a) The visit of Jules Isaac

Cardinal Bea's reference to various applications from the Jewish side doubtless included that of the French historian, Jules Isaac, the most important advocate, before the Council began, of Jewish concerns. In the early summer of 1960 he went to Rome, to make his wishes known to Pope John, with the support of the French branch of B'nai B'rith[1] and equipped with a letter of introduction from Mgr. de Provenchères, Archbishop of Aix-en-Provence, where he lived. After initial difficulties he succeeded in obtaining an audience on 13 June of the same year, with the help of the French Ambassador to the Holy See, M. de la Tournelle, and of the present Under-Secretary of the Secretariat for Unity, Mgr. G. Arrighi. The Pope began the conversation, with his characteristic ease of manner, by speaking of his great reverence for the Old Testament, especially for the prophets, the psalms, and the book of Wisdom. Isaac, on the other hand, was a man who believed he did not have much more time: he went straight to the point. He referred to the great hope that the measures taken by the Pope concerning the Jews had awakened in the hearts of the people of the old dispensation. "If we expect still more", he added, "what is responsible for that, if not the great 'goodness of the Pope'?" During the audience he gave the Pope a dossier in three parts: 1. A brief for the correction of false and indeed unjust statements about Israel in Christian teaching. 2. As an example, the theological myth that the scattering of Israel was a punishment inflicted by God on the people for the crucifixion of Jesus. 3. An extract from the catechism of Trent which in its treatment of the Passion emphasized the guilt of all sinners as the fundamental cause of Christ's death upon the cross, and thus, in Isaac's view, proved that the accusation of deicide raised against the Jews did not belong to the true tradition of the Church.[2] Towards the end of the audience, which lasted almost half an

---

[1] For details on the involvement of the *B'nai B'rith,* see *Hommage Solennel à Jules Isaac* (Salle des Centraux, 10 October 1963).

[2] The Tridentine Catechism, published in 1566 as one of the fruits of the Council of Trent under Pius V and often known as the *Catechismus Romanus,* is especially significant as a pastoral document. Unlike other catechisms it was designed to assist preachers and catechists and to lay down guide-lines for orthodox instruction. Since it was drawn up at an express resolution of the Council and advocated by many Popes, it must be treated as a pronouncement of the magisterium, despite the little use which has been made of it. From chapter V, which deals with the fourth article of the Creed, Isaac cites, among others, the following paragraphs:

hour, Isaac expressed his deep gratitude, asking anxiously at the same time whether he might take away with him a little hope. John XXIII reassured him with the words: "You have reason for more than hope." But he went on to say with a smile that even though he was indeed the head here, a matter such as this

"The first part of the article sets forth the truth of faith that Christ the Lord was crucified, and at the time when Pontius Pilate was administering the Province of Judaea in the name of the Emperor Tiberius. For it was then that Christ was arrested, ridiculed, loaded with every kind of insult and torment, and finally lifted up on the cross."

". . . The pastor of souls should not omit to speak frequently of the history of the Passion, so carefully recorded by the Evangelists, in order that the faithful may be well informed at least about the major points of this mystery which seem necessary for the securing of our faith. For on this article, as on their foundation, rest the religion and belief of the Christian; and if this has been laid, then the rest of the edifice will hold firmly together. If there is anything which creates difficulties for the human mind and heart, then certainly the mystery of the Cross is the most difficult thing of all. We are scarcely willing to comprehend that our salvation should come from the Cross, and from One who was nailed to the Cross for us. But it is precisely here, as the Apostle says, that we may wonder at the infinitely wise Providence of God."

". . . Anyone seeking . . . the principal reason [for the sufferings of Christ] will come upon sin, the original sin passed down from our first parents, and then all the possible sins which men have committed from the very beginning right up to the present and which will be committed up to the end of the world. That, indeed, was the intention of the Son of God, our Saviour, in his suffering and death: to take upon himself the sins of all ages, to wipe them out and to offer the Father superabundant satisfaction for them. The sublime magnitude of this expiatory suffering is made all the greater by the fact not only that Christ suffered for sinners, but also that these very sinners were themselves the authors and instruments of all his sufferings. The Apostle reminded us of this when writing to the Hebrews: 'Consider him who endured from sinners such hostility against himself, so that you may not grow weary or faint-hearted' (Heb 12:3). This is pre-eminently the guilt of those who repeatedly fall back into sin. It was our sins which drove Christ the Lord to his death on the Cross: those, therefore, who wallow in sins and vices are in fact crucifying the Son of God anew, in so far as it depends on them, and holding him up to contempt (Heb 6:6). And this is a crime which would seem graver in our case than it was in that of the Jews; for the Jews, as the same Apostle says, 'would never have crucified the Lord of glory if they had known him' (1 Cor 2:8). We ourselves maintain that we do know him, and yet we lay, as it were, violent hands on him by disowning him in our actions."

"Nonetheless, according to the words of holy Scripture, the Father, too, gave Christ the Lord, and Christ also gave himself up of his own accord. In Isaiah God says: 'I struck him for the trans-gression of the people' (Is 53:8). And shortly before this the prophet says, on seeing in spirit the Lord full of wounds and stripes: 'All we like sheep have gone astray; we have turned every one to his own way; and the Lord has laid on him the iniquity of us all' (Is 53:6). Of the Son himself it is said: 'When he has given himself up for sin, he shall see everlasting offspring' (Is 53:10). The Apostle has uttered this truth even more emphatically, though for another purpose, which is to show how much we are permitted to expect of God's immeasurable goodness and mercy: 'He did not', says Paul, 'spare his own son but gave him up for us all — how should he not also give us all things with him?' (Rom 8:32)"

". . . Men of every estate and rank 'took counsel together against the Lord and against his Christ' (Ps 2:2). Gentiles and Jews were the instigators, authors and executors of his sufferings. Judas betrayed him, Peter denied him, and all abandoned him."

". . . The reasons why all these great and supernatural benefits accrued to us from the sufferings of the Lord are as follow: First, his suffering was the complete and in all respects perfect satisfaction which Jesus Christ made to God the Father in a unique manner for our sins. Indeed, the

3

needed consideration and study in the appropriate quarters: "What you see here is certainly no absolute monarchy."[3]

b) The initiatives of John XXIII

That Jules Isaac's visit had a lasting effect on John XXIII cannot, in my opinion, be doubted. On the other hand, it is questionable whether his was the decisive influence in moving the Pope to act, as is sometimes asserted. What he did, however, was to cause the Pope's intentions, until then but vaguely formed, to mature. It was, after all, the measures taken by John XXIII before the audience to remove hurtful phrases from liturgical texts that had encouraged Isaac, as he himself acknowledged, to put his ideas before the Pope.

In 1959 John XXIII had given a new form to the Good Friday prayer for the Jews. He had deleted from the text the adjective *perfidus* in the exhortation *Oremus et pro perfidis Iudaeis* (let us pray also for the unbelieving Jews [that is, unbelieving in Christ]) and also the expression *perfidia Iudaica*. Both were often

---

price which he paid for us was not only equal to our guilt, but even exceeded it by far. — And then, his suffering was an offering infinitely pleasing to God. The Son himself brought it to the altar of the Cross, and thus it could not fail to reconcile the Father's anger and disfavour completely. This is the opinion of the Apostle, when he says: 'Christ loved us and gave himself up for us, a fragrant offering and sacrifice to God' (Eph 5:2). — Finally, his suffering was our ransom. Of this the Prince of Apostles says: 'You know that you were ransomed from the futile ways inherited from your fathers, not with perishable things such as silver or gold, but with the precious blood of Christ, like that of a lamb without blemish or spot' (1 Pet 1:18). And the Apostle declares: 'Christ redeemed us from the curse of the law by becoming a curse for us' (Gal 3:13)."

"There is still one other thing in addition to all the immeasurable graces mentioned, and it is perhaps one of the greatest: in this suffering alone we have the most resplendent example of every virtue: patience, humility, unequalled love, meekness, obedience, and supreme fortitude not only in his endurance of pain for the sake of righteousness but also in his submission to death — all this shows Christ's suffering in such perfection that we can truly say that the commandments which our Redeemer gave us in words during the whole time of his teaching activity he put into action during the one day of his suffering."

That the ignorance of those responsible for the crucifixion substantially mitigated their guilt even if it did not eliminate it altogether is a teaching with firm roots in the New Testament (Lk 23:24; Acts 3:17). On the other hand, it is exegetically unacceptable to adduce 1 Cor 2:8 in exoneration of the "Jews", i.e. of the Jewish authorities, as has been done in the Tridentine Catechism and elsewhere. The "rulers of this world (or aeon)" who would not have crucified Jesus, the "Lord of glory" (a name for God among the Jewish Apocalyptists) if they had known his wisdom, i.e. his design for salvation, are certainly not the high priests and the Sanhedrin, nor the Roman Emperor and his governor. The "rulers of this aeon" are the angelic powers hostile to God. Nonetheless, the passage can be used for this purpose insofar as it shows that, for Paul, the real adversaries of Christ, and hence also the authors of his death on the cross, would appear to be spiritual powers.

[3] For Jules Isaac's visit to John XXIII, see J. Toulat, *Juifs mes frères* (1962), pp. 152–4. Isaac's appeal is reproduced in *Du Redressement Nécessaire de l'Enseignement Chrétien Concernant Israël, Mémoire présentée par Jules Isaac* (1960).

misunderstood, through ignorance of the Latin of Christian antiquity, and reproduced in various modern languages by similar-sounding words like "perfidious" and "perfidy". At first the suppression of these wounding phrases, on 21 March 1959, seemed to extend only to the churches of Rome itself. But on 5 July in the same year the Sacred Congregation of Rites issued an instruction that expressly extended the papal decision, as had been its intention, to the liturgy of the whole Church.[4]

A further measure taken in the same year was the deletion of a part of the prayer dedicating humanity to the heart of Jesus.[5] In this prayer, originally from the hand of Leo XIII, various sentences were inserted during the pontificate of Pius XI, including the following: "Look finally full of pity on the children of the people who were once your chosen people. May the blood that once was called down upon them flow over them also as a fount of salvation and of life." The "once" of the first sentence is obviously a mistranslation. The word used in the original Latin text, *tamdiu,* means "for so long". But even this almost tender "for so long thy chosen people" is not in full harmony with the Pauline assurance: "For the gifts and the call of God are irrevocable" (Rom 11:29).

"The blood that once was called down upon them" is doubtless a play upon the words shouted by the crowd gathered before the governor's palace: "His blood be on us, and on our children" (Mt 27:25). The historicity of this cry is doubted by several exegetes. Nonetheless it is not unthinkable on the lips of a group composed largely of disappointed resistance-fighters. If this last interpretation is correct, then it can quite clearly be assumed that the zealots — blinded

---

[4] The edict had been passed on to the bishops through the Nuncios and Apostolic Delegates; cf. *Freiburger Rundbrief* 12, nos. 45–48 (1959), pp. 7 f. Since then the intercession has been revised to read as follows: "Let us pray also for the Jews, that our God and Lord will be pleased to look graciously upon them, so that they too may acknowledge our Lord Jesus Christ as the Redeemer of all mankind . . . Almighty and eternal God, who gavest thy promises to Abraham and his posterity, hearken to the prayers of thy Church that the people chosen by thee of old may attain the fullness of redemption: through our Lord Jesus Christ, thy Son, who liveth and reigneth with thee in the unity of the Holy Spirit, God, world without end. Amen." To appreciate the extent of this revision it is necessary to recall to mind the Good Friday intercession prior to 1966. Previously we prayed for the "unbelieving" Jews, i.e. who withheld their faith from Christ. Now it simply says: "Let us pray for the Jews." The simplicity of this petitition is the fruit of our newly-acquired *discretio,* our awareness that it is not for us to pass judgment on others. Earlier we prayed "that our God and Lord will remove the veil from their hearts", a negative expression which has been replaced by the more positive "that our God and Lord will be pleased to look graciously upon them". Formerly we spoke of Jesus Christ simply as "our Lord", which could easily lead to proprietary arrogance, as though the Lord were our own property. We now refer to him as "Redeemer of all mankind". Before 1966 the prayer spoke of the Jewish people as being blinded and living in darkness, whereas it is now recognized that they are still God's specially chosen people for whom we pray, with an ecumenical delicacy of feeling, that they may attain "the fullness of redemption". In other words, our wishes and even our faith must stand respectfully aside — it is for God to decide when and how his plan of salvation will be brought to completion.

[5] *A A S* 51 (1959), p. 595; *Freiburger Rundbrief* 12, nos. 45–48 (1959), pp. 7 f.

by their guerilla ideology, which sought only one thing: freedom from the Roman yoke — perceived neither the mystery of the person of Jesus nor the depth of his mission. His refusal to put himself at their head might have so enraged them that, at the decisive moment, they abandoned him and, sure of themselves, accepted the responsibility for his fate. But an impulsive acceptance of responsibility like this by a small group would be very different from that calling down of a curse upon themselves by the entire people which the words of Matthew 27:25 are taken to mean by the author of the prayer of dedication and by many others besides. Even if one took it that the evangelist was using the outcry of the crowd as an expression of the attitude which led, not only to the rejection of Jesus but also to the involvement of the Jewish people in a suicidal war with Rome, leading to the fall of Jerusalem and the accompanying blood-bath, it could not be understood as a permanent burden of shame upon the whole people. In any case, the exclusion of these two exegetically doubtful sentences from the prayer of dedication prepared the way — in fact, though not according to any preconceived plan — for the Council's understanding of the faith, corresponding as it does with the New Testament view of Israel's destiny.

The climax of this spontaneous, and in any case not purposely planned preparation for a Council Declaration on the Jews was a meeting between the Pope and a group of American Jews in October 1960. This party of well over a hundred, making a United Jewish Appeal study-trip through Europe and the State of Israel, stopped in Rome in order to thank the Pope for his many efforts to save Jews during the time of Hitler's persecution. As Apostolic Delegate in Turkey, the Pope had succeeded in saving thousands from the clutches of those who sought to exterminate them. Deeply moved, he sought to hold fast to the passing moment and to make it fruitful for the future. He greeted his visitors with the words, *"Son io, Giuseppe, il fratello vostro!"* ('I am Joseph, your brother!') This greeting, taken from the story of Joseph in Egypt (Gen 45:4), which gave him the opportunity to use his baptismal name Joseph instead of his official name John, shows clearly that the Pope wanted to break the chains that for centuries had divided Christians and Jews.

Pope John knew, of course, that there was an inevitable tension between the beliefs of Christians and Jews, but was convinced that this division must and ought not to degenerate into hostility. So he added to his greeting this reflection: "There is a great difference between the man who only accepts the Old Testament[6] and the man who joins to the Old the New as the highest law and teaching. These differences, however, do not extinguish the brotherhood that springs

[6] Pope John is here rather narrowing the breadth of Judaism. He was not alone in this, for Christians have often looked on Judaism as a religion which ceased to develop any further once the Bible had been completed. Post-biblical Judaism, however, is not determined only by the scripture of the Old Covenant; it takes its distinctive character also — and often even to a greater degree — from *Halacha,* the legal tradition formed by the Rabbis. Nonetheless, this overlooking of a distinct dimension of Jewish life by no means detracts from the force of the Pope's requirement which immediately follows.

6

from a common origin [of Christians and Jews]. We are indeed all children of the same heavenly Father and the light and work of love must always shine among us all. *Signatum est super nos lumen vultus tui, Domine!* (O Lord, thou hast put more joy in my heart!) (Ps 4:7)."[7] The Pope ended his address with a reference to the solidarity extending to all men, thus giving rise to the supposition that the brotherhood for which he had called at the outset was that which every man owes every other as his fellow-creature. However, the fact that on certain other occasions the Pope spoke of himself in the biblical phrase "I am Joseph, your brother!" shows that in John XXIII's view the relationship of Christians and Jews had above all a spiritual basis in the history of salvation.[8] His first encyclical, for example, was devoted to the three themes of truth, unity and peace. In the course of this document he turned towards all Christians separated from Rome, expressed his longing for their presence, and recommended urgently that they pray for the unity of the Church and the spreading of Christ's kingdom. Having also asked their leave to call them sons and brothers, he went on to say: "To all our sons and brothers . . . who are separated from the See of Peter, we address these words: 'I am Joseph, your brother!' "[9]

John XXIII, at the time when he was Apostolic Delegate in Bulgaria and Turkey, had had close experience of Jews and of Christians separated from Rome, especially those of the East — of their destiny, their sufferings, and their dire need. In Turkey he was kept informed, to an extent not generally realized, of the horrors of the National Socialist extermination-camps and the anguish of Jews threatened with deportation "to the East". He struggled to ward off these dangers wherever and however he could. Eye-witnesses testify to his constant alertness and never-failing activity. One of them speaks of the goodness of his intervention, his warmth, his dynamism and his sympathy.[10] Another explains that the Delegate's participation in the tragedy of the Jews in those days was no mere formality. "Deeply and sincerely moved by the suffering of the Jews, he showed a strong desire to help in every way possible." When reports of atrocities were brought to him, he received them "with hands folded in prayer and tears in his eyes". He always wanted to know all the details concerning

---

[7] *Osservatore Romano,* 19 October 1960.

[8] A statement made by Cardinal Suenens on the occasion of the tenth anniversary of the Jewish weekly, *Belgisch Israelitisch Weekblad,* is one proof of how the Johannine idea of the brotherhood of Christians and Jews has penetrated the Catholic consciousness. In his article of congratulations he said that fundamentally Christians have received everything through the Jews, both what they hold in common with them and what obviously separates them from each other. Everything that Christians have received obliges them to deep gratitude towards God for his purposes with the people of Israel. Moreover, all these gifts produce close ties, full of love and authentic brotherhood. In the eyes of God Christians and Jews are brothers (text in *Dialogue,* Montreal [May–June 1966], vol. V, 3, p. 7).

[9] *Ad Petri Cathedram,* IV. The encyclical is dated 29 June 1959, the feast of Sts. Peter and Paul, and was first published in *Osservatore Romano* on 3 July 1959.

[10] I. Hirschman, *Caution to the Winds* (1962), p. 185.

deportation orders, and noted them down carefully. These matters he never handed over to a member of his staff; he always saw to it personally that they were dealt with. In this way he succeeded in preventing deportations from Slovakia, Hungary and Bulgaria. He saved the lives of thousands and rescued them in their hour of direst need.[11]

Once one realizes how much the Apostolic Delegate regarded these rescue activities as matters of heart and conscience, one cannot help seeing as a continuation of this earlier work his measures as Pope when he purged liturgical texts of wounding or even merely misleading expressions, and commissioned Cardinal Bea to prepare a Council schema on the relationship between the Church and the Jewish people, with the help of the Secretariat for Unity. The work set in hand by Pope John then also appears as a response by the Church to Auschwitz, the epitome of Hitlerite atrocities.[12]

The actual source of the decision to propose that the Council issue a declaration on the relationship of the Church to the Jewish people lay therefore in the heart of John XXIII, in particular in his understanding of the suffering of the Jews. Compared with this, the action of Jules Isaac and other earlier or later interventions were of secondary importance. Nevertheless they deserve to be recorded here since, among other things, they disclose the position concerning this whole group of problems as it stood before the Council opened.

c) The petition of the Biblical Institute

The contribution of Rome's Biblical Institute to the Council's Central Preparatory Commission must be mentioned first. Dated 24 April 1960, it is signed by the then Rector, Ernst Vogt, S. J., on behalf of eighteen other teachers at the Institute, all Jesuits from various countries. The last paragraph of the dogmatic section contains a proposal to the Council fathers entitled *De antisemitismo vitando* (On the avoidance of anti-Semitism).[13] Its line of thought and manner of expression suggest that it was written by Fr. Stanislaus Lyonnet, S.J.

It contains the request that the Council include the problem of the people of Israel in its consideration of questions concerning ecumenism. It goes on to say that Christians are without doubt the true successors of the spiritual Israel, the

---

[11] Chaim Barlas in *Davar*, Jerusalem; reprinted in *Jewish Newsletter*, 29 December 1958.

[12] A similar view is taken by Cardinal König and Abbé Laurentin. Cardinal König writes: "As Apostolic Delegate in the Near East, John XXIII had come to know the distress and the mortal anguish of the Jews fleeing from their persecutors . . . He felt an urgent desire to set against the immeasurable and bottomless hate of those days a lasting word of love" (*Documents conciliaires,* vol. II [1965–66], p. 204). R. Laurentin interprets John XXIII's wish for a special conciliar declaration on the Jews as follows: "This intention had deep roots in his heart: his memory of the persecuted Jews and the powerlessness of an Apostolic Delegate in Istanbul, who could render no more than limited individual assistance" (*Bilan du Concile,* vol. IV [1966], p. 129).

[13] *Acta et Documenta Concilio Oecumenico Vaticano II Apparando* (Typis Polyglottis Vaticanis, 1961), series I, vol. IV, pars I, 1, pp. 132–4.

authentic heirs of the faith of Abraham "our patriarch" *(Patriarchae nostri Abrahae* — Canon of the Mass) and of the blessing of Jacob, "the Israel of God", as the Apostle says (Gal 6:16). And therefore the Christian profession of faith can fittingly and rightly be called "the dignity of Israel", as in the liturgy of Holy Saturday. Never should it be alleged that the Jewish people as such is "rejected". Already in the past, a part of the Jewish people turned to Christ (Rom 11:1–2). We know further that the part that does not believe in Christ will by no means remain for ever fixed in this position. In several passages, whose value as evidence cannot be doubted, the Apostle explains that that part also of the Jewish people will eventually turn to him. (Rom 11:15, 25). This teaching, which, in the opinion of the petitioners, belongs definitely to the deposit of faith, has, it is true, never been proclaimed by the teaching office of the Church. It does, however, seem capable of effectively countering many of the prejudices that promote anti-Semitism.

The petition then stressed particularly that all believing Christians should be warned to follow the example of ecclesiastical authority and to avoid most carefully those ways of speaking that could cause offence. To underline this point the instructions mentioned above for expurgating the texts of various prayers were then set out. The urgency of the petition arose from sermons and instructions which, on account of defective exegesis, taught the "accursedness", "rejection" and also the "collective guilt" of the Jewish people. For the true proclamation of the mystery of the Passion the Biblical Institute also and rightly pointed to the catechism of the Council of Trent with its emphasis that all sinners — all men — are to be reckoned as Jesus' crucifiers. A special reason brought forward for the petition was the "error of the ultimate rejection of the 'chosen people'" which rested on a false interpretation of such passages of the New Testament as Mt 27:25; 24:2; 1 Thess 2:16; Rom 9:22. Finally, the signatories of the petition saw in the Pauline teaching that a time would come when "the full number of the Gentiles come in" and "all Israel will be saved" (Rom 11:25, 26), the best weapon with which to put a stop to any theologically embellished anti-Semitism, or to make its revival impossible.

d) The request of the Institute of Judaeo-Christian Studies, U.S.A.

At about the same time that the Biblical Institute's petition was drawn up, another written request was being considered in the United States. As it was to express the common desire of a loose working-group scattered throughout the country, it took some time to draft, although the requests it contained were kept to a minimum. It was signed by John J. Dougherty, then Professor of Exegesis at the seminary in Darlington, New Jersey, today a bishop and President of Seton Hall University, and by the present writer as Director of the Institute of Judaeo-Christian Studies attached to the same university, together with thirteen priestly colleagues. On 8 June 1960, shortly after the nomination of Cardinal Bea as President of the Secretariat for Promoting Christian Unity became known in America, the present author was able to submit the petition, written in English, to him, and to ask him to take the necessary steps to satisfy the wishes expressed in it. The English draft, together with a Latin version, was sent to the Cardinal on 24 June 1960.

The petition's signatories saw it as a continuation of the work of reconciliation begun by Pius XI and Pius XII, but above all by John XXIII. The petition begins by referring to the measures of Pope John discussed above, but also to the words in which Pius XI rejected anti-Semitism at the time of the daily increasing persecution of the Jews by Hitler. He branded hatred of the Jews not, as one might have expected, as an injustice, a violation of the moral law — to him that was self-evident. He saw the hater of Jews much more as a rebel against the reality of saving history, which makes the Christian a supernatural descendant of our common father Abraham. In the words of the Pope: "Through Christ and in Christ we are of Abraham's spiritual stock. Spiritually we are Semites."[14] Social psychologists see in anti-Semitism, not without reason, a variant of xenophobia. But for Pius XI hatred of the Jews, especially of the National Socialist stamp, was the hatred of the apostate for whom God's plan of salvation had become a stumbling block. Thus he feared anti-Semitism as a danger to Jewish life and limb, but also as a threat to the existence of Christianity.

The petition adds to Pius XI's declaration a saying of Pius XII. On the occasion of the Holy Year, 1950, more precisely at its opening on Christmas Eve 1949, Pius XII invited all men to Rome. In particular he gave a welcome to Christians separated from Rome and, together with them, to the Jews. "We open the sacred gates to all who worship Christ — which is not to exclude those who await his coming in good faith, though in vain, and honour him as the one who is proclaimed by the Prophets though not yet come — and offer them a fatherly greeting and welcome."[15] There is a new spirit at work here, even though the "old" language is still being used. Today we give a more positive value than this to the Jewish expectation; we no longer venture to speak of a vain, and therefore senseless and fruitless waiting. We prefer to see the Jewish hope in its inner relation to that of Christians. But the Pope's invitation, despite its defective wording, is a great advance. It is the first ecclesiastical text that places the "Jewish question" in an ecumenical framework. The Jews are mentioned here in the same breath as non-Catholic Christians — the sub-title of the printed text speaks of "dissident Christians".

The signatories of the petition, supported by the teaching of the last three Popes, in particular by the "loving concern" of Pope John, formulated the following requests.

1. If the Council were to enquire into the nature of the Church in the course of its deliberations, it should proclaim that the call of Abraham and the deliverance

[14] *D C* 39 (October 1938), p. 1480.
[15] *A A S* 42 (1950), p. 126.

of Israel out of Egypt were part of the genesis of the Church, so that she can fittingly and rightly be called "the Israel of God" (Gal 6:16), the Israel renewed and exalted by Christ's word and blood. Such a proclamation would correspond entirely to the way the Church saw herself when, for example, she looked upon the wonderful acts that once accompanied Israel's Exodus as now present in a new way. Thus she acknowledges on Easter night that God, who saved Israel from Egyptian persecution, now accomplishes for all nations, through the waters of regeneration, what he did then for a single people. Thus it was possible for this prayer to end with a request that was characteristic of the Church's understanding of herself: "Grant that the whole world may become Abraham's children and share in the dignity of Israel."[16]

2. That the Council should give further liturgical expression to the unity of salvation history, which comes especially to life in the prayers surrounding the administration of the sacraments. This could be achieved if the Masses now peculiar to the patriarchate of Jerusalem were made into votive Masses of the whole Church, or if a universal feast of all the just of the Old Testament were introduced. Feasts celebrated by the Patriarchate of Jerusalem include those of St. Abraham, Patriarch and Confessor; of St. David, King, Prophet and Confessor; and of St. Jeremias, Prophet and Martyr. The signatories were confident that much would be gained by extending these feasts to the whole Church. In this way the marvel of the unbroken history[17] of our salvation would be actively experienced by the faithful, not mechanically learned. Together with the mystery of this unity they would incorporate into their lives the consciousness of God's unceasing guidance of mankind through his grace, and of the relationship of Christians and Jews. One could be sure that a liturgical renewal on these lines would lead to a growth in love and gratitude among the faithful.

3. Finally, the signatories asked — "for the love which Christ had for his kinsmen" — that misleading phrases, above all in the lessons of the Office, which distort the true teaching of the Church and her real attitude towards the Jews, should be changed. If the Council were to turn its attention to the problems of our own time, the petitioners continued, the Church should, as in the past, judge and condemn hatred of the people whose "is the human stock from which Christ came; Christ, who is God over all, blessed for ever, Amen" (Rom 9:5).

As has been mentioned already, these were minimum requests. As this appeal was the first advance into an area that had lain neglected for so long, and indeed seemed to be unknown territory for most people, it was advisable that it be

---

[16] The final sentence of this prayer, which follows the second reading for the preparation of the consecration of baptismal water, is without any doubt an echo of the theology of Rom 9 and 11, while the "transeat" of the Latin text is probably an allusion to the "transitus", the "pasch", the "Passover" of Christ (Exod 12:11).

[17] The manuscript and a number of texts based on it put this erroneously as "the uninterrupted *economy* of salvation".

limited to certain essential points. Furthermore, at the time it was drafted, the Council was still an unknown quantity — one did not know what could be expected from it. So the requests were put forward in a concise form, in part even more compressed than here. It is, however, astonishing what an influence the petition had on the work of the Council.

e) The memorandum of the Apeldoorn working group

Much more comprehensive and profound than the petition described above is a study carried out under the aegis of the study group of priests and lay people that met at Apeldoorn, in Holland, from 28 to 31 August 1960. This was an international group including, among others, Anton Ramselaar (Holland), Karl Thieme (Germany), Paul Démann (France), Jean Roger (Israel), and the author of this commentary, who lives in America. In the period before the Council, this group met every year in Apeldoorn for discussion of questions which preoccupied its members. Those taking part were all men and women who regarded it as their particular task in life to serve the cause of reconciliation between Jews and Christians. None of those listed above spoke for himself alone. Each represented also one of the periodicals or "centres" that were trying to reassess the problem of "Church and Synagogue": Ramselaar the *Katholieke Raad voor Israel;* Thieme (together with Gertrud Luckner) the *Freiburger Rundbrief;* Démann the *Cahiers Sioniens;* Roger the *Œuvre de St. Jacques;* and Oesterreicher the Yearbook of the Institute of Judaeo-Christian Studies, *The Bridge.* In retrospect one may well say that together they formed the prophetic element that over the years prepared a place in the Church, intellectually and spiritually, emotionally and theologically, for the Council Declaration of which they too as yet knew nothing. The meeting in the summer of 1960 was naturally influenced by the forthcoming Council. However, the memorandum drawn up in its name by Paul Démann, after thorough discussion by the whole group, was not addressed to any organ of the Council but to "those who in any way, direct or indirect, have a part in the teaching office of the Church or in the forming of opinion among the faithful, whether their field of work be the training of priests, catechesis, preaching, journalism or other writings".

The list of those to whom the memorandum is addressed is taken from the preamble, which recognizes, among other things, that the Church has never lost her interest in that part of Israel which did not follow Christ but has been preserved in continued existence by the hand of providence. The Church knows, the preamble goes on, that she is deeply rooted in the people of the old dispensation, and equally well that Jesus, the Christ, who stands as a sign of contradiction between her and the Jewish people of today, is at the same time the deepest bond between the two. The Church is fully aware of the inheritance she holds in common with the people of Israel in the writings of the Old Testament, and feels in her depths that solidarity which today still links her destiny to that of the

Jews. She lives, faithful to the Apostle's teaching, in unceasing hope of a reconciliation, a restoration of separated Israel to the unity of the one people of God. The Church well knows that Israel's continuance in history, with its richness in human loyalty and abundance of suffering, lays upon her great tasks and responsibilities. Not in the slightest degree can she pass over the torments that the Jews have suffered in the midst of the Christian peoples. She laments the ignorance, the deformities in thought and attitude on the Christian side which have, all too often, been the cause of those sufferings. She knows, finally, that the prejudices that gave rise to contempt and hatred have not yet disappeared.

On this basis the Apeldoorn meeting proposed the following guidelines for renewal in preaching and catechesis. As the group owed its existence to private initiative, and therefore held no official commission, it could only put forward suggestions. This, however, it did freely.

1. In the eyes of the Church the Old Testament advanced the same claim to be God's revealed word as the New. The revelation given in the Old Testament and the saving history recorded in it must keep their traditional place in Christian education and witness. Any attempt to reduce the value of the Old Testament Scriptures, any attempt to present its imperfections or the unfaithfulness of the Jewish people in a way that manifests contempt or even mere dislike, is contrary to the spirit of the Church.

2. As the Word made flesh, Jesus transcends the Old Testament, but as true man he belongs to his people and his country, and is steeped in their traditions. However much he goes beyond them, he yet continues the traditions of the patriarchs. He came "not to abolish them, but to fulfil them" (Mt 5:17). Neither he nor the Church can be understood outside this framework.

3. This is a framework that has many aspects, and our knowledge of it is imperfect. Nevertheless, we can say with confidence that at the time of Jesus, Jewry presented a picture of exuberant life, not of degeneration. One has to give the faithful a true picture of Judaism at that time, so far as the state of historical studies allows. It would be unjust to draw a caricature, in order that the greatness of Jesus and his teaching should stand out by contrast.

4. It would be contrary to the spirit of the Church radically to oppose the Old Testament to the New, as in speaking of a "God of wrath" on the one hand and a "God of love" on the other, or of a "law of fear" and a "law of love". It was the same divine grace that was progressively revealed throughout both Testaments and the same command of love that was present in them.

5. When seen historically, the dramatic conflict between Jesus and the leaders of his people, which led to his condemnation and crucifixion, is a complex problem. Certain facts have in any case to be borne in mind. In Jesus' time most Jews were already dispersed through the Mediterranean countries, and of those settled in Palestine only a fraction could have known him. Those who did meet him included not only his enemies and opponents but also the enthusiastic crowds and the disciples, who formed the Church. According to the Gospels,

13

the actual opposition came only from a group of spiritual and political leaders, and the condemnation of Jesus was their work also. Yet even they — whatever their personal responsibility may have been — acted, so Jesus declared and, following him, Peter and Paul, "in ignorance" (see Lk 23:34; Acts 3:17; 1 Cor 2:8).[18] If the events of this vital period are presented in a historically inaccurate way, then Christian instruction would itself be led into error.

6. Even more important is a theologically accurate understanding and explanation of the drama of Golgotha. Jesus suffered and died on account of the sins of all of us and for our salvation. No one stands outside the solidarity of sin, no man is excluded from the grace of salvation. (Mary, free of any sin, received an extraordinary favour in that she, in anticipation of the saving sacrifice, was preserved from all guilt.) All the participants in the drama of Golgotha, Jews and Gentiles alike, believers and unbelievers, represented mankind as a whole: they stood there in place of all of us. What made a man an accomplice of Christ's enemies and executioners was not his nationality or religion, but simply and solely sin, the rejection of grace.

7. In this connection it is of the greatest importance to avoid the fateful error that holds responsible for the death of Christ all Jews of that time — and indeed the Jews of all time and them alone. This gives rise to the absurd conception of a "deicidal people" and so works upon the feelings of the faithful in regard to the Passion as to instil in them revulsion from those immediately responsible, and not only from them but from the whole Jewish people. Such errors not only falsify the meaning of the Passion, they also deform the spirit of the faithful. The cross, this unique source of love, humility and expiation, then becomes a source of revulsion and hatred, and a reason for shifting the blame for one's own sins on to others. In the past such errors contributed to the nourishment of hostile feelings towards Jews among Christian people and roused them to scorn and persecution. These false ideas led to the Jews being crushed to the ground under the weight of the cross, and their appalling results also helped to hide the true meaning of the Passion from the Jews.

8. The central place of the Passion in the life of the Christian, the gravity of the errors already mentioned, the extent of the persecutions of the Jewish people in the midst of the Christian world, and the sheer depths of the roots of anti-Semitism — all these impel the Church to give solemn warning against these notions to her priests and catechists and indeed to all believers. The Church calls upon them to avoid, not only the errors themselves but also all forms of expression which reflect and nourish those errors: for example, generalizations such as *"the* Jews rejected Christ", *"the* Jews crucified Christ". In expounding St. John's Gospel one must be certain to take account of the fact that in a great many places the evangelist uses the expression "the Jews", by which he means simply and solely the Jewish leaders hostile to Jesus. The Church is the true

---

[18] See the end of n. 2, above p. 4.

"remnant of Israel", increased by the entry of those Gentiles who became sons of Abraham by faith: as such she must unite within herself both Jews and Gentiles. Therefore one should not say that henceforth the Jewish people were rejected or that, within the Church, the Gentiles had simply taken Israel's place. Nor should one depict the reality of salvation as if the Church had supplanted Israel, as one people might another. Certainly the change-over from the old to the new dispensation was accompanied by radical changes — institutions were superseded, a new all-embracing structure appeared — but what had happened was that the *same* people of God had been thus transformed in achieving the fullness of their vocation.

9. That part of Israel which remained outside this transformation has survived in present-day Judaism. Its preservation and presence in the world was a basic part of God's plan of salvation and therefore could not be without significance for the Church. Christians ought not to leave this present reality out of account, nor should they look at it from a purely human and political point of view, as do those who are not believers. They should rather draw nourishment for themselves from the Jewish world, with the insight and respect due to its past, its faith, and its trials. The Church expects it of her children that they leave nothing undone to tear down the wall of division between herself and the Jews, a wall which the misunderstandings of centuries have rendered almost impenetrable; and that they leave nothing undone to establish brotherly relations with the Jews, and to show them, at last, by their conduct the true face of the Church.

10. So far as the supernatural destiny of Israel is concerned, the teaching of the New Testament, especially that of St. Paul, leaves no room for doubt: "God has not rejected his people whom he foreknew" (Rom 11:1–2). Despite their resist-·ance to the gospel, "as regards election they are beloved for the sake of their forefathers" (11:28), and "the gifts and the call of God are irrevocable" (11:29). Finally the Apostle teaches that "all Israel will be saved" (11:26). Day by day the providential preservation of the Jewish people witnesses to the loyalty with which God holds to his plan for the salvation of the world. It would therefore be contrary to Scripture and to the true spirit of the Church if one were to assume, as often happens, that there lies upon the Jewish people a sentence of rejection, and indeed a curse. It would be absurd to give such a meaning to, for example, Matthew 27:25, "His blood be on us and on our children". As if God could ratify the outcry of a group of demonstrators, worked up by their ringleaders, and have it descend as a curse upon millions of innocent people! If one were to try to depict as a result of rejection by God the destruction of the Temple, the scattering of the Jews (which was indeed already a fact before the Crucifixion) and their sufferings and humiliations over the centuries, that would be contrary to the Church's teaching on the meaning of suffering. It is therefore advisable to warn seriously priests and the faithful never to adopt these inaccurate and far from Christian ideas about the destiny of the Jewish people.

11. The divinely guaranteed hope of the unification of Israel is an integral

part of Christian hope. At the same time it is the key to the mysterious destiny of the Jewish people, so that without it there can be no real Christian understanding of their destiny. When and wherever this hope is obscured or forgotten, the Christian vision is distorted. If, according to the teaching of the Apostle, the failure of many in Israel furthered the spread of the gospel and with it the salvation of the Gentiles, how much more would Israel's reunification reveal God's mercy and faithfulness? This revelation would be so glorious that the Apostle could portray it as *vita ex mortuis* (life from the dead) (Rom 11:15). This eschatological hope was always present in the Church. It required that believers let themselves be fired with this expectation in prayer and thought, and not least in their behaviour towards the children of the people of whose "race, according to the flesh, is the Christ, who is God over all, blessed for ever, Amen" (Rom 9:5).

A few weeks after its completion the Apeldoorn text was sent to the Secretariat for Promoting Christian Unity in the hope that it would have a favourable influence on its work. As, however, there prevailed from the start in leading Council circles a desire to keep the decree on the Jews short, the memorandum could not exercise the influence it deserved. For years it lay in the files of the Secretariat and in the drawers of those who took part in the conference. There, however, it underwent the test of time that tries all things. Its words have indeed not found their way into the Council text, but its spirit has. It contains nothing that needs to be altered on account of the Council Declaration. On the contrary, it reads like a commentary on certain significant passages of the Council document.

It is not possible to consider other attempts to gain a hearing for the cause of reconciliation between the Church and the Jewish people. It is enough to point out that there was also a lively interest in other quarters than those mentioned here. One example out of many was the enquiry by the publisher of *Wort und Wahrheit* into the question: "What do you expect from the Council?"[19] The démarches of Jewish organizations and individuals also deserve mention, even though they took place at a later stage, and had no influence to speak of on the discussion of the Council Declaration or the form of its text.[20] The reason may

---

[19] See the special supplement of *Wort und Wahrheit* 16 (October 1961) with the answers of Oesterreicher (pp. 646–8), Thieme (pp. 684–6) and the Dominicans of Walberberg (pp. 696–7). This questionnaire passed among German-speaking Catholics was certainly encouraging, though it is regrettable that, of about eighty answers, only three answers dealt in any detail with the subject of the Church and the Jewish people.

[20] I am thinking here of the memoranda of the "American Jewish Committee" — one on the image of the Jew in Catholic instruction (June 1961), and another on anti-Jewish elements in the Catholic liturgy (November 1961) — and of the memorandum of the rabbi and seminary professor Abraham Joshua Heschel (May 1962). The first gives a list of "slanderous statements which encourage hostility towards the Jews" to be found in school books, and requests the "serious support of the Vatican" in defeating all blind fanaticism and creating a prejudice-free climate of opinion, especially in the United States. The second shows from a series of liturgical texts how the Jews are represented as a worthless and morally contemptible people who have

well be that they were drawn up without knowledge of the possibilities open to a Council. Their proposals went too much into details, and the fulfilment of some of their requirements presupposed a mentality which the Council Declaration had first to create.

THE HISTORY OF THE TEXT

As has already been mentioned, Cardinal Bea announced at the first meeting of the members and advisers of the Secretariat for Unity on 14 and 15 November 1960 that Pope John had entrusted to the Secretariat responsibility for considering the problems posed for the Church in connection with the Jews. ("Problems concerning the Jews" is a rendering of the expression used for the item on the agenda

only one motive for their actions — vengeance and hatred. The signatories then go on to request "respectfully that the Church, in accordance with the precedents laid out, should take all available steps to correct those passages which . . . provoke and encourage the slanderous idea of the Jews as a cursed and despised people responsible for the death of God".

Professor Heschel rightly declares that anti-Semitism is an ancient evil and so complex that it is impossible to attribute it to any one cause or to make any one institution responsible for its persistence. Yet the Jews, in response to the prophets' call for justice and out of reverence for six million martyrs, are bound to request *all* institutions to investigate and block every possible source of anti-Semitism. Professor Heschel demands the extirpation of the religious roots of anti-Semitism and, in particular, makes four proposals for the improvement of relations between Catholics and Jews. First, that the Council should brand anti-Semitism as a sin and condemn all false teachings, such as that which makes the Jews as a people responsible for the crucifixion of Christ and sees in every Jew a murderer of Christ. Second: without wishing to impugn the rights of any religious group to win supporters by honest means, Jews do feel it as a spiritual torment that their sanctity as Jews, in their faithfulness to the *Torah,* is not accorded recognition. Genuine love, however, requires that the Jews be accepted as Jews, and it is their sincere hope that the Council recognize the integrity and the continuing value of Jews and Judaism. Third, in order to eliminate mutual ignorance every possible means should be used to make Christians truly familiar with Judaism and Jews with Christianity, e.g. through public discussions in which Christian and Jewish scholars could exchange opinions and tackle controversial and decisive issues; in this way Catholic theologians would learn much about Judaism. Plans should also be made for joint research projects and publications. The fourth proposal asks that a high-level commission should be set up at the Vatican, with the task of erasing prejudices and keeping a watch on Christian-Jewish relations everywhere. It would also be desirable to have similar commissions at the diocesan level to ensure that attention really was paid to the demands of justice and love.

A further memorandum of the "World Conference of Jewish Organizations" (February 1962) contents itself with the following plea — I quote a passage which, to my mind, sums up the essence of the whole document: "Encouraged by the historical initiative [John XXIII's removal from the liturgy of certain expressions susceptible of misinterpretation] and by many sympathetic actions of His Holiness, we turn to the Church with a respectful appeal that she may adopt such measures as appear appropriate to her to put all men, both inside and outside her ranks, who listen to her voice, on their guard against the great — religious and social — dangers inherent in racial fanaticism and in all teachings which stir up hatred and bring suffering upon defenceless people."

and for the title of the preparatory text, *Quaestiones de Iudaeis.)* The Cardinal had not yet decided, however, how to set to work. Fr. Gregory Baum, OSA, thereupon offered to collaborate in the task, for which he seemed to be well ·fitted by origin, experience and training. Cardinal Bea accepted this offer and commissioned Fr. Baum to produce a short survey, which was laid before the second meeting. This took place from 6 to 9 February 1961, in Ariccia in the Alban hills.

In his survey Fr. Baum put forward the thesis that the teaching of recent Popes made it clear by word and deed that the Christian approach to the "Jewish question" was a theological one, and also that certain patristic and medieval conceptions of the Jews were no longer to be defended. In order to make this "mystery" known (Rom 11:25) to the faithful and to give the Jews a correct picture of the Church, so that the flood of anti-Semitism would at last be stilled, it was of the greatest importance that the Ecumenical Council should issue authoritative Declarations on the following three points:

1. In the treatment of the origin and nature of Christ's Church, her close connection with the old Israel should be made unmistakeably clear. Thus it should be shown how the New Covenant confirmed, renewed and transcended the Old, and how the New Testament fulfilled and superseded the Old, but nevertheless did not render it invalid.

2. In order to correct the widespread notion that *the* Jews had rejected Jesus as the Christ, it should be made clear that the holy remnant of the Jewish people acclaimed and accepted the Saviour of mankind. It would therefore be unjust to regard the Jews as an accursed race or a people who had been rejected.

3. The Church's unceasing hope of Israel's final reconciliation with herself should be solemnly proclaimed and, no less important, until that day came the Christian's attitude to his Jewish neighbour should be one of love and respect. Anti-Semitism should be condemned.

a) The Sub-Commission for Jewish Questions

At the beginning of February 1961, Abbot Leo Rudloff (Jerusalem, Israel; Weston, Vermont, U.S.A.) was appointed a member, and the present writer an adviser, of the Secretariat. Together with Fr. Baum they formed the core of the "Sub-Commission for Jewish Questions", which was extended to include other members as occasion arose. The author was asked to prepare a study of the whole matter, on behalf of the sub-commission, for the forthcoming meeting.

The Secretariat for Unity had scarcely taken its first steps towards carrying out the papal commission when it ran into opposition. It seems that it was a confidential conversation with Cardinal Bea, innocently understood by a woman journalist to be an ordinary interview, that alerted the world, and with it the Arab governments, to the Secretariat's intentions. The anxiety and annoyance of the Arabs bore no relation to the facts. In the minds of the Arab leaders, a pronouncement intended as pastoral and theological was transformed in no time into a political document.

The line of thought of the Arab representatives may well have been as follows: if the Council did in fact proclaim the brotherhood of Christians and Jews, such a proclamation might well help the two to live together in peace in the countries of the West, but above all it would redound to the advantage of the State of Israel. Once Catholics began to take a friendly interest in Jews and Jewish matters, it would not be long before they extended their interest to the State of Israel. Thus the Council document would undeniably intrude into the sphere of politics and become a preparatory step towards diplomatic recognition of the State of Israel. It is not surprising that the Arabs, who could not for a single second forget the political tensions of the Near East, were determined to prevent a Council statement "in favour of the Jews". Before and during the Council they tried in every conceivable way to suppress any such Council Declaration.

It started with representations by diplomats accredited to the Holy See. Great efforts were made to make it clear to the representatives of the Arab countries that the Holy See was not planning a kind of chess game, let alone intrigue. Nevertheless I fear that they were never given to understand quite unambiguously that the proposed Declaration was a measure that was necessary for the inner life of the Church, and that she could not renounce it; nor that it was intended that the Council be kept free from any improper influence, and that, accordingly, no secular interference could be tolerated. The slanders that appeared from time to time in a section of the Arab press, and likewise the occasional threats, could have been met with the assurance that, rather than give way, an appeal would be made to world opinion. Historical accuracy, however, requires the admission that what is perfectly possible after the Council was unthinkable before.

In the period before Vatican II, the Vatican's permanent officials still expected to achieve much by diplomatic activities. When they were unable to convince the Arab leaders, they became uneasy and began to waver. Accordingly, a certain insecurity often prevailed in the Secretariat during the preparatory period and during the Council itself. It was sometimes not possible to be sure whether the Central Commission, as the highest organ of the Council, would permit an independent decree or whether the pronouncements on the Jews would be incorporated in another or several other documents. There were even times when it was doubtful whether there would be a Council pronouncement at all, to proclaim the Church's deep insight into the mystery of Israel. One must be aware of this situation in order to understand the ups and downs in the history of the text.

At the third meeting, which also took place in Ariccia, from 6 to 21 April 1961, Abbot Rudloff spoke, in his capacity of chairman of the sub-commission, of the seriousness and importance of the subject. He wanted, he said, simply to bring out certain points by way of introduction, and to define the extent of the problems involved. He shared the wishes expressed in the memoranda described above, and would add to them certain personal suggestions, for example, that the Easter week liturgy of the Byzantine rite be subjected to a fundamental reform, and also that there be removed from Church buildings all versions of the ritual murder legend in pictures and sculpture, together with other representations which insulted the Jews and did not stand up to historical investigation.

The main emphasis of his remarks lay in the proclamation — in his view unambiguously expressed in Romans 11:26–29 — of the reunification of the two Israels at the end of time. The Church had to live in the expectation of this event, which would be brought about by God's grace. There was, however, no doubt that the majority of her members were not inspired with this great hope. He therefore believed that a Council pronouncement on the relation of the Church to the Jews gave promise of a renewal of the true spirit of Advent.

After Abbot Rudloff, the present writer developed the thesis that the time of the Council was the God-given moment to speak in an ecumenical spirit of the people of whom Christ was born in his humanity. He gave the following reasons why it seemed to him to be the Church's duty precisely now to give expression to the role of the Jews in the working out of salvation, and also to put in its true light the relationship between the Church and the Jews, their ordination one to the other.

First: The biblical revival in our time and the accompanying rediscovery of semitic ways of thought and speech made possible, as never before, a perceptive and sensitive consideration of Jews living both before *and* after Christ. Certain exegetes had aroused from its long slumber the teaching of the Apostle concerning Israel's way of salvation given in chapters 9 to 11 of the Epistle to the Romans. In addition modern Popes had several times spoken of the Jews in a way that approached the idea that, despite their rejection of Christ, they were our "separated brethren". They were our brothers in Abraham, the father of our faith. It was therefore appropriate, indeed urgent that the Council continue the work of reconciliation.

Second: The Council would doubtless be dealing with the relationship of Catholics to Christians separated from Rome and with the Church's concern for non-believers. If, however, she were to keep silent concerning the Jews, then no regard would be paid to their place in God's plan of salvation and it might even appear as if it were the same as that of the pagans. Thus to ignore them or fail to single them out would be contrary to the spirit of Scripture and the tradition of the Church.

Third: If the Council fathers were to remain silent, they would be accused of having capitulated to the Declaration's opponents. The present writer recalls the meeting of the World Council of Churches at Evanston, U.S.A., in 1954, when even the slightest reference to Christian hope concerning the people of Israel, especially of an eschatological kind, was voted down by a coalition of Near

Eastern (or Near East-orientated) and American-liberal delegates, the first intimidated by the Arab governments and the others anxious about their Jewish neighbours and friends. The forthcoming Council, on the other hand, should not allow itself to be guided by a similar fear.

Fourth: As already mentioned, uncertainty prevailed as to whether it would be possible to break through the resistance to a special decree on the Jews. Since the sub-commission never took up a position of "all or nothing", the present writer was able to declare that it would not in all circumstances insist upon a special pronouncement. It did, however, earnestly beg the Council fathers to advocate certain essential truths concerning the Jews. If necessary these could also be incorporated in other decrees. If the Council were to proclaim that the Christian faith was rooted in that of the people of the Old Covenant and that we awaited a final reconciliation of Synagogue and Church, and especially if the Council were solemnly to condemn anti-Semitism, such professions would, without doubt, contribute to the atmosphere of friendship between Christians and Jews. The memory of the persecutions and oppressions of the past were most deeply imprinted in the consciousness of many Jews. All too often, these sufferings were, alas, caused "in the name of Christ". But if the Council statements gave true expression to the love of Christ and the fondness of the Church for the people of Israel, then they would do something to take away the burning sting of injustice and insult and help to bring peace.

Finally: A deep knowledge of Christ and the Church was impossible without a knowledge of God's dealings in the days of the patriarchs and prophets, without a loving awareness of the *magnalia Dei,* God's mighty acts (Exod 14:13). There would be no good news of salvation without the good news of creation. (This is no empty phrase: against the background of those pagan myths which represent the birth of the world as the outcome of a pitiless quarrel among the gods, the first chapter of Genesis, which sings the praises of the Creator who is good and by whose work there has come forth a world that is good, is truly a hymn, a gospel.) Jesus would not be God's Anointed and the Saviour of all mankind, without the promises and prefigurations of the Old Covenant, without those figures who in their lives in some measure foreshadowed his work and suffering. In conclusion, the Christian hope would not be fulfilled without the healing of the breach between Church and Synagogue. The restoration of their unity would be the "happy end" of the drama of salvation. In the words of St. Thomas Aquinas: *Ignorantia huius mysterii nobis esset damnosa* (Ignorance of this mystery would be to our spiritual harm).[21]

The writer finished with an appeal to all members of the Secretariat who were present: "On these grounds, and therefore not only for the sake of the Jews but also, and indeed much more, for the spiritual advancement of the faithful and for a testimony to the perfect unity of the Church which was, is, and always will be

---

[21] See his commentary on the Letter to the Romans.

the Church of Jews and Gentiles, we seek your agreement to our (yet-to-be-discussed) requests."

Thereupon Fr. Baum read out the preliminary study worked out by the present author and discussed by the whole sub-commission. At this stage, Fr. George Tavard, AA, was also a member of the sub-commission. The study had been drafted in English but was also available to the Secretariat's members in Latin and French translations. As was only to be expected, there were occasional differences of emphasis in these translations. In addition the study, like other documents, went through several drafts. First, handwritten improvements were made, for the sake of greater clarity or to meet objections. Later, it was re-copied for the fourth general meeting in August 1961 at Bühl, Germany. In the following summary, all stages in its development have been taken into account.

It should, however, be noted here, in advance, that its first reading in Ariccia was greeted with applause — contrary to all the customs of the Secretariat. Cardinal Bea was beyond doubt the ideal chairman. He steered the Secretariat's meetings firmly but gently. All discussions followed parliamentary procedure, but without rigid formality. During the preparatory period the Secretariat's members met for the most part away from Rome. They lived together in the same house, prayed and ate together, and met outside the formal sessions, so that the Secretariat took on the character of a community. Nevertheless outbursts of applause were not a daily occurrence. On the contrary, if my memory does not deceive me, the spontaneous clapping that greeted the preliminary study on 20 April 1961 was the only example of such a reception for a preparatory document. It seems to prove that this document expressed clearly matters that most had hitherto sensed only vaguely. What formerly had lain dormant in the subconscious was now brought out into the full light of day. The bishops, with their applause, here showed themselves true representatives of the people of God. The study accomplished for them what the subsequently promulgated Declaration was to do and would still do for the whole Church.

b) The preliminary study

I. 1. The study, which was intended to prepare the way for the carrying out of the Pope's commission, was divided into three parts. The first was entitled "Dogmatic Principles". It dealt initially with the *roots of the Church in the Old Covenant*. No one could truly understand the Church as Bride and Body of Christ, as the people of God and the community of believers, unless he was lovingly aware of the fact that the Church was rooted in the life and faith of ancient Israel. To St. Augustine, God's call and Abraham's response appeared as an *articulus temporis,* "a turning-point in time".[22] So much were this call and response a turning-point — the end of the dictates of idolatory and the birth, in

---

[22] *De Civitate Dei,* 12: *PL,* XLI, 492.

the pagan heart, of belief in the living God — that the *Pontificale Romanum* could speak of the Patriarch's life as the *seminarium fidei nostrae* (the seedbed of our faith).[23] Similarly for Augustine there were not only individual prophetic figures in Israel — the existence of the entire people seemed to him prophetic. For him the people as such was the divinely inspired herald of the Messiah and his Kingdom.[24]

On many occasions the Liturgy celebrated the proofs of Jahweh's mercy (Ps 88 [89]:2), as true elements in the history of the Church. Thus the *Exsultet* of Easter night proclaimed: "Haec nox est, in qua primum *patres nostros* filios Israel eductos de Aegypto, mare rubrum sicco vestigio transire fecisti" (This is the night when, long ago, thou didst cause *our forefathers,* the sons of Israel, in their passage out of Egypt, to pass dry-shod over the Red Sea). Thus it could be said without exaggeration that the Israel of the patriarchs and prophets was the Church in the making, while the Church herself is Israel fulfilled, renewed in the blood of Christ and spread over the whole earth. Just as the Israel of the time of Expectation was the matrix of the Church, so the Church represents Israel transformed by Christ's word and cleansed in the fire of the Holy Spirit.

Despite all their differences, the two covenants do not contradict each other. They are, rather, two stages in God's dealings with mankind. Doubtless the New in many respects transcends the Old. But it would show little honour to Christ to treat slightingly the stock from which he came and the order of grace into which he was born. St. Peter proclaimed that the God who had "glorified his servant Jesus" (Acts 3:13) was none other than the "God of Abraham and of Isaac and of Jacob, the God of our fathers". One and undivided was God's decree, one and indivisible the history of salvation, and therefore the Church prayed: "Ut in Abrahae filios et Israeliticam dignitatem totius mundi transeat plenitudo" (Grant that all men may become sons of Abraham and share in the dignity of Israel).[25]

I. 2. The second section of the first part spoke of *the Jews as those for ever favoured by God.* The enmities that were tearing mankind apart in our time made it necessary continually to recall the universality of the Church. For Christians at least this could be done in an impressive manner, were the Council to proclaim that in Christ the Church embraced Jews and Gentiles with a *single* love,[26] and

---

[23] *Pontificale Romanum,* De Alt. Consec.

[24] *Contra Faustum,* XIII, 4: *PL,* XLII, 283.

[25] Easter Vigil.

[26] Belief in the *"one love"* of God living and working in the Church should not be taken as meaning that this love is reduced to one particular level. It is not that God loves all men with the same love, but that he loves each individual with an infinite love. E. Peterson, in his invariably stimulating, though not always unbiased, book, *Die Kirche aus Juden und Heiden* (1933), gives the following commentary on Rom 11:32, where Paul speaks of the disobedience of all men and God's mercy upon all: "In the Christian religion the word 'all' has a mounting significance. It does not mean 'all' in the sense of the *Communist Manifesto,* which is addressed to 'all'. Its

that she was the Church of Jews and Gentiles alike. The separation and reconciliation of the two was of fundamental significance in Pauline theology. So long
as the division lasted, God's sovereignty was not fully acknowledged. In Christ,
however, the breach was healed, and thus the Apostle could rejoice: "He is our
peace, who has made us both one, and has broken down the dividing wall of
hostility, by abolishing in his flesh the law of commandments and ordinances"
(Eph 2:14). The necessary healing of this breach between Jews and Gentiles was
a sign of God's all-embracing love, and indeed it was more than that — it was
the proof that salvation had come in Christ, a proof that must be revealed and
made accessible to all men.

It was misleading to say "the Jews" had rejected Christ. First, one must not
forget that long before the Lord's coming, millions of Jews were living in the
diaspora. Secondly, the attitude of the people of Israel towards the gospel of
salvation had been divided. While those who held power had aimed at Jesus'
death, a remnant chosen by grace had welcomed him (Rom 11:5). While some
of the people, in their human weakness, seem to have accepted their leaders'
decision without protest, the first communities of the early Church consisted
almost entirely of men and women of Jewish origin and of proselytes. The
proselytes were Gentiles who had taken refuge under the wings of the God of
Israel (Ruth 2:12). Though of alien descent, they nevertheless were Jews by
belief and often also in their way of life. From these Jews of Jerusalem who had
become Christians·there came — to use a phrase of Bishop (now Cardinal)
Journet — the first heart-beats of the Church, which determined the whole
future rhythm of Christian life.[27]

Still more pernicious than the misconception that "the Jews" had rejected
Christ was the notion that God had rejected them, that they were an "accursed"
people. Quite apart from the indefensible assumption that the outcry of a raging
mob: "His blood be on us and on our children" (Mt 27:25) had bound God's
hands, so that this cry became his decree, the shouts of the crowd were not the
voice of the whole people.[28] In the same Jerusalem in which the shouts of the

concrete meaning is always Jews and Gentiles, but always in this gradational sense that *not only*
Israel *but also* the Gentiles are called upon to be the chosen people, and that not only the Gentiles
but also the Jews are included under disobedience, so that God may have mercy upon all, Gentile
and Jew alike. Here, too, the divine mercy can be seen essentially as something realized in
mounting stages. It is not a timeless benevolence imparted in the same manner to Jews and Gentiles, but a divine superabundance drawing Gentiles and Jews successively into its sphere. Only
if God's dealings are understood in this hyperbolic sense is it possible to see just why St. Paul
makes his treatment of the theme end in those words of praise: 'O the depth of the riches and
wisdom and knowledge of God!'"

[27] Charles [Cardinal] Journet, *Destinées d'Israël* (1944), p. 112.
[28] Attention must constantly be drawn to the fact that the cry, "His blood be on us and on our
children!" (Mt 27:25) was not, in itself, a curse. It was, rather, an asseveration of innocence and
is reminiscent of the words employed to warn witnesses in capital trials before they made their
statements. Footnotes and commentaries often refer to 2 Sam 1:16 and 3:29, but make no

"storm troopers" gathered before the Governor's palace resounded, there were also "a great multitude of the people, and of women" (Lk 23:27) who followed Jesus on his way to "the place which is called The Skull", and who "bewailed and lamented him".

If one separates the gospels from their historical context and takes no account of the fact that they originated under the influence of Semitic forms of speech, then they can, in certain passages, easily give rise to the impression that God repudiated the Jews, as if he were "finished with" the people he had chosen and made the original guardians of his revelation. If, however, we adopted the Pauline interpretation of Israel's destiny and read these passages in that light, then we know that they do not involve the inescapable finality which they seemed to express.

The Apostle often spoke boldly and impulsively but nevertheless he chose with extreme care the words with which he characterized those in Israel who did not know the time of their "visitation" (Lk 19:44). He did not hesitate to say of their efforts that they were made "in ignorance", they were "not enlightened", but at the same time he felt bound to testify that "they have a zeal for God" (Rom 10:2, 3). Had Paul so wished, he could have found in the prophetic tradition a whole series of violent expressions with which to castigate the leaders and the masses. He contented himself, however, with speaking of their "un-

mention of the criminal proceedings laid down in the *Mishna,* which is much more important. *Sanh.,* 4, 5, states specifically that it was customary to instil fear into witnesses as a means of encouraging them to keep to the truth. A reminder was given that capital trials were quite different from property disputes. In the latter it was possible for a person to make up for any false statement by paying an appropriate sum of money. But this was not so with capital crimes, where the blood of a man unjustly executed and his eventual descendants would be upon the perjurer until the end of the world. If this warning is kept in mind it can be seen why the crowd outside the governor's residence unhesitatingly declared their readiness to bear responsibility for Christ's execution at the hands of Pilate. They felt themselves, quite simply, to be without guilt. It is all the more easily explicable if it is assumed that the crowd was made up for the most part of members of the resistance movement. These "Zealots", as they are called, had long believed that Jesus was "their man". Even though Christ dissociated himself from their attempt to crown him king (Jn 6:15), even though he taught that the kingdom of God was incompatible with violence (Mt 11:12; Jn 18:36), even though he passionately rejected Messiahship as understood by the Zealots (Mt 6:8–10; Mk 8:33) and called those before him who had raised such a claim "thieves and robbers" (Jn 10:8), and even though he accepted Jerusalem's homage upon a gentle donkey and not on a battle-charger, the men of the resistance held to him in the illusion that he was simply waiting for the opportune moment to assume leadership. The moment, however, the Zealots realized that they had been mistaken and that Christ would not make common cause with them but proposed to go the way of the suffering Servant (Is 52:13–53:12), they dropped him in rage and fury. Obsessed as they were with their militarist ideology and their disillusionment, they thought themselves fully justified in abandoning Christ to "the Roman" and the shameful death of crucifixion.

For the question of Christ and the Zealots, see O. Cullmann, *The State in the New Testament* (1963), and the popular work of J. Pickl, *Messiaskönig Jesus* (3rd ed., 1939). For the liberation movement in general, its religious attitude and political orientation, see M. Hengel, *Die Zeloten* (1961).

receptiveness" towards the truths of God's grace, a word which most translators, however, render as "hardening" (Rom 11:7, 25).[29] With tender restraint he terms their failure to recognize Jesus a "trespass" and a "stumble" (Rom 11:11).

Paul did not, it was true, explicitly record the ignorance of Jesus' crucifiers, as Peter did, but it would not be wrong to attribute to them that "acting ignorantly in unbelief" which characterized Paul's own persecution of the Church (1 Tim 1:13) as also the work of "the rulers of this age" (1 Cor 2:8). Even if his kinsmen resisted God's plan of salvation and sought to thwart it, they still remained "God's favourites". "For the sake of their forefathers", "they are beloved" (Rom 11:28). Even when they are not aware of it, they testify to God's favour and his gracious rule among men, as it was revealed in Christ Jesus.

It was in this spirit that the Bishop of Lille, Cardinal Liénart, had written his Lenten pastoral of 21 February 1960. In it he rejects as unchristian the notion that the Jews are an accursed people, a race of deicides, who deserve our contempt, as if they, and not all men, bore the main responsibility for the Lord's death. "It is simply untrue", the Cardinal explained, "that Israel, the chosen people of the Old Covenant, became an accursed people under the New. In reality, the religious destiny of Israel is a mystery of grace, which Christians must ponder with respect and affection."[30]

I. 3. In its third part, this preliminary study with which the subcommission on questions relating to the Jews began its work, was devoted to *the final reconciliation of Church and Synagogue*. A view of the Church that did not include this imperishable hope seemed to the sub-commission's members to be incomplete. In the words of the Apostle, Israel according to the flesh[31] had been divided: the

---

[29] A modern translator — Jörg Zink, *Das Neue Testament* (1965), p. 358 — has translated Rom 11:25 with an excellent feeling for the text: "Part of Israel is *closed (verschlossen)* to Christ". The same translator renders Rom 11:7 as: "A part determined by God is [in harmony with him], the rest are as though *fettered" (gefesselt)*.

[30] *DC* 42 (1960), pp. 299f. This very significant final sentence reads in French: "En réalité, le destin religieux d'Israël est un mystère de grâce sur lequel nous, les chrétiens, nous avons à réfléchir avec une respectueuse sympathie."

[31] For inculcating a right understanding of the Jews in both pulpit and classroom it is important to note that the words "Israel according to the flesh" are not intended pejoratively. The expression does not stigmatize the Jews for any supposed carnality, sensuality or worldliness. It refers simply to the Israel which has come forth by natural generation, the offspring of the loins of Abraham. It is, therefore, a biological, not a moral designation. That the Church does not belittle procreation and birth in general and physical descent from Abraham in particular can be seen from the blessing she pronounces on a pregnant woman, in the following prayer: "O Lord, our God, Creator of all things, mighty and terrible, just and merciful, thou alone art good and loving. Thou hast set Israel free from all evil, thou hast made our fathers into thine own cherished people and sanctified them through the power of thy Spirit." The prayer continues by "reminding" God of the work of the Holy Spirit, who prepared the body and soul of the glorious Virgin Mary to be a

smaller part, "the elect" (Rom 11:7), was the means of the Church's growth and extension over the whole world, while the larger part, despite its disobedience, had been preserved as an object of God's mercy and a reminder of his faithfulness (Rom 11:30–32). God's steadfastness and pity went beyond Israel's mere physical preservation for "the gifts and the call of God are irrevocable" (Rom 11:29). Israel according to the flesh, at present far removed from Christ, would be united with him on the day foreordained by God.

It is true that some few exegetes had been so thrown off balance by the Apostle's penetrating but unexpected statements in his letter to the Romans that they believed that the assertion "all Israel will be saved" must be understood to mean that the Apostle was here speaking of all who, throughout history, had ever believed in Christ. But the overwhelming majority of exegetes, past and present, agreed that the Apostle was speaking here of the resurrection, the salvation, of the empirical Israel.

Among the Fathers of the Church, and also later, there were two ways of understanding the future "conversion" of Israel. One line of approach followed the opinion that with Israel's final turning to Christ, history would have reached its completion, and therefore Paul's phrase "life from the dead" (Rom 11:15) could mean nothing other than the resurrection of all flesh. The other approach, however, gave the words "life from the dead" — a phrase not found elsewhere in Scripture and therefore peculiar to Rom 11:15 — a spiritual meaning. The adherents of this interpretation saw in Israel's future conversion the signal for a new outpouring of grace, for a reawakening of love over the whole earth. It could not be the Council's task to choose between these two approaches.

Similarly one can only speculate on the ways and means of that "conversion" and its immediate results. Theodore of Mopsuestia assumed that the Jews of those days, like the Apostles, would be teachers of the Gentiles.[32] Gregory the Great saw them as imitating the passion of Christ, as martyrs who would deliver themselves up to insult and torture and take upon themselves the work of giving testimony in blood.[33] Photius's view was that the re-admission of Israel would bring with it the great kingdom of the future, "perfect and universal joy", as if the dead had risen.[34] But according to Origen it would actually transform this perishable world into an imperishable one.[35]

Little as could be known of the circumstances and consequences of Israel's final "in-gathering" — so that it could not be the subject of a conciliar decision —

---

worthy dwelling for his Son, and by asking him that he may watch over the child in the womb of the expectant mother — since the child, too, is his own work — and that the "hand of his mercy" may be with her at the time of her delivery, so that the child may come safely and whole into the world.

[32] K. Staab, *Pauluskommentare aus der griechischen Kirche* (1933), p. 156.
[33] *PL*, LXXIX, col. 108.
[34] Staab, *op. cit.*, p. 526.
[35] *PG*, XIV, col. 1190–1191.

the essence of this hope was certain (cf. Rom 11:21, 15, 25). As a divine promise and apostolic legacy, it was an essential part of the Church's never-failing expectation. A solemn declaration giving expression to this truth would certainly be a blessing for all.

II. 1. The "Dogmatic Principles" were followed by a second part — "Moral and Liturgical Considerations". In the first section of this part it was pointed out that a Christian who reflected upon the continuity of the old and the new order of grace and remained conscious of the links, as full of hope as of pain, that bound the Church to the children of Israel, could not maintain any attitude towards his Jewish neighbours other than that of respect and love. God chose his people without any merit of theirs, he gave his word to their ancestors and bound himself to their descendants for ever. Anyone who bears in mind God's constant faithfulness to his people will be conscious that he is still related to them, in their state of separation. This awareness of "belonging together" is included in the rejection of anti-Semitism by Pius XI (already dealt with here) and clearly expressed in the afore-mentioned address by John XXIII to a group of Jewish visitors.

While the Church holds in abhorrence any kind of racial fanaticism, hatred of the Jews has a special quality of evil. It not only violates the commands of truth, justice and love, but it also deals a blow to faith. Considered from without, anti-Semitism, like any other form of hatred, contradicts the doctrine of faith that every man is created in the image of God. At its heart, however, it wishes to deny, as if it had never been, the fact that at the Incarnation the eternal Son of God was made son of David and son of Abraham (Mt 1:1).

II. 2. In a further section it was said that for most of the faithful the liturgy was in fact their teacher in the spiritual life. In accordance with the old axiom, *Legem credendi lex statuat supplicandi* — here understood in the widest sense — the form prayer taken not only expresses the believer's convictions, it also gives shape to the life of faith. At the present time only one commemoration of Old Testament figures is known in the calendar of the Latin Church, that of the Maccabees (1 August). But the spiritual significance of the Maccabees is very much slighter than that of many other men and women of Israel. Would it not be of help to many believers — the study asked — if those feasts of the just of the Old Testament that are celebrated by the Latin Patriarchate of Jerusalem were in some way extended to the whole Church? This could be done, for example, in the form of a new feast of patriarchs and prophets. Yet, as it is the wish of the Church today to have the Saints' days give place to the Masses of the Christmas and Easter cycle, the signatories of the preliminary study suggested that the feasts of the Jerusalem Patriarchate be incorporated where possible in the Roman Missal as votive Masses.

Liturgical prayers, especially those bound up with the administration of the sacraments, do quite often show that the figures and events of the Old Covenant not only live on in the New, but also acquire a new significance. For many people, special Masses in honour of the various patriarchs and prophets would anchor yet more deeply in their hearts and minds this knowledge of the unity of saving history. Even if these Masses were celebrated only occasionally, their introduction into the Roman Missal would contribute, on the one hand, to a fruitful atmosphere in Judaeo-Christian relations. On the other, the life of grace among the faithful would undoubtedly be enriched by a prayer like the following — one of many from the Proper of the Jerusalem Patriarchate:

"God, thou hast revealed the riches of thy wisdom and thy knowledge to thy beloved servants, the Prophets. Grant that through their intercession we may never depart from the true wisdom, which is Christ, and may thus enjoy in heaven the everlasting revelation of thy majesty. Through Christ Our Lord."[36]

III. 1. A third part of the preliminary study put forward "Concrete Proposals". A number of books of religious instruction for various age groups have not yet absorbed the spirit that animates this report. It would therefore be of great value if the Council were to induce those responsible for the training of priests and for catechetics so to teach the role of the Jewish people in the history of salvation that their instruction stood in full harmony with God's marvellous saving will and with its execution.

III. 2. The signatories also requested that the work of creating a climate of respect and affection, begun by Pope John, be carried further. The Breviary still displayed examples of misleading and wounding expressions. To cite only a few instances: in the second Response of the third nocturn for Good Friday it says of Judas: "Iesum tradidit impius *summis principibus sacerdotum et senioribus* populi" (The wicked man betrayed Jesus *to the chief priests and elders* of the people). But the second Response of the second nocturn of Maundy Thursday contains the following sentence: "Denariorum numero Christum *Iudaeis* tradidit" (For a handful of coins he delivered Christ *to the Jews*). Similarly, the second Response of the second nocturn for Good Friday says: "Tenebrae factae sunt, dum crucifixissent Iesum *Iudaei*" (It became dark when *the Jews* crucified Jesus). This short list could be expanded with other examples.[37]

It is a commonplace among exegetes that the expression "the Jews" in St. John's Gospel very often does not mean the Jewish people as such but rather stands for Jesus' opponents, in particular for the establishment that rejected him.[38]

---

[36] Proper of the Patriarchate of Jerusalem.

[37] A further example is dealt with by P. Gordan, O.S.B., under the title "Die gottlosen Juden", *Freiburger Rundbrief,* 18 (1966), p. 54.

[38] It is totally false to see an anti-Semitic tendency in the Johannine use of the expression "the Jews". This view ignores the very largely Jewish character of the fourth gospel altogether. Various attempts have been made to give historical reasons for this usage, e.g. that of H. Kosmala,

Some modern translations of the New Testament contained footnotes which gave the non-specialist reader this essential information. It would be of great help to a correct understanding of the mystery of the Passion if such footnotes were also introduced into the people's Mass books everywhere, and if liturgical texts such as those mentioned above, which did not cite Scripture word for word, were altered so that they might be of better service to truth and love.

III. 3. Finally, Church buildings in various countries have immortalized the ritual murder legend in stone or paintings. Although several Popes have declared that the various accusations against the Jews that they killed Christian children in order to offer a sacrifice or to drink their blood, had their roots in the wickedness and greed of the accusers, reminders of these evil legends remain untouched. The appropriate authorities of the Anglican cathedral at Lincoln recently removed all memorials in honour of the alleged martyrdom of Little Hugh of Lincoln.[39] The incumbents of Catholic churches in which similar monuments are to be found should not let themselves be outdone by anyone. On the contrary, they should take the lead in striving to make good this historical injustice.

who thinks it may be part of the Qumrân tradition. "Israel", he says, is one of the cover-names of the Essene community, while "Judah", "land of Judah" or "house of Judah" denote the enemies of the community. Those who are "ready to repent" and therefore "the chosen of Israel" are those "who have gone out of the land of Judah" (*CD,* II, 5; IV, 2f., 3f.). Cf. H. Kosmala, *Hebräer — Essener — Christen* (1959), p. 345.

The Scandinavian exegete N. A. Dahl thinks the Johannine usage may be a trace of the biblical and rabbinic tradition concerning the representative role of Israel. "The Jews", he suggests, is not merely a synonym for the high priests and elders of the people, but stands for the hostility of the "world" towards Christ. In Jewish tradition Jerusalem, and especially Mount Zion, is the centre of the world. According to the rabbinic view Jerusalem, "in the latter days", will become the "mother city" of the human race. And for the prophets before them, Jerusalem was the place to which the nations would flow and from which the law and the word of the Lord would go forth (Is 2:2–3). The Holy City, accordingly, is the centre of salvation, the focal point of grace and the home of faith. The Evangelist saw Christ's mission to Israel as a mission to the whole world: it was there that he carried out his service to humanity. But the Evangelist added a negative aspect to all this. He also saw the resistance of the world as concentrated in Jerusalem: the resistance of man against his Redeemer is mirrored in concentrated form in that of the official clique of Jerusalem. Thus the authorities of the biblical city — "the Jews" — are made to stand for the permanent and ubiquitous resistance to the divine offer of renewal. Taking all in all, it is possible to say that the Johannine use of the expression "the Jews" is a literary device for bringing out a profound theological idea (cf. N. A. Dahl, "The Johannine Church and History", in W. Klassen and G. F. Snyder, eds., *Current Issues in New Testament Interpretation* [1962], pp. 134 f.).

Here is yet another example of the way in which the uninformed can take something as anti-Jewish which in reality forms part of Israel's so frequently ignored heritage.

[39] In Lincoln Cathedral is the burial place of an eight-year old boy named Hugh, who, according to legend, is supposed to have been "murdered by the Jews" in 1255 for ritual purposes. In 1955 — seven hundred years later! — a text reviling the Jews was removed from the walls of the cathedral. The following inscription was put up in its place in reparation:

Various *vota* were attached to the introductory presentation of the preliminary study discussed above, first at the end of each section, later at the end of the whole text. They were directed to the Council fathers, who were asked to consider earnestly the following matters.

First, in any definition of the nature of the Church they might also teach that, according to God's plan of salvation, the Church was rooted in the Israel of the patriarchs and prophets. They might likewise proclaim that the vocation of Abraham and the deliverance of the Jewish people out of Egypt formed part of the genesis of the Church. For the Church is the living continuation of the people of God who lived under the old order of grace, indeed she *is* Israel, exalted and renewed in the word and blood of Christ.

Second, they might teach that the Church is the Church of Jews and Gentiles, and that the reconciliation of the two in Christ prefigures and proclaims the reconciliation of all men in the Church, which therefore is the representative core of mankind. The Jewish people, however, even if far from Christ, does not in any way stand under God's curse. On the contrary, they remain forever dear to him, on account for their ancestors and the promises made to them.

Third, they might teach that the reconciliation of the two Israels was an integral part of Christian hope and that the Church awaited this hour of grace with longing and unshaken faith. It was true she did not know the day or the hour, but she knew, with Paul, that it would be an event full of grace, and indeed "life from the dead" (Rom 11:15).

Fourth, they might proclaim the dignity of every human being as an image of the Creator, and condemn racial fanaticism in all its forms. They might especially brand anti-Semitism not only as a sin against justice, love and the bond of human brotherhood, but also as an onslaught on the humanity of Christ, who was of the house of David.

Fifth, the feasts of the just of the Old Covenant, as they are at present celebrated in the Latin Patriarchate of Jerusalem, might be extended to the whole Church, either as votive Masses or as a feast of the patriarchs and prophets.

Sixth, guidelines and directives might be given on the best ways of teaching Israel's role in salvation history, and also the post-biblical history of the Jewish people, in seminaries and in adult religious instruction.

Seventh, the work of love begun by the Pope might be perfected by banning

---

"Trumped up stories of 'ritual murders' of Christian boys by Jewish communities were common throughout Europe during the Middle Ages, and even much later. These fictions cost many innocent Jews their lives. Lincoln had its own legend, and the alleged victim was buried in the Cathedral. A shrine was erected above and the boy was referred to as 'little St. Hugh'. . . Such stories do not redound to the credit of Christendom and so we pray — 'Remember not Lord our offences, nor the offences of our forefathers'." Asked about the reasons for the alteration a Dean of the Cathedral replied that no untruth had any place on the walls of a cathedral (cf. *Freiburger Rundbrief,* 12, nos. 45–48 [1959], p. 66).

statues or pictures that preserved the slanders accusing the Jews of ritual murder. Prayers, paintings and sculptures which are offensive to the people from which Christ came in his earthly life — "Christ, who is God over all, blessed for ever, Amen" (Rom 9:5) — should be removed.

c) The discussion of the preliminary study

In discussions of the individual petitions during the general meetings of April and August 1961 already mentioned, attempts were made to give greater depth to certain expressions, or to clear up misunderstandings. During the April plenary meeting great emphasis was placed, in connection with the first petition, on the *unity* of the two Covenants and on the impossibility of understanding the New Testament without the Old. The wish was expressed, that the terms "Old" and "New" Israel be dropped, as they only preserved the idea of opposition between the two. It would be far better to speak comprehensively of the "Israel of God".

In the second petition, in its original form, it was said that the Jewish people were in no way rejected by God, although the majority of them stood apart from Christ. A prominent member of the Secretariat protested against the word "majority" as going beyond what was stated in Scripture. In this connection another speaker recalled that at the time of Christ the dispersion of the Jews was already a fact. Two thirds of the Jews were already to be found in the Diaspora, and had therefore never heard Jesus' preaching and scarcely even that of the Apostles. So they could not have rejected him in their hundreds of thousands, much less in millions.

Another member found the expression "the Church of Jews and Gentiles" unsatisfactory. It did indeed describe the character of the Church in the time of the apostles, but not that of the Church today. As most Christians in Western countries sprang from a centuries-old Christian tradition, one could not properly call them "Gentile Christians". To that the answer was given that the phrase "Church of Jews and Gentiles" was not divisive, but was intended to proclaim the unity of all, that it described an event in saving history, not a personal or temporary situation. "Church of Jews and Gentiles" meant, among other things, that "God has consigned all men to disobedience, that he may have mercy upon all" (Rom 11:32).[40] It was also pointed out that the expression was not coined in modern times, but was to be found already among the Fathers of the Church, and furthermore, the art of Christian antiquity gave testimony to what it denoted.[41]

[40] For this, cf. the important statement of H. de Lubac in *The Catholic and His Church* (1960) that the Church, as regards the majority of its members, is descended above all from the Gentiles, *ecclesia ex gentibus;* but that the idea of the Church is descended pre-eminently from the Jews.

[41] For this theme, cf. E. Peterson, *op. cit.* — The witness provided by Christian art includes above all the mosaic at San Lorenzo in Rome depicting Christ as Ruler of the Universe (Pantokrator).

With regard to the truth of faith expressed in the third petition, it was said that it had largely fallen into oblivion in Catholic theology. The question was also brought up of whether the Jewish people still had a role in saving history. The questioner thought the answer was "No", while others replied "Yes".

The fourth petition stressed Christ's descent from the house of David. The wish was expressed that the envisaged Declaration should also give prominence to the fact that the Blessed Virgin and the apostles belonged to the people of Israel.

The fifth petition was originally addressed to the Sacred Congregation of Rites. It was stated in connection with it that, on the one hand, the Congregation of Rites did not like additional feasts, and on the other that there was already an invocation of the patriarchs and prophets in the Litany of the Saints, while Abraham occupied an important place in the Canon of the Mass.

The sixth petition, in its first draft, kept in general to the lines described in the account on pp. 30–2. In discussion, the importance of the instructions for seminaries indicated therein was underlined. In relation to the seventh petition, reference was made to the beneficial effect of the arrangements, already carried out, for the Good Friday bidding prayers.

At the plenary session of August 1961, discussion of the Declaration was resumed. The first comment concerned the origin of the Church. She was not simply rooted in Israel, for Christ was not only the son of Abraham but also the only-begotten of the Father. Thus the deepest roots of the Church lay in the triune God. The reply made to this was that this observation was undoubtedly correct in itself, but it did not constitute a relevant objection, since the theme of the first petition was only the origin of the Church in time.

One speaker found the words "a people of deicides", as they occur under I. 2 (p. 26), to be slanderous. It was true that the accusation was refuted, but one must explain that the expression was to be totally rejected. The second petition also gave rise to a far-reaching discussion, even though not to a decisive solution, of the problem of Israel's rejection of Christ. One speaker held that the New

Christ is seated on a globe, with Peter and Paul to his right and left, and at their feet are the holy cities: at Peter's feet Jerusalem, the temple of which had long been the place of God's special presence; at Paul's feet Bethlehem, the scene of his manifestation to the nations and their representatives, the wise men from the East. These two holy cities — the one of the Jews and the other of the Gentiles — constantly reappear in early Christian works of art; out of them went forth the flock of Christ, made up of twelve sheep, symbolic of the twelve apostles and the twelve tribes. Twelve was the number of universality, "sacramentum est cuiusdam universitatis" (Augustine, *In Psalm.: PL,* XXXVII, 1104). — The mosaic in the apse of S. Pudenziana shows Christ as Ruler and Teacher, enthroned in Jerusalem: the one to whom all authority in heaven and on earth has been given (Mt 28:18) and who bade his apostles to preach the gospel to the whole creation (Mk 16:15). At his right is the apostle who, on the day of Pentecost, urged his kindred to acknowledge Christ (Acts 2:36), at his left the one who brought the gospel to the Gentiles (Acts 15:7). Behind Peter stands the *Ecclesia ex circumcisione,* behind Paul the *Ecclesia ex gentibus.* The two women, who symbolize the twofold yet single Church, are about to crown the messengers of Christ with a garland.

Testament repeatedly presupposed a rejection of Christ by the *whole* people, another that Mt 27:25, "His blood be on us and on our children" was not correctly interpreted in the discussion preceding the petition. This passage was prophetic: in it the blood of Christ was called down "non in damnationem, sed etiam in salutem" (not [only] in damnation but also in salvation). It was answered that it was highly unlikely that the crowd before the praetorium were thinking of either salvation or damnation in what they shouted. Furthermore, Pope John had deleted from the prayer of dedication of mankind to the Heart of Jesus an expression along these lines. Also, the crowd which had gathered in front of the Governor's palace could not possibly represent the whole people. If the evangelist spoke of the "whole people" in this connection, then it was certainly not in order to report a fact, but to express a *theologumenon*. The nation as a whole was bound to feel the temporal consequences of the preference of Barabbas to Jesus — the loss of sovereignty. This preference should, then, be allowed to stand as a presentiment of the course upon which Jerusalem would later embark, and which was to lead to its destruction. One had also to distinguish between the Jews as a "corporate person" and the Jews as a sum total of individuals. Preachers who spoke of "the Jews" always gave the impression that they had in mind every individual.

A further protest was made against the notion that the view of the Church as the new Israel involved total rejection of the old Israel. It was much more a question of a new beginning and a "schism" within the people of Israel. Again, a leading member was of the opinion that one should distinguish between Israel as the economy of salvation under the Old Covenant, and Israel as a people. This economy had not been rejected but was brought to perfection in the New Covenant. The people, however, no longer belonged to the order of the Old Covenant. So far as the way of salvation was concerned, they were in the same position as all other nations. This view was, however, seriously doubted by another member. It could hardly be said that the Jews were in the same spiritual situation as other peoples. The special promises given to them had made them a special people in God's eyes, not, certainly, because of their own merit but solely through God's predilection and his faithfulness.

With regard to the third petition, objection was made to the phrase that the reconciliation of the two Israels was an integral part of Christian hope. "Integral" meant that "our salvation depended on this hope". It could, of course, be said in reply to this that the objection was perfectly well-founded if one understood by the words "our salvation" that of individual Christians. It was, however, quite invalid if one thought of the salvation of the world, that is, the full revelation of salvation, its ultimate unfolding and the final ripening of the fruits of that love which was at work upon the Cross and in the Tomb.

An English member raised the question of whether one was not bound to say that hope for the salvation of all peoples formed part of the Christian expectation. ·Whereupon another Englishman replied that Scripture said nothing about the conversion of the English, but most definitely spoke of the final turning of the Jews to Christ. It was also pointed out that the petitions were always speaking of the Jews because that was the subject of the Declaration. The lack of mention of others by no means implied an absence of interest in their welfare. The way out of the difficulty seemed to have been found when it was pointed out that a Christian's faith was not complete if he considered chapters 9 to 11 of the Letter to the Romans to be unimportant. This, of course, was not to lay down in detail what the three chapters taught. Thus it was decided that the petition must be so formulated as to leave aside all matters of theological opinion. It was not admissible to make theses that were still under discussion among theologians into the subject of a petition.

In the fourth petition, only one alteration was suggested. One could not simply say — as in the original text — that the anti-Semite "sinned against faith". One should attach to this categorical statement a "maybe", a "perhaps", a "possibly", so that the petition would read something like this: "Hatred against the Jews is not only a sin against justice, love and the bond of brotherhood, but may well be a sin against faith." This suggestion was in fact not directly accepted, but the final sentence of the petition was re-drafted in a more concrete form, so that it no longer said that the anti-Semite sinned "against faith" but against "the humanity of Jesus Christ, who was of the house of David".

Curiously, the fifth petition unleashed a very lively debate. It was pointed out that the Carmelites celebrated a Mass in honour of the holy prophet Elias, and equally that the Office for Advent was devoted to remembrance of the patriarchs and prophets. It should also not be forgotten that in so important an hour as that of death itself, the Church commended the dying man to God, that he might have mercy on him as he did on the just of the Old Testament. God was implored, in a whole series of liturgical invocations, to set free the soul of his servant from the agony of death, as he had freed — to mention only the most important prayers — Enoch and Elias from death, Abraham from the superstition of Ur, Job from his sufferings, Lot from Sodom and the flames of its destruction, Moses from the power of Pharaoh, Susanna from false accusation, and Daniel out of the lions' den. Another comment referred to the holy women, who ought not to be overlooked in our petition.

A bishop noted for his frankness held that the introduction of a special feast of the just of the Old Covenant was unnecessary since, as he summarily declared, "the feasts of Our Lord, the Blessed Virgin and the apostles are all 'Jewish feasts'." It was also objected that the feasts of the Jerusalem Patriarchate were largely of a local nature, and that it was not the custom of the Church to extend to the whole Church feasts thus linked to a particular locality. Besides, the present time, with its liturgical renewal, was not a favourable one for the introduction of new feasts.

Concerning the sixth petition, reference was made to the applications from Jewish organizations dealing with anti-Jewish expressions in Catholic textbooks.

The question was raised whether it would not be advisable to prepare a document concerning the Jews for the Commission on Seminaries and Studies. Another speaker suggested the following formulation for this proposal: "Everything is to be removed from schoolbooks, which is not in agreement with the teaching of the Church set out above." One member believed that it would be difficult to introduce the post-Christian history of the Jewish people into the already over-loaded teaching syllabus. Another enquiry read as follows: "Is the study of all Jewish history really necessary and required for an understanding of the plan of salvation?" The answer given was that there were false legends and "traditions" concerning the Jews which in no way advanced our understanding of history and must therefore be uprooted from our consciousness. The conclusion was then, as so often, that the petition could not go into details, but must be kept in general terms such as, perhaps: "In theological formation, care must be taken over all points that concern Jewish history."

In connection with the seventh petition, one speaker asked for Mary to be mentioned, she being also of Jewish stock. It was replied that the petition cited a text from the Apostle Paul in which Mary was not mentioned. The discussion of this petition again ended with the conclusion that — although it was true that there were many paintings and sculptures that must be removed — the Council fathers, in this as in other cases, could not go into details.

The whole discussion petered out in the admission of one bishop that he was indeed well satisfied with the general advice given, but that he found the excessively long and detailed presentation of this teaching not serviceable. The petition should be drafted so as to refer only to the teaching of the Church, while the practical applications should be reserved for directives to be worked out after the Council.

At the end of November 1961 there took place a fresh plenary session in Ariccia, at which problems relating to the Jews again stood upon the agenda. The discussion was concerned mainly with two points. First, the difference between Israel "according to the flesh" and Israel "according to the Spirit". In connection with this it was maintained that the promises given to Israel were of a spiritual nature, and their fulfilment was to be sought in the spiritual realm of the Church. There was not only a continuity, but also a discontinuity between the Old and New Covenants: the Church was a new creation. The question was also raised of whether it was correct to speak of the Jews as our "separated brethren", as the expression related to people baptized in the name of Christ but not united with Rome. Peter Canisius, the first to use it, was referring to Protestants, while Leo XIII applied it to evangelical and Orthodox Christians.

A well-known theologian spoke at this point in order, he hoped, to speed the matter up a little. In dealing with the entire problem one had to bear in mind two possibilities: 1. A Council proclamation against anti-Semitism. Here the theological basis was simple and the need obvious. 2. A Council declaration on the dignity of man which would testify that the world was the work of God the

Creator and that the true dignity of man lay in his likeness to God. Within this framework there could be made a special reference to the Jews, at which the Arabs could not take offence.

In connection with the theological position of the Jews one must again distinguish between two factors. First, there was personal salvation, which sprang from the relationship to Christ given by faith. Here people were to be regarded as individuals and not as representatives of a nation. Second, there was the question of belonging to a people, that is to say, whether and how far adherence to the Christian faith resulted in a dissolution of existing ties of nationality. Apart from the questions already posed, theology was further confronted with the following problems: 1. What is the significance of the Old Testament? 2. What is the status of the Jewish people up to the end of the world? 3. What significance have the promises given to the Jews? All in all, a Council Declaration could certainly much more easily condemn anti-Semitism than discuss controversial questions of theology, let alone solve them.

The discussion then turned to the ways and means of putting into effect the Pope's commission. One member put forward for consideration the point that anti-Semitism was such a complex historical problem that the Council could hardly go into it. It would be far better to affirm positively, before the whole world, the rights of the Jewish people. This objection met with agreement — a document from the Secretariat could not possibly deal with the history of anti-Semitism. Its task was much more to establish what were the duties of Christians and their mode of conduct towards the Jews.

A leading bishop said that he had no objection to the proposed approach, but wished to point out that the questions concerning the Jews still remained open. The Jewish people had endured through the ages and our salvation sprang from them. But what place did they hold in God's plan today, and what was the true attitude of the Church to this whole group of questions? It had also to be considered whether this question should be linked with that of tolerance. (The theme of "tolerance" was later dropped, as the "toleration" of people of other beliefs represented a phase in ecclesiastical attitudes that was superseded by the Council and did not accord with the religious freedom the Council proclaimed.)

Another suggestion was to prepare texts that could be built into the schemas *De Ecclesia* and *De Libertate Religiosa*. It was stated in reply that this would be well and good but one must not forget to propose to the Council a text on the Jews, bearing the seal of the Secretariat for Unity.

After a lively discussion in which a wide range of members took part, two questions were put to the plenary meeting:

1. Whether a theoretical and practical decree concerning the Jews should be worked out. The question was answered affirmatively by some three-fifths of the members.

2. Whether supplementary proposals should be made to the theological com-

mission and the Secretariat's sub-commission, "On Tolerance and Religious Freedom". This was agreed to almost unanimously.

I have dealt so extensively — though far from exhaustively — with the three general meetings which put problems relating to the Jews on their agenda because in my opinion the welfare and growth of the Church demanded such a presentation. On the one side there have been critics who have asserted, in a fit of bad temper and curious illogicality, that the length of the Council proceedings and the ebb and flow of debate proved that the "Declaration on the Jews" did not come from the heart. This type of criticism, it is true, was not universal. There were also people like the American Rabbi Moses Sachs (Minneapolis) who valued the Council fathers' efforts and declared that it required courage on the Church's side to probe into her position, tackle the problem amid full publicity and to show concern for the feelings of non-Catholics.[42] It was, however, common enough for a proof of its injustice to seem necessary. On the other side, the attempt to veil the Council's history in silence is doomed to failure. Also, it causes nothing but harm and gives encouragement to rumour-mongers. While the Council was meeting, it was a necessity of life to keep the preparatory work confidential, but now it would look like secretiveness. If one does not present the stages of the Council in a sober and objective manner, then one is only helping those who know how to transform the tiniest fact into a sensation and thus give a false emphasis to every word and event.[43]

In a treatment intended not to be of purely ephemeral interest but to serve as the first serious and scholarly research into the history of the "Declaration on the Jews", it would be out of place to treat as secrets facts that have long since ceased to be so. Pope John would give the lie to any kind of "secretiveness", as when he declared to a series of journalists accredited to the Council press office that the Church had nothing to hide and called on them to testify to this.[44]

The invitation to openness given to the men and women of the press applies

[42] *Catholic Bulletin* (Catholic Bulletin Publishing, St. Paul, Minn.) (1965), p. 115.

[43] The most alarming examples of "disclosures" which, for want of better information, are accepted by many as authentic reports, are *Der Pilger* by M. Serafian and an article on the history of the declaration on the Jews entitled "Vatican II and the Jews" (*Commentary,* January 1965) by the same author, this time under the other pseudonym of F. E. Cartus. The article contains, among other items, a prayer ascribed to Pope John, though in fact invented, in which he speaks of centuries-old blindness of Christians, of a cloak which has covered their eyes so that they have ceased to see the beauty of the chosen people or to recognize in its countenance the features of our "privileged brothers". The Pope is also supposed to have said: "We realize now that we bear the mark of Cain on our brows. Through the centuries our brother Abel has lain in the blood which we have shed . . . Forgive us for crucifying you a second time in the flesh [of the Jews]." The prayer has too clear an aim in view to be authentic. Every sentence is the exact opposite of some typically anti-Jewish remark. This tendency is carried so far that, unlike the Declaration of the Council, which rejects the collective guilt of the Jews, a universal guilt is laid on Christians for the wrongs and sufferings inflicted on the Jews. Here truth and justice have given way to sensationalism.

[44] Cf. below, n. 51.

with still greater force to the historian. In the long run frankness can only be of advantage to the Church in general and the purposes of the Council in particular. Together with the impression of a rather courageous conception, by the Secretariat for Promoting Christian Unity, of a problem that was not a simple one, I should like to convey to the reader two further impressions, though of a quite different kind. I hope that my somewhat detailed account testifies to the Secretariat's extraordinary concern to protect free expression of opinion. There was great care taken that everyone should have his say. While this was much to the Church's credit, there was another factor arising out of the reports of the discussions which was not at all beneficial. The public and press were inclined to see the démarches of the Arab governments as the main obstacle to the Declaration on the Jews. It would be wrong to underestimate the constant and indeed growing pressure from the Near East powers. But there was another factor that worked against the Declaration to the same, if not to a greater, extent: the theologians were not prepared for it in their own minds.

From the time of Christian antiquity up to that of Vatican II, there had been hardly any development of the Church's teaching on the mystery of Jewish existence. Many other mysteries had been subjects of meditation in prayer and intense intellectual activity, for example the great mysteries of the triune God, of the person and office of Jesus, and of the Eucharist. There was a constant clarification of concepts and continual refinement of language in order to represent supernatural realities as exactly as possible in human speech. But nothing of this kind had occurred with regard to the relationship of Church and Synagogue. The problem was really the Cinderella of theology.

From the point of view of the inner need of the Jews, caused by Hitler and scarcely understood by the surrounding non-Jewish world — including ecclesiastical circles — the Declaration came somewhat late: some, grief-stricken, say, too late. But from the point of view of the theologians and their quite different needs, the Declaration came rather soon, one is tempted to say — too soon. It seems to me admissible to reconcile the two extremes and to say that the Declaration came just at the right time. It is still possible to prevent the desperation of the present generation of Jews from becoming a further link in a long chain. Equally, the Declaration could rouse theology from its centuries-long sleep. To a small extent it has already done so. From the point of view of scholarship, the theological situation is today more ripe than it has ever been. Advances in philology, especially the unexpected penetration into the spirit of the languages of the Near East, an exegesis enriched by the researches of form-criticism, a growing appreciation of rabbinic literature and, not least, the insights conveyed by modern psychology — these all enable theology to come to a proper understanding of the post-biblical role of Israel and to express it in a valid manner.

d) The first draft: *Decretum de Iudaeis*

In accordance with the expressed wish of the plenary meeting and the vote taken, as mentioned above, the first draft of a *Decretum de Iudaeis* was already worked out during the general assembly held in Ariccia from 27 November to 2 December. For this purpose, and for this special task only, the following collaborators were added to the sub-commission on Jewish questions: Bishop Émile De Smedt, Bruges; Mgr., now Bishop, Johannes Willebrands, General Secretary of the Secretariat; and Mgr. Francis Davis, Birmingham.

Before the end of the session, the sub-commission had already tabled the following text:

"The Church, the Bride of Christ, acknowledges with a heart full of gratitude that, according to God's mysterious saving decree, the beginnings of her faith and election are already to be found in the Israel of the patriarchs and prophets. Thus she acknowledges that all Christian believers — Sons of Abraham by faith (cf. Gal 3:7) — are included in his call and, likewise, that her salvation is prefigured in the deliverance of the chosen people out of Egypt, as in a sacramental sign. (Liturgy of the Easter Vigil.) And the Church, new creation in Christ as she is (cf. Eph 2:15), can never forget that she is the spiritual continuation of that people with whom, in his mercy and gracious condescension, God made the Old Covenant.

"The Church in fact believes that Christ, who 'is our peace', embraces Jews and Gentiles with one and the same love and that he made the two one (cf. Eph 2:14). She rejoices that the union of these two 'in one body' (Eph 2:16) proclaims the whole world's reconciliation in Christ. Even though the greater part of the Jewish people remained separated from Christ, it would nevertheless be an injustice to call this people accursed, since they are beloved for the sake of their fathers and the promises made to them (cf. Rom 11:28). The Church loves this people. From them sprang Christ the Lord, who reigns in glory in heaven; from them sprang the Virgin Mary, mother of all Christians; from them came the apostles, the pillars and bulwark of the Church (1 Tim 3:15).

"Furthermore, the Church believes in the union of the Jewish people with herself as an integral part of Christian hope. The Church awaits the return of this people with unshaken faith and deep longing. At the time of Christ's coming only "a remnant chosen by grace" (Rom 11:5), the first-born of the Church, accepted the (eternal) word. The Church believes, however, with the Apostle that at the time chosen by God, the fullness of the sons of Abraham according to the flesh will finally attain salvation (cf. Rom 11:12, 26). Their reception will be life from the dead (cf. Rom 11:15).

"As the Church, like a mother, condemns most severely injustices committed against innocent people everywhere, so she raises her voice in loud protest against everything done to the Jews, whether in the past or in our time. Whoever despises or persecutes this people does injury to the Catholic Church."

With the completion of the schema on the Jews the preliminary work was concluded. There seemed to be no obstacle to discussion of this draft by the Council fathers during the first session. Accordingly, at the appropriate time, the Secretariat submitted the draft to the Central Preparatory Commission, whose task it was to see all documents destined for the Council fathers. In the summer of 1962, however, there exploded a bomb that seemed to demolish all these plans.

e) The "Wardi Affair" — The first setback

On 12 June Dr. Nahum Goldmann, President of the World Jewish Congress, announced that it was intended to despatch Dr. Chaim Wardi, a senior official of the Ministry of Religious Affairs in the State of Israel, to Rome as representative of the Congress. Dr. Wardi worked in the Ministry of Religious Affairs as an expert in Christian matters. Also, he had attended as official observer the World Council of Churches' third Assembly at New Delhi in the late autumn of 1961, and similarly the pan-Orthodox Conference in Rhodes during September of the same year. In the eyes of the leaders of the Jewish Congress, these duties seemed to equip him particularly well for his new task, while for others they strengthened their suspicions of such an appointment.

As the Jewish Congress later explained, it was a question of putting into practice the basic principle of having representatives in the world's most important capitals. Dr. Wardi was to serve the Congress as adviser on Christian affairs that also concerned Jews, without there being intended for him any special role in relation to the Vatican or the Vatican Council.[45] A section of the world's press, however, depicted the matter as if the Jewish Congress had attempted on its own account to send a diplomatic representative to the Vatican or a semi-official observer to the Council. It is difficult to decide whether the misunderstanding was caused by the journalists' quest for sensation, or by the (perhaps not unintentional) lack of clarity on the part of the leaders of the Congress, or by both together.

The announcement aroused general disquiet. Jewish organizations expressed consternation at the proceedings of the Congress. In Roman circles people were taken aback, as diplomatic representatives were never nominated without previous consultation and because no religious community had established officials at the Council without invitation. As it appeared from press reports, the imprudence of the Jewish Congress in appointing a government official as its representative made it seem as if they were attempting an impermissible interference. The Arab governments saw their worst fears confirmed and let loose a storm of protest against the seemingly preferential treatment of the Jews. It seems that at one moment they assumed that the Jewish Congress's decision

---

[45] J. Herschcopf, "The Church and the Jews", *American Jewish Yearbook* (Jewish Publication Society) (1965), pp. 111–12.

had Vatican approval. And they certainly believed that the State of Israel stood behind the plan and was trying to force its way under false pretences into the Council or at least into its "antechambers".

The result of this unhappy affair was that the Central Preparatory Commission decided, at their last session in June 1962, to remove the draft decree on the Jews from the Council's agenda, not, as Cardinal Bea later explained, on account of the teaching it contained, but simply and solely because of the unfavourable political circumstances then prevailing.[46]

The Central Preparatory Commission's decision to remove the *Decretum de Iudaeis* from the agenda could easily have led to the question never being taken up again, so that the first draft would instead have awaited rediscovery by a historian in the Council's archives. Once the question had been brought up, however, it could no longer be ignored. Often it seemed that it was of such weight and force that it created a hearing for itself. In any event it found persistent advocates.

On the eve of the Council's opening the Chief Rabbi of Rome addressed a message to the Council fathers, which said:

"The Jews are fully conscious of the great significance of this Council and of the effects that it would have on the spiritual and political life of many nations. The Jews express their wish that this assembly of the Church will take decisions which may establish peace, mutual understanding, co-operation and tolerance among men. Judaism and Christianity are today conducting a common and difficult struggle for religious freedom, one of the fundamental means of expression in civilization.

"The Jews hope that the Council, in accordance with the shining example given by Pope John . . . will understand the need to eliminate all expressions still in use in the Liturgy and in religious instruction which continue even today to evoke mistrust and ill-will towards the Jews. Likewise the Jews expect that the Council fathers will solemnly and without ambiguity condemn all forms of anti-Semitism and also those people who make use of Christian teaching to justify their hostile feelings and actions against the Jewish people and the Jewish religion."[47]

A further advocate in the matter was Mgr. Arceo Méndez, Bishop of Cuernavaca, Mexico, who broached the problem of Judaeo-Christian relations in the Council chamber at the beginning of December 1962. He wanted to know "whether pastors of souls, and the faithful, are following the example of the Pope and showing real love towards the children of our common father, Abraham, or whether they are not rather displaying an unconscious anti-Semitism."[48]

By far the most powerful advocate was Cardinal Bea. So convincing was his intervention that he should really be called the father of the Declaration on the

[46] *Relatio,* November 1963.
[47] *Neue Zürcher Zeitung,* 12 December 1962; reprinted in *HK* 17 (1962), p. 92.
[48] H. Fesquet, *Le Journal du Concile,* ed. by R. Morel (1966), p. 142 (7 December 1962).

Jews. He spoke with sympathy of the anxiety of Christians of the Near East who feared for their religious life. He held that, to judge from all appearances, this alarm was deliberately stimulated from a certain quarter. It would be bad policy to give way to the pressure of the opponents. If one stood firm against this pressure, it would probably crumble into nothing.

In consequence of what was called at that time the "Wardi Affair", he applied direct to Pope John with the request that he decide what was to be done. He reminded him in a memorandum that the Secretariat had striven, on the basis of a special mandate, to throw light upon the question of the bond between the Church and the Jewish people, and also that it had drafted a decree which declared, among other things, that the Jewish people, although separated from Christ, were not to be regarded as accursed by God, but were on the contrary exceedingly loved by him and must therefore be loved by the Church also.

He further recalled that the draft had been put before the last session of the Central Preparatory Commission on account of a special papal instruction, but had then been removed from the agenda because of the action of the World Jewish Congress and the excitement caused by the often exaggerated press reports. One had to consider whether reasons which were understandable at the time of the initial agitation still remained valid and were sufficient to remove the problem altogether from the Council's programme. He indicated judiciously that there were important reasons in favour of taking up the theme again:

This was demanded by the bond of brotherhood between Christians and Jews, which was far deeper than the bond which united all men.

Equally, the incredible and appalling crimes of National Socialism against six million Jews — atrocities for which the ground had been prepared by an extensive propaganda machine — required a purification of spirit and conscience.

In this connection one had also to acknowledge that even Catholic preachers had not always been inspired by the spirit of Jesus in their presentation of the Lord's passion. All too often the Jewish people as such, that is, all generations since Christ, had been accused of deicide and depicted as accursed by God. There was a real need for inner renewal here.

Finally, we should be spurred on by the decisive attitude of the World Council of Churches, which adopted a resolution on anti-Semitism on 3 December 1961, on the occasion of its third general assembly in New Delhi. The resolution began by repeating the stand taken by the first assembly of the World Council in the year 1948 in Amsterdam:

"We call upon all the Churches we represent to denounce anti-Semitism, no matter what its origin, as absolutely irreconcilable with the profession and practice of the Christian faith. Anti-Semitism is a sin against God and man. Only as we give convincing evidence to our Jewish neighbours that we seek for them the common rights and dignities which God wills for his children, can we come to such a meeting with them as would make it possible to share with them the best which God has given us in Christ."

The resolution then continued as follows:

"The (third) Assembly renews this plea in view of the fact that situations continue to exist in which Jews are subject to discrimination and even persecution. The Assembly urges its member Churches to do all in their power to resist every form of anti-Semitism. In Christian teaching the historic events which led to the Crucifixion should not be so presented as to fasten upon the Jewish people of today responsibilities which belong to our corporate humanity, not to one race or community. Jews were the first to accept Jesus, and Jews are not the only ones who do not yet recognize him."[49]

The question of whether the fathers could take upon themselves the responsibility of bringing new suffering down upon the Catholics of the Near East, was countered by the Cardinal with another question. Was it permissible to endanger the renewal of the whole Church and to leave out of account the problem of the Jews for reasons which were weighty in themselves, but were nevertheless conditioned and limited by temporary factors, especially if the arguments already discussed were valid?

The Cardinal made concrete proposals and summed up by saying that the Council should take its stand with apostolic frankness, and overcome obstacles fearlessly, though also with deliberation. It was necessary, and indeed absolutely urgent, that the Council discuss the matter.[50]

On 13 December 1962 Pope John replied with a short personal note to the Council, in which he said: "We have read Cardinal Bea's memorandum with care and entirely share his opinion that a profound responsibility requires our intervention." The Pope went on to say that the words: "His blood be on us and on our children" (Mt 27:25) did not relieve any believer of the duty laid upon him to work for the salvation of all the children of Abraham and similarly, that of every other being living upon this earth. He ended with the prayer from the Te Deum: "Help us, then, we entreat thee; help thy servants whom thou hast ransomed with thy precious blood."

The second part of the Pope's note at first makes a disconcerting impression. In my opinion it can only be understood if it is assumed that Pope John knew very well that certain circles wanted to use the difficulties in the Near East, and also the obscurity of some passages in Scripture, to persuade the Council to evade its responsibility at this point. Moreover, the prayer with which the Pope sealed his agreement with Cardinal Bea's memorandum shows that for him, the most human of all Popes, the Declaration on the Jews was not only a matter of the heart but also an act of faith and a work of piety.

[49] The exact text of this and other documents of the New Delhi Assembly are to be found in W. A. Visser 't Hooft, ed., *New Delhi Report. Third Assembly of the World Council of Churches* (1961).
[50] According to an unpublished memorandum to which the Cardinal himself referred at the end of his *relatio* of 18 November 1963. Cf. A. Bea, *The Church and the Jewish People* (1966), p. 159.

Public opinion, formed and in many ways guided by the press, proved unexpectedly helpful to the Declaration. It can be asserted without exaggeration that the efforts made on behalf of the Declaration, as in other Council matters, would have come to nothing, had not the press repeatedly directed the eyes of the world to them. The regular reports in the great daily newspapers of the Arab intrigues and attempted obstruction not only pilloried these activities but also torpedoed them. One can even go further and say: Had the Arabs not attempted, in various ways, to sabotage the Declaration, and had the Press not repeatedly unmasked these intrigues, and indeed repudiated them with indignation, the effect of the Declaration would have been significantly less than it was. Had the Declaration been accepted without further ado at the time of the first session, then it might have been forgotten long ago. The objections and attempts at intimidation by the Near East Governments and the consequent reverberations in the press made apparent the extraordinary importance of the Declaration and carried its proclamation to the uttermost ends of the earth.

On the other hand it must also be said, unfortunately, that the communications media did perceptible damage to the Declaration and to other plans of the Council as well. Certain misinterpretations have to be attributed to the journalists. Hard-pressed editors, nourishing their readers' eagerness for "sensation", composed headlines such as "Acquittal of the Jews by the Council" and "Church absolves Jews from guilt of Crucifixion". Here the emphasis of the Declaration is completely distorted. The Council's intention — to restore the Pauline view of the Jewish people and to put an end to certain interpretations of Scripture which contradicted its true meaning — is misunderstood in such a way that the humble revision of centuries-old stereotypes is transformed into a condescending gesture. If Christians in earlier times were so arrogant as to think that they were chosen by God to punish the Jewish people for their refusal of belief, now there is attributed to the Council the perhaps even more offensive arrogance of claiming for itself alone God's prerogative of forgiveness. The Church appears as a paragon of presumption, as she seeks to forgive a guilt which she at the same time teaches does not exist.

Despite John XXIII's call for "tact and discretion", "understanding and accuracy",[51] correspondents of major newspapers treated rumours as proven facts and their own guesses and constructions as if they were the firmly-based results of careful investigation. Journalists would doubtless reply that they were often forced to make guesses because full information was withheld from them. That is true. Nevertheless it must be said that some — to quote John XXIII again — "were more concerned about the speed than the accuracy of reporting", and that they were more interested in "sensations" than in truth.

To this category belongs the "Weigel incident". At the end of June 1963 the distinguished ecumenist, Fr. Gustav Weigel, S. J., spoke at the meeting of an

---

[51] Audience of 13 October 1963: F. Anderson, ed., *Council Daybook,* I, pp. 34, 36.

umbrella organization of Jewish associations, the National Community Relations Advisory Council, at Atlantic City, U.S.A., on a subject not directly connected with the Declaration. During the discussion that followed he was caught off-guard by a *New York Times* reporter, who asked what was the position concerning the condemnation of anti-Semitism by the Council. As Weigel himself later explained, he replied without sufficient reflection that such a denunciation had indeed been prepared, but that it had not been discussed during the first session, and probably would not be during the second, because of the opposition of the Arab states, who had interpreted a purely moral pronouncement as a declaration of political support for the State of Israel. At some points this answer did not correspond to the facts. To take only two: A mere condemnation of hatred of the Jews was never planned; also, Fr. Weigel was not aware of the most recent state of affairs, as he had not been present at the latest sitting of the Secretariat. His forecast was, however, blazoned forth to the world, and everywhere created great uneasiness. It was even feared that his answer would make the situation yet more difficult. This, thank God, did not happen. In fact, it even seems that this sensational report aroused men's consciences. Fr. Weigel frequently indicated that he deeply regretted his overhasty and ill-considered reply. All the same, he could not help seeing the favourable consequences of his "indiscretion".[52] At a meeting of the Secretariat during the second session we happened to sit next to each other. When he saw how well things were going, he went so far as to take some small credit for it upon himself and whispered in my ear that his thoughtlessness had proved "a blessing in disguise".

With this recollection I have somewhat anticipated the course of events in the Council. Cardinal Bea, after Pope John had assured him of his full agreement, took the necessary steps to bring the Declaration once more before the Co-ordinating Commission and thus into the Council *aula*. In his judgment the one great chance of achieving this lay in incorporating the Declaration in the schema on Ecumenism. At his suggestion there was inserted in front of the Declaration on the Jews a cautious reference to all other religions, reading as follows: "In dealing with the basic principles of Catholic Ecumenism, we do not wish to pass over in silence the fact that these principles are also to be applied, with due regard to the given situation, in dialogues and in acts of co-operation with those who are not Christians, but also honour God or, at least, impelled by God's will, try according to their conscience to keep the moral law implanted in human nature. This applies particularly to the Jews, who are indeed linked to the Church in a special degree."[53]

[52] *New York Times,* 1 July 1963; *The Advocate* (Newark, N. J.), 4 July 1963, interview with the present author concerning G. Weigel's statements.
[53] *Freiburger Rundbrief,* 16–17, nos. 61–64 (July 1965), p. 5; cf. also W. P. Eckert and E. L. Ehrlich, *op. cit.,* pp. 428 f.

f) The second draft: Chapter IV of the schema on Ecumenism

In addition to this modest introduction certain other changes were made in the text. Some were purely stylistic. The most important was certainly an additional passage rebutting the charge of deicide and warning catechists and preachers not to fall into an anti-Semitic exposition of the Passion story. This passage was inserted into the second draft between the statement establishing that the Jews were not a people accursed by God, but remained always dear to him, and the statement declaring that the Church kept it always in mind that her risen Lord was of Jewish origin, as were his Virgin Mother and his apostles, the pillars of the Church. The insertion read as follows: "(The chosen people cannot without injustice) be termed a deicidal race, as the Lord has expiated through his suffering and death the sins of all men — the (actual) causes of (his) Passion and (his) dying (cf. Lk 23:24; Acts 3:17; 1 Cor 2:8). His death was certainly not brought about by the whole people living at that time, much less by those of today. Priests must therefore take care that in teaching or sermons they say nothing that could create hatred of the Jews or contempt for them in the hearts of those listening."

In place of the last two paragraphs in the first draft the conclusion now read as follows: "As the Church shares with the Synagogue so great a common heritage, this holy Synod wishes expressly to demand and commend the mutual understanding and respect that is attained by theological studies and brotherly conversations. Further, just as the Church repudiates injustices committed against human beings everywhere, so similarly, and indeed even more, she deplores and condemns, in the spirit of a mother, the outbreaks of hatred and the persecutions of which the Jews have been the victims, in the past and in our own time."[54]

Although the new draft — as Chapter IV of the Decree on Ecumenism — was approved at the Secretariat's session of 25 February to 2 March 1963 and was later handed over to the Co-ordinating Commission, it was not sent in to the Council fathers, together with the first three chapters of the schema, before the Council opened, but was issued only on 8 November 1963, that is, two months after the second session had opened. The no less embattled Declaration on Religious Freedom, now Chapter V of the schema on Ecumenism, was delivered to the fathers only on 16 November of the same year. This delay, a consequence of the attitude prevailing in leading Council circles, was very regrettable, as it cut down the time available for study and discussion, but it was not able to stop progress in these two matters.

The impossibility of silencing the desire for clarification of the relation of Church and Synagogue was due also to the fact that within the first week of the second session bishops had stood up in the *aula* to urge that this theme be dealt

---

[54] The Latin text of the second version and a translation which differs somewhat from the one used here can be found in Eckert and Ehrlich, *op. cit.,* pp. 428 f.

with.[55] On 2 October 1963 Bishop Johannes van Dodewaard (Harlem) recommended, in the name of the Dutch hierarchy, that the schema on the Church give renewed expression to the close bond between the Church and the Jewish people. In an anticipation of the text, he depicted the children of Abraham as people who belonged in their God-given nature to the true olive tree (Rom 11:24) and for the sake of their fathers were especially dear to God. Whereas in the language that prevailed before the Council, the Jews were termed "perfidi" — "unbelievers" — and reckoned among the "infideles", Bishop van Dodewaard called them "populus ille fidelis" (that believing [or faithful] people). As he himself later declared, he saw beyond the people's unbelief in Christ, and the abandonment of the traditions of their fathers by many of them today, to their vocation as the people of faith. Above all, he saw in them the people to whom God had pledged his unchanging troth. Whatever Israel's shortcomings or failures might be, God was the faithful shepherd of this people.

On 3 October 1963 Archbishop (now Cardinal) Franz Šeper (Zagreb) asked that in the treatment of the mystery of the Church the place occupied by the chosen people in God's plan of salvation should be described as fully and precisely as possible. He stressed that Israel was not rejected by God and shared with the Church a common heritage. "The Jews have far more in common with the Church than all other peoples." The Archbishop has himself explained that, in order not to overrun the prescribed time-limit for speeches, he left unspoken the final sentence of his prepared text: "Nemo est qui non viderit populi Israelitici relationem erga Ecclesiam omnino specialem esse, cum nullo populo communam." (Anyone can see that the relationship of the people of Israel to the Church is a quite special one, unlike that of any other people.)

At the first possible moment, on 18 November, the leaders of the Eastern Churches rose up in a solid phalanx against Chapter IV. As this was not an organized discussion, those friendly to the cause of Chapter IV had hardly any say — they were waiting for the day reserved for statements on this matter. The opposition, however, made use of the general debate on the schema on Ecumenism to proclaim their rejection of this chapter. They fell into two groups: those who wished to give way to the pressure of the Arab governments, and others who in fact supported the statement as such but thought it a mistake to include it in the schema on Ecumenism.

Cardinal Tappouni, Patriarch of the Syriac rite at Antioch, objected to treating the questions of the Jews and of religious freedom together with that of Christian unity. He acknowledged that those who had worked for the text were guided by supernatural motives, but the current political situation was such that it could only too easily be misunderstood. In countries hostile to the Jews, Chapter IV would do the Christian Church serious harm.

---

[55] Unless stated otherwise, the official daily resumés of the various press offices were used for these and all the other interventions.

The Coptic Patriarch, Stefanos I of Alexandria, spoke in the same vein as Cardinal Tappouni. In a discussion of Christian unity it was completely out of place to devote a whole chapter to the Jews. Furthermore, such a chapter was unnecessary, since at the time of the (National Socialist) persecution of the Jews, the Church had given clear proof of her attitude. In other cases measures that might make the Church's position in various countries more difficult had been avoided. Why not here also? The difficulties under which the Church was living in the Near East were already great enough without the addition of a gratuitous provocation.

The Melchite Patriarch of Antioch, Maximos IV, was of exactly the same opinion as the previous speakers: "Ecumenism is the striving for reunion of the entire Christian family, that is, the reconciliation of all who are baptized in Christ. It is a question, therefore, of an intimate family matter. But if this is so, then it does not involve non-Christians." It was impossible to understand what the Jews could expect from a schema on Christian Ecumenism. If one really wished to speak of the Jews at the Council, that could be done either in the schema on the Church or in that of the Church in the Modern World.

Antoine Wenger, AA, in his account of the second session, heads the appropriate passage as follows: "When politics held theology in chains". He continues: "The unity of the three Patriarchs living in Arab countries was all the more remarkable as Patriarch Maximos did not usually agree with the other two in theological matters."[56]

On 19 November 1963 these three were joined by the Latin Patriarch of Jerusalem, Alberto Gori, and the Armenian Patriarch of Cilicia, Peter XVI. The former approved of the Council taking an interest in non-Christians, but maintained that it should mention either all non-Christian religions or none. Any favouring of the Jews would endanger Christian minorities in many countries. The Armenian Patriarch also held that the chapter on the Jews fell outside this framework. To quote Fr. Wenger again: "On hearing these interventions, we felt uneasy. It seemed to us that from a theological point of view, the schema on Ecumenism provided the natural context in which to set the Jewish question."[57]

There were of course also speakers, such as Cardinal Léger of Montreal (Canada) who welcomed statements on the Jews and religious freedom, but wanted these themes to be discussed in a different context. A special position was taken up by Cardinal Ruffini of Palermo, who declared as early as the first day that if one really wished to speak of the Jews, then one should also deal with other religions whose adherents were less hostile to the Church than the Jews.[58]

At first the objection of those who reacted against the inclusion of the Jewish question and that of religious freedom in the schema on Ecumenism seemed an obvious one. It is, however, noteworthy that theologically trained commen-

---

[56] A. Wenger, *Vatican II, Chronique de la Deuxième Session* (1964), p. 175.
[57] *Ibid.*, p. 175.
[58] Cf. *Council Daybook,* I, p. 271.

tators, like Fr. Wenger, and the experts whose special field was the relation of Church and Synagogue, approved the inclusion of the draft concerning the proper attitude towards the Jews in the schema on Ecumenism — the latter although they knew that the original reason for this was not theological but arose purely out of practical considerations of Council politics.

Thus I myself, when asked by the press why the Declaration on the Jews should not rather be attached to the expected schema on the Church in the Modern World explained that "human relations exist on various levels . . . The relation of Christians and Jews forms no exception. Its most obvious element is the social one. In the society of today Christians and Jews live side by side. They are neighbours . . . Their social proximity and equality as citizens — both characteristics of a pluralistic world — are without doubt of the greatest importance. Nevertheless it is not the task of an Ecumenical Council to discuss the constitutional privileges of Jews and Christians and their respective place in the political sphere.

"A much more basic and fundamental element in social and political relations between Jews and Christians is their personal nature. Every Christian, every Jew, is a person, and that means more than merely a member of a group . . . he is God's special creation in the flesh, unique and unrepeatable. Few things have to be so much emphasized today as the respect due to each single human being . . . He possesses a dignity that has no equivalent among the other living things on this earth. For this reason the Council, at the beginning of its first session, proclaimed the exalted status of each man in a solemn 'message to mankind'.

"The relation of Christians and Jews has, however, another, deeper dimension that is peculiar to it: a dimension rooted, not in their common human nature or nationality, but in a history in which both have taken part in a mysterious way — the history of salvation.

"Abraham, the father of the Jewish people, is at the same time the father of all who believe in the living God, in the 'goodness and loving kindness of God our Saviour' revealed to us in Jesus Christ (Tit 3:4). 'Mightiest Abraham, father of our faith', as the Roman liturgy calls him. All the patriarchs, prophets and psalmists, all the just of the Old Covenant, but also its sinners, are the spiritual forerunners of Christians. Thus it comes about that the world's salvation is most intimately linked to the majesty of Israel and also to its failure, to its election and also to its 'trespass'" (Rom 11:11).[59]

This dimension lies close to the ecumenical vision of the mystery of Israel, and justified the inclusion of the Declaration on the Jews.

Gregory Baum, O.S.A., also defended the schema on Ecumenism as the appropriate framework for the Declaration in the daily conference at the American Press Office. He said:

[59] Press office, *Handreichungen in deutscher Sprache*, 28, pp. 2/3 (20 November 1963).

. 1. We believe that the Church has her roots in the old Israel. To understand the mystery of the Church one must turn to Israel. The Church is supported by Israel, the true olive tree.

2. The division of the Jewish people into those who accepted Jesus as Messiah and those who did not accept him is a symbol of all the subsequent divisions within Christianity.

3. Christians believe that Israel is part of the eschatological dimension of the Church, in accordance with the saying of St. Paul who teaches that the Church and Israel will be a single people.[60]

In *The Ecumenist* Gregory Baum went deeper and developed these brief points into a vivid presentation of the problem.[61]

Those who approved the new framework for the Declaration also included René Laurentin, theologically one of the best-schooled commentators, who expressed himself as follows:

"It is said 'Ecumenism is the union of Christians. Jews are not Christians. Therefore they are not included in Ecumenism'.

"Now it is certainly true that Israel's position is not the same as that of the Orthodox and the Protestants, who explicitly profess their faith in Christ. Israel's position is unique ... It is important to recall certain fundamental facts:

"1. We have common roots or, to put it more exactly, the same roots as Israel:

"Common writings — the whole Old Testament which speaks of Christ. 'He wrote of me', said Jesus of Moses (Jn 5:46. Cf. 5:39; 8:58; 12:41; etc.).

"A common history — the whole history before Christ, but not that alone. Jesus lived within Judaism and its laws. He sought out 'the lost sheep of the house of Israel' (Mt 15:24). The Virgin Mary, the Twelve, and the principal witnesses to the faith of the first Christian generation all belonged to the Jewish people. At its beginnings the Church lived within the framework of Judaism. The problem of baptizing Gentiles seems to have arisen only some years later (Acts 11:19). For hundreds of years Jews (including proselytes) had a special position in this respect, corresponding to the practice recorded in Acts 8:36–38 and 9:18. They were regarded as fit for immediate baptism the moment they acknowledged Jesus Christ. Adherence to Judaism was equivalent to the catechumenate.

"One could accordingly speak of common roots in a quite special sense: 'It is not you that support the root but the root that supports you', says St. Paul to the community that had arisen among the Gentiles (Rom 11:18). Indeed it is not enough to speak of a root, it is much more a question of a common stem. According to St. Paul, Israel is still 'the true olive tree' into which we were grafted

---

[60] *Council Daybook,* I, p. 272.
[61] February/March 1963, pp. 37f.

'contrary to nature'. The 'natural branches' are summoned to return to life (Rom 11:17–25).

"2. There is a unity of goal and predestination. Israel is still the chosen people and 'all Israel will be saved' (Rom 11:26, 32, etc.).

"3. The split between Israel and the Church — which is, in any case, only partial — is nothing but a détour, an unnatural situation which at the deepest level forms part of the mystery of salvation and contributes to its realization (see St. Paul: Rom 11:14, 18–22, 30–31).

"4. There is a deep solidarity and even a certain unity between Israel and the Church in their expectation of union at the end of time. Christ has made Jews and Gentiles one 'and has broken down the dividing wall of hostility . . . that he might create in himself one new man in place of the two' (Eph 2:14–15).

"If it is the intention of Ecumenism to create a universal community based on the fullness of Christian values, then it cannot leave out of account the vocation of Israel — a vocation included so unambiguously within that of the Church that St. Paul cannot imagine the Church's eschatological fulfilment without Israel."[62]

So far as I know, the ecumenical theologian[63] who first dealt in detail with "Israel as an ecumenical problem" was Bernard Lambert, OP. He wrote:

"Judaism remains outside the Church: yet it never ceases to act on and in the Church. It acts in the Church through the Jewish origins of Christianity. It acts on the Church in virtue of a kind of shared destiny that brings Jews and Christians together at all the great crossroads of history. The Jew cannot lose sight of the Christian, the Christian cannot ignore the Jew. There is something very strange that both brings us together and separates us, as if neither of us can quite pass the other. The relations between us are governed by an odd alternation of rejection and acceptance.

"The Gospel gives the Christian the advantage of being able to guess at the true complementarity of these two parts that both seek and flee from each other. It is revealed to us in the great discourse of our Lord after the Last Supper, when Jesus prayed to his Father to bless the oneness of his Church. The literal sense of the passage shows that it is primarily and above all concerned with the oneness of Jews and Gentiles in Christ, which is given elsewhere as the motive for the Incarnation (Jn 11:52) and as the great secret hidden from older generations (Gal 4:28). In God's plan, Jews and Gentiles are seen as one: there is one election, one predestination, one vocation, one covenant, one glorification. And

[62] R. Laurentin, *Bilan de la Deuxième Session* (1964), p. 150.

[63] By an "ecumenical theologian" in this context I mean one who specializes in ecumenism, as distinct from those who limit their work to the relations between the Church and Israel. With regard to the latter, see (among others): K. Thieme, "Der ökumenische Aspekt der christlich-jüdischen Begegnung", *Freiburger Rundbrief,* 8, no. 29/32 (October 1955), p. 9; P. Démann, "Israël et l'Unité de l'Église", *Cahiers Sioniens,* 7, 1 (March 1953); C. F. Pauwels, O. P., "Ist das Mysterium Israels eine ökumenische Frage?", *Freiburger Rundbrief,* 12, nos. 45–48 (28 December 1959).

with the birth of the Church, the great design of the Lord has taken actual form. Jews and Gentiles have become one . . .

"So the problem of Israel is not extra-ecumenical. It concerns the reconciliation of the two parts of the *Oikoumene:* the Jews and the Gentiles. For measured by God's plan for man's salvation, this is the fundamental division of mankind: on the one hand, the Jewish people, the people of the covenant; and on the other, the pagans, the Gentiles. Neither the Old Testament nor the New gives us any other division of human society, in the economy of salvation: on one side, so very few — yet from them comes salvation; on the other, the mass of humanity. The question is not one of numbers, but of election and new birth. Abraham was chosen to be the father of all believers, the starting-point of the new humanity moving forward in faith to the promised land, gathering in as many Gentile peoples as it pleased God to lead that way. The covenant of nature was the root of the covenant of grace . . .

". . . An ecumenism which limited itself simply to the relations between Christians would be in principle condemned never to succeed, because it would be established on too narrow a foundation."[64]

There are two reasons why I have described in such detail, in this historical retrospect, the views of those who regard the relation of Church and Synagogue as an ecumenical, and indeed *the* ecumenical, problem. First, because these views show how much people's minds were influenced at that time by this question which might seem to be only one of method. And second, because they point the way for the future. For many people the question is still undecided. If one applies to the discussion of this question, as the only guide-line, the restrictive definition given at the beginning of the Decree on Ecumenism: "unitatis redintegratio inter universos Christianos" (the recovery of the unity of all Christians), then one will of course have to decide against the ideas put forward here.

Despite the help of theologians and journalists, and the support of bishops and bishops' conferences for the thesis it contained, Chapter IV of the schema on Ecumenism was denied success. Already on the second day of the general debate (20 November 1963), Cardinal Meyer of Chicago applauded the schema. He found especially praiseworthy the inclusion of Chapters IV and V. It was true there might be differences of opinion as to whether these two chapters were correctly placed, but it was the wish of many of the fathers, especially of those from North America, that the schema should here and now be dealt with as it stood.

Bishop Jelmini of Lugano, in the name of all the Swiss bishops, expressed his joy that the Church could be seen in this schema, not as a closed community, but

---

[64] B. Lambert, *Ecumenism. Theology and History* (1967), pp. 446–8. This first appeared in Paris in 1962 as the fruit of many years of study and discussion at the headquarters of the World Council of Churches in Geneva and at the Ecumenical Institute at Bossey under the title *Le Problème Œcuménique.*

as one open to the world. He thought it desirable to speak here not only about the Jews, but also about the adherents of Islam, and even about unbelievers. A succession of bishops greeted the schema as "an event, truly a gift of God's grace". This latter description came from the Mexican Bishop Méndez, who expressly emphasized the bond between the Jews and the Church in salvation history, and declared — no doubt in deliberate reference to the opposite opinion of the Near Eastern bishops: "It is extremely opportune to condemn anti-Semitism."[65]

All these interventions seemed to be of no avail. Although on 21 November 1963 the Council's Secretary-General, Archbishop Felici, offered the prospect of an early discussion ("in the immediate future"), none took place. To overcome the deadlock that seemed to have been reached, Bishop Helmsing (Kansas City) concluded his speech of 29 November concerning Chapters II and III of the schema with an urgent demand that in the few remaining days at their disposal the Council fathers proceed to a decisive vote on Chapters IV and V. "He thus gave expression to the growing concern and indeed anger of many Council fathers lest (the total silence concerning any discussion) might prove to be a well-planned attempt to delay a decision on these chapters and to bring the session to an end without their coming to the promised vote."[66] This fear was only too justified. The Council closed on 4 December without having taken the procedural vote on whether to accept or reject a given draft as a basis for discussion. Only such a vote would have made the two chapters into an unalterable part of the Council proceedings and have thus withdrawn them from the competence of the Co-ordinating Commission.

The discussion did not take place. At one point, when the possibility of such a failure had already to be taken into account, Cardinal Bea was, curiously, given the opportunity to expound Chapter IV of the schema on Ecumenism to the fathers. In his "plea" — in my opinion this is the most appropriate rendering for the type of statement called in the language of the Council *relatio* — the Cardinal began by pointing out that this chapter dealt, of course, with a question that was not political but religious. He said, *inter alia:* "The aim of this very brief decree is to call to the attention of Christ's faithful these truths concerning the Jews which are affirmed by the apostle and contained in the deposit of faith, and to do this so clearly that in dealing with the children of that people the faithful will act in no other way than did Christ the Lord and his apostles Peter and Paul."[67] Excellent as is the reference to the two apostles, who both stress that the people and their rulers had "acted in ignorance" during Christ's Passion (Acts 3:17; 13:27), the reference in this connection to our Lord's prayer on the Cross (Lk 23:34) is questionable.[68]

It was hardly the Jewish people for whom our Lord asked forgiveness here,

---

[65] Fesquet, *op. cit.,* p. 351.   [66] *Council Daybook,* I, p. 316.
[67] A. Bea, *op. cit.,* p. 156.   [68] *Ibid.*

but only those immediately concerned with the Crucifixion: that is, the high priests, the Governor, the soldiers and those who mocked. If the Lord's prayer for forgiveness for his tormentors is mentioned in connection with this issue in the Council discussion, then the impression could easily arise that Christians are called upon to display mercy towards the Jews, whereas what the Christian world in fact owes to Jewry and Judaism is, in the first place, justice. The Cardinal, however, ended his plea with these words: "For our purpose, of much more importance, in fact simply decisive, is the example of burning charity of the Lord himself on the cross, praying: 'Father, forgive them, for they know not what they do'. That is the example to be imitated by the Church, the Bride of Christ. That is the road to be followed by her. This is what the schema proposed by us intends to foster and promote."[69]

With the greatest respect for the Cardinal and his wisdom and goodness, I must say that this urgent request to the Council to imitate our Lord in its conduct towards the Jewish people, and to teach others to do likewise, supplied a possible starting-point for the misconception that the Council had, so to say, absolved the Jewish people from the guilt of the Crucifixion. A distinguished observer from the Reformed Churches, in a public discussion with me, misinterpreted this passage of the Cardinal's speech to mean that the Church was here presuming to forgive the Jews. This, of course, is a misunderstanding of the Cardinal's intention. His plea meant no more and no less than that the cause of Chapter IV represented not only the legacy of Pope John XXIII but also, and above all, the will of Christ.

The question of why it was so necessary to drive home yet again the truths set out in the draft was answered by the Cardinal, according to Fesquet, as follows: "Because they have been forgotten, and because there has been an old and extremely powerful anti-Semitic tradition in the Church, and because hundreds of thousands of Jews were executed by the Nazis."[70] In fact, however, the Cardinal's answer to this question, which he had himself posed, was that "some decades ago anti-Semitism, as it is called, was prevalent in various regions and in a particularly violent and criminal form, especially in Germany under the rule of National Socialism, which through hatred for the Jews committed frightful crimes, extirpating several million of Jewish people — we need not at the moment seek the exact number. Moreover, accompanying and assisting this whole activity was a most powerful and effective 'propaganda' as it is called, against the Jews."[71] The Cardinal went on to say that this propaganda might well have had a significant effect upon Catholic Christians also, especially as it often purported to draw its arguments from the New Testament and from Church history. He pointed out that the Declaration was principally concerned with the proper understanding of Scripture and a true interpretation

[69] *Ibid.*, p. 159. [70] Fesquet, *op. cit.*, p. 346.
[71] Bea, *op. cit.*, p. 157.

of the intentions of the Apostles and Evangelists, and thus with the rebirth of the Church.

The following sentence is certainly one of the most impressive and illuminating of the whole speech: "Since the Church in this Council is striving to renew itself by 'seeking again the features of its most fervent youth' as John XXIII of venerable memory said, it seems imperative to take up this question."[72] The quotation from Pope John comes from his address of 14 November 1960. In the original it reads: "ricercarne le tracce della giovinezza più fervorosa".[73] Following the will of John XXIII the Church sought, in the Declaration on the Jews as in the Council as a whole, to rediscover the traces of her new-born zeal, so that her countenance might again become as fresh and pure as in the days of her first love (cf. Rev 2:4).

g) The pilgrimage to the Holy Land

From all evidence available it seems that discussion of Chapter IV was postponed in order, on the one hand, not to make impossible Paul VI's pilgrimage to the Holy Land, and, on the other, because it was hoped that the pilgrimage might itself help to expedite the matter. The idea of such a pilgrimage, a return to the "cradle of Christianity",[74] was so brilliant that the postponement of the debate seems, in these circumstances, to have been fully justified. If inspiration were equivalent to success in this world, then the journey of 4 to 6 January 1964 would surely have cleared the way for the Declaration on the Jews. On 6 January the Pope declared, in Bethlehem, that the "mission of Christendom was one of friendship among peoples, of understanding, of encouragement, of progress, of exaltation and, we repeat, of salvation."[75]

Thus Paul VI — as *Le Monde* acknowledged with respect on 7 January 1964 — "was the first to dare to speak of peace on both sides of the Israel-Arab border". In the same spirit he quoted to King Hussein of Jordan, on 4 January, the words of the Psalm which St. Peter had already made his own (1 Pet 3:10–11): "He that would love life and see good days, let him keep his tongue from evil and his lips from speaking guile; let him turn away from evil and do right; let him seek peace and pursue it" (Ps 34:12–16). When the Pope entered the Holy City, he turned to the Governor, the mayor and the inhabitants of Old Jerusalem and called out: "Jerusalem! At this moment in which we stand within your walls, the joyful song of the inspired author comes to our lips: 'May they prosper who love you. Peace be within your walls, and security within your towers . . . peace be within you . . . I will seek your good'" (Ps 122:6–9). On taking leave of the people, and the King, in Amman, the Pope saluted them with the words "Salam

[72] *Ibid.,* p. 157.   [73] *AAS* 52 (1960), p. 960.
[74] Address at Rome airport: M. Maccarrone, *Il Pellegrinaggio di Paolo VI in Terra Santa* (1964), p. 25.
[75] Maccarrone, *op. cit.,* p. 104.

aleikum!" and warned with apostolic earnestness: "Let all bitterness and wrath and anger and clamour and slander be put away from you, with all malice, and be kind to one another, tenderhearted, forgiving one another, as God in Christ forgave you" (Eph 4:31–32).

On entering Israeli territory on 5 January, the Pope was greeted by the President of the State of Israel, Zalman Shazar. Paul VI closed his speech of thanks with a renewed call for peace: "As a pilgrim of peace we beg above all for the blessing of reconciliation of men with God and of deep and genuine concord among men and peoples. May God hear our prayer, God who, as the prophet proclaims, has plans for our "welfare and not for evil" (Jer 29:11). May He in His goodness pour forth upon the tormented world of today that incomparable gift, whose echo resounds on every page of the Bible. We are glad to sum up with it our greeting, our prayer, and our desire: 'Shalom, shalom'."[76]

During the penitential devotions led by him in the church of the Holy Sepulchre in Jerusalem on 4 January 1964, the Pope took up another theme — the inadequacy of Christian witness in the world, the manifold failures of Christianity in the course of its history. In his own name and that of many generations of Christians, he uttered this confession: "Lord Jesus, we have come here as guilty men to the place of our crime. We have come like the one who followed thee and yet betrayed thee. We have so often been both true and false. We have come to proclaim the mysterious link between our sins and thy suffering, between our deeds and thine. We have come to beat our breast, to ask for thy forgiveness, to implore thy mercy. We have come because we know that thou hast the power and the will to forgive us, because thou hast atoned for us, thou our salvation, thou our hope."[77]

No less significant were the numerous signs of the Pope's reverence for the Jewish people. His first words in Israel witnessed to the emotion he experienced on seeing and walking on the land "in which once lived the patriarchs, our fathers in the faith, in which the voice of the prophets resounded through the centuries in the name of the God of Abraham, Isaac and Jacob; the land which, finally and above all, the presence of Jesus Christ has blessed and made holy for ever for Christians and, one can truly say, for all mankind. From this land, unique in the grandeur of the events it has witnessed, our humble entreaty goes up to God, on behalf of all men, believers and unbelievers. We gladly include therein the children of the 'people of the Covenant', whose part in the religious history of mankind we can never forget."[78]

The highlight of the pilgrimage was, however, neither the encounter with the Islamic and Arab world nor that with Jewry, but the brotherly meeting of the

---

[76] Maccarrone, *op. cit.,* pp. 72 f.

[77] *Ibid.,* p. 41.

[78] Maccarrone, *op. cit.,* p. 72. It must without any doubt be considered a sign of the new view of Jewish life and religion, and also of the new relations between Christians and Jews, when Cardinal Tisserant, who accompanied the Pope on the journey, and an Orthodox dignitary lit candles at Israel's memorial of the martyrs, to honour the memory of the Jewish victims of Nazism.

Church of the West with that of the East. Late in the evening of 5 January 1964, the Ecumenical Patriarch of Constantinople, Athenagoras I, on the occasion of his visit to the Pope at the Apostolic Delegation in Jerusalem, said to Paul VI: "Venerable Brother in Christ ... for centuries the Christian world has been living in the darkness of separation. Her eyes are tired of straining into this darkness. May this meeting become the dawn of a bright and blessed day in which coming generations will partake of the same chalice of the Lord's holy body and precious blood, in which they will praise and glorify the one Lord and Saviour of the world in love, peace and unity."[79]

After an exchange of gifts and joint recitation of the Our Father in Greek and Latin, the Pope took the Patriarch's arm and led him to the door, at which the Patriarch exclaimed: "Oui, la main dans la main pour toujours" (Yes, hand in hand for ever).[80] As later became apparent, these words, the culmination of the great hope that fills the heart of Paul VI, were not without influence on the final form of the text of the Declaration on the Jews.

The immediate impression made by the Pope's pilgrimage to the Holy Land was a powerful one. "This Pope is a man of spirit. He is making history. Christendom is taking hold ... of new powers of action." Thus wrote a German newspaper,[81] while an American paper summed up the event as the rise of a guiding star and the setting of a goal.[82] Despite such manifestations of joyful approval, the pilgrimage did not fulfil the expectations of those who had hoped for a relaxation of the political situation in the Near East and with it an end to Arab opposition to the Declaration on the Jews. Although the Pope had come not only as a pilgrim but almost as a beggar for peace, the Jordanian radio repeatedly punctuated its reports in Arabic with hateful remarks, such as: Two thousand years ago, the Jews crucified Christ, and fifteen years ago, they attacked the people of Palestine, and: Truly, of all the world religions it is the Jews who are the enemies of God. Truly, the crimes of the Jews shall never be forgiven them.[83]

The Jordanian radio seemed to let no opportunity pass to stir up hatred against the Jews. On leaving the State of Israel Paul VI took up the defence of Pius XII against the crude and malicious attacks made by the German dramatist, Hochhuth. Some were alienated by this farewell speech. In my opinion the Pope's intention was to ask the Jews to pay no attention to those who were spreading slanders and trying to sow the seeds of discord. To many people, however, it seemed as if the Pope was holding the Jews and not the dramatist responsible for the play "The Deputy". A Jordanian newspaper, in its coarse way, wrote that Pope Paul's defence of his predecessor against the charge of not having

---

[79] Maccarrone, *op. cit.,* p. 90.
[80] X. Rynne, *The Second Session* (1964), p. 313.
[81] *Frankfurter Allgemeine Zeitung,* 4 January 1964.
[82] *New York Herald Tribune,* 6 January 1964; quoted in *HK* 18 (1964), p. 306. This number contains a detailed account of the friendly and hostile opinions in the world press.
[83] *New York Herald Tribune,* 5 January 1964.

stood by the Jews in the face of the Nazis' attempt to exterminate them, was a refutation of the accusations of the "Jewish propaganda apparatus".[84] This effort to poison the atmosphere by asserting that the Pope had rejected the products of the Jewish "propaganda machine" drew the following reply from the Israel paper, the *Jerusalem Post:* Whatever our opinion may be in this matter, one cannot but be deeply moved by the courage and frankness of the Pope's plea.[85]

It could be deduced from the statements of the Jordanian radio and press that the Arabs were not going to allow the Pope's pilgrimage to have any effect upon their propaganda machine, not to mention their further pressure on the Vatican. This pressure must have been greater than was publicly apparent. If it seemed to some that the Secretariat for Unity had slackened its grip on the reins and was letting itself be carried away, this was a false impression. Such a judgment of the situation leaves out of account the pressures to which the leaders of the Secretariat found themselves subjected, and betrays the irresponsibility of the armchair strategist, or of criticism based on hindsight. At any rate, at a plenary session of the Secretariat in Ariccia, from 24 February to 6 March 1964, to which, however, not all non-episcopal members and advisers were invited, a new text was produced. This revealed only too clearly the wounds inflicted by the Declaration's opponents. An attempt had been made, by omissions and by watering down many expressions, to appease its enemies. In order to take account of the formal objections to Chapter IV, the Declaration was now banished to the appendix of the schema on Ecumenism. The draft on religious liberty was similarly treated. The two drafts were now called the "First" and "Second" Declaration, corresponding to the time of their completion and delivery to the Fathers.

h) The third draft: Appendix to the schema on Ecumenism

In the "Second Declaration", that is, the third draft of the Declaration on the Jews, it was said that the Church gladly acknowledged that the beginnings of her faith and her election were to be found in the Israel of the patriarchs and

---

[84] From the very outset there have been Jewish voices expressing complete dissociation from the play and its thesis, though quite a number of Jews, still under the traumatic influence of the Hitler years, did welcome Hochhuth's attempt to shift the guilt from "the many" here and there and lay it on the shoulders of one man. It was not long, however, before they realized that the playwright was by no means a friend of the Jews. All the Jews who appear in the play are caricatures and freaks; not one of them is an upright man. One of them even speaks in accents which seem to have been taken from an anti-Semitic handbook. When Jacobson, who has "been in hiding" as Gerstein's librarian, hears that his parents have passed through the Nazi death-factory he bursts out: "I wish to go only in order to return as an avenger . . . I will come back — a murderer myself . . . as a bomber pilot. Murder for murder. Incendiary for gas, fire for fire." In a stage direction, Hochhuth describes this downtrodden man as speaking with a harshness that resembles that of the Old Testament.

[85] See *New York Herald Tribune,* 7 January 1964.

prophets. Nor could she forget that she — although a new creation in Christ — continued God's covenant with Israel. She further believed that her Lord had suffered and died freely for the sins of all men. She remained conscious that Mary, Mother of Christ, and the Apostles, the pillars of the Church, sprang from the Jewish people. For the sake of her common heritage with Judaism, the Council encouraged and promoted studies and discussion that would further mutual knowledge and respect. The Church rejected and deplored outbreaks of hatred and persecution against the Jews, whether committed in the past or in our own times. She warned (all to whom this applied) that in religious instruction, preaching and ordinary conversation, they should not represent the Jewish people as accursed or deicidal. Equally, nothing should be said that could produce hatred or contempt for the Jews in the hearts of those who heard it. All this was contrary to the will of Christ, who loved Jews and Gentiles with one and the same love.

In my opinion a solid framework had been left here, but only a framework. It lacked any links with Pauline theology. What the advocates of this draft expected from its meagreness of expression is not clear to me. The Arab governments' hatred of the State of Israel and fear of any reinstatement of the dignity of Judaism were so deeply rooted that no impression could be made on them by minor concessions. Despite all whittling down the Co-ordinating Commission was not satisfied with the new text and summarily re-cast it — an extraordinary and unprecedented proceeding. It was now entitled "On the Jews and Non-Christians".

The Evangelical pastor, Johann Christoph Hampe, an always intelligent and usually well-informed commentator, who occasionally makes mistakes of detail, was on firm ground in what he wrote about the period between the second and third sessions. "There must," he said, "have been, during the summer of 1964, a new and still more ominous phase in the history of the statement on the Jews, which called into question its whole future. The Co-ordinating Commission still did not approve the latest text and the State Secretariat was clearly once again impressed by the Arab opposition within the Unity Secretariat, under its leading spokesman, Bishop Mansourati. It was at this time that there appeared a plan to separate altogether the chapter on the Jews from the schema on Ecumenism and to hand over the task of producing it to the newly-formed 'Secretariat for Non-Christian Religions'. But since this Secretariat had nothing to do with the Council and was therefore not entitled to submit drafts to it for discussion, and a schema on all religions did not exist, this proposal amounted to an attempt to abandon completely any statement on the Jewish question. This attempt, however, was exposed by statements in the world's press and was defeated. It looked as if the statement as given above, in the form and place already indicated, would come before the Council at the beginning of the third session. Experts in this field hoped for a short debate and a positive vote."[86]

[86] Quoted in Eckert and Ehrlich, *op. cit.*, pp. 418 f.

Through an indiscretion the so-called "Second Declaration", in its revised form, reached the press, first in America and then throughout the world. The immediate reactions were anger, sorrow and protest. In many cases, this unconsidered response was all there was. It was often based upon inadequate translation. The Declaration was divided into three sections, of which the first spoke of the "heritage which Christians have in common with the Jews". Its wording was as follows:

"The Church of Christ gladly acknowledges that in accordance with God's mysterious saving decree, the beginnings of her faith and her election are already to be found in the patriarchs and prophets. Thus she professes that all Christian believers — the sons of Abraham by faith (cf. Gal 3:7) — are included in his call, and also that their salvation is prefigured, as in a sacramental sign, in the deliverance of the chosen people out of the land of bondage. For this reason the Church, "new man" in Christ (cf. Eph 2:15) and people of the New Covenant that she is, cannot forget that she is (at the same time) the spiritual continuation of that people with whom God in earlier times, in his inexpressible mercy and gracious condescension, made the Old Covenant, and to whom he entrusted according to his will the Revelation contained in the books of the Old Testament.

"Nor does the Church forget that Christ springs, according to the flesh, from the Jewish people; from them spring the Virgin Mary, mother of Christ; from them came the Apostles, the foundations and pillars of the Church.

"The Church also keeps, and will always keep, in mind the words of the Apostle concerning the Jews, that 'to them belong the sonship, the glory, the covenants, the giving of the law, the worship, and the promises' (Rom 9:4).[87]

"Since Christians have in this way received so great an inheritance from the Jews, this holy Synod wishes emphatically to promote and recommend the mutual knowledge and respect that is achieved by theological studies and brotherly discussion. In addition she strongly deplores and condemns outbreaks of hatred and acts of violence against the Jews, just as she strongly disapproves of injustices committed against human beings everywhere.

"In addition it is worthy of remembrance that the union of the Jewish people with the Church is a part of Christian hope. With unshaken faith and deep longing the Church awaits, in accordance with the Apostle's teaching, the entry of this people into the fullness of the People of God which Christ has founded (Rom 11:25–26).

"May all therefore take care, that in catechetical instruction, in preaching the Word of God and in daily conversation the Jewish people are not represented as

---

[87] It may, perhaps, be profitable once more to give the gist of J. Zink's German translation, which might well be described as a modern targum: "God gives them the prerogative to be his sons. Splendour and light, the kindness of God and his holy nearness are upon them. God has bound himself to them and put himself under an obligation to them. God's will and commandment have been entrusted to them. They know how they can worship God worthily in their celebrations and feasts. They have his promises for their future and know that he will be faithful to his people."

rejected, and equally that nothing is said or done that could alienate souls from the Jews. They should also guard against attributing to the Jews of our time what was done during Christ's Passion."[88]

The next two sentences of the "Second Declaration" were entitled "The Fatherhood of God over all men" and "The unacceptability of any degrading, prejudicial treatment". In the first section it was explained that the teaching of the Old Testament and insight of human reason that God is the father of all men had been confirmed and illuminated by the Lord Jesus. The Christian could not worship God as the Father of all if he refused to greet as brothers all men — created as they were in God's image. Every "no" to brotherly love among men was ultimately a denial of God who is no respecter of persons . . .

In obedience to the urging of love for our brethren we should consider with great attention the opinions and teachings (of non-Christians) which, though they differ from our own in many ways, nevertheless contain a ray of that truth which enlightens every man upon the earth. This consideration applies above all to the Moslems, who worship the one God and stand close to us not only in religion but also in many cultural achievements.

Going on to reject every kind of "discrimination", the schema said that the sense of brotherhood removed the basis of any theory or practice that made a distinction between one man and another, or one people and another, in relation to their human dignity and the rights resulting from it. All men of good will, therefore, especially Christians, should avoid every kind of degradation and persecution of others, whether on account of their origin, colour, religion or position. Furthermore the Council summoned all Christians with burning love to "maintain good conduct among the Gentiles" (1 Pet 2:12) and, so far as lay in their power, to live peaceably with all men (cf. Rom 12:18). The Council also enjoined upon Christians that they should love not only their neighbours, but also their supposed enemies, that they might be true sons of their Father who was in heaven and made his sun to shine upon all men (cf. Mt 5:44–45).[89]

On 25 September 1964 Cardinal Bea solemnly introduced the Declaration on the Jews and non-Christians. He began by saying that no other schema had so held the public in suspense and been so much written about. The interest was so deep that one could well say that many people would judge the Council by the stand it took on this question. This interest, however, was not the foremost reason why it was impossible to delete the "Jewish question" from the list of subjects to be considered by the Council. Its necessity arose much more out of the Church's faithfulness "in following the example of Christ and his disciples in love for the Jews".[90]

The Cardinal went on to say that the further work done on the draft submitted during the second session was to be explained by the fact that the Secretariat

[88] Eckert and Ehrlich, *op. cit.*, pp. 430–2; cf. *Freiburger Rundbrief* 12, nos. 45–48 (28 December 1959), p. 7.
[89] *Ibid.*   [90] Bea, *op. cit.*, p. 160.

had gone thoroughly into the suggestions made by the Council fathers and had made careful use of them. At the same time he gave a gentle reminder that the text now before the fathers by no means originated with the Secretariat, when he said: "The Co-ordinating Commission of the Council knows that it has had to spend a great deal of time on this short document."[91]

The central theme of that part of the Declaration which concerned the Jews was the question of the so-called deicide. Its treatment had been considerably altered. The question was whether and in what manner the Jewish people as such were guilty of the condemnation and crucifixion of Jesus. Many of today's Jews believed that this prejudiced idea of Jewish guilt was the main root of anti-Semitism and thus the source of many of the misfortunes and persecutions of the Jews over the centuries. The Cardinal emphasized that this assertion could not be sustained, but that it was nevertheless indisputable that, in the course of the history of various peoples, the notion of a universal Jewish guilt had led many Christians "to consider and designate the Jews with whom they lived as members of a race rejected and cursed by God for 'deicide' and so to despise or even persecute them."[92] For this reason the Jews now expected a solemn condemnation by the Council of such an attitude.

The question now arose whether the Council could declare that Jesus' death was not to be blamed upon the Jewish people as such and, if that were possible, how it should be done. There could of course be no question of impugning the findings of Scripture or of denying any point of doctrine contained in the gospel. The question was rather this: the leaders of the Sanhedrin in Jerusalem, though not elected by the people in a democratic manner, were doubtless to be regarded, according to the ideas of the time and of Scripture itself, as the legitimate authority.[93] Therein consisted, Cardinal Bea continued, the gravity and tragedy

---

[91] *Ibid.*, p. 160.   [92] *Ibid.*, p. 161.

[93] This statement, to my mind, needs qualifying to some extent. There is no doubt that the authorities were in possession of their offices, and the majority of the people of Judaea would hardly have questioned their legitimacy — such problems of political principle would have been far from their minds. But it should not be forgotten that the men of Qumrân — however insignificant they may have been in numbers — denied the legitimacy of the high priests of the time. The high priests descended from the Hasmoneans received their dignity by the grace of the Romans, not of God. The procurators, who were by no means averse to bribes, appointed and dismissed the high priests quite arbitrarily. Since these frequent dismissals were doubtless illegal — the office of high priest was for life — it is hardly possible to consider the subsequent appointments fully valid. Now and again one or other of the "aristocratic" families sought to snatch the high-priestly office with the assistance of armed bands. And it must be remembered that the people, to all appearances, had no confidence that the members of the various families, especially that of Annas, were exercising their offices properly; it would not be too much to say that the people hated the actual incumbents of this highest office.

At all events, the Talmud has preserved the words of Rabbi Joseph ben Hanin: "Woe is me from the family of Boëthos, woe is me from their cudgels; woe is me from the family of Hanin, woe is me from their whisperings; woe is me from the family of Kathoris, woe is me from their pen; woe is me from the family of Yismâél ben Phabi, woe is me from their fist. They themselves

of the decisions and actions of that authority, which led to the condemnation and death of Christ. And yet one must ask here, what order of gravity? "Did those 'rulers' of the people in Jerusalem fully understand the divinity of Christ and so become formally guilty of deicide?"[94] The answer to this question could only be "no", since the Lord had prayed for his crucifiers: "Father, forgive them; for they know not what they do" (Lk 23:34). If this prayer were not to be devalued to an empty formula — which heaven forbid — then it meant, without a doubt, that "the Jews" were by no means fully aware of what they were doing. Peter and Paul also excused the rulers on grounds of ignorance (cf. Acts 3:17; 13:27). And whatever might be the position concerning the knowledge of the Jerusalem authorities, could one accuse the *people* of that time of having killed Christ? At that date, the Jewish diaspora within the Roman Empire already consisted of some four and a half million people. Even assuming that one could indict the people of those times for the crimes of their leaders — which was in fact not acceptable — what right had one to blame these actions on the Jewish people of today?

Nothing that the Cardinal said hit the mark more exactly than this simple question: Is there any other case in which we reproach another people for the actions of their ancestors nineteen hundred years ago? Cardinal Bea went on to say: "Because of the difficulty of the subject, it is understandable that many different formulas were tried, one after the other, in the effort, also, to satisfy the wishes and the criticisms of the fathers."[95] On various occasions the "Council fathers and others, including non-Catholics and non-Christians, petitioned that the question of 'deicide' should receive some treatment. It would be

were high priests, their sons were treasurers, their sons-in law were lords of the temple, and their servants beat the people with cudgels" (*Pesachim,* 57a).

J. Klausner, *Jesus of Nazareth* (1943), p. 337, calls this song of woe a "street song". The "cudgels" refer to the violent methods used by the slaves of that house in gathering the tithes. The "whisperings" refer to the secret sessions where new suppressive measures against the people were devised. The "pen" is the instrument with which the exploiters' decrees were signed. The last lines, which may possibly have been added later, present a sorry picture of the financial machinations of the high-priestly clique. In view of all this it must be seriously asked whether the leaders of the Sanhedrin, these malevolent caricatures of *"high* priests", can really be looked on as the representatives of the people at all.

[94] Bea, *op. cit.,* p. 161. Is it really possible at all to ask whether the Jerusalem authorities *fully* grasped the divinity of Christ? Is it not more likely that they had no inkling whatever of the mystery of God made man? After all, the apostles themselves had to wait until the grace of Pentecost before the wonder of Christ's personality dawned on them. And even Mary and Joseph are said not to have understood the question asked them by the 12-year old Jesus in the temple: "Did you not know that I must be in my Father's house?" (Lk 2:49). Moreover, the assumption (so often recurring in the old polemics against the Jews) that belief in Christ as the incarnate Son of God was so "self-evident" that all failure to accept it could only have been bad will simply devalues the world-shaking mystery of the incarnation. This view of the matter reduces the mystery to nothing much more than the observation "what nice weather we're having" . . .

[95] Bea, *op. cit.,* p. 162.

tiresome to describe all the deliberations in detail ... These deliberations took a long time. Consequently we were unable to submit this part of the Declaration for examination by members of the secretariat. Since the secretariat had dealt with all its other business at its March sitting, it was decided not to recall the members to Rome, to discus this one section. All that now remains, Venerable Fathers, is to examine and discuss this schema."[96] It can be said in advance that the fathers made liberal use of this invitation.

Despite the Cardinal's efforts to win understanding for the new draft, it had a bad press. In many cases it was described as completely worthless — one of the many exaggerations of those days. Looking at the matter soberly, one has to say that the revisions had significantly weakened the Declaration and thus made it more palatable to its opponents. Nevertheless it was not a bad document. It was only when one compared it with its predecessors, and if one followed the principle that the good is the enemy of the better, that it came as a great disappointment. The most noteworthy alterations that the Co-ordinating Commission had made in the Secretariat's third draft were the following:

1. The unfortunate word "deicidal" was dropped from the summons directed to all Christians not to call the Jewish people accursed or "deicidal". There were various reasons for this which will be discussed later. It must, however, be said at once that the condemnation of this most deeply harmful expression had, indeed, certain tireless champions, but not many friends. Most bishops declared that they had never heard the accusation: "You are a Jew, therefore you are a deicide!" They were accordingly convinced that the proponents of a condemnation of this expression — whether they were Christians or Jews — were attaching much more importance to the problem than it actually possessed. They also felt an unspoken disquiet in using the very word "deicide", even as a negative example.

While the debate on this point was going on, there came up to me one day a certain bishop, who is widely known outside America and is by no means attached to the "bad old days". He said, "Look here, this won't do. One cannot simply declare, in public, that the Jews are not deicides." I answered, "Why not?" Upon which the bishop explained his objection like this: "Why not? Simply because it is insulting even to put the word into one's mouth. What would you say if someone suddenly announced, in public, 'Oesterreicher is no thief'? How would you like that?" "Your Excellency, that depends on the situation. If this 'defence' came like lightning out of a clear sky, I should of course be thunderstruck. But if, for years, I had been the victim of a slander, then I should feel that I had been set free by such a public vindication. I should in fact be pleased about it." The bishop was evidently impressed by this argument, as he asked me to prepare a memorandum for him on the matter. But I am not sure that I convinced him in the depths of his heart. This little incident shows how greatly we are tied to our emotions, and how much our judgment depends upon our experiences.

[96] *Ibid.*

The uneasiness of many friends of the entire Declaration that I have described enabled its opponents to win a victory on the deicide issue.

2. A further, much commented-on statement was the acknowledgment of the Church's eschatological hope for the union of Israel with herself. This passage was much warmer in tone than the rest of the Declaration, and this could give the impression to a hasty reader, especially if he were Jewish, that what was intended here was nothing but proselytizing. However, an unprejudiced reader who examines the statement carefully is bound to conclude that it does not recommend a mission to the Jews, but expresses simply and solely the belief that at the end of time God will gather into union with himself all who profess his name.

The statement was so greatly misunderstood that Rabbi Abraham Joshua Heschel — a man of deep insight whose blood, however, boils too easily — felt himself obliged to protest against it in the following terms: faced with the choice of conversion or death in the gas chambers of Auschwitz, he would choose the latter.[97] The imputation that the Church had kept alight the gas chambers of Auschwitz puts the Church's profession of faith in the union of all who worship the God of Israel in the same category as the most ghastly perversions of the Middle Ages, when Jews were more than once faced with the choice of, for example, baptism or exile. It is too fantastic to be refuted. Nevertheless Archbishop Heenan (Westminster) took it up at a press conference on 26 September 1964, and called Rabbi Heschel's declaration that he was ready to go to Auschwitz if he were forced to choose between conversion and death "pure rhetoric". True conversion meant the free acceptance of faith. It was, moreover, far from the intention of the Secretariat to use the Declaration on the Jews for an attack upon the convictions of our Jewish brethren.[98]

Three days later the Archbishop addressed the bishops in the Council. He said that the wording of the document that they had before them was not entirely theirs, and that he had no idea which theologians were entrusted with the drafting of this latest version of the Declaration. He went on to say that he in no way questioned the good will of these men, but it was probable that they had little experience of ecumenical matters. Such questions, however, required a special tact and sensitivity, particularly in matters concerning the Jews, whom frequent persecution has made quite sensitive. He stressed that the Jews were wrong if they regarded the text (of this profession of faith) as a demand that they give up their religion. But the fact that the Jews had taken this statement amiss was, he continued, sufficient reason for him to remove the relevant passage from the Declaration.[99]

One of the most curious misunderstandings in the history of the Declaration concerned the warning addressed to all the faithful not to say or do anything

---

[97] The exact words of Rabbi Heschel are quoted in *Time,* 11 September 1964.
[98] *Council Daybook,* II, p. 64.
[99] *Ibid.,* p. 82.

"quod animos a Judaeis alienare potest" (which could alienate souls *from* the Jews). Someone who had forgotten the rudiments of Latin or had read the text with great carelessness, read "animos Judaeorum" (the souls *of* the Jews) and understood it as follows: nothing should be said that could alienate the souls of the Jews (from the Church). As was to be expected, this mistranslation was regarded as a new proof of the Declaration's missionary character.

It was remarkable how the critics saw only the inadequacies of this draft and not its merits. But perhaps this failure is not so remarkable, but rather a symptom of the way in which many of us have lost all sense of theology. Were that not so, Christians and Jews alike would surely have pricked up their ears and rejoiced when they saw this insertion: "The Church also keeps and will always keep in mind the words of the Apostle concerning the Jews, that 'to them belong the sonship, the glory, the covenants, the giving of the law, the worship, and the promises' (Rom 9:4)."

In my opinion there are powerful starting-points here for a theology of post-biblical Israel. In future anyone who attempts to reflect on the role of Judaism in saving history or to express the relationship of Church and Synagogue in theological terms will have to draw support from the assurance given by the Apostle and recalled to Christian consciousness by the Council. It seems to me an encouraging feature of this addition that it did not originate among the members of the Secretariat. Although I have no sort of secret information or other proof, I cannot escape a feeling that the insertion derives from Pope Paul.

As so often in the history of the Declaration, real or supposed setbacks proved a spur to new efforts and helped to bring about a victory on the right side. The defects in the draft originating from the Co-ordinating Commission gave the bishops the opportunity for a far-ranging discussion not only of the wording of the Declaration, but also of its deeper meaning. The interventions were so much to the point and so well co-ordinated that one might have supposed a skilled hand directing from the rear. In fact, there was no plan, but only the lofty intentions of the speakers, their feeling for the signs of the times, their keen ear for God's message uttered through these signs, and their earnest devotion to the idea of the renewal of the Church. Many of the speeches on 28 and 29 September 1964 are so important that I reproduce large extracts from them, as they represent a climax in the history of the Declaration. They have not of course the status of the Council Declaration itself, as they always give only the opinion of an individual, but precisely in this lies their charm and value. They should really always be printed alongside the Declaration itself, as they support, explain and sometimes also develop it.

i) The great debate

At the beginning of the great debate, the Bishops of the Fulda Bishops' Conference assembled in Rome issued the following Declaration:

"We German bishops welcome the Council Decree on the Jews. If the Church in Council makes a statement concerning her own nature, she cannot fail to mention her connection with God's people of the Old Covenant. We are convinced that this Council Declaration provides an opportunity for renewed contact and a better relationship between the Church and the Jewish people."

"We German bishops welcome the Decree especially because we are conscious of the grave injustice done to the Jews in the name of our own people."[100]

The Swedish journalist, G. Vallquist, wrote in her report of 28 September 1964 as follows: "Today was the greatest day of the present Council session. The Declaration on the Jews was sped on its way with drums and trumpets in a succession of speeches, each more positive than the last."[101] Each speaker was frank and to the point, and the speeches formed a happy combination of prudence and warmth. There were moments when an atmosphere of awe lay upon the Council. It could be perceived that what was being dealt with here was not a matter of abstract principle, but the most concrete of all questions — the encounter of man with man, and of man with God.

The speech of Cardinal Ritter (St. Louis, Mo.) was a fine example of decisiveness.[102] He said:

"With all my heart I gladly make this Declaration my own. Quite clearly, it meets a need of our time. I speak of a need, not of some political or national pressure to be evaded or appeased, nor of some human approval to be sought for, but quite simply of a centuries-old injustice that cries aloud for reparation. For many centuries we Christians have been guilty of error and injustice towards the Jews. In many ways we have assumed that God . . . had abandoned this people. Christians, and even ecclesiastical documents, have charged the Jewish people with the suffering and death of Christ. In prayers they were called the 'perfidious', the 'deicidal' people, who 'once called down upon themselves the blood of the Saviour'. We who are gathered here in this Ecumenical Council have today been given an opportunity to root out such errors and injustices and to make reparation (for the injuries these have caused).

---

[100] *Freiburger Rundbrief* 16–17, nos. 61–64 (1965), p. 13.
[101] *Das Zweite Vatikanische Konzil* (1966), p. 292.
[102] The contributions to the great debate are reproduced here in mosaic form. In chronological order the speakers on the "Declaration on the Jews" on 28 September 1964 were: Cardinals Liénart (Lille), Tappouni (Syrian Patriarch of Antioch), Frings (Cologne), Ruffini (Palermo), Lercaro (Bologna), Léger (Montreal), Cushing (Boston), König (Vienna), Meyer (Chicago), and Ritter (St. Louis). Archbishops Jaeger (Paderborn) and Pocock (Toronto), and Bishops Nierman (Groningen) and Daem (Antwerp). On 29 September the speakers were Cardinal Bueno y Monreal (Seville, Spain), Archbishop Šeper (Zagreb), Bishops Plumey (Garoua), Méndez Arceo (Cuernavaca, Mexico), Satoshi Nagae (Urawa, Japan), Nowicki (Gdansk, Poland) and Hoa Nguyen-van Hien (Dalat, Vietnam), Coadjutor-Bishop Elchinger (Strasbourg), Bishop Leven (San Antonio, U.S.A.), Archbishops Heenan (Westminster) and O'Boyle (Washington, D.C.), and others.

"The schema is . . . a good start in this direction. It could, however, be much better constructed. It seems to me to require certain corrections . . . The Declaration should speak more fully and explicitly of the religious heritage which in our own day still binds Jews and Christians closely together. The promises which God who . . . can neither deceive nor be deceived made to Abraham still belong to the Jews. Jews and Christians are in a special way vessels of divine love, and a powerful unity of love and respect should therefore prevail between us and them. This spirit of love, which was alive in the original schema, should shine out more strongly in this Declaration also. It is a question of proclaiming with great joy our debt of gratitude and sincere attitudes the Jews, which in this schema are somewhat hesitantly and reluctantly acknowledged . . .

"Venerable Fathers, we must eradicate that error which holds a (whole) people guilty of the crime committed by individuals, that error which fills even the hearts of children with hatred of the people whom God so greatly loves. The last part (of the Declaration) should be removed and replaced by the following paragraphs, or something similar: 'For this reason all must take care that they in no way represent the Jewish people as rejected or deicidal, or throw the blame for all the crimes committed during the Passion of Christ upon the whole people then living and, *a fortiori*, upon the Jews of our own time. All these (crimes) are really the responsibility of all sinful men and especially of Christians who have fallen into sin. The catechism of the Council of Trent recalls this truth in all bluntness: the guilt of the Crucifixion falls above all upon those who repeatedly relapse into sin. For just as our sins brought Christ the Lord to death upon the Cross, so those who wallow in sin and vice in fact crucify the Son of God on their own account and hold him up to contempt (Heb 6:6)'."

Another American bishop, Cardinal Cushing (Boston) spoke even more frankly and firmly:

"The Church must proclaim, through this Ecumenical Council, her sincere concern, universal respect and true love for the whole world and for all men — in a word, she must show forth Christ . . . With regard to the Jews, I propose three amendments:

"1. We must draft the Declaration on the Jews in a much more positive form, not so timidly, but much more lovingly . . . For the sake of our common heritage we, the sons of Abraham in the spirit, must foster a special reverence and love for the sons of Abraham in the flesh. As sons of Adam they (the Jews) are our brothers, as sons of Abraham they are blood-brothers of Christ . . .

"2. So far as the guilt of the Jews in the death of our Saviour is concerned, the rejection of the Messiah by his own people is, according to Scripture, a mystery — a mystery given us for our instruction, not for our self-exaltation . . . We cannot sit in judgment on the one-time leaders of Israel — God alone is their judge. What is at any rate certain is that we cannot thrust upon later generations of Jews any guilt for the Crucifixion of the Lord Jesus, for the death of the Saviour of the world, for this is a common guilt in which we all share . . . Therefore we should deny, in clear and unmistakable language, that the Jews (as a whole) are guilty of Our Saviour's death . . . We must condemn especially those who seek to justify inequality of rights, hatred, and even persecution of Jews as Christian acts . . .

"3. I ask myself, venerable brothers, whether we should not humbly acknowledge before the whole world that Christians have all too often not shown themselves as true Christians towards their Jewish brothers, as true followers of Christ. How many (Jews) have suffered in our own time? How many died because Christians were indifferent and kept silent? . . . If in recent years, not many Christian voices were raised against those injustices, at least let ours now be heard in humility . . ."

Most of the fathers called for a return to the earlier text, in which the charge of deicide was explicitly rejected. In this sense spoke Cardinals Liénart (Lille), König (Vienna), Léger (Montreal), Meyer (Chicago), Shehan (Baltimore) and, with particular force, the suffragan Bishop of San Antonio, Texas, Stephen Leven, who said:

"In Chapter IV of the schema on Ecumenism, presented to us last year, it was said that the Jews were not guilty of deicide. Now, in the present text, this statement is missing. Some say that it has been suppressed because the word 'deicidal' is philosophically and theologically absurd, self-contradictory and therefore unworthy of a Council document . . . Fathers of the Council, we have to deal here not with a philosophical entity but with an infamous blasphemy that was invented by Christians for the sole purpose of bringing shame and disgrace upon the Jews. For hundreds of years, and even in our own century, Christians have flung the word 'deicide' into the face of the Jews in order to justify all kinds of excesses, and even the murder of Jews. It is not our task to deliver an explanation concerning some philosophical question. We are only obliged to condemn and reject a phrase that has so often provided the occasion and pretext for persecution. We must remove this word from the language of Christians, so that it can never again be turned against the Jews."

Altogether twenty-one bishops demanded the restoration of the text used at the second session.[103]

As has already been mentioned, Cardinal Meyer (Chicago) also regretted that in the Co-ordinating Commission's text the rejection of the pseudo-theological imprecation "deicide" was inadequate.

"Is it not much more our duty in this connection to present the fullness of truth concerning the Jews, in the spirit of St. Thomas (*Summa Theologica*, q. 47, a. 5 ad c.)? . . . Following the teaching of Scripture, St. Thomas brings out these two points: 1) No single individual Jew of Christ's time was guilty, formally

---

[103] W. Becker, "Die Erklärung über das Verhältnis der Kirche zu den nichtchristlichen Religionen", *Catholica*, 20 (1966), p. 120.

and subjectively, of deicide, since all acted in ignorance of Christ's divinity. That must be said explicitly in our text. 2) The bulk of the Jews should be acquitted of any formal guilt because they followed their leaders out of ignorance. As a proof of this, St. Thomas refers to St. Peter: 'I know that you acted in ignorance' (Acts 3:17). Finally, it must also be said where the real guilt for the torments of Christ lies — 'He died for us and for our salvation'!"

Archbishop (now Cardinal) O'Boyle (Washington, D. C.) expressly associated himself with Cardinal Meyer's view. He found the statement in the current text, which was limited to saying that the ill-treatment of Christ was not to be attributed to the Jews of our own day, too bald. Only a full vindication of the Jewish people would free them "from the insult laid upon them for centuries. The love of Christ impels us to make such a Declaration". Archbishop O'Boyle also addressed himself to other problems touched upon in the text. He said:

"It is true that this Declaration is conceived as a Declaration by the Catholic Bishops and is directed above all to Catholics. Nevertheless it must be ecumenical in spirit. The statements concerning the Jews will be carefully studied by them also. The spirit, the style and the words of the Declaration must accordingly be directed to this ecumenical goal. The love of Christ impels us so to formulate our thoughts that they do not give needless offence, and equally that they be expressed in a manner comprehensible to the Jews and that they be in harmony with the hopes and aspirations of the Jewish soul."

The first example of disregard for ecumenical style that struck him was the use of the expressions "union of the Jewish people with the Church" and "entry of this people into the fullness of the people of God". In the Jewish understanding both would seem to indicate a passionate desire on the part of Catholics for the "conversion" of the Jews:

"The word 'conversion' awakens in the hearts of Jews memories of persecutions, sufferings and the enforced denial of all the truths that a Jew loves with sincerity and good faith. So a Jew, when he hears that Catholics are seeking to further his 'conversion', thinks of the re-introduction of that type of proselytism that for centuries assaulted his rights and personal dignity ... The (spiritual) destiny of the Jewish people depends totally on the ways of divine providence and the grace of God. If therefore we express our hope (for the eschatological union) in words (that give the impression) that we are guided by the definite and conscious intention of working for their conversion, we then set up a new and high dividing wall, which makes any fruitful dialogue impossible. What is said in the Declaration on this point ... goes beyond the precise limits of doctrine. A text is in fact cited in the Declaration, from the Letter to the Romans (11:25), in which he uses words which are so uncertain and mysterious that the exegetes suggest quite diverse interpretations. It would therefore be better for us to remain within the limits of our knowledge and to respect the hidden ways of divine providence. It would be better if we were to express our hope for the turning of the Jews (to Christ) in such a way that they too can perceive with

71

respect its honesty and also our humble recognition that the mystery of salvation does not depend upon us, but upon God's transcendent act. I therefore suggest that we replace the section under discussion with the following words: 'Furthermore it is worthy of remembrance that the union of the Jewish and Christian people is a part of Christian hope. With unshaken faith and deep longing the Church awaits that union which God will bring about in his own time and in a way still hidden in his wisdom . . .' Finally I should still like to suggest that the Declaration include an act of humility and repentance, which alone moves men's hearts. Our Lord taught the Church to pray daily 'forgive us our trespasses'. A truly Christian Declaration concerning the Jews cannot leave to one side the fact that for centuries the Jewish people have been the victims of the injustice and cruelty of Christians. The best way of witnessing to our love for the people chosen by God in ancient times — the people from whom came Jesus and Mary, the people still dear to God on account of their virtues and their piety — would be for us explicitly to ask them for forgiveness for the pain and injustice with which certain Christians have dishonoured our history."

Archbishop Pocock (Toronto) began his speech which was, as he said himself, a short one, by on the one hand joining with appreciation in the praise of the other speakers, and on the other by making his own their demands concerning the deicide problem and the condemnation of the persecutions that had occurred. He continued:

"May I be permitted to add a few words in defence of the Declaration against those who object that in it the Jews are presented in a much better light than in Scripture itself. It is indeed true that the prophets of Israel not infrequently accused the people of being stiff-necked and hard-hearted. These accusations resound again and again, right into the New Testament. Christ himself sternly rebuked the high priests and Pharisees and sometimes the people also. The same way of speaking is to be found in the preaching of St. Stephen (Acts 7) and in St. Paul's First Letter to the Thessalonians (7:15f). In these passages the people of Israel are accused of repeated unfaithfulness. One should, however, not forget that these accusations against the Jews come from men who were themselves Jews. Christ, Stephen and Paul are indeed sons of the Jewish people. Their stern language is therefore nothing but a warning to the people, that they may be converted in their hearts — the people whom they love, to whom they belong, and with whom they know themselves in a certain respect to be one. Their statements should therefore not be understood as a literal description of the people. They were much rather a form of emphatic and impassioned preaching intended to stir the hearts of their hearers . . ."

Some of the fathers who took part in the great debate did not, in their criticism of the text, content themselves with pointing out its defects, but went further than the original draft. Cardinal König (Vienna), for example, demanded that, in connection with the warning to avoid any unjust judgment concerning the Jews in preaching and catechesis, one should not merely return to the original draft. He went on to say that it was not the task of Christian preaching to assess the exact degree of guilt of Caiphas, Pilate and others, as in fact all of us were the cause (of Christ's death on the Cross). The foremost task of Christian preaching was to show that in the Cross lies salvation. The Cross should be presented as the source of all graces, as the sign of love and salvation for all.

Cardinal Liénart (Lille), whose pastoral letter[104] in many ways anticipated the Council Declaration, suggested the following wording for the warning discussed above:

"All possible care should therefore be taken to exclude from catechesis and preaching of the word of God everything that could instil contempt and hatred for the Jews. In particular this Holy Synod commands that words which brand the Jews as a rejected and even deicidal people are to be most strictly avoided, because they in no way agree with the pronouncements of holy Scripture. Priests and catechists must instead take pains to show that the vocation of the Jewish people still continues and that they have a part in the present economy of salvation, according to the mysterious decree of God to which the Apostle Paul refers (Rom 11)."

Two German speakers, Cardinal Frings (Cologne) and Bishop Hengsbach (Essen) found it regrettable that in the text now laid before them, "that most beautiful and magnificent theology" of the Epistle to the Ephesians was completely absent. "According to it . . . Christ established peace between those who were far and those who were near, that is, between the (Gentile) peoples and the chosen people when He, the crucified, broke down the wall of hostility between Jews and Gentiles and created a new man in His body." Here, the Cardinal continued, was the classic scriptural passage concerning the relation between the people of the Old and New Covenant.

Bishop Hengsbach expressed his gratitude to Pope John for the mandate given to the Unity Secretariat to prepare a Declaration on the Jews. He was convinced that the Declaration represented a pre-condition for genuine contact and better relations between the Church and the Jewish people. He also mentioned the special satisfaction of the German episcopate, as already expressed in their statement at the beginning of the debate.

Among the outstanding speakers of the two-day debate were undoubtedly Cardinal Lercaro (Bologna) and Bishop Elchinger (Strasbourg). The Cardinal began with a notable affirmation:

"Other speakers have discussed the immediate grounds, the importance and the effective significance of this Declaration. I, however, should like to confine myself to one point only. I should like to throw some light on the ultimate reason, the deepest motive which, it seems to me, is leading the Church of Christ, in this historic hour, inescapably to such a decision. This deepest reason has nothing to do with political affairs and anxieties, nor with relations between States. It is

---

[104] See p. 26 above.

not even the events during the last great war — by which all men have indeed been deeply shaken — nor feelings of moral obligation and humanity — binding though these are — which are leading the Church to make this Declaration precisely at this time. It is much more due to inner impulses which have come to maturity at the deepest, supernatural core of the life and consciousness of Christ's Church, quite apart from any external event and stimulus. That the Church is only now taking into account these considerations (set out in the Declaration) is due to the fact that she has only now attained a deeper insight into certain aspects of the mystery of her existence and the fullness of her life. One should say, therefore, that the Declaration on the Jews is a result of the self-examination whose outcome is to be found in the Constitution on the Church and, especially, in that on the holy Liturgy . . . As my time is short, I should like above all to speak of the relation of the Declaration on the Jews to the Constitution on the Liturgy. When the Declaration speaks of the 'great spiritual heritage common to Christians and Jews', then it seems to look back, as is said in the Declaration itself, to the 'beginnings of her own election and faith', that is, to everything that the Church has inherited from the Jewish people, back to the days of the Virgin Mary, Christ Jesus and the Apostles . . .

"In the eyes of the Church the Jewish people has a dignity that has supernatural roots and a corresponding value, not only in the past, at the time of the Church's beginnings, but also in the present, and that with regard to the most basic and divine elements of her daily life. It is precisely this upon which the Constitution on the Liturgy is intended to shed light, and to make effective in the Church today. It is the culminating point of her action and the source of her strength. It is that upon which the Church is daily fed and lives — the Holy Scripture in the service of the word of God, and the Lamb of God offered in sacrifice. But these two blessings, this precious inheritance of the Church, come from the heritage of Israel — not only Scripture, as is obvious, but also the Eucharist, which is already pre-figured in the paschal meal and in mannah, and was introduced by Christ according to the pattern of the Paschal Haggadah of the Jews. In addition, the word of God and the Eucharist ('Behold, the lamb of God . . .') effect even now a certain union between the liturgical assembly, the Church, at the moment of her supreme action on earth, and the holy Kahal, the assembly of the sons of Israel. Likewise, they keep alive, at the deepest level, the exchange of word and life, so that at the most exalted moment of the divine liturgy, we can rightly call Abraham our Patriarch, that is, the father of our people: 'Deign to regard them (the gifts thou hast bestowed upon us) with a favourable and gracious countenance, and to accept them as it pleased thee to accept . . . the sacrifice of our father Abraham . . .'

"Even if this exchange is not at present fully disclosed to the Jews, it is still a powerful and ever present bond of a quite special nature and strength. It therefore seems to me necessary that *biblical* discussions should be explicitly mentioned and that the role here and now entrusted to the Jews should be honoured. Even in the present order of salvation, they are able to give a certain biblical, paschal witness, so long as they keep faith, humbly and loyally, with the ways of their fathers and preserve the pure religious sense of Scripture. This witness, even though still covered by a veil (2 Cor 3:15), can be of great use to us Christians, in that it promotes the spirituality of the Church, which more and more must be paschal and biblical.

". . . The reverence and respect which the Church owes and wishes to show to all men, all peoples, and every sincere religious belief, suffers no injury if our Council expresses a special veneration for the Jews, whom we here regard solely as a religious community . . .

"The 'union of the Jewish people with the Church', of which our Declaration speaks, could easily give rise to suspicion, that is, be understood in a crude and superficial sense. Our desire is, however, simply to profess the faith and hope of Paul, namely that God 'has not rejected his people whom he foreknew' (Rom 11:2), that 'the gifts and the call of God are irrevocable' (Rom 11:29), that (the Jews) are 'beloved' of God (Rom 11:28), and that 'their full inclusion' is not yet revealed (Rom 11:12). But in what ways will their full inclusion be revealed? Certainly in ways that are religious and mysterious, whose mystery we must respect. Those ways are hidden in the wisdom and knowledge of God. Therefore they should not be confused with the ways of men, that is with the methods of propaganda and the human arts of persuasion. (Jews and Christians) will be guided to the common, eternal, messianic paschal meal, not by changes in this world but by the eschatological destiny of souls."

Archbishop Elchinger (Coadjutor-Archbishop of Strasbourg) declared:

"Our Vatican Council is striving for a sincere dialogue with the men of this age. It is necessary and desirable, because appropriate to the time, that the Council promote especially the dialogue with the Jews. I should like to speak briefly about the meaning and conditions of this dialogue. After the last war, which was for the Jews a time of immense horror, a great Synagogue was built in the city of Strasbourg, of which I am bishop, and it was called the 'Synagogue of Peace'. There I often had the opportunity to talk with Jews. I therefore make so bold as to offer a modest testimony concerning two questions. 1. What is the significance of today's Jews for the Christians of our time? 2. What is the significance of our Declaration for the Jews of our time? Obviously we are concerned in this connection not with the citizens of the State of Israel, but with the Jews dispersed all over the world, in so far as they have preserved their biblical heritage.

"What is the significance of today's Jews for the Christians of our time? Not only the Jews of the Old Testament, but also the Jews of today deserve special attention, in as much as they remain living witnesses to the biblical tradition. This they are through their knowledge and understanding of the sacred books of the first Covenant. In many places, for example, Jewish children spend at least an hour every day studying the Holy Scripture — a very fine example for Christians. For those Jews the Bible is not a document that is dead and finished with,

75

but living history. I acknowledge that I have often been roused to a better understanding and more vital love for the Fathers of the first Covenant by some of these Jews.

"Quite certainly joint research into the law, the prophets and the other biblical books — common study, that is, by Jews and Christians well qualified in the subject — brings with it the greatest spiritual benefit. Many Jews of today testify to the biblical tradition by practising in their life certain religious virtues which are praised by the law and the prophets. Thus — to give only one example — they have an extraordinary sense of God's transcendence, so that they are often called in French 'les pélerins de l'Absolu' (pilgrims of the Absolute). They render obedience to the prescriptions of the divine law and in particular the Ten Commandments — an obedience that is not only moral but also most deeply religious. They trust in the liberation of God's people out of bondage. Divine worship and prayer, for which the liturgical setting is not only the synagogue but also the family itself, strengthen and sanctify the religious ties of family life.

"We believe with steadfast faith that God through all eternity does not recall his decrees. When he sealed the first Covenant he foresaw already, in his love, the Covenant to come. Hence the second Covenant does not annul the first. On the contrary, the Lord himself says, of the law and the prophets: 'I have come not to abolish them but to fulfil them' (Mt 5:17). We Christians are therefore not permitted to look upon the Jews as the rejected members of God's people. On the contrary, we are bound, so far as possible, to search out the treasures we hold in common, and together to put them to use in the present time. Anyone can see how effective this would be precisely now when atheism has spread and flourishes everywhere. Since Christians and Jews are witnesses to the word of God and to the history of salvation, they can no longer, as witnesses to the worship of the one God, present to the champions of unbelief that saddest of all testimonies, a grievous lack of mutual knowledge and love.

"What does our Declaration mean for the Jews of our time? Our late Pope of blessed memory, whom the Jews called 'John the Good', awakened an immense hope among them by his truly evangelical attitude. Today we must equally apply the same evangelical spirit in our Declaration, which presupposes sober humility and proper respect for the Jews. Without doubt the Declaration is of the greatest significance for the dialogue between the Jews and the Catholic Church that is so necessary. Our text, which is awaited by the Jews of the whole world, not without anxious questioning, will be a source and cause either of peace and joy or of deeper bitterness and grave harm. What then is required?

"The Jews expect, from our Ecumenical Council, a solemn word of justice. We cannot deny that, not only in this century but also in previous centuries, crimes have been committed against the Jews by children of the Church and, not infrequently, in the name of the Church, false though this was. We cannot overlook the fact that in the course of our history there have been inquisitions against the Jews, slanders, violations of conscience and forced conversions. Nor can we deny that right up to the most recent times there crept, all too often, into sermons and catechetical books, errors that are contrary to the spirit of the New Testament. Why can we not draw from the Gospel the magnanimity to beg for forgiveness, in the name of so many Christians, for so many and so great injustices? No doubt the Jews also have their faults and have committed errors and mistakes on their side. Nobody denies that. But regardless of this, the Gospel of Christ requires it of us that we should acknowledge our guilt, without expecting the Jews to do the same towards us. It is, besides, the office and bounden duty of our Ecumenical Council to purge our catechetical instruction of false teachings concerning the Jews, as our Declaration very properly demands. We must reject unconditionally that expression which makes out that the Jews are a deicidal people.

"Our Declaration must, however, avoid any kind of call for the conversion of the whole Jewish people, as has indeed in a certain sense already been done. At the present time it is simply impossible for the Jews to conceive that for them to pass over to the Gospel of Christ is no defection, but their true fulfilment. We do not and cannot yet know that hour appointed by God of which St. Paul speaks in his letter to the Romans, that is, the hour of the final union of the chosen people in its entirety."

In a similar spirit Archbishop (now Cardinal) Šeper (Zagreb, now Rome) regretted that the Declaration considered the Jews too much in the context of the Old Testament and applied itself far too little to the Jews of today. He called for a complete rearrangement of the text so that it might be not too didactic, but truly pastoral. In his opinion it should begin with a description of the "vis-à-vis" of the Church and the Jews of today, that is, their situation and mutual relationship. Then all their riches should be discussed: the sacred books of Israel; the hope of salvation — the idea of the coming Messiah is peculiar to Judaism and Christianity! —; the history of salvation, in part identical, in part intimately linked together. Then there should be a call for dialogue and sincere co-operation in eschatological studies, in the study of Jewish history and in scriptural exegesis. Now came the place to speak of the unacceptability of hatred for the Jews. "The Church's children are called upon to avoid with care everything that could prove offensive to the Jewish people." This new structure for the text was, however, not accepted. The Archbishop, with his emphasis on the present situation, seems to have been in advance of his time. In conclusion he spoke of the necessity of drawing up a detailed directive to regulate the dialogue with the Jews. In addition there should be established, within the framework of the Secretariat for Unity, a well-organized permanent department for relations with the Jews. Both proposals are still awaiting implementation at the time of writing.

Bishop Daem (Antwerp) introduced his contribution, which was highly relevant to the modern situation, on this special note:

"Let us condemn the injustices done to the Jews and likewise the outbreaks of hatred, tortures, murders and pogroms to which they have been subjected.

Let us hope for a speedy end to every kind of racial and religious hatred. Let us honour those Christians who, filled with love, are trying to establish and maintain better relations between Catholics and Jews . . . The Declaration on the Jews could take on greater pastoral value if historical and theological considerations were accompanied by a concrete account of the relationship of Christians to Jews in our countries. The Declaration lays great stress upon love. This would come to us more easily if we kept constantly before our eyes the positive value of the Jewish soul of our time. Is not the fact that today believing Jews are still mindful of the Covenant between their people and Jahweh a visible proof of this value? It is of great significance that believing Jews wish to be loyal to God's commands, even when these make demands that are difficult, as for example observance of the Sabbath. In their liturgical assemblies they read the sacred books which are also our own. They sing the same Psalms that we sing. They see and deplore the dangers of a growing materialism and combat it, so far as they are able. They implore God's mercy and forgiveness for their sins, especially when they celebrate the day of Atonement. They strive from the heart to give an example of loyalty to their traditions; they press onwards, filled with a great hope for the good things to come. Impelled by their vocation to a better world, they strive passionately (for this goal). These various human and religious values, so much prized in our times, are important because they determine the boundaries of the dialogue, which is, however, fundamentally conditioned for us by sacred Scripture. The Christian has to explain a certain paradox in sacred Scripture. The New Testament teaches that Jesus prophesied: 'I tell you, many will come from east and west and sit at table with Abraham, Isaac and Jacob in the kingdom of heaven, while the sons of the kingdom will be thrown into the outer darkness . . .' (Mt 8:11–12). This warning cannot be the final word of revelation concerning the fate of Israel. St. Paul says: 'As regards the gospel they are enemies of God, for your sake; but as regards election, they are beloved for the sake of their forefathers. For the gifts and the call of God are irrevocable' (Rom 11:28–29). The words of Jesus, like those of the Apostle, must be related to the historical realization of the divine decree. From the context of the former, it is clear that Jesus is speaking of the immediate consequences that its failure to recognize him would have for Israel. St. Paul, on the other hand, has in mind the ultimate destiny of Israel, its completion in God . . . This shows plainly that the two statements do not contradict each other. Christ did not exclude the Jews from eternal salvation. They are called, together with the rest of mankind, to be united with him in one body and to enter the Father's house. Loudly though the Apostle laments that 'they have stumbled over the stumbling stone' (Rom 9:32), he still rejoices over God's mercy which will save Israel. 'For God has consigned all men to disobedience, that he may have mercy upon all' (Rom 11:32).

"It will be very useful for the dialogue of Christians with Jews if the Christians follow the norms that the Apostle has laid down for their attitude.

"1. The Christian must avoid any kind of pride. He comes from the Gentiles and must acknowledge that he is a wild shoot, that he does not support the root, but the root him. '. . . You stand fast only through faith. So do not become proud but stand in awe. For if God did not spare the natural branches, neither will he spare you' (Rom 11:20–21).

"2. The Christian must be conscious of the divine decree revealed through the Apostle. If Israel has not so far grasped (it), even so the day will come when God's mercy takes its full effect. 'For if you (the Christian coming from among the Gentiles) have been cut from what is by nature a wild olive-tree, and grafted, contrary to nature, into a cultivated olive-tree, how much more will these natural branches be grafted back into their own olive-tree' (Rom 11:24).

"The Christian must bear in mind that in accordance with the divine decree the Jews and we Christians are moving towards the same fulfilment — the revelation of God's mercy in a common Covenant. We must follow this divine decree, not by means of an unseemly proselytism, but in plain dealing and complete humility . . . Let us therefore, reverend Fathers, choose this twofold standpoint of humility and of sharing in a common hope, in order . . . the better to walk in the light of Pauline teaching."

In order to bring to a meaningful conclusion this survey of opinions in the Council, or, more precisely, of the attitude of leading personalities to the Declaration on the Jews, I should like to cite a few more short and impressive statements. Bishop Leven repudiated the general indictment of the Jewish people in these words: "At the time of Christ so many Jews, especially in the diaspora, were completely unaware of him, and therefore could not in any way consent to his death. It is as senseless to blame all Jews of Christ's time for (having brought about) his death as it would be to accuse all the Romans of that time of being guilty of Jesus' death, because the Roman Pilate handed him over (to the soldiers) and Roman soldiers crucified him."

Archbishop Heenan, rejecting the use of the Declaration for attempts at conversion, declared: "The text contains these words: '(The Catholic Church) has a sincere respect for those ways of acting and living, those moral and doctrinal teachings which may differ in many respects from what she holds and teaches, but which none the less often reflect the brightness of that Truth which is the light of all men.' If then those (other religions) reflect the brightness of truth, how much more does the Jewish religion which is, at the same time, the root of our faith? As Pius XI said many years ago, '(Spiritually) we are Semites!'" On the question of collective guilt he expressed himself as follows: "In this century the Jews have endured grievous, and indeed inhuman injustices. In the name of our Lord Jesus Christ, who on the Cross forgave (his actual) persecutors, I humbly ask that our Declaration publicly acknowledge that the Jewish people as such are not guilty of the Lord's death. It would without doubt be unjust, if one were to blame all the Christians of Europe for the murder of six million Jews in Germany and Poland in our own day. In the same way,

I maintain that it is unjust to condemn the whole Jewish people for the death of Christ."

As was only to be expected there were, in the course of the great debate, one or two negative voices. The most prominent was the warning delivered by Cardinal Ruffini. He demanded that not only should Christians be enjoined to love the Jews — "this glorious stock, from which came Jesus Christ, the Virgin Mary and the Apostles" — but also that the Jews should be urged to love the Christians, especially the Catholics, or at least not to do them injury. As a basis for this last expression he referred to the Talmud, which taught the Jews to despise all other men, who were like wild animals, and also to the harmful influence they exercised through the Freemasons. "Is not this pestilential sect . . ., this continual conspiracy against the Church, sustained and promoted by the Jews?"[105]

[105] Cardinal Ruffini's view about Freemasonry seems somewhat out of date. In the past the designation "intriguers and agitators" may occasionally have corresponded to the facts, but can this still be maintained today? At all events, Catholics in the United States are coming round to the view that the Freemasons are not enemies and that it would be more than desirable to co-operate with them in social and, particularly, charitable work. There can, however, be no doubt that the Cardinal is vastly overestimating the influence of Jews on the world in general and on Free-masonry in particular. His intervention sees the Jews through the diseased eyes of the forgers of the Protocols of the Elders of Zion. Of course there have been, and always will be, conspiracies. But the attempt to represent conspiracies as a major historical factor is something which comes out of the darkness of the subconscious and not from the lucid sphere of knowledge. Anyone who is himself caught up in a web of inward conflicts will be very easily inclined to presume the existence of a web of conspiracies encompassing both Church and culture.

The source adduced by the Cardinal (*Baba Meziah,* 104, 2) contains, to the best of my knowledge, no vilification of non-Jews as "wild animals". In the rabbinic literature Gentiles were, in fact, compared with raging beasts, as in the comparison of the Gentiles with wolves and Israel with a lamb (*Pesik,* R. IX). But to understand the attitude of the rabbis towards non-Jews one must first try and understand all the hostile pronouncements in their contexts, i.e. in the light of the historical context and, so far as can be ascertained, the state of mind of the writer. Then again, isolated statements should not be generalized. The renowned Rabbi Akiba used to say: "Man is loved, for he was created in God's likeness; by a very special love, however, it was made known to him that he was created in God's likeness. As it is written: 'God made man in his own image' (Gen 9:6). The people of Israel are loved, for they are called children of the all-present God; it was a special love which made known to them that they are children of the all-present One, as is written: 'You are the sons of the Lord your God' [Deut 14:1]" (*Aboth,* III, 18). These words most successfully combine God's pre-eminent attachment to Israel with the favour with which he embraces all creatures.

Sometimes a highly disturbing sentence can be found in a context which eludes the reader unversed in the *Talmud,* while opening up broad perspectives to the trained reader. An especially instructive example is an utterance of Rabbi Simon ben Yochai (2nd century A.D.), which runs: "The grave of Gentiles causes no uncleanness of the tent, for it is written: 'And you are my sheep, the sheep of my pasture, you are man [Adam]' (Ezek 34:31). You are called 'man', the Gentiles are not called 'man'" (*Yebam.,* 61a). This statement is very disconcerting, coming as it does from a disciple of the Rabbi Akiba quoted above. Antisemitic writers have sometimes availed themselves of it to "prove" that the Jews despise non-Jews. Jewish apologists, however, have pointed out that Rabbi Simon had been a witness of his teacher's martyrdom. He saw the Romans tearing the

j) The October crisis

The panorama unfolding on these pages, and before that in the aula of St. Peter's, witnesses to a new awakening to the mystery of Israel in the hearts of many bishops. The question that occupied them was no longer that of better or worse relations between the Church and the Jewish people, but rather of a deep mutual bond. The initiative had now passed, in part, from the Secretariat for Unity to the bishops. In the revised draft put before the fathers towards the end of the third session, their influence was quite plain. The introductory sentence recapitulated an argument of Cardinal Lercaro, the final sentence was an echo of the plea made by Cardinal König. The images of the olive-tree, the return to the Pauline profession of Christ as the founder of peace between Jews and Gentiles, indeed as himself being that peace, the new conception of the Church's eschatological hope, the strengthened warning against a biased, one-sided interpretation of Scripture, the clear rejection of any Jewish collective guilt — all these vital changes, which gave the draft that followed the great debate its special character — derive from suggestions made by the bishops.

This new awakening thus proves that the Declaration on the Jews was not simply and solely the work of a minority or the product of an energetic and well-organized "lobby".[106] After the great debate one would have to be blind indeed

flesh off the body of the aged Rabbi Akiba. For his criticism of the Romans he himself was later condemned to death — though he avoided execution by taking to flight. Legend relates that he and his son remained twelve or thirteen years in hiding in a cave. No wonder, say a number of apologists, that he hated his and his teacher's persecutors, the Romans (for the Jewish people of those times the Gentiles *par excellence*), or that in his bitterness he denied them their humanity and branded them as brutes.

This interpretation appears extremely plausible if one tears Rabbi Simon's words from its immediate Talmudic context. But it can hardly escape the attentive reader that this context is a discussion on graves, and no judgment is passed on the metaphysical status of the Gentiles or their values as rational beings. As has been demonstrated by M. Guttmann, *Das Judentum und seine Umwelt* (1927), I. pp. 180f., the sole issue here was the extent to which graves caused ritual impurity. According to a cultic prescription in the Law, ritual impurity could be caused not merely by contact with a corpse but even by inhabitation of the same tent in which a corpse lay — hence "uncleanness of the tent". As a result of many wars graves were scattered all over contemporary Palestine (which, as a dwelling-place, was comparable to a large tent). This circumstance forbade priests to reside in certain localities and also made it difficult for them to go to and from the temple, and thus to carry out their duties, since any priest who — intentionally or otherwise — walked across a grave became unclean and was incapacitated from divine worship until his "cleansing". To remove this burden from the priests Rabbi Simon reinterpreted the regulation in question. Since occasionally (e.g. Ezek 34:31) "man" was used of Israel alone, it is a probable assumption that the expression was confined to the "children of Israel" in the Levitical law of impurity too. The argument used by the Talmudic rabbi was of this kind; it is confined exclusively to the sphere of cultic law and has nothing to do with morality. It implies neither hostility nor friendliness towards the Gentiles. (An objective and detailed account of the rabbinic attitude towards the Gentiles can be found in the *Jewish Encyclopedia*, V, pp. 615, "Gentiles".)

[106] There was indeed a Jewish lobby at the Council, which often drew considerable attention to itself. Whether it should be described as "energetic and well-organized" is another question. At all

to attribute the Declaration solely to the influence of lobbyists. In a communiqué published after the third session, Patriarch Maximos attributed the progress of the Declaration to the skill of the Jews in the art of propaganda, and even went so far, it was said, as to make the assertion (which he later regretted) that the powerful intervention of the American bishops in favour of a strongly-worded Declaration was the consequence of the commercial interests of many Americans, who maintained close business relations with the Jews.[107]

The Patriarch apparently did not content himself with this attempt to depict a section of the Declaration's advocates as having been "bought". In the same communiqué he disassociated himself from the Declaration by explaining, in opposition to the great majority of the Council, that "so long as the Jewish people stand apart from Christ the Saviour, there rests upon the brow of that people a mark of shame, as the prophets of the Old Testament foretold. This mark of shame is not, however, equivalent to a personal crime."[108] The Patriarch, who is otherwise an excellent theologian, omitted to give a scriptural reference. He would have found it difficult to produce in evidence an appropriate passage from the prophets.

The Patriarch's dishonourable imputations date from the period following the third session. Already in October 1964 it was reported that the Arab Supreme Committee for Palestine had sent a deputation to the Vatican, in order to counter the efforts being made at the Council "to declare the Jews innocent". A communiqué issued by this Committee saw behind the Council's efforts "imperialist-Zionist manoeuvres to lead the Church to take up a position in the Palestine conflict favourable to international Jewry".[109]

It can be supposed from these desperate attempts to bring the Declaration on

events, its influence on the form taken by the text was minimal. Only the hypersensitive who are afraid to look the facts of life straight in the eye could be scandalized that such lobbyists should wish to assert their wishes and opinions. There was a lobby of pacifists, one for equal rights for women in the Church, and any number of others. It is only natural that particular interest groups should want to get a hearing at so unusual an event as an Ecumenical Council.

[107] See G. S. Higgins, "Christian-Jewish Relations", *The Yardstick*, N.C. Features (25 January 1965), p. 3. This essay contains several quotations from the Patriarch's communiqué and Higgin's own reply.

[108] *Ibid.*, p. 2. The text has also been reprinted (in French) in *L'Église grecque melkite au Concile. Discours et notes du Patriarche Maximos IV* . . . (1967), p. 455, dated 30 November 1964. See *ibid.*, pp. 443–59, for all the expressions of Melchite opinion on the "Declaration on the Jews". However much I regret the injurious remarks of the Patriarch, fairness requires that certain other words of his should be recorded. After Maximos IV's return from Rome he confronted the Muslims who were worked up over the Declaration with the following argument: It is a contradiction to speak of deicide in the case of someone who does not believe in the divinity of Christ; the fact that the Council has repudiated the accusation of deicide should present no difficulties for a Moslem, for the Koran itself states that the Jews believed they had killed Jesus, whereas in reality they had crucified not him but a double (cf. 4th *Surah*). Cf. R. Laurentin, *Bilan de la Troisième* Session (1965), p. 82.

[109] Fesquet, *op. cit.*, p. 578.

the Jews into disrepute, with the help of pseudo-theological and pseudo-historical arguments, how strong were the repeated remonstrations of the Arab governments with the State Secretariat. It is no wonder that the elderly State Secretary, Cardinal Cicognani, felt himself driven into a corner. To do him justice, it must be borne in mind that he was coming under pressure not only from the Arabs, but from many sides. In this tense situation, the idea may have come to him, not to untie the knot, but to cut it.

Late in the afternoon of 9 October 1964, a Friday, the Secretariat for Unity held a plenary meeting. As usual, Cardinal Bea was in the chair. At the time fixed he came in, took two letters out of his pocket, and read them out without comment or explanation. They came from Archbishop Felici, the Secretary-General of the Council, who purported to write "on higher authority". This aroused the impression that he was communicating the wishes of the Pope. In reality, it seemed he was acting only in the name of Cardinal Cicognani who, to all appearances, had neglected to ask the other members of the Co-ordinating Commission for their opinions. At any rate, one letter contained the information that the Declaration on Religious Freedom must be examined again by a mixed commission. What this "examination" would be like one could see from the fact that the majority of the members already nominated consisted of outspoken opponents of this Declaration. The second letter related to the Declaration on the Jews. It required that this Declaration should also be submitted to a renewed examination by a Commission of Six (three members were to be nominated by Cardinal Bea, and three others by Cardinal Ottaviani, the Chairman of the Theological Commission). The object of this examination and recasting was an abbreviation which was to make it possible to incorporate the Declaration in the Schema on the Church.

These two letters struck like a bomb — and within a few hours the explosion was heard all over Rome. There was general consternation. The instruction was seen as a clever manoeuvre to bid defiance to the authority of the bishops, to circumvent the rules of the Council,[110] and, not least, to cripple the Secretariat for Unity, that is, to rob it of its Conciliar status by withdrawing from it further responsibility for the Council documents that had originated within its province.[111]

It is said that Cardinal Bea spoke with Archbishop Felici and demanded to know whether he had acted on papal authority. The Secretary-General answered this question in the negative, but at the same time gave to understand that he had acted according to the mind of the Pope. To this Cardinal Bea is supposed to have replied, "Well, I cannot accept that as the last word." It is said that he

---

[110] According to the regulations only the Moderators or the Pope himself could transfer the competence for a conciliar document from one commission to another; *Orientierung,* 31 October 1964, quoted in X. Rynne, *The Third Session* (1964), p. 64.

[111] Valquist, *op. cit.,* p. 319.

then applied directly to Pope Paul, who informed him that a mixed commission had in fact been discussed, but that no definite decision on its establishment had been reached.[112]

Cardinal Bea's intervention was, however, not the only one. On the evening of Sunday, 11 October, at the invitation of Cardinal Frings (Cologne), there assembled at his residence in the "Anima" a group of leaders of the Council, among them Cardinals Alfrink (Utrecht), Döpfner (Munich), König (Vienna), Léger (Montreal), Lefèbvre (Bourges), Liénart (Lille), Meyer (Chicago), Richaud (Bordeaux), and Ritter (St Louis). The fourteen Cardinals present drew up a letter to the Pope, beginning with the now famous words *"magno cum dolore"*: "Holy Father, we have learned with great sorrow that the Declaration on Religious Freedom, although it stands in harmony with the wish of the

---

[112] Rynne, *op. cit.*, p. 64. Hampe thinks that the measures which led to the October crisis were a sudden move on the part of the "conservatives". "It is, in fact, probable that the attempt then made by the Secretary of State, Cicognani, and the Secretary General of the Council to push through a new version was brought on as the result of the long pent-up misgivings of the conservative group in the Curia about the Declaration on the Jews. It is generally assumed that they turned an offer of reconsideration supposed to have been made by Pope Paul into a directive and informed the Secretariat of Church Unity that the Declaration on the Jews would have to form part of the schema on the Church" (Eckert and Ehrlich, *op. cit.*, p. 420). This is a possible explanation of Archbishop Felici's demand, though it is more probable that the suggestion to incorporate the "Declaration on the Jews" into the schema on the Church was an attempt to demonstrate the non-political character of the statement. It was thought it might in this way be possible to convince the Arabs that the Council's motives were of a purely spiritual nature.

On 12 October the Vatican was awaiting the visit of President Sukarno of Indonesia; there was every reason to assume that he would come not only as head of state but also as a champion of "Arab interests". And shortly before the crisis the four Patriarchs of the Near East had called on the Pope, doubtless to implore him urgently for support. Even during the great debate the Patriarch of Antioch, Cardinal Tappouni, had entreated the Council in the name of all the Near Eastern Patriarchs as follows: "I most earnestly request that this totally inopportune Declaration be completely abandoned. It is not that we are hostile to the Jewish religion or in favour of discrimination against a particular nation. Nearly all of us are ourselves Semites. If we do not want this Declaration it is because we desire to avoid the great difficulties which it would without any doubt put in the way of our pastoral activity. It will be said that the Declaration is pro-Jewish, and this would be seriously prejudicial to our work. After giving the matter due consideration in all conscience we submit once more that this Declaration is not opportune and request that it be struck off the agenda of the Council."

In his intervention during the great debate, Bishop Tawil, Melchite Patriarchate Vicar for Syria, went even further: "Although it is necessary to condemn antisemitism there are other persecutions. It is forgotten that millions [*sic!*] of refugees were driven out of Palestine. The Jews have already forfeited the friendship of the Arab world — the Declaration will shut all doors for good. For this reason it is extremely inopportune: it will have grave consequences and make whole nations enemies of the Church." The Patriarchs probably came up before the Pope and the Secretary of State with the same heavy artillery. I speak of "heavy artillery" because such emotionally charged arguments make all arguments to the contrary appear like lack of feeling and disarm the other side. If I see things rightly, it was mainly the regrettable, if understandable, failure to resist this pressure which brought on the October crisis.

majority of the fathers, is to be entrusted to a mixed Commission. Three of its members seem to be hostile to the sense of the Council in this respect."[113] The letter, which dealt only with the Declaration on Religious Liberty, spoke of the extreme concern and great disquiet of the signatories in whose opinion even the "appearance of a violation of the Council's rules and its freedom" would compromise the Church before world public opinion. They asked the Pope "with the utmost urgency" for a return to the normal procedures of the Council and for all questions to be dealt with in accordance with the existing rules, in order to avoid great harm to the whole people of God. The letter was subsequently also signed by several Cardinals who were unable to take part in the meeting. In all it bore seventeen signatures.

According to R. Laurentin[114] this letter was delivered to the Pope on Monday 12 October. J. Schmitz van Vorst[115], however, reports that Cardinal Frings handed it personally to him in his one hour audience on Tuesday 13 October. It is probable that the Cardinal chose the more polite way and gave the Pope time to examine the matter and to consider his further steps. The Pope was pained, not to say deeply disquieted. It is difficult to tell how far he was offended by the hidden abuse of his authority (as has been mentioned before, the Secretary General's letters to Cardinal Bea were written "on higher authority", which made it probable that the Pope himself was involved.) In any case, he quickly restored both his own and the Council's threatened authority by assuring Cardinal Frings that the Secretariat for Unity would remain responsible for both declarations. Moreover, the mixed commission was appointed in exact correspondence with the rules of the Council, it was also deprived of the right of direct intervention and restricted to making suggestions.

The changes in the "Declaration on the Jews" forecast in the second letter would hardly have been rejected if they had not been combined with the proposal to cut it to one paragraph. Many fathers and theologians had always held that the Constitution on the Church was the right place for a statement on the relation between the Church and the Synagogue. But an abridgment which would have left only a fraction of the original text would have been unacceptable. In the early stages of the crisis Paul VI is supposed to have assured Cardinal Bea that the "Declaration on the Jews" would be "neither amputated nor diminished".[116] It is also difficult to see how a smooth incorporation of the "Declaration on the Jews" could have been possible at such a late stage, when the Constitution on the Church was already completed. In any case the Theological Commission which was responsible for the Constitution on the Church refused to consider the proposal of Archbishop Felici's letter; thus in the end the Declaration was not even made — as had also been proposed — an appendix of *Lumen Gentium,* but

---

[113] Cf. Fesquet, *op. cit.,* 17 October 1964; Rynne, *op. cit.,* pp. 65–6.

[114] *Troisième Session* (1965), p. 140.

[115] *Frankfurter Allgemeine Zeitung,* 14 October 1964.

[116] A.-M. Henry, ed., *Vatican II,* Unam Sanctam 52–53 (1966), p. 62.

became the heart of a separate declaration on the relation of the Church to the non-Christian religions.

k) The enlargement of the Declaration

During the great debate and even before several fathers had expressed the wish that the "Declaration on the Jews" should be given a wider application, so that the new spirit of encounter would extend not only to the Jews, but to all non-Christians. During the second session in 1963 this was suggested by Cardinals Bueno y Monreal of Spain and Doi of Japan, but most emphatically by Bishop Da Veiga Coutinho of India. In the third session in 1964 the idea of a graduated declaration which would, however, include all religions was represented mainly by Bishops Plumery of the Cameroons, Sfair (Maronite), Descuffi of Turkey, Nagae of Japan and Nguyen Van Hien of Vietnam. A number of African bishops desired that animism should be expressly mentioned.

Thus many fathers emphasized the value of all spiritual experience; nevertheless the leading men of the Secretariat refused for a long time to express this view in greater detail, and not only quite generally. Not, indeed, because they believed that God did not speak at all to those outside the sphere of the biblical revelation, but because they felt that the Secretariat for Unity was not authorized to produce such a declaration; it had neither competence nor the experts needed for drafting a declaration on the all-embracing salvific will of God and his saving work among the nations. After the great debate, however, the Secretariat for Unity began to appoint a number of special temporary commissions to which belonged among others Georges Anawati, O.P. (Egypt), Yves Congar, O.P. (France), Canon Charles Moeller, and Josef Neuner, S.J. (India).

In February 1964 the American Institute for Jewish-Christian Studies had submitted a memorandum drawn up by Dr. Barry Ulanov of Columbia University, New York, to the Secretariat for Unity and several bishops. According to this memorandum it was not only extremely suitable but indeed necessary that the Council should "celebrate" the variety as well as the essential unity of the inner experiences of mankind. In his view it was the task of the Church gladly to praise every just deed, every just man, every loving deed and every loving man, every opening of a soul to God, every movement of the heart, however weak, which announces the goodness of God and the goodness of men towards each other. The recognition of religious experiences outside its own sphere does not mean that the Church does not realize the great differences between itself and those who do not believe in Christ. But by affirming the work of the Spirit who blows where it wills it can also deepen its own asceticism and piety, its own sympathy and its own incessant prayer. At the same time it shows itself as the faithful companion and intercessor for all those who seek permanent peace.

From the very beginning of his pontificate Paul VI has defended this wider outlook of the Church and thus encouraged a larger declaration in part consciously, in part without realizing it. He had first sounded this theme in his opening speech for the second session:

"The Catholic Church, however, looks beyond the frontiers of Christianity. How could she limit her love, as she is to imitate the love of the divine Father, who gives his good things to all men (cf. Mt 5:48) and so loves the world, that he gave his only son for its salvation? (cf. Jn 3:16). Thus she looks beyond her own sphere to the other religions which have preserved the sense of the Divine and the idea of the one supreme and transcendent Creator and Preserver. These religions venerate God by sincere acts of piety, a piety which, like their convictions, form the foundations of their moral and social life. The Catholic Church sees — not without regret — in these religions gaps and errors. But it cannot but turn also to them in order to tell them that the Catholic religion gives due respect to whatever truth, goodness and humanity she finds in them, and to assure them that she is in the forefront of those who, among our contemporaries, protect the sense of religion and worship, both the conditions and the obligations of the earthly common good in order effectively to defend, as it were, the rights of God over men."[117]

Since then this theme has been recurring again and again. In his Easter Message of 29 March 1964 the Pope proclaimed: "Every religion contains a ray of the light which we must neither despise nor extinguish, even though it is not sufficient to give man the truth he needs, or to realize the miracle of the Christian light in which truth and life coalesce. But every religion raises us towards the transcendent Being, the sole ground of all existence and all thought, of all responsible action and all authentic hope. Every religion is a dawn of faith, and we await its full realization in the light of noon, in the splendour of Christian wisdom."[118]

Paul VI's first encyclical, *Ecclesiam Suam* of 6 August 1964 was devoted to the task of the Church to enter on the dialogue with "the others". He says there:

"Then we see another circle around us. This, too, is vast in its extent . . . It is made up of the men who above all adore the one, supreme God whom we too adore. We refer briefly first to the children of the Hebrew people, worthy of our affection and respect, faithful to the religion which we call that of the Old Covenant. Then to the adorers of God according to the conception of monotheism, the Moslem religion especially, deserving of our admiration for all that is true and good in their worship of God. And also to the followers of the great Afro-Asiatic religions."

The Pope says further that evidently the members of the Church cannot share in these various forms of religion, nor could they pretend that all are of equal value and that these religions absolve their followers from the duty to seek God

---

[117] Cf. *HK,* 18 (1963), pp. 82f.
[118] *Vatican II* (see n. 116 above), *loc. cit.*

in the perfect and definitive form in which he has revealed himself and in which he demands to be known, loved and served. The Pope continues:

"But we do, nevertheless, recognize and respect the moral and spiritual values of the various non-Christian religions, and we desire to join with them in promoting and defending common ideals of religious liberty, human brotherhood, culture, social welfare and civil order. For our part, we are ready to enter into dialogue on these common ideals, and will not fail to take the initiative where our offer of discussion in genuine, mutual respect, would be well received."

The idea to give the "Declaration on the Jews" a Catholic framework embracing the earth was tremendously advanced by the Pope's plan to attend the Eucharistic Congress at Bombay after the third session. The new declaration was passed "in the first reading" even before the end of the session. On 3 December 1964 the Pope delivered a speech before the representatives of non-Christian communities in Bombay. It was a programmatic statement applying the declaration of the Council to a concrete situation.

"Your country", he said, "is a country of an old civilization, the cradle of great religions, the home of a nation which has sought God in constant desire, in deep meditation, in silence and in ardent hymns. Only rarely has this longing for God been expressed in words so full of the Advent spirit as those in your holy books written many centuries before Christ: 'From unreality lead me to reality, from darkness lead me to light, from death lead me to immortality!' (*Upanishads, Brihadaranayaka* 1). This prayer is relevant in our time. Today more than ever before it should ascend from every human heart. Mankind passes through profound changes; it is groping for principles and new forces which are to lead it into the world of the future."

Going on to the special problems of India the Pope continued:

„You, too, are struggling with the evils which darken the lives of innumerable men throughout the world, such as poverty, hunger and disease. You fight an inexorable battle for more food, clothing and houses, for education, for a just distribution of the riches of this world. Are we not all united in this struggle for a better world, in the effort to give to all men those things that are necessary so that they can fulfil their human destiny and lead a life that is worthy of the children of God? Hence we must come nearer to each other, not only through the modern means of communication, through press and radio, through ships and aeroplanes. We must come together with our hearts, in mutual understanding, in respect and love, we must meet each other, not only as tourists, but as pilgrims who have set out to find God not in temples of stone, but in the human heart. Men and nations must meet each other as brothers and sisters, as children of God. In such mutual understanding, in such friendship, in this holy fellowship we must begin to work together in order to build the common future of the world . . . May (the Lord) transform us into the one family of his children!"

The speech of the Pope was evidently inspired by the enlarged declaration with its confession of unity and of the all-embracing brotherhood of mankind as well as of the dignity of the non-biblical religions. The Church has always believed and taught that mankind is one. But it is one thing to grasp a truth with the mind, and quite another to experience it in life. The technological inventions of the last decades from the aeroplane to radio and television with their consequences such as the fight against hunger and disease, illiteracy and unproductive methods of labour, all these have made the one world a personal experience of many through caring for the needs of others.

The speed of the means of transport and communication has transformed our vast planet into a village with many newcomers. In the view of the Council the geographical neighbourhood is not enough; the newcomers must also become neighbours mentally and spiritually. Just as the Church-in-Council has rethought its connection with the people from which it sprang, so also that with the peoples among which it lives. Thus it could examine its relations to the world in which it is placed and which it is meant to serve. As man is both an individual and a member of a community, the Church is meant to care not for isolated individuals, but for individuals who are also members of religious bodies and thus for these bodies themselves.

In her longing for unity and love among men and nations the Church "gives primary consideration in this document to what human beings have in common and to what promotes fellowship among them", as the final text of the Declaration expresses it, speaking of the one origin and goal of mankind. The metaphysical situation of man is everywhere the same. Everywhere he asks the same existential questions, but he does not receive everywhere the same answer to the riddle of his existence. Wherever men are, they ask what is the meaning and the end of life, what is the good and what is sin, what is the way to true happiness and what is the primeval and ineffable mystery of our existence from which derives our being and for which it longs. Different cultures give different answers to these basic questions. The Council is not at all discouraged by this variety, but it sees the finger of God also in these religions. Though God is not present in them in all his glory, which is the sign of the biblical revelation, he is nevertheless present there, too. Otherwise the Council would not have been able to express its reverence for those who believe, worship and live according to the light of the religion in which they were born.

It was a great moment when the ecumenical gathering of the bishops said for the first time, and a year later solemnly proclaimed, that the Church despises nothing that is genuine and good in the various spiritual traditions of the peoples. "The Catholic Church rejects nothing which is true and holy in these religions" — this is the key formula of the first section, which treats of the various religions of mankind. Timid souls were afraid that the Council fathers had come close to indifferentism when pronouncing this principle. But the truth is exactly the opposite. The bishops did not think at all that it made no difference what men considered to be true and what they worshipped. They only confessed what is perfectly, if not exclusively, Catholic: namely that whoever proclaims a religious truth has received his thought and his word from the Holy Spirit. Wherever goodness is taught and lived God is well pleased. Whoever conquers selfishness can only do so because his victory had already been achieved on Golgotha. Wherever there is grace, there is the Church.

Exponents of relativism assert that all traditions are true and at the same time none, that every tradition is only true for the believer. The respect for the values present in the non-Christian religions such as the Council fathers affirmed was so far removed from such a mentality that they could claim the authority of Christ himself for their view. As soon as they had affirmed that the Church rejects nothing she finds to be true and holy in other religions they continue: "Indeed, she proclaims and must ever proclaim Christ, 'the way, the truth, and the life' (Jn 14:6), in whom men find the fullness of religious life, and in whom God has reconciled all things to Himself (cf. 2 Cor 5:18–19)." He is so obviously the way, the truth and the life of those who follow him, but he is also, even though in a hidden way, the power of those who do not yet know him. Thus the openness of the Council, too, has no other source than Christ's work of reconciliation.

When the Apostle expressed his joy because Christ had reconciled the world in Christ he wrote that "God gave us the ministry of reconciliation" (2 Cor 5:18). Thus because the bishops were the ministers of reconciliation they acknowledged the groping of the primitive religions for the power hidden in all things and events and their search for the supreme Being. As servants of this reconciliation they valued the deep longing for ultimate validity of Hinduism and Buddhism and their desire to be free from the cares of the human situation or of the transitoriness of life. As servants of this reconciliation they respect the Moslems, who "adore one God, living and enduring, merciful and all-powerful, Maker of heaven and earth, who speaks to men" and acknowledge the submission of pious Moslems under the will of God which resembles the obedience of Abraham. As servants of the work of reconciliation the bishops implore all, both Christians and non-Christians, to forget the past with its dissensions and hostilities and to "strive sincerely for mutual understanding", asking to make common cause in fostering justice, peace and freedom among all men.

EXCURSUS: THE OMNIPRESENCE OF GRACE

Centuries ago Pius V, Innocent XI and Clement XI condemned the following frightening theological opinions: All works of non-believers are sin and the virtues of the philosophers are vices; pagans, Jews, heretics and others are doomed to perdition because they are under the dominion of vice. They are outside the Church, and God's grace does not work outside the Church (*D* 1025, 1295, 1379). The enlarged Declaration — in its provisional form of 1964 and even more in its final form of 1965 — is not content simply to reject the pessimistic view of God expressed in the condemned propositions. On the contrary, "she looks with sincere respect upon those ways of conduct and of life, those rules and teachings which, though differing in many particulars from what she holds and sets forth, nevertheless often reflect a ray of that Truth which enlightens all men (cf. Jn 1:9)."

This raises a question: If the power of God breaches the wall that separates the Church from the non-Christian world, if there are communities outside the Church which are touched by God's Spirit in one form or another, do these nevertheless remain alien to the order of grace established by Christ, are they unrelated to the Church, which is the sacrament of salvation on earth? Or does the presence of the Church extend to all men? The Church is an enclave of prayer and mercy within the world; but at the same time it is somehow one with the world. The world subsists through the Church's *diaconia,* through its service, just as the Church lives because of the *diaconia* of Jesus Christ, the great Servant of God, who represents God to men and men to God, who reveals the meaning of human existence as belonging with him to God and also to his fellow men. The Church mirrors the fact that Christ represents humanity throughout history, that is to say between his ascension and his second coming. Being the community of believers, the Church is destined to witness, explain and praise the service of Christ the Saviour not only through her preaching but through her whole existence, her action and her visible reality.[119]

The non-Christian world, too, has a function within the sphere of salvation history, even though it is unaware of it. According to J. Feiner it consists first of all in this that the non-Christian section of mankind constantly causes the Church to experience its own existence as a gift of grace. Furthermore, the part of mankind that lives outside — and apparently without — the Church, represents "a question, a call, a 'provocation' which the Church needs in order not to become unfaithful to its true function." The challenge of the "non-Church" becomes all the greater, the less the whole life of the Church is distinguished from it. Moreover, non-Christian mankind helps the Church "to a more comprehensive historical presentation of its own essence and the means of salvation that are given to her" as well as "to a more clearly reflected comprehension of its own message and service." Finally, the world outside the Church reminds her time and again of the sovereignty of God who is quite independent of the institutions and means of grace he has himself established.[120]

No doubt the desire of the Buddhist to be freed from the burden of existence is foreign to the thought of the Bible. But no Christian would dare to take a completely negative view of this desire, especially when looking at the serenely smiling Buddha, no Christian would regard the multitudes of pious Hindus who wash in the sacred river to be cleansed of their sins as merely victims of an illusion.

---

[119] Cf. J. Ratzinger, "Stellvertretung", in H. Fries, *Handbuch theologischer Grundbegriffe,* II, pp. 566–75, esp. pp. 574 f.; J. Feiner, "Kirche und Heilsgeschichte", in H. Vorgrimler and others, ed., *Gott in Welt* (1964), pp. 317–45, esp. pp. 324 f.

[120] Feiner, *loc. cit.,* pp. 339–44.

Nor could any Christian be so stupid as to imagine that the Moslem's invocation of Allah is not heard anywhere. The Moslems perform every action in the name of him who has pity and compassion. Thus the Koran begins with the following brief prayer:

"In the name of Allah, the All-Merciful!
Praise be to Allah, the Lord of the worlds,
The gracious All-compassionate,
The Lord of the Day of Judgment.
We wish to serve You alone, we ask You alone for assistance,
Lead us in the right way,
The way of those to whom you are gracious,
With whom you are not angry and who do not go astray."

Though the last line seems to be directed against Jews and Christians, the whole song of praise is a fruit of biblical spirituality. This Mohammedan *Te Deum* echoes the voice of revelation.

There is no question that Islam has been influenced by Judaism and Christianity. But what about the aforementioned signs and prayers where such an influence is excluded? These, too, have been transformed into ways leading to God through Christ's dwelling among men. God in his mercy has restricted his grace neither to those prayers that the Church has received from Christ, from the singers of Israel or from her own poets, nor has he restricted it to the Sacraments. Already the Schoolmen taught "Deus virtutem suam non alligavit sacramentis" — "God has not tied his power (to vivify and to sanctify) to the sacraments" (cf. *Summa Theologica*, III, q. 64, a. 7). The non-Christian religions, too, have a certain measure of sanctifying power, they are near to salvation because they share unconsciously in the grace of Christ which is ever active in the Church. As has been said, they are a challenge to the Church, reminding her that she owes all she is and has to God's goodness alone. In this way the non-Christian world assists the Church and becomes, as it were, the servant of the serving Church.

In the opinion of some Christians this view of the non-Christian world is a symptom of the fact that the Church has lost the conviction of her own identity and has capitulated to the "world". But this is a most pernicious error. On the contrary, the view of the Council is a sign of new life which has nothing in common with the contemporary spiritual malaise nor with the modern passion for indifference. "Therefore let us be grateful for receiving a kingdom that cannot be shaken, and thus let us offer to God acceptable worship, with reverence and awe; for our God is a consuming fire" (Heb 12:28f.). Today these words are as true as they were yesterday and as they will be tomorrow. Idolatry is still an abomination (Deut 7:25; 27:15), and fornicators, murderers and idolaters will always remain outside the City (Rev 22:15). The prophets' and apostles' curse on the worshipers of Baal has not been annulled, nor has the Church, in a fit of indecision suddenly made peace with godlessness. What has happened, and what is expressed in the Declaration, is the overwhelming realization that mankind bears the seal of Christ, even if it is far from being Christian. He came into the world, and this merciful event can never be undone. All men are images of the eternal Word made flesh, however blurred their contours. Whether they know it or not, all have been offered a share in the divine life, all are infinitely loved and have their being only in the love of God. The traces of God are everywhere, and we must open our eyes to them.

Though all these considerations are not expressed in the Declaration in so many words, they are nevertheless basically there. They owe much to the work of Karl Rahner, even though substantially this theology is by no means new. It has been formulated most clearly by Henri de Lubac:[121] "Without closing our eyes to the needs of all those who are 'in the shadow of death', we nevertheless believe with Irenaeus that from the beginning the Son reveals the Father to every creature in a more or less hidden way, and that he can 'become salvation also for those who have been born outside the Way'.[122] We believe with Cyprian, Hilary and Ambrose that the divine sun of justice shines on all and for all men.[123] We confess with John Chrysostom that grace is poured out everywhere and excludes no soul from its wooing. We deny with Jerome and Cyril of Alexandria that any man is born without Christ.[124] Finally, we are inclined to assume with Augustine, the strictest of all the Fathers, that the divine goodness has been at work always and among all the nations, and that even the heathen had their 'hidden saints' and their prophets."

The Council has imparted new strength to these opinions which have often been forgotten. But we must not be satisfied with some general knowledge of them; the Declaration rather demands a deeper knowledge of the ways of God and men. The more we penetrate into the convictions and religious practices of non-biblical origin, the more we shall perceive God's gentle, almost shy action everywhere, even in the jungle, in the mountains and the temples that have not yet been marked with the Cross. It is the greatness of those sections of the Declaration dealing with the various non-Christian religions that they praise the omnipresence of grace.

l) The fourth draft

A new stage was reached when the Declaration was extended to the whole sphere of man's thirst for the Absolute and his awareness of the primeval mystery of the

---

[121] See *The Catholic and His Church* (1960).

[122] *Adv. Haer.*, II, 22, 4; III, 18, 7; IV, 20, 6–7; IV, 22, 2: *PG,* VII, col. 784, 937, 990, 1036f., 1947. Demonstratio 34: "The invisible presence of the Logos is diffused everywhere ... Through it everything is made subject to the working of the economy of salvation, and the Son of God ... has imprinted on each thing the sign of the cross" (*PO,* XII, 773). Fragment 1 (*PO,* XII, 732).

[123] Hilary, *In Ps.,* 118, 8, 5 (*Z.,* 459). Ambrose, *In Ps.,* 118, s. 8, n. 57: "The mystical Sun of justice rises upon all, has appeared for all, has suffered for all" (*P.,* 186); cf. s. 19, n. 39 (442).

[124] *In Io. hom.,* 8, n. 1 (*PG,* LIX, col. 65); *In Rom. hom.,* 5 (*PG,* LX, col. 427).

world.[125] When the Council recognized the religious experience which is the foundation of the non-Christian religions of the world, it did not mean to deny the tremendous difference between the way of Israel and the ways of the heathen. The difference consists ultimately in this that the God of Abraham, Isaac and Jacob, the God of revelation, seeks men, and that the God of the pagan world is sought by men. Hence it is strange that such an alert observer as Johann Christoph Hampe should write: "It is not only in the Catholic style, but in the special style of the Council, that distinction and separation are hardly mentioned, or if so very irenically. The Declaration does not mention that the gods of the Hindus and the attempts at redemption of other religions or the Buddhist pessimism with its demand to get rid of any conception of God are incompatible with the Christian faith, just as it says nothing of Israel's historical protest against the Messiah Jesus of Nazareth."[126]

To allege that it is "Catholic style" to formulate distinctions not at all or at best very irenically is something new in the criticism of the Church. But the Secretariat for Unity has anticipated Hampe's complaint that the Council had committed a sin of omission. For the last version of each draft was accompanied by a justification *(expensio modorum)* in which the relevant commission explained how it had dealt with the objections and proposals of the fathers. In this justification it is said expressly: "The aim of the Declaration is not an exhaustive presentation of the religions and their faults and weaknesses, it is rather to point to the connections between peoples and their religions which serve as a basis for dialogue and co-operation. Hence it takes more notice of that which unites (Christians and non-Christians) to one another."[127]

The Declaration does not in the least indulge in a blind optimism which would pass by any problems; it is rather the sign of a great hope. Its depth cannot be discovered at first sight. It has rightly been said that the Council is the end of the Counter-Reformation. It may be said equally truly that the Declaration marks the end of the Reformation. More exactly: the main concern of the Reformation is no longer of interest to us. Today the pious Christian is no longer worried by the question: How do I obtain a gracious God? The question that concerns him is: How does God accomplish the salvation of all creation?

This throws new light on the connection of the Declaration on the Jews with its attitude to the religions of mankind. The whole Declaration makes it clear that all singularity exists for the sake of universality and all separation for the sake of the community. Israel's election, too, is directed towards the allembracing kingdom of grace. Thus the Declaration on the Jews has taken on a dimension far surpassing its original importance. It proved its value by becoming the nucleus round which old-new insights could gather.

[125] E. Schillebeeckx, *Vatican II: The Real Achievement* (1966), p. 38.
[126] Eckert and Ehrlich, *op. cit.*, p. 424.
[127] *Schema Declarationis de Ecclesiae Habitudine ad Religiones Non-Christianas* (1965), Expensio modorum ad I, 2, p. 13.

Abbé Laurentin, who has already been quoted frequently, seems to be one of the few men to have grasped the depth of this new attitude. He says of the new text that it has drawbacks as well as advantages: "The drawbacks: the Jews are no longer included in the ecumenical concern. If this were really so the Decree on Ecumenism would have been mutilated. Whether we like it or not, the separation of the Church from the people of Israel was the consequence of the Christ-event, hence it took place on the Christian plane. The disadvantage (of separating the Declaration on the Jews from the Decree on Ecumenism) is, however, mitigated by the fact that the Declaration — or, more precisely, the responsibility for the dialogue with the Jews — is still in the hands of the Secretariat for Christian Unity. The advantages: The difficulties the Church encountered concerning the text on the Jews had a positive result. They made it necessary to be open to entirely new horizons . . . What must be emphasized is the importance (which the concern with all religions, i.e. with hundreds of millions of men throughout the world has) for the problem of the Jews: 'Their failure means riches for the Gentiles', as St. Paul says (Rom 11:12). This principle seems to have found an unexpected application when the Decree on the Jews was enlarged to become the Declaration on all non-Christian religions."[128]

Before continuing it seems advisable to reproduce the Council fathers' proposals for emending the text. 1. The overwhelming majority of speakers emphasized the absolute necessity of the Declaration on the Jews, but insisted on the return to the spirit and content of the text that had been submitted at the second session. 2. Five fathers demanded that the loving spirit of the former draft which was absent from the text placed before the third session should be restored. 3. Twenty-one fathers demanded a special rejection of the accusation of deicide. 4. Ten required a strong condemnation of the persecution of the Jews in the past as well as in the present. 5. Four enlarged on the bad consequences of prejudiced teaching, which might easily lead to hatred or scorn. 6. Six fathers wanted an emphasis on the fact that the sins of all men had caused the death of the Saviour. 7. Two asked that the Declaration should include a confession of guilt on the part of the Christians because of the persecutions of the Jews. 8. Three speakers pleaded to introduce the image of the good olive-tree and its branches in order to explain the relation of the Christians to ancient Israel. 9. Four wanted the words about Christ, the peace between Israel and the nations (Eph 2:15) to be included. 10. Twelve speakers wanted the eschatological hope of the Church expressed in such a way that even the semblance of any proselytizing among the Jews would be avoided. 11. Three considered it necessary to emphasize more strongly the common heritage of Christians and Jews. 12. Six fathers regarded it as very important that the Declaration should take due notice of the religious values of contemporary Judaism.

[128] R. Laurentin and J. Neuner, *The Declaration on the Relation of the Church to Non-Christian Religions,* Vatican II Documents (1966), p. 35.

Besides these positive proposals there were only several critical *modi*. The extreme demand to abandon the Declaration altogether has already been mentioned (see footnote 112). Three fathers wanted the negative tendencies of Judaism mentioned. Some wanted it made clear that Rom 9:4 referred only to the past, not to contemporary Jews; another demanded more prudence when speaking of the common heritage, and a third warned against the dangers of dialogue. One bishop thought the warning to teachers and preachers not to abuse Christian instruction too strong.[129] In a similar context Fesquet quotes a remark of Bishop Lamont (Southern Rhodesia), a member of the Secretariat for Unity: "It would be offensive to insinuate that anti-Semitism is rampant (also) among Catholics (sic)".[130] I am afraid the bishop, who is a very kind man, has judged the world by his own heart.

If we compare the negative with the positive voices the former appear very thin and timid. The "conservative" opposition to the Declaration on the Jews came from the same quarter as the "conservative" opposition to other schemata: from those who were afraid to admit that there had been errors in the Church and who held that the first task of a Catholic as well as of the Council was to defend tradition, all that is *called* Catholic, rather than bearing witness to the good tidings of Jesus Christ and that service of the Gospel which makes it a leaven.

After the great debate the subcommission for Jewish problems was temporarily enlarged so that the wishes expressed on the Council floor might be more easily put in order and incorporated into the new text. At first Barnabas Ahern, C. P. (U.S.A.), Pierre Benoit, O. P. (École Biblique, Jerusalem), Bruno Hussard, O. P. (Israel) and the seminary regent Nicolaus Persich, C. M. (U.S.A.) were coopted as advisers, later also Thomas Stransky, C. S. P. (from the Secretariat of Unity) and Mgr. Ramselaar (Holland). Bishop Holland presided at the last meetings of the enlarged subcommission, when the text was transformed bit by bit.

It was generally considered one of the great advantages of the new version that it emphasized the charity which had caused Pope John to order the Secretariat for Unity to produce such a document. According to the opinion of most critics the clear rejection of hatred of the Jews was another advantage. Most emendations have been mentioned in connection with the great debate of September 28 and 29 1964. Hence a brief discussion will suffice.

What is new is especially the statement that the Declaration on the Jews belongs essentially to the Church's self-realization, which was the principal task of Vatican II. The Church knows herself to be called by God because Abraham, Isaac and Jacob had been called. Her mission is the fruit not only of the mission of Christ, but also of that of Moses and the prophets. But this fact that the Church is implanted in the Israel of the patriarchs and prophets is now expressed in a different way. The Church is no longer called the "new creation in Christ, the

---

[129] Bruno Hussard, *Le Religioni non cristiane nel Vaticano II*, pp. 38f.
[130] Fesquet, *op. cit.*, p. 506.

people of the New Covenant", nor as the continuation of the people of the divine mercy and revelation. Rather is the pagan world seen as branches from a wild olive tree grafted onto the good olive tree, so that the whole Church draws its nourishment from the root of the tree. Even in the past the faithful had been reminded of the Jewish descent of Jesus, Mary and the apostles, now they are also told that the first messengers of the good tidings of Jesus who were sent into the world came from the Jewish people.

The new version repeats the Pauline testimony according to which the rejection of Jesus by a large part of Israel does not invalidate its special vocation. Thus it differs from the third draft. The same had in fact already been said in the second, though in other words. It continues to be the people loved and called by God. Thus it necessarily occupies a special place in the eschatological hope of the Church. But the new version emphasizes this hope and its universality more strongly, and it avoids even the shadow of a doubt as if the confession of a future unity were a hidden call to convert the Jews. A common study of Scripture is counselled as a way to further mutual knowledge and respect.

After present and past persecutions have been rejected (that is to say the bloodbaths initiated by Christians and the gas chambers invented by anti-Christians) the Council document exhorts all never to give religious instruction or preach the Word of God in such a way "that hatred or scorn of the Jews could develop in the hearts of the faithful". The document warns further never to represent the Jewish people as a nation rejected or condemned by God or as guilty of deicide. The fourth draft culminates in the impressive message: "Whatever happened at the Passion of Christ can in no way be blamed on the people then living and even less on the people of today. For the rest, the Church has always maintained and maintains it still that Christ has freely accepted his passion and death for the sins of all men out of his infinite love. Hence it is the task of Christian preaching to proclaim the Cross as the sign of the all-embracing love of God and the source of all grace."

After the subcommission and the four working committees had finished their respective texts the five sections were combined into the "Declaration on the Relationship of the Church to Non-Christian Religions". The Declaration on the Jews remained the centre of the whole document, though the other parts were not reduced to secondary importance. In his *relatio* of 20 November 1964, Cardinal Bea applied the parable of the mustard seed to the growth of the Declaration: the seed, that is the brief statement on the right attitude of the Christians to the Jewish people, had become a tree in which many birds built their nests; in a certain sense all non-Christian religions had found a place in it.[131] After innumerable individual votes on a paragraph, a sentence or even an expression the document was accepted by all bishops belonging to the Secretariat. The last voting took place on 30 October.

[131] Bea, *op. cit.,* p. 166.

Many critics unfamiliar with the many problems of the Declaration and the difficulties of having to work in common have asked why the drawing up of the document took so much time and why endless discussions within the Secretariat should have been necessary. Some have even doubted the sincerity of the Declaration. They argued that something that had caused so many difficulties could scarcely have been genuine. Spontaneity is certainly a wonderful gift; but it can never be the working method of a team, let alone the style of a Council.

A brief passage from the discussion on the schema of religious freedom might illustrate how lively and lengthy teamwork can be. At a certain stage of the evolution of the text one of the sentences dealing with the dignity of man ran as follows: "Homo, *qui* persona est, in eadem instantia est ens sociale — man who (by his nature) is a person, is at the same time a social being." After the sentence had been read out one of the members asked to speak: "No", he said, "not so! In my view the idea underlying this ought to be expressed like this: 'Homo, *quia* persona est, in eadem instantia est ens sociale' — Because man is a person he is at the same time a social being." Here the alteration is so minimal — a single letter has been added — that it could easily be overlooked. But however small the change, it holds many philosophical consequences. Another speaker wanted even to say: "Homo, *qua* persona, est ens sociale — Inasfar as man is a person, he is also a social being." After a memorable discussion of more than half an hour the original version was accepted, because it could not be the task of the Council to solve philosophical problems. Not every problem was so intricate, not every discussion was so concerned with niceties of expression. But the difficulties of team work — which, by the way, has more advantages than disadvantages — were not the only element that delayed the final shaping of the text. It was the resistance of the Arab governments — which has already been mentioned and will have to be mentioned again — that produced repeated delays of the final decision.

It was probably due to the same indecision that three weeks went by before the revision of the text that had been criticized in the great debate and which had been decided on 30 October was handed to the fathers. Only very few people know where the draft which the Secretariat transmitted to the president of the co-ordinating commission remained for three weeks. But, as happened so often in the history of the Declaration, here too strong nerves conquered exaggerated caution, though surely hesitation was not overcome by natural courage but by grace.

The Declaration was distributed to the fathers on Wednesday, 18 November 1964. At the same time the secretary general announced that the voting on it would take place on Friday, 20 November. Hence the time allowed for the study of the document was short. There was reason to fear that the Declaration on the Jews would meet with the same fate as that on religious freedom, that is to say that the minority hostile to it would demand a delay of the voting because the time was so short. But such a delay would have meant a transfer to the fourth session, since the solemn final meeting of the third session was to take place on 21 November. Thus on the morning of Friday there was a false rumour that the Declaration on the Non-Christian Religions had again been removed from the schedule. We are probably not wrong to suppose that no one wanted to take the blame for yet another delay.[132]

Before the voting Cardinal Bea did all he could to convince the fathers that the Secretariat for Unity had done its best to comply with the wishes of the Council whose organ it was. At the beginning of his *relatio* he declared: "Our Secretariat has taken pains to consider all suggestions honestly and sincerely in order to produce a document which would be, as far as possible, worthy of the discussion which led to it, and worthy of the Council."[133] A little further on in his speech he returned to this subject and said that the Secretariat had done everything to comply as far as possible with the wishes of all. He quoted the words of the apostle of the Gentiles: "Remain at peace with all men *so far as it depends on you*" (Rom 12:18), and added: "It was impossible to draw up a Declaration which would not, in any passage, be open to misinterpretation by one side and at the same time satisfy the other side. Besides, it must be borne in mind that it is more important to have such a solemn Declaration by the Council than to satisfy everyone, even if that were possible."[134]

Besides emphasizing that the Secretariat had done everything to meet the wishes transmitted to it Cardinal Bea was even more concerned to stress the paramount importance of the Declaration: "What is at stake is to acknowledge the saving counsel of God and his benefactions, to condemn without exception hatred and injustice and to avoid them in the future. The Church and thus also the Council must therefore fulfil their task and may not be silent." He said emphatically: "No Council in the history of the Church, unless I am mistaken, has ever set out so solemnly the principles concerning them [non-Christian religions] ... We are dealing with more than a thousand million men who have never heard of, or never recognized Christ."

In this connection he makes two points: one, that this immense multitude can

---

[132] X. Rynne relates two interesting occurrences. The first took place in the study of the Pope, who had summoned a number of Cardinals there in the late afternoon of 19 November to hear, among other things, a report on curial reform. On this occasion two American cardinals and one German are supposed to have intimated that, in the event of a postponement of the vote on the Declaration, they would see themselves obliged to absent themselves from the solemn final sitting. The second is stated to have taken place on 20 November in the aula of the Council. A messenger was sent by the minority in the Curia to Archbishop Felici, the Secretary General, with a petition requesting a postponement of the vote on Cardinal Bea's Declaration on Non-Christian Religions "for purposes of further study", whereupon Felici was seen to shrink back as though he had been presented with something unclean. With a wave of his hand he signified to the unfortunate messenger that he should turn to Cardinal Tisserant, who simply let the petition fall on to the presidential table, and that was the end of the matter. (Cf. Rynne, *op. cit.*, pp. 261 f., 66.) Whether the two events actually took place in this way or are apocryphal, I am unable to determine. At all events, even should they prove legendary they give a very good idea of the atmosphere prevailing.
[133] Bea, *op. cit.*, p. 166.   [134] *Ibid.*, pp. 167–8.   [135] *Ibid.*, p. 168.

achieve salvation if they follow their conscience; two, that it is the duty of the Church to begin a dialogue with those who do not believe in Christ. It would have been marvellous if the Pope had been able to present this Declaration to India as a gift to his hosts. But as this was unfortunately no longer possible it was very important that the Council should still do as much as it could, because this Declaration was as it were a passport of the Church in the eyes of all nations which were far from Christ.[136]

Thus the voting took place, as announced, on 20 November 1964. The situation in the Council hall was not favourable. The atmosphere in St. Peter's had been tense ever since Cardinal Tisserant, the chairman of the presidial council, had announced the day before that the voting on the schema on religious freedom had to be delayed because there was not enough time to examine it. When the Pope did not comply with the most urgent request to allow the (by no means final) voting during the third session, because he did not want to reject the decision of the presidial Council and the judgment of the Council court that had confirmed it, there was profound discouragement. This may have been one of the reasons for the rather small vote. Moreover, voting took place towards midday, that is at a time when the vigour and interest of the fathers were always at a low ebb. 2129 fathers had voted on the Decree on Ecumenism, rather early in the session, while only 1996 took part in the voting "On the Relationship of the Church to Non-Christian Religions". This was a difference of 113 votes, which was remarkable, even if not overwhelming. It should also be remembered that the opponents of the Declaration were almost without exception violently opposed to it, hence did not stay away from the voting, whereas not all those in favour of the Declaration were passionately attached to it. But we will say at once that on the day of the solemn voting (28 October 1965) 2313 fathers cast their vote.

Voting took place in three stages: the first vote was concerned with sections 1–3 (Preamble: the unity of mankind; the natural and the great religions, especially Hinduism and Buddhism; Islam), the second with sections four and five (the Jews, rejecting any discrimination), the third with the Declaration as a whole. The first three articles received 1838 affirmative and 136 negative votes; thirteen were invalid. On the last two articles 1770 fathers voted Yes, 185 No, again fourteen votes were invalid. In the vote on the whole the proportion was 1651 Yes, 99 No, 242 Yes with reservations and four invalid votes.

The reaction to the result was not long in coming. An American daily had the headline "History is Written" for one of its articles.[137] The Catholic press in Switzerland welcomed the Declaration as a "new beginning of the Church's encounter with the Jews".[138] A leader of the Hamburg daily *Die Welt* said that the

---

[136] *Ibid.,* pp. 168–9.

[137] *New York Journal American,* 21 November 1964.

[138] This headline forms the title of an exhaustive article by Dr. Willehad Eckert, O. P., in the *Basler Volksblatt,* 7 November 1964.

Council had given back to the Jews their theological dignity.[139] Xavier Rynne saw in the provisional acceptance of the Declaration a justification of the long activity of Cardinal Bea and his collaborators.[140] The frequently critical Swedish journalist Gunnel Valquist wrote simply that the voting was the happy event of the day, the text was wholly positive. She only hoped that it would not be tampered with between the sessions; it was certain that the Arab States would be working for this end.[141]

m) The "Holy War" against the Declaration

The fears of Mrs. Valquist were only too justified. Though the Declaration on the Jews had been given a new framework and though the new Declaration "On the Relationship of the Church to Non-Christian Religions" was to be appended to the Constitution on the Church[142] the Arab reaction was very unfriendly, to put it mildly. The attempt to include the Declaration on the Jews in the Constitution on the Church or to append it to the Constitution had been made not least in order to reconcile the Arabs. A Catholic weekly in the United States wrote that since for the Arabs, living still in the theocratic age, religion and politics were almost the same, the Council fathers had tried to place the Declaration in a context which would emphasize its theological meaning.[143] But all this was of no use. On 18 November two days before the voting, the Syrian radio in Damascus stated that the new text said nothing new about the Jews. It was the same old Decree which had been given a facelift that could deceive no one. For twenty centuries the Church had held on to the view that the Jews are deicides who were responsible for the death of Christ. Why did she change her opinion just now, when the Arabs were involved in a bitter struggle with their Jewish aggressors — those aggressors who had invaded Palestine and had expelled a million Arabs from their home, whom they now allowed to perish in refugee camps? Why did the Church not have the courage to display the same favourable attitude when millions of Jews were persecuted by the Nazis? Could the Church find no better moment to rehabilitate the Jews than when these were persecuting the Arabs? If the Council wanted to absolve the Jews from the murder of Christ this was its own affair. But the Arab world was horrified that it should have chosen just this moment for the purpose. The co-ordination of time proved that political factors were at work behind the façade of religion. Instead of approving a document that absolved the Jews of the murder of Christ the Council should rather have approved those documents that accused the Jews of massacring and expelling thousands of innocent Arabs.[144]

---

[139] *Die Welt,* 21 November 1964.

[140] Rynne, *op. cit.,* p. 226.   [141] Valquist, *op. cit.,* p. 416.

[142] When the Declaration was provisionally accepted on 20 November 1964 it was still considered as an appendix to the Constitution on the Church (Bea, *op. cit.,* p. 167).

[143] *America,* 31 October 1964, p. 305.

[144] According to *Herder Correspondence* (March 1965), p. 80.

While the Syrian authorities responsible for this radio commentary were content with bitter complaints, the Jordanian prime minister Bahjat Talhouni threatened "punitive measures". During a session of the Jordanian parliament on 25 November both Christian and Moslem members condemned the Declaration. The prime minister then said he did not want to be involved in the religious implications, but from a political point of view he could only deeply regret the Declaration. His government would blacklist those cardinals, archbishops and bishops of the Vatican Council who signed the Declaration.[145]

It seems that the entire Middle East was drawn into the whirlpool of these hostilities, governments and people, Moslems and Christians, Orthodox and Catholics, laymen, priests and bishops. Shortly after the end of the Council two bombs were placed in the Christian quarter of Aleppo for which the "Moslem Brotherhood" seems to have been responsible. The leaders of the Catholic community of Damascus sent a telegram to the Pope in which they stated that despite its religious character the decision of the Council had inevitable political consequences which would harm the Arabs, whether Catholics or Moslems. The greatly excited Christian young people were about to organize demonstrations; hence they asked His Holiness to preserve them from this calamity.[146]

One of the saddest accompaniments of the Arab fight against the Declaration was the attempt of some Orthodox Christians to exploit the difficult situation of the Church in the Middle East in their own favour. On 25 November the Orthodox bishopric of Latakia organized a demonstration against the Council's work of reconciliation. In the service following the demonstration the Greek-Orthodox bishop, one of his priests and the Protestant parson all preached.[147] On the same day the Jacobite Patriarch of Antioch and the Orient, Ignace Jakub III, delivered a theological exposition which should rather be called a scornful protest. The Patriarch began as follows:

"In these days when Christendom complains bitterly against the so-called Ecumenical Council which declares the Jews to be innocent of the blood of Christ — a declaration which is nothing but a fruit of the "night work" of the chief and the members of the Council — in these days, when Rome has sinned by its Declaration against holy Scripture, the apostolic tradition, the truth of history and the teaching of the Fathers and Doctors, We consider it Our inescapable duty to proclaim the true, centuries-old belief concerning this question before the whole world. We do this as the legitimate successor of St. Peter and head of the first apostolic see of Christendom, indeed as the head of the whole Oriental Church."

The patriarch then indulged in an exegesis of the New Testament completely unaware of any modern biblical scholarship. Thus he asserted that it was

---

[145] *New York Times,* 26 November 1964.

[146] *Herder Correspondence* (March 1965), p. 80; likewise *The Catholic Messenger* (Davenport), 24 December 1964, on the basis of reports of the N. C. W. C. News Service.

[147] *Herder Correspondence* (March 1965), p. 80.

certainly not the lower classes who had shouted: "His blood be on us and our children", but rather "the high priests, the Pharisees, the scribes, the teachers of the Law, the elders (sic!), the heads of the people, the Sanhedrin and the whole people, the inhabitants of Galilee and Judaea and those scattered over the other countries." For at every Easter just as at Pentecost Jews from every nation under · heaven were in Jerusalem. "Jews" from all countries, Galilaeans and Judaeans certainly went on pilgrimage to Jerusalem at these sacred times, but not *the* Jews, *the* Galilaeans, *the* Judaeans, nor could they possibly all be gathered before the palace of the governor. This would have been physically impossible. And how can the assertion that the lower classes were not implicated in the death of Jesus be reconciled with the statement that the whole nation was guilty?

But even the implication of all the Jews then alive does not satisfy the patriarch. According to his view, which he believes to be the faith of the whole Church, Israel's "crime affects all its descendants, just as Adam's sin affected his descendants". One could fill a book with the exegesis of this speaker and its refutation. Here we can only reproduce the conclusion of the radio talk of the Jacobite patriarch who considers himself the true successor of Peter:

"From the crucifixion of Jesus until our own days (the Jews) seek to declare their people to be innocent of the blood of Christ. Indeed, they seek to destroy Christendom with the help of the Christians. Their last effort in this direction was their influence on the Second Vatican Council, which has provided them with a document asserting their innocence. All this in order to satisfy them and with regard to a definite policy. We, and all the venerable episcopal members of Our synod express our disapproval of this Roman heresy, which contradicts the clear truth of the Bible and the teaching of the Christian Church throughout the centuries. The belief of the Church according to which the responsibility for the crucifixion of Christ remains with the Jewish people until the end of the world will remain deeply embedded in the spirit of Christianity, whatever changes may occur in the ideas, views and customs of mankind . . ."[148]

Already on Sunday, 22 October, a message was read in all the churches of Damascus warning the faithful against believing all the rumours, explanations and commentaries that would reach them. It affirmed that the Ecumenical Council had not yet come to a decision and that in any case it was not a question of absolving the Jews from being guilty of the death of Christ, as some people were trying to persuade the public. There was no question of that. The only point was to make it clear to Christians that they should show good will to all men regardless of race and religion, including the Jews.[149] An Arab Anglican prelate, Bishop Najib Atallah Cuba'in, said that the declaration of the Vatican Council was due only to Jewish machinations. These, he alleged, followed faithfully the

---

[148] From a French translation of the radio talk distributed in Rome; cf. *Herder Correspondence* (March 1965), p. 81.
[149] *Ibid.*, p. 80.

Protocols of the Elders of Zion, which he — like the Czarist secret police and Adolf Hitler — believed to be a genuine historical document.[150]

There were, however, other Arabs who did not succumb to these attacks. On 6 December *L'Orient* (Beirut) published an article by Hassan Saab, "Christianity and Islam vis-à-vis Zionism". These are the most important passages on the Council: "The Arabs ought to be happy about such an awakening of the Christian conscience . . . It is a pity that the fear of Zionist exploitation of the Declaration prevents them from closely examining its contents. Investigating its own truth, the Church experiences a great change: for the first time she sees the reflection of truth in other religions. (In the Declaration) Islam is presented as a sister religion. The Christian is exhorted to end all disrespect not only of the Jews, but of all non-Christians. This new attitude of the Church deserves to be imitated rather than to be criticized." Somewhat triumphalistically the author continues: "Here (the Church) approaches the idea of the Koran of the unity of God's family as well as the other idea of the Koran that the people of the book is one, the people that consists of Jews, Christians and Moslems, of all who worship God, Allah, the Father of Abraham, who is the Father of all who believe in the one God. Christianity and Islam must be reconciled in this Declaration and congratulate themselves on its spirit . . ."

The same edition of *L'Orient* printed parts of an article by Mohammed Naccache which had appeared in an Arab weekly. Its original heading was: "Does the declaration that the Jews are not guilty of the blood of Christ diminish our rights?" *L'Orient* entitled it: "The Revision of the Attitude of the Catholic Church towards the Jews Corresponds to the Arab Standpoint". Neither author is free from the clichés of Arab propaganda, hence it is to be appreciated all the more that they should have written so clearly and objectively about everything connected with the Declaration. Mohammed Naccache writes:

"I ask myself in what way the Jews' innocence of the blood of Christ could affect us. We have never accused the Jews of having crucified Jesus. The Declaration is a manifestation of the tolerance of the Catholic Church. (The term 'tolerance' does not belong to the vocabulary of Vatican II — the author.) And this tolerance is not only practised towards the Jews but extends to all religions . . . It is in the interests of all mankind if tolerance conquers in those religious circles which were formerly centres of fanaticism, especially in an age of peaceful co-existence and the unanimous desire for fruitful co-operation among men . . . The decision of the Council with regard to the Jews abolishes all inferiority of one religious group to another. It ends — at least in principle — the wars pretending to be crusades. Now men will be able to live as brothers, and it will be left to God to ask them to justify their faith on the day of the last judgment."

Unfortunately these two authors were voices crying in the wilderness. The

---

[150] *Catholic Star Herald,* 18 December 1964.

Declaration continued to be overwhelmed with reproaches, even with slanders. Even before its provisional acceptance in October 1964 a Syrian newspaper called the schema "ridiculous and inspired by the Zionists". At the same time the state-controlled Syrian radio declared that when the Jews dipped their hands into the innocent blood of Christ they actually wanted to murder the principles and teachings of Christ.[151] After the acceptance of the Declaration the language of the Syrian press became even more violent and malicious. The Council was called a second Judas who betrayed Christ for Jewish money, and the statement that the Church sold Christ once more, not for thirty pieces of silver, but for American dollars, became a constant refrain.[152]

In Jordan the *Jerusalem Times* became the spearhead of all attacks on the Council: "Who crucified Christ? The Vatican in the year 1964." A number of Christian members of the Jordanian parliament declared they would ask the government to take over the control of all Catholic schools. They even asked Jordanian Catholics to break with the Vatican. An Orthodox member of parliament invited them expressly to join the Orthodox Church.[153] The 88-year old Greek Orthodox Patriarch of Alexandria and Africa, Christophoros, believed that the decision of the Council would place new obstacles in the way of the present efforts to achieve unity.[154] The Coptic Patriarch Kyrillos VI, on the other hand, was convinced that the action of the Council was due to a conspiracy. He would protest together with all the archbishops and bishops of his Church against the imperialist plan of exploiting the Second Vatican Council.[155] On 25 November a manifesto of the "Constituent Council of the Islamic World" was read on Radio Cairo, in which the Catholic Church was reminded that its hostile policy would produce enmity between the Islamic and the Christian worlds. The interests of the Vatican in the Islamic states would also be endangered, as it had institutions and communities there.[156]

All this shows that the Arab attitude was not only governed by misunderstanding and opposition; its leaders, the political as well as the religious ones, were so passionately attached to their cause that they carried on a "holy war" against the Council. True, it was conducted *mostly* with words; nevertheless, it was a war with all its wickedness.

n) Surrender?

In the realm of nature a thunderstorm is usually followed by calm and a purified atmosphere. But nothing like that happened here. On the contrary, the thunder of public propaganda was replaced by showers of secret diplomacy. No end of complaints, criticisms, discussions and proposals were to achieve what

---

[51] *The Providence Visitor,* 9 October 1964, on the basis of reports of the N. C. W. C. News Service.
[52] *Herder Correspondence* (March 1965), p. 80. [153] *Advocate,* 3 December 1964.
[54] *The Providence Visitor,* 11 December 1964, on the basis of the Religious News Service.
[55] *Frankfurter Allgemeine Zeitung,* 24 Nov. 1964. [156] *The Jewish World,* Dec. 1964, p. 19.

the fury of press and radio had been unable to accomplish. R. Laurentin describes the activities of the Arabs in the period between the third and fourth sessions unsparingly:

"The famous Declaration . . . was causing agitation in Arab countries; as a result, persecutions, perhaps serious, were threatening Catholics in those countries. The Arab States, which had more or less officially agreed to recognize the exclusive religious nature of the texts already voted upon, found themselves outflanked by their own troops. Diplomatic offensives multiplied with the support, advice and help of the bishops and patriarchs of these countries, who furnished biblical objections and other religious motives to counter the Declaration. Let us not forget that two of the bishops from these countries were members of the Secretariat for Promoting Christian Unity, where opinions were thus divided."[157]

Laurentin goes on to say that the Israelis gave grounds for the Arab propaganda without meaning to do so. For part of the Israeli press had given a political, that is to say a zionist, interpretation to the Declaration's rejection of the accusation of deicide. This ran counter to the repeatedly expressed intentions of the Secretariat for Unity and thus called in question the statement that the Jewish people was not guilty of deicide. Laurentin gives no reference for his statement that Israel's effort had been counter-productive, that is to say that it had achieved the opposite of what had been intended. True, there had been rumours in Rome that the Israel radio had misused the Declaration to further its political ends, and a number of people were only too ready to take this at its face value. Actually, however, I am afraid that such rumours originated in Cairo or another Arab city. At least I have never had any evidence that the accusation was based on fact. True, there had been isolated voices, mostly those of self-appointed Jewish spokesmen, which declared the Church should crown the Declaration with the diplomatic recognition of the state of Israel. However imprudent, indeed irresponsible, these private statements are far from a semi-official, let alone official statement that the Council Declaration guaranteed, as it were, the dignity and rights of the state of Israel.

Laurentin is right, however, when he says in the course of his description: "Some interventions even left the impression that, by renouncing deicide, the Church was beginning to dissociate herself from the divinity of Christ, etc. Arab diplomacy had a fine opportunity to exploit facts of this kind and the Arabs deduced from them irreproachable theological arguments that hit the bull's eye. What a scandal for the Orthodox if deicide were excluded! It would convert the Catholic Church to Nestorianism![158] It would be as if the Church were to

---

[157] Laurentin-Neuner, op. cit., p. 37.

[158] Nestorianism is the teaching, ascribed to the then Patriarch of Constantinople, Nestor, and condemned by the Council of Ephesus (431), according to which only an acquired, "moral" unity of divinity and humanity subsisted in Christ, not a union of the two natures in the one Person of the Eternal Word. But if Christ was simply a perfect human being, upon whose human

abandon the phrase 'Mother of God' in referring to the Virgin Mary. The whole argument developed around the slogan introduced by Cardinal Ruffini, which Maximos IV had tried to take up to calm Arab opinion: 'To speak of deicide is absurd, since one cannot kill God.'[159] Whatever the case might be, the Secretariat, already internally divided on this question, found itself forced to modify the text far beyond what the fathers' vote required and allowed."[160]

But the situation was not as simple as that. What had forced the Secretariat as a commission of the Council to take up again the problem of deicide was, in fact, certain *modi* suggested by the fathers. One of these *modi* especially, which was signed by thirty fathers, most of whom had not been prominent in the discussions, demanded that the warning not to call the Jewish people rejected, condemned and guilty of deicide should be changed in the sense that "never should all the Jews *individually* be represented as rejected and guilty of *formal deicide*". This was based on the view that the Jewish people as a people had been guilty of material deicide through the actions of its leaders, as was clear from 1 Thess 2:15; moreover, some of its leaders had undoubtedly been guilty of deicide, since Jesus himself had said: "If I had not done among them the works which no one else did, they would not have sin; but now they have seen and hated both me and my Father." (Jn 15:24.)

Thus the problem was posed. The experts who had to deal with the *modi* did not find it difficult to make a decision. Their conviction emerges from the words with which their account, the *Expensio modorum,* begins: "Textus a Concilio approbatus quoad substantiam mutari non potest. Praeterea argumenta quibus culpam deicidii et reprobationem populi iudaici probare conantur, valida non sunt." — "A text approved by the Council cannot be substantially altered. Moreover, the texts by which the guilt of deicide and the reprobation of the Jewish people are attempted to be proved are not valid."

As to the arguments produced by the *modi*, the *Expensio modorum* says that in 1 Thess 2:15 Paul did not speak of the Jewish people as a whole, but of the authorities in Jerusalem and Judaea, which persecuted Jesus and those who believed in him and who are the descendants of the murderers of the prophets (cf. Mt 23:30–32; Acts 7:51f.). The words of Christ in Jn 15:24 refer to the sin of those who sought to kill him. John frequently calls these men "Jews" ("Judaeans" would perhaps be a better translation). It might have been added that by this was not meant the whole people, which emerges from the fact that

ty the divine reality was "superimposed" and to whom the divine attributes were accorded as a sign that he had proved himself, then it is impossible to say that God-in-the-flesh suffered and died on the cross for men's sins.

[59] Cardinal Ruffini's exact words were: ". . . [Iudaeos] vocare deicidas non possumus, eo magis quod nomen 'Deicida' insulsitatem quamdam exprimit, nemo enim Deum occidere unquam valeret."

[60] Laurentin-Neuner, *op. cit.,* pp. 37f.

the same evangelist records that "many of the people believed in him" (Jn 7:31)
and also that "many of the Jews . . . believed in him" (Jn 11:45). Other evangelists
report that the opponents of Jesus did not dare lay hands on Jesus because they
feared the people (cf. Mk 14:2), that when the high priests and scribes made
plans to lay hold of him they were terrified, saying: "Not during the feast, lest
there be a tumult among the people" (Mt 26:5). After clarifying the opposition
between leaders and people the *Expensio* continued with the equally important
statement that the sin of those who engineered the death of Jesus and of those
who actually caused it was never characterized as formal deicide — neither in
the Fourth Gospel nor elsewhere. And not only that. According to Scripture the
enemies of Jesus, however great their guilt, did not know that they had killed
"the Holy One of Israel" (cf. Acts 3:17; 13:27; 1 Cor 2:8), even though their
deed may be ascribed to their blindness and hardness of heart. In the parable
of the householder who planted a vineyard, which the more than thirty fathers
had also quoted in support of their proposal, the Lord's threat was addressed to
the leaders of the people, not to the people; at least his original hearers had
understood it in this way, for the Gospel continues: "When the chief priests and
the Pharisees heard his parables, they perceived that he was speaking about
them" (Mt 21:45).[161]

This reply shows the definite attitude of the experts. The attitude of the
bishops, however, was more doubtful. Some found it difficult to give up ancient
prejudices which so easily disguise themselves as the sacred tradition of the
Church. They would not accept that the reading of the Vulgate: "Auctorem
vitae interfecistis" — you have killed the author of life (Acts 3:15) was wrong,
that according to the original text and the context it should be translated: "You
have killed the leader towards life", that is him who rose first and has prepared
the way for others and led them into life. Others again wanted to avoid possible
controversies or were very much in sympathy with the Arab bishops.

When, during the plenary session of the Secretariat at Ariccia in March 1965,
those, who wanted to abolish the expression "guilty of deicide", seemed to be
in the ascendancy, Cardinal Shehan intervened. Full of almost prophetic zeal
he said that he had not asked to be assigned to the Secretariat when he became
a cardinal, nor was he one of its members when the Declaration on the Jews
was first drafted. He had, therefore, no part in it; but now he was a member and
therefore responsible for its text. Hence he felt he must say that the rejection of
the accusation of deicide ought not to be omitted. "Deicide" had become a key
word, a symbol of all the Jews had ever been accused of. It was a word which
might only too easily be misunderstood. He was also firmly convinced that by
excising these words the document would be emasculated and its effect would
be seriously weakened. He asked from his heart that the text should be retained

[161] For the whole argument see M.-M. Cottier, O. P., *Vatican II. Les Relations de l'Église avec les
Religions non-chrétiennes* (1966), pp. 73 f.

as it stood and as it had been approved by the overwhelming majority of the bishops of the Council. This summary cannot reproduce the vigour and ardour of his speech; unter its influence the attempt to change the text was rejected, but not, as it then seemed, for ever.

The accounts reaching Rome from the Middle East became ever more frightening. It was said that the final acceptance of the Declaration on the Jews would lead to serious attacks on the Christian minorities. The inevitable result would be the closing of the Catholic schools and the burning of churches, in fact the destruction of Christian life. Its friendly gesture towards Islam had evidently not impressed the Arabs. It seemed that only the complete omission of the Declaration could satisfy their obstinacy. In order to investigate the rumours and ascertain the facts Paul VI sent Bishop Willebrands and Father Duprey, P.A., to the Middle East. The result of this journey with its visit to all the leading Christian personalities in question was not encouraging. Both confirmed that the fears existed and were probably justified. In any case, they had not dared contradict the Arab bishops who were worried about the future of the Church. Some people might be tempted to speak of "pusillanimity", but no one who has not been in a similar situation had a right to do so.

The account of Bishop Willebrands's and Father Duprey's impressions was given to the last plenary session of the Secretariat, which took place some months before the fourth session in May 1865. Its largely pessimistic outlook was shared by not a few members and consultants of the Secretariat. In those days it could often be heard that one could not pass a declaration which might result in tumult, killings and misery, and the immediate fruit of which would be the physical and psychological persecution of Christians in the Middle East. Thank God the Jews were not exposed to direct danger, but the Christians in the Arab countries were so exposed. One could not heal wounds on one side and inflict them on the other. Here it was a question of a piece of paper — after all, a document was nothing else — but there of living men and women. (The opposition of human beings to paper is wrong, however well it may sound. A document such as the Declaration on the Jews is part of a psychological and spiritual restitution, an "incarnated" will to reconciliation and brotherhood, a living testimony of God's faithfulness.) Such a mood naturally produced several plans.

It was considered, for example, if it might not be better not to publish the Declaration at all. Instead the fathers should be told that because of the tensions in the Middle East it was in danger of being misinterpreted. Hence the commission thought it better to leave the Declaration in the hands of the Secretariat for Non-Christians or of the Secretariat for the Unity of Christians as a basis for their work. Its content might then prudently be published at the appropriate time. These and other proposals were roundly rejected, as well as a new version of the Declaration which refrained from making any specific statements or even allusions with regard to "disturbing" problems. It was an unsigned draft of one page which contained hardly more than a high-flown paraphrase of the command:

"Children, love one another!" On the lips of the venerable old Apostle John these words must have been a striking testimony, on the lips of the Council fathers, however, from whom the world was expecting concrete statements, they would have been regarded as an excuse, an "escape into piety", that is into a false piety that rejected any clear-cut commitment. The anonymous proposal met the worst fate possible: it was not taken seriously at all but completely disregarded.

Nevertheless, there remained the possibility that the Declaration would be quietly dropped. In this situation a number of bishops and advisers asked to speak. One of the most stirring interventions was that of the otherwise rather silent Bishop of Würzburg, Josef Stangl, who spoke on 12 May. He said, among other things: "The question of the acceptance or rejection of our decree is of decisive importance for the Council. Will the Church walk in the way of incorruptible truth and justice or in that of tactics, diplomacy and the least resistance?" The bishop confessed that he came from the country of Hochhuth, the author of *The Deputy*. He was surrounded by a flood of publications, of a violent discussion of Pius XII, the German bishops and the Church in the Third Reich. The customary explanation of past attitudes no longer reached the hearts of men. Contemporary Christians no longer took seriously considerations of prospective dangers and pastoral prudence. "The question is always: Has the Church been walking in the way of the children of this world who calculate and follow earthly considerations? These questions are asked by the faithful, especially by young Christians who are unsure." Growing more intense the bishop continued: "If we speak in the name of God, in the name of Jesus Christ, as representatives of the Lord, our speech must be yea, yea — no, no, that is to say truth, not tactics, for 'anything more than this comes from evil' (Mt 5:37)." What was at stake was, as Bishop De Smedt had said in another context, the credibility of the Church. The whole world knew that the Decree had already been accepted by the fathers, the whole world was waiting for its promulgation. The whole Council was enjoying an extraordinary reception and the greatest respect, because of its openness, its honesty, and because it was no respecter of persons. If our Decree were not to be promulgated everybody would be asking: Why not? The reply "diplomatic considerations or something" would appear as a sign of weakness, it would be a defeat of the Church before the whole world.

Bishop Stangl continued: "It is not only a question of the credibility of the Church but also of her claim to moral leadership. The Council wants to present the Church as *Lumen Gentium*, the Light of the Nations, it wants to be a new Pentecost (John XXIII). We must be absolutely honest and lay our cards on the table . . Many doubters, seekers, Christians of the various denominations need the witness of fearless truthfulness and justice which will give back to the Church the claim to moral leadership which it has lost in the opinion of many. Perhaps this experience of the Church as grace is needed precisely by the Arabs, by the land of Israel and by the Orient. Do not the words of St. Paul concern us too

'I charge you in the presence of God and of Christ Jesus who is to judge the living and the dead . . . preach the word, be urgent in season and out of season' (2 Tim 4:1–2) and 'Take the whole armour of God, that you may be able to withstand in the evil day . . . having girded your loins with truth!' (Eph 6:13–14). In this decisive hour of the Council we shall not be made free by diplomacy, tact, too much pastoral prudence, but by justice in the straight way and by truth" (cf. Jn 8:32).

The speech of the Bishop of Würzburg had a sobering effect in the deepest sense of the word. It revealed perfectly the difficult situation of the bishops and the importance of their decision. Now they could no longer flirt with easy solutions, and no one would try to get rid of the obstinate problem by dropping the Declaration altogether. But the struggle about individual phrases went on. Time and again the theologians tried to get rid of the condemnation of the deicide formula, but all efforts came to nothing until one day a two thirds majority was actually found in favour of eliminating the relevant words. The majority had become convinced that an obstinate clinging to the text would endanger all ecumenical efforts in the Middle East and would destroy all hope of a reunion of the Churches of East and West or at least of closing the wounds of centuries (the dream of Paul VI). If after the vote somebody had told the bishops: "Now you have capitulated to the Arabs after all! More, you have done violence to your own conscience", one of those who had voted for removing the words "guilty of deicide" would certainly have answered: "Not at all! We have made a *verbal* compromise for the sake of a higher good; we have removed four words without touching the sense for the sake of the well-being of our Christian brethren in the Middle East, but above all for the sake of the unity of the Church."

Thus at least things were seen in the account of the Secretariat for Unity. According to its conviction the Secretariat, it says there, could remove the relevant words *(verba)*, because they did not belong to the actual substance of the text. For the idea was already contained in the preceding sentences, in which a collective guilt of the Jews is expressly denied and the view that they are rejected or cursed by God is decisively rejected. The following reasons are given for the omission of the phrase "guilty of deicide":

"Whatever the context in which the word *deicidium* occurs, it has a hateful sound *(odiose sonat)*. Hence terms like *deicida* and others must be removed altogether from the Christian vocabulary. Besides, the term *deicidium* might lead to wrong theological interpretations. These have already occurred and caused difficulties in pastoral work as well as in the ecumenical dialogue with some Churches."

Some commentators consider the first reason unsatisfactory.[162] Whether a commentator considers it satisfactory or not, he ought to support the rejection

---

[162] *Ibid.,* p. 75.

of words like "Godkiller" as much as he can and besides see to it that the ban be carried out everywhere, so that all might realize the tragic effects of this epithet. Only thus can the Declaration on the Jews lead to the purification of religious language which preaching and catechizing so badly need.

o) Alarm about the Declaration

The struggle for a just "Declaration on the Jews" within the Secretariat was accompanied by public requests that the Council should emphasize its profession of God's constant love for Israel. There were repeated rumours in the world press that the Declaration was going to be suppressed or at least considerably weakened. Sometimes such a rumour was only a journalistic strategem for acquiring information. Looking back, however, it may be said that the false reports, too, have contributed to keeping the discussion alive. Both well founded and unfounded reports brought about reactions which cannot have been without influence on the Council fathers.

On 20 June 1964 the Jesuit periodical *America* published a leader which mentioned the widespread disquiet which the news of a weakened Declaration on the Jews had caused, and which therefore asked for a sincere and unmistakeable declaration. Many readers' letters welcomed this editorial. James C. Tower, Jersey City, N.J., thought that the opposition of the Orientals to a Declaration on the Jews was in the last analysis only a provincial reaction. According to this reader the Orientals see the matter from a point of view that allows only a caricature, produced by local Israeli-Arab tensions. They should realize that their demand that the universal Church should take over their limited point of view is not co-operative (with the Council) but rather obstructive. They sought to prevent a proper gesture of Christian contrition for the massive and cruel persecution the Jews had suffered at the hands of nominal Christians.[163] The Paulist editor of *The Catholic World* in New York, John B. Sheerin, thought that the leader had cast much light on a very urgent question. The Declaration on the Jews such as it had been presented to the second session did not only show prophetic foresight, but also contrition for the injustice the Jews had suffered for two millennia.[164]

The author of this commentary emphasized the view of the leader "that the great question was that of deicide". The killing of Jesus is undoubtedly deicide, for it is the murder of God incarnate. But does this mystery make formal deicides of the actors in the drama of the Passion — the Jerusalem judges and the Roman hangmen, the Jewish crowd before the palace of the governor and the (probably Syrian) soldiers who mocked, crowned and crucified Jesus? The answer is obviously No. None of the people concerned knew whom they crucified. This, after all, was the testimony of the victim himself: "Father,

[163] *America,* 4 July 1964, p. 1.　　[164] *Ibid.*

forgive them, for they know not what they do" (Lk 23:34). Nevertheless there are people who insist on calling deicides not only the actors in the drama of salvation but the whole Jewish people. But we are all sinners and thus also spiritually guilty of the crucifixion just as we are its beneficiaries. Thus we have become brothers in guilt just as we have become brothers in mercy — why should therefore a Christian — a sinner who has been forgiven — want to burden the Jews with his bitterness, even his hatred? Why should he want to accuse at all, instead of rejoicing that his own and the world's sin "deserved such a great Redeemer"?[165] I must own I should be much more easily convinced of the purity of the motives of the persistent defenders of the accusation of deicide if they were equally anxious to give the Jewish people credit for being, as it were, the womb of Christ. The consequence seems inevitable to me: If the whole Jewish people bears the guilt of the few who tried and condemned Jesus, they must also be named in the same breath as the Mother of Jesus. But I have never heard anyone who calls the Jews deicides say that they brought forth God and that the Jewish people should be called: "Israel, the Godbearer". Could it be that the source of their accusation is not their faith and their love of Christ, but their love of self or an even more sinister power (*America*, 4 July 1964, p. 1)?

These examples of a public discussion of the Declaration and its then still uncertain fate stem from the early time when the first news of the draft launched by the co-ordinating commission or its president reached the public. The examples might easily be multiplied by some of the same time and by even more from later days. They all belong to the history of the text, because they are visible proof of the fact that the whole Church has been thinking and feeling during the Council, even though only the bishops were able to express her convictions and emotions.[166]

The months between spring and autumn 1965, that is the time before the fourth session of the Council, were particularly depressing. One piece of bad news followed the other. In March of the same year an obscure Italian bishop was made famous by the world press far beyond the borders of his own tiny diocese and indeed of his country. In an Italian clergy review Bishop Luigi Carli had opposed the Declaration which had been approved by the Council fathers with an overwhelming majority during the first reading. According to him there was a collective guilt of the Jews concerning the crucifixion of Christ, and this

---

[165] *Exsultet,* liturgy of Easter night.

[166] However often the expression "deicide" may have been employed by Christian writers and preachers, it does not form part of the authentic tradition of the Church. This was demonstrated, for example, by Cardinal Journet as early as 1945 in his book, *Les Destinées d'Israël* (p. 153) with the following quotation from Augustine: "The Lord rose again and many [Jews] believed in him. Without understanding [what they did], they had crucified him. Yet later they believed in him, and this so great sin was forgiven the *homicides.* I do not speak of *deicides,* for had they realized it they would not have crucified the Lord of glory (see 1 Cor 2:8). The killing of an innocent man was forgiven them: through grace they drank the blood which they had shed in folly" (*Enarrat. in Ps.,* 61, 5: *PL,* XXXVI, 791). See also J. M. Oesterreicher, "Deicide: A Theological Problem", *Unitas* (Autumn 1968).

guilt endured because the Judaism of today was "the free, willed continuation" of the Judaism of the time of Jesus and its No to him. Thus it must indeed be called "rejected, cursed and deicidal". As if this frontal attack on the Declaration on the Jews were not bad enough, it caused all kinds of rumours such as that the Pope had established a commission of four, to which Bishop Carli belonged, in order to examine the Declaration. But such a commission would have meant the cassation of the document.

This rumour seemed to be confirmed by a sermon of the Pope. On Passion Sunday 1965 Pope Paul conducted the principal service in a Roman suburb on Mount Mario, Santa Maria della Guadalupe. Explaining the Gospel (Jn 8:46–59), he said, according to the *Osservatore Romano,* that the Gospel of the day was "a serious and sad page, giving an account of the conflict between Jesus and the Jewish people. This nation, chosen to receive the Messiah whom it expected for thousands of years . . . does not only not recognize him at the right moment in Christ who came, spoke and revealed himself, but even fought, slandered and insulted him, and finally killed him." Turning his attention to the present, Pope Paul stated that this drama continued to be repeated even to this day through the works of all those who offended and denied Christ.[167]

For a time it seemed as if all sound communication had broken down. Paul VI had spoken in pre-conciliar language. This was regrettable, because it was hardly compatible with the spirit and letter of the "Declaration on the Jews" to say that the Jewish people, that is all the Jews, had fought, insulted and killed Jesus. It seems as if the content of the Declaration had not yet reached the Pope's subconscious, so that in this probably spontaneous sermon he used still the "old" language without knowing it. Most journalists did not realize what the Pope was driving at and suppressed his application to the present. But this was the chief point of the homily. No wonder that it caused consternation. Most students of the homily thought to discover a retrograde movement in it. Some saw in the

---

[167] Cf. *Frankfurter Allgemeine Zeitung,* 9 April 1965; *New York Times,* 11 April 1965. The following are the main points made by the Pope about the connection of the mystery of the crucifixion with the modern world:

"This drama . . . is being repeated in our own times: a large part of the human race is proud of acting in contradiction to God; there are men who think themselves superior to others simply because they assail Christianity and its message of peace and brotherliness . . .

"Christ did not curse his crucifiers, but prayed the Father to forgive, for they did not know what they were doing. And in our own time, too, opposition to God is more than anything else a sign of ignorance, of a lack of knowledge of Christ and his teaching. For this reason it is necessary to be honestly and exactly informed as to what Christ's message consists in. It is necessary for our own sake and for the sake of our souls that we should remove ignorance . . .

"It is necessary that we should believe in him, that we should put our trust in him, that we should accept him totally, and that in the midst of all our cares he should remain the centre of our lives. We must not be afraid of Christ, but must give him our faith and our love."

These words prove that the tenor of the sermon has been to a large extent misunderstood. This does not change the fact that the way the Pope expressed himself was unfortunate, though it does prove that all anti-Jewish intentions were far from his mind.

gaffe — which could have happened to the best speaker, especially in a state of fatigue — a well calculated plan: Paul VI wanted to examine the reaction to his words in order to see how the elimination of the Declaration would be received. These people did not realize that such a calculation was quite foreign to the character of Paul VI, who is also far removed from any anti-Semitism[168] — a final element of what I have called the breakdown of all sound communication.

Two leading Jews, chief rabbi Dr. Elio Toaff and the president of the union of Israelite congregations, Sergio Piperno, sent a telegram of protest to the Cardinal Secretary of State Cicognani, in which they expressed their "painful astonishment" that the Pope had renewed the ancient accusation of the guilt of all the Jews in the death of Christ after the Declaration of the Council seemed to have put an end to it.[169] In the United States Rabbi Balfour Brickner, the director of interdenominational work of the Union of Reform Congregations, among others, objected to the sermon of the Pope. He found it difficult to believe that the same man who, even a week ago, had spoken of the removal from the Liturgy of all offensive expressions about Jews and Judaism[170] could be the same who now renewed the disputed question of deicide.[171] (Incidentally, the inexact use of "deicide" here and by other Jewish speakers or writers as well as similar thoughtless phrases have contributed to the demand for greater precision which was answered by the Secretariat so that several changes were made in the text.) Several Catholic and Protestant periodicals were no less vociferous in their protests against the "lapse" and "bigotry" of the Pope.

In such an atmosphere disquieting rumours were almost inevitable. On 25 April the *New York Times* reported that the Declaration on the Jews had been exposed to renewed attacks, this time not from the Arabs, but from conservative elements in the Church. It now seemed more than probable that far-reaching verbal changes would have to be made. Thank God this prognosis was wrong, though it is true that the Declaration had been under fire from some (not from "the") conservatives. It is one of the ironies of life that an even very subtle anti-Judaism often leads to an attitude extraordinarily similar to that which is attacked. So it may well be said that certain opponents of the Declaration on the Jews resemble Annas and Caiaphas, those lovers of the status quo. Because they were afraid of renewal they held on to the old state of things.

Nevertheless, the alarming news continued to mushroom. On 20 June the London *Observer* declared simply that the Declaration had been removed from the agenda of the last session of the Vatican Council. The *Frankfurter Allgemeine Zeitung* reported the next day that the Pope had sent an instruction to the Co-ordinating Commission in which he had demanded the removal of the Declaration

---

[168] See Paul VI's words in the Promulgation of the Declaration, below, p. 129.
[169] *Frankfurter Allgemeine Zeitung*, 9 April 1965, and *New York Times*, 11 April 1965.
[170] See above, n. 4.
[171] See *American Jewish Yearbook* (1966), p. 48. There and on the following pages various opinions about the whole affair are collected.

from the discussion. On 20 June the correspondent of the *New York Times* alleged to have learned from a highly placed authority that the final fate of the Declaration was again to be thoroughly examined. These partly very wild rumours caused the German Co-ordinating Council of the Societies for Christian-Jewish Co-operation to appeal to the German bishops to do all they could that the Declaration should actually be promulgated essentially unchanged before the conclusion of the fourth session.[172] This happened on 25 June. Exactly a month before German Catholics had addressed a magnificent petition to the Pope. (I call it magnificent because the request is expressed clearly and without circumlocution; the language is humble without being obsequious, urgent without being arrogant.) It says there:

"The undersigned have read with great interest and joy the present Declaration of the Council of 20 November 1964 on Non-Christian Religions including section 4 on the Jews, which they regard as the basis for a new relationship between Christians and Jews.

The importance of this Declaration cannot be overestimated because all Christians who have desired it welcome the fact that ancient and unjustified reproaches against the Jews can no longer be continued (e. g. the corporate guilt in the crucifixion of Christ). Thus the ground is cut from under Christian anti-Semitism. After the sad events of the past this must be a profound satisfaction for all Christians who are aware of the situation. For innumerable advocates of a reconciliation between Christians and Jews this achievement is one of the finest results of the Council. At the same time we hope that the new relation to the ancient People of God will also open new ways towards the unity of Christians, because the Old Covenant is evidence of the saving grace of God and thus the common heritage of all Christians and a means towards the unity of the whole people of God. Therefore the undersigned welcome the fact that the Council has now spoken in this manner and look forward to the future promulgation as a historical task of our time."[173]

---

[172] The entire text of the letter has been reprinted in *Freiburger Rundbrief*, 16–17, nos. 61–64 (July 1965), p. 4.

[173] *Ibid.*, pp. 3–4. The names of the signatories (without titles for the sake of simplicity) are: Rupert Angermair, Franz Xaver Arnold, Diego Arenhoevel, O. P., Clemens Bauer, Alfons Beil, H. Bockel, Linus Bopp, Franz Büchner, Walter and Marianne Dirks, Alois Eckert, Willehad Eckert, O. P., Richard Egenter, E. Eiffler, Paulus Engelhardt, O. P., Gertrud Ehrle, Gerhard Fittkau, Heinz Fleckenstein, Karl Forster, Heinrich Fries, Rupert Giessler, Paulus Gordan, O. S. B., Robert Grosche, Richard Hauser, Emmanuel Maria Heufelder, O. S. B., Fritz Hofmann, Georg Hüssler, Erwin Iserloh, Hedwig Klausener, Gertrud Luckner, Gustav von Mann, Johann Michl, Franz Mussner, Engelbert Neuhäusler, Wilhelm Neuss, Wilhelm Nyssen, Marianne Pünder, Walter Rest, Ernst Rösser, Angela Rozumek, Maria von Rudloff, Elisabeth Rüttenauer, Karl Hermann Schelkle, Karlheinz Schmidthüs, Michael Schmitz, Joseph Solzbacher, Bernhard Stasiewski, Albert Stehlin, Franz von Tattenbach, S. J., Johannes Vincke, Eugen Walter and Elisabeth Zillken.

p) Anti-Semitism on the periphery of the Council

A very different accompaniment of the Council were the libellious pamphlets that were distributed on the periphery of the Council. Already during the first session of the Council the fathers received a book of several hundred pages entitled *Complotto contra la Chiesa* ("Conspiracy against the Church"). Maurice Pinay was given as the name of the author. Despite this French-sounding pseudonym and the fact that the first edition appeared in Italian the book is of Spanish origin, as is evident from the bibliography. References are normally to Spanish translations, even if the original had been published in another language. (In the Austrian edition, the only translation accessible to me, this error has been corrected.) Though the book refers frequently only to one author, for example: "All rights reserved by the author", a preface states that the book "has been written by a group of idealists who are strict Catholics" and who are firmly convinced "that the Catholic Church passes at present through one of the most dangerous periods of its history". The Church is threatened by international communism, whose secret driving forces are Jewry and freemasonry, whose hidden strength is Jewry again, which in itself is the "synagogue of Satan". These are the first three sections of this concoction, while the fourth is devoted to the "fifth column in the clergy". This "fifth column" is a creation of the Marranos, though both the Gnostic and the Arian heresies had been the work of Jews, Arius having been a Jew. One chapter treats of the Jews as the most dangerous enemies of the Church, another calls them the betrayers of their most faithful friends and protectors, yet another states that they spread the cult of Satan. Thus it goes on and on: The barbarian invasion was a Jewish triumph; the Albigensian heresy had been instigated by the Jews; the Jews have at all times attempted to infiltrate into the clergy so as to accomplish their work of destruction more easily. The same is going to happen at the coming Council. That the author speaks of the Council as in the future shows that the book had been in preparation for a long time; that the words were not removed from the translation shows how carelessly the "information" had been gathered.

The author(s) write(s): "We know from a reliable Jewish source that this statute will regulate the relations between Jews and Christians and will be presented to the next ecumenical council by agents of Jewry in the higher echelons of the clergy, which was planned in dark synagogues and high masonic circles. Its aim is to oblige Jews and Christians not to attack one another and thus to prevent Catholics from defending their nations or their Catholic families from the destructive activity of Jewry, which on its part does not appear to attack the Church and the Catholics directly, but will do so according to the classic system of casting the stone while hiding the hand that throws it."[174] Most bishops thought the book so disgusting and — boring that they threw it into the waste-paper basket.

---

[174] *Verschwörung gegen die Kirche* (Austrian edition, 1963), pp. 730f.

While "Pinay" considers conversion (which, according to the nature of the Jews, can only be feigned) the secret weapon of the underground activity of the Jews, "Bernardus", another agitator who conceals his name, regards the conversion of the Jews as the only way by which they can get rid of the curse that lies upon them. In a pamphlet written in Italian, "Gli Ebrei e il Concilio alla luce della Sacra Scrittura e della Tradizione", distributed during the second session of the Council, Bernardus defends the view that the Jews are indeed a deicide, damned and pernicious people. The Church must defend herself against them even today, as she has done in the past. He asserts that the suppression of the Jews as well as belief in their rejection belong to the binding tradition of the Church. According to Bernardus past laws restricting the freedom of the Jews (or rather restraining the freedom of Christians and Jews to meet each other) and demanding their social separation are not conditioned by the times — whether they are just or unjust — but are eternal norms. He considers a decree on the "Inquisition for the Jews" of 1751, for example, a sacred law.

This decree teems with directives; we shall quote only a few which will show what happens when the Church imitates a police state. According to the decree Jews may not buy or receive any books whatever unless they have been presented to the competent censors. During the burial of their dead Jews may not observe any rites, and on the way to the cemetery they may neither sing nor carry lights, under pain of financial or corporal punishment. Jews of either sex must wear a yellow badge. There is no dispensation from this; if a clergyman of inferior rank were to grant it, he must be punished by his superiors as they think fit. Jews are forbidden to distribute, give or sell meat of any animal killed by them to Christians; the same applies to milk and milk products. The punishment of a fine of 100 "Kronen" and imprisonment is incurred by both, Jews and Christians, involved in such transactions. No Jew may spend the night away from the ghetto, that is to say he must return before 1 a. m. and may not leave it before daybreak. Those who infringe the order are threatened with flogging, three strokes with the rope for men and with the whip for women, administered in public. Jews are forbidden to play, eat, drink or otherwise converse with Christians. Nor are they allowed to visit places of entertainment, castles, farms and other places for any reason whatsoever, even if they needed a change of air.[175]. One must really be insane to regard such precepts as the law of Christ.

During the crisis of October 1964 the bishops received by post another scurrilous publication entitled "The Jewish-Masonic Action at the Council". This purported to have been written by (anonymous) priests and religious of an unnamed diocese; two of them who also refuse to give their names were said to have been members of the Council. Since the gentlemen enjoyed the protection of anonymity their statements could not be examined. They wrote that their

---

[175] The Inquisition Edict is reproduced in detail by Laurentin (*Declaration on the Relation of the Church to Non-Christian Religions* [1966], pp. 24–48).

hearts were heavy when they saw the audacity prevailing at the Council. Some of the fathers had evidently lost the faith. As had happened so often in history, Jewish converts were trying to destroy the divine work.

International Jewry, made proud by its temporal triumphs, was now staging a new attack on the Catholic Church, pretending to honour the Jewish people before mankind, an attempt contradicting the traditional teachings of the Church. Jews who had attained a high rank in the hierarchy had fraudulently persuaded John XXIII to create a Secretariat for the Unity of Christians. This had served them as a platform from which to launch their propaganda "in favour of the Jews, the eternal Antichrists". This work was in the hands of the following Jews: Cardinal Bea, Monsignori Oesterreicher and Baum, together with Walter Kempe (all from the country of Luther) and Bishop Méndez Arceo, Mexico.

Here two things are interesting. First the authors evidently do not know which card to play, that of fear of the Jews or of Lutherophobia. Secondly, the carelessness in making statements. Cardinal Bea is as little of Jewish descent as the authors are Congolese. Gregory Baum is an Augustinian, hence not a monsignor. I myself do not come from the land of Luther. The bishop called "Kempe" is evidently Auxiliary Bishop Kampe. Neither he nor Bishop Méndez Arceo had anything to do with the authorship of the Declaration on the Jews. If one has no real cause one must fabricate one. Hence the authors boldly state that the many fathers who supported the "theses of the Jews" had done so only because they had been deceived by the aforementioned agents of international Jewry "who have so far been able to conceal their identity". The authors who concealed their own identity failed to realize that they deprived a number of prominent ecumenists of their merit of having prepared the Secretariat, and that they implied that the fathers who had supported the Declaration on the Jews had not obeyed the voice of conscience but rather the blandishments of Antichrist. No wonder Fesquet could write that these statements made their authors ridiculous in the eyes of every reasonable person.[176]

Another pamphlet also complained about the "Jewish-masonic conspiracy". "If now", we can read there, "the Roman Curia, the Pope himself and especially the fathers assembled in the Second Ecumenical Vatican Council no longer realize what is behind the pretended reforms of Cardinals Bea, Suenens, Frings, Döpfner and their associates when they want decentralization of the formation of a parliament around the Pope, and if it is impossible energetically to frustrate such plans, then the Catholic Church and the Pope will suffer the same fate as the Christian monarchs, who were first deprived of their authority and then deposed. Then the Vatican can be turned into a beautiful museum such as the Louvre, Versailles and many other European palaces."[177] According to this pamphlet

---

[176] Fesquet, *op. cit.,* p. 504; cf. *Frankfurter Allgemeine Zeitung,* 15 October 1964.

[177] Both here and at other points in this section I am omitting exact page references, etc., since the pamphlets discussed here are not obtainable through the legitimate book trade. Moreover, most of them appeared without any publisher's name.

these palaces were taken away from their owners through the machinations of Jews and freemasons, because the monarchs did not oppose them in time.

It was further alleged that the name of Cardinal Bea was not of German, but of Jewish-Spanish origin, it was derived from the sephartic Beja or Beha (it actually derives from Behaim). According to the pamphlet, "the principal author of the Decree on the Jews, the allegedly converted Jew, nowadays Monsignor Oesterreicher", is alleged to have said verbatim in a sermon preached in New York Cathedral: "We no longer read the many statements of Jesus Christ against his people which are contained in the gospel." Hence Monsignor Oesterreicher dared to "censure the gospel of our Lord Jesus Christ". I can only repeat here what I already said in Rome, namely that the authors are not only cowards who do not dare to give their names to their slanderous writings, they are also deliberate forgers. In 1961 I preached in New York Cathedral in connection with the octave of prayer for Christian unity, taking as theme the action of the Holy Spirit in the Church of our own days. I went on to say that owing to this action of the Holy Spirit we no longer read the woes of Jesus, all his harsh sayings against the leaders of his people and against the crowds, recorded by the Evangelists, in such a way as if they were words of scorn, as had been done so often in the past, but as words of care, not as general condemnations but in the way they were meant, as calls to return, as merciful warnings. From this passage the authors took about a third, presenting it as the complete thought and omitted the rest.

A man called Giorgio Trillini produced a pamphlet under the name Fra Giorgio da Terni — in order either to give his statements an ecclesiastical character or to feign a special commission, for he was neither a priest nor a monk. There he wrote that all famous priests, saints and Fathers of the Church had warned against the Jewish disease which was more catching than the black death or one of the venereal diseases. Jews had been everywhere, from the first freemasons' lodge to the Bolshevik revolution, from Rome to the bestial bloodthirsty Marx, Engels, Lenin, Trotsky, Stalin, Krushchev and Breshnev (of the above-mentioned seven five are not Jews! — the author). The six million Jews gassed in the concentration camps had never existed except in the lies of the clever children of Israel. The truth had just begun to appear in the press of Egypt, Syria and Jordan, and the authors exhorted their readers to learn from the Arabs who the Jews are and how they hate Jesus.[178] In my view the mental connections between the Nazis, the authors of the anti-Semitic pamphlets and the Arabs are here quite evident.

The connection between the last two is even clearer in a publication of the year 1965 with the lengthy title: "The Declaration in favour of the Jews lays the foundation for a new form of racism which impairs the right to the legitimate defence of other nations." The author calls himself Dr. Edoardo di Zaga. He

[178] Cf. *American Jewish Yearbook* (1966), p. 55.

manages to reproduce a correspondence between the leader of the Palestinian-Arab delegation in New York, Issah Nakley, and Cardinal Bea. As the Cardinal refuses to comply with the wishes of his correspondent he is at once compared with Machiavelli. "The Jewish problem", the author writes, "is not only serious — it is *the only problem* of the world today, because all other problems which have brought our present age to the threshold of death are the result of the unnatural fertility of this serious problem. To be free or not to be free, to have a fatherland with all that the word implies, or to be part of the world of Leviathan, the world that is controlled and enslaved by Zionism — *that is the question!*"

Here are a few gems from the pamphlet: the Council seemed to assert that the blood of Abraham made the Jew into a sacrament, that "he as an individual and as a community is *ex opere operato* the end and subject of the divine promises and the divine blessing." Cardinal Bea had condemned the Church in order to satisfy Jewry. He condemned all persecutions of the Jews, not only in our own days but in all ages of the Church. "It is a condemnation *en masse;* it is a condemnation of more than thirty Popes who have raised their voice against the excesses, the intrigues and crimes committed by the Jews, that is by the Maffia (sic!), who are without sin, because Abraham's blood flows in their veins." With this general condemnation of the fictitious crimes of the Jewish people (meaning probably: against the Jewish people — the author) a new, sacred racism was to be introduced, "A Jewry protected by the Church and the Council". Two Messianisms had to be distinguished: 1) the Jewish one, which is political and nothing but the desire for power and for the subjection of the world, and 2) the divine one, that is the redemption and salvation of all men through the sacrifice of Christ on Calvary.

The authors live in a primitive world, in which there is only black and white, no grey, no transitions, no concert of colours, in a world of angels and devils, not of men, where all justice is on one side and all wrong on the other. Indeed it may be asked what kind of God they worship. Certainly not the God of Abraham, Isaac and Jacob, the God of the living, the God of astonishing deeds, of grace, of the incalculable, whose ways are not the ways of men. Peter thought it enough to forgive seven times seven — certainly a good measure — but Christ expected a man to forgive seventy times seven, that is again and again. Dr. Zaga, on the contrary, thinks that "we", that is to say the Christians, "may not love a people that is the incarnation of the war against Christ and his Church". It is complete nonsense to assume, as does our author, that today as always Zionism "seeks to eliminate and destroy Christ, its rival". That Christ and Zionism should be rivals is truly the height of absurdity. That would mean taking Zionism much more seriously than it takes itself. But supposing Dr. Zaga's view of Zionism were right, ought we to follow him in his hatred? This sentence, indeed the whole paragraph, tells the reason why I have treated the anti-Semitic campaign *ad nauseam*. This anti-Semitism threatens the Church much more than the Jewish people, because it preaches an alien God. However much anti-Semites like Dr.

Zaga may speak of Christ, their God is the God of dark, irreversible fate. The God of Israel who shows mercy unto the thousandth generation (Exod 20:6) is foreign to them. It is a scandal to such anti-Semites that the Lord should be faithful to Israel, that he has not rejected it, even though it does not recognize Christ.

The obstinacy with which the anti-Semitic opposition was carried on to the end can only be explained by a profound *ressentiment* against the incomprehensibility of God's grace and the election of Israel. In mid-October, that is a few days before the final vote, the fathers received a last warning, this time signed by about thirty so-called Catholic or Christian organizations. Most were unknown to the *periti,* a few were certainly fictitious. One of the few identifiable groups who had supposedly supported the manifesto in the eleventh hour was the "Traditionalist Movement of America". The leader of this ultra-conservative group, Father Gommar De Pauw, was in Rome when the document appeared and simply denied that his movement had anything to do with the attack. When he was asked first to make sure what was behind the signature of his movement he decided to telephone. On the same afternoon he announced that the spokesmen of the Traditionalists who had remained in the States asserted neither to have seen nor to have approved nor to have signed the manifesto. This should suffice to show how reliable were the authors of the document.

Once more the bishops were adjured to reflect that their approval of the Declaration on the Jews would make them heretics and the Council a kind of "robber synod", while the Pope would show himself an anti-Pope if he were to promulgate it. The authors considered themselves empowered to issue such a warning, because their only motive was "to save the Catholic Church from such a disgrace". Moreover, they only followed Christ and his apostles: "(The authors) bear witness that Christ and the Apostles John and Paul were the first anti-Semites, and that the New Testament was the first pamphlet (sic!) of our era." Neither the Pope nor the bishops were frightened by the voice of the adversary masquerading as God's advocate.[179] A few days later the Declaration was accepted and shortly afterwards promulgated.

q) The end of the way

On 28 October 1965 the day of the promulgation, the difficult journey had come to an end. Despite certain faults the "Declaration on the Jews" was a triumph over the law of inertia which had carried certain prejudices through the centuries. One defect, the dropping of the express condemnation of the accusation of deicide, has already been mentioned. Another, which derived from the same source, was

[179] Referring to the anti-Jewish pamphlets, A. Wenger, A. A., also says that "their arguments were so vile, their allusions so repulsive, their origin so uncertain and even suspect" that the fathers allowed themselves to be influenced by them in no way whatever (quoted from J.-P. Lichtenberg, O. P., *L'Église et les religions non-chrétiennes* [1967], p. 18).

the heading of Article 4 in the whole Declaration. One *modus* had suggested to say "On Judaism" instead of "On the Jews", in order to make it clear that Article 4 dealt with the religion and not with the people. The proposal was accepted, but unfortunately not in the form suggested. The heading chosen was "on the Jewish Religion". But the Jewish religion without the Jewish people is a fiction, it exists only in a "History of Religions", that is to say, in books. Those who chose the heading were simply unaware of the fact that the Jewish religion cannot be separated from the Jewish people. For it is undoubtedly a people *sui generis,* that is, a community of experience and destiny which can hardly be called anything but "people", whether or not it has a State of its own and lives in its own country. It is a question of Jewish existence which is not the existence of individuals but of a community, of an incarnate vocation. The change was made principally for the sake of the Arabs, and the only mitigating factor is that all titles were provisional, because they only served to find one's way about in the documents more easily. In the final edition all subtitles, including that "On the Jewish Religion" have been eliminated.

The provisional version of 1964 and even earlier ones had the phrase: "The Church of Christ acknowledges with grateful mind *(grato animo)* that the beginnings of its faith and election are to be found already in ancient Israel." A proposal signed by only two fathers suggested to eliminate the words "with grateful mind" because they sounded as if gratitude were owed to the Jews of today for the graces mediated by the patriarchs. It could surely not be denied on the one hand that the present generation of Jews are responsible for the evil done by (or in) an earlier one and on the other asserted that the present generation should be credited with the merits of the past. This objection was possible only because philosophers and psychologists had not yet worked out the difference between the solidarity which binds the members of a community to one another and the concept of collective guilt, and because biblical theologians especially had not differentiated sufficiently between the Scriptural teaching of the unity of the patriarchs and their descendants and of their coalescing into one personality on the one hand, and collective thought on the other.

But apart from this elementary distinction, ought not a contemporary Catholic be grateful to the Jews of our time also for those gifts that they have not merited themselves? It is not part of the Catholic spirit to cry: "Honour to God alone!" in other words to fear to diminish God's sovereign honour by honouring his creatures.

What is even more important in our context is the Church's constant veneration for the Holy Land which has borne Christ and for the holy places, even though they were not conscious of the great deeds God accomplished in them. If the Church lovingly greets these dumb and lifeless witnesses, should the Christian not do the same for the living witnesses, through whom the revelation of the Old Testament has come to us, according to the Declaration? The elimination of thanks is regrettable, not only because the affectionate tone of the

Declaration has thus been diminished, but also because the fullness of faith and the courage that stems from it have been harmed.

In the draft of 1964 the disapproval of the hatred of the Jews was expressed by the verbs *deplorare* (deplore resolutely) *et condemnare* (condemn). In the final version the text was shortened so that only *deplorare* was left. The explanation that in the language of Councils "condemn" was applied only to heresies and not to sins or crimes did not convince anyone. For, first, the Constitution on "The Church in the Modern World" condemned, among other things, expressly the inhumanity of total war.[180] Secondly, anti-Semitism is not only sinful but also heretical. It is true, however, that the first drafts did not contain the term "condemn", since Pope John had told the Council particularly not to issue condemnations but to announce the good news of the Gospel. Moreover, "the special mission of the Secretariat is one of dialogue, formation and education, not the issue of anathemas".[181]

One *modus* had asked to reject persecutions in a stronger and more general manner, so that a particular rejection of anti-Semitism appeared unnecessary and could therefore be eliminated. The Secretariat rejected the second proposal while accepting the first. The fact that the majority preferred the shortened form must have been due to pity for the Arabs. The Arab representatives felt all the time neglected and complained constantly that the "Arab cause" was at a disadvantage: the injustices done to the Jews had been duly considered, but the wrong done to the Arabs in Palestine had been passed over in complete silence. The lengthy debates on the alterations had finally two positive results: 1) Anti-Semitism was no longer given different designations but was for the first time called by its name. 2) Its rejection acquired a new depth. In the words of Laurentin: "If the Jews are here mentioned among the other persecuted peoples this does not make them less important; on the contrary, they appear as the prototype of the persecuted people, from the Egyptian genocide of Exodus to that of Hitler in the Second World War."[182]

Some obvious "changes" in the final version deprive the Declaration on the Jews of some of its vigour, but give it greater precision. This is the case with the three additions which precede the relevant sections of the old text: 1) Jerusalem's failure to recognize its extraordinary hour of grace; 2) The fact that the Jewish authorities and those who followed their lead pressed for the death of Christ; 3) The Church as the new people of God. They all strengthen and clarify the relevant passages and thus the whole Declaration. They are, as it were, the answer to the frequent objection that the Secretariat had rewritten the Gospel, that it had modified Scripture in favour of the Jews and quoted only those passages or parts of them that flattered them but not those that criticized them.

---

[180] *Gaudium et spes,* art. 77, 2; 72, 2; 80, 3–4.
[181] Cf. M.-M. Cottier, P. P., *Les Relations de l'Église avec les religions non-chrétiennes,* Unam Sanctam 61, pp. 72f.
[182] Laurentin, *Bilan du Concile* (1966), p. 303.

Thus on the eve of the promulgation, when even the slightest change was out of the question, a papal delegate from the Middle East asked that the statement on the character of the Jews as a people always beloved by God should be modified. For this statement only reproduced the positive half of the Pauline text, not the negative one on Israel's hostility to the Gospel. He was only pacified on being told the obvious, namely that the Declaration did not mean to quote Paul verbatim, wherefore there were no quotation marks; that, further, the negative aspect was expressed by the addition that not a few had rejected the propagation of the Gospel, and finally, if one had to split hairs, one could rather say that the Council text was not as clear and plain as that of St. Paul, because the Apostle said quite simply that the Jews are beloved of God, whereas the Declaration adds an "adhuc": that they are still beloved. Thus the Council Declaration loses something of the naturalness and sureness of the Letter to the Romans. Here was a bishop — true, an opponent of the Declaration from the beginning — who could not get over his theological difficulties. What would happen to ordinary Catholics if the anti-Jewish machinations should continue even after the Council? The additions were inserted to prevent them from being helpless victims of anti-Semitic campaign.[183]

Despite all the modifications the text is a triumph of truth and justice. This is the sober judgment of all competent critics. Mario von Galli, S. J., could write: "On the whole, I think, it may be said that the new version has not drawn back an inch in all essential statements, but it reflects the violent attacks to which it had been subjected in the meantime. This is a relative weakness, but it would be foolish if this were to spoil our joy in a Declaration which corresponds essentially to the ecumenical turning point marked by this Council."[184]

To quote once more Abbé Laurentin: In a meditation on 15 October 1965, the day of the final acceptance of the Declaration by the Council fathers, he reminded the readers of the *Figaro* that he had said in the year before that this text, which was so compact, clear and attractive to the men of our time, was perhaps the finest success of Vatican II. He went on to say that he maintained this judgment despite the alterations: "I have just read the text again such as it is, trying to forget what it had been before. I do not take back my judgment of the year before: the text is still beautiful. It resembles one of those women who are still admired though they are about to fade; those who had known them before still whisper: 'If you only knew how beautiful she once was!' A stiff look has replaced the candid smile with which the Church, in a moment of extraordinary grace, had regarded the people from which she had sprung . . .

[183] Prompted by the criticisms of those who were trying to make out, both to themselves and to everyone else, that the modifications had robbed the Declaration of all its value, the present writer once attempted an exegesis of the most important of them and delivered this before the Goethe-Institute in Rome. It appears with certain alterations in the fourth chapter of vol. III of J. C. Hampe, ed., *Autorität der Freiheit* (1967).
[184] *Die Furche* 43 (1965), p. 12.

Some people are bitter about this. However, at first glance this stiffness is not noticeable."[185]

In another context and almost a year later Abbé Laurentin repeated this judgment, adding that the transition from centuries-old hostility to warm friendship could not be made in a day. In such a situation it might even be dangerous if words and gestures were too much in advance of the feelings on which they must be based. Perhaps the present modest and cautious text was the most appropriate first step. The text on the Jews opened locks that had not been in use for centuries. The door had not been opened in the opposite direction without difficulty or pressure. Now the dialogue and the friendship between the Catholic Church and Israel could develop on a sound foundation.[186]

I have anticipated events in speaking of the triumph of truth and justice. Before the Declaration could be promulgated some difficulties had still to be overcome. In order to facilitate the voting and make it as reliable as possible the Secretariat had arranged that several individual points should be submitted to the vote. These were: 1) the preamble, 2) the various non-Christian religions, that is to say, nature religions, Hinduism and Buddhism, 3) Islam. Four questions were devoted to the section on Judaism. Point 4 concerned the spiritual connection between the peoples of the Old and the New Covenant, the Church's roots in the Israel of the patriarchs and prophets, the graces given to Israel and their irrevocability, the common heritage of Jews and Christians and the encouragement of brotherly conversations and common studies. Point 5 dealt with the rejection of the collective guilt of the Jewish people in the death of Christ. Point 6 examined the views of the fathers concerning the alleged curse on Israel and its rejection by God. Question 7 concerned the need for sermons and catechetical instruction to be free from prejudice, the incompatibility of anti-Semitism with Christian love and the special relationship between Christians and Jews; it also included the paragraph on the redemptive death of Christ and the Cross as the sign of the all-embracing love of God. Vote 8 concerned universal brotherhood which must exclude none. The final vote was on the Declaration as a whole.

The voting took place on 14 and 15 October 1965. On 11 October, as it were at the eleventh hour, the bishops received a letter from the "Coetus (or: Comitatus) Espiscoporum Internationalis" instructing them how to vote. This international committee of fathers was an organization of ultra-conservatives, almost a Council within the Council. The instructions purported to have been drawn up at the request of Council fathers seeking advice and were dated 11 November (sic!) 1965. They were signed by Bishop Carli and Archbishops Lefèbvre and Rigaud. Questions 1–3 were to be answered in the negative (non placet). As a reason for the negative first votum the authors gave among

---

[185] *Le Figaro,* 16/17 October 1965.
[186] *Declaration on the Relation of the Church to Non-Christian Religions* (1966), p. 54.

others that for centuries the apostles and their successors had not followed the suggested principle; on the contrary, they had fearlessly rejected errors and plainly confessed the truth of Christ. The authors seemed to be unaware of the fact that the time in which we live requires new, no less courageous methods. The defenders of the status quo could not understand that the Church was no longer the ruler, but had become the servant of mankind.[187] Nevertheless they dared to assert that "the vision of the draft" was that of "a professor in his study", because it considered "only religious notions or rather a comparative 'ideology'. The *faith* that justifies us, however, is not merely an intellectual system in which . . . one might think out a so-called 'terrain d'entente' with others or a so-called 'common denominator' or at least a certain 'apertura'. Through faith the Catholic does not 'adhere to' certain propositions as if he were a philosopher, but he submits to a revealing Person, believes on his authority and gives himself completely to him".[188] It is interesting to see how the leading men of the "Coetus" here make use of a theology of faith which does not fit at all into the framework of their other ideas.

On Question 4 the spokesmen of the "Coetus" say that they like the first five paragraphs apart from what is said of God's friendship for the Jewish people and the eschatological hope of the Church. The Pauline text of Rom 11:28 was mutilated and changed; the words "according to the election" were missing and "carissimi sunt propter patres" had been changed into "adhuc carissimi manent propter patres". Moreover, the critical part of the Pauline text had been suppressed. This objection has been dealt with above (see p. 125). Instead of speaking of multilation one could say more correctly that the Council document was weaker than the Pauline words. For these say simply that the Jews *are* beloved of God, whereas the Council text, which had to oppose a centuries-old prejudice, said that the Jews continue to remain the beloved of God. The opposition to the ghastly prejudice that the house of Jacob is a people hated by God is sufficient justification for the alteration which leaves the meaning completely unchanged.

The second objection shows the same narrow outlook. According to this it was "unworthy of the Council" to have changed the suggestion of "the future conversion of Israel" in such a way as to exclude any proselytizing. The authors were evidently incapable of understanding that a pastoral Council devoted to renewal and reconciliation had to avoid giving any unnecessary offence to others, and that after centuries of injustice it was particularly necessary to speak of the Jews (both inside and outside the Council) with deliberate "délicatesse du cœur".

[187] It would be well to recall the significant words addressed by Paul VI to the non-Roman Christian observers when he first received them in audience. Professor Skydsgaard, in his words of greeting, had quoted Augustine's "we seek in order to find, and find in order to seek". The Pope gratefully took this up and made the stirring comment: "Le vrai Chrétien ne connaît pas l'immobilisme", "the true Christian does not 'stand still'" (L. Cardinal Jaeger, *Das Konzilsdekret über den Ökumenismus* [1965], p. 139).

[188] The script is not paginated.

Their objections were directed not so much against the Secretariat for Unity and its text as against Pope John and his "theology of the heart".

The directive says that Question 5 might be answered with *placet* if the term "the Jews" was understood in its ethnic, not in its religious sense. This suggests Bishop Carli's argument. Question 6 receives a *non placet*. Of the text which concerns Question 7 the signatories say that it would have been acceptable if the Secretariat had approved the *modus* that demanded the rejection of an anti-Semitism "of race or religion". This limitation agrees partly with the demand of the pamphlet with the long title which has been discussed above and which had been distributed in the first half of October. According to this it was not permissible to call persecutions and anti-Semitic outrages "those just measures of the legitimate defence of the Church and of so many nations which had been taken by Popes, Councils and political leaders against the conspiracies, attacks, and other crimes of the Jews which had done the greatest damage to the Church and so many peoples".[189]

Question 8, too, did not meet with the approval of the three bishops who had signed the document, because the section on the brotherhood of all men had not distinguished clearly between natural and supernatural brothers, that is natural men and those reborn through Christ in baptism — as if it were the duty of a brief conciliar document to spell out every distinction. The last question which concerned the document as a whole was simply answered *non placet*. This directive undoubtedly caused uncertainty to a few, but it had no effect on the majority and did not produce the result its authors had intended, namely to prevent the Declaration from being accepted.

The result of the voting was decisive. The first question received 2185 votes of which 2071 were positive and 110 negative.

The figures for the other questions are as follows:

	Votes	*Placet*	*Non placet*
Question 2:	2183	1923	184
Question 3:	2105	1910	189
Question 4:	2099	1937	153
Question 5:	2072	1875	188
Question 6:	2080	1821	245
Question 7:	2118	1905	199
Question 8:	2128	2064	58

2023 fathers took part in the final voting on the whole draft; 1763 voted in favour, 250 against it, and ten votes were invalid. These figures must briefly be

[189] This reference to a *certain* similarity in the wording of the two circulars — the anti-Semitic and the conservative — is not intended as a suggestion that the "Coetus", in particular Bishop Carli, and the anti-Semitic forces at work outside the aula — not to say an "International" — had been working in concert. This has often been insinuated. But it is much too facile to identify the opposition of the conservatives with the crude hostility of the pamphleteers.

analyzed. 250 negative votes seems a comparatively high figure; but it should not be forgotten that this comprises not only the opponents of the section on the Jews but also those dissatisfied with the text on Islam or Buddhism, or even those missionary bishops who had wanted a special mention of animism. The 245 negative votes on Question 6, too, are more than those on the other questions of the Declaration on the Jews. This was the question where the affirmative vote meant the approval of eliminating the words "guilty of deicide". In the days before the voting took place Bishop Leven and Abbé Laurentin had asked for a negative answer to Question 6, the former through a brief circular letter, the other through an important essay. At first many fathers were inclined to protest against the change, but finally most were convinced that it was better to leave the matter alone, since the Declaration was now at such an advanced stage. A vote of protest could easily have turned out to favour the opponents, who were excellent canonists and could therefore have used the fact that a high number of negative votes — over a third — was required for the restoration of the original text, to demand yet another delay. This might have made it impossible to pass the Declaration in the fourth and final session of the Council. Hence all those in favour of the Declaration preferred one with some defects to none at all.

On 28 October, the day of the promulgation, another solemn vote was taken. 2312 bishops voted for, 88 against the Declaration and three votes were invalid. Whoever had witnessed all the crises and vicissitudes of the Declaration on the Jews from close by could only regard the triumph of that day as a miracle. As usual the Pope made a speech on the occasion of its solemn promulgation. He saw a sign of new life in the change represented by this Declaration. "The Church is alive", he exclaimed. "Well then, here is the proof, here the breath, the voice, the song . . . The Church lives. The Church thinks. The Church speaks. The Church grows. We must take account of this astonishing phenomenon. We must realize its messianic significance." Paul VI hoped that the world, too, especially the Christians separated from Rome, would contemplate the growth of the Church and its new face that had become more beautiful. The same applied to the followers of other religions, among them especially those "who are united to us in Abraham". He continued with much warmth: ". . . maxime Hebraei, quibusdam sic agitur, ut non reprobentur neque iis diffidatur, sed ut erga eos reverentia et amor adhibeatur spesque in iis collocetur", ". . . especially the Jews, of whom we ought never to disapprove and whom we ought never to mistrust, but to whom we must show reverence and love and in whom we must place our hope." The Jews were not only the sole non-Christians mentioned, but these words were spoken with obvious ardour. It can only be hoped that all those who had accused Paul VI of anti-Semitism because of his sermon on Passion Sunday 1964, as well as those who thought the section on the Jews would be eliminated at his request, now realized that they had wronged him. Nothing was heard about this in public. But the sincere words of the Pope did indeed crown the work on the Declaration; they were the perfect "end of the way".

r) A new beginning

Beginning and end belong together. The Declaration had scarcely been completed when voices were heard asking that it be realized in the life of the Church. On 20 November 1964 Cardinal Bea demanded: "The Declaration ought to lead to effective action. Its principles and spirit should inspire the lives of all Christians and all men, so that the dialogue explained by the Pope in the encyclical *Ecclesiam Suam* may be begun. It is here, in the fruits which this Declaration should and will have after the Council, that its main importance lies."[190] At the time of the promulgation, on 20 October 1965, the Cardinal gave an explanation to the news agency ANSA in which he said: "The Declaration on the Non-Christian Religions is indeed an important and promising beginning, yet no more than the beginning of a long and demanding way towards the arduous goal of a humanity whose members feel themselves truly to be sons of the same Father in heaven and act on this conviction."[191]

The theme of a new beginning sounds again and again and on the lips of the most varied speakers. Jacques Madaule, the president of the "Amitié judéo-Chrétienne" spoke along similar lines as the Cardinal: "In my opinion the Declaration should not be regarded as an end, but as a first attempt, a new beginning. After so many centuries of bitterness the Church at last resumes the authentic dialogue with the Jews. Now this dialogue must be made as fruitful as possible. I am convinced that it initiates a new era in the relations between Christians and Jews and also between Christians and all non-Christian religions, especially with Islam."[192]

J.-P. Lichtenberg, O.P., goes into greater detail: "A first stage of the difficult, but necessary dialogue between the Church and Israel; a first invitation to Christians and Jews to understand each other better in order to love each other more sincerely, that is the true meaning of the present text. Another stage could have been reached when the Church acknowledges Judaism as a living and effective religion . . . Finally as a third stage the Church would have to recognize the State of Israel."[193]

This third stage is opposed to the attitude which the champions of the "Declaration on the Jews" displayed during the Council. They stated time and again that the Declaration was in no way meant to prepare the diplomatic recognition of the State of Israel; sometimes it was even suggested by some that such a measure was out of the question for a long time. Nevertheless among Catholics this demand is made again and again, and there are many signs that it will continue to become stronger. It seems the Arab attack on the Declaration with its threats and blandishments has turned into a boomerang; the conduct of the Arabs during and after the Council has deprived them of the sympathies which they

---

[190] Bea, *op. cit.,* p. 168. [191] Quoted from Fesquet, *op. cit.,* p. 1020.
[192] *Ibid.,* pp. 988 f. [193] *Esprit* (June 1966), p. 1178.

had enjoyed before, and thus the hearts of Christians turn to the forward-looking State of Israel. All this must be said in order to show beforehand that the increasing desire for the recognition of Israel does not amount to a breach of promise but springs from the realization that it is the duty also of the Christians to confirm the sovereignty, freedom, even the mere existence of the country that has given its Jewish citizens a home and has strengthened a healthy self-esteem of Jews everywhere.

Lucien Lazare, the Jewish partner in conversations held at Strasbourg after the Council had ended presented the new outlook of the Declaration in this way: "Two thousand years of enmity, the Second World War and twenty years of thought were needed to achieve the Declaration. Nevertheless we sincerely welcome the signs of change without any reservations. It is something new that the Church has remembered that Jesus was a Jew and that the apostles were Jews and that she also teaches this. It is new for the Church to acknowledge the vigour of Jewish spirituality and that the rich religious life of Judaism possesses a dignity of its own."[194] But the whole old-new teaching is by no means restricted to these two aspects of the "Declaration on the Jews". The brief remarks of Lucien Lazare are much more than a reflection of the awakening of the Church. His joy in the Declaration has not been affected by the bitterness of the past; his simple acknowledgement has been free from condescension or pride, secure in the change that has taken place he has refrained from making demands, because this would have amounted to a vote of no confidence; and thus the Jewish partner in the discussions of Strasbourg seems to have expressed the necessity of putting the Declaration into effect much more strongly than many doubters who keep repeating that only future actions can prove the real value of the Council document.

The truth of the last sentence cannot be denied, but "c'est le ton qui fait la musique". I hope I myself shall find the right tone in order to sharpen the theological sense and the feeling, indeed the conscience of all concerned. For the demand of the Declaration that the Jews ought not to be exposed to the hatred of the faithful is not only a question of elementary justice but also of the Christian consciousness. A few examples from popular missals should illustrate my meaning. I choose these missals for two reasons. First, because I know at least some of their editors sufficiently well to realize that their commentaries are not inspired by vulgar anti-Semitism, and that therefore the inherited misunderstanding of the Jews appears all the more clearly; secondly, because in future the liturgical life and hence the missals will be the principal source of religious instruction.

On the Ninth Sunday after Pentecost the Church reads a text from chapter 10 of 1 Corinthians: "Brethren, these things are warnings for us, not to desire evil as they did . . ." (vv. 6–10). Since the paragraph was evidently taken out of its

[194] *Ibid.*

context the editor of Schott's missal (the most popular German missal which has gone through several editions and carries more explanations than the ordinary English missals — Tr.) rightly thought it proper to identify the "they". Only he did not choose an expression like "the people in the desert" or "those freed from the slavery of Egypt", or, following St. Paul "our fathers in the desert",[195] but simply: "the Jews in the desert". This explanation was added in square brackets. Taken by itself "the Jews" — the whole for the part — is a legitimate figure of speech, since both literary and colloquial languages recognize its use. It is not in the least dangerous to say "the Swedes" instead of the "Swedish football team" — hardly anyone would assume that the good or bad qualities of these few Swedes are those of all Swedes. It is different in the case of the Jews. Centuries of errors, last of all the genocidal attempt of Auschwitz and all the other places of mass murder have taken away the legitimacy of such an expression. But every alert Christian should be warned against such global terms not only by the events of recent history. An attentive reading of 1 Corinthians ought to have the same effect. For though St. Paul first says that with most of those Jews who had passed through the sea and were baptized in it "God was not pleased", he later says again and again "some of them". Some became idolaters, some indulged in immorality, some put the Lord to the test and some grumbled (10:7–10). The punishments inflicted on them were an example: "Therefore let any one who thinks that he stands take heed lest he fall" (10:12). Here is a great danger for the honest self-knowledge of the Christian. If he constantly hears "the Jews", he will fail to appreciate the delicate distinctions of the passage, and thus fail to acquire the humility this Letter to the Corinthians ought to instill in him.

On the Tenth Sunday after Pentecost the Church reads the parable of the Pharisee and the Publican (Lk 18:9ff.), an incomparable opportunity to emphasize some fundamental truths of the Christian life. But unfortunately this opportunity is mostly passed by, because the historical circumstances of the parable are stressed too much and are, moreover, misrepresented. A characteristic example is the *Missel de l'Assemblée Chrétienne,* edited by the monks of the abbey Saint André, which is in many ways excellent. Here a publican is defined as "a Jew who through his profession as a tax collector was in constant touch with the pagans and therefore unable to fulfill the many prescriptions of (ritual) purification and the inexorable forms of sanctification demanded by the Pharisees".[196] The commentator does not mention that these tax collectors not only had relations with some pagans but that they were in the service of the Roman authorities and, protected by the occupying power, exploited their own people

---

[195] It seems to me that much too little attention is paid to Pauline usage. For the Apostle, the spiritual ancestors of the Christians are not only the servants and friends of God — like Abraham who entrusted himself entirely to God's guiding hand, and Isaac who submitted to the will of the Lord, and Jacob who wrestled for God's blessing — but also the stiff-necked Jews, the men and women who resisted God's grace in the wilderness.

[196] *Missel de l'Assemblée Chrétienne* (1964), p. 831.

for the sake of idolatrous Rome and for their own advantage. Can one call a definition unprejudiced which overlooks that the publicans must appear to their own people as cheats, blackguards and traitors? One would have thought the editors, who belonged to a twice occupied country and a former colonial power, would better understand the tension between the suppressed people of the Jews and the tax collectors who trampled on their own countrymen while kotowing to their foreign masters. They were not criticized for entertaining friendly but harmless relations with the Romans — the publican knew very well what he meant when he asked: "God, be merciful to me, a *sinner!*" (Lk 18:13).

Another footnote concerns the Pharisee: "Member of an integralist sect which had added petty prescriptions to the Law in order to preserve the Jews from contact with the pagan world; this supercilious care for religious purity was accompanied by total contempt for other spiritual families and other people." Here almost every statement is wrong.[197] The Pharisees were a lay order separated from the people, not a sect, which means a community cut off from Judaism. It is true that they did everything to regulate life in great detail, nevertheless we do them wrong if we regard them as punctilious legalists who believed that the religious life consists in nothing but the external, minute obedience to rules. The idea that the Pharisees were only concerned with their own salvation contradicts even the Gospel, since it is stated in Matthew that they traversed sea and land to make a single proselyte (23:15). They clung to the oracle of Isaiah that out of Zion should go forth the law and the word of the Lord from Jerusalem, that in the latter days all the nations should flow to the mountain of the Lord (Is 2:2–5).

[197] The description of the Pharisees as a *secte intégriste* is certainly in keeping with the idea, current among Christians, that they were a static element, as would seem to be suggested by their conflict between them and Christ; but it does not correspond to the actual role played by the Pharisees in Jewish history. I take it that the expression "secte intégriste" — what a *contradictio in adiecto!* — has been borrowed from modern Catholic usage, according to which integralists are people who are convinced that Catholics, to safeguard the integral substance of their faith, must shut themselves off from the movements of history, oppose all innovations and persist in the old ways. It is true that the Pharisees were in favour of a certain measure of isolation for the Jewish people, but they were certainly no advocates of immobility. While the Sadducees, the real conservatives at the time of Christ, admitted only Scripture as the source of Jewish life, the Pharisees believed in the resurrection of the dead, even though there is no clear indication of this in Scripture. Pharisaism was most certainly not the total opposite of Christianity, as can be seen from Paul, who, without any fear of compromising his faith, was able to declare before the Sanhedrin: "I am a Pharisee, a son of the Pharisees; with respect to the hope and the resurrection of the dead I am on trial" (Acts 23:6). While the Sadducees held rigidly to the old ways (for which reason they vanished, after A.D. 70, from the face of the earth), the Pharisees did their utmost to ensure the survival of Judaism into the new era of exile. To this end they were prepared to reinterpret the precepts of the Torah in order to bring them into line with the reality of Jewish life, with its needs and its possibilities. After the destruction of the temple and the decline of the priestly cult they taught simply that fasting, charitable acts and prayer — the "worship of the heart" — made up for the cult required in the Torah. They were no integralists in the anti-modernist sense of the word; it would be much nearer the truth if we acknowledged their *genius* for combining the old and the new, fidelity to tradition and openness to present needs.

133

I know of no Pharisee teacher who rejected the prophecy of the same biblical author that there would come a day "when the idols of Egypt will tremble at his (the Lord's) presence" (19:1). On that day the Lord will make himself known to the Egyptians and they will know him. He will smite them and heal them, and they will return to the Lord (19:21 f.). On that day the Lord will say: "Blessed be Egypt my people, and Assyria the work of my hands, and Israel my heritage" (19:25). A Christian concerned with the truth ought not to disregard this Gospel before the Gospel, this confession of love for the whole earth, for Israel as well as for her hereditary enemies.

The American *Bible Missal*,[198] a kind of pendant of the Belgian *Missel Biblique* and the *Missel de l'Assemblée Chrétienne,* not to say their offspring, has the same interpretation with negligible alterations. What worries me is not so much the errors I have mentioned as the fact that the priests and laymen responsible have evidently not realized that the parable does not speak of *the* Pharisees and *the* publicans but of *a* Pharisee and *a* publican. Hence it is not a description of Pharisees nor of the role of tax collectors, but a call to repentance to all, whether Jews or Christians, individuals or communities. How is it that when the authors were compiling these notes they did not think of those canonists to whom a paragraph of canon law seemed more important than the Gospel or of those moral theologians who pretended to know the heart of God and unhesitatingly declared that reading thirty pages of a book on the Index is a venial sin, but thirty one a mortal sin which separates a man from God for all eternity? How is it that they did not remember the many Catholics who never forgot to confess that they had eaten meat on a Friday but were not conscious of any fault against justice or charity? How is it that they were apparently not worried by the fact that the care for the purity of the faith led to the perversion and caricature of the Gospel which was called the "holy Inquisition"? The explanations ought to speak of these things, I mean of our own sins. By concentrating exclusively on an even inexact treatment of the contemporary scene of the parable the commentators bar their readers from a true understanding of the spirit of Jesus, indeed they foster — though certainly without realizing it — in their listeners or readers the ghastly attitude: "I thank you, God, that we Christians are not like those conceited Pharisees."

The mistaken exegesis of the parable is on the same lines as the misunderstanding of Judaism at the time of Jesus and after. Many Christians assume *a priori* that the Judaism after Christ is without life or grace. Here, too, a new attitude is needed. Whoever meditates on the prayers of the synagogue cannot possibly imagine that God has left his people to its own devices. One of the most touching of these prayers is the "prelude" to morning prayers:

---

[198] *Bible Missal* (1962).

Lord of all worlds,
We approach you with our petitions
Not because of our own justice,
But for the sake of your great mercy.

What are we,
What is our life,
What is our love,
What our justice,
What our salvation,
What our strength,
What our power?

What shall we say before you,
The Eternal, our God and the God of our fathers,
Are not all heroes as nothing before you,
The famous, as if they did not exist,
The wise as if without wisdom,
The reasonable without reason?
For their many deeds are as nothing,
And the days of their life are as a breath before you . . .

And yet we are your people, children of your covenant.
Children of Abraham, your friend, to whom you have sworn on
    Mount Moriah,
Descendants of Isaac, his only son, who was bound on the altar,
The congregation of Jacob, your son, your firstborn —
In your love, with which you have loved him,
In your joy, in which you have rejoiced in him,
You called his name Israel and Jeshurun.

Therefore we are bound
To love to praise, to glorify you,
To bless and to sanctify you,
To give praise and glory to your name.

Blessed are we, how good is our portion,
How lovely our lot, how beautiful our inheritance!
Blessed are we, that we may speak in love early and late,
In the evening and in the morning:

Hear, Israel, the Eternal, our God,
The Eternal is the Only One.[199]

---

[199] The translation is patterned after that by Else Schubert-Christaller in *Der Gottesdienst der Synagoge* (1927), pp. 9 f.

Can the close relationship between Judaism and Christianity be proved more clearly than by this prayer, with its surrender to the Lord, with its consciousness of its own nothingness and its God-given mission? The new thought inaugurated by the Declaration does demand a mental change, and this is not easy. Indeed, the Declaration was never meant to be a document favouring ease and comfort. On the contrary, it is, in the words of the editor of these commentaries a revolutionary document in the good sense, a document intended to change a centuries-old mentality in the spirit of reconciliation. As once the sins of Israel were sent out into the desert, so now, through this Declaration, "the sins of Christendom are expelled into the desert, whether they have been committed horizontally, among the peoples, or vertically, throughout the centuries of history. Not for nothing is the figure resulting from this a Cross."[200]

[200] From an unpublished letter.

Excursus on Hinduism

by
Cyril B. Papali

"In Hinduism men contemplate the divine mystery and express it through an unspent fruitfulness of myths and through searching philosophical inquiry. They seek release from the anguish of our condition through ascetical practices or deep meditation or a loving, trusting flight toward God."[1] These words of the Council are not meant to be a description of Hinduism, but an indication of some of its outstanding spiritual values which may serve as spring-boards for a dialogue with it. And such a dialogue is of the utmost importance to the Church, for Hinduism is a religion that has moulded the spiritual destinies of a large part of humanity for thousands of years and still remains a living force. Having absorbed, during its long lifetime, the peoples and religions of the Indian subcontinent, and spread its philosophy and spirituality over the greater part of Asia, it now stands knocking at the portals of the Christian world. Since the turn of the century, Hinduism has grown increasingly missionary and keen on entering into dialogue with Christianity. Ananda Coomaraswamy has expressed this attitude in eloquent terms: "Our position in relation to Christians and other faiths can be stated by saying that 'even if you are not on our side, we are on yours; and that is something all your zeal cannot take away from us'."[2] A dialogue, therefore, has become inevitable, which in its turn demands a deep understanding and sympathetic appraisal of this extremely complex religion. In the following pages we propose to present a picture of Hinduism in the broadest outlines, emphasizing those aspects of it which may serve as common ground for dialogue.

The word Hindu is derived from the name of the river Indus, originally 'Sindhu", beside which the ancient Aryans settled about the middle of the second millennium before Christ. The Persians designated them by the name of the river, pronouncing it "Indu" instead of "Sindhu", and the name stuck. Today, however, the term Hindu has a religious significance, the people of the subcontinent now being known as Indians. Hinduism, therefore, is the religion

Vatican II, *Nostra Aetate,* art. 2.   [2] Cf. *Orientalia* (1946), p. 33.

of that ancient people which, through millennia of evolution from within and absorption of elements from without, has grown into the immense religio-social system that it is today.

Let us admit at once that Hinduism baffles definition. Viewed from the outside, it is a confusing mass of everything from religion and philosophy to myth and magic. Probing deeper, however, one finds that these divergent elements are held together by certain principles and practices which may be considered the essential features of Hinduism. They may be reduced to the following: acceptance of the *Vedas* (sacred books of the Hindus) as infallible truth; faith in *Karma-saṃsāra* or the transmigration of souls in accordance with the law of retribution; and the practice of *Varṇa-āçrama-dharma*, that is, the law of life according to the caste and condition of each individual. But all this does not reveal the true significance of Hinduism which is this: Hinduism is the cumulative expression of the religiosity of a people whose long history has been one interminable search after God, and whose whole thinking has been characterized by an other-worldly attitude and the primacy of the spirit.

The long evolution of Hinduism may be compared to the progress of a snowball gathering everything on the way and growing as it goes. In its capacity for absorbing everything, even irreconcilables, lies the secret of the continual growth and longevity of Hinduism. It reached its full stature and definitive form in the first centuries of the Christian era. Its history, therefore, easily falls into two periods: the pre-Christian and the post-Christian.

The pre-Christian period embraces three distinct stages corresponding to the three successive portions of the Vedas. The first, based on the earliest books, the *Samhitas,* was a popular form of religion and, like popular Hinduism even today, was practically polytheistic, though the scriptures sounded repeated warnings against this tendency. Thus in the *Ṛig-Veda* we have statements like these: "What is but One, wise people call by diverse names";[3] "priests and poets multiply with words that Reality which is truly one only."[4]

In the second stage, corresponding to the Vedic books called *Brāhmanas* we have a very elaborate form of ritualism. The idea of sacrifice was developed to a remarkable degree. The expiatory function of it was clearly expressed in some of the formulae. Sacrifice is even represented as having been instituted by God as a substitute for an immolation of himself: "To them (i. e. the celestial beings) the Lord of Creation gave himself; He became their sacrifice ... Having given himself for them he made an image of himself which is sacrifice ... By means of this sacrifice he redeemed himself from them."[5] But, as with many other doctrines of Hinduism, the idea of sacrifice was soon overdone and became a species of magic, supposed to be efficacious by itself even against the will of the gods. This

[3] *Ṛig-Veda,* i, 164, 46.
[4] *Ibid.,* x, 114.
[5] *Çatapatha Brahmaṇa;* cf. K. N. Banerjee, *Aryan Witness,* pp. 203, 204.

138

naturally raised the priests to a position even above the gods and set into motion a process of social stratification which gradually crystallized into the caste-system. This stage of religion did not last very long, but it left an indelible mark on Hinduism with its sacred rites, the caste-system and elaborate socio-religious legislation.

The third stage was partly due to a reaction of the intellectuals against the excessive ritualism of the preceding phase. The result was the extraordinary collection of books known as the *Upanishads* which, being the final flower of the Vedas, are also called the *Vedānta* (the end of the Veda). It was an age of intellectual awakening all over the world, an age that produced a Pythagoras in Greece, a Zoroaster in Persia, a Confucius in China and a Buddha in India. But an intellectual awakening in India must needs result in an intense search after God. Among the opening verses of the greatest of the Upanishads is found this famous prayer: "From the unreal lead me to the real; from darkness lead me to light; from death lead me to immortality!"[6] Another commences with this insistent query: "Whence are we born? Whereby do we live and whither do we go? O ye who know Brahman, (tell us) at whose command we abide whether in pain or in pleasure."[7] All the Upanishads carry on this relentless inquiry. And it has not been in vain. In fact, outside the Christian revelation we find nothing to compare with the speculations of those ancient sages about the nature and attributes of God. Here are a few specimens: "The eye cannot reach him, nor the voice, nor the mind. We do not know him, nor can we describe him. He is different from all that is known, and beyond all that is unknown";[8] "He knows him who comprehends not; but he who comprehends him knows nothing. For he is the *Unknown* to the wise; to the ignorant on the other hand He is the *known*";[9] "He moves all things, but is Immovable, is far and near at once; is within everything and beyond all things":[10] "The immortal Brahman is the abode of the world and all that there is. He is the Life, the Word, Intelligence, Reality, Immortality."[11] The Vedantic definition of God is *Sat-Cit-Ānanda* (Existence-Intelligence-Beatitude). The mind of man has not conceived anything more worthy of God.

But the speculations on the world proved disastrous. Without the notion of creation *ex nihilo,* which, as a matter of fact, man has learned only through revelation, those ancient thinkers were faced with three alternatives: to admit a real world co-eternal with God, compromising thereby the absolute sovereignty of God; or to regard the world as a real emanation or evolution of God sacrificing his immutability; or to finally maintain the absolute perfection and immutability of God and deny the reality of the world. All these explanations are suggested in the Upanishads; but metaphysics in the main chose the last alternative, absolute monism, which will remain for ever at the heart of Hinduism. But even in this fatal mistake we must recognize a certain merit: forced to choose between the

---

[6] *Bṛhad. Up.,* i, 3, 27.   [7] *Çvetāçvatara Up.,* i, 1.   [8] *Kena Up.,* i, 3.
[9] *Ibid.,* ii, 3.   [10] *Īça. Up.,* 5.   [11] *Muṇḍ. Up.,* II, ii, 2.

reality of the world and the absolute perfection of God, those ancients, as it were, sacrificed the world in order to save God.

It was during this period that the orthodox schools of philosophy developed within Hinduism and the heterodox sects like Jainism and Buddhism broke away from it. At the same time the various races of India with their diverse religions and cultures were gradually drawn into the Hindu fold, with the result that Hinduism grew into a veritable epitome of many religions. About the 3rd century B.C., there appeared certain scriptures that played a decisive role in the final shaping of Hinduism. The most important were: the *Brahma-sūtra* of Bādarāyaṇa in which were systematized for the first time the theological specula- tions of the Upanishads; the *Dharma-çāstra* of Manu which laid down in the minutest detail the socio-religious laws of the Hindus; the epic *Mahābhārata* which is an encyclopœdia of Hinduism written in the language of myths and fables for the benefit of the common folk; and the famous *Bhagavat-Gīta* (the Lord's Song), a short poetical work of exquisite beauty, philosophico-mystical in character, lying imbedded in the above mentioned epic, but altogether a unity by itself. This last Scripture, which has even been called the New Testa- ment of Hinduism, has been mainly instrumental in introducing the religion of love and the doctrine of grace into Hinduism, and remains to this day the richest source of Hindu spirituality.

In the early centuries of the Christian era, we notice a reawakening and a profound transformation in Hinduism, touched off in the first place by the chal- lenge of Buddhism. From the 3rd century B.C., when the Emperor Asoka turned Buddhist and missionary, Hinduism had been almost driven underground. But it did not admit defeat, and when it finally emerged it literally devoured Bud- dhism. It adopted all the good points of Buddhism and allotted Buddha himself a niche in the Hindu pantheon, till the Buddhists found themselves unwittingly back in the bosom of Hinduism.

But the most important achievement of Hinduism during this struggle for survival was the unification of the many conflicting currents of philosophy, religion and mythology that make up Hinduism. *The Bhagavat-Gīta* had already pointed the way by slightly modifying the various sectarian doctrines of salva- tion and arranging them around its own religion of love. To be sure, it was not strictly a synthesis, but a loose compromise that lets even contradictory doctrines live side by side — a spirit that has characterized Hinduism ever since. By the fourth century A.D., Hinduism had attained its full stature and the classical form it still retains. In this unified Hinduism one may distinguish three strata. At one end stands high metaphysics, radically monistic. But as the unreality of the world does not fully convince the philosophers who propound it, monism in practice behaves like pantheism, a subtle shade of which pervades the whole of Hinduism. At the other end we have the popular religion based on my- thology, practically polytheistic, though in principle all the gods are admitted to be manifestations of the one God. Besides, popular religion has also to deal with demons, not indeed as objects of love and devotion, but as objects of fear, evil spirits that have to be kept out of mischief with gifts. Between these two extremes lies the Hindu religion proper with all its spiritual values. It is avowedly monotheistic without, however, being able to shake off the yoke of either metaphysical pantheism or mythological polytheism.

The noblest and most characteristic feature of post-Christian Hinduism is its doctrine of *Bhakti* (religion of love). When the *Bhagavat-gīta* appeared in the 3rd century B.C., there were three outstanding theories about the essential means of salvation: Vedānta held that *Jñāna,* the intuitive realization of one's identity with the Absolute, was the only means; for *Mīmāmsa* the essential means consisted in the performance of the vedic rites; while Yoga proposed as the only way of liberation, the practice of asceticism and mental abstraction until the spirit discerns itself as being different from matter and withdraws into itself. The *Gīta* does not deny the validity of these ways under certain conditions for certain categories of people, but the one universally valid and easily accessible means of salvation is *Bhakti,* that is, love and devotion to God, and humble dependence on His grace. Thus says *Bhagavat* (the Lord) to his devotee: "On me alone fix thy mind, let thy understanding dwell in me. In me alone shalt thou live thereafter . . . Whosoever offers to me with devotion a leaf, a flower, a fruit, or water, that offering of love of the pure of heart I accept . . . Whatever thou doest, whatever thou eatest, whatever thou offerest, whatever thou givest away, whatever austerities thou dost practise — do that as an offering to me . . . I am the same in all beings. None is hateful or dear to me. But those who worship me with undivided love are in me and I in them."[12]

We may say that this doctrine restored to the Hindus their soul, which metaphysics had rudely suppressed. The response was spontaneous and universal. From the sixth century onwards we have an almost unbroken line of mystics and minstrels of God singing of His love. Thiru-Mūlar sounds almost like the Beloved Apostle:

"The ignorant say that Love and God are different;
None know that Love and God are the same.
When they know that Love and God are the same
They rest in God's Love."[13]

The spiritual experiences of some of them come very close to that of Christian mystics. Here are a few lines from the confessions of Māṇikka-Vāsag:

"My inmost self in strong desire dissolved, I yearned,
Love's river overflowed its banks;
My senses all in Him were centred; 'Lord' I cried,
With stammering speech and quivering frame
I clasped adoring hands, my heart expanding like a flower."[14]

---

[12] *Bh. Gīta,* xii, 8; ix, 26, 27, 29.   [13] Cf. Carpenter, *Theism in Medieval India,* p. 353.
[14] *Ibid.,* p. 356.

A woman mystic, Kāraikāl Ammaiyār, gives this advice:
"If one desires the path that leads to God
And wishes to deserve his grace, and asks:
'Where dwelleth he?' — Even in the heart of those
Like my poor self, it is easy to find."[15]

From the tenth century onward we have elaborate treatises on the spiritual life and the doctrine of grace which, though essentially different from the Christian doctrine, bears amazing similarities to it. Particularly interesting is the controversy on grace and human co-operation which followed lines closely parallel to those of the famous controversy on the same subject which divided Catholic theologians some three centuries later.

The doctrines of Hinduism are grouped under three heads: God, the world and the soul. Unified Hinduism accepts both the metaphysical notion of the Impersonal Absolute and the religious idea of a Personal God. Considered in Himself God is Impersonal, in relation to the world He is Personal. At this point mythology steps in to complete the idea. In his relation to the world, God assumes three distinct forms suited to the respective functions of Creator, Conserver and Consummator. This is *Trimūrti*, the divine triad. The idea is essentially different from the Christian dogma of the Trinity, for Trimūrti is merely the outward expression of God, not His inward nature. It is not 'Three Persons in One Substance', but rather 'one essence in three substances'; but how deceptively close it can come to the Trinity may be gauged from the following lines of the famous poet Kālidāsa:

"In these three Persons the one God was shown,
Each first in place, each last — not one alone;
O Siva, Vishnu, Brahma, each may be
First, second, third among the blessed Three."[16]

Another doctrine, equally central to Hinduism, is that of *Avatāra*, the descent of God, commonly called Incarnation, but better termed theophany.

Whenever the world is beset by some spiritual disaster, Vishnu the Conserver descends in visible form to save it. There have been several such descents, some of them in sub-human forms. Rama and Krishna are the most popular of the Avatāras. The religion of love received a strong impetus from this doctrine. A complement to it is the doctrine of *Arcāvatāra,* the indwelling of the divinity in the consecrated idol. There is no idea of Transubstantiation here, but of a type of incarnation, the divinity assuming the idol as his body. All the same the sentiment of a devout Hindu about it may be very like that of a Catholic about the Eucharist.

One should not be surprised at this extraordinary parallelism between Christian mysteries and Hindu myths, for these myths are the expression of certain

---

[15] *Ibid.*, p. 358.
[16] Cf. Monier Williams, *Brahmanism and Hinduism,* p. 45.

deep-seated cravings of the human soul. And when God deigned to answer these aspirations, the marvels He worked infinitely surpassed man's wildest dreams.

To Hinduism the cosmos is eternal, but periodically appearing and disappearing in endless cycles. God is Creator in the sense that it is his power that draws the cosmos out of a potential state into an actual one. At the close of one cosmic cycle He reduces it back to potentiality, where it continues to exist invisibly in Him until He draws it out at the next cycle. Mythology enumerates fourteen worlds, seven of the higher order and seven of the lower. Our earth is the lowest of the higher order of worlds, but has this distinction: while all the others are *Bhoga-bhūmi* (worlds of reward or punishment), the earth alone is *Karma-bhūmi* (world of probation).

Perhaps the most cardinal of the doctrines of Hinduism is *Karma-Samsār*, the transmigration of souls according to the law of retribution. Souls are eternal, passing through an interminable succession of births and deaths. The condition of a new birth depends on the merits or demerits acquired in the past. Though the soul can assume any species of animal body, only in the human body can it acquire merits. For salvation, therefore, one must be born as man, but it is not enough. In the ordinary way of living, one invariably amasses more debt than one expiates, with the result that at the end of its life the soul finds itself even more deeply involved in transmigration than at the beginning. There is no escape from this iron ring without the special aids that religion alone can provide. And Hinduism has a comprehensive system of rites and regulations to this end.

If Hinduism is hardly consistent in its doctrines, it is exceptionally so in its laws. In this sense it is an integral religion embracing the whole man with all his individual and social activities. In one of the early Scriptures we read: "Man is a sacrifice. His first twenty-four years are the morning libation ... In hunger, thirst and abstinence from pleasure consist his initiation rites ... In laughter, banquets and pleasures he sings a hymn of praise ... Penance, liberality, righteousness, kindness, truthfulness, these are his offerings ... His death is the ablution that concludes the sacrifice."[17] It is this ideal that the Hindu *Sanātana-dharma* (eternal law) proposes to incarnate. This law in its entirety is called *Varṇa-āçrama-dharma*, the duties of the caste (varna) and condition (āçrama). The first regulates the social, the other the individual life of the Hindu. The caste is the framework that holds together Hinduism, giving it a vague, indefinable but strongly-felt unity and individuality, in spite of the absence of a central authority and the presence of an infinite gamut of races and traditions. But its twenty-five centuries of history have not been altogether glorious.

The other institution, Āçrama (state of life), is less known, but far more sober and beneficial. To reach perfection a Hindu must pass through four stages of progressive spirituality. The first is that of the Vedic student which all boys of the first three castes must go through. The next is the family state which is obligatory

17 *Chhaṇḍ. Up.*, iii, 16, 17.

on all. The last two, the state of the hermit and that of the wandering ascetic, are not of obligation but strongly recommended to the brahmins and the nobles, provided they have fulfilled the obligations of the family life. In practice, however, one who feels called to a life of perfection embraces it immediately after the vedic studies.

Intimately related to these stages there are twelve sacraments (Samskāra), four religious vows (veda vrata) and detailed laws to regulate everything in life. The family is the heart of Hinduism and the home a veritable temple, for in it are performed the essential rites of religion. Marriage is considered the second greatest of the sacraments, the first being the initiation rite at the beginning of the vedic studies. It is deserving of mention that the high esteem in which marriage and family are held in no way detracts from the great reverence accorded to celibacy and asceticism, and the people instinctively discern and venerate a true ascetic, whatever his race or religion. A sense of spiritual values is inborn in them, which is yet another opening for a dialogue.

We conclude with words of the great Orientalist Sir Monier Williams: "The Hindu race affords perhaps the only example of a nation who, although apparently quite indifferent to the registering of any of the great facts of their political life, or even to the recording of any of the most remarkable events of their history — as, for example, the invasion of the Greeks under Alexander the Great — nevertheless, at a very early period, regulated their domestic rites and customs according to definite prescribed rules, which were not only written down, but preserved with religious care and are many of them still in force."[18]

---

[18] Monier Williams, *Indian Wisdom,* p. 197.

Excursus on Buddhism

by
Heinrich Dumoulin*

I. The Declaration

It is especially difficult to give a succinct description of Buddhism because of the great differences between the various forms of the Buddhist religion. The Council text sets out in the first place certain essential common characteristics, above all the awareness, present in Buddhism as a whole, of "the radical insufficiency of this shifting world", an awareness already expressed in one of the oldest and most sacred Buddhist texts, the Sermon of Benares attributed to the Founder *Shâkyamuni*.[1] A further essential common feature that can be claimed for Buddhism is its religious attitude.[2] In this connection the Council text speaks of the "path" by which the Buddhist strives to attain the goal of salvation "in a devout and confident spirit". This religious character is particularly prominent in the *Mahâyâna* branch of Buddhism, but is present also in the more rationalistic *Theravâda*.[3] Religious practice in all forms of Buddhism has been profoundly enriched and strengthened by many links with the native religions of the countries in which Buddhism has spread.

The "either . . . or" in the second half of the statement [in the Council text] is not to be understood as indicating mutual exclusion. For the "supreme enlightenment" characteristic of the *Mahâyâna* branch and mentioned at the end of the sentence means, for those who reach the goal, the "state of absolute freedom"; while in Buddhism as a whole "absolute freedom" includes an experience of enlightenment in the broad sense.

The second part of the statement in the Council text recognizes the special

---

Translated by Simon and Erika Young
Cf. H. Oldenberg, *Buddha,* ed. by H. v. Glasenapp (13th ed., 1959), pp. 133 ff.; see also the interpretation of the four sacred truths in *Dîgha Nikâya,* XXII, 18 ff.
On the religious character of Buddhism and for further bibliographical data, see below, I. Starting-Point for a Theological Dialogue with Buddhism.
In view of Buddhist attempts at unity, the former designation *Hînayâna* is avoided by Buddhists today because of the pejorative meaning of the word.

features of the two main branches of Buddhism, *Theravâda* and *Mahâyâna*.[4] The goal of *Theravâda,* whose sacred scriptures are set down in the *Pâli* canon, is known in Buddhist terminology by the Sanskrit word *Nirvâna* (Pâli: *Nibbâna*). The word chosen to translate this in the Declaration — "freedom" — indicates the negative character of the original Pâli or Sanskrit word, but also makes it clear beyond doubt, in accordance with the general Buddhist exposition of this doctrine, that the goal of salvation here denoted has a positive content. The first draft of the Council's Declaration contained, as a rendering of *Nirvâna,* the expression "state of permanent rest" *(status permanentis quietis),* which is indeed closer to the idea of "extinction", but does not express the positive content of the final goal and could therefore easily give rise to misunderstanding.

Any attempt at a short summary of *Mahâyâna* Buddhism runs into insuperable difficulties if it has to take into account all the known *Mahâyânistic* schools of China and Japan and, in addition, Tibetan Lamaism and the new styles of religion dependent upon *Mahâyâna* Buddhism that have arisen in our own time. The Council text gives "the supreme enlightenment" as a general description of the goal of all forms of *Mahâyâna* Buddhism, without specifying its content, and goes on to distinguish between the paths to salvation "by their own efforts" and "by higher assistance". These distinctions arose in China, were transplanted to Japan, and were developed to the full in the widespread schools of *Zen (jiriki =* by one's own power) and *Amida* piety *(tariki =* by the power of another).

II. Starting-Points for a Theological Dialogue with Buddhism

Buddhism, in the course of its 2500-year history, and in its present-day manifestations, presents a complex picture, containing elements of both a religious and a philosophical world-view. It plays a large part in the formation of society, art and culture among the peoples of Asia.[5] The statement concerning Buddhism in the "Declaration on the Relation of the Church to Non-Christian Religions" indicates the most important religious elements that have developed within Buddhism. The unity of the Buddhist religion,[6] in its various branches, rests in the first

---

[4] The improved and enlarged version of the sentence about Buddhism, which takes into account Japanese Buddhism by means of the insertion of the distinction between Theravâda and Mahâyâna Buddhism as well as by the scanty description of the latter, had been recommended by the Japanese bishops at the fourth session of the Council and approved by the Council fathers without discussion.

[5] Nearly all accounts emphasize the basically religious character of Buddhism. See E. Conze, *Der Buddhismus. Wesen und Entwicklung* (1953); C. Regamey: *Christus und die Religionen der Erde II,* ed. by F. König (1951); see also *LTK,* II cols. 752 ff., III, cols. 1341 ff.; H. v. Glasenapp: e.g., *Die Fünf Grossen Religionen I* (1952); F. Heiler: e.g., *Die Religionen der Menschheit* (1959); E. Schlinghoff, *Die Religionen des Buddhismus,* Göschen, vols. 147, 770.

[6] The Council statement evidently assumes an ultimate, comprehensive unity of the Buddhist religion. On this subject cf. H. Nakamura, *Unity and Diversity in Buddhism: The Path of the Buddha. Buddhism Interpreted by Buddhists* (1956), pp. 364–400. On strivings for unity and the international

place upon the historical personality of the Founder, *Shâkyamuni,* and also upon an agreement concerning certain basic conceptions and themes; for example, the fundamental transitoriness of the created world and of man's existence; the vital importance of meditation and inwardness; the ordination of human life to an ultimately decisive liberation, or completion. The Council text, in referring to essential elements in the Buddhist religion that are bound up with the nature of man, indicates at the same time possible starting-points for a dialogue with Buddhism. This dialogue, as the Council statement implies, will take on a different direction and development according to the particular standpoint of the Buddhist partner (*Theravâda* or "with help from above").

The universal Buddhist awareness of the "radical insufficiency of this shifting world" is one of the basic human religious experiences, and may be found in the life of any man of religious feeling. It arises from the very nature of human existence. Man sees his life, as it is actually lived, once and for all, in this shifting world, as unsatisfying, full of suffering, constrained and transitory. These four characteristic features of the Buddhist understanding of existence denote qualities that differ in the abstract but are bound together in the actual experience of the Buddhist who is alive to religious values. If any one of them, above all liability to suffering, is transferred from the concrete to the abstract order of being, and is looked at independently from the others and in isolation, Buddhism turns into a form of philosophical pessimism. Rationalistic interpretations (both by Buddhists and by others) have often led to this kind of misunderstanding. On the other hand it is important to understand that the fundamental Buddhist experience is that of the man who realizes the insufficiency of his own painful and transitory existence. In this way the correct basis for a religious dialogue with Buddhism can be established.

The characterization of the Buddhist as a religious man who advances along the "path" in a "devout and confident spirit" is valid for all forms of Buddhism. The "path" as understood in the Eastern sense, is conceived as a way of spiritualization and salvation. The man following this path strives towards perfection. The religious character of the Buddhist path, affirmed in the expression "in a devout and confident spirit", can be seen in the various forms of the Buddhist religion under different aspects and with varying clarity. Although Buddhism does not acknowledge God the Creator, it is aware of the awe-inspiring mystery of existence and can by no means be equated with Western atheistic materialism. Many texts in the Buddhist Canon, both the *Pâli* Canon of the *Theravâda* school and the *Mahâyâna* Canon which has been handed down in Sanskrit and Chinese, witness to the religious attitude of the Buddhist towards reality, an attitude most convincingly expressed in the fundamental Buddhist virtues of kindness (Pâli: *mettâ,* Sanskrit.: *maitrî,* sinojap.: *ji*) and compassion (Pâli and Sanskrit.: *karunâ,*

movement in Buddhism see H.Dumonlin, *Der Buddhismus: Weltgeschichte der Gegenwart,* II (1963), pp. 626–46.

sinojap.: *jihi*), which are related to the Christian love of one's neighbour.[7] There are considerable differences between Buddhists in their religious customs and in the practices that most nearly correspond to prayer as Christians know it. In addition, some characteristic attributes of Buddhism stand out in sharp contrast to the customs of other religions, in particular of Christianity. These points must be dealt with carefully in the dialogue, with concern for mutual understanding.

In the second part of the statement in the Council Declaration two distinctions are introduced that are important for the dialogue. First, in the characterization of the two main branches of Buddhism, *Theravâda* and *Mahâyâna*, neither of which is mentioned by name, the State of Perfection is considered from different points of view, being named at one point "State of Absolute Freedom" and then "Supreme Enlightenment". A second distinction is raised within the *Mahâyâna* by the two possible paths to salvation, "Through one's own Efforts" and "By higher Assistance".

The final state aimed at in *Theravâda* Buddhism is called in Sanskrit *"Nirvâna"* (Pâli: *Nibbâna,* literally "extinction"). Despite the negative form of the word, however, its meaning is that of the highest positive value, beyond all that can be expressed in human concepts and human speech.[8] The description of ultimate perfection (which Buddhists always refer to in negative terms) as "a state of absolute freedom" brings out the core of positive meaning in the word *Nirvâna* and shows that Buddhism, as seen by its followers, is a religion of salvation. The theme of salvation, which is central to many texts in the Buddhist scriptures,[9] provides an important starting point for the dialogue between the two religions.

At the same time, the negative formulation of the ultimate goal in the Buddhist expression *Nirvâna* has to be taken into account. Buddhist negativism is not philosophical nihilism. This preference for the negative approach is an essential characteristic of Asiatic thought, native both to India and to the countries further east — China, Korea and Japan — and it runs all through the various forms of Buddhism. In all variants there can be seen an orientation to transcendence, and the theology of negation within Christianity should therefore be

---

[7] Not explicitly mentioned in the Council statement, but certainly implied in the emphasis on the religious character of the Buddhist attitude. Although the metaphysical foundation of Buddhist compassion differs essentially from that of Christian love of one's neighbour (cf. H. de Lubac, *Aspects of Buddhism,* 1953, pp. 15–52), the two attitudes come close to each other in actual practice.

[8] The inexpressible peace of *Nirvâna* is extolled in the following verses from the Pâli Canon:
"There is no measure for the man who has gone to that rest,
There are no words to speak of him.
Gone is all that thought can grasp.
And every path is closed to speech."
(*Sutta Nipâta,* quoted in H. Oldenberg, *Buddha* (1959), p. 298.

[9] According to H. Oldenberg's analysis of the Sermon of Benares, there stands "at the centre of the whole a single concept: the concept of salvation" (op. cit. p. 139). The theme of salvation stands out no less clearly in *Mahâyâna* Buddhism, especially in the *Amida* schools.

brought into the discussion at this point from the Christian side.[10] In this way thinking resembling that of the East in its style, though Western and neo-Platonic in essence, can form a bridge. The Greek Fathers of the Church who, in their dialogue with neo-Platonism, opened their minds to the influence of the Platonic spirit without sacrificing any of the treasures of Christian faith, serve as an example of the attitude required from Christians in the contemporary encounter with Buddhism. The speculative, dialectical constructions of the theology of negation in East and West, in neo-Platonism and Christianity, differ widely from each other, but the fundamental concern of this way is everywhere the same — to arouse in the religious spirit a response of wordless adoration before inexpressible mystery.

The *Mahâyâna* branch of Buddhism, unlike the *Theravâda*, provides no uniform system of doctrine, worship and conduct. The Council text, in describing the ultimate goal of *Mahâyâna* Buddhism as "supreme enlightenment", allows for two essential features of *Mahâyâna,* its metaphysical and gnostic tendency[11] and its practice of meditation in search of enlightenment. For many centuries Christianity was familiar with the spiritual attitude of Gnosticism. Today the West is experiencing in many places a revival of this style of thought, which is poised between mysticism and rationality. The concept of "meditation" has many meanings. The feelings of approval and even of longing that the word evokes in the Western Christian require some explanation. Serious meditation certainly represents a spiritual value. All types of Buddhism develop and practise meditation, though in different ways and with varying intensity. Often there is bound up with it a long and gradual process of purification that includes a moral transformation of one's life and demands as well the abnegation and inner purification regarded as indispensable pre-conditions for attaining the desired spiritual concentration and enlightenment. Meditation can be seen to be the common possession and central concern of Buddhism as a whole. For this reason serious attention to the way of meditation is indispensable for a deeper understanding of the Buddhist religion.[12] The meditative approach is also of vital importance in inter-religious dialogue with Buddhism.

The Council text does not attempt to describe the many variants within the *Mahâyâna* branch, but contents itself with indicating the distinction, especially important to religion and relevant also to theology, between salvation "by one's own efforts" and "by higher assistance". In fact this distinction denotes two forms of *Mahâyâna* Buddhism which have succeeded in spreading most widely in Eastern Asia, especially in Japan. The Sino-Japanese school of *Zen* Buddhism is

[10] On the significance of the way of negation in Eastern (Buddhist) and Western Christian mysticism, cf. H. Dumoulin, *Östliche Meditation und christliche Mystik* (1966), pp. 98–124.

[11] Cf. J. A. Cuttat, "Östlicher Advent und gnostische Versuchung": *Kairos* 2 (1960), pp. 145–63.

[12] Cf. the section on Buddhist forms of meditation in *Östliche Meditation und christliche Mystik* pp. 192–216, which gives an account of specialist literature concerning meditation in *Theravâda, Amida* Buddhism, the *Zen* school and the new Burmese method of meditation.

representative of the Buddhist way of salvation "through one's own efforts". It has developed an original and valuable technique of meditation, and seeks in its method for enlightenment which, in the *Zen* Buddhist understanding, means an extra-sensory, intuitive, immediate awareness of the Self and the All.[13] On the other hand, adherents of the schools of *Amida* Buddhism, which have likewise achieved their fullest flowering in Japan, are confident of receiving help from above through the practice of unceasing devout invocation of the name of Buddha *Amida*.[14] These two characteristic mahayanistic ways of salvation, significantly termed *jiriki* (literally "own power") and *tariki* ("another's power") represent different religious attitudes and therefore stand in contrast to each other. Both, however, lead to the same goal of enlightenment and in practice overlap in the religious life of the Japanese and hardly ever occur in their purest form. This situation is rooted ultimately in human nature itself, which cannot reach salvation either by "its own power" alone or by "another's power" alone, but is in fact polarized between these two realities and necessarily gives expression to both in actual religious life. This distinction between the two goes to the heart of religious anthropology and comes up against the central problem that confronts all believers and invites discussion by them all.

Besides the themes of dialogue that are indicated in the Council statement devoted directly to Buddhism, other pronouncements of the Council, above all in the declaration on religious freedom and in the decree on the missionary activity of the Church, as also in the Dogmatic Constitution on the Church, provide fruitful material for discussion with Buddhists. The Council, in statements of a thoroughly pastoral and practical nature, addressed to all men, has opened up for those outside the Church new possibilities for their understanding of Christianity and the Catholic Church. Generally speaking, the anthropological aspects and structures of religious behaviour provide the most important starting-points for theological dialogue with non-Christians.

---

[13] An account of the significance of *Zen* meditation for Christian spirituality is given in H. M. Enomiya-Lassalle: *Zen — Weg zur Erleuchtung* (1960), and *Zen-Buddhismus* (1966).
[14] The religious value of *Amida* Buddhism is made clear in H. de Lubac, *Amida* (1955); cf. *LTK,* I, cols. 436 f.

Excursus on Islam

by
*Georges C. Anawati**

Three questions concerning the text of the Declaration on the Moslems will be considered here: 1. Does it mean a change in the Church's attitude to Islam? 2. To what extent does it present a concise account of the essential teaching of Islam? 3. What basis does it supply for a dialogue between Islam and Christianity?

1. The answer to the first question is especially easy for those who know a little about Church history since the seventh century, that is, since the emergence of Islam. One can say that up to the beginning of the twentieth century the constant attitude of the Church towards Islam was one of condemnation, insofar as Islam appeared to be a "new" religion, which sought to supplant Christianity and denied its principal dogmas: Trinity, Incarnation and Salvation. Moreover, the revelation completed with the death of the last apostle could not be further extended by a new prophet. During the Middle Ages, in view of the political dangers presented by the Moslem countries and of the exhaustion of the secular powers of Europe, none of which had the strength to defend the frontiers of the Christian West single-handed, the Popes made themselves the foremost champions of the Christian countries and the instigators of the Crusades. For the various opinions of scholars and the general attitude of Christianity over the centuries, see the documented work of N. Daniel, *Islam and the West, The Making of an Image* (1960), and the more general, outstanding survey by P. Southern, *Western Views of Islam in the Middle Ages* (1962).

With the Renaissance, and above all since the nineteenth century, there arose a new science — Oriental studies. The Koran was translated into the various Western languages. Research was carried out into the life of Islam's founder. The vast religious and secular literature of the Arabs became known. Attempts were made to draw an objective picture of Islam. But on the strictly dogmatic plane attitudes continued to be "classical": Islam was necessarily condemned, Mohammed was a false prophet, the Koran was a collection of errors, the truths contained in it had been taken from the Bible, and so on. The decline of the

* *Translated by Simon and Erika Young*

151

Moslem countries from the nineteenth century onwards and their occupation b
the European powers strengthened the opinion held in the West that the Mos
lems were victims of the "fatalism" preached by their religion.

The revival of enquiry into the subject of Islam is due to the work of Professo
Louis Massignon, a believing Catholic and one of the best-known of contempo
rary orientalists. He was brought back to the faith of his childhood throug
studying the Moslem mystic al-Hallāj, and devoted his long and fruitful life t
discovering the riches of Moslem culture and to efforts to track down what h
saw as true and valid in the Moslem religion. It was his opinion that Christian
should embark upon a "spiritual Copernican revolution" and return to the origir
of Moslem teaching, "to that point of virgin truth that is found at its centre anc
makes it live". In the formulation which he made his own, the three mono
theistic religions were characterized as follows: Israel is the religion of hope an
Christianity is the religion of love, but Islam is the religion of faith. To som
extent he adopted the Moslem concept that the three monotheistic religion
derive from the same source, and he acknowledged the Moslems' connectio
with Abraham through Ismael: they were the heirs of his blessing and of hi
vocation as the Chosen One. Islam, in its emphasis on the sovereign rights o
God over men had, in a certain sense, a vocation in relation to Christianity
Some more or less direct pupils of Massignon tried to draw conclusions from hi
premises which were not free from exaggeration (cf. G. C. Anawati, *Vers u
dialogue islamo-chrétien*. Chronique d'islamologie et d'arabisme: RThom 64 [1964
pp. 280–326, pp. 585–630). In any case, however, thanks to him and his pupil
there appeared in the Church a trend favourable to the "islamic-christia
dialogue". This explains how a declaration concerning Islam such as that mad
by the Second Vatican Council was possible, and how it represents an advanc
in the Church's attitude to Islam.

2. In giving a precise answer to the second question — how far does th
description of Islam in the Declaration correspond to what it actually is? — i
must be made clear that criticism of this description proceeds from two opposing
standpoints. Some reproach it with being "minimalistic", especially because i
does not mention that in the Koran Jesus is called "the word of God" *(kalima
Allāh)* (IV, 171) and "spirit of God" *(Rūḥ Allāh)* (IV, 169). Others, on the othe
hand, find that the Declaration maintains a significant silence concerning certai
features of Moslem morality (polygamy, and repudiation of the wife by a mer
declaration of intent on the part of the husband). It could be said that the tw
critical approaches neutralize each other. The theologians with special knowl
edge of Islam, who drew up the Declaration, had in fact to avoid two dangers
It would not have been right for them to make use of phrases which are indee
to be found in the Koran but could lead to misunderstanding if they are no
explained and understood in the Moslem sense (as is the case with Jesus a
Kalima and *Rūḥ*). But the very narrow limits that were set to the Declaration di
not permit even the smallest explanation. The second danger was that a declara

ion intended to be sympathetic to the opening of a dialogue might yet give prominence to serious weaknesses, in which case there arose the risk that the two sides might then no longer have any desire for this dialogue. Of course, polygamy and the repudiation of wives are the two most serious defects in the morality of the Koran. But — and this also could not be said in the Declaration — these defects are very clearly perceived by reformers among the Moslems themselves. In most Moslem countries today a serious effort is being made to moderate the effects of both these provisions of religious law, if not to abolish them altogether. (Cf. the prohibition of polygamy in Tunisia and the plan for strict regulation of it in the United Arab Republic, etc.)

It is a fact, however, that the first draft of the Declaration was, so to speak, still "more favourable". The old text said: "Moreover they (the Moslems) honour God above all through prayer, alms-giving and fasting. They strive also, in obedience to God, to lead a moral life both as individuals and in the family and society" ("vitam quoque moralem tam individualem quam familialem et socialem in obsequium Dei ducere conantur"). This draft evoked numerous objections from bishops who live in contact with the Moslem population of Africa. Polygamy and the repudiation of wives must not be allowed to appear in any way acceptable to a community that was concerned about the morality of family life. In order to avoid possible objections, it was preferred in the new draft to leave out the reference to family morality.

With this reservation it can be said that the Council's Declaration gives an account, in the shortest possible form, of the Moslem theodicy, but not of the essence of the Moslem faith, which includes among its most important elements belief in the prophetic mission of Mohammed. To be convinced of this, one need only think of the sentence in the Koran which expresses the true "righteousness" that makes the good Moslem as follows: "The righteous man is he who believes in Allah and the Last Day, in the angels and the Scriptures and the prophets; who for the love of Allah gives his wealth . . .; who attends to his prayers and pays the alms-tax . . ." (II, 172). Islam has summed up its dogma still more concisely in the "Profession of Faith" *(shahāda)*: *"Lā ilāh illā Allāhwa Muḥammed Rasūl Allāh"* (There is no God but Allah, and Mohammed is his prophet). That the Church has declared, in a solemn and official document like that issued by the Council, that the God of Islam is the one, living and true, merciful and Almighty God, the creator of heaven and earth, is a fact of the first importance in the field of relations between Christians and Moslems.

The Declaration is most cautious of all, however, with regard to the question of the Moslems' historical link with Abraham and thus with true revelation. Louis Massignon worked very hard to secure acceptance in Christian circles, as in Islam, of the conception of the three religions, Jewish, Moslem and Christian, as three branches of a single monotheist revelation. So far as Islam is concerned, such a conception is not truly illuminating without a further proviso: if it must be acknowledged that in the history of salvation Islam occupies a special position

153

above that of other religions, this must not detract from the unique originality of the great biblical revelation. Moreover the historical descent from Ismael that the Moslems claim for themselves is as yet far from proved in the light of the documents available to us. These considerations explain the very careful language of the Declaration on this point and also its silence concerning the second part of the *shahāda:* "Mohammed is his prophet". Obviously this is the most sensitive point for the Moslems, and the Catholic experts have chosen to deal with it — by ignoring it. Once the dialogue is under way, this central point will have to be considered in more detail.

3. This leads to the answer to our third question: What basis does the Declaration provide for Islamic-Christian dialogue?

The final section of the Declaration gives a very precise answer to this question and sets out the course to be followed. It might be said that this is the really constructive part of the Declaration concerning Islam. It must meet with the approval of all men of good will. And in fact there is already to be seen on the Moslem side open satisfaction that the Church should be thus outlining an area of effective co-operation outside that of dogmatic and theological differences. This, however will require great effort and patience, above all on the Catholic side. For if on the Western side ecumenical and intellectual progress has made it possible to regard past events with equanimity of spirit, the same does not apply to the Moslem countries. These are still engaged in a struggle against Western pressure, which they all too often equate with "Christian" pressure. The wounds of the past are still far from healed and some leading Moslems who are directing this struggle find it difficult, in mobilizing the people and arousing their fighting spirit, not to recall the "aggressions" of the West at the time of the Crusades as well as those of "colonialism" and "imperialism". Many concrete situations have to be cleaned up (for the Arab countries especially the problem of Israel and the liberation of some of their peoples) before the conflicts of the past can also be forgotten. The Christians of the West must arm themselves with inexhaustible patience and live in the faith that moves mountains.[1]

---

[1] I have pointed out certain possibilities for the beginning of the dialogue in my lecture, "L'Islam à l'heure du Concile. Prolégomènes à un dialogue islamo-chrétien", *Angelicum* 4 q (1964) pp. 145–68. Literature published after the appearance of the Declaration, R. Caspar, "Le Concile et l'Islam", *Études* (January 1966), pp. 114–26; G. C. Anawati, "La religione musulmana", in *Le religioni non cristiane nel Vaticano II* (1966), pp. 171–99.

For the already very extensive literature on the Islamic Christian dialogue cf. my article *Revue Thomiste* (see above) which analyses some important reactions on the Islamic side, and above all R. Caspar, *Le dialogue islamo-chrétien.* See bibliography in *Parole et Mission* 33 (April 1966) pp. 312–22, p. 34 (July 1966), pp. 475–81.

Dogmatic Constitution on Divine Revelation*

Origin and Background

by
Joseph Ratzinger

The idea of having a Constitution on the themes of revelation, Scripture and tradition goes back to the early beginnings of the preparations for the Council. Work on the text continued through all stages of the Council, so that Archbishop Florit was able to introduce his *relatio* on its first two chapters, given on 30 September 1964, with the words: "Because of its inner importance, as well as the many vicissitudes that it has undergone, the history of the draft of the Constitution on Divine Revelation has fused with the history of this Council into a kind of unity."[1] The obviousness with which the theme presented itself, as well as the keenness of the struggle over it, show both the degree to which it expresses an urgent question of our present situation and also the fact that, in contrast to the reform of the liturgy or even to many questions of ecclesiology and ecumenism, no kind of mature conclusion had been reached, so that the discussion of the Council took place in an atmosphere of restless theological ferment and sometimes almost risked being overwhelmed by it.

More specifically, there were three motifs that came together in the struggle for a Constitution on Revelation. The first was the new view of the phenomenon of tradition, which had been developing, for various reasons, from the beginning of the last century. The first impetus towards a new attitude to tradition came with the Romantic movement, for which tradition became a leading philosophical and theological idea. In the one case it was seen as an organically evolving process, and in the other appeared to be practically identical with the voice of the Church as living tradition. The controversy concerning the dogma of 1854 was a further milestone, for which — in default of biblical proof — tradition was made responsible, which could now, however, no longer be under-

Translated by William Glen-Doepel
[1] Quoted from the fascicule *Revelationes super schema Constitutionis De Revelatione Divina*, which also contains the minority *relatio*, presented on the same day by F. Franič and the *relatio* on Chapters III–VI presented by J. van Dodewaard. Cf. also E. Stakemeier, *Die Konzilskonstitution*, p. 9; id., Hampe, *Die Autorität*, I, p. 174. Hampe also prints on pp. 122–6 most of the *relatio* of Archbishop Florit and on pp. 126–9 that of Bishop Franič, in German translation.

stood as the simple passing on of something that had been handed down once and for all, but had to be understood in terms of the categories of growth progress and the knowledge of faith that Romanticism had developed. The ideas that were developed in this connection by the Jesuit School in Rome[2] not only had a decided influence on Newman's idea of development, which in turn gave rise to a very varied literature on the subject of the development of dogma,[3] but were also the basis of the later discussion that arose, in similar circumstances concerning the dogma of 1950 and now placed the idea of the Church's knowledge through faith in the forefront of the idea of tradition.[4] If here the idea of material tradition was abandoned more and more in favour of that of tradition as a process and the question of factual proof changed to that of the criteria of the testimony the ecumenical reflection which had begun about the same time also, strangely enough, developed in the same direction. In the ecumenical dialogue the positive meaning of the idea of *sola scriptura* had appeared more and more clearly (together with the incontestable results of historical research), that Scripture can be the only concrete counter-weight to the teaching office and is the only place where the truly apostolic tradition is clearly and distinctly to be found. But had not Trent barred once and for all the road to a Catholic version of *sola scriptura?* After E. Ortigues' epoch-making research into the question of the Tridentine dogma, it was chiefly the Tübingen theologian J. R. Geiselmann who concerned himself with it and endeavoured to find an answer in the spirit of the nineteenth-century Catholic Tübingen school. He pointed out that the Tridentine formula had been changed from the original words "partim in libris . . . partim in . . . traditionibus" to "in libris scriptis et sine scripto traditionibus". He considered that this resulted from the fact that some of the Trent Fathers had supported the *sola scriptura* idea and concluded from this that the Council of Trent had not desired to make any statements about the relation between Scripture and tradition and had also left open the possibility of *sola scriptura,* i.e. of a material completeness of Scripture. Geiselmann's views were greeted immediately with both enthusiastic acceptance and violent rejection;[5] the literary polemic reached its height during

---

[2] Cf. W. Kasper, *Die Lehre von der Tradition in der Römischen Schule (Die Überlieferung in der neueren Theologie,* V) (1962).

[3] Cf. H. Hammans, *Die neueren katholischen Erklärungen der Dogmenentwicklung* (1965); K. Rahner "Dogmenentwicklung": *LTK,* III, pp. 457–63; Ch. Boyer, *Lo sviluppo del dogma: Problemi orientamenti di teologia dommatica* (1957), pp. 359–86 (pp. 381–6: Bibliography by C. Colombo).

[4] Cf. esp. M. D. Koster, *Volk Gottes im Wachstum des Glaubens, Himmelfahrt Mariens und Glaubens sinn* (1950); C. Dillenschneider, *Le sens de la foi et le progrès dogmatique du mystère marial* (1954) further literature in Colombo, *loc. cit.,* p. 386 (see note 3); cf. also my summary in *LTK,* pp. 293–9 (under *Tradition*).

[5] All the important literature is listed in J. R. Geiselmann, *Die Heilige Schrift und die Tradition* (1962) and in J. Beumer, "Die mündliche Überlieferung als Glaubensquelle" (*HDG,* I, p. 4). Much endeavours to reconcile conflicting points of view. The strongest opposition against Geiselmann is to be found in a number of articles by H. Lennerz, especially "Scriptura sola?" *Gr* 40 (1959), pp. 38–53. The most important historical treatments are E. Ortigues, "Ecriture e

he Council, with theologians of both schools seeking to influence the course
of the Council in their own direction by publications that were often hastily
launched against the other side.[6] But above all the problem of tradition had found
he form which dominated the Conciliar discussion: it was concerned with the
ignificance of replacing "partim — partim" by "et", i.e. in concrete terms, with
he question of the material completeness of Scripture. The so-called conservative
group sought with all possible emphasis to obtain a condemnation of this idea,
gainst which the progressive school put up a no less energetic opposition, calling
or both possibilities to be left open (nobody had thought of canonizing the
'new" position). It achieved this aim through the approval of the open draft,
efended by Archbishop Florit in the *relatio* we just referred to, whereas the
nore conservative group, which had now clearly dwindled to a minority, was
propitiated by an addition to the text of Article 9, made at the request of the Pope,
which does not positively teach that Scripture is materially supplemented by
radition, but on the criteriological level accords a specific value to tradition (cf.
he commentary on Article 9). Looking back it is possible to say that this particular
ormulation of the question was not a very happy one; perhaps it was a necessary
ransitional stage, but it had scarcely yet dealt with the real problems. Fortunately,
we can say that, although the text grew in the shadow of this formulation, it
nally left behind and led on to a new level.[7]

One may fairly say that the second source of the Constitution on Revelation
was what emerged ever more clearly as the theological problem of the application
of critical historical methods to the interpretation of Scripture. The question
ad already played an important part in the modernist crisis, since when it had
ever been resolved. Indeed, despite the big step forward of the encyclical
Divino afflante of Pius XII, which appeared in 1943, it reached a new climax
with the banning of professors at the Biblical Institute from teaching and with
he exceptionally sharp polemic of Mgr. Romeo against modern Catholic exe-

'raditions apostoliques au Concile de Trente", *RSR* 36 (1949), pp. 271–99; P. de Vooght, *Les
urces de la doctrine chrétienne* (1954); B. Decker, *Sola scriptura bei Thomas von Aquin: Festschrift
1. Stohr,* I (1960), pp. 117–29; the summary by H. Holstein, *La Tradition dans l'Église* (1960) is a
esult of careful historical research; cf. also Y. Congar, *La Tradition et les traditions, I: Essai
istorique* (1960), II: *Essai théologique* (1963).

For example, R. Rusch, "De non definienda illimitata insufficientia materiali Scripturae",
'KT 85 (1963), pp. 1–15; H. Schauf, *Die Lehre der Kirche über Schrift und Tradition in den Kate-
hismen* (1963); J. Ratzinger, "Zur Katechismenlehre von Schrift und Tradition", *ThRv* 60 (1964),
p. 217–24.

This is probably owing to the work of Y. Congar, the second volume of whose monograph on
'adition (cf. note 5) clearly extended the field of vision. As far as the understanding of Trent is
oncerned, the narrow controversy between Lennerz and Geiselmann was overcome by M. Béve-
ot, "Traditions in the Council of Trent", *The Heythrop Journal* 4 (1963), pp. 333–47; J. Ratzinger,
On the Interpretation of the Tridentine Decree on Tradition" in K. Rahner and J. Ratzinger,
evelation and Tradition (1966), where I have also endeavoured to give a systematic outline of the
uestion. As regards the Tridentine text, it can be said that these investigations have made the
ositions of Lennerz and Geiselmann out of date.

gesis. It is hard to say to what extent John XXIII himself influenced these events, either by his approval or disapproval. It seems certain that he too felt some concern, as can probably be seen from the fact that the *Quaestiones Commissioni theologicae positae* presented by Archbishop Felici as the wishes of the Pope, contained the following sentence: "Iuxta ea, quae a Summis Pontificibus recentius edita sunt, exponatur doctrina catholica de Sacra Scriptura (i.e. de sacrorum librorum historicitate; de obsequio, quo Exegetae erga Traditionem sacram et Magisterium ecclesiasticum tenentur): novi de hac re errores damnentur; simulque congruentes edantur normae, quibis exegetae in Sacris Litteris iuxta sensum Ecclesiae interpretandis ducantur."[8] Even now, after the Council, it is not possible to say that the question of the relation between critical and Church exegesis, historical research and dogmatic tradition has been settled. All that is certain is that from now on it will be impossible to ignore the critical historical method and that, precisely as such, it is in accordance with the aims of theology itself. Another feature of the conciliar discussion of this point is worth mentioning. It was inevitable in the new formulation of the theological categories of inspiration and inerrancy, which are the basis of the definition of the idea of "sacred Scripture", that the modern approach would put strong emphasis on the human factor in Scripture, from which then follow both the possibility and the necessity of investigating it according to critical historical methods. This emphasis was theologically legitimate on the basis of the Christian conception of God, which has been shaped by the idea of the incarnation, and which is centred precisely on the idea of the historical and human mediation of the eternal in the revelation of Christ. On the other hand, the traditionalists insisted on an idea of inspiration that was conceived entirely in terms of the divine author which involved an untenable view of the negligible human contribution in the transmission of revelation, but the positive value of which should be recognized, namely, the strong sense of the sacredness of Scripture, so that this shows, at any rate, how much even the "traditionalists" were, in their own way, filled with concern for the dignity of Scripture and how close the basic concerns of both sides were, despite the different ways in which they were formulated and the contrast in their actual positions.

The third motivating element in the move towards a Constitution on Revelation is the most positive one: namely, the biblical movement that has grown stronger and stronger since the turn of the century and has already brought about a fundamentally new attitude to Scripture in large areas of Catholic Christendom giving rise to a new familiarity with it and an ever-increasing tendency, both in theology and piety, to go back to it. As in the case of the liturgical movement, a new spiritual fact had become a reality within the Church in the decades before

---

[8] Quoted from Betti, *Commento,* p. 61; with regard to factual detail for the whole of the following account, cf. the extraordinarily careful account of the history of the Constitution by Betti *Commento,* pp. 33–67.

the Council, a fact which the Council only had to take up, deepen and extend to the whole Church (insofar as this lies in the power of a Council).

As far as the history of our Constitution immediately before the Council is concerned, we can see its main tendencies, as well as the main points of the Conciliar debate, from the comments that were made by the bishops'conferences, the Holy Office and the Roman University faculties. Thus the Holy Office had called for a clear and emphatic statement on the question of the inspiration and inerrancy of Scripture and its interpretation by the Church, and especially emphasis on the historicity of the Gospels, as well as a statement that tradition contained more, in terms of content, than Scripture.[9] Bishops requested doctrinal, defensive and pastoral sections; the wishes of the Roman universities showed a clear concept of a "Constitutio de fontibus Revelationis".[10]

In the preparatory Theological Commission, with Cardinal Ottaviani as president and S. Tromp, S. J., as secretary, the idea of including the problems of revelation in the schema on the Church was considered, but immediately dropped. Thus there first emerged a *Schema compendiosum Constitutionis de fontibus Revelationis,* developed in 13 points, which was presented to the Praeparatoria on 27 October 1960. The work proceeded in a special sub-commission, and on 13 February 1961 the result of this work was a schema in six chapters which was presented to the Papal Commission. After further revisions, which led to a reduction to five chapters on 4 October 1961, the whole was handed over to the Central Commission, which proceeded on 10 November of the same year to examine the text, for the improvement of which numerous suggestions were made, the legal validity of which, however, was not clarified, so that the working sub-commission remained largely autonomous and its members used the suggestions as they thought fit. The result of all this work was a *Schema Constitutionis dogmaticae de fontibus Revelationis* in five chapters, which was sent to the fathers in a large volume together with six other schemata in the course of the summer of 1962. Much has been written about this text, which amounted to a canonization of Roman school theology; we do not need to discuss it again here in detail.[11] All the relevant questions were decided in a purely defensive spirit: the greater extent of tradition in comparison with Scripture, a largely verbalistic conception of the idea of inspiration, the narrowest interpretation of inerrancy ("in qualibet re religiose vel profana"), a conception of the historicity of the Gospels that suggested that there were no problems etc. In the struggle about all these questions in which Catholic theology had been involved, this would have meant that the attempt to understand the idea of tradition in a new way, as well as a large part of the modern work on exegesis, would have been condemned; the burden that this would have meant for the future course of Catholic theology was not

[9] *Acta et documenta Conc. oec. Vat. II apparando III,* pp. 5 and 8 f. (cf. Betti, *Commento,* p. 34).

[10] The documents from *Acta et documenta* in Betti, *Commento,* p. 61, note 8, cf. p. 34 f.

[11] It is sufficient to mention the well-known chronicles of the Council by Wenger, Laurentin, Congar, and Ratzinger.

easy to estimate: it would probably have been still more serious than the difficulties that resulted from the one-sided condemnation of modernism. As it is in accordance with the best conciliar tradition that the Church's teaching office should not decide academic controversies at a council, anger and resistance against the intended mode of procedure grew as soon as the texts became available. This, however, was a completely new experience for those theologians concerned in the preparatory stages of the Council. They were not aware that their text decided academic controversies. By academic controversies they understood the classical differences, canonized for centuries, between the various theological schools that had emerged in the late Middle Ages and the early modern period. Something that could not be fitted into the antitheses of "Thomism", "Scotism", "Molinism", etc., was not known as a "theological school", but simply as an innovation and therefore did not come under the protection enjoyed by the differences of the "schools", the number of which, however, appeared to be settled. It is probably not an exaggeration to say that it was only the Council that brought home the fact that the classical "schools" have today become as unimportant as the conflicts between them: it has also emerged that Catholic theology has remained alive, that new "schools" and conflicts have formed within it and that these new groups and their questions are also legitimate forms of Catholic theological work. It is really only in this way that critical historical exegesis has come to be recognized as an independent theological partner in the dialogue within the totality of Catholic theology.

When the debate on the schema was introduced by the *relatio* presented by Cardinal Ottaviani and Mgr. Garofalo on 14 November 1962, at the nineteenth general congregation of the Council, the inevitable storm broke that had been building up in a private counterdraft, circularized by the presidents of the bishops' conferences of Belgium, Germany, France, Holland and Austria. Cardinal Liénart stated laconically: "Hoc schema mihi non placet."[12] The same view was taken at that session by Cardinals Frings, Léger, König, Alfrink, Suenens, Ritter and Bea, while Cardinals Quiroga y Palacios, Ruffini and Siri defended the text. Bishop De Smedt of Bruges from the Secretariat on Christian Unity, made an important intervention on November 19. He pointed out, among other things, that the Pope had assigned to the Secretariat the task of advising the other commissions on ecumenical questions. The Theological Commission, however, had refused to accept this advice. The result of their work made no contribution to the ecumenical dialogue. "The schema is a step backwards, a hindrance, it does damage. The publication of the theological schemata in the form of the drafts we had before us would destroy all the hope that the Council could lead to the drawing together again of the separated brethren."[13] A vote was taken on

[12] Cf. D. A. Seeber, *Das Zweite Vaticanum. Konzil des Übergangs* (1966), p. 89; *ibid.,* pp. 88–94, is a fine account of the course of the discussion. See also H. Jedin, *Kleine Konziliengeschichte* (7th ed., 1966), pp. 142ff.
[13] Seeber, *op. cit.,* p. 92.

20 November, in a rather unfortunate form. It was not asked, as would normally have been the case, whether the text received the general *placet* of the fathers or not, but whether they were for or against an interruption of the discussion. Whoever was against the schema now had to vote "yes", and who was for it "no". Whether this was clear to all those voting, we cannot say. The more important point is that this procedure reversed the legal basis of the question of acceptance: if the *placet* question had been asked of the schema then it would have required two-thirds of all votes to have been saved; but now, with the question put the other way round, those who were against the text (who were now voting "yes") had to produce a two-thirds majority; they did not succeed in doing so: 1368 fathers voted for interruption, 822 against, and 19 votes were invalid.[14] By reversing the procedure the situation had arisen whereby a good third of the votes was enough to have the text accepted.

The anger and the fears for the further fate of the Council which resulted from this procedure were assuaged when, on 21 November, the General Secretary of the Council, Archbishop Felici, announced that the Pope had removed the text from the agenda and handed over its revision to a specially created Mixed Commission, of which he appointed Cardinals Ottaviani and Bea to be chairmen; Fr. Tromp, the Secretary of the Theological Commission, and Mgr. Willebrands, Secretary of the Secretariat for Christian Unity were appointed secretaries. Of the College of Cardinals, Cardinals Liénart, Frings, Ruffini, Meyer, Lefèbvre and Browne were appointed to the Commission. In sessions between 25 November and 7 December 1962, general agreement was reached on the structure of the *schema* as well as on a new title, *"De divina revelatione"*. Subsequent work was constantly dominated by the problem of what tradition had to offer over and above Scripture. A noteable advance was achieved when on 23 February 1963 a vote was taken in which the majority supported the view that this problem should be left open, and when the formula that was then drawn up was approved, at the end of February, both by the President of the Co-ordinating Commission and the Pope himself.[15] There were now no further barriers to the revision of the rest of the text. On 27 March 1963 it was approved by the Co-ordinating Commission, printed in April and distributed to the fathers (Form D).

The draft had been composed with some skill; it avoided the controversial questions and was in many respects a step forward: the *Preface* presented an outline of the idea of revelation, in which strong emphasis was put on salvation history; new forms were found for the question of Scripture and tradition; the problem of inspiration and interpretation were treated in a relatively open way; and a number of positive things were said about the use of Scripture in the Church. Nevertheless, no one was very happy with this new draft. It was too inadequate and vague, recognizable at first sight as a product of resignation. The

---

[14] These are the definitive figures given in Betti, *Commento,* p. 40; cf. Stakemeier, *Die Konzils-konstitution,* pp. 66f.; Jedin, *loc. cit.,* p. 143.
[15] Betti, *Commento,* p. 42.

Church could not express itself before the world in this way on a subject which should have been a heartfelt concern. Instead of this, one had the impression that it caused embarrassment. The impression spread that it was best to leave the whole subject alone. A group of French and Italian bishops led by Archbishop Florit of Florence, who was eager to act as mediator, endeavoured to win friends for the suggestion that the chief themes of the draft be incorporated in the Constitution on the Church. The surprise was all the greater when Paul VI, in his closing speech at the end of the second session of the Council on 4 December 1963, mentioned the schema on Revelation as among the tasks of the third session. In retrospect one can see that this decision was absolutely right. The Council would otherwise have risked falling victim to a kind of ecclesio-monism in its texts, whereas the Constitution on Revelation now stressed the importance of listening, thus moving beyond everything that was said at the Council in order to take up an attitude of listening, an attitude in which the Church transcends itself, for it is not there for its own sake, but only to lead to him to whom all honour is due, God the Lord.[16]

On the basis of the written wishes that had been received in the meantime from the Council fathers, the Theological Commission resumed its work on the text. On 7 March 1964 a special Sub-Commission was set up with Bishop Charue of Namur as chairman, and Bishops E. Florit, F. Barbado, G. L. Pelletier, J. van Dodewaard, J. Heuschen and Abbot Butler as members. The secretary was the Roman Franciscan U. Betti, and the *periti* were G. Castellino, L. Cerfaux, C. Colombo (who was made a bishop on the same day), Y. Congar, R. Gagnebet, S. Garofalo, A. Grillmeier, A. Kerrigan, C. Moeller, A. Prignon, J. Ramírez, K. Rahner, J. Ratzinger, B. Rigaux, H. Schauf, O. Semmelroth, P. Smulders, L. Turado. Of course the two secretaries of the Theological Commission, who had played an important part in the growth of the text, S. Tromp and G. Philips, also sat on it.[17] After the preliminary work of the *periti* the Sub-Commission was able, between 20 and 25 April 1964, (divided for the sessions into two sub-groups) to produce that version of the text which was then presented to the full Commission. Here also the main difficulty remained, the problem of the material completeness of Scripture. Apart from the normal *relatio* on Chapter II, provided by U. Betti, the sub-commission had two special *relationes,* written by K. Rahner (presenting the majority view) and H. Schauf (presenting the minority view). From 1 to 5 June 1964 the Theological Commission examined this draft. It found it easy to reach agreement on the whole of the text, but again became involved in a heated discussion on the question of the extra material provided by tradition.

---

[16] An impressive warning of the danger of an ecclesiological positivism is given in H. de Lubac in G. Baraúna, ed., *De Ecclesia,* I (German ed., 1966), pp. 15–22, French edition: *L'Église du Vatican II,* vol. II (1966), pp. 25–31.

[17] These details were taken from Betti, *Commento,* p. 63, note 30. The number of *periti* consulted, however, seems to vary. An unprinted *relatio* on Chapters I and II (a document circulated within the Commission only) also mentions the *periti* Salaverri, Schmaus and Trapé as collaborators.

17 fathers voted for the text and 7 against. As it was impossible to reach agreement, it was decided to present two *relationes* to the Plenary Assembly, one presenting the majority, and the other the minority view. We can see how much the situation had changed, compared with 1962, by the choice of *relator* for the majority *relatio,* namely Archbishop Florit of Florence. Florit, formerly Professor of New Testament exegesis at the Lateran, belonged by background and his theological views to the traditional group. Although opposed to all radicalism, he had attempted, from the start, to reconcile the two views and had come to see that abandonment of a positive definition of the relationship between Scripture and tradition with regard to their material extent was possible without endangering the teaching of the Church, and that, in view of the two opposed views, this would be desirable for the sake of peace and the further work of theology. In view of the high reputation that he enjoyed as one of the most popular and respected theological teachers of the Lateran University (for example, he had been one of the first Catholic theologians to consider the question of form history, although his own attitude was very traditional),[18] it was of decisive importance that he made himself the interpreter of that version of the schema approved by the majority and defended it with warmth against the minority, whose language he spoke and whose confidence he possessed. His *relatio,* presented to the Plenary Assembly on 30 September 1964, can be considered as one of the most important events of the Council. Its solid theological content, its clear logic, and its consideration of all the reservations that were felt did not fail to produce an appropriate effect on the fathers. Just as in the debate on collegiality it had been decisive that a member of the Holy Office, Archbishop Parente, had been the warmest protagonist of the idea of collegiality and supported it in a *relatio* before the Plenary Assembly; here, too, the presentation of the text by a representative of Roman theological tradition was of great assistance in allaying the fears of those Council fathers who were hesitant and uncertain. The Bishop of Spalato, F. Franič, a friend of Cardinal Ottaviani and a firm ally of the minority, acted as *relator* for it. With detailed arguments he pleaded for the necessity of explicitly anchoring the primacy of tradition in the text as Catholic teaching, but he admitted that the *schema* did not contain any error, but only "defectum notabilem". This also helped to take the drama out of the situation.

The discussion of the text that occupied the Council from 30 September to 6 October 1964 proceeded quietly, but it became clear that as well as the previous main controversial point there were two further critical points of prime importance: the question of a more detailed account of the "inerrancy" of Scripture and that of the form in which the historicity of the Gospels was to be anchored in the text. The Theological Commission, or the appropriate sub-commissions began immediately on the revision of the text, on the principle that the substance

---

[18] E. Florit, *Il metodo della "Storia delle forme" e sua applicazione al racconto della Passione* (1935).

163

of the draft could no longer be interfered with. The revised text was sent out to the fathers on 20 November 1964, but was only put to the vote in the Plenary Assembly of the Council in the last session. On 20, 21 and 22 September 1965, 20 votes were taken on the text. It was accepted in general at every vote with a great majority, but there were, in the details, a large number of *modi*, which were then dealt with in a small technical commission, in which S. Tromp, G. Philips and U. Betti were the most active members, but of which A. Grillmeier, A. Kerrigan, B. Rigaux and O. Semmelroth were also members. Of the Council fathers it included A. M. Charue, E. Florit and J. van Dodewaard.[19] In the full session of the Theological Commission on 29 September 1965 there was again a heated discussion on the question of tradition; in the votes the so-called *Comitatus internationalis Patrum,* which had acquired between 100 and 250 supporters, had produced uniform *modi* expressing the view of the minority, which the representatives of this view now called on the Commission to consider. After violent arguments, however, it was decided to reject these requests, which, despite their relatively large number, were opposed to the clear will of the majority. The same thing happened on 4 October, in the discussion on Chapter III (the question of inerrancy), for which the way had been paved by a number of hectographed comments from both sides, and with the consideration of Chapter V (the historicity of the Gospels) on October 6. The final stage of these controversies was reached when Cardinal Cicognani sent a letter to Cardinal Ottaviani on October 18, at the request of the Pope, calling for additional clarification on all three questions (tradition, inerrancy, historicity). Comparative freedom, however, was allowed in the formulation, and so, in its session of 19 October, the Commission was able to work out statements on all three questions, thus complying with the request of the Pope, but without shutting doors that one had struggled for four years to keep open. That the minority was still not satisfied was shown by a pamphlet that was circulated shortly before the vote on the *Expensio modorum,* which was explained by Archbishop Florit and Bishop van Dodewaard. It had no effect: of the 2115 fathers who voted on 29 October 1965, 2081 voted *placet,* 27 *non placet,* and 7 votes were invalid. Thus on 18 November 1965, in the eighth public session of the Council, the final vote was taken with the following result: 2350 voters, 2344 *placet,* 6 *non placet.* This provided an amicable conclusion for an important part of the Council's history. The text, which was solemnly proclaimed by the Pope on this day, naturally reveals traces of its difficult history; it is the result of many compromises. But the fundamental compromise which pervades it is more than a compromise, it is a synthesis of great importance. The text combines fidelity to Church tradition with an affirmation of critical scholarship, thus opening up anew the path that faith may follow into the world of today. It does not entirely abandon the position of Trent and Vatican I, but neither does it mummify what was held to be true at those Councils,

---

[19] Betti, *Commento,* p. 65, note 48.

because it realizes that fidelity in the sphere of the Spirit can be realized only through a constantly renewed appropriation. With regard to its total achievement, one can say unhesitatingly that the labour of the four-year long controversy was not in vain.

Note: The various stages of the text, the history of which has been briefly outlined in the foregoing, are designated in the commentary by the abbreviations which A. Grillmeier has elaborated in his contribution "Die Wahrheit der Heiligen Schrift und ihre Erschließung. Zum dritten Kapitel der Dogmatischen Konstitution 'Dei Verbum' des Vaticanum II" *(Theologie und Philosophie =* *Scholastik* 41 [1966], pp. 161–87, here p. 162f.). The following is a summary of his nomenclature:

Form A: *Constitutio de Fontibus Revelationis,* prepared by the *Commissio Theologica* *Concilio Oecumenico Vaticano II Apparando* (1961). Incipit (= Inc.): Revelatio; Explicit (= Expl.): conscriptis. Five Chapters: I. *De duplici fonte Revelationis;* II. *De S. Scripturae inspiratione, inerrantia et compositione litteraria;* III. *De Vetere* *Testamento;* IV. *De Novo Testamento;* V. *De Sacra Scriptura in Ecclesia.*

Form B: The same text with slight alterations presented to the *Pontifica Commissio Centralis Praeparatoria Concilii Vaticani II* (1961).

Form C: The text sent, in folio, to the Council fathers for the first session: *Schemata Constitutionum et Decretorum de quibus disceptabitur in Concilii sessionibus,* Series prima (1962), pp. 9–22; *Schema Const. dogmat. De Fontibus Revelationis.*

Supplementary Text I: In the same volume: *Schema Constitutionis dogmaticae de deposito Fidei pure custodiendo,* Cap. IV: *De Revelatione publica et de Fide catholica* (pp. 36–44); Cap. V: *De progressu Doctrinae* (pp. 45–47). — Form C was discussed in the Assembly of the Council from 14 to 19 November 1962, and after a queried vote at the end of the general debate was given back by Pope John XXIII to be revised by a *Commissio mixta* (Theological Commission, Secretariat for Christian Unity and specially appointed members; the chairmen were Cardinal Ottaviani and Cardinal Bea). The particular point of the discussion was the relation between Scripture and tradition. The work on the new draft began during the first session.

Supplementary Text II: The *Schema decreti pastoralis De Verbo Dei* (1962), drawn up by the Secretariat for Christian Unity, with 13 Articles. Inc.: *Verbum Dei;* Expl.: "manet in aeternum" (Is 40:8). This text was later important for the Constitution (Chapters I and VI).

Form D: The new text distributed to the fathers from 22 April 1963: *Schema Constitutionis dogmaticae De Divina Revelatione:* Inc: *Sacrosancta Synodus;* Expl.: sperare licet. The text had a preface (Articles 1–6) and 5 chapters: I. *De Verbo Dei revelato;* II. *De Sacrae Scripturae divina inspiratione et interpretatione;* III. *De Vetere Testamento;* IV. *De Novo Testamento;* V. *De Sacrae Scripturae Usu in Ecclesia.* — The text was not discussed at the second session of the Council. But in his closing speech Pope Paul VI, on 5 December 1963, announced the following (after he had spoken of the texts to be presented during the third session, for which suggestions for alterations could still be submitted: "Huius generis est, ut exemplum supponamus, quaestio de divina Revelatione, quam Concilium eo modo persolvet, ut hinc sacrum depositum veritatum a Deo traditarum tueatur adversus errores, abusiones dubitationes, quibus vis earum subiectiva infringatur, illinc studia Sacrorum Bibliorum, ope Patrum ac theologicae disciplinae recte dirigat, quae docti catholici viri, magisterio Ecclesiae fideliter inhaerentes et quibusvis aptis huius aetatis subsidiis usi, alacriter, prudenter, fidenterque promovere pergent" (*AAS* 56 [1964], p. 36).

Form E: A new version of D on the basis of the suggestions submitted from June 1963 to 31 January 1964 (Spring 1964; available for sending to the fathers from July 3), prepared by the Theological Commission and its Sub-Commission. Inc. and Expl. as in D (64 folio pages, double columns, Form D on the left, and Form E on the right, including *relationes* on the text). A new preface and 6 chapters: I. *De ipsa Revelatione* (taken partly from the preface of Form D): II. *De Divinae Revelationis transmissione* (previously chapter I, with extensive additions); III. *De Sacrae Scripturae divina Inspiratione et Interpretatione;* IV. *De Vetere Testamento;* V. *De Novo Testamento;* VI. *De Sacra Scriptura* in Vita Ecclesiae. The discussion in the Assembly lasted from 30 September to 6 October 1964.

Form F: A revision of E on the basis of the discussion in the Assembly (1964). Inc.: *Sacrosancta Synodus;* Expl.: verbi Dei "quod manet in aeternum") (Is 40:8; cf. 1 Pet 1:23–25) (47 folio pages, double columns, Form E on the left, Form F on the right, with relationes). The title of Chapter III is: *De Sacrae Scripturae divina Inspiratione et de eius Interpretatione.*

Form G: In the fourth session of the Council a vote was taken on Form F from 20 to 22 September 1965, with *placet, non placet, placet iuxta modum.* The text received a two-thirds majority, but was supplemented by the submitted *modi* which the Theological Commission had accepted, and on 29 October 1965 it was again put to the vote — "utrum placeat expensio Modorum", and was accepted. It was completely reprinted for the promulgation of the Constitution in the *Sessio Publica* of 18 November 1965. Inc.: *Dei Verbum;* Expl.: "manet in aeternum" (Is 40:8; cf. 1 Pet 1:23–25). 19 pages.

Preface

by
Joseph Ratzinger

Article 1. The brief form of the Preface and the barely concealed illogicalities that it contains betray clearly the confusion from which it has emerged. The opening phrase "Dei verbum religiose audiens et fidenter proclamans", which did not appear at the beginning until Text G as a result of the *expensio modorum,* is certainly one of the happiest formulations in the text: the dominance of the word of God, its sovereign supremacy above all human eloquence and activity of the Church is given due prominence. The Church itself is depicted in its double role of listening and proclaiming. The connection between the Constitution on Revelation and the Constitution on the Church thus becomes quite clear programmatically. If sometimes it might appear that the Council was tending towards an ecclesiological mirroring of itself, in which the Church moved completely within its own orbit and made itself the central object of its own proclamation, instead of constantly pointing beyond itself, here the whole of the life of the Church is, as it were, opened upwards and its whole being gathered together in the attitude of listening, which can be the only source of what it has to say. What it says, however, is described as *"proclamare"*, as the call of a herald, which paradoxical situation is undoubtedly expressed in the adverb *"fidenter"*, which R. Latourelle rightly connects with the biblical idea of παρρησία.[1] This also expresses the trust and confidence with which the Church bears its word into the world, as well as the knowledge of the "folly" of the word, which quality, in the eyes of the "world", it does not possess for the first time today, in the situation of the "city without God", in the face of a consciousness dominated by the idea of "death of God",[2] but which belongs to it by nature, even if the challenging contradiction between the "folly of God" and the "wisdom of the world" emerges in varying degrees of sharpness, thus putting far greater pressure on the

[1] R. Latourelle, *La Révélation,* p. 8.
[2] H. Cox, *Secular City* (1965); cf. J. A. T. Robinson, *New Reformation* (1965). Of the large body of Catholic literature on the subject see E. Borne, *Dieu n'est pas mort* (1965); Concilium 6, no. 2 (1966); 3, no. 3 (1967).

παρρησία of him whose speech is moved by the word of God than in other situations.

The quotation from the first chapter of St. John's Gospel has probably been chosen because it presents, in a brief summary, first of all the formal structure of the *Kerygma,* identifying it as an announcement that is based on historical witness — on oral and visual evidence — and thus points to the essential manifestation of Christian revelation, grounded as it is in the incarnation, and to the faith in it. But it also makes clear the significance of the Christian proclamation, whose word leads to fellowship with God the Father and his Son Jesus Christ. In the particular context this quotation from the text does not appear to be completely logical insofar as the Council uses this text to describe its own activity, i.e. to classify, in terms of Scripture, the significance of the Constitution. For the scriptural text is dealing with the actual (material) proclamation, in which the Church passes on the good news of the salvation of God in Christ Jesus, whereas the conciliar text investigates the formal conditions of the proclamation: revelation, tradition, inspiration which, as basic categories, certainly dominate all theological and kerygmatic utterance, but only become clearly conscious in reflection on what has been said, and thus become accessible to investigation.[3] Thus the claim made by the text, compared with the actual intention of the Council, is too great. Nevertheless, we can consider its inclusion in the text as valuable, in so far as it states the situation which gives meaning to all theological reflection and to all the utterances of the teaching office, thus providing the co-ordinating point in relation to which this Constitution also must be interpreted. The following *propterea,* however, suggests again that uncritical parallel of the conciliar *proponere* with the *annuntiamus* of Jn 1, which we have just had to describe as inappropriate.

In the last sentence the most important thing is the relation that is established here to the two previous Councils, Trent and Vatican I. Is this not a rejection of any attempt to move forward beyond these two Councils? Does it not mean that the Council calls for a retrogressive interpretation of the text? After examining the development leading to the text, to which the reference to Trent was added only in Text G, we are compelled to say that the formula ". . . inhaerens vestigiis" was in fact chiefly intended to allay the fears of the "conservative" group and bring out the continuity of the Church's teaching, the continuity of Vatican II with the previous Councils — but a continuity that is not a rigid external identification with what had gone before, but a preservation of the old, established in the midst of progress. It so happens that Chapters I and II of the text, in particular, can only be properly understood if constantly compared with the parallel text of Vatican I and Trent, and only if this is undertaken carefully in every instance can we know fully what is meant concretely by *inhaerere vestigiis.* We could probably

---

[3] Latourelle, *La Révélation,* p. 36: "This is the first time that a council studies in such a conscious and methodical way the fundamental and primary categories of Christianity, i.e. those of revelation, tradition and inspiration."

best summarize its significance by using the term that has become common in exegesis: this Constitution is a *relecture* of the corresponding texts of Vatican I and Trent, in which what was written then is interpreted in terms of the present, thus giving a new rendering of both its essentials and its insufficiencies. Thus we can entirely agree with Karl Barth's suggested translation of this formula as "moving forward from the footsteps of those councils".[4] This suggests that we might perhaps see the relation of this text to its predecessors as a perfect example of dogmatic development, of the inner *relecture* of dogma in dogmatic history.

The last clause "ut salutis praeconio mundus universus audiendo credat, credendo speret, sperando amet" was chosen, according to the *relatio* for Text E, because it *pulchre innuit* the pastoral intention. One cannot help thinking that the Council is once more tacitly identifying its *propositio* with the service of the *kerygma* as such and is thus qualifying it in an inappropriate way. Thus the whole Preface is marked by the dilemma of the kerygmatic and doctrinal intention which can be explained, as we have already said, by the previous history of the text: an extensive kerygmatic Preface from Text D, which described the process of revelation in salvation history according to substance, was, from Text E on, challenged in a brief foreword and thus robbed of its logical coherence. At a deeper level, of course, there is the dilemma of the Council itself, with the discrepancy between its pastoral intention and its doctrinal obligations, so that the structure of this short text throws a surprisingly clear light on the structure of the Council as such, the magnitude and limitations of which have been concentrated into these few sentences.

K. Barth, *Ad limina apostolorum* (1967), p. 49. Note the difference here in the way in which Vatican I had formulated its continuity with Trent: "Nos idem decretum renovantes hanc illius mentem esse declaramus . . ." (*DS* 3007 = Cap. II *De revelatione*).

Revelation Itself

by
Joseph Ratzinger

Article 2. Chapter I attempts to describe what Christian faith means when it speaks of revelation or appeals to revelation. There was no chapter of this kind in Text C, which began immediately with the question about the nature of the "double source of revelation", thus tacitly restricting "revelation" to a teaching that one acquires from different "sources" — a view typical of the age of historicism and its emphasis on the "positive", which here, however, unconsciously appeared in the garment of ecclesiastical traditionalism. One of the most important events in the struggle over the Constitution on Revelation was undoubtedly the liberation from this narrow view and the return to what actually happens in the positive sources, before it was crystallized into doctrine, when God "reveals" himself, and thus a re-appraisal of the whole nature and basis of Christian existence. In Text D this endeavour is still concealed in the Preface, which is, admittedly, fairly long. From Text E on there appears a special chapter headed *De ipsa revelatione.* Only by going back to the comprehensive reality of the deeds and words of God it is possible to do away with the positivistic idea of the *duplex fons;* only by going back to the common foundation of all Christian discourse, could the question of the individual elements of the passing on of revelation be removed from the field of controversy and placed within the appropriate framework. If one compares the text of Article 2 with what was said at Vatican I *(DS* 3004f.), it becomes clear how much Catholic theology has benefited in the last fifty years from the theology of Karl Barth, which itself was influenced by the personalistic thinking of Ebner, Buber and others. The first thing for us to note is the quite different structure: whereas Vatican I starts from the natural knowledge of God and considers "supernatural" revelation only in close connection with this idea, in order to proceed immediately to the question of its transmission in scripture and tradition, here the question of the natural knowledge of God is put at the end and God's revealing activity described within a comprehensive survey of salvation history. If we examine the details of the text, the progress since 1870 becomes even clearer. Latourelle has pointed out here the following significant correspondences in the two texts:[5]

Vaticanum I	Vaticanum II
. . placuisse eius sapientiae	Placuit Deo in sua bonitate
et bonitati . . . se ipsum ac	et sapientia seipsum
eterna voluntatis suae	revelare et notum facere
decreta humano generi revelare . . .	sacramentum voluntatis suae
	(cf. Eph 1:9) . . .

Here, instead of the abstract values "sapientia et bonitas" we first have a reference to God himself "in his wisdom and goodness", thus giving a far greater emphasis to the personal and theocentric starting-point when compared with Vatican I: it is God himself, the person of God, from whom revelation proceeds and to whom it returns, and thus revelation necessarily reaches — also with the person who receives it — into the personal centre of man, it touches him in the depth of his being, not only in his individual faculties, in his will and understanding. The second difference between the two texts is more important: instead of the words "the eternal decree of his will" we have the "sacramentum" of his will. Instead of the legalistic view that sees revelation largely as the issuing of divine decrees, we have a sacramental view, which sees law and grace, word and deed, message and sign, the person and his utterance within the one comprehensive unity of the mystery. The idea of mystery in the Epistle to the Ephesians, with all its associations, should echo here: this idea includes the universality of salvation ("unite all things in him", i.e. Christ; 1:10), the unity of mankind in the one Christ, the cosmic dimension of what is Christian, the relation of revelation to history, and finally its Christological centre. For the mystery of God is ultimately nothing other than Christ himself — it is the person (Col 1:27). From this there follows an understanding of revelation that is seen basically as dialogue, as is indicated in the words *alloquitur* and *conversatur*. In Article 25 this idea is taken up again when the reading of Scripture is described as a *colloquium inter Deum et hominem*.[6] This also indicates the element of actuality that is contained in dialogue: the dialogue of God is always carried on in the present; his address "no longer do I call you servants . . . but . . . friends" (Jn 15:15) is given here and now with the intention of forcing us to reply. Thus we can see how the idea of revelation also outlines a conception of man: man as the creature of dialogue who, in listening to the word of God, becomes contemporaneous with the presentness of God and in the fellowship of the word receives the reality which is indivisibly one with this word: fellowship with God himself.

Another important thing in our text is the markedly Trinitarian conception:

Latourelle, *La Révélation*, p. 40.
Cf. also Chapter II, 8: ". . . Deus . . . sine intermissione cum dilecti Filii sui Sponsa colloquitur.
Cf. also H. Ott, "Die Offenbarung Gottes nach dem Konzil", in Hampe, ed., *Die Autorität*, I, pp. 169–74, esp. p. 170.

171

the movement of revelation proceeds from God (the Father), comes to us through Christ, and admits us to the fellowship of God in the Holy Spirit. Thus although our text has been composed in definitely Christological terms — Christ is described finally as the mediator of revelation and the fullness of revelation itself — it does not present a one-sided Christocentric view. If, however, one wished to consider it as Christocentric, then this should, at any rate, be understood wholly in the original Pauline sense: Christ stands in the centre as the mediator, his "place" is characterized by the mediating word *per;* he enfolds us in the dimension of the Spirit, and our being in him means at the same time that we have been led to the Father.[7] Thus, on the one hand, the pneumatological dimension is not overlooked here, this emerging naturally from a Christology of the resurrection as a correction to a one-sided Christology of the incarnation, and at the same time the theocentric position is given appropriate emphasis, towards which the Christocentric view, properly understood, is necessarily orientated.

There is a final point which our text wants to make: it offers a new view of the relation between the word and the event in the structure of revelation. The Council's intention in this matter was a simple one, scarcely touched by the many distinctions that the problem has undergone in contemporary theological discussion. The fathers were merely concerned with overcoming neo-scholastic intellectualism, for which revelation chiefly meant a store of mysterious supernatural teachings, which automatically reduces faith very much to an acceptance of these supernatural insights.[8] As opposed to this, the Council desired to express again the character of revelation as a totality, in which word and event make up one whole, a true dialogue which touches man in his totality, not only challenging his reason, but, as dialogue, addressing him as a partner, indeed, giving him his true nature for the first time. This takes up the new ideas that emerged in theology between the wars; the more recent controversy between the theology of salvation history (Cullmann) and the theology of the word (Bultmann, Ebeling) is not considered.[9]

Article 3 attempts to give, in a very brief form, something like a compendium of revelation and salvation history before Christ. It again emphatically asserts the historical character of revelation, which comes to man not as a timeless idea, but

---

[7] For a scriptural understanding of Christocentric theology mention should be made of th important study by W. Thüsing, *Per Christum in Deum. Studien zum Verhältnis von Christozentrik und Theozentrik in den paulinischen Hauptbriefen* (1965). There is also a notable criticism of K. Barth' Christo-centrism in E. H. Amberg's *Christologie und Dogmatik. Untersuchung ihres Verhältnisses i der evangelischen Theologie der Gegenwart* (1966). Cf. also J. Ratzinger, "Christozentrik in der Ver kündigung", *TTZ* 70 (1961), pp. 1–14.

[8] One cannot deny that there is a tendency in this direction in Vatican I, even if counter-tendencie are not entirely absent. Cf. on this esp. H. Fries, "Kirche und Offenbarung Gottes", in Hamp *Die Autorität,* I, pp. 155–69, esp. pp. 158 ff.

[9] Cf. the bibliography given in O. Cullmann. *Heil als Geschichte* (1965); cf. also J. Ratzinge "Heilsgeschichte und Eschatologie", *Theologie im Wandel* (1967).

s the historical operation of God in our own time and sets man in the context of his history as the place of his salvation. So far we can see here a certain approximation to the position of Cullmann and his school, without necessarily speaking, n a technical sense, of a theology of salvation history. Actually, in the major questions of the knowability of divine saving action and its realization the Council departs from the path mapped out by Cullmann, as we shall see in Chapter II. Thus on this question also the Council has remained outside all echnical theological positions, and this is all the more important as it was nfluenced by the observers almost exclusively in the direction of a theology of aving history and was scarcely confronted with the other positions of modern heology.

The first problem the text is faced with could be described in the words 'creation and revelation" or "creation and salvation". The Council's answer again confirms its cautious, hesitant attitude. By first making the firm point that God had perfected his creation "through the Word", through the Logos, the Christological nature of creation is made clear, and the self-testimony of God in creation, which is mentioned immediately afterwards, is placed in a Christological context, an important point for the question dealt with in Article 6, which emphasizes the unity of divine action, thus excluding from the start any false extrinsicism. Also the point is made that creation was already orientated towards salvation, but then the revelation to the patriarchs is separated from the creation and treated as a new action (indicated by the use of the word *insuper*). Thus the idea of the duality of the orders is combined with that of the unity of Logos-determined divine action and a dialectic connection between the two levels of statement.

The second main concern of the text was to bring our changed historical perspective, which has immeasurably extended the range of human history beyond the scriptural span of 6,000 years, into the historical understanding of salvation. Again it was a matter of achieving a dialectic combination of two apparently contrary series of statements, in that the particularism of salvation history and the universalism of the divine saving will have to be seen as related one to the other. Although one can appeal to Scripture itself in support of this intrinsic relationship, the new task is to ensure to universalism the full breadth given by our changed conception of history. It is worth noting, however, that the change of view induced by our new knowledge refers, as it were, only to the quantity, but not to the structure as such, which even in Scripture still has the particular and the whole combined in an indissoluble unity? The text sees the whole of history, on the one hand, under the sign of the Fall, i.e. as fallen history, but, on the other, under the sign of the promise and the care of God, who alone makes possible "the patience of good works" and thus eternal life. Here we can scarcely suppress the question as to whether the Council did not start from an over-optimistic view in its account of revelation and salvation history, losing sight of the fact that divine salvation comes essentially as a justification of the *sinner;* that grace is given through the judgment of the cross and thus itself always retains the character of judgment; that therefore the *one* word of God appears in the double guise of Law and Gospel — a statement that is still true even if we consider the specifically Lutheran theology of Law and Gospel as too narrow and inadequate.[10] If Rom 2 was quoted as a testimony for the universal possibility of salvation, should not also mention have been made of the terrifying context of this passage of Scripture, that belongs to an indivisible line of thought which runs from 1:17–3:20, ending finally, in 3:20, in the statement that is directly contrary to the text quoted (2:6f.): "For no human being will be justified in his sight by works of the law . . ."; cf. also 3:23: "since all have sinned and fall short of the glory of God . . .".[11] When salvation is being treated should not the mystery of the anger of God also have been mentioned, that weighs so heavily upon these chapters? The whole vast subject of sin, law, and the anger of God is gathered together here in the one little word *lapsus (Post eorum lapsum . . .)* and thus is given neither its full weight nor is it taken seriously enough. The pastoral optimism of an age that is concerned with understanding and reconciliation seems to have somewhat blinded the Council to a not immaterial section of the testimony of Scripture.

This lack is also noticeable in the third subject treated in this section, which may be described as the attempt at a brief Christian theology of the Old Testament (a task that is taken up again in Chapter IV). This would have been the place to consider the double nature of revelation as Law and Gospel, which is so characteristic of the whole structure of Christian revelation, that it cannot be resolved either into Gospel alone, or into Law alone. In the text, however, we have the Christological account of the Old Testament seen from just two points of view: it appears as a whole, as παιδεία (an idea that in Paul expresses the punitive function of the Old Testament, but here appears in the more friendly light of modern pedagogics). This again serves to lead us to the one God (monotheism), to his caring and rewarding power; it is also the preparation for the promised redeemer. Here we have once more the extension of the perspective from which the text started: the last clause *(atque . . . praeparavit)* obviously means that the whole period of time before Christ, also outside Israel, was the preparation for the Gospel, which occurs in Israel in the more specific form of expectation of the redeemer and the gradual accustoming of Israel to faith in the

---

[10] Cf. G. Söhngen, "Gesetz und Evangelium", *LTK,* IV, cols. 831–5 (bibliography).

[11] Cf. O. Kuss, *Der Römerbrief,* p. 29, esp. pp. 64f. On p. 64, Kuss agrees with Lietzmann, who had said of the passage: "In vv. 5–12 Paul was still arguing from the pre-evangelical standpoint which knows nothing of justification by faith and expects a judgment on the basis of one's own achievements. But because in this context he seeks to reduce the idea of the justification of the world *ad absurdum,* to be strictly logical this whole discussion must be regarded as hypothetical: this is how it would be if, first, we did not have the Gospel and second, it were possible to fulfil the law." Cf. Kuss, p. 65: "The Apostle cannot seriously mean that there was a realizable possibility for man — apart from the salvation that has come through Christ — . . . of attaining . . . eternal life" on the basis of good works (v. 7).

one God. This expresses again very happily the unity of the whole of pre-Christian history and the special nature of God's mission for Israel.

Article 4 speaks of Christ as the last word of God and belongs, even externally, in the very middle of Chapter I, so that the structure of the text is an impressive indication of its Christological orientation. The quotation from Heb 1 shows, on the one hand, the continuity of divine history with men: the word of God in Christ continues his words through the fathers and the prophets; but at the same time it reveals what is truly new in the New Testament: instead of words, we have *the* Word. Christ no longer speaks merely of God, but he is himself the speech of God; this man is himself and as an entity the Word of God that has made himself one of us.[12] Thus the perfection of revelation in Christ is here removed from the domain of positivist thinking: God does not arbitrarily cease speaking at some point of history and at some point of his discourse, although there would be much more to say, but Christ is the end of God's speaking, because after him and beyond him there is nothing more to say, for in him God has, as it were, said himself.[13] In him the dialogue of God has attained its goal; it has become a union.

We can see again here how little intellectualism and doctrinalism are able to comprehend the nature of revelation, which is not concerned with talking *about* something that is quite external to the person, but with the realization of the existence of man, with the relation of the human "I" to the divine "thou", so that the purpose of this dialogue is ultimately not information, but unity and transformation. At the same time we can see how far the Christ event, precisely as an end, is also a beginning that necessarily continues, remaining through the whole of history a presence and a promise of what is to come. We said before that Christ was the end of God's speaking, but this end is nothing but man's being constantly addressed by God, it is the constant relating of man to the one man who is the Word of God himself. Thus subsequent history cannot surpass what has taken place in Christ, but it must attempt to catch up with it gradually, to catch up all humanity in the man who, as a man coming from God, is the man for all others, the area of all human existence and the one and only Adam. And if we made the point that Christ was the end of God's speaking because after him there was nothing more to say, then that also means that he is the constant address of God to man, that nothing comes *after* him, but that in him the whole extent of God's word begins to reveal itself. Thus we are able to regard this as the basis for the following treatment of revelation and tradition, and at the same time the true nature of revelation and its truth becomes apparent: it does not reveal *something,* nor does it reveal various kinds of things, but in the man Jesus,

---

[12] Cf. Latourelle, *La Révélation,* p. 18 f.

[13] Cf. K. Rahner, "The Development of Dogma", *Theological Investigations,* I (1961), pp. 39–78; p. 49: "Nothing new remains to be said, not as though there were not still much to say, but because everything has been said, everything given in the Son of Love, in whom God and the world have become one . . ."

in the man who is God, we are able to understand the whole nature of man. The truth and deception of human existence appear in the light of the man who is truly man because he comes entirely from God and is *una persona* with God himself.

For the understanding of the text R. Latourelle has pointed out a parallel with Vatican I which was certainly not intended by the fathers, but is for that reason all the more enlightening. When Vatican I speaks of the Church as a testimony of revelation, it uses formulations that are similar to those employed by Vatican II when it talks of the function of Christ *(DS* 3012f.).[14] Vatican I said that the Church itself was an unshakeable witness of its own divine mission because of its miraculous extent, its holiness, fruitfulness, unity and constancy. Vatican II says that Christ, through his own presence and revelation, through his signs and words, his death and his resurrection, is the fullness of revelation, which he himself guarantees with his divine witness. Of course this does not mean that the text of Vatican I is cancelled out or questioned, but the centring of everything on Christ, which leaves any ecclesio-monism far behind it, is very clear. The Church can fundamentally only be a sign because and insofar as it lives from Christ, who is himself the sign and content of revelation, the great divine σημεῖον and μυστήριον, which alone gives power and significance to all the other signs and testimonies. Thus this text was also able to open up a new phase in the problem of fundamental theology. All the individual miracles are here set within the one decisive divine miracle that Jesus Christ himself exists, the true witness of God. The witness cannot be separated from what is borne witness to, the attestation from the attested content, and the final point is made that the whole stands in an eschatological context: Christian faith is essentially also hope and thus can find its final attestation only in the fulfilment of hope. What is daring about it is less the intellectual paradox than the trust with which it sets out on a path the end of which cannot yet be seen.[15]

The final paragraph again emphasizes the definitive character of the revelation that has taken place in Christ, which cannot be supplanted by any new development in the history of religion or of mankind. This brief passage of text first appears in Form D, where it concluded a chronological outline of salvation history and was summed up in the statement that Christianity ("Christianism"— an un-

[14] R. Latourelle, Le Christ signe de la révélation selon la constitution 'Dei Verbum'", *Gr* 47 (1966), pp. 658–709. An exact comparison of the text is found on pp. 686 and 688. There is an apt formulation on p. 689: "It is precisely, it seems, because the Church has endeavoured to define itself better that it has, in a sense, moved away from its centre in relation to itself in order to centre itself more on Christ."

[15] Cf. J. Moltmann, *Theologie der Hoffnung* (5th ed., 1966), e.g. p. 13: "Doctrinal statements find their truth in their verifiable correspondence with the reality that is present and can be experienced; but the statements of hope, on the basis of the promise must contradict the reality that can be experienced in the present"; p. 14: "The contradiction in which hope places man in relation to the given reality of himself and the world is precisely the contradiction from which hope itself is born, it is the contradiction of the resurrection to the cross."

theological word that was dropped in later versions of the text because of its theological obscurity, being replaced by the patristic idea of *oeconomia)* was not a transitory period in the history of religion *(historia religiosa)*, but its absolutely final and definitive stage. The extremely concrete point that the text expressed, in this confrontation with the intellectual awareness of our century, has been sacrificed to the exactitude of technical theological language. On the other hand, the Christological foundation for the Christian claim to finality has become clearer and the eschatological relation brought in, which now shows from within faith the provisional nature of Christianity and hence its relatedness to the future, which exists together with the connection with the Christ event that has taken place once and for all, so that it is impossible to state the one without the other. Perhaps the dimension of hope and promise that is here indicated and is essential not only for the faith of the Old Testament, but also, in a transformed way, no less for that of the New, should have been brought out more clearly, because it probably offers the only way of stating the significance of the Christian claim to finality as against the questioning of our age that is attuned to progress and change, at the same time distinguishing it from the merely retrogressive thinking of Romanticism and the Restoration. In an age that conceives of man more and more as a being that is still coming into existence and is scarcely capable of making statements about being and the claim that this involves, a proper definition of the finality of Christianity, which at all times claims to be a "New" Testament, is of fundamental importance. The starting-point is given here with the Christological anchoring of the idea: faith proclaims Christ as the one who has come and as the one who is to come and thus bears within itself both the infinite openness of man and the finality of the divine answer that does not put an end to man's development, but makes him conscious of his true, infinite nature.

Article 5. The section on faith presents what is essentially a contraction of the corresponding passages of text of Vatican I *(DS* 3008–10). It derives its significance as a further development of the 1870 Council both from the new context in which it places the analysis of faith and from the nature of the selection which it makes from the preceding document. The context is determined, as we have seen, by an understanding of revelation that is wholly Christological and that sees the dualism of word and reality reconciled in him who, as the true Logos, is at the same time the true ground of all that is real, and that consequently sees the antithesis between intellectual dogmatic faith and the yielding-up of one's whole existence in trust as overcome through the total acceptance coming from the person, which recognizes Jesus Christ as, indissolubly, both the truth and the way. Thus the total character of faith inevitably emerges strongly here; it is expressed in the scriptural idea of obedience in faith, "by which man entrusts his whole self freely to God".

The perspective that is presented in this context is supported by the omission in the text compared with *DS* 3008–10. Vatican I had mentioned three elements in the genesis of faith: the inner aids of the Holy Spirit, the external *argumenta revelationis* (with which the main part of the section *DS* 3009 was concerned), and, finally, inner illumination by the Holy Spirit (which, as the active working of grace, must be differentiated from the aids to understanding). This structure of the acceptance by faith gives a dialectic quality to faith itself, in that it is described both as *donum Dei* and as *opus ad salutem pertinens,* which is of course ultimately a description of the "work" as a "present", and an illumination of God's way of making a gift as something that makes us free for the true nature of this operation. The text does not go into this last question; rather it takes over the description of the *Genesis fidei,* from which, however, it omits the "external arguments" and limits itself to the interior aids of the Holy Spirit and *gratia praeveniens.* This is certainly not a denial or rejection of the teaching, so firmly insisted on by Vatican I, that revelation is attested through exterior signs, such as miracles and prophecies, but it is given a notably more modest place; faith appears as more inwardly orientated, and no further attempt is made to make the certainty of faith measurable by positivist criteria so that it may compete with the positivism which dominates all contemporary thinking. Here again there emerges the particular manner of the certainty of faith, which we have already encountered in the section on Christology.

The second omission is of a similar nature. Vatican I had defined the obedience of faith as "believing as true what has been revealed by God" (*DS* 3008). This definition, which comes in the first section of the chapter on faith, gives to all the following statements a strongly intellectual tone, which is confronted again and again with elements, but without cancelling out the general tendency that had been already given. Vatican II has simplified this statement by speaking simply of an acceptance of *revelationi ab Eo datae.* This change from *revelato* to *revelatio* opens up a new vista, which again in no way removes the intellectual component of faith, but understands it as a component in a wider whole.

Another innovation, compared with Vatican I, is the final sentence, which speaks of a constant perfecting of faith through the gifts of the Holy Spirit and sees the effect of these as an ever deeper insight into revelation. The sentence shows surprisingly clearly how automatically, despite all the stimulus that they received from Protestant theologians, the authors moved within the tradition of Catholic theological thought. For it would have been very difficult for Protestant theologians to use an expression such as the "perfecting" of faith. For them faith is a decision between "yes" and "no", which is made either entirely or not at all, but which cannot be conceived of in terms of different degrees. The fundamental point here is the extent to which one regards faith as a "possession" of man himself or merely as God's paradoxical action in relation to man, which cannot then be regarded as a "virtue" that gradually takes over wider areas of man's existence, but is rather the total nature of his existence and cannot be thought of as being on the same level with human practices and virtues. Thus the problem of the dialectics of *donum* and *opus,* more explicitly considered by Vatican I, nevertheless comes to the fore here. Contrary to first impressions, we may say that this dialectic is fully sustained here, for it is the Holy Ghost that appears as the effective subject of the *perfectio* that is related to the *opus*. Thus God remains here the one who is really acting, but his activity penetrates man steadily and increasingly.

In order to understand this brief sentence completely, it is important to take note of the explanation given of it in the *relatio* on Text E (cf. p. 13, C). This says: ". . . ita innuitur continuitas inter primum assensum et progressum, non solum pro singulis fidelibus . . ., sed etiam pro communicate." This means that already here there is the intention to provide a foundation for the idea of tradition developed in Chapter II: tradition takes place essentially as the growing insight, mediated by the Holy Spirit, into revelation that has been given once and for all; it is the *perfectio* of faith which the Spirit brings about in the Church. This is the crux of the difference between Catholic and Protestant theology in the question of tradition, which emerges in the discussion on Chapter II. As this sentence shows, it can be reduced to the varying understanding of the relation between God's acts and the acts of man, the different attitude to the dialectics of *donum* and *opus*. But this also raises the question that will have to be considered in more detail in the commentary on Chapter II as to whether, despite the fundamental view which it is impossible for Catholic theology to abandon, the question of the criticism of tradition or the impossibility of a rectilinear idea of *perfectio* should not be more fully considered here.

Finally it must be said that it is not without significance that the attempt to present the total character of faith primarily makes use of the idea of obedience and only secondarily takes up the idea of trust. This makes it clear that self-abandonment in faith is not without direction, but includes commitment to the word, and that this self-abandonment of faith means a readiness for the concrete manner of the encounter with God and his claim, as these are brought to me historically through the preaching of the Church. That this view is entirely in accordance with the Pauline *kerygma* has been shown impressively in the works of R. Bultmann.[16]

Article 6. The last section of this chapter repeats, in abridged form, the first two sections of the chapter *De revelatione* from Vatican I (*DS* 3004f.). The only new thing that has been added to the text is the substitution of *manifestare ac communicare* for *revelare,* which again emphasizes the character of revelation as a reality that goes beyond the merely doctrinal, revelation which does not merely present "divine ordinances", but is the dialogue of salvation, the communication from person to person that takes place in the word. The development from Vatican I, however, is seen again in a different context. In 1870 people had started with the natural knowledge of God and had moved on from this to "supernatural" revelation. Vatican II has not only avoided the technical term

---

[16] Cf. G. Hassenhüttl's account in *Der Glaubensvollzug* (1963), pp. 189–96, with extensive references from Bultmann's works.

supernaturalis, which belongs too much to the world of physical thinking (however indispensable the term may be for the time being), but followed the reverse procedure. It develops revelation from its Christological centre, in order then to present the inescapable responsibility of human reason as one dimension of the whole. This shows that the human relation to God does not consist of two more or less independent parts, but is indivisibly one; there is no such thing as a natural religion in itself, but each religion is "positive", though because of its very positivity it does not exclude the responsibility of thought, but includes it. Vatican II had no reason to suppress this basic idea developed with such care by Vatican I; on the contrary, in dealing with the onslaughts of atheism it will have increasing importance.[17]

[17] For the concept of nature at Vatican I, cf. the excellent account in H. U. von Balthasar, *Karl Barth* (1951), pp. 314–35.

The Transmission of Divine Revelation

by
Joseph Ratzinger

Article 7. Chapter II of the Constitution still bears the marks of the bitter struggle from which the final version of the text emerged. Article 7 is consciously based closely on the Tridentine text (*DS* 1501), and the direction in which it is moving can be understood only when compared with the latter and in terms of the new accents that we find here. Two new additions in the sentence that begins with the words "Ideo Christus Dominus . . ." continue the line of Chapter I and now bring out its significance for the problem of tradition. After the words "ante per Prophetas Ipse" we find "adimplevit", not found in the Tridentine text, and at the end of the sentence the phrase "eis dona divina communicantes" is also new. The common purpose of both additions is easy to see. By describing the activity of Jesus in relation to the Gospel not only as "promulgating", but also as "fulfilling", it plays down the narrow legal aspect to which the categorization of the Christian message under the idea of *nova lex* had ultimately led, which is what lies behind the concept of promulgation. An outline is given of the unity of the history of salvation in the Old and the New Testaments, thus giving an historical and sacramental, and not a juridical and legal account of the Christian reality, pointing out the reality and saving character of the word of Christ, which is not only a summons, but primarily the plenitude from which the saving activity comes and from which alone the nature of the Christian summons is to be understood. That this is its intention is made clear by the second addition: the preaching of the Apostles is explained by the ideas of *donum* and *communicare;* again, instead of the legal concept, we have the idea of grace and the principle of dialogue: proclamation as communication in the giving activity of God. This provides an essentially new starting-point for the question of tradition, for if the origin of tradition — that which stands at the beginning and must be passed on — is not a promulgated law, but communication in the gift of God's plenitude, then the idea of "passing on" must mean something different from before.

The next sentence ("Quod quidem fideliter . . ."), which now directly describes the beginning of the process of handing down, continues along the same lines. If Trent had seen this starting-point only as the preaching of Christ and the

181

Apostles, the present text sees three different kinds of events: the "exempla" and "institutiones" of the Apostles are placed beside the *praedicatio oralis* and accordingly, as far as the Christological origin is concerned, above and beyond the word of the Lord, both living with him and seeing what he did are described as origins of tradition. The same process of extension is seen also in the mention of the new pneumatological component of the origin of revelation, as when the Tridentine phrase "Spiritu Sancto dictante" is changed to "Spiritu Sancto suggerente" — which is also more in accordance with Scripture (Jn 14:26, Vulg.). Again it is not hard to see the basic purpose of this. The point is certainly not to play off the theology of salvation history against word theology, but in place of a narrowly doctrinal conception of revelation, as had been expressed in the Tridentine word theology, to open up a comprehensive view of the real character of revelation, which — precisely because it is concerned with the whole man — is founded not only in the word that Christ preached, but in the whole of the living experience of his person, thus embracing what is said and what is unsaid,[1] what the Apostles in their turn are not able to express fully in words, but which is found in the whole reality of the Christian existence of which they speak, far transcending the framework of what has been explicitly formulated in words. And finally the guidance of the Paraclete promised to the disciples is not a "dictation", but "suggestio", the remembering and understanding of the unspoken in what was once spoken, which reaches down to the depths of a process that cannot be measured by the terms "praedicatio oralis" (Trent had "ab ipsius Christi ore"), and the transmission of which cannot therefore be merely a process of the handing-down of words. It must also be pointed out that at the end, when the origin of Scripture is mentioned, "apostolic men" are purposely mentioned as well as the Apostles, in order to keep open the question of the authorship of the Gospels (cf. Chapter IV of the Constitution).

A further point that is new in comparison with Trent is the connection between the principles of succession and tradition, first made by Irenaeus, which is found in the next sentence ("Ut autem Evangelium . . ."). In fact for Irenaeus both principles are indissolubly one: "The succession is the visible manifestation of tradition, tradition is the manifestation of succession."[2] Tertullian expressed in a different way the same idea in his *Praescriptio,* which together with the anti-gnostic texts of Irenaeus provided the basis for the idea of tradition.[3] "Tradition" appeared in both cases (in contrast to the gnostic idea of tradition) not so much as a material principle as a formal one. Primarily, it means a fundamental herme-neutical decision, namely that faith is present in no other way than in the historical

---

[1] Cf. H. Schlier, *Besinnung auf das Neue Testament* (1964), p. 50, and in general pp. 7–62, E. T.: *The Relevance of the New Testament* (1968), p. 59, and in general pp. 1–75.

[2] I have tried to give a summary of this position in K. Rahner and J. Ratzinger, *The Episcopate and the Primacy* (1962), pp. 51 f.

[3] Of the large body of literature see O. Kuss, "Zur Hermeneutik Tertullians", in J. Blinzer, O. Kuss and F. Mussner, *Neutestamentliche Aufsätze (Festschrift J. Schmid)* (1963), pp. 138–60.

continuity of the believers and must be found in it and not against it.[4] But this question is simply touched on here, by connecting the foundation of tradition with that of succession.

Before we consider another basic terminological difference in this chapter compared with the Tridentine Decree on Tradition, let us consider the last sentence of Article 7, which introduces the eschatological element: All knowledge in the time of the Church remains knowledge seen in a mirror — and hence fragmentary. The direct relation to reality, to the face of God itself, is kept for the *eschaton* (cf. 1 Cor 13:12). This is the only place in this chapter in which one can hear a gentle note of criticism of tradition, for when everything is seen and read only in a mirror, one must expect distortions and shifts in emphasis. In any case, this is *theologia negativa,* which necessarily involves the setting of a certain limit to both kerygmatic and ecclesial positivity, without this line being further developed. We shall come back to it again later on.

In considering the next sections, we shall have to concern ourselves with what is perhaps the most important terminological difference between our text and that of Trent. It is, incidentally, probably the least conscious shift in emphasis, which, for this reason, is particularly characteristic of the new nature of the question from which both sides of the conciliar dispute departed. Whereas Trent had used the idea of tradition only in the plural — as traditions — Vatican II, except for one quotation from .Scripture (2 Thess 2:15), uses it only in the singular: *traditio.*[5] This makes clear, however, the difference in the two positions, never consciously realized. Vatican II starts from an abstract concept, whereas Trent was concerned with the concrete phenomenon, the actually existing traditions, by which it meant the form of the Church's life as it was actually practised: the Lord's Supper was celebrated as a sacrifice in the form of the Mass, there were days of fasting, one baptized children, prayed facing east, crossed oneself while praying etc.[6] In short, there was no question of discussing the particular form of the Church's life, which could not always be

---

[4] At the same time we should not fail to note the limit that Irenaeus set in his conception, which in no way wanted to give the Church's teaching office unlimited freedom, when it was a question of avoiding the arbitrary nature of gnostic speculation. N. Brox, in particular, brought this out well in his article "Charisma veritatis certum", in *ZKG* 75 (1964), pp. 327–31. On p. 327 he writes: "The office does not give the authoritative statement of a truth and unit of doctrine that would otherwise not be known as such, but rather the unbroken chain of testimony is seen as a good reason for the unchanged handing down of the kerygma (III, 24:1). In the gnostic *diadoche* it is the asserted encounter of authority with the Apostles ... that has to authorize the *gnosis,* which remains in its origin ... inaccessible and, as a secret teaching, ... unverifiable ... In the Church the legitimate authority of the bishop is shown in the fact that, because of the *diadoche* of the teaching, he is able to cite the apostles, for he is preaching the same thing as the Apostles. But that he is teaching the same thing is proved, according to Irenaeus, from Scripture ..."

[5] Cf. M. Bévenot, *Traditiones in the Council of Trent* (cf. note 7 to the Introduction); P. van Leeuwen, "Der Reifungsprozess des Zweiten Vatikanischen Konzils in der Lehre über die göttliche Offenbarung und ihre Weitergabe", *Concilium* 3 (1967), pp. 2–8, esp. p. 6.

[6] On the collection of *traditiones* in relation to the Council of Trent, cf. Y. Congar, "Traditions

derived from Scripture in its details, or the actual form of Christian life as it had developed in the Church. Thus for the fathers of Trent, the question of tradition was more a question of the reform of Church life than a question of Church teaching.[7] One saw the question of tradition as the actual problem of the Church's existence, not the problem of the historical justification for each of the statements to be found in its catechism, as happened during the controversy of Vatican II. That people were incapable of realizing this is shown by the lamentable weakness and the impossibility of any inner solution to the bitter dispute on tradition, which ever since 1962 has divided the fathers on a question that must be regarded as fundamentally fruitless.[8] What has in fact, however, been achieved was the return to a more comprehensive view of the problem by the new understanding of revelation and a more general view of the phenomenon of tradition which results from it, but both the conception of tradition as an accumulation of statements and, consequently, the quantitative way of looking at it remained to the end an explosive source of controversy.

Article 8 appears for the first time in Text E under the heading. *De sacra Traditione* and is an attempt to meet the widely expressed need for a clear and positive account of what is meant by tradition. It is not difficult (as in the additions in which Article 7 goes beyond Trent) to recognize the pen of Y. Congar in the text and to see behind it the influence of the Catholic Tübingen school of the nineteenth century with, in particular, its dynamic and organic idea of tradition, which in turn was strongly impregnated by the spirit of German Romanticism.[9]

The first section points out the total nature of tradition: primarily, it means simply the many-layered yet one presence of the mystery of Christ throughout all the ages; it means the totality of the presence of Christ in this world. Again the three divisions of Article 7 are taken up, which had outlined the perspectives of the reality of origin. Teaching, life and worship are named as the three ways in which tradition is handed on. It has its place not only in the explicitly traditional statements of Church doctrine, but in the unstated — and often unstatable — elements of the whole service of the Christian worship of God and the life of the Church. This is the basis of the final comprehensive formulation of tradition as the "perpetuation", the constant continuation and making present of everything that the Church is, of everything that it believes. Tradition is identified, and thus

apostoliques non écrites et suffisance de l'Écriture", *Istina* 6 (1959), pp. 219–306, esp. pp. 289 ff. ; J. Ratzinger, *Revelation and Tradition* (1965), pp. 57–62. [7] Ratzinger, *op. cit.,* pp. 59 f.
[8] In his intervention at the Council on 5 October 1964, Archbishop Edelby expressed this from the viewpoint of the Eastern Church, in a manner that was both brilliant and highly enlightening for both sides of the conciliar controversy. It is printed in Hampe's *Die Autorität,* I pp. 119–122.
[9] Cf. the two-volumed work by Congar, mentioned in note 5 on the Introduction, in which he sums up the findings of numerous earlier works on this theme. On the idea of tradition in German Romanticism, especially in the Tübingen School, cf. the various writings of J. R. Geiselmann, and in particular, *Lebendiger Glaube aus geheiligter Überlieferung* (1942); *Die lebendige Überlieferung als Norm des christlichen Glaubens* (1959).

defined, with the being and the faith of the Church. The danger that lurks in this statement (as altogether in the dynamic idea of tradition held by the Tübingen School) had been pointed out by Cardinal Meyer in an important speech on 30 September 1964: not everything that exists in the Church must for that reason be also a legitimate tradition; in other words, not every tradition that arises in the Church is a true celebration and keeping present of the mystery of Christ. There is a distorting, as well as a legitimate, tradition. As examples of this negative kind of tradition Meyer mentioned a kind of piety that is opposed to the spirit of liturgy and a casuistic and untheological moralism. He asked that the text should state not only that *in statu viatorum* tradition proceeds in a spirit of progess and ever deeper insight into faith, but that there is also the possibility of a *deficere,* and in fact, this possibility is constantly being realized. Consequently, tradition must not be considered only affirmatively, but also critically; we have Scripture as a criterion for this indispensable criticism of tradition, and tradition must therefore always be related back to it and measured by it.[10]

As a result of these objections the middle clause *(omne quod habet)* was deleted from the original formulation in three parts — in tradition the Church passes on *omne . . . quod ipsa est, omne quod habet, omne quod credit.* On this point, the *relatio* in Text F states that this omission is intended to make clear that all that, and only that, proceeds from the apostolic tradition "quae substantialia sunt Ecclesiae . . ." *(ibid.,* p. 19). This concession, to which there is no reference in the present text, must be regarded as unsatisfactory, and it is to be regretted that the suggestion of the American Cardinal was not, in fact, taken up. Even Trent had not been able to give a positive account of the criticism of tradition, the need for which was not questioned (the necessity of reform was one of the reasons for the Council, and this reform was concerned with the *traditiones*); it is hidden away, hardly discernible for someone who is not historically informed, in the phrase *ad nos usque pervenerunt.* This was an attempt to formulate at that time, in the multiplicity of the *traditiones* that had passed away and that still remained, a criterion of valid tradition. It was found in the reception by the whole Church — only traditions received by the Church were described as important for faith. A second criterion was apostolicity, which again was supposed to help in differentiating between true and merely factual tradition. In practice, however, the reception of a tradition by the Church was taken as a criterion of apostolicity, so that the latter was largely excluded as a separate yardstick.[11] Nevertheless, an attempt had been made to make a distinction among traditions, unsatisfactory though it was, inasmuch as criticism of reception by the Church was scarcely possible. On this point Vatican II has unfortunately not made any progress, but has more or less ignored the whole question of the criticism of tradition. By doing this, it has

---

[10] Cf. A. Wenger, *Vatican II,* III (1965), pp. 145f.; L. A. Dorn and G. Denzler, *Tagebuch des Konzils. Die Arbeit der Dritten Session* (1965), p. 103. Unfortunately this important speech was not included in Hampe's collected volume.

[11] Cf. J. Ratzinger, *op. cit.,* pp. 57ff., p. 63 (cf. note 6); Bévenot, *loc. cit.,* p. 338.

missed an important opportunity for ecumenical dialogue. In fact, it would have been ecumenically more fruitful to work out a positive possibility and to stress the necessity of the criticism of tradition within the Church than to engage in what must be called an unreal controversy about the quantitative completeness of Scripture.

The second paragraph of our text points out the dynamic character of tradition, thus arousing lively opposition on the part of the Canadian Cardinal Léger. It states that tradition, which stems from the Apostles, develops under the assistance of the Holy Spirit in the Church, i.e. that there is a growing understanding of the words and realities that have been handed down to us. Again, three factors of this growth are listed: contemplation and study on the part of believers; inner understanding, which comes from spiritual experience; and the proclamation by the teaching office. The final point is made that the Church and its understanding of revelation is moving forward towards the fullness of the divine word in the Church in the *eschaton*. It is important that the progress of the word in the time of the Church is not seen simply as a function of the hierarchy, but is anchored in the whole life of the Church; through it, we hear in what is said that which is unsaid. The whole spiritual experience of the Church, its believing, praying and loving intercourse with the Lord and his word, causes our understanding of the original truth to grow and in the today of faith extracts anew from the yesterday of its historical origin what was meant for all time and yet can be understood only in the changing ages and in the particular way of each. In this process of understanding, which is the concrete way in which tradition proceeds in the Church, the work of the teaching office is one component (and, because of its nature, a critical one, not a productive one), but it is not the whole.

The dynamic concept of tradition, with which the Council here develops its positive conception of *traditio,* was strongly attacked from two quite opposite directions. On the one hand, Cardinal Ruffini rejected it from his position of traditionally neoscholastic theology, but on the other, Cardinal Léger attacked it from an ecumenical standpoint.[12] In spite of the sharp division in their general theological orientations, the arguments of these two Council fathers were astonishingly similar.[13] Ruffini firmly emphasized the idea of revelation being concluded with the death of the last Apostle, rejected the idea of including disciples of the Apostles among the origins of revelation, and opposed the idea of a living and growing revelation, for, in accordance with the text of Trent and Vatican I, he considered that this should be mentioned only in connection with a strong

[12] The text of the speeches can be found in Hampe's *Die Autorität,* pp. 112ff. (Ruffini) and pp. 114ff. (Léger).

[13] Cf. the comment made by G. Maron on the discussion on tradition in his *Evangelischer Bericht vom Konzil* (1965), p. 32: "Again — as so often during this Council — the strange situation has arisen that many Protestant observers of this development are (relatively!) closer to the traditionalists than to the progressives."

emphasis on the strict unchangeability of a revelation that had been concluded once and for all, with which he referred to an appropriate text by Vincent de Lérin, quoted at both Councils. In the concept of the schema, and especially in its emphasis on spiritual experience as a principle of the growing knowledge of revelation, he detected theological evolutionism, condemned as modernism by Pius XII. In another tone and with other reasons Cardinal Léger insisted on the same point. He found that the Schema, especially in its idea of progress, which seemed to refer not only to the knowledge of tradition, but tradition itself (*Haec . . . Traditio . . . proficit*), blurred the strict distinction between apostolic and post-apostolic tradition and endangered the strict transcendence of divine revelation when it was confronted with the statements and actions of the teaching office of the Church. The Cardinal was concerned that the Church should bind itself firmly to the final and unchangeable word of God, that does not grow, but can only be constantly assimilated afresh and cannot be manipulated by the Church. The Theological Commission considered the question carefully, but decided not to make any major alterations in the text. It pointed out that the clause ". . . Traditio . . . proficit" is explained by a second clause "crescit . . . tam rerum quam verborum . . . perceptio", i.e. the growth of tradition is a growth in understanding of the reality that was given at the beginning.[14] It formulated the idea of religious experience more cautiously, without abandoning it, but it refused to quote again the text of Vincent de Lérin, cited by past councils, in view of the dubious light in which this Church writer is now seen by historical research.[15] He no longer appears as an authentic representative of the Catholic idea of tradition, but outlines a canon of tradition based on a semi-Pelagian idea. He attacks Augustine's teaching on grace as going beyond "what had always been believed", but against this background this proves to be an inappropriate attempt to express the relationship between constancy and growth in the testimony of faith.[16] The rejection of the suggestion to include again Vincent de Lérin's well-known text, more or less canonized by two councils, is again a step beyond Trent and Vatican I, a productive revision of their texts, a phenomenon that we have come across several times already. It is not that Vatican II is taking back what was intended in those quotations: the rejection of a modernistic evolutionism, an affirmation of the definitive character of the revelation of Christ and the apostolic tradition, to which the Church has nothing to add, but which is its yardstick, but it has another conception of the nature of historical identity and continuity. Vincent de Lérin's static *semper* no longer seems the right way of expressing this problem. This kind of new orientation simply expresses our

[14] Thus in the volume published after the votes of 20 to 22 September 1965, with the *Expensio modorum,* pp. 20 f.

[15] Ibid., p. 21: "Interpretatio autem Vinc. Lirin. controvertitur."

[16] Cf. B. Altaner and A. Stuiber, *Patrologie* (7th ed., 1966), p. 454 f. (and bibliography); K. Baus: *LTK,* X, cols. 800 f. (and bibliography); J. Ratzinger, *Das Problem der Dogmengeschichte in der Sicht der katholischen Theologie* (1966), p. 9.

deeper knowledge of the problem of historical understanding, which is no longer adequately expressed by the simple ideas of a given fact and its explanation, because the explanation, as the process of understanding, cannot be clearly separated from what is being understood. This interdependence of the two, which does not remove the ultimate basic difference between assimilation and what is assimilated, even if they can no longer be strictly isolated, is well expressed by the dialectic juxtaposition of the two clauses *Traditio proficit* and *crescit perceptio*.

After the Council the objection of Cardinal Léger (and thus indirectly also that of Ruffini) was again taken up by Protestant theologians — cautiously by J. C. Hampe[17] and emphatically by O. Cullmann[18] and J. K. S. Reid,[19] who says of the statement about the development of tradition that it is "both unclear and untrue".[20] He considers that this is to make the commission of the Lord identical with its actual fulfilment and continues: "Here we stand before the broadest and deepest gulf that separates the Reformed Churches from the Roman Catholic."[21] Cullmann referred, in this connection, to his well-known theory, according to which the establishment of the canons of Scripture and the self-submission of Scripture to this canon "were decisive events in the history of salvation and an essential part of it — in fact, its climax".[24] The Bible itself, however, knows nothing of this climax of the history of salvation, and there is nothing to show that the Church of that time saw it as such. This thesis is rather the expression of a special theological theory, a conception of the history of salvation developed by Cullmann, but by no means generally shared, even by Protestant theologians.[23] If one wanted to pursue a comprehensive and proper discussion of the problem, one would also have to take account of the many other positions that are to be found in Protestant theology on this question, and above all the whole would have to be placed within the wider framework of the fundamental question of the possibility and nature of historical understanding altogether. This cannot be the purpose of our commentary. The important problem raised by Cullmann is not the question of development, but that of the relation between Scripture and Church, which we shall have to consider in detail in our commentary on Articles 9 and 10. Let it suffice here to say that both Cullmann and Reid, like Ruffini and Léger, ignored the problem of understanding, the emergence of which over the last decades has dissolved the clear antithesis of object and subject, without leading to an identification of both, in a way that is simply not in accordance with the present situation in hermeneutics and that, both historically and theologically, makes things too easy for itself. This was also clearly shown by the conference on

17 Hampe, *Die Autorität,* I, p. 116, note 3.
18 *Ibid.*, pp. 189–97.
19 *Ibid.*, pp. 223–31, esp. pp. 229 ff.
20 *Ibid.*, p. 229.   21 *Ibid.*, pp. 230 f.
22 *Ibid.*, pp. 192 f. Cullmann has elaborated this view in *Die Tradition* (1954), pp. 42–56.
23 Cf. Cullmann's treatment of the Bultmann school in *Heil als Geschichte* (1965).

faith and the nature of the Church at Montreal in 1963, which was concerned, at many different levels, with the same problem.[24]

The last paragraph of Article 8 *(Sanctorum Patrum . . .)* presents in concrete form the preceding general definition of the idea of tradition and at the same time tries to formulate from the new position the particular importance of the Church Fathers for the faith of the Church. They can no longer be seen, as in the static conception, as the bearers of individual apostolic traditions in the form of statements, but rather their importance is to be revalued in the light of the dynamic understanding of tradition. Their writings testify to the living presence of tradition and are, as it were, a living expression of the perpetuation of the mystery of Christ in the life of the Church. This raises, rather than answers, the question of the special position of the fathers, for the same thing could be said about the theological and spiritual writings of all the other periods of the Church's history. Nevertheless, the purpose of the statement is to declare that the fathers are a specific source of tradition, not in the sense of settled individual statements, but as an expression of the act of understanding, which assimilates what has been passed down and holds it for the present. Again there is a reference to the "practice and life" of the "believing and praying Church", in which the wealth of tradition effectively realizes itself. It is important to note the concrete way in which the effects of tradition are described: through it the canon of Scripture is made known and made active, in a constant dialogue of God with men — not in the sense of a pietistic and individualistic conception — but as the converse of the Son with his bride, the Church. That in no way excludes converse with the individual — he will be affected in this dialogue by the word that is spoken to him in a new and highly personal way — but it places the individual dialogue within the dialogue between the Son and his bride, thus presenting in a wholly scriptural way the irreplaceable importance of the Church for the process of understanding Scripture. In this context we can now finally see the pneumatological character of the idea of tradition. Tradition is ultimately based on the fact that the Christ event cannot be limited to the age of the historical Jesus, but continues in the presence of the Spirit, through which the Lord who "departed" on the cross "has come again" and through which he "reminds" his Church of what had happened, so that it is led, as it remembers, into its inner significance and is able to assimilate and

---

[24] Cf. the profound remarks of E. Dinkler in his article "Theologische Aufgaben der ökumenischen Arbeit heute" in *Ökumenische Rundschau* 14 (1965), pp. 116–32, esp. 117–27. On the connections between the Constitution and what was said at Montreal cf. Schutz and Thurian, *La parole*, pp. 101 ff.; E. Stakemeier in Hampe, *Die Autorität*, pp. 182 f. Both refer to nos. 44–46 of the official report of the conference, where we find the important sentences: "Thus we can say that we exist as Christians through the tradition of the Gospel, to which Scripture testifies and which is passed on to the Church through the Church in the power of the Holy Spirit. Thus we understand tradition as actualized in the preaching of the word, in the administration of the sacraments, in the worship of God, in Christian instruction, in theology, in missionary work, and in the testimony that the members of the Church give for Christ through their lives . . ."

experience it as a present event.[25] Only if this pneumatic dimension is taken into consideration, can Christology be seen in its full New Testament breadth, and at the same time the scriptural equivalent of our modern problem of understanding become apparent. In this necessary correction of a Christocentric view that had become too narrowly incarnational the Council was able to learn much from the views of those fathers who stood in the tradition of the Eastern Church.[26]

With regard to the objections by Protestant theologians mentioned above, it seems important that our text sees the function of tradition as wholly related to Scripture. First it guarantees the canon, not simply in terms of an act of salvation history that has taken place in the past, but also in that acceptance of the canon that necessarily involves accepting tradition, and if there is a fundamental rejection of tradition — tradition as the dynamic realization of faith, not as a propositional statement by the Apostles —, the canon also would cease to exist as such, and there would no longer be any reason why this particular selection of writings is to be regarded as "Scripture". Tradition is further described as the process whereby *Litterae* are a *colloquium*. Both these functions of tradition are concerned wholly with Scripture, but at the same time Scripture is placed within the framework of tradition. This will no longer appear strange if we remember that the Montreal Conference, at the suggestion of the Orthodox theologians, thought seriously of replacing *sola scriptura* by *sola traditione*.[27]

Article 9 takes us to the focal point of the controversy, the question of a mutual relation of Scripture and tradition. The text shows clear signs of the firm position taken during the discussion against the idea of "two sources" of revelation. Two objections were made to this idea. The first was that, in a typically

---

[25] Cf. F. Mussner, *Die johanneische Sehweise* (1965); id., "Die johanneischen Parakletsprüche und die apostolische Tradition", *BZ* 5 (1961), pp. 56–70. This idea is firmly expounded by the Bultmann school — partly overshooting the mark — as, for example, when E. Käsemann attacks J. Jeremias, who had made the point that revelation has been concluded by saying: "The proclamation of the Church is not itself revelation. To put it in an extreme way, revelation does not take place on Sundays from 10 to 11 o'clock." Käsemann maintains that the difference between Gospel and kerygma, which has no foundation in the New Testament, avenges itself here, "by separating the testimony, produced by the Spirit, from the gospel of Jesus, and thus ultimately separating the Spirit and Christ. Do not the farewell discourses in St. John's Gospel teach that Christ, Spirit and preaching are one in the promised Paraclete and that the revealing function of the Spirit is manifested in preaching? ... If revelation is limited to the years from 1 to 30 A.D., this creates, in my opinion, a new dogma" (E. Käsemann, *Exegetische Versuche und Besinnungen*, II [1964], pp. 38 f.).

[26] The speech of Archbishop Edelby mentioned in note 8. Cf. also the criticism of the Constitution on Revelation made by N. A. Nissiotis who again takes up this idea: "Report on the Second Vatican Council", *Ecumenical Review* 18 (1966), pp. 190–206, esp. pp. 193 f. The idea of a more pneumatological view found a firm supporter among the *periti* in H. Mühlen, see his *Der Heilige Geist als Person* (2nd ed., 1966).

[27] Cf. E. Dinkler, *loc. cit.*, p. 118 (cf. note 24).

modern spirit of positivism, it identified revelation with its historical presentation and thus falsified the original idea of "sources" in the theological sense in favour of an historical idea of "sources". One could here point to Trent, which still used the term "source" exclusively in the singular to refer solely to the "Gospel", which, as the word of Christ, precedes and is the basis of all historical forms of traditions. The second objection was that the idea of *partim — partim,* which is contained in the idea of the two sources, distributes revelation in a mechanical way between two vessels of revelation that are independent of each other and thus again fails to recognize its true nature, which is not a collection of propositions that can be divided up at will and sheered out between two different compilations, but a living organic unity which can only be present as a whole. Following the Tübingen theologians of the nineteenth century, Geiselmann had thrown into the debate the formula "totum in sacra scriptura — totum in traditione" as an antithesis to "partim — partim" and asked that the relation between Scripture and tradition should not be understood in terms of a mechanical juxtaposition, but as an organic interpenetration.[28]

Both points have been incorporated in the text. It is emphasized that both Scripture and tradition flow from the same sources. However, in order to avoid the clash between the singularist and pluralist understanding of the word *fons,* the word *scaturigo* is used, and then it is possible to continue to speak of the *duo fontes.* In fact, however, the comprehensive theological view of Trent is restored, as compared with the superficial approach of neo-scholastic theology and is even given a deeper dimension, insofar as the idea of *revelatio* behind it, as was shown in Article 7, is conceived more personally and less legalistically than in the text of 1546. Also, the idea of unity, of organic interpenetration is formulated in strong terms both here and again at the end of Article 7 *(unum sine aliis non consistat).*

One may ask, however, whether this was really a gain and whether the Catholic idea of *sola scriptura,* which it intended to make possible in this way (an idea that must now, in this formulation, always be thought of as combined with that of *totum in traditione*), has not been bought at a rather high price. While the first of these two points, the pre-eminence of revelation over the concrete forms in which it is presented, was able to be accepted by Protestant theologians without any difficulty, the firm emphasis on the unity of Scripture and tradition has aroused the strongest opposition and shown that the Protestant idea of *sola scriptura* is less concerned with the material origin of the individual statements of faith as with the problem of the judging function of Scripture in relation to the Church. This emphasis, however, on the indissoluble interpenetration of Scripture and tradition, or (according to Article 10) of Scripture, tradition and teaching office, seems to have excluded this idea even more fully than would a

[28] Geiselmann, *Die Heilige Schrift* . . . (1962), p. 282; id., Das Konzil von Trient über das Verhältnis der Heiligen Schrift und der nicht geschriebenen Traditionen in M. Schmaus, *Die mündliche Überlieferung* (1957), pp. 203 ff.

more mechanistic conception, which still preserves the difference between the individual entities. Thus we have the paradoxical result that today it is precisely those formulations of our Decree which were the product of the attempt to take into account, to the widest possible extent, the points made by the Reformed Churches and were intended to keep the field open for a Catholic idea of *sola scriptura* that have met with the strongest opposition on the part of Protestant theologians and seem to have moved dangerously away from the meaning and intention of the Protestant idea of *sola scriptura*. The critical voices of Cullmann and Reid, mentioned above, have also been directed precisely against the vision of the unity between Scripture and tradition as developed by Articles 9 and 10 of our text.

If we try to make up our minds about this question, the first thing to be noted is that such an end to a dramatic attempt at ecumenical encounter is not of course simply an unhappy mischance or the result of misunderstandings. Rather, it indicates the factual divergence of the starting-points on both sides, which is the origin of the schism in the Church — a schism which can by no means be simply regarded as the result of a misunderstanding.[29] This does not, however, mean that both positions must rigidly confront each other, awaiting the capitulation of the other side. In the first place, it is generally recognized that, despite the fundamental difference that emerges in Articles 8–10, the Constitution as a whole marks a great step towards reconciliation, in that both the fundamental understanding of revelation and faith as well as the actual function of Scripture in the Church are interpreted in a way that largely takes the sting out of a number of controversial issues. K. Barth has rightly pointed out that as against one chapter on tradition, in which in any case tradition is considered entirely in relation to Scripture, there are four chapters which are concerned more or less exclusively with Scripture. Thus even the external structure shows what importance the text accords to Scripture in the life of the Church and the building-up of its faith.[30] Scripture is factually presented as a yardstick, and that is even stated in a well-known passage in Article 21, which says that all the preaching of the Church and the whole Christian religion must be nourished and ruled by Scripture ("nutriatur et regatur oportet"). There is a similar statement in Article 10, which declares that the Church's teaching office does not stand above the word of God, but serves it. (It is true that here the idea of the word of God is not expressly limited to Scripture, so that it can also include tradition and thus is, to some extent, indeterminate.)

As far as the more important objections of Cullmann and Reid are concerned, let us make, briefly, two points.

a) As stated above, we shall have to acknowledge the truth of the criticism that

---

[29] Dinkler stated this correctly, if exaggeratedly *loc. cit.*, p. 117. His treatment of the problem shows that both positions are not as rigid and irreconcilable as one would have thought from the Introduction.

[30] Barth, *loc. cit.*, p. 51 f. (note 4 to Chap. I).

there is, in fact, no explicit mention of the possibility of a distorting tradition and of the place of Scripture as an element within the Church that is *also* critical of tradition, which means that a most important side of the problem of tradition, as shown by the history of the Church — and perhaps the real crux of the question of the *ecclesia semper reformanda* — has been overlooked. In particular a council that saw itself consciously as a council of reform and thus implicitly acknowledged the possibility and reality of distortion in tradition could have achieved here in its thinking a real achievement in theological examination, both of itself and of its own purpose. That this opportunity has been missed can only be regarded as an unfortunate omission.

b) On the other hand, Cullmann's position does not offer any real alternative, and we can see here the inner difficulties of the Protestant position. To contrast Scripture strictly with the Church, as it demands, is not only impossible from the start (as shown above) because the writings gathered together in the Bible are, and can be, a "Bible", "Scripture", only within the Church, but it would also involve the absurdity of making faith the function of historical research and expose it to scientific criteria, the certainty of which cannot go beyond a very moderate form of probability and is on quite another level from that of faith. This kind of position can be basically maintained if we disregard our fundamental hermeneutical situation. On this point the Bultmann school has clarified the situation once and for all in such a way that we can no longer return to the situation that existed before. When Cullmann says that there can be mistakes in exegesis, but that they can be "reduced to a minimum" by means of the historical literary method that we must also regard as a gift of God, then we only have to read what E. Käsemann has said, with biting irony, against the same argument by J. Jeremias. Jeremias had stated that there had been errors in exegesis, but that ever more exact methods would give ever more effective protection against them, so that it would become more and more reliable. If we make ourselves dependent on exegesis, we do not need to fear "that we are setting about a dangerous undertaking to which there may be no end". Käsemann's comment on this is: "On the contrary, it seems to me safer to walk through a minefield blindfold. Is it possible to forget for a second that we are daily concerned with a flood of doubtful, even abstruse ideas in the fields of exegesis, history and theology, and that our scholarship has gradually degenerated into a world-wide guerilla warfare . . .? Can we free ourselves from the *massa perditionis?* Can we pursue our craft in any other way than in the knowledge that those who will carry us out have long been standing outside the door?"[31] How ever much we may *materialiter* agree with Jeremias and Cullmann and disagree with Käsemann and Bultmann, the latter have seen more clearly the point of the basic formal problem. There is no recourse to history against *kerygma,* and (we must add) *kerygma* does not exist in

---

[31] Käsemann, *loc. cit.*, pp. 36f. (cf. note 25).

any other way than as Church *kerygma*. Historical research has done away with the Reformation idea that Scripture itself has one clear meaning, or, rather, that this meaning can only have a relative character, namely within the framework of the *kerygma*. This means that an opposition between Scripture and the Church is ultimately not possible, and this is why we cannot accept as a whole the objections of Cullmann and Reid, however much they contain that is essential and necessary. Moreover, there is no solution without risk and without trust. When Cullmann tells us to put our faith in the exegetes, i.e. in their being led by the Holy Spirit, then we must say that fear of the terrifying possibilities of the teaching office can equally be dispelled only through confidence in the Spirit that guides his Church. This is, however, in no way intended to devalue or remove the place of vigilance.

If we return to our text, we shall see that, following the stress on the unity of Scripture and tradition, an attempt is made to give a definition of the two entities. It is important to note that only Scripture is defined in terms of what it *is:* it is stated that Scripture *is* the word of God consigned to writing. Tradition, however, is described only functionally, in terms of what it *does:* it hands on the word of God, but *is* not the word of God. If this makes clear the nature of Scripture, we can see from the more detailed characterization of tradition, whose task it is to "preserve (it), explain it, and make it more widely known", that it is not productive, but "conservative", ordained to serve as part of something already given.

The next part of the sentence *quo fit . . . hauriat* is the result of a *modus* suggested by 111 fathers. They had wanted, with small variations, something like the following addition: *quo fit ut non omnis doctrina catholica ex (sola) Scriptura (directe) probari queat.*[32] Clearly, the problem of the material completeness of Scripture once more crops up here, the problem that had caused fierce debate in the Council in its first and third sessions. When the question was treated in the Theological Commission on 6 October 1965, a dispute flared up. Mgr. Philips, its secretary, made a conciliatory proposal, which met with no success, so that finally the idea of any addition of this kind was rejected. On 18 October, the President of the Commission, Cardinal Ottaviani, was given a letter written by Cardinal Cicognani at the request of the Pope, which, apart from a few improvements in Chapter III, also stated that it would be desirable *(magis opportunum)* to have an addition at this point. The letter included seven textual suggestions, on which the Secretary of State commented in his letter: "His enim formulis ii etiam assensum ac suffragium praestaturi esse censentur, qui in maiore Concilii parte pollent." After careful deliberation the Council decided on the third of the suggested formulations, which was probably the work of C. Colombo. It now stands in the text. From the ecumenical point of view there can be no objections

---

[32] *Expensio modorum,* pp. 23 ff. (modus 40) (cf. note 14).

o it. H. Ott says: "Moreover, it is surely also true for a Protestant who has not forgotten the basis of the Reformation that we do not acquire certainty about God's revelation only from Scripture, but also through preaching and the inner testimony of the Holy Spirit."[33] Actually, there would have been nothing to object to in the text of the 111 fathers, for no one is seriously able to maintain that there is a proof in Scripture for every Catholic doctrine. The ecumenical difficulties of the text lie, as we have seen, in quite different points. Emotions had become attached to a point where they were completely superfluous. Furthermore, when one analyses this text calmly, it appears as a positive contribution towards the clarification of the problem of tradition. The function of tradition is seen here as a making certain of the truth, i.e. it belongs in the formal and gnoseological sphere — and, in fact, this is the sphere in which the significance of tradition is to be sought.

More difficulties for ecumenism, however, are presented by the last sentence, which repeats the formula of Trent, according to which Scripture and tradition are to be accepted and revered *pari pietatis affectu ac reverentia*. This phrase had already been discussed at Trent with some warmth. Probably the only reason why it was accepted then was that, handed down through the *Decree of Gratian* (D XI c 5), it was considered to be a text of Basil's, to whom it does go back in substance.[34] In Basil, of course, the statement refers to the εὐσέβεια, to the realization of faith in its affirmation and the worship of God, not to a doctrine distinct from this. This was also the starting-point for the fathers at Trent, who were primarily concerned with the sacredness of the canon of the Mass, as the centre of the *consuetudo ecclesiae*. In the present Council the text was not reconsidered. It was, for a minority, a symbol of the fidelity to Trent, to the totality of the Church's faith. For this reason it was inevitable that those attempts undertaken at the third session of the Council to achieve a progressive revision of what had been said at Trent, were doomed to failure. But this also allows us to state precisely what the text means in the context of the Constitution. It is not a total

---

[33] In Hampe's *Die Autorität,* pp. 173 f.

[34] Cf. Bévenot, *loc. cit.*, p. 336 (cf. note 7 to the Introduction). The text in Basil reads:

Τῶν ἐν τῇ ἐκκλησίᾳ πεφυλαγμένων
δογμάτων καὶ κηρυγμάτων τὰ μὲν ἐκ τῆς
ἐγγράφου διδασκαλίας ἔχομεν, τὰ δὲ ἐκ
τῆς τῶν ἀποστόλων παραδόσεως
διαδοθέντα ἡμῖν ἐν μυστηρίῳ
παρεδεξάμεθα· ἅπερ ἀμφότερα τὴν
αὐτὴν ἰσχὺν ἔχει πρὸς τὴν εὐσέβειαν

(*De Spiritu Sancto,* XXVII, 66: *PG,* XXXII, 188).

In Gratian we read in D 11 c 5: "Inviolabilis est consuetudo, quae nec humanis legibus nec sacris canonibus obviare constat." Basil is quoted as *auctoritas* in the following: "Ecclesiasticarum institutionum quasdam scripturis, quasdam vero apostolica traditione per successiones in ministerio confirmatas accepimus; quasdam vero consuetudine roboratas approbavit usus, quibus par ritus et idem utrisque pietatis debetur affectus . . ."

description of the relationship between Scripture and tradition, but simply a profession of faith in the unassailability of dogma, the outward form of the Church's faith. Certainly, ecumenically speaking, a line has been drawn here, but it is not different from the one that is presented by the different starting-points of the contesting parties, which we have come up against several times in the foregoing.

Article 10. The last section of Chapter II describes the relation of the Church to Scripture and tradition as the heritage which has been entrusted to it. It first makes the point that the preservation and active realization of the word is the business of the whole people of God, not merely of the hierarchy. The ecclesial nature of the word, on which this idea is based, is therefore not simply a question which concerns the teaching office, but embraces the whole community of the faithful. If one compares the text with the corresponding section of the encyclical *Humani Generis* (*DS* 3886), the progress that has been made is clear. The latter had stated, in a strictly antithetical way, that the divine saviour had "entrusted his word neither to the individual believers, nor to the theologians as such for its authentic explanation, but solely to the teaching office". This idea of *solo magisterio* is taken up here in the next paragraph, but the context makes it clear that the function of authentic interpretation which is restricted to the teaching office is a specific service that does not embrace the whole of the way in which the word is present, and in which it performs an irreplaceable function precisely for the whole Church, the bishops and the laity together. Thus this short section presents us also with an important achievement of a renewed theology of the laity, seen here in connection with the theology of the word and making clear not merely the secular function, but also the truly ecclesial and spiritual function of the layman. It is to be regarded as a fortunate decision of the Council that, in emphasizing the share of the laity in the work of keeping the word pure, it did not become involved with the theory of the consensus of faith, which, in connection with the dogmas of 1854 and 1950, resulted in the acceptance of the view that the whole Church has a share in the making manifest of the word.[35] For there is still too much that needs clarification in this theory before it can be regarded as a safe expression of this particular point. It is difficult here to regard entirely as unjustified the doubts of the Tübingen dogmatic theologian J. E. Kuhn, who feared that the theory of the consensus of faith would favour arbitrary and secondary traditions.[36] The function of the total Church lies rather, as history teaches, in the idea of *perseverat,* to which the text gives a central place: in the power of persistence, which recognizes as such the false innovation that is contrary to faith and condemns it, while holding firmly, on the other hand, to the original truth.

The essential contents of the second paragraph of Article 10 were already

[35] Cf. the bibliography mentioned in the Introduction, note 4.
[36] Cf. Geiselmann, *Das Konzil von Trient über das Verhältnis* . . ., pp. 201 f. (cf. note 28).

mentioned when we dealt with Article 9. Again a comparison with the previous text from *Humani Generis* (*DS* 3886), which underlies it, shows the progressive nature of the revision that the Council has carried out here.[37] For the first time a text of the teaching office expressly points out the subordination of the teaching office to the word, i.e. its function as a servant. One can say, it is true, that there could never have been any serious doubt that this was in fact the case. Nevertheless the actual procedure often tended somewhat to obscure this order of things, though it had always been acknowledged in principle. Thus the risk of a false orientation cannot be dismissed when *Humani Generis* (which incidentally quotes Pius IX on the point) declares that it is obviously wrong to seek to clarify what is clear by the help of what is obscure — which means in the context that it is not the teaching office that can be clarified by Scripture, but only, on the contrary, Scripture by the teaching office. This is then developed to the point at which the task of theology is described as that of showing how what the teaching office has established is contained in the sources — "and that precisely in the sense in which it has been defined". One can hardly deny that the point of view which sees only Scripture as what is unclear, but the teaching office as what is clear, is a very limited one and that to reduce the task of theology to the proof of the presence of the statements of the teaching office in the sources is to threaten the primacy of the sources which, (were one to continue logically in this direction) would ultimately destroy the serving character of the teaching office.[38] When seen against this background, the explicit emphasis on the ministerial function of the teaching office must be welcomed as warmly as the statement that its primary service is to listen, that it must constantly take up an attitude of openness towards the sources, which it has continually to consult and consider, in order to be able to interpret them truly and preserve them — not in the sense of "taking them into custody" (to which sometimes the activity of the teaching office in the past may have tended), but as a faithful servant who wards off attempts at foreign domination and defends the dominion of the word of God both against modernism and against traditionalism. At the same time the contrast between the "listening" and the "teaching" Church is thus reduced to its true measure: in the last analysis the whole Church listens, and, *vice versa,* the whole Church shares in the upholding of true teaching.

The last paragraph of the text is a summing-up, in that it gives expression to the reciprocal and inseparable functional relationship of Scripture, tradition, and the Church's teaching office, none of which could be conceived independently of the other. The objections to this position, as well as their insurmountability, have probably been pointed out adequately in what was said about Article 9. It is true that Scripture simply cannot be conceived separately from tradition, nor

---

[37] Cf. Latourelle, *La Révélation,* p. 34.

[38] Cf. J. Ratzinger, "Das Problem der Mariologie", *Theologische Revue* 61 (1965), pp. 73–82, and on this point, pp. 80 ff., which discusses J. A. de Aldama, *De quaestione mariali in hodierna vita Ecclesiae* (1964), pp. 77–99.

tradition separately from the Church, nor the latter separately from either of the two others, without the specific function of these three entities being thereby called into question. This has also been made sufficiently clear in the foregoing. Again the whole is placed within the pneumatological context, which avoids the danger of being seen in terms of a merely ecclesiastical functionalism. The last clause brings in the idea of the "saving power of the word" and thus again contributes an important element to a theology of the word, which, in the dialogal conception of the Constitution of necessity no longer appears merely as a preliminary condition for the actual sacramental reality of salvation, but itself as the dialogue of salvation.[39]

[39] This idea was dominant in the schema prepared by the Secretariat for Christian Unity called *Decreti pastoralis De Verbo Dei* (supplementary Text II, according to A. Grillmeier's classification). Of the growing number of Catholic attempts at a theology of the word see H. Volk, *Zur Theologie des Wortes Gottes* (1962); O. Semmelroth, *Wirkendes Wort* (1962); L. Scheffczyk, *Von der Heilsmacht des Wortes* (1966).

The Divine Inspiration and the Interpretation of Sacred Scripture

by
Alois Grillmeier

PART ONE

The growth of the text and of the theological statement of Chapter III of the Constitution

Chapter III of the Constitution gives a short account of the Church's doctrine on the inspiration of Scripture, its truth (inerrancy) and the principles of Catholic exegesis. In the course of the growth of the text as a whole, the position, title and text of this chapter underwent important changes. At a cursory glance they may seem unimportant; but in their development they reveal a particular intention of the Council that cannot be found directly in the actual words of the text. Hence it is essential to indicate the different stages of the growth of the text in order to have an historical basis for the interpretation of its final form.

I. The inspiration and inerrancy of Scripture

1. The teaching on Scripture in Form C (1962)

The text of Chapter III presented to the Council fathers in the first session was, like the previous Forms A and B, strongly influenced by the attitude of the whole schema. Hence the twin sources of revelation were also a major issue in the preceding Chapter II, "De Scripturae Inspiratione, Inerrantia et Compositione litteraria". The introductory Article 7 shows this: "Praeterquam viva Prophetarum et Apostolorum voce, Deus in Scripturis quoque sanctis Veteris ac Novi Testamenti, quae alterum ac praeclarum constituunt supernae revelationis fontem, verbum suum hominibus tradere et accuratius conservari voluit. Haec est Scriptura 'divinitus inspirata' (2 Tim 3:16), ab Apostolis catholicae Ecclesiae tradita atque in sacro canone rite agnita et recepta, ad perpetuum eiusdem Ecclesiae usum, ut munus suum adimpleat docendi, ad christianae vitae moderamen et ad omnium hominum salutem."

It is right that two different points are made about revelation: 1) its emergence into history through the *viva vox* of the prophets and apostles, with the preaching, person and life of Christ as the climax and completion of this sequence of events; 2) Scripture as a way of transmitting God's word to men and of preserving it in a special way *(accuratius conservari)*. It is not concerned with "Scripture and tradition" which was the kernel of the draft of 1962. This Form C then goes on to give a fairly detailed account of the nature and definition of inspiration (Article 8) of God as the only *auctor primarius* and the large number of human authors, both of the whole of Scripture and even of individual books (Article 9). But they all function as servants chosen by the Holy Spirit to write down God's word *(ministri divini verbi scribendi, a Spiritu Sancto assumpti)* — a formulation which would have conformed well to the gradually emerging intentions of the Council, but was not taken up. It is of special interest to look at the version of the teaching on the inerrancy of Scripture, as it is set out in the former Article 12:[1]

"Ex hac divinae Inspirationis extensione ad omnia, directe et necessario sequitur immunitas absoluta ab errore totius Sacrae Scripturae. Antiqua enim et constanti Ecclesiae fide edocemur nefas omnino esse concedere sacrum ipsum errasse scriptorem, cum divina Inspiratio per se ipsam tam necessario excludat et respuat errorem omnem in qualibet re religiosa vel profana, quam necessarium est Deum summam Veritatem, nullius omnino erroris auctorem esse."[2]

Thus the "absolute inerrancy" of Scripture is stated here in very strong terms, and is applied to the whole range of religious and secular statements, being presented as the ancient and constant conviction of the Church. With this text, in contrast to the final form of the Constitution, the question of the development of teaching on inerrancy at Vatican II must begin. It is only in this way that one can estimate the difficulty of the struggle for a purified conception of inspiration and inerrancy and see what has been actually achieved. We can see how important the problem of inerrancy and the solution indicated is for the detailed Chapter II (Form C), from the following Article 13 and its title, "The Interpretation of *Inerrancy*" (Quomodo *inerrantia* diiudicanda sit). The question of inerrancy thus becomes the primary theme also of the section in which the principles of the interpretation of Scripture are to be set out. Thus the rules of exegesis are to serve in the defence of the absolute inerrancy of Scripture: "Haec tamen *inerrantia* diiudicanda est ex modo quo *veritas* in libro sacro attingitur." "Truth" does not mean the same thing here as in the final text. The actual background to this is the problem of "truth in secular matters", as it was posed in the 19th century. In order to answer the objections against the inerrancy of Scripture in

---

[1] Article 10 of Form C of the text dealt with the "Inspiratio personalis hagiographi et communitas"; Article 11: *De extensione Inspirationis*.

[2] There is a reference in note 7 to Pius XII's *Divino afflante: EB*, 539, which again quotes Leo XIII's *Providentissimus Deus* (*EB,* 124). Other references for the doctrine of inerrancy are: *EB,* 44, 46, 125, 420, 463. As against these papal texts the teaching on inerrancy in Schema C is obviously more strictly formulated.

his area hermeneutical rules are developed, in a narrow interpretation of the encyclical *Divino afflante* (*EB* 560). We shall have to return to the aim of the hermeneutics of this encyclical. The schema of 1962 presents, on this point, very general hermeneutical rules: the general character of a book, on which the Church has to make judgment in case of doubt; the particular circumstances of the time in which the hagiographers were writing; and contemporary forms of thought and behaviour are named as ways of defending the truth of Scripture. We then return to the theme of inerrancy, and the point is made that whatever human forms of expression became the garment of the divine word, they damage the inerrancy of Scripture as lightly as similar forms of expression in daily life, that are hardly considered to be a falsification of, or hindrance to, intercourse between human beings. This mantling in human terms of the divine word of revelation is then (as in *Divino afflante*) in Article 14 likened to the "condescension" of the Logos in the incarnation. As in the incarnate Word sin and ignorance were excluded, despite all the humbling of the Godhead, so all error (error in secular matters is what is chiefly meant) was avoided when divine revelation passed into the written human word. Later we shall have to ask, as it was asked at the Conciliar discussion, what is the value of this kind of parallel, already found in *Divino afflante*.

Many formulations and motifs of this text of 1962, which covers three folio pages, will continue into the final stages of the Constitution. As a whole it was already abandoned by the *Commissio mixta* (1962–63), even though there was no completely new orientation. In any case the highly defensive and strict tone of the long Chapter II of 1962 was not likely to provide a solution to the problems of exegetes, theologians and believers generally. Rather, the tension is increased to the extreme: on the one hand we have the insistence on the absolute inerrancy of all parts of Scripture, even the most insignificant, in its religious and secular statements, and on the other the knowledge of the many human, historical and geographical limitations of the written word! Does it still have any meaning to speak of the "humanity" of the word of God if inerrancy is interpreted in such narrow way? The parallel drawn in Article 14 between Scripture and the incarnation tempts one when looking at the history of Christology to speak of a "monophysite" doctrine of inerrancy. The "humanity" of God's word in Scripture is not understood at a deep enough level. With this kind of interpretation of inerrancy it risks being absorbed by the divine.

It was the Council's concern not to shut doors too soon, but to enable a solution to be reached that would preserve the essential traditional nature of the doctrine of inerrancy and at the same time ensure that the exegetes, theologians and faithful would not have to examine their consciences. The search for a new concept and formula was unfortunately affected by the pressure of time from which the Council suffered, particularly from the third session on. During the second session no work had been done on the schema — probably because of a certain anxiety about once more taking up the thorny problem of Scripture and tradition, and it was a surprise for everybody when at the end of the second session Paul VI put the schema on Revelation on the agenda of the third session. This greatly increased the pressure on the Theological Commission for the next two years. For it had not only the long schema on the Church to deal with, but also — together with the Commission for the Lay Apostolate — the Pastoral Constitution on The Church in the Modern World. Before we consider the new orientation that came at the beginning of 1964, we must consider the results achieved by the Mixed Commission on the schema on Revelation set up by Pope John.

2. Form D (Spring 1963)

The new version of the text combined the long Articles 7 — 12 of the C version in a short Article 11 which dealt with Scripture as the mediator of revelation, its inspiration and inerrancy. It was preceded by a fuller account of the reality of revelation and its transmission in the Church (Introduction and Chapter 1). We can detect here the influence of the Secretariat for Christian Unity. Whereas Form C still continues to work on the basis of the *distinction* between the "two sources", now, without failing to see the different nature and function of Scripture and tradition, the Article emphasizes their inter-relationship in the transmission of revelation (Articles 8 — 10). With the new orientation of the Constitution, the chapter on Scripture also acquired a new emphasis. Mention of inerrancy was omitted from the title, and only the inspiration of Scripture and its interpretation were named. These two themes, stressed in this way, were now more clearly distinguished from each other. Article 11 was concerned with inspiration and inerrancy *(inerrantia)*, and Article 12 with the principles of the interpretation of Scripture. The arrangement and numeration of these articles was to remain the same from now on, although a Chapter III emerged from Chapter II. The inerrancy of Scripture was no longer presented as the leading motif of all hermeneutical rules. Instead the positive point emerged that we should "see clearly what God wanted to communicate to us" (ut pateat quamnam *veritatem* nobis communicare voluerit) (Article 12:1).

Because, for the sake of harmony, it had been agreed to avoid anything that would decide the question of the "material sufficiency of Scripture" in a positive or negative sense, the formulation of the role of Scripture in the transmission of revelation was made particularly difficult. It became obvious here also that there was no deep understanding of the relationship between Scripture and tradition. Thus the difficulty was circumnavigated by silence and the avoidance of positive statements, which certainly was not to the benefit of the whole. In contrast to the lengthy formulations of 1962 the inerrancy of Scripture was now stated quite briefly in traditional language.[3] The statements on the principles of the inter-

---

[3] Form D, Article 11, 2: "Cum ergo totius Scripturae Deus principalis auctor affirmetur et sit inde totam Scripturam divinitus inspiratam ab omni prorsus errore immunem esse consequitur."

pretation of Scripture were not yet inspired by the total theme of the Constitution (revelation and its presence in the word). In short, neither text D nor the criticism that followed the second session augured well for a new version of the teaching on Scripture. In any case, many fathers found that Form D said less than the corresponding sections of *Divino afflante* and *Humani generis*.

3. Form E (July 1964)

Given the predominance of the theme of the Church at the Council, in the Theological Commission and in theological publications during the Council, work on the schema on Revelation could not proceed with the desirable speed. Above all there was an absence of enlightening theological writing on inspiration, inerrancy and biblical hermeneutics. This was due to the internal Catholic attacks on modern exegesis during the Council. It seemed wiser to remain silent than to speak. Thus new proposals on the schema on Revelation, and especially for the chapter on Scripture, came only with some hesitancy. One thing had been shown: the account of inspiration was now less scholastic and "apersonal" than in Form D (1963). The hagiographer was no longer described as an "instrument", and God no longer as the *"principalis* auctor", but simply as *auctor*. This was formulated in such a way that a true causality was ascribed to God, which embraced the hagiographers too, but that the activity of the writer was emphasized more. Nevertheless, God achieves everything with man. At the same time everything that belongs to the *auctor litterarius*[4] can be sought in the sacred writer. It is not explained how this co-operation of the genuine influence of God and the activity of the sacred writer comes about. The text does not go into any psychology of inspiration. The main thing was to be the *theological* interpretation. This also required that the idea should be briefly expressed that inspiration does not mean the exclusion of human capacities, neither of all of them taken together, not of single ones. Hence in this form of the text it was expressly stated: "In sacris vero libris conficiendis Deus homines elegit, quos *omnibus* (italics mine) facultatibus ac viribus suis utentes adhibuit, ut Ipso in illis et per illos agente ea

---

[4] Incidentally, no Church document requires that God should be described as the *auctor "littera-rius"* in the narrower sense. J. Beumer, in *Die katholische Inspirationslehre zwischen Vatikanum I und II* (1966), p. 86, note 11, expresses doubts about this statement, as also about the different translation of *auctor* in Article 11: God is described as the "originator", and the sacred writers as the true "authors". The application of one and the same idea *auctor* to the sacred writers and to God is, of course, an analogy. With the tradition of the Church, the Council wants to accept the idea of a true influence of God on the sacred writers. At the same time, however, it is said that God chooses men to "compose" the sacred books, men who are to bring their own capacities and powers to this task — and thus become "genuine authors" of the books. Thus the analogy compels one not to apply the German expression "Verfasser" (author), which has a strictly limited meaning, to God. If the same word is to be used to translate *auctor,* then the German word "Urheber" is better (like the French *auteur*). In German we speak of *Urheberrechten* ("copyright", lit. "the rights of the originator"), but not of the "Urheber" ("originator") of a book.

omnia eaque sola, quae Ipse vellet, scripta traderent." These words about "the use of *all* capabilities and powers" could be understood also as being *exhaustive* in a concrete case. That could not, and cannot, be proved. That is why the word *omnibus* was omitted. Instead in Forms F and G it was again emphasized: ". . . quae Ipse vellet ut *veri auctores* traderent." What the formula just discussed really meant was now stated more clearly: inspiration does not mean the exclusion, repression or replacement of the human activity of the hagiographers. Any memory of old theories of verbal inspiration was to be omitted, and hence any form of an impersonal, mechanistic interpretation of the origin of Scripture.

The formulation of inerrancy also had a more positive form: ". . . Scripturae libri integri cum omnibus suis partibus veritatem sine ullo errore docere profitendi sunt" (Form E, Article 11, Conclusion). The formula was actually pleonastic or even a tautology. Whoever teaches truth is free from error, and whoever teaches without error offers truth. Here, as so often in the growth of the conciliar texts, a new positive suggestion was included and combined with the formula hitherto used, which was generally *in possessione,* without establishing complete unity. But this little word *veritas* that intruded here proved to be a living cell that continued to grow. But what did it mean? Only "religious" or even "secular" truth, to use the language of the 1962 schema? This was the real problem that now had to be taken up with full force both inside and outside the conciliar discussion. This did not happen, and new suggestions for the solution of the inerrancy question, as modern research posed it, could be made only hesitantly. The development of Article 12 was also to contribute something to this question.

4. Form F

Form F was worked out in the third session of the Council. The first change that strikes us is in the title of Article 11: "Statuitur factum inspirationis et *veritatis* S Scripturae." *Inerrantia* is replaced by the positive term *veritas,* which is notably extended in the text. In the course of the discussion on the schema in the autumn of 1964, various fathers from the Eastern and the Western Churches made important speeches on the necessity of an interpretation of the inerrancy of Scripture that would be in harmony with the latest findings of exegesis. It was variously pointed out that the doctrine of inerrancy received its particular and narrower formulation in the 19th century, at a time when the means of secular historical research and criticism were used to investigate the secular historical accuracy of Scripture, and this was more or less denied — which had inevitable consequences for its theological validity. The teaching office of the Church sought to concentrate its defence at the point of immediate attack: i.e. to defend the inerrancy of Scripture even in the *veritates profanae*[5] with the ultimate intention of

[5] Cf. P. Grelot, *La Bible Parole de Dieu* (1965), pp. 98–101; pp. 210–13; p. 99: "Here again, critical rationalism and traditionalist apologetics, though starting from opposite premisses, found themselves on common ground."

generally defending the claim of the Bible and of Christianity to be revelation. To defend scriptural inerrancy in this sphere of secular truths various theories[6] were employed which sought to prove the absolute inerrancy of Scripture on the basis of these conditions and attitudes. Because of the apologetical viewpoint from which they started, they were in danger of producing a narrowness and a false accentuation[7] in the doctrine of inerrancy. Also in the area of the interpretation of Scripture and the rules pertaining to this we can see a similar phenomenon, which the Council observed in different spheres of theology and endeavoured to nullify: namely, the tendency to an apologetical isolation and the claim to absolutism of a partial view. With this kind of motivation for the defence of the inerrancy of Scripture in the 19th and the beginning of the 20th centuries, there was a weakening of the awareness that Scripture as the inspired, written word of God is supposed above all to serve the preservation and expansion of the saving revelation and reality given through Christ in the world. Of course it was always realized that this was the real purpose of Scripture. In the question of inerrancy, however, the emphasis was placed on the one-sided and isolated accentuation of the *veritates profanae*. This tended to create uncertainty rather than a joyful confidence that God's truth and salvation remain present in the world in an unfalsified and permanent form — namely through the inspired word. It was necessary to reawaken this awareness. The doctrine of inerrancy needed its own centre and the right accentuation.

In this respect the most important contribution was undoubtedly the speech by Cardinal König on 2 October 1964. Several other fathers who took part in the discussion from 2 to 6 October either verbally or in writing came back to this point. The Cardinal first of all pointed out the new situation that exists in relation to the question of inerrancy. As a result of intensive Oriental studies our picture of the *veritas historica* and the *fides historica* of Scripture has been clarified. Many of the 19th century objections to the Old Testament in particular and its reliability as an account of historical fact are now irrelevant. But Oriental studies have also produced another finding: ". . . laudata scientia rerum orientalium insuper demonstrat in Bibliis Sacris notitias historicas et notitias scientiae naturalis a veritate quandoque deficere." Thus Cardinal König admitted that not all the difficulties could be solved. On the contrary, in certain cases they have an urgency that is borne out by scientific research. His speech mentioned a few examples: according to Mk 2:26 David had entered the house of God under the high priest Abiathar and eaten the bread of the Presence. In fact, however, according to 1 Sam 21:1 ff. it was not under Abiathar, but under his father Abimelech. In Mt 27:9 we read that in the fate of Judas a prophecy of Jeremiah was fulfilled. In fact it is Zech 11:12f. that is quoted. In Dan 1:1 we

---

[6] *Ibid.,* pp. 99f.

[7] *Ibid.,* p. 96: "The task of defending the Bible against the rationalists who claim to discover errors in it is not without dangers, for there is a risk of enclosing the apologist within the narrow confines of a problem, whereas the first thing he ought to do is to be critical of this limitation . . ."

read that King Nebuchadnezzar besieged Jerusalem in the third year of King Jehoiakim, i.e. 607 B.C., but from the authentic chronicle of King Nebuchadnezzar that has been discovered we know that the siege can only have taken place three years later.[8] Other geographical and chronological points could be quoted in this connection.

The fact that this speech could be held in a plenary session without any protest being made is surely significant. It shows that the total and absolute inclusion of the *veritates profanae,* as they are called, under the inerrancy of Scripture cannot yet be regarded as definitively decided by the Church's teaching office. Cardinal König chose a cautious phrase in order to describe the situation: "Notitias historicas et notitias scientiae naturalis a veritate quandoque deficere." Thus he indicates a psychological and theological way of coping with this situation:

1) In the question of inerrancy we should speak sincerely, unambiguously and directly (sincere et sine ambiguitate loquendum est, non artificiose nec cum timore). This is an admonition which the Melkite Archbishop of Edessa, N. Edelby, also made in the course of the discussion on 5 October 1964. He spoke of the *timiditas* which dominated the Western Church in this field. The Eastern Churches as well as the young Churches of Africa and Asia did not have these anxieties. "Pro tota autem Ecclesia, finis ponendus est huic obsessioni, ut denuo ingrediamur totalitatem Mysterii Ecclesiae!" The fact that the Bible is set within the context of history and of what was possible at the time is actually too profoundly realized for one to be able to deduce from the fact of inspiration as such that the sacred writers were absolutely independent of the limitations of their statements because of the time in which they were living. By adopting an unhistorical attitude in these matters one does not, for Cardinal König, save the authority of Scripture, one only makes exegesis incredible. For the modern mind this kind of *deficere a veritate* in historical and scientific questions in no way endangers the authority of Scripture.

2) In all this, from a theological point of view, we can see only the *condescensio Dei,* as brought out in Article 13. God takes the human author with all his weaknesses and his failures and still achieves his aim: namely, of teaching us the "truth" with which the whole Constitution is concerned, the truth of revelation or salvation. Thus Cardinal König implicitly gives up that premise that comes from the aprioristic and unhistorical thinking that has dominated teaching on inerrancy since the age of the Fathers: if one admits that a sacred writer has made a mistake, then one is necessarily admitting that God has made a mistake with the human author. The actual aim of inspiration allows us to find a better solution: one can still maintain the true influence of God on the human authors without making him responsible for their weaknesses. These relate only to the

[8] See D. J. Wiseman, *Chronicles of Chaldaean Kings (626–656 B. C.) in the British Museum* (1956) pp. 70–71, lines 21–23. It is the second year of the reign of Nebuchadnezzar (21 April 603–19 May 602) and the sixth year of the reign of Jehoiakim. The text of the chronicle has been damaged here but is vouched for in pp. 64–65 ff. — See also *The Interpreter's Bible* (1956), pp. 360 f.

form or the outer garment of the Gospel, and not the latter itself, however much the two might be inwardly connected — indeed, without this genuine humanity, with all its limitations, Scripture would appear like a foreign body in our world. But God speaks to us in this way, in our language, from out of our midst.

A number of Council fathers followed the example of Cardinal König and refer to him as an authority: others, admittedly in the minority, produced the traditional statements, without, however, dealing with the new points raised by Cardinal König. On 5 October 1964 Cardinal Meyer of Chicago called for both a more profound doctrine of inspiration and, within the framework of the teaching on the word of God presented in the Constitution, a subtler understanding of inerrancy, which went "beyond the teaching of the encyclicals *Providentissimus Deus* and *Spiritus Paraclitus*": "Etenim facilius intelligemus, quomodo divina revelatio componi possit cum humanis debilitatibus, et limitationibus, in instrumento humano, sicut constat ex haud paucis exemplis ipsius Scripturae ad quae etiam Em. Card. Koenig ultima sessione se retulit."

Archbishop João J. da Mota e Albuquerque von S. Luís do Maranhão of Brazil made the same point (in writing). He said that one must detach oneself from a polemical doctrine of inerrancy directed against the rationalists and speak of the "truth" of Scripture, which he sees under the aspect of salvation or revelation: "Haec mutatio (namely of replacing *inerrantia* in the text with *veritas*) proponitur ut clarius ostendatur id quod sancitur charismate inspirationis reapse esse verbum Dei, quod et in quantum hominibus communicat divinam revelationem. Ceteroquin, sic resumeretur doctrina Concilii Vaticani I, quod dixit libros sacros continere 'revelationem sine errore' (*D* 1789): in hac formula, vox 'error' clare contraponitur 'revelationi', et non qualicumque veritati exactae qualis indagatur a peritis historiae profanae vel ab iis qui scientiis positivis incumbunt." The Council father closes his remarks on Article 11 of the Constitution with the words: "Criterium veritatis Sacrae Scripturae non est illa accurata adaequatio cum factis praeteritis, quam periti scientia historicae profanae obtinere conantur; sed est intentio auctoris inspirati, quae semper aliquo modo se refert ad revelationem salutis."

The Archbishop of Lubumbashi (formerly Elisabethville) in the Congo, J. F. Cornelis, referred even more decisively to Cardinal König in a written criticism on all the articles of the Constitution: "In sua enim ad Patres oratione diei 2. oct., Em.mus Card. Koenig iure ostendit et contendit S. Scripturam errores de facto *exhibere*. Verum quidem est, quod Scriptura illos errores *non docet*. Aliis verbis: si textus sacer materialiter consideratur, adsunt errores, si vero intentio, qua libri sacri conscripti sunt, conspicitur, errores non docentur ... Expressio 'sine ullo errore' non est tantum mere negativa, sed etiam ambigua, ut idem Em.mus orator ostendit. Multum iuvaret rem proponi modo claro et positivo."

The president of the Colombian Bishops' Conference, Archbishop Aníbal

Muñoz Duque, called for a more open and more fundamental account of the doctrine of inerrancy in his written statement on the *schema:* "Ex una parte principium generale inerrantiae asserendum est; ex alia parte eius elaboratio theologica aperta debet manere, ut ex studio positivo Sacrae Scripturae perficiatur; valde enim periculosum est hoc principium evolvere *methodo pure deductiva* (italics mine), ignorata prorsus realitate biblica. Ideo proponitur formula certissima et indiscussa et quidem ex Concilio Vaticano I desumpta. Insuper, ex evolutione semantica, terminus 'error' hodie late patet, et si non accurate definiatur, eius indiscriminatus usus grave scandalum generare potest."

The written statement by the Bishop of Bilbao, P. Gúrpide Beope, made a similar point: ". . . Inspirationem divinam promovere positive Opus salvificum, ducere ad sanctitatem et veritatem. Ponimus hic iterum observationem quam fecimus Schemati De Revelatione in eius secunda forma: Inerrantia non est nisi una, et quidem in forma negativa expressa, inter proprietates ex divinae Inspirationis natura promanantes; finis vero primarius Spiritus Sancti inspirantis, nempe supernaturalis hominum salus, per veritatem et sanctitatem divinam Sacris Litteris communicatas directe intenditur."

Finally, we may mention the written statement by Alberto Devoto, Bishop of Goya in the Argentine: "Affirmatio inerrantiae Sacrae Scripturae aliis verbis fieri debet (as in Form D, of July 1964). Proponitur haec formula: Cum ergo omne id quod auctor inspiratus sive hagiographus dicit retineri debeat dictum a Spiritu Sancto eo modo quo ab hagiographo dictum est, inde libri Sacrae Scripturae veritatem exhibere dicendi sunt in omnibus suis partibus, diversimode tamen pro qualitate affirmationis hagiographi. Ratio est quia textus prout iacet non videtur considerasse diversum valorem veritatis inesse diversis Sacrae Scripturae sententiis, iuxta communem exegetarum doctrinam."

If we examine the speeches given in the assembly from 2 to 6 October 1964, or the written submissions, we discover that there were actually two Council fathers who saw no reason to alter the doctrine of inerrancy as hitherto expounded, especially in *Providentissimus Deus* and *Spiritus Paraclitus*. E. Martínez, Bishop of Zamora in Spain, who made his remarks first in writing and then, on 6 October 1964, verbally, rejected, on the well-known traditional grounds, any possibility of error, for it would then fall back on God! Bishop F. J. Whealon, in a written submission, admitted the difficulties of scriptural inerrancy, but considered that they could all be solved in the course of time: "Revera adsunt difficultates praesertim in rebus historiae, sed Spiritu Sancto adiuvante studium et labor et oratio exegetarum etiam has difficultates in futurum solvent."

This view revealed a lack of insight into the problems and methods of exegetical research. It is no solution to comfort oneself with the thought of the future. The overwhelming majority of the fathers who expressed themselves on the question were, on the contrary, in favour of the Council's allowing a more open treatment of the question, in the spirit of the speech by Cardinal König, or even itself presenting in its formulations a new version of the doctrine of inerrancy that would correspond to this new situation, the state of research in relation to the *veritates profanae* in Scripture, and a more profound theology of revelation and inspiration. We have quoted these points made by the Council fathers in some detail, for we must be aware of this background if we are to understand the final formulation of the nature of the truth of Scripture. In accordance with the legitimate method of the interpretation of conciliar documents in general, here also the whole discussion in the Council and the Theological Commission must be used as sources for a better understanding. Moreover we must also consider the vote on the *modi* of 22 September 1965. But before we go into that, we must give a short account of the fate of Article 11 in the autumn of 1964.

The new form of the text (F) contained two changes. First, it was to be made clearer (from the object) that the "truth" which Scripture "teaches without any error" (Form E) is not only the *veritates profanae* and truth in the philosophical sense (as the *adaequatio intellectus ad rem*), but is truth in the fullness of the scriptural idea,[9] i.e. primarily the truth of revelation, which is to say the full self-communication of God, his truthfulness and fidelity, but also the life of men. That was why the wish was repeatedly expressed that this rich concept of truth should be expressed, as against the intellectualistic formulation of the defensive doctrine of inerrancy of the nineteenth and early twentieth centuries. Many fathers, as we have seen, wanted to make this clearer by saying "veritatem seu revelationem", referring to Vatican I.[10] Others had pointed out the parallel between the infallibility of the teaching office and the inerrancy of Scripture. God had given the Church the guarantee of infallibility only in questions of faith and morals, i.e. in relation to salvation in Christ. The same thing was true of the inerrancy of Scripture. Its significance lay in the fact that the truth of revelation and salvation was written down and thus handed down untouched to the men of all ages. This was in the spirit of Chapter II of the Constitution, which speaks of the transmission *(transmissio)* of revelation in Scripture and tradition (cf. also Chapter VI, Article 21). We can see clearly that the old account of inerrancy did not fit in with the general trend of the whole Constitution. Thus the basic idea of Chapter II was to be further developed. This was attempted in a new formulation on the inerrancy of Scripture: "Therefore, since everything asserted by the inspired authors or sacred writers must be held to be asserted by the Holy Spirit, it follows that the books of Scripture must be acknowledged as teaching firmly, faithfully,

---

[9] Cf. J. de la Potterie, "Vérité", *Vocabulaire de Théologie Biblique* (1962), pp. 1092–8. P. Grelot takes the scriptural idea of truth as his starting-point for the interpretation of inerrancy, *loc. cit.*, pp. 103–34; cf. also C. H. Ratschow, *Lutherische Dogmatik zwischen Reformation und Aufklärung,* I (1964), pp. 96 and 121.

[10] Vatican I, *Constitutio Dei Filius,* Cap. II: De Revelatione, *EB* 77: "Eos (= Veteris et Novi Testamenti libros) vero Ecclesia pro sacris et canonicis habet . . ., nec ideo dumtaxat, quod revelationem sine errore contineant . . ." In the mind of the council the fact that the sacred books contain revelation without error cannot be the *only* reason for the fact that the Church regards them as sacred and canonical. But this fact can and must be regarded as a *positive* reason, as was also the case in the early Church.

and without error the truth of salvation." (Veritatem salutarem inconcusse et fideliter, integre et sine errore docere profitendi sunt.) This gives a positive expression to the doctrine of inerrancy: it is a question of truth, namely the truth of salvation. This is the content and the motif of inerrancy. But inerrancy is not a static quality, communicated in a unique fact once and for all. Rather it is now seen as a continual act of God, who stands by the revelation, saving truth and promise of salvation set out in Scripture, in truth and fidelity to his covenant. Precisely in its inerrancy inspired writing becomes the expression of the truthfulness and fidelity of God to his covenant, whose word is to remain forever in the world.[11] Thus the gift of inspired Scripture is conceived now in terms of the whole Church, as is often expressed — even if, ecclesiologically speaking, it is not fully stated.[12]

In order to bring out still more clearly the salvation significance of inspired Scripture which had been expressed in this way, the reference to 2 Tim 3:16-17 was added at the suggestion of a Council father. Thus the effect of inspiration is that in all the books of Scripture and in all their parts the truth of salvation is taught unshakeably and faithfully, wholly and without error.[13]

This new view and motivation of the doctrine of inspiration and inerrancy, although actually in the logic of the Constitution, especially of Chapter II,[14] was unfortunately insufficiently prepared in theological writing,[15] and therefore unfamiliar to the majority of the fathers. Hence they were unable to grasp the full implication of the new formulation. In fact, it would have been the *relator's* task to present a detailed theological interpretation of this formula and give answers to possible objections. Unfortunately the new formula was left more or less unprotected. The first difficulty was not long in coming: if it was only and

---

[11] The *Schema Decreti pastoralis De Verbo Dei* (Supplementary Text II, p. 8), closed with the words: "Verbum autem Domini nostri manet in aeternum" (with reference to Is 40:8). From there they were taken over, in somewhat altered form, as the final words of the *Constitution "Dei Verbum"*. Bishop Hermann Volk, in particular, brought out the connection between "truth and fidelity to the covenant" in his speech on 6 October 1964. But this aspect of inerrancy should not be taken in isolation and over-emphasized, a position to which O. Loretz tends in his *Die Wahrheit der Bibel* (1964).

[12] Cf. "Dei Verbum", esp. II:10, VI:21. Actually the first form of the *schema* had good formulations of this point, which were later overlooked. Thus Chapter V (now VI) was originally called *De Sacra Scriptura in Ecclesia*. In it Article 24 says that the Holy Spirit had presented the treasure of the sacred books to men through the Church (per Ecclesiam hominibus tradidit); or Article 29: these books were "written for the Church for the salvation of all". On this cf. K. Rahner, *Über die Schriftinspiration* (1958), pp. 47-62; P. Lengsfeld, *Überlieferung, Tradition und Schrift in der evangelischen und katholischen Theologie der Gegenwart* (1960).

[13] The expression *"veritas salutaris"* is already found in the decree of the Council of Trent of April 8 1546; *EB*, 57.

[14] Cf. *Dei Verbum*, II, 7 (see above).

[15] Cf., however, P. Grelot, "L'inspiration scripturaire", *RSR* 51 (1963), pp. 337-82; id., *La Bible Parole de Dieu*, pp. 96-134 (with biblio.) (cf. above, note 5); id., "La Constitution sur la Révélation", *Études* 324 (1966), pp. 99-113, 233-46; cf. above note 9.

exclusively the *veritas salutaris* that was intended as the material object of inerrancy, then the *veritates profanae* are simply placed outside this truth. Would this not mean that the Council was coming close to an interpretation of the extent of inspiration that had been rejected in the nineteenth century, namely as being limited to doctrines of faith and morals?[16] It was in this way that a solution had been attempted to the problem of inerrancy, which at that time had been so pressing. The vote of 22 September 1965 showed, in the *modi* submitted, that the fathers feared this false interpretation of the *veritas salutaris*. Hence a large number of fathers suggested simply returning to Form E, i.e. cutting out *"salutaris"* and speaking now of "truth". Their reasoning was that the expression "truth of salvation" would, as against the documents of the teaching office, limit inerrancy to matters of faith and morals. But how is it with the other statements of Scripture?[17] It was still desired to make a distinction in the statements of the sacred writers, by saying that the sacred books contained the truth, but in different ways, according to the particular character of the statement of the sacred writer ("diversimode tamen pro qualitate affirmationis hagiographi"). Or *veritas salutaris,* as the primary object of the effect of inspiration, should be presented positively with the words "veritatem *super omnia* salutarem . . .", so that the secular truths also perhaps, in "their way", would share as it were in inerrancy at one remove. Other fathers wanted to acquire a new perspective on the question of inerrancy from the "intention" of God. Everything "that God intends to communicate to us" (quae Deus nobis communicare intenderit) is to be free of error because it is inspired. This was intended as an alternative suggestion to another one, which was then definitively adopted, as will immediately be shown. The same search for a new formulation of inerrancy gave rise to other suggestions such as "the books of Scripture contain *divine* truth", or "the truth *revealed by God,* or *taught,* or *stated* by him" (veritatem divinam, a Deo manifestatem, edoctam, vel assertam). Another way of avoiding a misunderstanding of *veritas salutaris* seemed to be the addition of a note in the official text. This was to give sources for the expression (such as Augustine and the Council of Trent), as well as to protect it against abuse and wrong interpretation by references to the encyclicals *Providentissimus Deus* and *Divino afflante.* The final text contains these references, in note 5 of Chapter III, supplemented by a quotation from St. Thomas. Yet the collation of these quotations, which have different tendencies, presents a special problem of interpretation. The interpreters of the conciliar text would have had to face this problem, with or without explicit quotation. Thus we must ask how the new conciliar text is to be interpreted against the background of the earlier statements on inerrancy.

In its reply to these *modi* of 22 September 1965, the Theological Commission

---

[16] Cf. P. Grelot, *La Bible Parole de Dieu,* pp. 99–103.

[17] Thus the text presented to the fathers for the vote on the *expensio modorum,* p. 33: *(expressio "veritatem salutarem")* "contra documenta Magisterii inerrantiam ad res fidei et morum restringere videtur: quid ergo de inerrantia aliarum assertionum Scripturae?"

had to go into the main difficulty: "the truth of salvation" *(veritas salutaris)* restricts inerrancy to statements on faith and morals *(res fidei et morum)* and is thus contrary to the documents of the teaching office. At this moment Paul VI intervened by means of a letter from the Secretariat of State to Cardinal Ottaviani as the president of the Theological Commission. From the discussion of these *modi* which now followed in the Theological Commission and the suggestions made in the letter from the Secretariat of State, we find important material for the understanding and extent of the final formula.[18] First of all the Theological Commission dealt with the *modi* submitted. Neither the sub-commission charged with dealing with them nor the full commission considered that they should depart from the expression *veritas salutaris* that was so important for the whole Constitution, despite the objections made. According to the full account given in the "Civiltà Cattolica", the so-called *expensio modorum* had three different forms: 1) the first version, which was merely mimeographed, said: "The word *salutaris* is added (to *veritas*) in order to express the scope *(scopus)* of inspiration, not to limit *inspiration* (italics mine) to matters of faith and morals . . . Thus the expression is to be understood in a positive and not exclusive sense." 2) In the printed sheets *(bozze)* of the *expensio modorum* intended for the assembly the formulation was more detailed: "The word *salutaris* is not intended in any way to suggest that Scripture is not wholly inspired and the word of God (non esse integraliter inspiratam et verbum Dei) . . . These words in no way suggest a material limitation of the truth of Scripture, but states its formal nature *(nullam* inducit *materialem limitationem* veritatis Scripturae, sed indicat eius *specificationem formalem)*, which must be considered when deciding in what sense not only matters of faith and morals and the events connected with the history of salvation are true . . ., but everything that is stated in Scripture (in diiudicando quo sensu non tantum res fidei et morum atque facta cum historia salutis coniuncta . . . sed omnia quae in Scriptura asseruntur sunt vera). Therefore the Commission has decided that the expression *(veritas salutaris)* should be retained." Thus, before the letter to Cardinal Ottaviani, the previous version of the doctrine of inerrancy was defended. It was realized that in the question of inerrancy "truth" had a different meaning according to whether it was a statement of salvation or a "secular truth", without affecting the unlimited extent of inspiration.

On 12 October 1965, however, the Pope was presented with an opinion on this question. On 14 October the papers *(bozze)* of the *expensio modorum* were given to him. Obviously the attitude of the Theological Commission had already become generally known; for on 8 October 1965, a group of fathers, probably the same who had suggested cutting out the word *salutaris,* had sent a memorandum to the Pope via a Cardinal stating that *veritas salutaris* was purposely put

---

[18] More details will be found in G. Caprile, S. J., "Tre emendamenti allo Schema sulla Rivelazione", *La Civiltà Cattolica* 117 (1966), pp. 214–31, esp. pp. 223–7: II La *"Verità della Scrittura"*. This gives an exact account of the proceedings in the Theological Commission on the question of *veritas salutaris.* The details given in the following are taken from this article.

nto the text in order to limit the inerrancy in Scripture to the supernatural things that concerned faith and morals; this was obviously contrary to the consistent preaching of the Church; it left the field open to exegetical arbitrariness; f it was accepted, this would be a heavy blow against the Church. Nor was there a lack of positive voices which encouraged Pope Paul to accept the formula *veritas salutaris*. Others wanted to retain it, but have it explained. The Theological Commission had actually already done this and thus replied to the objection that t was working towards a limitation of inspiration. This accusation was undoubtedly without justification.

On 17 October 1965, the Pope sent the letter mentioned above via the Secretariat of State to Cardinal Ottaviani as the President of the Theological Commission (dated 18 October), in which, apart from two other important points, he also discussed the question of *veritas salutaris*. He suggested that the Commission "should consider in fresh and serious deliberation the advantage of omitting the expression *veritas salutaris*". The Holy Father's concern *(perplessità)*, it stated, was greater in this respect than with the previous observation (namely the formulae on the relation of Scripture and tradition in Chapter II). For it was a doctrine which was not yet general in the scriptural and theological instruction of the Church; nor had the formula been adequately discussed in the assembly of the Council — although it was notable that during the break between the third and fourth sessions no criticism was made of it. This formula, moreover, did not avoid the danger of a false interpretation. Thus the time was apparently not yet ripe for a Conciliar decision on such a delicate question. The Council fathers were not perhaps able to estimate the extent and the possible abuse of this formula. By omitting it, however, there would be no barrier raised to a further study of the question.

We can see that *veritas salutaris* was not simply considered as false by the Pope. His position was very cautious and left a free hand to the Theological Commission. The "Civiltà Cattolica" reports the dramatic struggle that this letter occasioned in the Theological Commission. Because of lack of clarity in the voting, an appeal even had to be made to the Administrative Tribunal of the Council. The formula that finally emerged from this struggle was all the more valuable theologically. *Veritas salutaris* became "veritatem, quam Deus nostrae salutis causa litteris sacris consignari voluit". Thus the *expensio modorum* for this section, already in print, was rewritten. The Theological Commission now makes the final point: "The expression *salutaris* should in no way imply that Scripture is not, in its totality, inspired and the word of God: cf. what was stated in the text . . . (of 1964, Form II) in the spirit of the encyclical *Providentissimus*, *EB,* 127. It is impossible that 'the word of truth, the Gospel of your salvation' (Eph 1:13; cf. 2 Cor 4:2 etc.) should not teach the 'truth of salvation' (non potest fieri ut 'Verbum Veritatis, evangelium salutis vestrae . . .' non doceat 'veritatem salutarem')." In order, however, to avoid any misunderstanding in the interpretation, the Commission accepted a suggestion, presented by 73 fathers, to

213

improve the text so that it reads as we have it now (cf. the final text). There follows a reference to the expansion of note 5 by quoting the encyclicals *Providentissimus Deus* and *Divino afflante*.

A number of observations are important if one is to estimate the theological value of this final position of the Theological Commission: 1) we must note the different point at which the *modi* were aimed which called for the removal of the words *veritas salutaris* and which the Theological Commission chose in its answer: the complaint of the *modi* (like the memorandum submitted to Paul VI, which probably had the same authors as the *modi*) was that *veritas salutaris* limited "inerrancy" of Scripture to matters of faith and morals. Against this the Commission rejects the limitation of the "inspiration" of Scripture which might follow from this formulation, on the basis of the pronouncements of the teaching office in the nineteenth century and later. For at that time it was proposed that the solution of the pressing question of inerrancy should be the limitation of inspiration.[19] This was not an avoidance of the issue, but a clarification of the chief interest of the documents cited and also of the mind of the Council. There can be no doubt that all the books of Scripture, in all their parts, are inspired. But since the Commission now approaches the question of the "truth" of Scripture, it starts with a quotation from *Providentissimus Deus* ("Deum ipsum per sacros auctores elocutum nihil admodum a veritate alienum ponere potuisse": *EB,* 127). This statement is, however, immediately explained in relation to *veritas salutaris,* with reference to Eph 1 :13 — and, one might say, *authentically* explained. Thus the Theological Commission — as well as clearly emphasizing the universal extent of inspiration — keeps the way open for a new interpretation of inerrancy. It was firmly of the opinion that *veritas salutaris* could remain. Only in order to avoid a misuse of this expression — in the direction of a limiting of inspiration — a new formula is chosen. *Veritas salutaris* thus becomes "veritas, quam Deus salutis nostrae causa litteris sacris consignari voluit". At the same time the material submitted by the 73 fathers was significantly altered by the Commission, as was their right. Instead of "veritatem, quam Deus, nostrae salutis causa, libris sacris consignare voluit" it reads: "veritatem, quam Deus nostrae salutis causa litteris sacris consignari voluit". "Nostrae salutis causa",[20] in apposition with *Deus,* became a final adverbial qualification of *consignari,* which, moreover, was conceived passively and not actively, in accordance with the Constitution's

---

[19] Cf. J. Beumer, *Die katholische Inspirationslehre* (cf. above note 4), pp. 21–31; N. Lohfink, *Katholische Bibelwissenschaft und historisch-kritische Methode* (1966).

[20] In the first Italian translation of the Constitution, which appeared immediately after its publication in "Osservatore Romano", the apposition was, however, again retained: "Deus, nostrae salutis causa, litteris sacris . . ." The Theological Commission immediately protested against this change. The volume published by the General Secretariat of the Council containing all the Conciliar documents (1967) explicitly indicates the accepted text typographically: *"nostrae salutis causa"* ! — It is also to be noted that instead of the suggested active form *consignare* the Theological Commission chooses the passive *consignari,* in order to put more emphasis on the human authorship, in the spirit of the other changes in Article 11.

conception of inspiration (in order to put more stress on the human authorship under inspiration).

Here the Theological Commission has followed a particular aim — in opposition to the marked activity of a particular group in the Council and the attitude of Paul VI to it — namely, to present the doctrine of the inerrancy of Scripture in a way that was in harmony with the concept of Chapters I and II of the Constitution on Revelation and took more account of the modern difficulties than was possible in the strict formulation of the papal encyclicals on Scripture, and especially the schema of 1962. But the resistance of the fathers mentioned and the reservations of the Pope undoubtedly had their effect; for the formula that was found is a much happier one than the hotly contested *veritas salutaris.* This will be seen when we come to its theological interpretation.

Some other changes in Article 11 are of lesser importance. Such phrases as, for example, "unshakeable and complete" to describe the teaching of Scripture on the truth of salvation *(inconcusse . . ., integre . . . docere),* could be criticized: *inconcusse* on philological grounds (it was replaced by *firmiter); integre,* because it seemed to express the idea of the material insufficiency of Scripture. Originally it was intended to express the idea that Scripture is a special guarantee that the full saving truth would remain among men, which Chapter VI then expresses in its own way (cf. Article 21). Various objections had already been made to *docere:* that it sounded too intellectualistic and didactic; "it seemed to have a flavour of the period of the struggle over the question of inerrancy (only that could be included under inerrancy which Scripture really "taught"). It finally remained in the text. The Theological Commission added an explanation: "The expression *docere* is to remain because it refers to what is really stated" (quae agit de illis quae proprie *asseruntur).* "To teach" does not, then, have a strictly technical meaning.

II. The history of the text on scriptural hermeneutics (Article 12)

1. From 1961 to 1963 (Forms A — D)

This text was concerned with scriptural hermeneutics. Form C (1963) is on this point, interestingly enough, very different from the two first Forms. It is notable that these first two versions only give a very short account of the long statements of the encyclical *Divino afflante (EB,* 558 – 62). The words *litterarium genus,* so important in the encyclical, no longer appear. Was this still the old mistrust against this progressive encyclical of Pius XII? *Divino afflante,* which had distinguished between the meaning of the words which can be discovered by means of the laws of grammar, philology and from the context, and what the writer had actually desired to express, had met with fairly strong opposition in some quarters. There were also declared opponents of research into the literary forms of Scripture. Many desired that the "principles of interpretation that the encyclical put forward should at least be limited to the ancient Eastern world and the Old Testament, which the actual words of the encyclical seemed to justify". It was typical of the situation that still existed during the Council that the important *Instructio de historica Evangeliorum Veritate* of the Papal Commission on Scripture, of 21 April 1964, had to give a firm warning: "the exegete is to follow the binding instruction of Pope Pius XII 'to investigate carefully to what extent a phrase used by a writer or a literary form is important for a faithful interpretation. Let him know that he cannot neglect this part of his task without doing great harm to Catholic exegesis.' "[2] Nevertheless, Form A sought to present more or less the substance of the lengthy pronouncements of *Divino afflante* with a clear reference to a particular part of the text and with a reference to the whole (*EB,* 558–62) in the notes: "Haec tamen inerrantia diiudicanda est ex sensu, quem in determinatis adiunctis expressit hagiographus pro sui temporis conditione. Veritas enim et fides historica sacrae Scripturae recte probantur, si rite attendatur ad suetos nativos cogitandi, dicendi vel narrandi modos, qui tempore hagiographorum vigebant, quique tunc in mutuo hominum commercio passim adhiberi solebant. Cum igitur haec omnia, salva Scripturae auctoritate et sanctitate, in eodem divino eloquio, quod pro hominibus modis verbisque humanis exprimitur, inveniantur, non magis erroris argui debent, quam cum paria ac similia in quotidiano usu haberentur, immo habeantur."[3] Let us give the parallel from *Divino afflante* (*EB,* 560): "Non raro enim . . . cum Sacros Auctores ab historiae fide aberasse, aut res minus accurate rettulisse obiurgando nonnulli iactant, nulla alia de re agi comperitur, nisi de suetis illis nativis antiquorum dicendi narrandique modis, qui in mutuo hominum inter se commercio passim abhiberi solebant, ac reapse licito communique more adhibebantur. Ista igitur mentis aequitas postulat, ut haec, cum in divino eloquio, quod pro hominibus verbis humanis exprimitur, inveniantur, non magis erroris arguantur, quam cum eadem in cotidiano vitae usu habeantur." Obviously there was pressure even in the Preparatory Commission to use *Divino afflante* more fully and prepare a rather more comprehensive account of scriptural hermeneutics for the coming Constitution *De Fontibus Revelationis.* The new form of Article 14 of Form C of 1962 (Quomodo inerrantia diiudicanda sit) is interesting for more than one reason: "Haec tamen inerrantia diiudicanda est ex modo quo veritas in libro sacro attingitur. Qui modus imprimis elucet ex indole generali libri, de qua casu dubii, definitivum iudicium soli competit Ecclesiae. Aliter enim veritas exprimitur in libro historico vel didactico; aliter in prophetico, poetico, allegorico, parabolico.

Quo autem ad singula spectat, modus attingendi veritatem diiudicetur oportet

---

[1] Semmelroth-Zerwick, p. 35. Cf. *Divino afflante, EB,* 558.
[2] Cf. J. A. Fitzmeyer, *Die Wahrheit der Evangelien* (1965), p. 39; *ibid.,* p. 35, where there is mention of the resistance to *Divino afflante.* Cf., however, the resistance also within Protestant research, mentioned by K. Koch, *Was ist Formgeschichte?* (1964), pp. 72 f.
[3] In Form C (1962) this Article 13 was altered in various ways, as shown.

tiam ex sensu quem in determinatis adiunctis pro sui temporis condicione expressit hagiographus."[4]

The subject, as in all the previous forms, is the inerrancy or the "truth" of Scripture, but by this it does not mean what the Constitution *Dei Verbum* finally meant by this. "Truth" here means, as Form A clearly shows, the *veritas et fides historica,* the historical truth and accuracy of Scripture. Everything is still conceived in terms of the problems of the nineteenth and early twentieth centuries. Hermeneutics is enlisted in the service of the defence of the inerrancy of Scripture. To this end we must first of all note the way in which truth is "approached" in the sacred book *(attingitur).* According to Form C what has to be established is: 1. the general character of the book (whether historical, didactic, prophetic, poetic, allegorical or parabolic). Obviously it is not considered here that in a single book one may find different literary forms according to the material to be presented. *(Divino afflante* was rather more differentiated on this point.[5]); 2. the meaning *(sensus)* which the sacred writer has expressed or sought to express according to the particular circumstances of the situation of his time. This also applies to the individual statements *(singula).* As we have seen this second mode of establishing the truth refers clearly to *Divino afflante.*

It is clear that Form C sought to indicate a progress in thinking and to give a clearer structure to this very difficult question of scriptural hermeneutics with a certain hidden reference, probably, to *Divino afflante.* For the differences are, for the most part, quite clear: 1. Form C (1962) also avoids from now on — like Forms A and B — the expression *genera litteraria.* 2. It makes the distinction between the "general character" of the book and the individual questions *(singula).* The general nature of a book, however, is determined by whether it is historical, didactic or any other form. Form C gives no indication whether it would describe this as the *genus litterarium.* Unfortunately there was not complete clarity on this point in the encyclical *Divino afflante* either. Apparently it identifies the literary forms first of all with "modes of speech" *(formae, modi discendi) (EB,* 558). Then suddenly the phrase "old forms of speech" is mentioned, as employed in the presentation of poetic subjects, conditions and laws of life, and finally in the narration of historical facts and events. Here the capacity of the people of Israel to present historical material is especially praised. Nevertheless, like other ancient peoples, it has certain *artes* in presentation and narration, idioms which are peculiar to the semitic languages, also approximate accounts *(approximationes),* hyperbolic and paradoxical ways of writing which provide the real point in

There then follows, briefly extended, the text of Form A, quoted above (veritas enim . . .); it is to be noted that it now states: *"Veritas enim et fides S. Scripturae."* The word *"historica"* is dropped. There is, however, no definite extension of the idea *veritas.*

Divino afflante: EB, 560: "Haec porro, postremis hisce decenniis maiore, quam antea, cura et diligentia peracta, clarius manifestavit, quaenam dicendi formae antiquis illis temporibus adhibitae sint, sive in rebus poetice describendis, sive in vitae normis et legibus proponendis, sive denique in enarrandis historiae factis atquo eventibus."

expression. In the summary which *Divino afflante* finally offers to exegetes *dicendi forma* is identified with *litterarium genus* (*EB,* 560). This is further explained as "nativi antiquorum dicendi narrandique, modi, qui in mutuo hominum inter se commercio passim adhiberi solebant". If exegetes are familiar with the "ways and arts of the ancients in speaking and writing" then many doubts concerning the inerrancy of the Bible can be solved. This study also leads to a fuller knowledge of the *mens Sacri Auctoris*.

In a statement that goes even further (*EB,* 561) we have the final warning that exegetes should not overlook anything "quod novitatis attulerint, cum archaeologia, tum antiqua rerum gestarum historia priscarumque litterarum scientia, quodque aptum sit, quo melius veterum scriptorum mens, eorumque ratiocinandi, narrandi, scribendique modus, forma et ars cognoscatur". After this undoubtedly open and progressive instruction in *Divino afflante* there is some difficulty in knowing how the various hermeneutical points are to be balanced against one another. Finally, however, there are two tasks for the exegetes that are clearly distinguished: 1) They must take account of the findings of archaeology, ancient history, the history of ancient literature, and in fact of everything that can be a help to their particular work, which is, namely, 2) to understand the mentality of the ancient writers, the nature of their reasoning (*modus ratiocinandi*), the form of their narration (*narrandi . . . forma*), and the art of their writing (*scribendi . . . ars*). It is to be noted that the encyclical lays strong emphasis on the different forms of expression, but less on the pre-given forms of thought or the modes of feeling and experience. Only a slight hint of this is given in the mention of the "nature of their reasoning". What Form C (1962) sought to achieve, as against *Divino afflante* with its distinction of the "general nature" of a book and the "individual questions" was not an advance in hermeneutics. It almost seems as if to establish this "general nature" of a book had already settled the question of the literary genus. This kind of statement would have been a big step backwards from *Divino afflante*. This had already been corrected in Form D (1963). The question of the "general nature" was omitted, even if the distinction of the *singula* remained. But now the emphasis was put on what the writer intended to express. Moreover it is no longer a *liber* historicus, etc., that is spoken of, but the historical, didactic, prophetic "text". Thus the possibility is recognized that we may find within the same book different literary modes or forms. Also, the purpose of all hermeneutical endeavour is better expressed: it is a question of the "truth" which God desires to communicate to us. It is true that in the closing section of Article 12 in Form D the emphasis in hermeneutics is still on the question of inerrancy. Let us quote the first sentence of this article in this form: "Cum autem Deus per homines scripserit, hac de causa, ut pateat quamnam veritatem nobis communicare voluerit, interpres Sacrae Scripturae attente investigare debet quid reapse hagiographus significare intenderit. Aliter enim veritas in textu historico et aliter in textu didactico, prophetico, poetico, allegorico aut parabolico proponitur et exprimitur."

2. The growth and final form of Article 12 (1964–1965)

After Pope Paul, in his final address to the second session of the Council, had again put the schema on Revelation on the agenda,[6] work on it was renewed in the winter of 1964. Form E (1964), in accordance with the opinions submitted by the fathers up to January 1964, had changed this introduction to Article 12 in the following way: "Cum autem Deus *in Sacra Scriptura* per homines *more hominum locutus sit,* interpres Sacrae Scripturae, ut perspiciat, quamnam veritatem *Ipse* nobis communicare voluerit, attente investigare debet, quid hagiograph*i* reapse significare intender*int* et *eorum verbis manifestare Deo placuerit.*"

There are two important points here for scriptural hermeneutics: 1) there is a connection established between "the literal meaning" and "the intention of the statement", and yet both are distinguished. We have already noted that on this point *Divino afflante* had opened up new paths. In the spirit of the encyclical, the Council now clearly demands that the actual contents of the statement be discovered in the "literal meaning" (which is to be established philologically, grammatically and from the context). But this involved another problem: 2) the question of the so-called *sensus plenior*[7] of Scripture, or: what is the relation between what the sacred writers intended to say and what God intended to say? Is the *sensus divinus* wholly identical with the *sensus hagiographi,* i.e. with the content of the statement that can be shown historically to be the content that the sacred writer himself was aware of, or does what God intends to say go further? In the discussion on the text two tendencies emerged: one wanted to give precedence, as far as possible, to the *sensus historicus* and to see exegetical work as the discovery of this, the other saw the *primary* task of the exegete as the discovery of this very *sensus historicus hagiographi.* It also recognized that in the sacred writer's intention, discovered in this way, the particular intention of God in the situation of that time becomes apparent. But it also wanted the conciliar text to express the point that the full *sensus divinus* points beyond what was conscious at the time and must be rediscovered in a constantly renewed exegetical effort.

With Form F (autumn 1964) and finally even in the vote on the *modi* on 21 September 1965, attempts were made to preserve the now established juxtaposition of what the sacred writers and what God intended to express from a misinterpretation, by putting them on exactly the same level or even identifying them, thus working out a clear distinction in the formulation (in the sense stated above). Thus the text was to read: "quid hagiographi ... intenderint et *quid* verbis manifestare Deo placuerit". This repetition of *quid* — doubtless also a linguistic improvement — would have given the protagonists of the *sensus plenior* a greater chance. In order to make it easier for their opponents they suggested in the *modi*

---

[6] Paul VI, "Allocutio Secunda SS. Concilii Periodo exacta", *Sacrosanctum Oecumenicum Concilium Vaticanum II* (1966), p. 938. The Pope directs that the exegetes should pursue scriptural studies 'magisterio Ecclesiae fideliter inhaerentes et quibusvis aptis huius aetatis subsidiis usi".

On the question of the "sensus plenior" cf. the bibliography in J. Beumer, *Die katholische Inspirationslehre,* pp. 96–97 (see above I, note 4).

a slight weakening: the *et quid* was to become *quidque*. This formula seemed, on the one hand, to unite closely the intention of the sacred writers and that of God, and on the other, to leave open the possibility of a *sensus plenior*. The Theological Commission, however — with Form F as with the final text of 1965 —, decided against accepting the repetition of the *"quid" (et quid* or *quidque)*, but instead, in the *relatio* on the text (1964, II) and finally in the *expensio modorum* (1965) decided to point out that the question of the *sensus plenior* is by no means resolved, either negatively or positively. "Si scribitur quidque, quaestio in sensum positivum (i.e. in the sense of the *sensus plenior)* dirimeretur. Expressio *et* est neutralis", runs the *expensio modorum*. So each of the two views can be defended. In the exegesis of the text (see below) we shall again have to return to this problem and to the connection between Articles 11 and 12 and the consequences that ensue from this for hermeneutics. The question will be what is meant in both sections by "truth" *(veritas)*.

The main concern of Article 12, however, is what hermeneutical rules are to be given to the exegete and the theologian. As we have seen, Form C (1962) sought to divide up the rules of scriptural hermeneutics into a simple system: 1. the establishment of the general nature of a book of Scripture; 2. the interpretation of the ' *singula*. Both formulations disappeared, and first of all the question of the *indoles generalis* of a book. Already Form D (1963) started from the keyword *text* and left it open to accept different literary forms or types within the one book, even if the words *genus litterarium* have not yet appeared. This is not the case until after July 1964.

After this, Article 12 is chiefly concerned with the *genera litteraria,* placing this question in the service of the establishment of the sacred writer's intention. Effort was concentrated more and more on a further version of the principles for the *genera litteraria*. From Form E on it is stated that research into the literary types or forms is only one way *(inter alia etiam)* of investigating the *sensus* of the sacred writers. Thus other ways remain open, which are not further defined. It was neither possible nor wise to list here all the individual hermeneutical rules or ways that contemporary exegesis has already developed or constantly suggests. The openness of the text to any legitimate method of interpretation of Scripture must suffice. Certain points from Chapters IV and V (as, for example, Article 19) belong here.

Within the *genera litteraria* listed, the Constitution, after the autumn of 1965, expressly refers to the fact of "how widely the idea of 'history' is to be taken when defining types, in as much as it says: 'in texts that are historical in various ways (in textibus vario modo historicis)' . . . it is also notable that the Commission's reason for adding 'historical in various ways' and extending the text with the words 'other literary types' is that there should be no step backwards by the Council into the time before *Divino afflante* and *Humani generis.*"[8]

[8] Semmelroth-Zerwick pp. 36–37. I am indebted, in the following, to P. G. Schelbert, S.M.B. (Schöneck, Switzerland) for many suggestions.

Thus the investigation of literary types is not seen as the only method of hermeneutics, nor are these various types all listed. Even within an established *genus* there can be further differentiation.

Article 12 speaks with a "moreover" clause *(porro)* of another method of scriptural hermeneutics. "The interpreter must investigate what meaning the sacred writer intended to express and actually expressed in particular circumstances as he used contemporary literary forms in accordance with the situation of his own time and culture." These words "determinata adiuncta . . . pro sui temporis conditione" already appear in Form A and have been retained through all the forms of the text, even though their position has changed. For from A to D everything was put under the heading of the defence of inerrancy. *Divino afflante* also presented its account of hermeneutics chiefly from this aspect, which is important to note if we are to understand the full extent of the final text of the Council. This idea of saving scriptural inerrancy (as far as the "secular truths" are concerned) was finally abandoned and scriptural hermeneutics given a fully positive significance that must still be more closely defined exegetically (cf. II).

The "moreover" clause indicates that it is no longer a question of literary types and forms. The Theological Commission especially emphasized this when, in the vote on the *modi* on 21 September 1965, a Council father wanted to have this word removed: "*porro* is to be retained because a new idea *(nova idea)* is introduced concerning the various circumstances of the composition of the books." This is true, although at the particular wish of influential fathers the literary types are again mentioned in this "moreover" clause — not in order to place the whole section again within the framework of this subject, but only to express the connection between the new material and what had been said before.

It is the *determinata adiuncta,* the particular circumstances, the situation from which the sacred writer speaks or in which the text has grown, that is the starting-point. This must all be established by historical critical methods. *Divino afflante* firmly urged this. The phrase about the "influence of contemporary conditions" *(temporum conditio)* is taken from Augustine's *De Doctrina Christiana.* In Book III of this work he was concerned with the *ambiguitates* of the Bible, the doubtful passages, the awkwardnesses, the ambiguities that arise from the immediate literal sense and can become a scandal for Christians, especially when it is a matter of ethics. In order to solve these problems it is necessary to note the "influence of contemporary conditions" on the use of the words "permitted" and "forbidden", so as not to draw wrong conclusions from the letter of Scripture for the moral life of the Christians of the particular generation: "Item cavendum est, ne forte quo in scripturis veteribus pro *illorum temporum conditione,* etiamsi non figurate, sed proprie intellegatur, non est flagitium neque facinus, ad ista etiam tempora quis putet in usum vitae posse transferri."[9]

But the text of 1962 (C) does not apply these words about the influence of

---

[9] Augustine, *De Doctrina Christ.,* III, XVIII 26, ed. by H. J. Vogels, *Floril. Patr.,* XXIV, 58.

contemporary conditions so much to ethics, but to the question of the truth and the intention of the sacred writer in general. If the conciliar text, in all its forms, refers here to Augustine, this is only in order to formulate the point about *temporum conditio*. Critical historical work requires not only the investigation of the situation, the temporal and cultural milieu, the literary forms, which are here mentioned again, but research into all the other things which are now named: "Ad recte enim intelligendum id quod sacer auctor scripto asserere voluerit, rite attendendum est tum ad suetos illos nativos sentiendi, dicendi, narrandive modos, qui temporibus hagiographi vigebant, tum ad illos qui illo aevo in mutuo hominum commercio adhiberi solebant."

If we are to understand the present form of the text we must briefly consider its history. From Forms A to F (1961–1964, I) the text spoke of the "sueti nativi cogitandi, dicendi vel narrandi modi, qui tempore hagiographorum vigebant, quique tunc in mutuo hominum commercio passim adhiberi solebant". If one reads the text of *Divino afflante* immediately behind this, we find there in rather more detail what is summed up in the short sentences of form A: ". . . omnino oportet mente quasi redeat interpres ad remota illa orientis saecula . . ." (*EB*, 558); ". . . dispicere enitatur, quae propria fuerit sacri scriptoris indoles ac vitae condicio, qua floruerit aetate . . ." (*EB*, 557).

In this connection comes the request that all this historical knowledge should help the exegete to establish the literary types that were in use *at that time*. They cannot be determined *a priori (in antecessum)*, but only from an exact study of Oriental literature.

Compared with *Divino afflante* this text in one point, brings a differentiation. The aim is no longer solely the establishing, by critical historical means, of the *genera litteraria*. The *porro* clause gives to the "nativi sentiendi, dicendi, narrandive modi . . ." a special importance in the discovery of what the sacred writer meant, however much the *genus litterarium* may be conditioned by this. It is a question of modes of feeling, experiencing, thinking and understanding. This can all be understood by the phrase *sentiendi . . . modi*. *Divino afflante* had said too little about this. It was concerned too hastily or too exclusively with the (literary) *mode of expression*. Forms of feeling and thinking, as well as the pre-literary ways of speech and narration, must be given their own value. They are expressions of a total understanding of the world and life, even though they may not be conscious. They express themselves in the whole life of a man, in his views and moral valuations, in the history of a people and a particular cultural field, even in the daily round. These forms of thinking, feeling and speaking may penetrate all literary forms, they precede the written presentation. *Divino afflante* took too little note of this. In modern times much has been written about forms of thought, the spirit of a language, which can differ from people to people, culture to culture, and also from epoch to epoch. But all this determines the content of the ideas that are to be expressed or the way in which a message is understood and received. Although they have become clichés, expressions like the "judaizing", "hellenizing", "latinizing", etc. of the Christian message are the proper subjects of research.[10] One and the same thought, one and the same event acquire a different aspect according to whether they are expressed in Hebrew, Greek, Latin, or in a modern language. This is shown by the history of Bible translations (cf., for example, Exod 3:14 in the Hebrew and in the Septuagint and the very different ideas of God contained therein![11]).

Thus the history and first exegesis of the Conciliar text show us that the final text of Article 12 distinguishes the *nativi sentiendi, dicendi, narrandive modi* from the *genera litteraria*, however closely they may belong together. A fuller interpretation of the text is given below; but first there is another interpretation problem to be clarified in Article 12. In the vote on the *modi* of 21 September 1965, seven fathers had requested "ut clarius distinguantur illa quae ad genera litteraria pertinent ab illis quae ad *mutuum hominum commercium* respiciunt. Varias suggerunt *additiones,* v.g. 'dicendi *scribendive* modos ... *in arte litteraria* ... ad *expressiones* quae ...' etc." The Theological Commission wanted to grant this request and recommended as a solution: "Scribatur: 'rite attendendum est *tum* ad suetos illos nativos sentiendi, dicendi, narrandive modos, qui temporibus hagiographi vigebant, tum ad illos qui hoc aevo (finally altered to *illo* aevo) in mutuo hominum commercio passim adhiberi soleant'." Thus special mention is made of the habits of daily human intercourse as a source of knowledge of what the sacred writer wanted to say. As a hermeneutical approach they now acquire greater independence — in comparison with *Divino afflante* and the first forms of the Constitution. The original placing of the words *mutuum hominum commercium* was determined by the question of inerrancy. Let us refer again to the texts quoted above (II, 1) of Form A and of the encyclical *Divino afflante*. The impressive heading of what was Article 13 at that time, containing the hermeneutical rules, must always be remembered: "Quomodo inerrantia diiudicanda sit!" The question about the general character of the book helps to decide the question of inerrancy. In the interpretation of individual passages *(singula)* it is helped by the fact that what is being said is affected by the particular accompanying circumstances, which are again to be seen in terms of the conditions of the time of the writer. For every age has its own ways of thinking, speaking and narrating, which are expressed even in everyday events. Thus we must note here that forms of thinking and speech are not intentionally contrasted with the habits of daily intercourse. It is only stated that the customary ways of thinking and speaking are expressed and applied to everyday intercourse *also*. The purpose of all these points was expressed in the final section of the old Article 13: "Cum igitur haec omnia, salvis Scripturae Sacrae auctoritate et sanctitate, in eodem divino eloquio, quod pro hominibus modis verbisque humanis exprimitur, inveniantur, non

---

[10] Cf. A. Grillmeier, "Hellenisierung-Judaisierung des Christentums, *Scholastik* 33 (1958), pp. 321–55 and 528–58.

[11] Cf. *ibid.*, pp. 528–38 (on the studies of C. H. Ratschow and T. Boman); cf. also A. Gélin in *Sacra Pagina,* I (1959), pp. 303–15.

magis erroris argui debent quam cum paria ac similia in cotidiano usu adhibebantur, immo adhibentur, proindeque Scripturae sacrae auctoritati ac sanctitati
minime officiunt."

It is not hard to see that parts of this section were retained in the final version,
but here they are placed in another context. This explains the mention of "the
ordinary habits of daily human intercourse", and this in a double sense: in order
to judge a statement of Scripture one has to take account of the forms of daily
human intercourse that were customary then and still are now. Today too we use
expressions which are wrong, if taken literally, but are understood correctly by
everyone (e.g. the sun rises, sets, etc.). One cannot make an attack on the "truth"
of Scripture on this basis, and certainly not a second Galileo affair, as the first
forms of the text tacitly inferred. This double reference to the everyday expressions of that time and of today was originally intended to be included in the
final text, even though in the context of the new basic position of the section. Thus
the text was supposed to read: "If one wishes to understand correctly what the
sacred writer sought to express in what he said, one must ultimately take careful
note of the native forms of thought, speech and narrative that were customary in
the writer's time, as well as of those which are found *today* in human intercourse."

Thus the modes of speech and thought of that time and of today were to be
distinguished through the words *tum — tum —*, a faint reminder of the words just
quoted of Form A of the text *adhibebantur, immo adhibentur*. In the final text the
temporal contrast of then and now became a *factual* distinction between the
inherited ways of feeling, thinking and narrating, and the forms of daily human
intercourse of *that* time — both for the time of the sacred writers or the origin of
Scripture. There is no longer any reference to the customary forms of today.
Unfortunately, the language has not been chosen carefully enough.[12] Work on
the tough dough of the previous texts had an adverse effect on this particular
section on the rules of hermeneutics. In spite of this the whole thing did not
become simply a rule to remove doubts about scriptural inerrancy — a purpose
that they can continue to fulfil — but finally an indication of how to discover the
truth content of Scripture to its fullest extent, for which naturally the rules of
Divino afflante could and should also be applied. In this first part of the hermeneutical rules the Constitution recommends ways of establishing what the sacred

[12] The Latin text would read more clearly as: "Rite attendendum est tum ad suetos illos nativos
modos sentiendi, dicendi, narrandive, qui temporibus hagiographi vigebant, tum ad illos qui in
mutuo illius aevi hominum commercio adhiberi solebant." The reference to everyday colloquial
language was originally intended to serve in defence of the inerrancy of Scripture, as shown
already in the text of Article 13 quoted following: "Cum haec omnia in divino eloquio, quod pro
hominibus modis verbisque humanis exprimitur, inveniantur, non magis erroris eadem argui
debent quam cum paria aut similia in quotidiano usu habita sint, immo habeantur, proindeque
auctoritati et sanctitati Scripturae minime officiunt." Now that the rules of hermeneutics have
been freed from the narrow goal mentioned, it has also become possible to use the speech of
everyday life as a source of knowledge of the *sensus auctoris*. A good example of what is meant here
is given by K. Koch, *Formgeschichte,* p. 1, note 18.

writers intended to say — and hence ways of critical historical research: 1) *"inter alia"* the investigation of the literary forms in the various texts; 2) the establishing (a) of the particular situation (of the *determinata adiuncta*) in which the writer and his statement are placed; (b) the particular temporal and cultural conditions of this statement, which can be expressed in various literary forms; 3) the study of inherited or native ways of feeling and thinking (forms of thought), of language and the spirit of the language, the various modes of narration; 4) attention to the forms of ordinary daily social intercourse.

Up to now there had been talk only of the critical historical methods of establishing the meaning of Scripture. It was not until Form E (1964, I) that mention was made also of the principles of *theological* exegesis. The meaning of Scripture was to be investigated in the light of the whole, i.e. within the unity of all the books, but especially of the Old and the New Testaments within each other, and further with the aid of tradition and the analogy of faith. These principles had only been hinted at previously in the chapter on the New Testament in connection with a warning to exegetes (Chapter IV, later V, n. 19). Text E states briefly: "Sed ad recte sacrorum textuum significationem eruendam, respiciendum est etiam ad contentum totius Scripturae, in viva Ecclesiae traditione, sub analogia fidei."

Form F (1964, II) makes only slight stylistic changes. More important, however, is the final version of the text, which was worked out on the basis of the *modi* of 21 September 1965: "since Scripture must be read and interpreted in the spirit in which it was written, the proper discovery of the sense of the sacred texts requires that one should attend with equal care to the contents and unity of all of Scripture, while taking account of the living tradition of the whole Church and the analogy of faith".

This final form of the text contains the express references to the pneumatic character of Scripture. Hence the Holy Spirit must be the real guide to the understanding of Scripture, either for scientific work on it or for its religious study. This is supported by reference to the encyclical *Spiritus Paraclitus* (*EB*, 469) and by quotation from St. Jerome. From Forms E and F to the final text there was a visible attempt to describe the role of the Church in exegesis (as also the task of the exegetes themselves). *Traditio* (with a capital letter, "quia non agitur tantum de traditionibus ecclesiasticis"[13] was to be given its full weight in exegesis, as this is now presented in the Constitution as a source of the life of the Church (cf. below, Chapter VI). In the "living tradition of the whole Church"

---

[13] A *modus* on Article 12 of 21 September 1965, signed by 13 fathers, read:". . . scribatur *Traditio* cum maiuscula quia non agitur tantum de traditionibus ecclesiasticis." The Theological Commission added: "Insuper (hi 13 Patres) addere volunt *Magisterium* et *sensum fidei Populi Dei*. Alius vult citari *Patres Ecclesiae*. Unus denique Pater proponit *longiorem additionem* de normis quae imperant exegesi ut disciplinae *theologiae*." The Commission suggested: "Scribatur: '. . . vivae totius Ecclesiae Traditionis et analogiae fidei'. Ita in totius Ecclesiae Traditione iam cointelliguntus Patres et sensus fidei . . ."

the teaching office, the mind of all believers, and especially the scriptural interpretations of the Church Fathers are included. In addition the *analogia fidei* is
mentioned, which is nothing but the consciousness of the unity of the revelation
of God in its whole history and in its development in the Church.

The task of exegetes

During the preparatory period and in the first sessions of the Council mistrust
had become evident against the more modern-minded exegetes.For this reason
it was not easy to get the fathers to say a good word for the representatives of
scriptural studies. In Form E their task was described in Article 19 within a
rather narrow framework: "Exegetarum autem . . . est, servatis rationalis et
catholicae hermeneuticae normis, sub ductu magisterii Ecclesiae adlaborare, ut
Evangelii loci, qui expositionem certam et definitam adhuc desiderant, bene
intelligantur, ita ut quasi praeparato studio, iudicium Ecclesiae maturetur."

Form E (1964, I) had included this text in the present Article 12. This definition of exegetical work comes from *Providentissimus Deus*, which assigns to the
doctor privatus as a special area of investigation those "passages" of Scripture
which are still in need of an exact and certain explanation (*EB*, 109). With this
point the encyclical wanted to show that the teaching office of the Church in no
way hinders scriptural research, but leaves it a wide field. Nevertheless behind
these words we can detect a quite inadequate conception of exegesis, as if it was
only concerned with individual "passages" of Scripture that had hitherto been
obscure, the number of which would grow ever smaller as the "*loci iam definiti*"
grew. These ideas of the explanation of Scripture have today long been out-
moded. A fuller description of the task of exegetes was rightly called for several
times, and for the last time in the vote on the *modi* of 21 September 1965. Exegetes
must constantly address themselves to Scripture as a whole, in order to discover,
at an ever profounder level, its meaning. Now we read: "It is the task of exegetes
to work according to these rules toward a better understanding and explanation
of the meaning of sacred Scripture, so that through preparatory study the
judgment of the Church may mature. For all of what has been said about the way
of interpreting Scripture is subject finally to the judgment of the Church, which
carries out the divine commission and ministry of guarding and interpreting the
word of God." Scripture must ultimately be read in the Church. Even the exegesis of scholars should see itself only as serving the life of the Church. Chapter VI
will develop these ideas in a special way.

III. The growth of Article 13

Chapter III closes with a short epilogue on the "condescension of God" *(condescensio)* which is revealed in the word of God passing into the human word. The
analogy with the incarnation of the Logos in this connection was already made by

Divino afflante. Up to Form E (1964, I) inclusively this comparison between the incarnation (the passing of the Logos into human form) and the Holy Spirit (the passing of the divine word of revelation into the form of Scripture) had been interpreted in a quite concrete sense: the incarnation of the Son of God guarantees the sinlessness of the humanity of Jesus. God's word of revelation in the human written word has, because of its inspiration, the guarantee of infallibility or inerrancy. Thus the sinlessness of Jesus and the inerrancy of Scripture are regarded as parallels, as already in *Divino afflante* (*EB,* 559): "Sicut enim substantiale Dei Verbum hominibus simile factum est quoad omnia 'absque peccato' (Heb 4: 15), ita etiam Dei verba, humanis linguis expressa, quoad omnia humano sermoni assimilia facta sunt, excepto errore . . ."

Although this strict parallelism was expressly desired by some fathers, it was rightly criticized by others and consequently dropped. For — to argue dogmatically — the sinlessness of Christ in his humanity follows from the hypostatic union. Just as the connection of the Church with the Holy Spirit cannot be regarded as a parallel with the divine humanity of Christ,[14] Scripture too, as the word of God in the human word, cannot be seen as a parallel to the incarnation. There is an important analogy between the two, but it is only an analogy. The whole argument was conceived in terms of the problem of the inerrancy of Scripture. The Constitution *Dei Verbum* finally broke through this narrow framework and for this reason dropped the reference to Heb 4:15. Certainly the incarnation and the inspiration of Scripture are seen as two modes of the condescension of God and his accommodation of himself to us. At the suggestion of Cardinal König the emphasis on this condescension acquired a meaning which was precisely opposite to that given it in the schema of 1962: it is not the absolute inerrancy of Scripture which is deduced from it, but, on the contrary, the admission that this condescension also accepts the human failings of the writers.

PART TWO

Exegesis of the contents of Chapter III of the Constitution

Chapter II of the Constitution showed the close connection between Scripture and tradition in their function of preserving revelation within the world, and, more particularly, in the Church. Chapter III deals with the theological character of Scripture. Because it is inspired it is especially qualified to mediate the truth of revelation. It is the saving word of God that has passed infallibly into the weak human word, and its contents must be ascertained by various means under the direction of the Church. This chapter goes on to speak of the relation of Scripture to revelation; of the inspiration of the sacred books, which represent a special

[14] Cf. A. Grillmeyer's commentary on Article 8 of *Lumen Gentium* in vol. I of this work, pp. 146–52.

working together of divine and human activity; of the guarantee, because of this inspiration, of the fullness and living force of the truth set down in Scripture for our salvation; of the ways and rules for deriving this divine truth of salvation from the written human word; and of the "humanity" of God, which reveals itself in this passing of his word into our word.

Article 11. Scripture is in a special way the vessel of the divine revelation of salvation, of which Chapter I spoke. This relation to revelation determines the whole. It was somewhat difficult to give it complete expression, because no decision was to be made on the question whether Scripture contained the whole of revelation or not. The vexing question of the material adequacy of Scripture, which made the text of Chapter II so difficult to write, prevented here too a fuller account of the relation between Scripture and the revelation of salvation.[1] Nevertheless, this importance placed on the revelation of salvation was the dominant note, especially for the doctrine of the inerrancy of Scripture, but also in laying down the principles of exegesis. Although the first sentence is cautiously phrased, it contains an important statement: the working of the Holy Spirit which takes place in the inspiration of Scripture is concerned with the preservation of revelation in the Church and the world. In order to preserve and make fruitful for men the *divinitas revelata* "once and for all".[2] Inspiration and its results, the inspired books, belong to the area of the *assimilation* of revelation and the saving reality of God, not of the *historical constitution* of revelation and salvation. Hence also the particular relation to the Holy Spirit and to the Church, the exponents and mediators of "the assimilation of salvation". Scripture belongs to the "age" of the Holy Spirit and the Church, even though Scripture existed before Christ. The assimilation of salvation and the Church begin with the first realization of salvation. "The Church exists from Abel on", as the Constitution *Lumen Gentium* says, with the fathers.[3]

The statement on the inspiration of Scripture, its extent *(extensio)* to all books and all their parts and on the well-known fact in the Church that it was their admission to the Canon which was the criterion of their inspiredness simply presents traditional teaching. Thus the relationship between inspiration and canonicity is seen as Vatican I saw it, as the references in the text show. Neither the question of the extent of the canon nor of the nature of canonicity (the relation between inspiration, canon and Church)[4] is taken up again here. This would have required extensive theological preparatory work and discussion in the Council. These problems did not appear to be so acute. Even the "observers" did not, or

---

[1] Previously, in Forms E and F, the sentence read: "Divinitus revelata, quae afflante Spiritu Sancto litteris consignata sunt, in Sacra Scriptura continentur et prostant." This would have raised the question whether other (lost) inspired books might have existed apart from the canonical books that have been preserved.

[2] Cf. *Dei Verbum*, VI, 21. [3] *Lumen Gentium*, I, 2.

[4] Cf. K. Rahner, *Inspiration in the Bible* (2nd ed., 1964).

this point, act as catalysts for the Conciliar discussion, although in Protestant circles the question of the canon is today receiving new attention. Hardly anything is said here about inspiration — perhaps because, as in orthodox Protestantism also,[5] there is little one can say about it. The Council made a tentative effort to provide a certain clarification of the idea of inspiration and, above all, to show its real meaning.

The development of the text shows that teaching on inspiration was to be purified of certain mechanistic ideas. That is why some effort was directed towards conceiving the relation between the authorship of the sacred writers to the divine origin of Scripture in a more personal way. God is not described as *auctor litterarius* in the literal sense.[6] There is, however, ascribed to him a true influence on the sacred writers.[7] Thus the old tradition is clearly firmly retained.[8] But the Council gives no more detailed explanation and particularly avoids a psychological interpretation of inspiration. It is satisfied with a stronger emphasis on the human share in the creation of the sacred books, with a particular reference to the interpretation of the inerrancy of Scripture and the hermeneutical rules of Article 12. Everything that belongs to the *auctor litterarius* in the strictly technical sense is to be sought on the side of the human authors. This is actually obvious. The share of the sacred writers is more strongly emphasized primarily by avoiding a terminology that could be interpreted in a onesided way: they are no longer described as "living *instruments*" (as in Form C, Article 8 and Form D, Article 11). Also the description of God as the "auctor *principalis*" (Form D, Article 11) is dropped. Instead, the sacred writers are described as the "true authors", which is precisely what *auctores litterarii* is intended to convey. A further change in the text made room for a recognition of differences and limitations in the human authors. In order to bring out their share fully, it had been suggested that it might be stated that they were involved with all their capacities and powers in the composition of the books. Thus Form D, Article 11 stated: "omnibus nempe humanis facultatibus praediti"; or Form E: "omnibus facultatibus ac viribus suis utentes". Both statements went too far. The final text, therefore, speaks simply of the "use of their own powers and abilities". The sacred writers have differing talents and use their powers in different ways. There was to be plenty of room left to appreciate the humanity and hence also the limitations of the inspired writers.[9]

---

[5] On the Protestant view of inspiration cf. J. Beumer, *Die Inspiration der Heiligen Schrift* (in the press), Ch. 5, §9 (older Protestant theology); Ch. 7, §12 (modern Protestant theology).

[6] Thus on the question of the *sensus plenior* in the *relatio* in the *expensio modorum* to Article 12 it is stated: "Omnes concordant de non dirimenda hac quaestione."

[7] The suggestion of a Council father, in the vote on the *modi* of 22 September 1965, that inspiration should be understood in terms of general providence, was firmly rejected.

[8] Cf. J. Beumer, *Die Inspiration der Heiligen Schrift,* §10 and 11.

[9] Thus the *relatio* on Form F, Article 11 under D states: "Deletum est 'omnibus' . . . quia de facto de singulis hagiographis edici non potest, illos 'omnibus' facultatibus suis usos esse. E/3222 loco 'omnibus' proponit 'humanis', quod videtur superfluum . . . Neque admissa est propositio ut dicatur: 'facultatibus *limitatis*'."

In spite of this, God achieves his aim with them: under his influence and his directing power they write everything, and only what is his will.

This is as much as is stated directly in the text. The Council leaves it to theologians to consider, on the basis of the history of the text, the nature of the co-operation of the divine authorship or influence with the human literary authorship. It is possible to ask whether the new nuances in the account of the divine and the human share in the sacred books allow one to give a new account of the nature, goal and effect of the divine influence and then to describe the human share in the writing of the books in such a way that God retains, in relation to them, his true authorship — and yet does not have the limitations of these authors laid to his account, whether in the form of the narrative or in its contents; in the latter it is a question of what they are contributing from the purely human, secular sphere and hence by their own powers. This is not intended to introduce a division between inspired and non-inspired parts of the sacred books. This idea was expressly rejected by the Council, as we have already shown. Without endangering the idea of full inspiration, however, the new version of the divine and human co-operation in the writing of Scripture leaves more room for human limitation. A critical examination of the patristic statements on the nature and working of inspiration would be necessary in order to establish its essential nature, independently of the conceptions of any particular age. *Divino afflante* (*EB*, 556) already suggested this, something that had unfortunately not been done before the Constitution was finally passed.[10] The result of this investigation also affects the premisses of the teaching on inerrancy in *Providentissimus Deus*. Thus, starting from the Council, one is able to move along a path of balanced "demythologization" and "depsychologization" of the teaching on inspiration, which still preserves the essentials of tradition, precisely in order to give a new account of its meaning and make it more acceptable to modern man. Obviously the Council was only able to prepare the way for this kind of work, but was not in a position itself to give any new formulation.

Its contribution to a new doctrine of inspiration consists, however, primarily in what it says on the relation of inspiration, inerrancy and the meaning of Scripture as a whole in terms of the theology of salvation. The relation of Scripture to the revelation of salvation became more and more consciously recognized, combined with a more sharply defined doctrine of revelation and its transmission in the first two chapters of the Constitution.[11] It is the relation of Scripture inspired as a whole and in all its parts to the revelation of salvation that properly shows for the first time its *theological* genus. To have given us a new awareness of this is undoubtedly the real contribution of the Council to a deeper understanding of inspiration and, above all, of the manner in which "truth" is contained in Scripture. This brings us to the problem of inerrancy.

[10] Cf. now J. Beumer, *Die Inspiration der Heiligen Schrift*.
[11] Cf. J. Ratzinger in this commentary, pp. 167–98.

230

The sacred books teach surely, faithfully, and without error the truth that God wanted to have written down in sacred writings for our salvation. From the process of growth of the text, as described above, it emerges that it was the clear will of the Council to formulate more openly its teaching on the inerrancy of Scripture — also under the influence of the irrefutable results of modern research. It should also be noted that this very research in many respects also counters liberal criticism and thus has made the problem of inerrancy in the area of the secular truths less pressing. At the same time, however, it has made possible a fuller picture of the historical and human conditionedness of Scripture. A purely a priori and "absolute" doctrine of inerrancy, as the text of 1962 sought to present, is scarcely compatible with the facts. The Council has not solved the problem by undertaking a purely material investigation, but endeavoured to achieve a solution by pointing out the real meaning of scriptural inerrancy and finding a positive expression for it.

Teaching on inerrancy was to be formulated more positively and given a new emphasis. Hence instead of merely saying *sine (ullo) errore* it speak of the "truth" that "God had written down in Scripture for the sake of our salvation". The *modus* on which this was based was somewhat differently phrased and expressed less clearly the intention of the fathers who were seeking for a new solution.[12] There is a conscious strengthening of the final text. "To have truth written down for the sake of our salvation" is stated to be, not merely here but throughout the whole Constitution,[13] the purpose of the origin of Scripture and its inspiration. These words, "for the sake of our salvation", mean the same thing as the deleted phrase "truth of salvation" *(veritas salutaris)*. But the new formulation is more felicitous and goes further than the one first suggested. The words *salutis causa* remove the possibility of the misinterpretation that *veritas salutaris* was exposed to: namely that Scripture was materially divided into inspired (and inerrant) parts on the one hand, and non-inspired parts (and thus from the start liable to error) on the other. The main point to note is that inspiration and inerrancy are to be understood primarily from the will of God, who desires to communicate

---

[12] The question here is that of the already-mentioned *modus* of the 73 fathers who claim that they said, instead of "veritatem salutarem": "veritatem, quam Deus, nostrae salutis causa, libris sacris consignare voluit." The difference between this and the final version has already been explained.

[13] Cf. Article 7: "nuntiam salutis scriptis mandaverunt"; Article 8: "praedicatio apostolica, quae in inspiratis libris speciali modo exprimitur"; Article 10: Conclusion. A theology of Scripture, above all, must work with these facts. Thus P. Grelot in *La Bible parole de Dieu* (1965), p. 103: "Rather than starting, like Father Benoit, from the psychology of the sacred author, we are going back, in two different respects, to the definition of Scripture as the *word of God addressed to men through the intermediation of the inspired writers*. God speaks to men only to give them his revelation: thus the truth of Scripture is of the same order as that of this revelation. God does not speak to men except by other men: in Scripture his teaching passes through that of the sacred writers in order to reach us. To clarify the present problem it is necessary to reflect on two points: the *truth* of the divine revelation and the *teaching* of the sacred authors." This, in fact, restates the intention and the division of Articles 11 and 12 of Chapter III.

to men his saving truth, and this in such a way that this truth is taught "firmly, faithfully and without error". "Firmly" and "faithfully" describe the special function of Scripture of guaranteeing the permanent existence in the world of the truth of salvation and thus of bearing witness to the special fidelity of God to us in his covenant. Chapter III argues only from inspiration, as a way of imparting to the Church through the Holy Spirit the revelation made and completed in Christ (including both the Old and New Testaments). Chapter VI also refers to the particular elements of its "being written down", especially to the fact that it is written down "once and for all".[14] Here the general human element of "scriptural testimony" is incorporated in the theology of Scripture. This gives to Scripture the character of a "rule of faith". The post-apostolic age discovered the "scriptural character" of the New Testament at a time when Christian doctrine threatened to be more and more dissolved by wildly proliferating *traditiones*. The defenders of "tradition" at Vatican II, who were sometimes so rigid, were too little aware of this connection. The words *firmiter-fideliter* of Chapter III and *semel pro semper* of Chapter VI have their particular importance. Here we have a clear *typos* of doctrine. At the same time, in this fuller view inerrancy is a particular expression of fidelity to the covenant and of the permanent saving will of God. The "truth" and "truthfulness" of God are inseparably bound up with each other. The new version of the inerrancy of Scripture seeks to avoid the danger of intellectualization. Hence the emphasis on its full saving function in the words *firmiter-fideliter*. It seeks to give back to this doctrine its true content: the significance of the inerrancy of Scripture is that it is a special guarantee of the permanent existence and effectiveness of the saving truth of God among men.

We should also say a word about the formulation *"teaching* firmly, faithfully and without error". The word *docere* is not meant in the sense of a particular theory of inerrancy or inspiration, as had been the case before.[15] The new meaning given to the doctrine of inerrancy makes such theories more or less superfluous since they had been elaborated in order to answer the criticisms of the idea of biblical inerrancy. They were more or less unconvincing and unreal solutions. The final editing of the text and the vote on the *modi* reveal various attempts to substitute *exhibere* ("offer") or *exprimere* ("express") for *docere,* in order to exclude the didactic and intellectualistic ring of the word "teach" or to prevent a limitation of inerrancy (or inspiration) to actual "doctrinal statements". The Commission replied that "the word 'teach' is to be retained, as it is concerned with what is actually *said*". Thus it involves no commitment to higher theories connected with it. "Even by speaking only of what is (firmly) stated, the Council certainly does not desire to declare that those views are false which see the hints, surmises, metaphors, attitudes and emotional contents of the scriptural text as

---

[14] Cf. *Dei Verbum,* VI, 21: "semel pro semper litteris consignatae".
[15] Cf. Beumer, *loc. cit.,* ch. 7, § 13 (on Benoit and Grelot, *loc. cit.,* pp. 101–2).

ransmitting communication from God to man.''[16] Taken in the whole context
of the sentence and having the same meaning as *asserere,* this word "teach"
acquires the sense of a fixed and truthful statement and promise, which corre-
ponds to the scriptural *veritas.*

Excursus on Article 11

The relation between saving truth and secular statements in Scripture according to Vatican II

Beyond this positive new orientation of teaching on the inerrancy of Scripture
he Constitution gives no more detailed account of the relationship between the
ruths of salvation and secular statements and their inerrancy. Hence we need to
consider in a separate section what the Constitution has stated positively and
vhat it has left open. This task can only be achieved by looking at the background
of the whole development of the text.

1. The first intention of the Constitution is not to present a *theory* by means of
vhich the well-known difficulties of the doctrine of inerrancy could be solved.
ts primary concern is to regain the larger perspective and real meaning of
criptural inerrancy. It is expressly emphasized that God is concerned with
passing on, unfalsified and imperishable, the truth of salvation and hence to
maintain his eternal covenant with men. What we are to regard as such a truth of
alvation is described broadly in Chapter I of the Constitution. It is also the actual
content of "transmission" *(transmissio),* the organs of which are Scripture and
radition, closely bound up with each other and yet different in their function
cf. esp. Articles 7 and 8). In Chapters IV and V the same truth of salvation is
hown to be the actual content of the Old and New Testaments (cf. esp. Articles
5, 17 and 20). It is always a question of the *thesaurus revelationis,* which is entrusted
o the Church, and through the Church to mankind.[1]

2. Now the question arises: is the strong emphasis on *salutis causa* in the question
of inerrancy a licence to exclude the so-called *veritates profanae* from it? In our
answer we must distinguish between what can be established as the direct or
ndirect statement of the text (against the background of its history), and what
s presented to us as a "theory" or hint of such.

a) From the sources we can see that the majority of fathers who spoke on the
ubject of inerrancy tended towards a more open attitude to the difficulties.
The statement of Cardinal König, ". . . in Bibliis Sacris notitias historicas et
notitias scientiae naturalis a veritate quandoque deficere", was not opposed or
ejected either in the assembly or in the Theological Commission. It was not
neld to be contradictory to earlier statements by the Church's teaching office.

---

³ N. Lohfink, "Die Wahrheit der Bibel und die Geschichtlichkeit der Evangelien", *Orientierung*
°9 (1965), p. 254.
  Cf. above note 13.

b) The Council firmly rejects any limitation of inspiration to particular truths or particular parts of Scripture. When, on the vote on the *modi* on 21 September 1965, objections were raised against the expression *veritas salutaris* because it seemed, as opposed to the documents of the *magisterium,* to limit inerrancy to teaching on faith and morals and the question was raised of the inerrancy of the other statements of Scripture, the Theological Commission replied in its *expensio modorum* again with the two points that the *whole* of Scripture is inspired and therefore the word of God, and that the word of truth does not teach anything other than the *veritas salutaris.*[2] The words quoted from the encyclical *Providentissimus Deus* (see above) are also interpreted in relation to this "truth of salvation". Only in order to avoid any misuse of the expression "truth of salvation" (in the sense of a limitation of inspiration, as we can see from the context), is the change made from *veritas salutaris* to "the truth that is written in sacred books for the sake of our salvation". Hence nothing is said about the claim that inerrancy is being limited. This shade of meaning in the final answer of the Theological Commission should be carefully noted. It is not accidental or a mistake, but intended. The Theological Commission did not want to make a decision on this point — this was also in the spirit of the intervention of Paul VI, at least insofar as he did not want to put anything in the way of a new investigation of the question.

c) In interpreting the doctrine of inerrancy we must start from this point: "veritas, quam Deus nostrae salutis causa Litteris Sacris consignari voluit". "To have the truth written down in the sacred books for our salvation" is thus presented as the motive (formal object[3]) of inspiration. Whereas *veritas salutaris* had rather the character of a material object from which *veritas profana* was distinguished, the words "to have written down for the sake of our salvation" show a more careful approach, which makes possible a new solution of the problem of inerrancy, and this is intentional. It would be a simplification of the Council's position if one were to say that the inerrancy of Scripture applied only to the material that contained truth of salvation *(veritates salutares)* as opposed to secular truths *(veritates profanae)*. This would be to confront Scripture again with the 19th-century position. It would also be a misunderstanding of the Council's intentions if one said that it had not produced anything new on the question of inerrancy beyond the position of the well-known scriptural encyclicals. The Council starts from a profounder understanding of the nature of Scripture, which

---

[2] Thus the Theological Commission in its first answer to the *modi* of 22 September 1965, which called for the removal of the expression *veritas salutaris*. Since, however, this expression was changed to *nostrae salutis causa,* this version was again dropped.

[3] Cf. O. Loretz, "Die Wahrheitsfrage in der Exegese", *Theologische Revue* 63 (1967), 1–8 (7–8). Here Loretz is criticizing the distinction between formal and material object, taken over by P. Grelot *(op. cit.,* pp. 79–81) and A. Grillmeier *(loc. cit.,* p. 181), and its application to the interpretation of inerrancy in Scripture. This expression, however, does not need to be rejected simply because it belongs to the language of scholasticism, since it in no way affects the nature of the language of Scripture (cf. the commentary on Article 12).

presents an inseparable combination of divine and human activity and yet leaves to each its own area. The development of the text has shown us that "mono-physitism" in the understanding of inspiration and inerrancy is to be given up, as presented in the thesis of verbal inspiration, but also in the version of the teaching on inerrancy found in the form of 1962 (and in the scriptural encyclicals). So much can be said on the basis of Article 11. It remains for theology to examine inerrancy even more thoroughly on the basis of the new approach.

d) In the area of theological reflection P. Grelot presented an attempt at interpretation during the Council which is worthy of discussion. He starts practically from the idea of *salutis causa* and says that in Scripture not only are truths of salvation communicated as "a material object", but that "the communi-cation of saving truths" is the whole "formal object" of Scripture. Thus the so-called secular truths or narratives also acquire through this a relation to salvation. They are chosen and presented not as saving truths in themselves, but as the medium of the communication of salvation.[4] They serve as a framework to what is essential, "locating" saving truth and the history of salvation (cf. e.g. Dan 1 or Lk 1). They are chosen and presented only in so far as they fulfil this purpose.[5]

It is especially important today to emphasize this subsidiary function of the "locating" of saving truths and saving history. In all its documents the Council starts from the clear conviction that God has spoken and acted in the world. For the Church the saving revelation and action of God in Christ is a reality that certainly, in the first place, speaks personally to man, but that must not be in any way reduced to an existential interpretation, however much the latter might be understood as the process of salvation (in self-understanding in Christ). It is not important that in order to locate the saving actions or words of God exact historical or geographical data should be supplied. We know today too much about the way in which the sacred books were conditioned by the time in which they were written to be able to apply the 19th-century conception of historical truth to them. But both the opponents and the defenders of the inerrancy of Scripture had done this. The authority of Scripture today is no longer threatened from this quarter. On the contrary; the ever fuller knowledge of the way in which the saving statements of Scripture are embedded in history shows their

---

[4] Cf. P. Grelot, *op. cit.,* p. 81: "None of the particular elements which figure in the sacred books is integrated in an unconditional way. Even if it holds an important or even the first place, the sacred authors are never interested in anything but one particular point of view, connected with the life of faith: *its relation to the mystery of salvation.* In scholastic language, useful here for its precision, we could say that this is the *formal object quo* of their witness, whatever the material object might be."

[5] Thus the *Interpreter's Bible,* VI, for example, noted on the above-mentioned question of the date of the siege of Jerusalem in Dan 1:1 in a calm and factual way: "Since they are but literary devices, strict historical accuracy in such particulars is not important, for they are there to provide a setting for this story, not to give historical information". For similar remarks cf. *ibid.,* pp. 375–6 (on Dan 2:1) and pp. 419–20.

truly genuine character. Here we can see fully that "condescension" of God which was mentioned in the discussion on inerrancy and in the text itself.

In the light of the *salutis causa* we can see Scripture as a complex entity with many levels — analogous to the way in which the Church as a whole saw itself at the Council.[6] There are direct statements and accounts of salvation in which this formal object *salutis causa* is clearly verifiable. But there are also parts of Scripture which have only an auxiliary function in relation to these direct truths of salvation. Here, from the point of view of the secular sciences, somewhat less than the truth can be expressed. Here we must accept facts without prejudice and without anxiety. The question of inerrancy is not to become a matter of a bad conscience or false attitudes but should open one's eyes to the full nature of Scripture. God's word communicates itself to us unfalsified in the fragile vessel of human language and human writing. God's purpose is that his word of salvation is received in all its fullness. To it he gives the guarantee of full authority. This is the true meaning of inspiration, the assistance of the Holy Spirit. Everything else only serves the truth that is written down without error "for the sake of our salvation". It is a meaning or framework of the statement that is actually intended and thus only has a part-share in inerrancy, namely to the extent required in its service of the saving word. Thus one can accept inerrancy in a true sense of the whole of Scripture, as inspiration also applies to all the books and their parts. Everything in Scripture has a share in the "truth that God wanted to have written down for the sake of our salvation", either directly and in content or indirectly and by reason of its service for the statement of salvation. This gradation is also the guarantee of the point about *firmiter, fideliter et sine errore docere*. What secular science regards as the material mistakes and inaccuracies in Scripture should not be considered in isolation and simply described as "error". It should all be seen within the total framework of Scripture and judged in terms of its service for the word of salvation.

The question of the inerrancy of Scripture has passed into a new stage. The questions of criticism are no longer directed so much at the *veritates profanae,* but at the validity of the way in which Scripture understands salvation itself, about the justification of the scriptural ideals and moral demands. We are now wrestling with the *theological* content of Scripture, with the reality of the deeds performed by God for the sake of our salvation, as, for example, the resurrection of Jesus in particular. It is a question of the interpretation of the person, the mission, the work, the whole life and death of Jesus and his story. We are also concerned with the facts connected with the foundation of the Church and with its nature — and no longer with a given historical date, or given geographical or scientific details. The question of the nature of biblical Christianity is asked in a particularly radical way. Thus the Constitution rightly emphasizes that Scripture teaches the *truth of salvation* "surely, faithfully and without error". Hence in Chapters IV and V the

---

[6] *Lumen Gentium*, Chapter I, Article 8 *(realitas complexa).*

question of the interpretation of the Old and the New Testaments is raised and finally the imperishable living value of Scripture emphasized in Chapter VI.

Thus one may say that the question of the "truth" of Scripture has found an expression in the Constitution which is appropriate to our own age. This can be seen further in the hermeneutical rules of Article 12. They retain their connection with the question of inerrancy, even if in another sense than that of *Divino afflante* and the first versions of the text of the Constitution.

Article 12. On the basis of the account given above on the history of the text of Article 12, let us briefly sum up the basic features of scriptural hermeneutics presented in *Dei Verbum*. In order to see what has actually been achieved we must place the new text against the background of *Divino afflante* and the first forms of the text (A–C). It is not correct to say that Article 12 does not offer anything more than that the hermeneutics of *Divino afflante* has been raised to the level of a Conciliar pronouncement.[1] This will emerge from the exegesis of the various sections.

1. The introduction to Article 12

This deals with the *purpose* of exegesis and the scriptural hermeneutics developed in the following sections. In content it is more comprehensive than *Divino afflante* and the first forms of our text (A–C). In these documents all hermeneutics was conceived exclusively in terms of the solution of the problems of scriptural inerrancy, as they were understood at the time. Not without reason did Form A state the goal of the rules of scriptural interpretation to be: "Veritas enim et fides historica sacrae Scripturae recte probantur . . .", and this with reference to *Divino afflante* (*EB,* 558–62). In Form C everything was conceived in terms of the problem: "How are we to understand inerrancy?" "Truth" had a very narrow meaning and was only concerned with the historical truth *(fides historica)* of the Bible.[2]

Now it is concerned with the discovery of the "truth . . . that God wanted to have written down in sacred Scripture for the sake of our salvation". This *salutis causa* also applies to the introduction of Article 12, which is concerned with what God intended to convey and what the writer intended to convey: "The interpreter of sacred Scripture, in order to see clearly what God wanted to communicate to us, should carefully investigate what meaning the sacred writers really intended, and what God wanted to manifest by means of their words."

---

[1] N. Lohfink in *Orientierung* 29 (1965), p. 255; id., *Katholische Bibelwissenschaft und historisch-kritische Methode* (1966), p. 14.

[2] Of course *Divino afflante* and the first forms of the Constitution *Dei Verbum* speak of the significance for salvation of Scripture as a whole. But it still remains true that the rules of scriptural hermeneutics are presented from the point of view of saving the inerrancy of the *veritates profanae*. Thus particularly in Form C (1962).

a) The truth of Scripture is bound up with what the sacred writer or writers intended to convey, in which what God desired to convey expresses itself. This point is important primarily for the understanding of the inspiration of Scripture. The Church is not committing itself to the idea of a verbal inspiration that can be understood more or less "mechanically". The truth of Scripture is contained in meanings that have first to be discovered in the single words and sentences. This gives to the idea of inspiration itself a new depth and a particular relation to the revelation of salvation. However much the Church's understanding of inspiration is related to the "written" word and Scripture is, through this inspiration, "the written word of God", it is not the letter or the sentence, but the intention of the sacred writers that decides the meaning of Scripture. But because of inspiration what they desire to express is the same as what God desires to express. Because, however, the statement of God, according to Article 11, is a statement of salvation, the *salutis causa* is the formal point of view from which the sacred writers compose their writings. Hence even after *Dei Verbum* — as in *Divino afflante* — the truth of Scripture and inerrancy is bound up with what the sacred writers desired to express. It is not separated from this.[3] We have shown how the so-called *veritates profanae* are also included, though in their own way. Thus Scripture becomes — despite all its humanity and its conditioning by the age in which it was written — God's address to us in the human word, *propter salutem nostram!*

b) This clearly determines theologically the goal of exegesis, even if there are various ways towards it. The introduction to Article 12 makes this theological aim clear. In considering the development of the history of the text we have already referred to the controversial question within Catholic exegesis which is often described by the phrase the *sensus plenior* of Scripture. If the intention of the sacred writers and that of God are so likened to each other, the question of their full and complete identity is still not settled in any way. The Council consciously did not want to decide this, but wished to leave it to further discussion. Without going into the various ramifications of the problem in the discussion hitherto, let us just take up a cautious position on the basis of Article 12. The question is: does God want to say only what the author of a book or a scriptural text can be proved historically to have had in mind and what he understood his statement to express according to the conceptions of his own time? Or does the expressive intention of God go further, so that each generation is justified in interpreting Scripture according to its own situation? — i.e. interpreting it and not simply applying it. Historically-minded exegetes might like to reduce the divine meaning of Scripture to what can be proved historically to have been the meaning in the mind of the sacred writer and see only this as truly scientific exegesis. Other, more theologically orientated exegetes or scriptural theologians or even dogmatic theologians defend the idea of a graded exegesis: as a first step, they

---

[3] N. Lohfink is of a different opinion in *Orientierung* 29 (1965), p. 255.

want to discover by critical historical means — like the others — what it was the sacred writers intended to say. They consider this also as the *sensus divinus,* but only to the extent to which the sacred writer of the time grasped it. They do not, however, simply identify what God desired to express with this historically conditioned understanding of the writer, but extend it beyond this. For example, they emphasize that it was not necessary, nor even possible, that an Old Testament author should know the full objective contents of his words, as this only became apparent in the further succession of the various books, but above all fully in Christ and the New Testament. The Old Testament interprets itself through its own history, "et Novum Testamentum in Vetere latet, et Vetus Testamentum in Novo patet".[4] Moreover, in the scriptural statement of salvation ideas are used whose general human meaning can only be analogous to the reality that is actually intended. But the history of theology and also exegesis lives from the fact that both the ideas and their human content are constantly being understood more profoundly and enriched, and also from the fact that the mystery expressed is more deeply understood from a new starting-point. We do not need to give a more detailed account of the various forms of this intellectual process. Nor are we entitled to interpret the conciliar text in any one particular way.[5] Let us, however, make two further points: 1. Because everything is seen from the point of view of the *salutis causa* of inspired Scripture, any scriptural statement which has been arrived at by critical historical work is a genuine *sensus pneumaticus.* The pneumatic meaning of Scripture must not be separated from the historically established *sensus auctoris.* 2. All searching for the *sensus plenior* must start with the findings of critical historical research, which must proceed according to legitimate methods of theological scholarship. An interpretation that is detached from the genuine *sensus auctoris* is eisegesis, not exegesis.

This is our starting-point for the interpretation of the hermeneutical rules of Article 12. They are divided into two groups. First, it is concerned with the different ways of critical historical work, which is the prerequisite for the discovery of the *sensus auctoris* and thus also (at least in a preliminary way) of the *sensus divinus.* But it then goes on to develop rules of hermeneutics which depend on a fuller *theological* evaluation of Scripture in the light of tradition and as the property of the Church. Various Council fathers distinguished here between so-called "rational" and actual "theological" exegesis. This distinction is not a happy one. As it is always a question of the *sensus divinus* in the *sensus humanus* it is always concerned with theological exegesis. Since Scripture must always be read in the Church no distinction can be made between the first and the second way, inasmuch as both are correctly followed. A better division would be between the technical exegetical rules of hermeneutics (in the modern sense) and the dogmatic theological rules of the interpretation of Scripture.

[4] See below, Chapter IV, 2 (Augustine).
[5] See above, Article 11, note 6.

2. The hermeneutical rules of Article 12

a) The first group (the technical exegetical rules)

(i) The first method of understanding the intention of the sacred writers is the investigation of literary forms. There are three points to be noted here: 1) The investigation of literary forms or types is only one way "among others" *(inter alia etiam)*. By the "alia" one can understand any legitimate method of hermeneutics, whether tried or untried.[6] Certain points from Chapters IV and V of the Constitution belong in this context (especially Article 19). 2) To speak of the various types enumerated, the historical account is mentioned first, though it can, however, have very different forms, as is correctly, but rather infelicitously, put: "whether a text is history of one kind or another". "There is 'early history', which covers the span between Abraham and the beginnings of the human race, without naturally being able to base itself on actual sources. There is 'religious history', which sovereignly ignores all secondary sources and reduces everything to the direct intervention of God. There is the religious national epic. There is the historical novel. There is, above all, the remarkable fact that we describe as historical those books of the Old Testament that were considered by the *ancient Jews* as *prophetic literature* . . ."[7] If now — in contrast with the fuller lists of earlier forms of the text — only prophecy and poetry are mentioned apart from history, this follows from the view that a complete list is not necessary. The main thing is that the literary investigation of types of literature is given conciliar authority and scholars are free to consider "some other types of speech" as well. — 3) The Constitution distinguishes more clearly than *Divino afflante* the idea of the *genus litterarium* from other methods of discovering the meaning of Scripture, as we shall now see.

(ii) Further *(porro)* the intention of the sacred writers is to be discovered by considering the particular situation or the circumstances, i.e. the general cultural conditions of the time that might have a bearing on the way that a particular situation is grasped by the mind. The *determinata adiuncta* are the concomitant circumstances, the situation from which the writer writes or in which a text has grown that he takes over. Let us consider the various situations from which the individual psalms have emerged. The words "the situation of his own time and culture" do not refer so much to the objective conditions or the historical and

---

[6] An excellent account of the present standpoint on this question is to be found in K. Koch, *Was ist Formgeschichte? Neue Wege der Bibelexegese* (1964) (cf. the review by N. Lohfink in *Theologie und Philosophie* 40 [1966], pp. 112–15; important observations on the problems raised in Article 12 are given by J. A. Fitzmeyer in *Die Wahrheit der Evangelien* [1965], pp. 18 ff., following the instruction of the Papal Commission on Scripture of 1964). Koch deals primarily with the determination of the type, with type history, with the *Sitz im Leben*, with the history of tradition and editing as separate stages of exegetical methods. In the second part of his work he analyses selected scriptural examples according to this method.

[7] Semmelroth-Zerwick, pp. 36–37.

cultural milieu of the writer, as their influence on the way in which he experiences and understands reality, which seeks in him its own expression. If there is here another reference to the literary types, it is in order to establish a unity with what has gone before. For the concrete situation, the particular understanding of life, all the various subjective preconditions affect the choice of the literary genus in the writer's account. But the main thing here is not the literary expression, but the mental, subjective modes of understanding and evaluating reality or a situation, which depend on the circumstances, the milieu and the age (in his reference to the *temporis conditio* Augustine was primarily concerned with the development of moral judgments). In any case these judgments and evaluations take precedence over the written accounts, however much influence they may have on them.

In connection with what is said here, especially concerning the *determinata adiuncta* the phrase coined by Hermann Gunkel, which has subsequently become so significant, *Sitz im Leben* was quoted, even during the work on the text.[8] Whether this parallel is a legitimate one depends on a precise definition of the *determinata adiuncta* in our text and on the exact meaning of the expression *Sitz im Leben*. Gunkel wanted to use the idea of *Sitz im Leben* in order to explain the choice of the literary type. He meant by this a recurrent situation or function that determined this choice, as is the case, for example, with the psalms in worship and liturgy. Marriage, birth, death, family funeral-rites, the coronation of a king, marching into battle, the celebration of a victory, can undoubtedly be included in the idea of the *determinata adiuncta*. If one considers the close connection between this mention of the "particular circumstances" and the whole influence of the age and culture and the second mention of the literary types, Gunkel's phrase *Sitz im Leben* would not be inappropriate, and this all the more as it has acquired a further significance in contemporary usage.

The text of the Constitution, however, does not see the context of the writer's statement only in terms of Gunkel's idea of such recurrent situations, nor only in terms of the cultural conditions of the time; it sees the real medium through which the cultural milieu of the time affects the author as being the modes of feeling, speaking and narrating and the forms of everyday human intercourse. All this precedes the written account. It can affect the choice of the literary type, but does not have to. In any case, however, these modes of feeling and thinking, the spirit of the language and the forms of narration and daily social life, are of the greatest importance in understanding the meaning of Scripture. If one desires to express all this by the one phrase *Sitz im Leben,* then the latter is being used in a more developed sense than that in which Gunkel used it. It is a question of all the factors which make up the concrete historical conditionedness, i.e. in a word, the "historicalness" of the scriptural statement. These may be unique conditions of time and place, recurrent situations, or permanent conditions within a particular epoch or cultural area.

[8] Cf. K. Koch, *op. cit.,* pp. 30–44.

In calling upon scholars to investigate and evaluate the historical conditions of the statements of Scripture, the Constitution is according a more comprehensive and profound task to critical historical research — if not so fully elaborated — than in *Divino afflante*. The actual scope of all these endeavours emerges more clearly in the Constitution than in the encyclical. Here the theme of inerrancy dominates the statements on hermeneutics. Now the goal of critical historical work is seen as the *sensus divinus* in the *sensus humanus* or the discovery of the message of salvation. Two stages are differentiated in work on Scripture: 1. History; 2. Interpretation.[9] The discovery of the historical connections between the statements of Scripture and history is the task of critical historical research. Our conciliar text, like *Divino afflante*, marks out this area adequately. But all this is only a means and a way to interpretation and hermeneutics. The conciliar text presents this task of interpretation in a far more impressive way than the encyclical: "... the interpreter of sacred Scripture ... should carefully investigate what meaning the sacred writers really intended and what God wanted to manifest by means of their words ..."; "those who search out the intention of the sacred writers ..."; "further, the interpreter must investigate what meaning the sacred writer intended to express and actually expressed ..."; "for the correct understanding of what the sacred writer wanted to assert ...": it is always concerned with the *sensus auctoris,* which, however, is always subject to the *salutis causa* of Article 11. This search for the intention of the writer and that of God is a search for the fullness of revelation — and is no longer seen as merely a way to save the inerrancy of Scripture. But this search is not completed with critical historical work as such. It is only after this that the interpretation proper begins.

According to the Constitution, all legitimate methods of critical historical research to establish the historical conditions of the writer's intention are to be acknowledged, whether it is a question of the literary genus, the history of forms, traditions or themes, the *Sitz im Leben* or any other influence. This does not mean, however, that the Constitution is welcoming a relativization of the scriptural statements to the point where their content is removed. For in everything it is a question of the *sensus divinus,* which has been written down in the human word and for all (Article 21) for the sake of our salvation under the influence of the spirit of Christ. Whatever is demonstrably the *sensus* of the human author must always be the starting-point for the question of the divine message of salvation. All the efforts of the exegete must be directed primarily towards establishing this meaning.

b) The second group (The rules of dogmatic theology)

The second group of the rules for the interpretation of Scripture is introduced by a reference to the pneumatic origin of Scripture. It asks that any concern with it be governed by the same spirit. Scripture must be read and interpreted in the

[9] Cf. N. Lohfink, *Altes Testament, Historisch-Christliche Auslegung* (1967); id., *Katholische Bibelwissenschaft und historisch-kritische Methode* (1966).

spirit in which it was written. Perhaps the place chosen to make this point could lead to a misunderstanding. This "interpretation in the Holy Spirit" takes place naturally primarily along the lines of the method indicated. This is why the term "rational" exegesis that was coined for it is ambiguous. What is "rational" about it is primarily the application of the critical historical method. The actual interpretation on the basis of history may also be, in some measure, "rational", namely, to the extent that rules are applied here that are also valid for other non-scriptural texts. But because the whole endeavour is concerned with the *sensus divinus* in the *sensu humano,* we are already involved in "theological" exegesis. We are concerned with the revelation of God's salvation. On the other hand, we do not leave the area of "science", when hermeneutical principles are now established that are derived from the full *theological* character of Scripture *and* its place in the *Church* and its *tradition.* It is true that this is not the area of technical exegetical work in the narrow sense, but that of the biblical and dogmatic theologian. Both the professional exegete and the theologian are to collaborate, according to Chapter VI of the Constitution, in order that everything that Scripture has to offer be made available to the life of the Church.

1) Because of the inspiration of the canon of Scripture by the one Holy Spirit, the Church sees Scripture as a unity. This in no way prevents the individual nature of the sacred books or traditions being investigated and differentiated by critical historical means. This unity of Scripture is not affected by the fact that Scripture inspires or supplements itself, thus, in a sense, correcting itself. At all events, the theologian who proceeds from this premiss of the unity of Scripture will always be obliged to establish the nature of the individual statement in its context and in its particular significance, entirely according to the first group of hermeneutical rules given in Article 12. But a synthesizing of the knowledge that has been acquired in this analytical way is legitimate. Since Schleiermacher it has been considered necessary to take account of the context in the scientific exegesis of texts.[10] Modern hermeneutics has already developed a method that can be used to serve this synthetic view: the "history of tradition", introduced by G. v. Rad. The "history of themes", developed by M. Noth, can perform a similar service. Both methods are able to act as a bridge between the historical and the Christian interpretation of Scripture. "We must interpret *historically,* because we must enquire, for the sake of intellectual honesty, what was originally meant. We must interpret in a *Christian* way, because we are concerned with Scripture as the word of God, but because we cannot assume that God himself will contradict his own all-embracing word spoken in Christ."[11] This "unity" of Scripture is, of course, a dogmatic premiss. But Scripture itself works with it, as we can see from the place

---

[10] Cf. L. Alonso Schökel, *The Inspired Word. Scripture in the Light of Language and Literature* (1965), pp. 217–18. The first Spanish version of this work did not appear until 1966 under the title *La Palabra Inspirada* (1966).

[11] Cf. N. Lohfink, *Altes Testament,* p. 16; id., *Katholische Bibelwissenschaft* (cf. above note 9), p. 25.

of the Old Testament in the New or from the relation of individual books to others within both Testaments.

At this point it is possible to take up again the theme of *sensus plenior*. The history of tradition itself and an examination of the unity of Scripture show that the historical interpretation has to reckon with the fact that it is not necessary for the particular author to have been fully conscious of the full implications of his statement in relation to the total revelation of God in Christ or to the *eschaton*. It follows from the historical nature of the statements of an author, which is so strongly emphasized in the rules of the first group, that he himself has a definite and therefore limited understanding of what he is writing down. But if the critical historical content is to have an ultimate validity as a "theological" statement, reflection about its implications is justified and even necessary. This reflection grows with the finer methods of the analysis of ideas, the procedures of philology, but also of philosophy and finally of theology. Only through this reflection on the implications contained in biblical ideas and statements is a development of the knowledge of faith, theology and the history of dogma possible. At the same time, however, the scriptural origin of the later dogmas and of systematic theology becomes visible. According to the will of the Council, theology has to reflect on this anew,[12] in order itself to retain that unity that is the property of Scripture.

2) Modern hermeneutics also has a more positive attitude to the significance of tradition in the interpretation of texts. This is particularly true for "sacred writings", which, like all other Christian ones, refer in such a comprehensive way to saving revelation and events, especially the Christ event. Scripture is the book of life for those who believe in Christ. But Christianity is not a book-religion. It is not bound to the letter. Article 12 shows this by the fact that the goal of exegesis is stated to be the discovery of the *sensus divinus* in the *sensu humano*. The reading and interpretation of Scripture is a thoroughly intellectual process, which centres, however, on the Christ event, that must itself always be more profoundly extended in proclamation and theology and assimilated by the Church. This intellectual process is the tradition of the Church, from which Scripture — under the special influence of the Spirit of Christ — has emerged. This process continues, but must, as the Council emphasizes, be inspired by Scripture itself (cf. Chapter VI). The age of the Fathers, considered so important by the Council, was supremely a time of the re-reading of Scripture (cf. below on Chapter VI).

3) If the interpretation of Scripture is to consider the whole of revelation, as presented within the one body of Scripture and lived in the Church, then one statement can be seen in the light of another. They can be combined to yield new knowledge. This is the analogy of faith. Even if historical exegesis retains its

---

[12] Cf. Chapter VI of the Constitution *Dei Verbum* and the Decree on Priestly Formation, Article 16.

place and must be a constant corrective, the theologian is able to take the original individual statements of Scripture, e.g. on the Father, Son and Spirit, on the person and mission of Jesus, see them as a synthesis and relate them to the trinitarian and Christological dogmas. This all the more as these dogmas do not seek to be anything other than the maintenance of the genuine doctrine of Scripture in contrast to its evaporation into heresy. There is here a reciprocal relationship: the living tradition of the Church helps us through its growing understanding of faith to a deeper understanding of Scripture. An ever renewed re-reading of Scripture, however, must become the soul of theology and of the whole of tradition, so that everything can be led back to the unified fullness of the beginning, where everything was still "together".

4) Thus what *Dei Verbum* says about the transmission of Scripture is part of Church hermeneutics: "This tradition which comes from the Apostles develops in the Church with the help of the Holy Spirit. For there is a growth in the understanding of the realities and the words which have been handed down. This happens through the contemplation and the study made by believers, who treasure these things in their hearts (cf. Lk 2:29, 51), through the intimate understanding of spiritual things they experience, and through the preaching of those who have received through episcopal succession the sure gift of truth. For, as the centuries succeed one another, the Church constantly moves forward towards the fullness of divine truth until the words of God reach their complete fulfilment in her."[13] This maturing of the Church is, for the Constitution, also to be a maturing of its judgment on, and understanding of, Scripture. Thus the Council recommends a combination of technical exegetical hermeneutics and total theological method with a living Church understanding of faith, which leaves everyone with their necessary individuality, but points the common goal to all: the ever fuller understanding and assimilation of the reality of salvation.

Article 13. The conclusion of Chapter III again takes as its starting-point the idea of the word of God as it passes into the written human word. The depth and uniqueness of this process can be seen from that analogy of faith which Article 12 had presented as the source of the understanding of Scripture. The humanity of the word of God in the word of Scripture is understood from the greater mystery of the humanity of God, which he showed in the incarnation. This would have been an opportunity to adduce another analogy and refer to the connection of the divine and the human in the Church, thus giving Scripture its place within the whole of the being and history of the Church and the divine economy of salvation. In Scripture the Church possesses the living treasure of revelation, which, by reason of its being inspired, imperishably remains, although set down in the fragile vessel of the human word (cf. 2 Cor 4:7). This humanized ex-

[3] *Dei Verbum,* Article 8.

pression of the word of God in our language aroused — like the mystery of the incarnation of the word and the Church — the amazement of the fathers.[14] In all these mysteries the divine appears — even though each time in a different way — "in our form", the word of the Father in the flesh of our weakness,[15] the spirit of God in a community that is "at the same time holy and in need of purification",[16] the word of God clothed in our words.

Conclusion

We have endeavoured to understand Chapter III of the Constitution *Dei Verbum* from the history of the whole text and the tendencies which emerged through its various transformations. If one only knows the final text of the Constitution or of its third chapter, one cannot understand its intentions and implications. Here too there must be a combination of a critical historical method and interpretation. The many vicissitudes that the history of this Constitution has undergone point to a direction in which the Church hopes for a renewal. This is not a break with the past, but a rendering fruitful of an older and richer tradition. It is true that exegetes are now given, after long periods during which their work was severely restricted,[17] greater freedom for the future, a freedom that corresponds to the nature of the word of God as it has emerged in history, and to the nature of the Church. The Constitution brings home to us in this very Chapter the way in which the Church must concern itself with Scripture. By pointing the way to a clearer understanding of the co-operation of God with men in the inspiration of Scripture, it also frees us from false attitudes in the search for the truth in Scripture. We are not to devote our energies to the defence of positions that were set up against an enemy that has long since departed, but rather to the discovery of the fullness of truth that God caused to be written down for the sake of our salvation. In declaring the purpose of all hermeneutics to be the discovery of the *sensus divinus* in the *sensu humano* and the purpose of the inspiration of Scripture the sure, faithful and the infallible making known to us of the truth of salvation, the Constitution is presenting the word of Scripture as the medium of a constant spiritual dialogue of God with men. To contemplate the "living word of God" — the theme of the Constitution from beginning to end — leads to a deepening understanding of inspiration, to a positive understanding of the doctrine of inerrancy, and at the same time to its humanization and to a comprehensive concern with Scripture. The age of anxiety in relation to Scripture is to be regarded as over — a new life with it is to start.

[14] Cf. on this question A. Grillmeier's commentary on Chapter I of *Lumen Gentium* in vol. I of this work, pp. 146 f.

[15] Cf. *Lumen Gentium,* Article 9.

[16] Cf. *ibid.,* Article 8.

[17] Cf. J. Beumer, *loc. cit.*, ch. 7, §13.

CHAPTER IV

The Old Testament

by
Béda Rigaux

It would be useful to make a few short preliminary observations before commencing the commentary.[1] The first thing to note is that the general ideas that are used in the headings of Chapters IV and V indicate the intention of the Council. It regards both orders of salvation in their totality and does not simply limit itself to the books which are their testimonies. Moreover, the brevity of the chapter that is devoted to the Old Testament may be surprising. The reason for it is twofold. On the one hand, the encyclical *Divino afflante*[2] brought peace to Catholic exegesis of the Old Testament. On the other hand, the literary and historical problems presented by the books of the Old Testament are less urgent than before. Finally, the Constitution is clearly different from the statements from earlier Councils. It does not return to the question of the canon of Scripture and leaves the literary questions of the authenticity of the various writings undiscussed. Its novelty, as regards the Old Testament, consists in the emphasis with which it both differentiates and combines the economy of salvation and the inspired books. Thus the goal clearly emerges: salvation history is a preparation for the fulfilment of the ways of God in Jesus Christ, who is the "end of the law" (Rom 10:4); as the word of God, however, the Old Testament retains its permanent importance. This places the Constitution on the level of that theology which dominates the contemporary endeavours of the Christian churches. All apologetical or polemical aspects are missing.

[1] J.-J. Weber and G. Martelet, "Constitution dogmatique sur la Révélation divine 'Dei Verbum'", *Concile Œcuménique Vatican II. Documents conciliaires* 4 (1966), pp. 27–28; P. Grelot, "La Constitution sur la Révélation", *Études* 324 (1966), pp. 241–2; A. Penna, *La Costituzione dogmatica sulla divina rivelazione* (1966), pp. 216–46; Semmelroth-Zerwick, pp. 40–42; Stakemeier, *Die Konzilskonstitution* pp. 164–9; N. Lohfink, *Die Kirche und das Wort Gottes* (1967), pp. 77–94.
[2] On the importance and range of the encyclical cf. A. Bea, "Divino afflante Spiritu. De recentissimis Pii PP. Litteris Encyclicis", *Biblica* 24 (1943), pp. 313–23; J. Bover, "La verdad histórica della Biblia según la Enc. 'Divino Afflante Spiritu'", *Estudios Eclesiásticos* 18 (1944), pp. 429–43; H. Haag, *Das Rundschreiben Papst Pius' XII. über die zeitgemäße Förderung der biblischen Studien. Authentische Übersetzung mit Kommentar* (2nd ed., 1950). *Questione bibliche alla luce dell'enciclica 'Divino Afflante Spiritu"* (1949); J. Beumer, *Die katholische Inspirationslehre zwischen Vatikanum I und II* (1966), pp. 56–69.

Article 14. Like the Constitution *Lumen Gentium* on the Church, Chapter IV of *Dei Verbum* begins with a survey of the divine plan of salvation. God, who is boundless love, has lovingly desired and prepared the salvation of all mankind. This theocentric and soteriological character of the Old Testament is brought out through the whole chapter. In the versions of the text of the Theological Commission, Article 14 had the title: "The History of Salvation as presented in the Old Testament". In order to avoid any obscurity in the meaning of the controversial idea of "salvation history" this was changed in the text to "the economy of salvation", which is a good description of the active and evolutive character of divine action. The election, the vocation, the covenant, the promise, the mission represent its more important and lasting elements. The law could also have been mentioned among these various phases of the divine plan of salvation. It represents, however, an element of transition, however important it was in the old economy of salvation. Election is the original deed through which Yahweh places himself in contact with his people; it is the lasting reality that combines all the revelations of the Godhead and develops them; it embraces the fall, the separation, the fashioning into a people, the interest and care on the part of God. The election finds concrete form in the covenant and gives to it a dynamic character. The covenant is a gift of God through which a bond of community is created and commitments are laid down that assume the shape of laws. By a process of intellectual extension this is described as a covenant of Yahweh with Abraham and the Patriarchs (Gen 15:17–18; 17: 7).

In fact, tradition tells us of a promise of land and of issue, together with its realization. It emphasizes, above all, the irrevocable fidelity of Yahweh to the covenant: Yahweh will be their God (Gen 17:1–8); he has committed himself to this through an oath (Gen 22:16–17; 26:3). But this is to be seen only as a preparation for the solemn conclusion of the covenant on Sinai (Exod 19–24). The covenant consists essentially of election, commitment and obedience (Exod 15:18; Num 23:21; Deut 33:5; Jg 8:23). It is a unique element and essential theme in the religion of Israel. The prophets refer to it and give it a profounder meaning. Jeremiah proclaims a new covenant (31:31–34), in which the Holy People are restored by the reconciliation granted. Ezekiel emphasizes the inner renewal and ascribes it to the working of the Spirit (36:23–28). The second Isaiah declares that the servant of Yahweh will be the covenant of the people (Is 42:6) and the light of the people (42:7). This universalistic accent of the prophets is taken up again in Ps 22 (21), 28–29 and 96 (95), 1–3 and they combine the proclamations of the great prophets Isaiah (2:1–4) and Jeremiah (3:17). In the covenant of the prophets the covenant is extended to a mission of light and salvation.

The initiative of God and its realization are just as much the object of a sacred history and of a proclamation of the prophets and wisdom as the object of a sacred and official prayer. Thus the Israel of God is built up. The event, the proclamation, the more profound intellectual understanding and the whole of

248

religious life become part of an economy, the building up and the proclamation of a fourfold power: one people, one law, one temple, one God. This dynamism is supported by the word of God that is constantly renewed from the patriarchs and the prophets to the prescriptions for worship and songs. The living word of God passes into the books which have been handed down and which, grouped according to types, are received as the norm of faith, worship and personal life. In clear and unanimous awareness they are declared to be holy, and religious life is affected by them to its deepest roots. This is probably what Paul meant in Rom 15:4: "For whatever was written in former days was written for our instruction, that by steadfastness and by the encouragement of the Scriptures, we might have hope." Scripture itself is the bearer of salvation.

Article 15. This article takes up again the distinction made in the previous article between the old economy of salvation and the sacred books. Its purpose is to bring out the permanent validity of the Old Testament for Christians.[3] Its economy of salvation retains its importance because it was a preparation and a prophetic proclamation of the Messiah who was to redeem all men and of the establishment of the Messianic kingship. In it we find a great number of symbols, images, words and events that assume the importance of models. The link between the two economies goes beyond the historical events. It is part of the movement that God imparts to the whole through his Spirit. The expression "Redeemer of the universe" is not a scriptural phrase. It is inspired by the phrase: "God of the universe" in 2 Macc 14:35 and in the idea of the universality of redemption (Mt 20:28; Phil 2:7; 1 Tim 2:6). In this way the Christological content of the Old Testament is illuminated. The text quoted shows that this Christian significance of the Old Testament was clearly understood by the early Church. Luke states that everything that had been written on Jesus in the law of Moses, in the Prophets and the Psalms by an infallible decree of God, must be fulfilled (22:24). Jesus says in Jn 5:39 that it is the Scriptures that bear witness to him. 1 Pet states: "The prophets . . . searched and inquired about this salvation" (1:10). This is only a first attempt to outline the problem of the relations of the Old Testament to the New; it could have been continued at every level of the New Testament writings. These texts, however, are sufficient to indicate the unity of the message of Scripture from its centre. Referring to 1 Cor 10:11, the Constitution emphasizes the typological significance of the Old Testament.

Of the many works on this question cf. P. Lestringant, *Essai sur l'unité de la révélation biblique* (1949); J. Coppens, *Les harmonies des deux Testaments* (1949); C. Larcher, *L'Ancien Testament dans l'église* (1962); J. Schildenberger, *Vom Geheimnis des Gotteswortes. Einführung in das Verständnis der heiligen Schrift* (1950); P. Grelot, *Sens chrétien de l'Ancien Testament. Esquisse d'un traité dogmatique* (1962); id., *La Bible Parole de Dieu. Introduction théologique à l'étude de l'Écriture Sainte* (1963). Apart from these main works cf. also G. v. Rad, *Theologie des Alten Testaments* II (1960), pp. 370–401, (E. T.: *Theology of the Old Testament*) with an account of the views of Protestant theology; A. Jaubert, *La notion d'alliance dans le Judaïsme aux abords de l'ère chrétienne* (1963), pp. 445–68; L. Cerfaux, *L'exégèse de l'A. T. par le N. T.* (1951); G. A. F. Knight, *A Christian Theology of the Old Testament* (1959).

The quotation from 1 Cor 10:6, which the second text contained, would have been better. The events of the Old Testament contain instructions and examples, so that we "must not indulge in immorality . . . upon whom the end of the ages has come". Whatever the importance and validity of the "typos" in Christian instruction, it is to be noted that the Council expressly refused to go into the problems of the *sensus plenior*. The *relatio* in Chapter III, Article 12, stated: "Abstrahitur autem a solvenda quaestione de 'sensu pleniore'."

The second part of the article is concerned with the permanent validity of the books. In a subordinate, but important clause, the Constitution states that the Old Testament's writings contain "some things which are incomplete and temporary". This applies less to events than to teachings.[4] With regard to the events, *Dei Verbum* had already outlined the hermeneutical principles that make it possible to judge texts of "history of one kind or another" (Ch. III, Article 12). Here we are concerned with complete teachings, which cannot be described more exactly but deal *inter alia* with the idea of a Messiah and his eschatological dominion, the individual reward after death, personal responsibility, the love of one's neighbour, etc. The temporary elements refer to the prescriptions of the law in questions of worship, purification, and social and political organization. The positive and lasting elements of the Old Testament present a genuine art of education, which assumes that humanity before Christ received progressive instruction and was engaged on an ascending path before it reached a stage of mature adulthood.

But also in the age of revelation through the Son these first steps towards the light offer revelations that retain their validity forever. The texts preserve their actuality, by being written in the present tense, as if presenting a manifestation. It is a light for all men and goes beyond the people for whom Scripture was written. In its penultimate formulation the text had stated even more explicitly that the books "retain the value of true education even for Christians".

The Council emphasizes five great areas, the importance of which will always remain: 1) a living sense of God and of the human situation in the face of God as he draws near to us; 2) sublime instruction on God, the absolute Lord of infinite love and boundlessness; 3) a wisdom of life that brings salvation and is normative for human behaviour; 4) a treasure-house of prayer, to be found in the sacred books, especially in the Psalms; 5) finally, the mysterious realization of our redemption, which is always present and effective for the Christian reader. Let us sum up briefly the essential point of this list. Already in Article 14 the Council had declared that God had revealed himself as the one true and living God through words and deeds. The God of the Old Testament is the highest being, the ground of all things, through which all things exist. His existence is accepted as a principle

---

[4] Cf. A. Gelin, *Morale et Ancien Testament* (1952), pp. 71–92; J. M. Aubert, *Loi de Dieu, loi de hommes* (1964), pp. 116–50; N. Lohfink, "Über die Irrtumslosigkeit und die Einheit der Schrift" *Stimmen der Zeit* 174 (1964), pp. 161–81; *J. Coppens,* "Comment mieux concevoir et énoncer l'inspiration et l'inerrance des S. Écritures?" *NRT* 86 (1964), pp. 933–47.

that needs no proof. His first characteristic is that he is the *living* God. The Israelite went so far in his description of this life that he fell into eloquent anthropomorphisms, but on the other hand, he saw in his God the God of holiness, the one true God, the Almighty, who acts in infinite mercy. This teaching on God was without any shadow. It demanded of the believer that he should accept a genuinely religious attitude in worship and prayer; it taught him humility and obedience; it is the source of salvation and saving truth; it leads to the acceptance of the promise, the contents of which are revealed by the word of the Son, for the rock, from which the living water springs, is Christ (1 Cor 10:4). This is the significance of the old texts. The word of God lasts for ever (Is 40:8).

Article 16. The short sentences of this article are a kind of summary. They bring out the relations between the Old and the New Testaments and emphasize their unity. Repeating a very old anti-Gnostic and anti-Manichaean formula, *Dei Verbum* states that God is the founder of both economies, of both covenants. By reason of the inspiration of the human author by the Holy Spirit God becomes the author of all the books in the sense that Chapter III of the Constitution set out in more detail. Here, as before, the Council is careful not to use the idea of the primary and the secondary author. Each is, within his own sphere of action, the whole author. This co-operation involves a close connection between the two Testaments and their mutual illumination. Although the old economy of salvation is fulfilled and surpassed, it still retains elements that retain their validity in the new one. All the revelations of God are eternal. They contain new truth, the light of which can never be extinguished. The New Testament can only be understood with certainty if one grasps the themes that go through the Old; it often takes from the latter its language, its ideas, and its modes of expression. Into the old bottles it pours new wine (Mk 2:22), so that the Augustinian formulation is profoundly true: "The new covenant is hidden in the old; the old is revealed in the new" (Novum in Vetere latet, Vetus in Novo patet). It is as true in the area of exegesis, as in that of the deep realities with which we are here concerned. In their preaching the apostles quote, use and constantly work with the Old Testament in order to make their gospel clearer and deeper. The Church Fathers do the same thing. They work through the old books, showing that this procedure is justified, and finally elaborate on the basis of a spiritual understanding[5] a system of hermeneutics that makes possible to Christians a heightening of their religious life through impregnation with the word of God.

The spiritual meaning of Scripture must not be confused with the *sensus plenior* of modern research. "The only 'fuller' meaning, the idea of which fits fully into the context, will definitely not be the one that many authors have recently wanted to play with": H. de Lubac, *L'Écriture dans la Tradition* (1966), p. 194.

251

The New Testament

by

Béda Rigaux

The commentary on this important chapter of *Dei Verbum* calls for a short account of its history.[1] The text presented to the fathers in 1961 before the opening of the Council, which was already the third version of the draft, was divided into four articles: The Gospels and their Authors; The Truth of the Acts of Christ in the Gospels; The Truth of the Word of Christ in the Gospels; The Reliability of the Teaching of the Apostles in the Canonical Writings. This text required complete revision. It retained features of a polemical attitude that reflected the conflict in Roman circles at the time.[2] It contained condemnations of errors which, it was said, had found their way into Catholic exegesis. It contained formulations that can hardly be regarded as matters of settled fact: e.g. that the Church has always held to the view, and does so, still that the human authors of the Gospels are those men whose names the Gospels bear: Matthew, Mark, Luke and John. The truth of the Gospels is described in terms from the *monitum* of the Holy Office of 20 June 1961 (*AAS* 53 [1961], p. 507): "germana veritas historica et obiectiva"; all the events of the childhood narrative in the Gospels were placed, without any differentiation, on the same level as the miracles, the resurrection and the ascension. There were other formulations which were equally inacceptable to the members of the Theological Commission. The whole document seemed to be an expression of distrust in Catholic exegetes. In May 1963 the fathers were sent a new text. The fourth chapter on the New Testament had been completely revised. It began with an article (no. 17) on the special position of the Gospels; Article 2 (no. 18) dealt with the particular

---

[1] Cf. J. J. Weber, "La Révélation", *Concile Œcuménique Vatican II. Documents conciliaires* 4 (1966), pp. 28–30; P. Grelot, "La Constitution sur la Révélation", *Études* (1966), pp. 242–5; E. Galbiati *La Costituzione dogmatica sulla divina rivelazione* (1966), pp. 247–63; Semmelroth-Zerwick, pp 43–50; J. Beumer, *Die katholische Inspirationslehre zwischen Vatikanum I und II* (1966), pp. 90–92 Stakemeier, *Die Konzilskonstitution*, pp. 169–91; M. Zerwick, "De S. Scriptura in Constitutione dogmatica 'Dei Verbum'", *Verbum Domini* 44 (1966), pp. 37–42; A. Vögtle, *Die Kirche und das Wort Gottes* (1967), pp. 27–44; R. Schnackenburg, *ibid.*, pp. 95–108.
[2] The situation is well described by J. Beumer, *loc. cit.*, pp. 70–75.

historical nature of the Gospels; Article 3 (no. 19) contained, under the heading "Catholic Exegesis" an encouragement for exegetes; Article 4 (no. 20) dealt with the books of the New Testament. In the observations sent to the Secretariat of the Theological Commission, about 300 fathers expressed modified satisfaction and made further observations to be taken note of in the revision stage. This text was never discussed in the assembly. In the course of April 1964 the final text was worked out. Fundamental changes brought about an improvement in the suggested text. First, a new article was added to the chapter under the heading "The Pre-Eminence of the New Testament"; the article called "The Apostolic Origin of the Gospels" omitted that section of the previous text which had contained a declaration on the doubts widespread among Christian exegetes concerning the "historical faith" and the "divine authority" of the Gospels. The article on the historical nature of the Gospels had been greatly altered in the light of the instruction *Sancta Mater Ecclesia* of the Scriptural Commission, 14 May 1964 (*AAS* 56 [1964], pp. 712–18). The final article on the other writings of the New Testament had been expanded in order that the message of the New Testament be better understood in its totality.

Following the discussion of this text in the assembly from 30 September to 6 October 1964, the examination of the *modi* after the vote of 20 to 22 September 1965 and after the intervention of the Pope in his letter to the Theological Commission on 18 October 1965, this text was again changed. In our commentary we shall discuss the development of Chapter V.

Concerning the heading cf. the remark on the heading of Chapter IV.

Article 17. *The fullness of time.* This article was included in 1964 at the request of certain fathers. The earlier texts had treated almost exclusively of the Gospels, and yet the chapter was entitled "Concerning the New Testament". The writers' intention, as with the foregoing chapter, had been to see the connection of the new economy of salvation with the writings, but also to sum up, beyond the mere letter, the reality proclaimed. Hence the Council enumerates the great elements of the new covenant; the incarnation, the proclamation of the dominion of God, the revelation of the person of Jesus, the death and resurrection, the ascension and the descent of the Holy Spirit, that crown the work of Christ. Further, the article points to the eternal validity and actuality of the events. The Lord Jesus draws all the men of the earth to him (Jn 12:32, in the Greek). He is the only one who possesses the words of eternal life. Finally, the text refers to the unique situation and novelty of the new age: the mystery was revealed to the Apostles and the Prophets in the Holy Spirit so that it might be preached, so that faith in Jesus as Christ and Lord should be spread, so that the Church could be gathered together. The article concludes with the idea that the eternal and divine testimony to these events is to be found in the writings of the New Testament.

The content of the article requires some clarification. The first two words simply repeat the Latin title of the Constitution. They were not chosen by chance. The unity and deepest concern of the Council is to be found in its return to the theme of the word of God. It gives to this idea the importance that the whole New Testament and especially Paul[3] gave to it, when there is mention either of "the word of God": in Luke four times, Acts twelve times, Paul eleven times, Hebrews and 1 Peter once, or of the "word of the Lord": Acts six times, Paul twice, or simply of "the word": forty times in the New Testament. Since the Son is the uncreated word (Jn 1:1), he is at the same time the revealer of this word and the object of the revealed word. The Council does not speak in the language of exegesis or of the historical sciences. Its teaching is proclamation. It combines the divine word that enlightened the Prophets of the Old Testament with the perfect word which is the Son and speaks (Heb 1:1). It sees in him the revelation in God of Jesus Christ, who is the way, the truth and the life (Jn 14:6); power, wisdom and salvation (1 Cor 1:24; 3:20). Just as it is part of being a Christian to believe in the Lord, follow him and be in him, so too the believer trusts in his words, accepts his testimony and remains in his word. Since the Council is here taking up the theme of the New Testament, the supreme expression of the word of God, these words acquire a special significance.

This word of God, this *evangelium*, that is at the same time the economy of salvation and the Gospel, is "the power of God for salvation to everyone who has faith" (Rom 1:16). This power is now made present and proves today as ever, its power, its working and effective strength (2 Thess 3:1). The text had first contained the adjective "effective" and connected the lasting, effective power with the inspiration of Scripture: "The word of God that works in the Gospel for the salvation of every man who comes to faith has a unique effective presence in the inspired writings of the New Testament." The text was altered at the last moment because it was desired to keep it closer to the Pauline text (Rom 1:15), namely, to bring out explicitly the eternal actuality of the word and its ever potent strength, the testimony of which the last sentence of Article 17 speaks is an active witness, an authorized statement, a constant proclamation, and so also are the writings that transmit it.

There are a few other points to be underlined. When the text states that the word of God is set forth in a unique way in the New Testament, *praecellenti modo,* this is not intended to be a less important comparison with tradition. This question is the object of Chapter II, Article 4, and is not what is under discussion here. The formulation: "Christ established the Kingdom of God on earth" must be understood in the light of the Constitution *Lumen Gentium,* Article 5. The kingdom is already there, but not yet realized, since the eschatology of the New Testament describes a reality that is still in the process of coming to be. The scriptural quotations of Jn 12:32 (Greek text 6:68); Eph 3:4–6 (Greek text) are all introduced by a "cf.". The synthesis that Article 17 endeavours to achieve called for scriptural language. In a conciliar text the use of Scripture does not

---

[3] ὁ λόγος τοῦ θεοῦ: Rom 9:6; 1 Cor 14:36; 2 Cor 2:17; 4:2; Phil 1:14; Col 1:25; 1 Thess 2:13 (twice); 1 Tim 4:5; 2 Tim 2:9; Tit 2:5; ὁ λόγος τοῦ Χριστοῦ: Col 3:16; ὁ λόγος τοῦ κυρίου: 1 Thess 4:15; 2 Thess 3:1; Tim 6:3.

necessarily have to involve the literary meaning, if one is only seeking a starting-point or an allusion in the sacred text. Thus Jn 12:32 (Greek text) refers primarily to the kind of death which was destined for Jesus (cf. 12:32), but the fourth Gospel likes playing with the ambiguity of words. "The crucifixion and glorification of Jesus are so close that they appear to fuse."[4] The question raised by Eph 3:4–6 is more difficult. The majority of commentators assume that the Prophets mentioned here are the Prophets of the New Testament (cf. Eph 2:20; 4:11) and that the "saints" refer to the apostles[5] and the prophets, not as a description of holy life, but in their quality as those chosen and consecrated to the service of God (cf. Cor 1:2; Heb 3:1; Acts 3:21), "for building up the body of Christ" (Eph 4:12). The proclamation and the dissemination of the Gospel are the work of the Holy Spirit, who reveals the mystery and entrusts it to those who are chosen for an apostolic or prophetic mission. In the reference to Eph 3:4–6, without violating the text, it is possible to see the Council's desire to bring out the twofold aspect of the active presence of the Spirit. The Constitution on the Church contains and develops the same teaching (Article 35). The Pauline idea becomes clear when compared with Eph 1:19–20: "You are fellow citizens with the saints and members of the household of God, built upon the foundation of the apostles and prophets, Christ Jesus himself being the cornerstone." Paul ascribes to Christ this function, as he is the foundation (1 Cor 3:10–11). The Church is built up on the mission and the proclamation of the apostles and prophets (Mt 10:40–41; 23:34; Lk 11:49). By retaining the word "mystery" in the singular, as in the scriptural text, and linking with it the events and mysteries of the appearance of the saviour, the Council is not exhausting the richness of the Pauline idea of mystery.[6] By referring to it, it has simply opened access to it.

Article 18. *The apostolic origin of the Gospels.* The article is divided into two parts: the first brings out the pre-eminence of the Gospels and justifies this by saying that the books of the New Testament are the chief witness to the life and the teaching of the incarnate word, our saviour; the second states that the apostolic origin of the four Gospels belongs to the tradition of the Church's faith. The Gospels preached at the direction of Christ were written down under the inspiration of the Holy Spirit. The apostles and apostolic men have transmitted the fourfold Gospel according to Matthew, Mark, Luke and John as the basis of faith.

The teaching of this article does not go beyond the declaration of the extraordinary and ordinary teaching offices of the Church, which go back to the

---

[4] F.-M. Braun, *Jean le Théologien. Sa théologie. Le mystère de Jésus-Christ* (1966), p. 175.
[5] On the word "apostle" in the Pauline epistles cf. P. Bläser, "Zum Problem des urchristlichen Apostolates", *Unio Christianorum (Festschrift Erzbischof L. Jaeger)* (1962), pp. 92–107.
[6] For the opposite view see E. Galbiati, *loc. cit.*, p. 252: "Si noti bene che la Constituzione conciliare reafferma bensì la convinzione tradizionale sull'identità degli autori ed anche sull'ordine cronologico dei quattro Vangeli, ma non intende definire in modo particolare questo punto, altrimenti lo avrebbe fatto intendere più chiaramente."

second century. When the Church says that the Gospels *are* the testimony, i.e. when she does not say that they only *present* it, this is to indicate the written character of the testimony and emphasize that, as written documents, they offer a solid basis for historical work and theological penetration. The life and teaching of Jesus are founded in them in truth and reality.

When, in the second section, the Council retained the words *tenuit et tenet* instead of *credidit et credit,* this is because both phrases have an identical meaning as an expression of the faith of the Church; the words *semper et ubique* (always and everywhere) bring out the solemnity of the proclamation. It seemed necessary to retain the further formulation *tenuit et tenet* because the Church holds to this doctrine, both from human conviction and certainty as also from the consciousness of the need to remain faithful to the revealed tradition of faith.

This second section simply takes up again the statements of a solid tradition, but purposely disregards the problems of literary criticism and the chronological order of the Gospels. The Council does not state more exactly just how the Apostles are related to the origin of the Gospels. These contain the apostolic proclamation, but the measure of the apostolic influence in the preparation of the final version of the writings is not stated. Cf., for example, the remark of P. Grelot: "It is often assumed in criticism that the first Gospel was edited by a Christian catechist, who was not necessarily St. Matthew, and that the disciples of St. John had an active share in the final version of the fourth Gospel (cf. the postscript to St. John's Gospel, 21:24). The true connection of a text with a particular man in the framework of a tradition should not be confused with literary authorship in the narrow sense in which we use the word today."[7]

Using the beautiful phrase of Irenaeus, the Constitution here once more returns to the connection between the economy of salvation and the sacred books. The Gospel message is more comprehensive than the Gospels. St. John's Gospel (21:25) itself states that Jesus did many other deeds. Up to Justin this concept was not used of the writings (*Apol.,* I, 66; *Dial.,* 10, 2; *2 Clem* 8, 5; Theophilus, *Ad Autol.* 3, 14). On the other hand the content of the economy of salvation and the proclamation of this new covenant is common to the writings of the New Testament, as with the *Didache* (15, 3–4) and Polycarp (9, 2). Irenaeus brought both traditions together. Eusebius (*Ecclesiastical History,* V, 24, 61) and Augustine (*In Io. Ev.,* 36) take up again the ideas of Irenaeus.

Article 19. *The relations between history and the Gospels.*[8] This article is the heart of the chapter. When compared with what was stated at previous councils, it

---

[7] P. Grelot, *loc. cit.,* p. 243.

[8] In recent years this question has given rise to a great deal of writing. See here a few Catholic studies: F. Mussner, "Jesus und der Christus des Glaubens", *BZ (NF)* 1 (1957), pp. 224–52; B. Rigaux, "L'historicité de Jésus devant l'exégèse récente", *RB* 65 (1958), pp. 481–522; R. Schnackenburg, "Jesusforschung und Christusglaube", *Catholica* 63 (1959), pp. 1–17; A. Descamps, "De historiciteit van de synoptische evangelien", *Collationes Brugenses et Gandavenses* 2 (1960), pp. 145–62; F. Mussner, "Der 'historische' Jesus": *TLZ* (1960), pp. 321–37; A. Vögtle, "Jesus Christus", *LTK,* V, cols. 922–32; F. Mussner, "Leben-Jesu-Forschung",

comes as something truly new. We must note first of all that this article is to be understood in the light of the statements of Chapter III, Article 12, on the literary types and the possibility of the text being historical in various different ways. The golden rule of exegesis requires that one seeks to discover the meaning that the sacred writer sought to express and actually has expressed. Our version of the text is inspired by the encyclical *Divino afflante* and by the instruction of the Commission on Scripture on the historical truth of the Gospels.[9] The Council had to move with caution between two positions. An excessive clinging to the literal meaning led to unreal results.[10] On the other hand it was necessary to face the risks that arose from the questioning of the historical value of the Gospels as happens in various schools of contemporary exegesis. The Council considers that it was not enough to make a straightforward condemnation of this kind of dangerous scepticism. It is better to move beyond the present situation and treat the problem in its own right, while taking note of the results of contemporary research. Negatively, it appeared necessary to avoid a terminology which is influenced by the infiltration of philosophical existentialism into the sphere of exegesis. If one uses the words "history" or "historical", it is easy to forget that the meaning of these ideas is controversial. The romance languages have no way of expressing the difference between the two words "Geschichte" and "Historia". In present-day terminology "Geschichte" is not the event in itself, but what the proclamation conjures up in the mind, irrespective of its actual content. *Historia* is the grasping of the event through reason according to the laws of historical criticism. Faith means committing oneself to *Geschichte*.[11] Other authors use the word "Geschichtlichkeit" instead of "Geschichte". Because of this kind of terminology the Council thought it better not to use these words, so as to avoid all ambiguity. The important positive point that it wanted to make was that Christian faith is bound up with a rational affirmation of the facts. Moreover, it states quite clearly that between the events and the original account of them in the Gospels there is a gap which, without the reality of the events being affected, has given to the version of the text a particular form.

LTK, VI, cols. 859–64; A. Bea, "La storicità dei Vangeli Sinottici e il carattere storico dei Vangeli Sinottici come opere isparate", *La Civiltà Cattolica*, II (1964), pp. 417–36 and 526–45; J. R. Geiselmann, *Jesus der Christus. Die Frage nach dem historischen Jesus* (1965). An objective and critical account of the situation concerning this question, which takes in all the publications, is given by W. G. Kümmel, "Jesusforschung seit 1950", *Theologische Rundschau* 31 (1966), pp. 15–46 and 289–315.

[9] A good commentary on the instruction will be found in J. A. Fitzmyer, *Die Wahrheit der Evangelien* (1965).

[10] J.-J. Weber, *loc. cit.*, p. 36.

[11] R. Bultmann's interpretation of the New Testament was the object of a great deal of comment. On the significance of *historia* and *Geschichte* cf. G. Greshake, *Historie wird Geschichte. Bedeutung und Sinn der Unterscheidung von Historie und Geschichte in der Theologie Rudolf Bultmanns* (1963). On Bultmann's interpretation of Scripture cf. also the two studies: R. Marlé, *Bultmann und die Interpretation des Neuen Testaments* (1959); F. Hohmeier, *Das Schriftverständnis in der Theologie Rudolf Bultmanns* (1964) (bibliography).

The first sentence of Article 19 contains a clear and solemn statement that must be borne in mind throughout the whole account: namely, that the Church has decided, has firmly and confidently held, and still continues to hold the same formulation as in Article 18, but still more emphatically expressed, that the four Gospels hand on *reliably* the events of the human life of Jesus, what he really *(reapse)* did and taught. This reliability and reality are later re-affirmed. After describing the editorial activity of the evangelists the text goes on to say: "but always in such fashion that they told us the honest truth about Jesus *(vera et sincera)*". These last two adjectives had caused a strong reaction, as in an earlier text they had followed the word *non ficta* (not invented, made up, fabricated), and also in the version which preceded this text, to which had been added the words "proceeding from the creative power of the early Christian community". In the course of the revisions of 1964, at the request of a number of highly qualified fathers, the Commission dropped both these additions. The latter clearly referred to the ideas of R. Bultmann. That meant that in a single sentence one had dealt with a complex and controversial problem. The radical view that the New Testament's teaching and events had all been created solely by the early Church is now on the decline. The sentence would have been the only polemical reference to a system which had been rejected firmly as a whole in the text. As far as the words *non ficta* are concerned, it had very little meaning once the sentence had been dropped which it had explained more clearly.

In the assembly vote on 22 September 1965, Article 19 received 61 *non placet* votes. The vote on the whole chapter showed that there were 313 fathers who desired improvements. The formulation that the evangelists had used a kerygmatic form in their Gospels was criticized — we shall return to this point — and above all the statement "that what they tell us about Jesus was true and honest" was too weak. The *relator* had stated, without success, that the word *vera* referred to the agreement between the statement and the reality described and that the word *sincera* had been added in order to emphasize the integrity of the witnesses, who had had no intention to deceive.

The resistance against the proposed text did not affect the Commission, two-thirds of which voted for the preservation of the formula. The fears of the minority of the fathers who opposed it, however, reached the Pope's ear, and on 19 October 1965, the latter had a letter sent to the Theological Commission.[12] The papal suggestion was that the words *vera et sincera* should be replaced by *vera seu historica fide digna* (true, i.e. worthy of historical belief). The Pope's reason for the change was that the proposed formulation had not guaranteed the true historicity of the Gospels. On 18 October 1965, the Theological Commission

---

[12] The proceedings are described by G. Caprile, "Tre emendamenti allo Schema sulla Rivelazione", *La Civiltà Cattolica* 117 (1966), pp. 214–31, esp. pp. 223–9. Cf. also N. Lohfink, "Die Wahrheit der Bibel und die Geschichtlichkeit der Evangelien. Erste Randglossen zur dogmatischen Konstitution 'Dei Verbum' (Über die göttliche Offenbarung), verkündet am 18. November 1965", *Orientierung* 19 (1966), pp. 254–6.

examined the papal suggestion together with the proposed alterations in Chapters II and III. Despite the recommendation of Cardinal Bea, who advised the acceptance of the text proposed by the Pope, the Commission objected that the word "historical" could have a double meaning and that the words *fides historica* had a real Bultmann flavour about them. Thus they finally decided to retain *vera et sincera*, but in order to conform to the wishes of Paul VI, they added after the word "Gospels" at the beginning of Article 19 the words "whose historical character the Church unhesitantly asserts". The abstract noun *Geschichtlichkeit* ("historicity") is not so controversial in the literature of exegesis and theology as "Geschichte" ("history") and *geschichtlich* ("historical"), and if this addition was able to overcome the resistance to the text of the Commission, on which the Assembly had voted, the conciliatory gesture was justified. In his account of these events the correspondent of *Time*[13] concluded his article with the words: "The problem: what precisely is meant by historicity." The text of Article 19 says this quite clearly. Throughout all these discussions and misgivings we can see the clear will of the Church to accord to these synoptic Gospels their value as testimony to the reality of the events that they narrate and to the certainty with which they present us with the person, the words, and the acts of Jesus.

The second part of Article 19 describes the procedure of the sacred writers in composing the Gospels. The history of the text helps us to appreciate the novelty and importance of the text. The text of the schema of 1962 said: "Although the Gospels sometimes betray *(resonent)* the manner of preaching *(praeconii)* and do not agree in all things with the requirements *(modis)* of historical writing that we are accustomed to in our own day, nevertheless they hand down to us a true and honest story", *veram et sinceram historiam*. Despite their extremely anxious form and the conditional clause in which they are expressed both statements were necessary and opened the way to clearer explanations: the synoptic Gospels contain features of the preaching situation from which they emerged, and their way of writing history is not in accordance with the methods that we employ today.

During the discussion on this text in July 1964 something happened which was of benefit to the Theological Commission. In April 1964 the Papal Commission on Scripture had published its instruction on the historical truth of the Gospels. It is a rule of conciliar methodology not simply to repeat the texts of the official teaching office. In this case, however, whole sentences of the instruction passed into the text of *Dei Verbum*. The instruction clearly distinguished three levels in the coming into being of the Gospels: the stage of the emergence of tradition in the deeds and words of Jesus and in the understanding of his hearers and of the disciples; the stage of apostolic preaching in the foundation of the first churches; and the stage of the compilation of the Gospels. The Constitution distinguishes in even more detail the situation of the apostles and the sacred writers. It does not

[13] *Time,* 5 November 1965, p. 52.

analyse the literary form of the words and sayings of Jesus, nor does it treat further the characteristics of the apostolic proclamation. It acknowledges that this was retained. It starts by showing that it was the glorification of Christ, his resurrection, ascension, and sending of the spirit of truth (Jn 14:26; 16:13) that especially enabled the apostles to understand more profoundly what Jesus had said and done and to proclaim it. The note refers to several Johannine texts, but the text itself is concerned with all the Gospels.

This declaration of *Dei Verbum* is important and requires illustration. The text also refers to the resurrection and ascension of the Lord, as well as to the light of the Spirit; it says that the writers had acquired from these things a deeper understanding. This statement is taken from the instruction and is there significantly explained. The instruction states clearly that the resurrection and the faith in the divinity of Jesus — both clearly grasped — had not obscured the memory of the events, but rather fortified it. Thus all risk is excluded of seeing the faith of the apostles as negatively affecting their testimony in the rational sphere. Taken together with the statements of the Council, there can be no doubt that this is also the conciliar view. On the other hand, the Constitution describes this deeper understanding not only as following from the *events* of the resurrection and ascension, but also from the power of the faith in the Lord being always alive and present in the apostolic work of teaching and in the apostolic mission (Mt 28:18–20). Finally, it must also be said that the influence of faith in the glorification of Jesus obviously found greater resonance in St. John's Gospel than in the Synoptics.

The compository work of the sacred writers is described as having four features: 1. They made a selection from the large amount of material that was at their disposal and that was offered them by both oral and written tradition. 2. They combined synthetically the words and deeds, as in the Sermon on the Mount, in the miracle stories, the polemical discourses, the parables, etc. 3. They adapted their testimony to the particular state of the Churches, since they were genuine writers and not simply compilers. 4. It was always their purpose to give words of instruction and encouragement. The basis and authority of their writings are their own memory and recollections; in places where there are no eye-witnesses, their testimony is confirmed by that of those who were from the beginning eye-witnesses and servers of the word (Lk 1:2–4). Although the texts are very short and must be supplemented by the more didactic exposition of instruction, they bring out well the uniqueness of the literary, didactic and historical aspects of the Gospels. They open a wide field for exegetical research. They combine history and theology in a constructive and living vision. By emphasizing the importance of the glorification of Christ, the living presence of the risen and ever-living Lord, the function of the spirit in the instruction and the remembering of the things that Jesus said (Jn 14:2–6) *Dei Verbum* belongs to the true dimension of the evangelical tradition: its testimony is true and honest; it explains, illuminates, makes more profound and brings to life what, in the pre-Easter stage, was mysterious and hidden. The unity between the events and their written account, between hope and faith, is guaranteed by the will of the writers to teach the truth and to give their readers complete certainty. The word "truth" in Lk 1:4 means both certainty and objective truth. The emphasis of "truth" in the printed text points to the Greek word translated from the Vulgate.

Article 20. This final Article of the Chapter reminds us of the rest of the New Testament literature: of the Pauline letters, the other apostolic writings, the Acts and Revelation. These books confirm the testimony of the Gospels on Jesus Christ as the Lord and the Son of God, they throw a new sanctifying light on his authentic teaching, without falsifying its intentions and imbuing it with an alien *gnosis,* they continue the proclamation of Jesus and the apostles in the power of God that is contained in their message to continue the saving work of Christ. Thus the general view of the Constitution is maintained. The person of Jesus is combined with his words, his deeds with what he did both before and after Easter; the apostolic message rests on the truth of the events, on their authentic interpretation, and on the missionary power of the salvation proclaimed. The books transmit to us the living word of tradition, they preserve it and give it a form that is at the same time profoundly unified and yet diversified in its ramifications. The eternal presence of the living and active Jesus and the activity of the Spirit guarantee the eternal continuance of what the word of God, sovereignly set down in the New Testament, intended to convey to us.

Sacred Scripture in the Life of the Church

by
Joseph Ratzinger

The last chapter of the Constitution on Revelation emerged within the Council from two different sources: Texts A, B and C had a chapter called "De Sacra Scriptura in Ecclesia", which endeavoured to give an account of the importance of Scripture and its interpretation both for the Church and for individual believers and also contained a section on the function of exegesis. Despite its positive basic intention its limitations and reservations were so numerous that no one was satisfied by this draft document. There was also a short schema from the Secretariat on Christian Unity which, under the title *De Verbo Dei,* pursued a much wider goal: namely, to present an outline of a theology of the word and thus fill in a gap within the statements of the teaching office, that had become ever more apparent in the total structure of Catholic theology. In this text the reference to Scripture also had, inevitably, an important place. Thus elements could be taken from both texts and used in the schema *De Revelatione* (Text D), which emerged after the turning point of November 1962, from whose chapter "De Scripturae usu in Ecclesia", after much reshaping, the final text eventually emerged.

Article 21 bases the statements of the chapter on an image of great power and depth which was common in the Latin tradition from Jerome and Augustine down to the *Imitatio Christi:*[1] the Church receives the bread of life from the table of the word and the body of Christ and thus reveres the sacred writings "like the body of the Lord itself". The fears of some fathers that this idea furthered the break-down of faith in transubstantiation were acknowledged by the Theological Commission, inasmuch as it changed the word *velut,* which was open to misinterpretation, to the clearly co-ordinating phrase *sicut et.* It was not, however,

---

[1] Cf. the detailed investigation by T. Stramare, "Mensae tuae. Studio biblico-patristico su s. Scriptura ed Eucaristia", *Seminarium* 18 (1966), pp. 1020–34. In the *Expensio modorum,* p. 60, the Theological Commission answered the objections that were made by referring to Jerome, *Comm. in Eccl.,* 3, 13; *PL,* XXIII, 1039; Augustine, *Sermo,* 56, 10; *PL,* XXXVIII, 381; 57, 7; *PL,* XXXVIII, 389; 58, IV, 5; *PL,* XXXVIII, 395; 59, III; *PL,* XXXVIII, 401. Cf. for the whole theme of this chapter, H. de Lubac, *L'Écriture dans la Tradition* (1966).

prepared to give up the basic conception, nor even to water it down. In this way the text emphasizes again what had already been made clear in the Constitution on the Liturgy: namely that the liturgy of the word was not just a preliminary part of the Mass that could be more or less dispensed with, but of fundamentally equal value with the liturgy that is sacramental in the narrower sense; that the Church, as the community of the body of Christ, is definitely also the community of the Logos, living on the word, so that the "flesh" and "word" in which the "body of Christ", the word made flesh, comes to us becomes our "bread". One can see that this is a statement that is of equal importance for the concept of the Church, the concept of liturgy, the understanding of faith, and the theology of the word and the sacraments. It shows the necessity of extending a concept of the Church that had been structured in an over-exclusively sacramental way.

The next sentences of this section pursue three main ideas: the particular character of Scripture as opposed to tradition resides in the fact that, as it were, it breathes "the smell of the earth" of the land of the patriarchs; it gives us the unmistakable tone in which the prophets talked, the way in which Israel prayed in its great and its sorrowful days; it gives us the voice of Jesus Christ — in the various and particularly striking Aramaic phrases that were handed down untranslated; we hear him speak his native language; we meet him across the gulf of centuries, as he lived, a man among men.[2] We also encounter the passionate temperament of Paul; the peaceful voice of Luke — in short, the humanity of the word of God, its original historical shape, remains close to us through this document and through it alone. But the Council did not rest satisfied with this statement, which can easily degenerate into romanticism; the resonance of the voice of the apostles and prophets throughout Scripture is important to it because the voice itself resounds with the Holy Spirit, because in them we encounter the dialogue of God with men. Thus the reference to the original colour of Scripture is placed in the context of the idea of dialogue, and the latter again is to be seen against the background of the original dialogue of the Spirit of God, which created men, with them.[3]

From this follow the three further points of Article 21. One is the specifically normative character of Scripture, while the other is the reference to the *vis et virtus* of the word of Scripture: what is said of the word of God in general in the Bible is especially true of Scripture, which preserves for us the basic dialogue of God with man and constantly renews this possibility. This word is life which builds up man; it is not empty talk, but power that nourishes man, who does not live from bread alone, but from the word of God that gives meaning to him, as it comes to him in the open reading and hearing of Scripture.

The reference to the specifically normative character of Scripture, which follows from all that has been said, brings us once more to the problem of the

---

[2] Cf. J. Jeremias, *Abba. Studien zur neutestamentlichen Theologie und Zeitgeschichte* (1966), pp. 33–67 and pp. 145–52.

[3] Cf. H. Ott: Hampe, *Die Autorität*, I, p. 170.

relation between Church and Scripture that was discussed in detail in connection with Chapter II, Article 9. Thus it is clear that there was a protracted struggle before the final form of this text was arrived at and that it appears somewhat subdued when compared with the vigorous form that the text had taken in Form E. The latter had stated that all the preaching of the Church and the Christian religion in general had to "semper respicere (scripturam) tamquam ad normam et auctoritatem quibus iudicantur et reguntur". When, in Text F, only the completely noncommittal formula "Omnis ergo praedicatio ecclesiastica sicut ipsa religio christiana Sacra Scriptura nutriatur oportet" survived, the final text still went back to the claim of *regere,* while the words *regula* and *auctoritas,* made so much of in the traditional textbooks, were not included. The view was taken that this would have meant embarking, in an inexact way, on terminological discussions of theology, which could not be the purpose of a conciliar pronouncement. One will perhaps regret the loss of both these terms less than the disappearance of the idea, that had also been expressed in Text E, of Scripture possessing in a specific form the quality of a *regula,* as a self-contained, clearly delimited entity, a *regula* which, precisely because it stands so unalterably and indestructively in itself, requires that man constantly measures himself against it. The kernel of this point is still to be found in the abbreviated form of the final text and thus supplements happily the formulations of Chapter II.

Article 22. The call to open wide the gates of Scripture to all believers acquires its particular emphasis when seen against the background of its history. The barriers that had been erected from the 13th, and especially from the 15th, century against the Bible in the vernacular and the reading of it by those who were not theologians,[4] are here firmly removed. Our text represents the final and definitive overcoming of the restrictions set up in the various forms of the index of Paul IV, and from Pius IV, Sixtus V, Clement VIII down to Gregory XVI, and proves itself here to be a revision of the Tridentine decisions: the *inhaerens vestigiis* again proves to be an advance. If at that time the fight against the Reformation had led to a sequestration of Scripture, now the concern for dialogue led to a return to it in the most intensive way.

The next sentences take up again in the same spirit the Tridentine Decree on the Vulgate (*DS* 1506–8) and change it in two ways, placing it in a new, and this time truly ecumenical, context:

a) Instead of the statement, liable to misinterpretation, that the Vulgate must be "considered authentic", the simpler and clearer formula is chosen that it has always been held in honour by the Church. But this statement is no longer made merely about the classic Bible translations of the Latin West, but is also extended to the great translations of the various other branches of the Church — the Eastern and Latin —, with particular weight being given to the importance of

---

[4] Cf. A. Stonner, "Bibellesen", *LTK* (1st ed.), II, cols. 290 ff. The article of the same name by this author in the new edition of the *LTK* (II, cols. 366 f.) is unfortunately heavily abridged in respect of the historical material.

the Septuagint for the early Church and for the Greek New Testament and its Christian re-reading of the Old Testament. In the phrase *ut suam suscepit* the fundamental event of the reception of the Bible of the ancient people of God, also in its form as the Bible of the Greek-speaking Jews, as the sacred Scripture of the new people of God is indicated. This new context now also expresses the reason for the value that the Church places on the Vulgate: it is the Bible of the Fathers, and as a translation it is inevitably also in part an interpretation, it shows us the way in which the ancient Church of the West read, understood and accepted the Bible. Hence it is not simply Scripture, but a piece of the Church's interpretation of Scripture and hence "part of tradition". To declare it alone as authentic would be to place tradition above Scripture; to "give it a place of honour" and at the same time to insist on a return to the original text means, on the contrary, a restatement of the relation between Scripture and tradition, so that the step that Vatican II has taken on this point is seen perhaps more clearly in this concrete example than in the formal fundamental statements of Chapter II. But above all it should also be noted that we have here the practical effects of the basic ideas of the Constitution on the Church and the Decree on Ecumenism, in that the isolation and the virtual absolutization of the Latin Church has been done away with, and it is seen together with the non-Latin Churches again as the one total Church, so that one cannot speak of the Latin tradition alone, though before they are mentioned, the same things must also be said about the traditions of the East. The extension of the horizon that Vatican II has brought about, as opposed to Trent and Vatican I, proves here to be not only a human, but a truly theological phenomenon.

b) As has already been indicated, as well as honouring tradition by acknowledging the permanent value of the early Christian Bible translations,[5] the document calls for a return to the original text in order that it may be used for God's word to be made available in the languages of today. It helps to illuminate the whole structure of reform in the Church to note here how "going back" is at the same time, and from within, a moving forward, and how the unity in the original text, uniting all men, at the same time makes variety possible: to go back beyond the classical translations to the original text involves re-translation and hence moving forward. To go back to the one basic text is, at the same time, to make the Bible available in every modern language. This unity in the one text has even further implications: if both the Catholic and the Reformed Churches are going back beyond the classical translations of their own tradition to the source that unites them all, the way is opened up for new translating in common, and with translating, reading and understanding in common. The encouragement of translations of Scripture in co-operation with non-Catholic Christians is a call

---

[5] There is a parallel phenomenon in the special value placed on the Luther Bible in German Protestantism. It was characteristic that, for example, Bishop Dibelius, according to newspaper reports, gave the revised version of Luther's translation to the German Evangelical Church with the words: "Here we have our Luther again."

to re-read the Bible together in terms of our contemporary Christian situation, a call to understand together the word of God that supports us all. If anything can, this can be the starting-point of a new common understanding of the Gospel that sustains us all. Here Trent is indeed left far behind, and the pragmatic statements of this text are, in fact, theological events of great significance.

Article 23. Whereas Article 22 treated the basis of the constant presence of the word of God in Scripture and its process of being opened up to us through appropriate translations, Article 23 is concerned with the question of interpretation as the next stage of making the Bible available in every age, and hence with the subject of exegesis, which in this chapter is considered under the aspect of its character as servant of the Church, while Chapters III–V had dealt with the basic problems of its intermediate position between history and theology. Thus the very first sentence outlines the fundamental ecclesial place of exegesis: it follows from the constant duty of the Church to immerse itself ever anew and more deeply in the word of God, in order to be able to offer ever anew the water of life that it contains. If the Church is described, in this context, as the "Sponsa Verbi", the Bride of the Word, this indicates the inner orientation of the Church to the word and also makes the point that inner congeniality, which is the prerequisite for understanding, comes from love, which alone can open our eyes to the other and to God.[6] One might mention that the history of this sentence shows that in the successive versions of the text there was a gradual reduction of the idea of progress, which the idea of exegesis easily suggests: Text B states that the Church "profundiorem in dies Sacrarum Scripturarum intelligentiam assequitur", which in Text E had become "ad profundiorem . . . intelligentiam assequendam procedit". This remained the same in Text F, whereas the final text reads "ad profundiorem . . . intelligentiam assequendam accedere satagit", thus describing the task of the Church as a constantly renewed one, without making this to a continuous line of progress. This is, in fact, much nearer the Church's concern with Scripture: where one is dealing with the essentials of man, the model of progress breaks down because the essentials have always to be found anew, and progress is conceivable fundamentally only within collective orders, which do not reach down into what is specific to a person. Moreover, from an ecumenical point of view the only sensible thing is to give up the idea of progress: the Reformation was based on the denial of any continuous linear progress and on the constant direct return to Scripture; the Eastern Churches are based on a strict adherence to the position of the Church in the time of the Fathers.

---

[6] The idea that love engenders knowledge has probably been most firmly expressed in the tradition that followed Pseudo-Dionysius. Thus Thomas Gallus of Vercelli says in his paraphrase on the *Mystica theologia*: ". . . per unitionem dilectionis (quae effectica est verae cognitionis) unitur Deo intellectualiter ignoto" (*Dionysiaca,* I [1937], p. 710b). As opposed to this, the view of Augustine appears much more "intellectualistic": cf. M. Schmaus, *Die psychologische Trinitätslehre des hl. Augustinus* (2nd ed., 1966), pp. 736 ff.

The following encouragement to study the Fathers and various liturgies is not to be found in Text D; it exists in E and F in a quite rudimentary form, and has found its full expression only in the final text. It grew from the attempt of a minority to avoid an isolated biblicism and to preserve for tradition its proper place in the life of the Church. Even if one does not share the view of this minority, one must still admit that its concern was justified; to separate Scripture from the total tradition of the Church leads either to biblicism or modernism or both. For, given the way the human mind works, it would not result in a more immediate relation to Scripture, but would rather allow itself to be fitted into one's own particular intellectual tradition. Thus it is factually justified to recommend the Fathers and the liturgies as helps in understanding Scripture. It is true that this presents a task, of which the next sentence goes on to speak: the development of theological studies has led to the situation that the various disciplines have grown far apart from one another and become so specialized that, in many cases, they are scarcely able to understand one another. The lack of inner connection between various branches of knowledge that the university has had to submit to as a result of the modern form of scholarship is reflected in theological work also and presents one of its chief problems in the present situation.

The rest of this section is concerned with the works of exegetes. First, they are urged to co-operate with the other theological disciplines, which raises the dilemma of contemporary theology that we have just been considering, standing as it does between specialization and unity.[7] The problem exists with all the theological disciplines (the relation between exegesis and patrology, dogmatics and moral theology, etc.), but it is most clearly seen in the relation between exegesis and systematic theology, as the basic form of the relation between critical historical method and statements, supported by faith, about the whole of Christian reality. The actual task will fall to systematic theology, which must attempt to speak of the whole and, in doing so, include and assimilate the more specific statement of the interpreter of Scripture. This is just as fundamental a task for contemporary theology as the dialogue with the modern world — in fact, the latter can have no basis if the former task is not performed in a satisfactory way. The disagreements which had arisen in Rome just prior to the Council between the Lateran and the Biblical Institute and which were only the particular climax of a crisis that had been building up since the beginning of critical historical work, are an expression of this dilemma, which, in other ways and other forms, is also shaking the Reformed Churches as well. If the last sentence of Article 23 is an express encouragement of exegetical work, it consciously rejects the methods still being tried in 1962 as unsuitable means for solving the problem: the difficulty that the critical historical method presents for theology cannot be removed by denying it or more or less banning it. Certainly it is stated

[7] Cf. Semmelroth-Zerwick, pp. 55f. Cf. the various works on the subject of exegesis and dogmatics, esp. *Exegese und Dogmatik,* ed. by H. Vorgrimler (1962).

that this method should be set within the context of the faith of the Church; the work of exegetes must proceed *secundum sensum ecclesiae* and *sub vigilantia Sacri Magisterii*. *Vigilantia* was used in Text F to replace the previous term *sub ductu*, in order to express the fact that the function of the teaching office is not to lead the way — progress is the concern of scholarship; basically, the teaching office has the negative function of describing impenetrable terrain as such. The juxtaposition of the phrases *sub ductu Magisterii* and *aptis subsidiis,* i.e. a reference to the ecclesial nature of exegesis, on the one hand, and to its methodological correctness on the other, again expresses the inner tension of Church exegesis, which can no longer be removed, but must be simply accepted as a tension.

As well as this double involvement of exegesis — both in the totality of theology and in the context of the Church's teaching proclamation — a third point is made about it: its kerygmatic function. It is not self-sufficient, but ultimately serves the transmission of the word of God. Just as the Bible comes from preaching, work on the Bible must lead back to preaching.[8]

Article 24 is devoted to the function of Scripture in theology. It starts by describing this function as that of the foundation of theology, with the element of constancy very much in the foreground. However much may grow within the one house, its foundation remains and is the constant prior requirement, without which the rest could not exist. Just as when Article 21 spoke of the *suprema regula* of the Church and supplemented it with the reference to Scripture by the words *una cum traditione,* so here also the idea of its function as foundation is placed within this context. The reason for this in each case may have been the taking into consideration of the wishes of a Council minority, but it corresponds also to the spirit of Chapter II and, properly understood, to the facts of the case as well. The fact that even for the Reformed Churches the idea of *sola scriptura* does not in fact exclude, but includes, the understanding of Scripture and the determining of its hermeneutical centre by the use of confessional writings,[9] is a clear indication that Scripture ultimately always only exists *una cum traditione* — which formulation also expresses the fact that not only is Scripture related to tradition, but also that tradition, in its turn, is based upon Scripture.

The static character of the image of the foundation is supplemented in the second half of the sentence by the words *"roboratur"* and *"iuvenescit",* describing the activity of Scripture on theology. The "house" of theology is not a building that has been erected once and for all, it stands only because theologizing continues to go on as a living activity, and so the foundation is also something that is always actively founding and hence the constant starting-point for the possibility of theology's existence. Hence the image is changed into one of the organic sphere, and Scripture is described as the rejuvenating force that keeps theology alive. This thought had already been expressed in the encyclical *Humani Generis,*

---

[8] Cf. H. Schelkle, "Von der Predigt zur Predigt", in *Theologie im Wandel* (1967).
[9] This has been made quite clear by E. Dinkler, *op. cit.* (cf. chapter II, note 24), pp. 123 ff.

to which the point had been added that experience showed that, without the constant return to the *sacrum depositum,* speculation would be unfruitful (*DS* 3892); but there it had been stultified by the particular limitation of exegetical work to proving what had already been laid down by the teaching office (cf. the commentary on Article 10) and gains its full weight only by the immediate relation to Scripture which our text demands of theology.

In a third image that goes back to Leo XIII Scripture is finally described as the "soul of sacred theology".[10] The full force of this statement can be seen when it is examined in connection with the Decree on Priestly Formation, which employs the same term *(S. Scriptura anima theologiae)* in order to draw from it a practical consequence which could be of almost revolutionary importance for the systematic shape of Catholic theology. In previous handbooks of dogmatics it was the body of the Church's teaching that formed the starting-point of the discussion. Following this proof was offered from Scripture and tradition, and then the attempt made to achieve a theological synthesis. The result of this was that Scripture was considered basically only from the aspect of the proof it offered for already existing statements, and even when this was done with great care and with modern exegetical methods, this mode of procedure hardly allowed for a theme to be developed from the perspective of Scripture itself or questions from the Bible to be raised that were not covered in the body of the Church's teaching. When new questions were treated, they generally resulted from the work of systematic theology itself, and not as a response to the stimulus of Scripture. In the Decree on Priestly Formation, however, it is stated that dogmatic theology must be pursued in such a way "ut ipsa themata biblica primum proponantur".[11] This means that in future the Bible must first be seen, considered and questioned on its own terms, and that only then can the development of tradition and dogmatic analysis take place. The consequences that this has for the methodology of Catholic theology still have to be considered — it is quite clear that this idea gives a quite concrete content to the formula that Scripture is the soul of theology.

The last sentence of this article places preaching and all forms of the Church's proclamation under the same law that we have just seen applied in theology: its chief concern must be conformity to Scripture. Here again we can see the unity that runs throughout the work done by the Council: the call for the regular homily, which had been made in the Constitution on the Liturgy (Chapter II, Article 52) is taken up again here and expanded into the demand that the whole work of proclamation be orientated towards Scripture. There is work to be done in plenty here also, considering the primarily systematic orientation that existed

---

[10] Cf. L. Leloir, "La Sainte Écriture, âme de toute la théologie", *Seminarium* 18 (1966), pp. 880–92.
[11] No. 16, official edition (1966), p. 376; cf. also C. Vaggagini, "La teologia dogmatica nell'art. 16 del Decreto sulla formazione sacerdotale", *Seminarium* 18 (1966), pp. 819–41; in addition the studies by P. Benoit ("Stellung des Schriftstudiums in einer neuen kirchlichen Studienordnung", *ibid.,* pp. 842–53); P. Grelot "Bibelunterricht", *ibid.,* pp. 853–79 and Pellegrini ("Stellung der Väter im Theologiestudium", *ibid.,* pp. 893–902), which are all included in this important volume.

hitherto, but of course the intention is not to engage in archaism, and the vision of the totality and unity of Christianity which the system seeks, as well as the binding of the whole into the faith of the Church, continue to remain necessary tasks.

Finally, let us draw attention to the statement in this section that "the sacred Scriptures contain the word of God and, since they are inspired, really are the word of God". This formulation, which was intended to state in a quite central place the essential difference between Scripture and tradition and the special pre-eminence of Scripture, unexpectedly caused doubts among exegetes, whose constant concern with Scripture brings home to them in a particularly clear way the indissoluble difference between the mediating word of man and the word of God. Scripture, too, is the word of God only as and in the human word; it also includes an element of mediation and cannot be dissolved into a direct immediacy of the divine.[12] It is to be noted that our text does not state anything like this either. It is not concerned with the problem of mediation and immediacy, but is attempting to bring out the special importance of Scripture that is ultimately based on the fact that it is as a whole, the word of revelation, because it is inspired, which cannot be said of any other document of the Christian past, and thus proves Scripture to be the fundamental form of "tradition".

Article 25 draws the practical conclusions on the new attitude, formulated in Article 22, to the original text, the translation and availability of the Bible. Bible-reading is placed in the centre of Christian life, which gives to Catholic piety a new orientation. The prayer life of the Catholic Christian hitherto, apart from participation in the liturgy, had been determined chiefly by the various forms of devotion — rosary, stations of the Cross, veneration of the Sacred Heart, etc. — which had arisen since the late Middle Ages and during more recent times. Private reading of Scripture played no important role and even for meditation and for preaching was not considered of prime importance. It may thus be regarded as an event of special importance for the development of the spiritual life, when our text gives a central place to the personal acquaintance with Scripture as a fundamental form of the relation to God and emphasizes its importance with the emphatic utterance of St. Jerome: "for ignorance of the Scriptures is ignorance of Christ". It is important to see that the Council is not here concerned with a purely intellectual or informative knowledge of Scripture, or one that is motivated by cultural and educational considerations, but it means the reading of the Bible as prayer, as entering into that dialogue with the Lord, for the living realization of which in faith, in prayer the pages of Scripture, are, as it were, waiting. It is fair to say that Catholic piety has still largely to discover the Bible properly and that, *vice versa,* this process will also be important for exegesis, which otherwise may easily find itself in a merely intellectual climate

[12] It is not necessary here to go into the profounder objections of an extreme actualistic theology, according to which the word of God only takes place in the word of Scripture as a new event each time it is read.

and will ultimately be lacking in depth, however much it may gain in historical knowledge. Obviously the call for the reading of Scripture and for a corresponding development of spirituality is addressed especially to the preaching of the word (whether by priests or not) and to those men who, as members of religious orders, have given themselves in a specific way to a life for the word and from the word.

It would be foolish to deny that the reading of Scripture, too, can be misunderstood and lead to dangers: no one found that more than Luther in his struggle against the enthusiasts, against whom he asserted the authority of his interpretation, which was inevitably, in fact, a limitation of the idea of *sola scriptura*.[13] After all the Bible is a book which reflects all the problems of historical understanding, however much it is able, in the immediacy of faith, to overcome and transcend them. Hence the fact itself of reading Scripture as well as the nature of faith require that there be suitable aids to understanding in order to be able to understand Scripture meaningfully. The reading of Scripture, however, reaches its highest point when the Church listens to the word of God in common in the sacred liturgy and within this framework itself experiences the active presence of the Logos, the Word in the words. The private reading of Scripture points ultimately towards this reading of the Bible that is in the fullest sense "ecclesial", but this ecclesial reading would lose its soul, were it not constantly nourished by total personal immersion in the word of God. In the daily enthronement of the Gospel the Council gave to the liturgy of the word a particularly solemn quality and thus endeavoured to place itself, as the "listening Church" (which it wanted, and had to be, precisely as the "teaching Church": cf. Article 10), entirely under the dominion of the Gospel. This dominion of the Gospel should last beyond the Council and can do so only if the Church lets itself be increasingly penetrated by the word of Scripture.[14]

The last section of the article extends what has already been said to the missionary-field as well and thus takes another new step which will be of some importance for the basic understanding of mission work. What Protestants had been doing for a long time is now made the business of the Catholic Christian and the Catholic Church: the dissemination of Scripture among non-Christians. This brings a new element into the idea of missionary activity, which had hitherto been too hierarchically and institutionally-minded: namely, confidence in the self-active power of the word, which by no means makes the Church's preaching superfluous, but which means that the word is brought, as part of the presence of Jesus Christ, among the peoples, far beyond the area of the hierarchical Church. Perhaps we could try to give a higher theological value to the presence of Christ, which is made possible in this way among the unbaptized and those

---

[13] Cf. P. Hacker, *Das Ich im Glauben bei Martin Luther* (1966), pp. 65–96; H. Schütte, *Protestantismus* (1966), pp. 451–61; R. A. Knox, *Enthusiasm* (1950).

[14] On the history and significance of this rite, cf. R. de Maio, *Il libro del Vangelo nei Concili Ecumenici* (1963).

who will largely remain unbaptized: what it means when men are perhaps only able in this way to touch, as it were, the fringe of the garment of the Lord as he passes by (cf. Mk 6:56), ultimately only he himself can know. We can see here a particularly fine example of that spirit of openness that has become increasingly characteristic of the Council. "It seems to me incontestable that with this statement of the Council the Church has more or less renounced the monopoly of alone being able to read and 'be in charge of' the Bible. In this simple way it has provided a yardstick for the renewal that it introduced in the incredibly short period of three years."[15]

Article 26 returns again to the comparison with the eucharistic mystery with which this chapter began: the word of God and the body of Christ, word and sacrament, belong together and are the threefold, and yet one, way in which the incarnate Logos is with His Church and gives life to it. At the same time the spiritual intention of the whole Constitution is firmly expressed, which certainly clarifies a number of doctrinal and theoretical problems, but ultimately could not have as its purpose the pursual of theological discussions, but rather the service of the life of faith in the Church. To this end the idea of the Preface is again taken up and its meaning made clear. Though we found that the Preface expressed the pastoral aim in somewhat extravagant terms and did not integrate it into the theological concern of the whole, we find here more convincingly and more happily expressed the inner unity of both intentions and the relation of the theological work to the basic spiritual intention: to renew the Church from the word of God, which is its true bread of life. The universalistic idea of the Preface comes in here again also: "Let the word of the Lord run and be glorified" (2 Thess 3:1). What has immediately gone before, the readiness to sow the seed of the word of God in Scripture generously and fearlessly, even where one is unable to supervise or check what grows out of it, is a full affirmation of the universal meaning and the inner power of the word of God, that does not return without fruit (Is 55:10f.). The Constitution, which began with the idea of universalism, ends with it: the word of God is intended for men, and the service of the word which the Church attempts in this Constitution, cannot, for this reason, be limited simply to reform within the Church; it is ultimately related to mankind as a whole, for not only the Church, but every man lives in his ultimate depths more from the word of God than from the bread that is granted him by his mortality on earth.

[15] J. M. González Ruiz, "Der Gebrauch der Bibel in der Kirche des Konzils", in Hampe, *Die Autorität,* pp. 232–9, quotation p. 238. Cf. Schutz-Thurian, *La parole,* p. 184: "It is also a sign that the Catholic Church considers also that the written word of God can speak for itself and touch the hearts of men who do not believe. In this way the Council is manifesting the desire for complete confidence and submission of the Catholic Church to the word of God contained in Scripture, which makes the voice of the Holy Spirit resound where it wills."

Decree on the Apostolate of the Laity

by
*Ferdinand Klostermann**

History of the Text

The text of the Preparatory Commission

The Decree on the Apostolate of the Laity, approved by the Council on 18 November 1965, was the product of five years' work almost to the day, the Preparatory Commission for the Apostolate of the Laity having held its first plenary session on 15 November 1960. This Commission was charged by the Central Papal Commission to develop the following topics selected from the numerous *vota* requested of various instances: 1) the Apostolate of the Laity: its extent, its goals, its relation to the hierarchy, its nature interpreted in the light of present-day needs; 2) Catholic Action: its nature, its extent, its relation to the hierarchy, its organization, conformity to present needs, its difference from other groups such as the Marian Congregations, pious societies, professional groups, etc.; 3) societies: the adaptation of their activities according to present needs and present aims. Special mention was made here of charitable works and social action.[1] By 17 November 1960, 3 subcommissions were formed to help ease the burden of the work: one for Catholic societies and Catholic Action, one for social action, and another for charitable works. This division was later to prove a source of difficulty for the Commission.

After barely a year and a half of work the first text of a "Constitution on the Apostolate of the Laity" was presented which was then approved during the 7th general session of the Preparatory Commission from 2 to 8 April 1962, the most important discussions taking place on 18 and 19 June 1962.[2]

---

* Translated by John M. Jakubiak
[1] Pontificia commissio centralis praeparatoria Concilii Vaticani II, *Quaestiones Commissionibus praeparatoriis Concilii Oecumenici Vaticani II positae* (Typ. polygl. Vat., 1960), p. 23. If no sources are indicated in what follows, references for the preparatory period and the general congregation of the first session are based on the reports of *Orbis Catholicus (Herder-Korrespondenz)*; for the last three sessions on the CICath (Centrum informationis Catholicum) publications, an information service for Council fathers of the Working Committee of Catholic news-agencies: W. Seibel and L. A. Dorn, eds., *Tagebuch des Konzils* (1964, 1965, 1966). The remaining references are taken from the *Acta Commissionis Conciliaris "de fidelium apostolatu"* (mimeogr. 1966) and from private notes of the author.
[2] *HK* 16 (1961/62), pp. 514f., i.e. the source quoted in n. 6.

In the Central Commission, besides many minor changes, radical abbreviations as well as considerable expansions of other parts of the text were proposed. Complaints were made on its unclear and faulty principles, its overly negative concept of the laity, and also on its insufficient stress on the dependence of the apostolate upon the hierarchy which must support every form of apostolate; questions were raised with respect to the use of the concept of the priesthood, as well as other common expressions for priests and laity; similarly, some complained of the "unsuitability" of speaking of the charisms of the laity.

One cardinal sharply criticized the text in its treatment of Catholic Action and proposed a change after the manner of the "suggestion" which "had been communicated" to Pius XII with respect to the terminology and structure of Catholic Action and which he passed on in his address at the Second World Congress for the Apostolate of the Laity on 5 October 1957;[3] it is certain that the same person was involved then. This suggestion had received very divided reception at that time and the Secretary of State thought it necessary one day to explain that there was really nothing to be changed in the life of Catholic organizations. This topic was also a source of divided opinion in the Central Commission as well. It was not clear to what extent the ideas of the cardinal referred to were shared by others. A serious discussion does not appear to have taken place. In any event, at the voting two cardinals were found to urge circumspection on this question.

The Central Commission sent its criticisms to the Commission for the Apostolate of the Laity which was already at work in July with a small circle of Roman members of the Commission. Several minor changes, abbreviations, as well as some amplifications of the text were accepted and incorporated into it, while other suggested changes, especially the more radical ones, were put off for various reasons which were given in each case. With respect to Catholic Action the suggestions of the cardinal already referred to were unambiguously rejected. One or other smaller changes, nevertheless, were proposed: the *genus proximum* for all apostolic lay organizations should be called "the apostolate of the laity"; the *species* should be called the *apostolatus officialis laicorum,* among which would also be counted Catholic Action. The latter would include the *organisationes religiosae apostolatus,* the *organisationes caritativae* and the *organisationes sociales.* On the level of the whole Church the Apostolic See should be responsible for the co-ordination of the actual organizations, and in matters concerning local bishoprics only the individual bishop should be responsible. A final formulation of this suggestion is to be found in a note in the edition of the text printed in 1963.[4] Six small changes were also proposed which did not seriously affect the substance of the material but these were nevertheless later again withdrawn by

---

[3]   Address of Pius XII, 5 Oct. 1957: *AAS* 49 (1957), pp. 929 f.

[4]   *Sacrosanctum oecumenicum Concilium Vaticanum secundum, Schemata constitutionum et decretorum ex quibus argumenta in Concilio desceptanda seligentur. Series quarta* (Typ. polygl. Vat., 1963), p. 73 (*nota* 3).

the Commission. They did not appear in the 1953 edition of the text just mentioned as they had already been withdrawn by the time it went to print. Similarly, there was no sign in this edition of those suggested transfers of topics to other documents which we shall now consider.

With regard to the structure of the whole text, questions referring to broader aspects of culture and public morals were too large to be treated by one Commission on the Apostolate of the Laity, especially in an appendix to the second title of the second part; they require separate chapters of their own. Hence those sections were to be omitted which dealt with the mass media, the apostolate for the promotion of Christian unity, the apostolate in those countries overrun by materialism — especially of the Marxist stamp —, and the apostolate in the mission-fields of the Church, since they were all to be treated by other commissions. Among the last mimeographed copies of the text of the Preparatory Commission there was also a plan for the second part of the "Constitution on the Apostolate of the Laity" (*DAL:* De Apostolatu Laicorum 2), which in its second part, titled *"De Diversis Modis et Saeptis"*, contained a Chapter 7 *"De Cultura"* and a Chapter 8 *"De Publicis Moribus"*. At the end of these chapters it was already noted that Chapter 6 "On the Participation of the Laity in the Apostolate for the Promotion of Christian Unity" and Chapter 8 "On the Apostolate of the Laity in Mission Countries of the Church" no longer belong to our schema since they were to be treated by the schemata of the Commission on the Missionary Activity of the Church and the Secretariat for the Promotion of Christian Unity. In spite of this, both chapters were again to appear in the same place in the text which was later printed.

The Commission for the Apostolate of the Laity again sent their criticisms and recommendations to the Central Commission; they were all examined by the Subcommission for the Improvement of the Schemata on 27 November 1961 and were incorporated into the text accordingly.[5]

The corrections of the Central Commission just mentioned appeared in a printed brochure of 52 pages, together with the answer of the Commission on the Apostolate of the Laity. At the end of this document a request was made that those cardinals who were members of the Central Subcommission for the Improvement of Schemata should examine everything and then indicate whether the text of the Constitution had been sufficiently corrected, and if not which corrections were still desirable.[6]

On 22 November 1962, during the first session of the Council, Cardinal Cento, the president of the Tenth Conciliar Commission engaged in the Apostolate of the Laity, called together the members of the Commission (bishops) under his chairmanship who had already taken part in the preparatory work. Present

---

[5] Cf. *declaratio* of Cardinal C. Confalonieri in the 12th general congregation on 5 Nov. 1962: *Sacrosancto Concilio Oecumenico Vaticano II., Declarationes die 5. nov. 1962* (mimeogr.).

[6] *Pontificia subcommissio centralis de schematibus emendandis praeparatoria Concilii Vaticani II., De emendatone schematis constitutionis de apostolatu laicorum* (Typ. polygl. Vat., 1962), cf. pp. 2 and 52.

among these were Castellano, Larraín, Hengsbach, Ménager, Guano, and the Secretary. The Cardinal related all the events which had led to the corrections in the schema. Great satisfaction was expressed over the minor extent of the changes; only those corrections on the subject of Catholic Action were still found wanting. The Secretary was charged to inform the General Secretariat of the Council of the difficulties which were being encountered with the text, which now represented a tolerable compromise laboriously achieved between parties which were in part diametrically opposed. He also urged that the text be kept as it was, and this in fact was achieved.

Before the plenary session of the Commission on 5 December 1962, the four fascicles prepared by the Preparatory Commission were actually distributed without any essential changes; the text on Catholic Action remained completely unchanged.[7] This text is still to be found, with only a few alterations and with some appendices, in the fourth of the drafts of Conciliar Constitutions and Decrees which appeared in 1963.[8] The *relatio* which the Secretary read in conjunction with this text on 5 December 1962 referred to those difficulties which the text presented: i.e. that baptism and confirmation are not the basis of a specific apostolate of the laity; that the different types of the apostolate in the world make general remarks on the subject difficult to formulate; that laymen themselves could not take part in the work of the Commission although certain contacts with international organizations were being cultivated; that the threefold division of the Commission partly threatened to undermine the unity of the apostolate. Some of these difficulties were referred to in the declaration which appeared at the head of the text in the 1962 edition and which formed the first part of the preface in the 1963 edition.

With its four parts the text still comprised 131 pages and had 272 articles in the large format edition of 1963. The 74 articles of the first part, following a five-page General Introduction *(prooemium generale)*, are divided into 10 chapters of General Considerations *(notiones generales):* the laity in the apostolate of the Church; its relation to the hierarchy; the task of the priest in the apostolate of the laity; the apostolate of the individual; the laymen who serve the Church in positions of special rank; the family as a subject of the apostolate; the forms of the common apostolate; the co-ordination of all forms of the apostolate; the apostolic spirit; the formation and preparation of the laity for the apostolate. The 77 articles of the second part treat in 2 sections of "the apostolate of the laity in the service of the direct promotion of the reign of Christ" (de apostolatu

[7] Pontificia commissio centralis praeparatoria Concilii Vaticani II., *Quaestiones de apostolatu laicorum. Schema constitutionis de apostolatu laicorum propositum a competenti commissione. Prooemium generale et pars I. Notiones generales; pars II. De apostolatu laicorum in actione ad regnum Christi directe promovendum; pars III. De apostolatu laicorum in actione caritativa; pars IV. De apostolatu laicorum in actione sociali* (Typ. polygl. Vat., 1962).

[8] *Sacrosanctum oecumenicum Concilium Vaticanum secundum, Schemata constitutionum et decretorum ex quibus argumenta in Concilio disceptanda seligentur. Series quarta* (Typ. polygl. Vat., 1963), pp. 43–173.

276

laicorum in actione ad regnum Christi directe promovendum): the forms into which this apostolate is organized, and the different methods used and the fields in which it is carried out. The first section has 3 chapters: the apostolate of the laity in the different communities of the Church; Catholic Action; other forms of the apostolate for the direct promotion of the reign of Christ. The second section has 8 chapters: the apostolate of the word; of the family; of youth in the Church; in one's own professional and social milieu; in international and supra-national spheres; the participation of the laity in the apostolate for the promotion of Christian unity; the apostolate in those countries which are subjected to materialism and especially those dominated by Marxism; the apostolate of the laity in the mission areas of the Church. An appendix treats in addition of culture, public morals, means of social communication, and the right use of leisure. The 36 articles of the third part deal with "the apostolate of the laity in charitable works" (de apostolatu laicorum in actione caritativa) in 7 chapters: the nature and range of charitable works; justice and charitable works; the duty of performing charitable works; charitable works and the apostolate of the laity; the charitable works of the individual; the formation of the laity for the practice of charitable works. The 85 articles of the fourth part deal with "the apostolate of the laity in social work" (de apostolatu laicorum in actione sociali) in two sections: social works in general and in particular. The first section comprises 5 chapters: the activity of the laity in directing and perfecting the natural order; the relation of the laity to the hierarchy; the various forms of social works; the formation of the laity for social works; the glorification of God and the natural perfection of the Christian. The second section comprises 9 chapters: the family; education; the position of women in employment and in social life; the order of economic and social matters; the order within the community; the sciences and the arts; order in technological society; order within the State; the development of a universal order of all peoples.

Development of the text
from the beginning of the first session of the Council to the beginning
of the second session (11 October 1962 — 29 September 1963)

To distinguish it from the Preparatory Commission for the Apostolate of the Laity in Everything which concerned Catholic Action, Religious and Social Action,[9] which was called for short the "Commission for the Apostolate of the Laity", the tenth Council Commission was given the title "Commission for the Apostolate of the Faithful; for the Editing of Printed Material and the Mass Media".[10] It was at that time, namely, not only the Secretariat for Press and

---

[9] Cf. motu proprio of John XXIII, *Superno Dei nutu*, 5 June 1960: *AAS* 52 (1960), pp. 433–7: 'Commissio de apostolatu laicorum in omnibus qua ad actionem catholicam, religiosam atque socialem, spectant."

[10] *Sacrosanctum oecumenicum Concilium Vaticanum secundum, Ordo Concilii Oecumenici Vaticani II celebrandi* (Typ. polygl. Vat., 1962), p. 18: "de fidelium apostolatu; de scriptis prelo edendis et de

Theatre, as it was known for short[11] then incorporated into the Tenth Conciliar Commission, but was also according to its title not only the *apostolatus laicorum* but an *apostolatus fidelium*. As early as September 1962 the General Secretary of the Council was asked by the Secretary of the Tenth Council Commission to replace the word *fidelium* by *laicorum*. The reply which was given to this was that the word "laity" has an anti-clerical ring to it; and also it was to be made clear that the schema was to be addressed to the faithful in the Church and not to Christians of other confessions. The schema itself, nevertheless, retained the name "Apostolate of the Laity" as was expressly noted in the third session of the Commission on 5 December 1962, although the name of the Commission was not to be changed again. In fact, it was spoken of from that time on as the Commission for the Apostolate of the Laity.

On 12 November 1962, on the occasion of the first meeting of the Tenth Council Commission, a mandate was received from the Central Commission, or rather from the Secretariat for Extraordinay Affairs which in some matters had taken over the duties of the Central Commission, that the text of the Declaration should be considerably shortened before being presented to the Council. The General Secretariat, which had also supported the mandate, likewise gave to the Commission at the end of November an outline of the "schemata treated by the Preparatory Commissions which nevertheless were still to be given to the Council Commission so that when necessary they might be made to conform to general principles, and where similar or overlapping material required it, to bring the material into a greater unity".[12] Among the 20 conciliar documents contemplated here — previously there were 72[13] — the twelfth was listed as "the draft of a decree on the laity", the rough divisions of which were given as follows:

General Principles: a) the apostolate of the laity in the service *(actio)* of the direct promotion of the reign of Christ; b) the apostolate of the laity in charitable and social works; c) societies of the faithful.[14]

In spite of the name of the Commission the document here referred to is titled "Decree on the Laity", which the Commission itself, however, was trying to have changed to "Schema on the Apostolate of the Laity". Similarly, the title was given here for the first time as a "Decree" and not a "Constitution". According to these new directions, then, only the general principles were to be developed on the basis of the text as it had come from the Preparatory Commission. And

---

spectaculis moderandis"; Segretariato della stampa e dello spettacolo — what was meant were the mass media, especially press, radio, film, and television.

[11] Cf. motu proprio of John XXIII, *Superno Dei nutu, ibid.*: "Secretariatus quaestionibus omnibus expendendis, quae, cum hodiernis vulgandarum sententiarum rationibus (ut sunt folia typis impressa, radiophonicae et televisificae transmissiones, cinematographica spectacula, etc.) quoquo modo conectuntur."

[12] *Sacrosanctum oecumenicum Concilium Vaticanum secundum, Schemata constitutionum et decretorum ex quibus argumenta in Concilio disceptanda seligentur* (Typ. polygl. Vat., 1962), p. 3.

[13] Cf. *HK* 17 (1962–3), pp. 103 f.

[14] Cf. index 8 of schemata and themes in n. 12.

so the 4 fascicles they then had were to be reduced to only one: the third and fourth parts were to be joined together and the Decree "On the Societies of the Faithful" which was prepared by the Preparatory Commission "for the discipline of the clergy and the faithful" was to be included within the decree. At the request of the Secretariat for Extraordinary Affairs the section on social works was to be given to a commission composed of members of the Theological Commission and the Commission for the Apostolate of the Laity so that a new schema could be drawn up on this topic together with the text prepared by the Theological Commission on the social order[15] and on the social community.[16] The theological aspects of the schema on the Apostolate of the Laity were to be treated in connection with the schema on the Church.

Meanwhile, at the conclusion of the first session of the Council on 5 December 1962 the Cardinal Secretary of State published the *Ordo agendorum* for the period between the sessions;[17] a general "examination and improvement of the schemata" was recommended which was to be carried out by "special and mixed subcommissions". "From the various themes which were contained in the last edition of the schemata[18] the most important are to be selected, and they are to be critically examined with a view to those things which are of concern for the whole Church, the faithful, and mankind. The schemata are to be so drawn up that they treat mainly of more general principles. Particular questions which do not belong in a discussion of these principles are to be omitted. We must keep before our eyes the fact that the Ecumenical Council has the interest of the entire Church before it and that its decrees are to have a lasting significance. For this reason excessive verbiage and repetitions are to be avoided. Those things which belong to the future revision of the *CIC* are to be referred to the Commission in charge. Likewise, there are some special topics which are to be treated by commissions to be formed after the Council." Another directive of the *Ordo* was also important for our text, namely in that it gave permission "to consult other experts in different fields as well, especially those who are experienced in the activities of the public apostolate". The General Secretary of the Council requested the fathers at the end of the first session to hand in their recommendations to the various schemata by 28 February 1963, so that they could be incorporated into the texts by the commissions.

By the end of November work was in progress to determine the method and principles to be used in excising and compressing the schemata, and these were

---

[15] *Sacrosanctum oecumenicum Concilium Vaticanum secundum, Schemata constitutionum et decretorum ex quibus argumenta in Concilio disceptanda seligentur. Series tertia* (Typ. polygl. Vat., 1962), pp. 5–44: Schema constitutionis doctrinalis de ordine sociali.

[16] *Ibid.,* pp. 45–66: Schema constitutionis doctrinalis de communitate gentium.

[17] *Sacrosanctum oecumenicum Concilium Vaticanum secundum, Ordo agendorum tempore quod inter conclusionem primae periodi Concilii oecumenici et initium secundae intercedit* (Typ. polygl. Vat., 1962), nn. 13 f.

[18] The reference is to the index of schemata and themes in n. 12.

then adopted by the Commissions. The most important of the 4 fascicles was to be selected; each part which belonged to the work of other commissions or which was to be treated by a mixed commission was to be sent to these commissions. All repetitions were to be eliminated, and the present schema was supposed to form the basis for a Directory for the Apostolate of the Laity to be set up after the Council.

In the period from 21 December 1962 until the beginning of January 1963, several theologians belonging to the commissions who were resident or present in Rome (the *Coetus Romanus*) set to work according to the principles fixed upon for excising the texts. This work was then continued from 14 to 19 January 1963, in smaller commissions. In the preparatory work for the combining of parts 3 and 4, a German sub-commission was made chiefly responsible. After many preliminary drafts the commission produced a new and radically abbreviated text which was presented together with a corresponding *relatio* on 20 January 1963 — still as a draft for a *constitutio* — to Cardinal Giovanni Urbani who was the *relator* on the schema on the Apostolate of the Laity for the "Commission for the Co-ordination of Conciliar Work" created by the *Ordo agendorum* of 5 December 1962.[19]

In the meantime other problems had arisen, and it was agreed that the vote on the Schema for the Apostolate of the Laity was to be held together with the vote on the chapter on the Laity in the Schema on the Church, since much of what was treated in the latter belonged to the former schema. These wishes were relayed to the Theological Commission which had been requested to assist the Commission for the Apostolate of the Laity in this work. At the same time the Commission for the Apostolate of the Laity was asked by the Commission for the Discipline of the Clergy and the Faithful to work with it in a mixed commission on the societies of the faithful. Likewise, proposals were agreed upon for a detailed chapter on "cultural activity" *(de actione culturali)*: first, general principles were to be set forth and then particular aspects were to be treated in respect of culture, science, art, technology, leisure, tourism, sport, and public morals. But in the course of this work the question arose as to how many of these and similar topics treated in the schema on the Apostolate of the Laity belonged rather to the Schema on the Church in the Modern World which was then being planned. The Commission was soon asked to assist in the work on this new schema as well. The Co-ordinating Commission was expected to settle those problems which were still left open.

The question of lay participation in the work of the Commission, which the Preparatory Commission had already tried to settle though without results, was also taken up anew. A reference to this question in the 33rd general congregation of 4 December 1962, and in the new *Ordo agendorum*[20] again raised the Commission's hopes in this matter. Thus it was proposed to decide by vote

---

[19] *Ordo agendorum . . ., loc. cit.,* n. 4.   [20] *Ibid.*

whether a separate commission of laymen was to be established or whether it would be better to engage lay consultants only as the topic required; the majority of those present voted for the latter proposal in a session on 19 January 1963.

In January a positive report was received from Cardinal Urbani on the abbreviated text; it had received the general approval of the Co-ordinating Commission at a meeting from 21 to 27 January 1963.[21] The approval was given on 27 January 1963. This approbation expressly recognized the importance of the schema on the principles and the activities of the Church for the promotion of the welfare of society *(de Ecclesiae principiis et actione ad bonum societatis promovendum)* which had been proposed by the Commission for the Apostolate of the Laity. A new mixed commission was to be formed for the work on the new schema, to be composed of members of the Theological Commission and the Commission for the Apostolate of the Laity. The decree on the societies of the faithful was to be abandoned; only general principles were to be treated in the schema for the Apostolate of the Laity and the rest was to be treated by the Commission for the Reform of Canon Law: laymen were to be consulted in connection with the schema for the Apostolate of the Laity.

After a last revision by several Conciliar theologians present in Rome, the new mimeographed text was sent to the members and consultors of the Commission on 5 February 1963. The text was also sent to the ecclesiastical assistants of the Organisations Internationales Catholiques (O.I.C.) and the members of the board of directors of the Comité permanent des Congrès Internationaux pour l'Apostolat des Laïcs (COPECIAL). The Co-ordinating Commission had also orally agreed to the assistance of laymen on the re-editing of the text.

The new text, amazingly enough, again contained four parts even though a preliminary draft was prepared[22] which proposed a first part "de apostolatu laicorum in actione ad regnum Christi directe provehendum" and a second part "de apostolatu fidelium in actione caritative et sociali" and which explicitly referred in the preface to the second part to the mandate of the Central Commission and the approbation of the Commission of the Apostolate of the Laity. Of this first part only the title remained; Part II is given complete and contains a general introduction and two headings. The first part, "de apostolatu laicorum in actione caritativa", comprises 16 articles in 2 chapters; "de natura actionis caritativae" (7 articles); and "de variis formis actionis caritativae" (11 articles). The second part, "de apostolatu laicorum in actione sociali", originally comprised 17 articles in 5 chapters: "de laicorum actione in ordine naturali christiane perficiendo" (3 articles), "de relatione laicorum ad hierarchiam in eodem ordine" (4 articles), "de actionis socialis formis" (3 articles), "de laicis ad actionem socialem efformandis" (4 articles), and "de applicatione doctrinae socialis

---

[1] *HK* 18 (1963–64), p. 33.
[2] *De apostolatu laicorum (Schema alicuius Decreti)*, 14 pages (mimeogr.).

Ecclesiae ad varios campos negotiorum" (3 articles). The new "Draft of a Constitution(!) on the Apostolate of the Laity"[23] contained 98 articles in only 32 pages of text and 8 pages of notes.

After a general introduction in 4 articles, the first part proposes some "general considerations" in 4 sections and altogether 7 chapters. The first section "on the various ways of realizing the apostolate of the laity" contains two chapters: the apostolate which is exercised by all and everyone (4 articles), and the social form of the apostolate (4 articles). The second section "on the right order in the apostolate of the laity" also contains two chapters: the relation of the laity to the hierarchy in the apostolate (8 articles), and the mutual co-ordination of all in the apostolate (3 articles). The third section "on some special problems of the Church in regard to the apostolate of the laity today" again contains 2 chapters: the apostolate of the laity in respect of various states of life (6 articles: on youth, men, women, families, laymen in the special service of the Church, diaspora and the missions); special areas of the apostolate which are especially to be recommended in the present world-situation (6 articles: work, culture, leisure, areas dominated by materialism, especially by Marxism, the moral sense and public morals, public life, the international and supra-national levels). The fourth section contains a chapter on the education of the laity for the apostolate (5 articles). The second part "on the apostolate of the laity in the service of the direct promotion of the reign of Christ" contains 3 chapters: the apostolate of the laity in various communities of the Church (6 articles); Catholic Action (5 articles); other forms of the apostolate for the direct promulgation of the reign of Christ (3 articles). In the last-mentioned it was pointed out that by decision of the Co-ordinating Commission the schema "on the Societies of the Faithful" would be dealt with by a mixed commission (composed of members of the Commissions for the Apostolate of the Laity and for the Discipline of the Clergy and Faithful), but that the general principles would probably be found in this chapter. The third part "On the Apostolate of the Laity in Charitable Works" contains an introduction (3 articles) and two chapters: the nature of charitable works (7 articles) and various forms of charitable works (9 articles). The fourth part "on the apostolate of the laity in social works" also contains an introduction (4 articles) and 4 chapters: the activity of the laity in the Christian perfection of the natural order (4 articles); the relation of the laity to the hierarchy in this order (2 articles); the formation of the laity for social works (5 articles); the application of the social teaching of the Church in various fields (3 articles).

The fourth part was thus reduced from the 85 articles of the first published draft to 18 articles. By March a mixed commission was to prepare a single schema on social action. At the wish of Cardinal Ottaviani, Cardinal Cento was to act as President and Cardinal Browne as Vice-President; in addition four bishops were appointed from the Theological Commission, three from the Commis-

---

[23] *Schema constitutionis de apostolatu laicorum* (mimeogr.).

sion for the Apostolate of the Laity and some *periti* from both commissions. On 18 and 19 February 1963 the Mixed Commission for the Societies of the Faithful met; to this commission the Commission for the Discipline of the Clergy and the Faithful had given three bishops and three theologians, the Commission for the Apostolate of the Laity two bishops and four *periti*. At this point those difficulties arose which inevitably arise when several special types of organization are treated in a general text.

From 1 to 4 March 1963, groups of theologians from the pertinent commissions prepared the material for the plenary session of the Tenth Council Commission scheduled to convene from 4 to 10 March. It was to occupy itself with the study of the new text and the proposals and criticism which had been expressed up to that time. Up to the deadline which was set by the General Secretary of the Council at the end of the first session, i. e. 28 February 1963, 40 pages of proposed corrections had been received by the members and consultors to the Commission. To these were added detailed written recommendations from the O.I.C. and from COPECIAL, which had held a separate meeting in Rome from 26 to 28 February 1963.

The Plenary Commission studied the new text from 6 to 10 February 1963. The repetition of the fourfold division was criticized and a twofold one was proposed: the apostolate of the laity in general and in particular. Opposition was aroused by the inclusion of the new chapter on the societies of the faithful at the instigation of the Co-ordinating Commission, as it had to have a more juridical character which did not correspond to the character of the document as a whole. This material was given to the Commission for the Apostolate of the Laity already in the preparatory phase of the Council, but it was then thought to belong rather to the province of the Commission for the Discipline of the Clergy and the Faithful; the Commission for the Apostolate of the Laity had again to resign itself to this new development. It seemed better at that time to assign the whole matter to the consideration of the Commission for the Reform of Canon Law, and it was then resolved to inform the Co-ordinating Commission of this opinion. There was much discussion of the text on the topic of Catholic Action. The members of the Commission were reminded that the treatment of this theme at the Council had been requested by very many bishops, even those from countries in which neither the name Catholic Action was used nor the concept itself very widely known. Reference was made to the heated discussions which took place during and after the preparatory period. The new difficulties had come chiefly from the Anglo-Saxon countries where the word "Action" could all too easily be taken in a political sense as a "groupe de pression", as well as from Cardinal Suenens, who sent an inofficial note to all the members of the Commission in which he pointed out that the schema had not been improved in spite of the correction which had been proposed in the Central Commission on this topic. The difference of the two positions was clear: those in the first group wanted to omit the use of Catholic Action, and those in the other wanted to have it used

283

much more freely. In the end, several proposed changes from a commission of theologians were accepted, which left the substance unchanged but which helped to remove some of the difficulties. It was suggested that the name Catholic Action be more restricted in use but that the four characteristic features which together constitute genuine Catholic Action whether it be given that name or some other be retained unchanged. In the second part, therefore, Chapter 2 "on Catholic Action" and Chapter 3 "On the Other Forms of the Apostolate for the Direct Promotion of the Reign of Christ" were to be combined to form one chapter "On the Different Forms of the Social Apostolate for the Direct Promotion of the Reign of Christ". The first two articles of this chapter at that time treated of the variety of the forms of the social apostolate and the various relations it had to the hierarchy; it was taken in its essentials from what was then Chapter 3. The third article included almost unchanged what was up to then contained in Article 5 on Catholic Action; it was only pointed out in addition that Catholic Action could be carried out as well by organizations which bear other names. The last article treated of the furtherance of forms of the social apostolate on the part of the bishops. In the notes as well several explanations were given. At the end of the session it was agreed that the new text should be given to the General Secretary as soon as possible. This was done on 16 March 1963. On 20 March the text was presented to the Co-ordinating Commission — still under the title "Draft of a Decree on the Apostolate of the Laity".

The new draft consisted of 29 mimeographed pages of text in 92 articles and a concluding section with almost 10 pages of notes.[24] The decree contained a general introduction (5 articles) and two parts: the apostolate of the laity in general (43 articles) with 4 sections, and the apostolate of the laity in particular (44 articles) with three sections. In the first part the number and titles of the sections and chapters were retained just as they were in the previous text. The first section thus again had 2 chapters and 4 and 5 articles respectively; the second section also had the same 2 chapters consisting of 8 and 4 articles respectively; the third section had 2 chapters with 6 and 7 articles. Article 35 now only treated of materialism as such, with no "special mention of Marxism"; the fourth section had one chapter with 9 articles. The second part contained three sections which corresponded to the previous last three parts: the apostolate of the laity for the direct promotion of the reign of Christ; the apostolate of the laity in charitable works; the apostolate of the laity in the temporal order. The first section comprised only two chapters, which represented a compression of the previous Chapters 2 and 3: the apostolate of the laity in the various communities of the Church (5 articles); various forms of the social apostolate for the direct promotion of the reign of Christ (4 articles). Like the last text, the second section comprised again an introduction (3 articles) and two chapters consisting of 5 and 9 articles

[24] *Schema decreti de apostolatu laicorum* (mimeogr.); cf. the previous version, *Schema constitutionis de apostolatu laicorum* (n. 23).

respectively under the same titles. Similarly, the third section had an introduction (4 articles) and the same four chapters: the activity of the laity in the Christian perfection of the temporal (!) order (4 articles); the relation of the laity to the hierarchy in this order (2 articles); the formation of the laity for temporal (!) activity (5 articles); the application of the social teaching of the Church in various fields (3 articles).

The Co-ordinating Commission which met from 25 to 29 March 1963,[25] gave its affirmative response to the new plan in the first days of April 1963, only adding a few suggestions for improvement. The new Article 14 "on the societies of the faithful in present and future canon law", totalling 11 lines, was explicitly approved; the question was also to be treated in the Schema on Pastoral Care and on the Episcopate. The Commission for the Apostolate of the Laity, on the other hand, was to prepare an "appendix" which was to embody the elements for the revision of canon law, and an instruction on the formation of the laity for the apostolate. The Secretariat took this work upon itself. In the early months of 1963 members of the Commission had worked on a detailed "Appendix ad schema decreti de apostolatu laicorum — quaedam elementa pro revisione Codicis Iuris Canonici". This also formed the basis for the conferences of the sub-commissions appointed on 29 October 1963 by the Commission for the Apostolate of the Laity which met on 7, 14, and 21 November 1963. Since the Commission for the Reform of Canon Law had asked for a document treating of this topic there was no longer any question of an appendix to the decree itself. Members of the sub-commission were the Bishops Castellano, Herrera y Oria and De Vet; the consultors Hirschmann, Klostermann, and Papali; and the auditors of the Roman Rota, Ewers, Lefèbvre, and Sabattani. This preparatory work was also made use of in the later contacts of the post-Conciliar Commission for the Apostolate of the Laity with the Commission for the Reform of Canon Law.

Under the date of 22 April 1963, the "Draft of the Decree on the Apostolate of the Laity" was printed with the approval of the Pope and with very few changes, most of which were only stylistic. It was then sent to the Council fathers for their response. The Decree comprised 48 printed pages and contained 92 articles with a concluding section.[26]

Development of the text from the beginning of the second session to the beginning of the third session (29 September 1963 — 14 September 1964)

In September a number of critical remarks and suggested corrections of the fathers had already been received; these were then printed together in a fascicle and were given a preliminary examination by a small commission of Roman *periti*. The commission itself met for the first time during the second session of

---

[25] *HK* 18 (1963–64), p. 33.

[26] *Sacrosanctum oecumenicum Concilium Vat. secundum, Schema decreti de apostolatu laicorum* (Typ. polygl. Vat., 1963), cf. n. 24.

the Council on 3 October 1963. The members were given the 37 pages of recommendations which had been received up to that time. At the beginning of this work there were four lay auditors, later joined by two more. The first 6 auditors were: De Habicht, Inglessis, Norris, Sugranyes de Franch, Vázquez, and Veronese. The lay auditors were moreover empowered to enlist the help of other persons, providing the president gave his approval. Bishop Hengsbach (Essen) was chosen as sole reporter to the aula. To deal with the suggested improvements of the fathers, two sub-commissions were formed for the two parts of the Decree, which met on 8 and 10 October 1963 and whose recommendations were examined in the following plenary session of the Commission on 15, 17, and 22 October 1963. Much effort was expended in the formulation of a positive conception of the laity; even the title of the schema was reconsidered. On 22 October 1963, the *relatio* was approved which Bishop Hengsbach was to read in the aula.

In the plenary session of the Commission on 26 November 1963, there was some concern that the schema for the Apostolate of the Laity should not be treated again in the second session, since the discussion on the schema on the Church required more time than was expected, and since the Decree on Ecumenism was yet to be brought forward.

Preparations were made for a general discussion of two or three days and for this an introduction by Cardinal Cento, a *relatio* by Bishop Hengsbach and a fascicle of "suggested corrections" were prepared; but this document was never printed. There was general agreement that the schema should be revised for the third session. Since up to this time only a seventh of the fathers had submitted their *modi,* about 300 in all, it was urged that a definite deadline be set by which time all the criticisms were to be sent in. The Secretary was to try once more to arrange for a short debate in the aula.

On 1 December 1963 a statement from Cardinal Cicognani was sent by the Co-ordinating Commission to Cardinal Cento in which it was suggested that the schema should definitely be postponed until the third session of the Council and that the following principles be adhered to for the future: a new and shorter text was to be prepared in observance of the wishes of the fathers corresponding to the pastoral goals of the Council and it was to be entrusted to the Co-ordinating Commission until March. Everything else was to be referred to the Commission for the Reform of Canon Law. The General Secretary, Felici, expressed himself in the same vein in the 79th general congregation, the last of this session, on 2 December 1963, in a reference to all the schemata that had not been completed. The fathers were to hand in their objections and corrections up to 31 January 1964, after which date the Commissions were to commence their work. Similarly, in his concluding address on 4 December 1963, Paul VI expressed the wish for "proposals profoundly studied, accurately formulated, suitably condensed and abbreviated, so that the discussions, while remaining always free, may be rendered easir and much briefer". Schemata were to be composed "which are short and so worded that it will not be difficult to obtain a judgment of the Council on certain fundamental propositions. It will be left to the post-conciliar commissions to explain these principles more fully and to work out their practical implications".[27]

Towards the end of the last general congregation on 2 December 1963, the 79th of the Council, Bishop Hengsbach finally delivered his *relatio* to the draft of the Decree on the Apostolate of the Laity. In it he gave a short history of the draft and a sketch of its contents, with indications of the pertinent criticisms of the fathers which had been received up to that time. He presented in some detail the difficulties which were encountered on the subject of Catholic Action. Finally, Bishop Hengsbach asked the fathers to present the rest of their criticisms and remarks on the text.[28]

On 3 December 1963 the Commission met again to discuss the continuation of their work according to the new guidelines. They expected new criticisms from the fathers on the basis of the *relatio,* and from the *periti* of the Commission as well. 31 January 1964 was the deadline set for the handing in of the criticisms. It was also suggested that a directory be added to the short text which was not to be discussed in the general congregation. But the relation between this directory and the text could not be made sufficiently clear. The instruction prepared by the Secretariat on the Formation for the Apostolate was also distributed for criticism.

Already on 13 December 1963 a recommendation for an abbreviation of the draft of the Decree on the Apostolate of the Laity was sent by Bishop Hengsbach to the members and assistants in the Commission, which was to be commented upon by 6 January 1964. A new text was to be issued before the plenary session which was scheduled for February.

From 13 to 25 January 1964, the *Coetus Romanus* examined the recommendations for which they had asked and drew up a draft dated 1 January 1964 for a general directory on the Apostolate of the Laity, which was divided into two parts: the activity of the laity in the life of the Church, and the mission of the laity in the world. There were also two appendices: one on the formation of the laity for the apostolate, and the other on the duty of the priests in the apostolate of the laity. The material was to be taken from the previous text.[29] Another result of the efforts made at this time was the "Draft of a Decree on the Apostolate of the Laity" dated 25 January 1964.[30] The draft had 17 printed pages and contained 47 articles, of which all but three were already prepared. They are divided into an introduction (2 articles) and three chapters: 1) vocation, responsibility, and formation for the apostolate (7 articles); 2) different forms and areas of the apostolate of the laity (27 articles): on the apostolate which is to be exercised by all; on the social forms of the apostolate, on a special form of the social apostolate,

---

[27] *AAS* 56 (1964), p. 36.
[28] *Sacrosanctum oecumenicum Concilium Vat. sec., Relatio super schema decreti de apostolatu laicorum* (Typ. polygl. Vat., 1964).
[29] *Directorium generale "de apostolatu laicorum"* (mimeogr. dated 20. 1. 64).
[30] *Schema decreti "de apostolatu laicorum"* (redactio 25. 1. 64).

the Catholic Action; on the exercise of the apostolate of the laity in Church and lay bodies; 3) the preservation of the proper order in the apostolate of the laity (11 articles): on its relation to the hierarchy; on mutual co-ordination; on the co-operation of Catholics with other Christians.

However, even before the letter accompanying the new draft of the text, dated 25 January 1964, could be distributed to all the members and theologians of the Commission together with the plan for the directory and a request that comments would be accepted until 25 February 1964, a message was received from the Cardinal Secretary of State Cigognani by Cardinal Cento on 23 January 1964. In the name of the Co-ordinating Commission which had met in a session on 1 January 1964, it directed everyone "to reduce the draft on the apostolate of the laity to its essential points and to present it in the form of propositions upon which the fathers would be able to vote after a short debate. All the rest was to be given to the Commission for the Reform of Canon Law or to be left to special Instructions from the Holy See." At the same time a detailed *relatio* was to be prepared outlining the work which had been done up to that time, the method of procedure, the examination and selection of the criticisms received, all of which was to be printed as an appendix. The new text was to be presented in March. There was no mention of a directory. Nor was there any indication in the letter as to what "in forma *propositionum*" really meant; one of the four moderators of the Council who was also a member of the Co-ordinating Commission, Cardinal Döpfner, interpreted it as a "draft of 10 to 12 pages".

On 5 February 1964, the *Coetus Romanus* discussed the unhappy situation. They were of the opinion that a final position could be adopted toward the draft only when it was known what was contained in the chapter on the laity in the draft of the Constitution on the Church, as well as in what was then known as "Schema XVII" on the Church in the Modern World. They were also of the opinion that the exercise of the apostolate should once again be separated into charitable and social works. With this in mind, a new and even more abbreviated draft was drawn up and again all the documents were sent with an accompanying letter to the members and consultors of the Commission on 6 February 1964.[31] The divisions were the same as those in the draft of 25 January 1964, apart from the separation into charitable and social works. The text comprised 24 articles and was compressed into 10 pages.

In three plenary sessions of the Commission on 2 and 3 March 1964, the new state of affairs and the new text of 5 February 1964 were discussed. In these discussions it was stressed that a mangled and too general decree would disappoint the fathers and the laity, and also that the question of the directory would have to be solved by the Co-ordinating Commission; it was felt that in such a situation a completely new draft could scarcely be considered. It was also urged that the new work be based as much as possible upon the text already approved

---

[31] *Propositum ulterius abbreviatum*, 5 Feb. 64. *Schema decreti "de apostolatu laicorum"* (mimeogr.).

by the Commission and the fathers, and that the end of March was to be the latest deadline for the new text. A private communiqué from Cardinal Cicognani was then received which stated that "the propositions could also be organized into chapters". Thus, the work proceeded on the basis of what had already been done, though it was decided in a plenary session on 4 March 1964 that the material should be divided into 5 chapters and for this work 5 subcommissions were organized which were to work on the new "Draft of a Decree on the Apostolate of the Laity" in the next few days. This draft was approved in 6 plenary sessions on 7, 9, 10, 11 and 12 March 1964. The new text which was produced in such a short time was again somewhat corrected and revised by the *Coetus Romanus* on 18 March 1964; it was then distributed to the members and consultors of the Commission on 24 March 1964,[32] and given to Latinists for improvements in style. On 14 April 1964 Bishop Hengsbach sent in the revised *relatio*. The text of the new draft was already in the hands of the Co-ordinating Commission for their session on 16 and 17 April 1964, and was approved so that it could already be issued for printing with papal approval on 11 May 1964 and was then distributed to all the fathers.[33]

The text itself agrees completely with the "revision of 2 to 12 March 1964", save for a few stylistic changes, and comprises 14 printed pages; it includes an introduction, 21 articles, and a concluding admonition, with an additional 2 pages of notes. Appended to this there is a detailed 36-page *relatio,* containing a short history of the text, a table of contents, and a detailed report on the treatment of the suggested corrections which had been sent in by the fathers. The 21 articles are grouped into 5 chapters: the apostolic vocation of the laity (3 articles); different communities and social milieus (5 articles); the goals to be achieved (4 articles); different social forms of the apostolate (5 articles); the order to be preserved (4 articles). Throughout the summer various recommendations and criticisms were sent in which were then printed together. On 12 September 1964 the General Secretary informed the President in the name of the Co-ordinating Commission, the presidents of the Council, and the moderators, that the *relatio* which was to be read in the aula should refer to the written recommendations which had been received and also that it should contain the proposed or approved corrections.

The development of the text from the beginning of the third session
to the beginning of the fourth session
(14 September 1964 – 14 September 1965)

In the 82nd general congregation, on 17 September 1964, General Secretary Felici announced that requests to speak on the Schema on the Laity were to be

[32] *Schema decreti de apostolatu laicorum (redactio* 2.–12. 3. 1964; mimeogr.).
[33] *Sacrosanctum oecumenicum Concilium Vat. sec., Schema decreti de apostolatu laicorum* (Typ. polygl. Vat., 1964).

received by 28 September 1964; in the 88th general congregation on 25 September 1964, the deadline was extended to 2 October 1964. On 22 and 29 September 1964, the Commission met in plenary session to discuss the work of the coming session. The 5 subcommissions responsible for the last printed text (27 April 1964) were increased in number. The Commission decided that it would serve no useful purpose to examine the recommendations so far received before the debate in the aula. A welcome was extended to the new lay-auditors. One of them was to speak on the schema in the Council. On 29 September 1964, Bishop Hengsbach presented his *relatio* for approval. During the debate he was asked to answer the criticism, then loudly voiced, that the schema was too short, with a declaration that the Commission for the Apostolate of the Laity was nevertheless the only one which had not followed the request of the Co-ordinating Commission for a reduction to a few propositions; other commissions regretted now that they had not acted in the same way.

In the 95th general congregation, on 6 October 1964, Cardinal Cento introduced the draft on the Apostolate of the Laity, the debate upon which was finally to be begun the following day, after so many new drafts and revisions. In the 96th general congregation on 7 October 1964, Bishop Hengsbach presented his report on the course of the work on the draft and all the revisions and the way in which it was abbreviated to a quarter of its original size by the elimination of material treated in the chapter on the laity in the Dogmatic Constitution on the Church and the Pastoral Constitution on the Church in the Modern World. In the description of the apostolate of the laity an effort was made to avoid unclear terms or those which could be used in several different senses, e. g. the apostolate in the narrow and the wider senses, direct and indirect apostolate, the apostolate of the evangelization and the *consecratio mundi*. Nevertheless, it was still maintained that the efforts of the Christian to infuse the temporal order with the Christian spirit belonged to the apostolate. Clericalist formulations were eliminated, and realistic and objective study of the various milieus concerned was recommended. With respect to the differences of opinion surrounding the question of Catholic Action, the adoption of a middle way was attempted. It was decided that whatever was to be said upon the topic of social works could be dealt with only after the debate on the draft of the Constitution on the Church in the Modern World. In spite of rather severe criticism at the very outset of the debate, the draft was accepted in the 96th general congregation as the basis for the debate after only four speeches from the floor. Five other fathers were also able to address the assembly. At the end of the 99th general congregation on 12 October 1964, the debate on the apostolate of the laity was terminated by an informal majority vote. In the 100th general congregation on 13 October 1964 the first to speak was a layman, the President of the International Catholic Workers' Movement, Patrick Keegan. He spoke in the name of the lay auditors on this draft and stressed among other things the need of close contact between priests and laity. This was the first time a layman had addressed the Council. After this there followed three more interventions which were each supported by at least 70 fathers. In all, 66 fathers addressed the Council, of whom 6 were cardinals, 48 diocesan bishops, and 12 were suffragans; 36 of these were from the Continent (France and Italy with 8 each, Spain 5, Poland 3; Belgium, Germany, Ireland, Yugoslavia, the Netherlands with 2 each; England and Austria with one each). South America had 8 speakers (the Argentine 3, Chile 2, Brazil, Ecuador and Peru one each); Africa had 7 speakers (South Africa 2; Egypt, Algiers, Mozambique, Tanzania and Zambia one each); Asia also had 7 (India 3, China-Taiwan 2; the Lebanon and Syria each with one); North America had 6 (Canada 4, U.S.A. 2); Indonesia and Panama each had one.

43 fathers had already taken part in the general debate which was terminated with the end of the 98th general congregation on 9 October 1964. It was stressed that the schema was still too clerical in tone, too juridical in concept, too diffuse and general, too abstract, and that it did not correspond to modern needs; it was claimed that the layman's Christian state was not fully recognized and that his specific spirituality, vocation, and apostolate was not understood (Ritter, De Roo, Carter). The apostolate of the laity was still interpreted in too narrow a way due to the acute lack of priests or in such a way that it was based upon participation in the apostolate of the hierarchy and under its direction. There was too much emphasis on the organized apostolate; there was as much danger from an exaggerated institutionalism as there was from a world-alienated angelism (Larraín). Because of these severe criticisms some thought that the schema should be completely re-written (Sani, Hurley). It was considered to be of special importance to set out the dogmatic basis of the apostolate of the laity much more clearly (Charbonneau, de Vito, Fernandes, Leven, Rugambwa, Rastouil, Pironio, Quarracino, McGrath, Tenhumberg); the Church's new conception of itself and the new Christian evaluation of the worldly sphere should be of decisive importance in this conception (De Vet); it was only through the activity properly exercised by the laity that the Church would become the leaven of the world. It was necessary to accord first place to the family and professional calling as areas of apostolic activity. In doing this the Christian's solidarity with all other men must naturally be invoked (Duval, De Smedt). "The apostolate is the realization of the charisms of the people of God" (Leven). Likewise, it was asserted that the spiritual life of the laity was not to be patterned upon that of the religious (Bettazzi, Mosquera, Corral). In the education of the laity in general, union with Christ and our relationship to the world must be seen together. In another vein, others stressed participation in the entire universal mission of the Church (Barela, Enrique y Taracón); laymen could be given responsible positions even within the Roman Curia and in the diplomatic service of the Church (D'Souza). In the apostolate religious freedom must be respected and moral coercion avoided (De Smedt). Likewise, a clearer definition of the apostolate and of Catholic Action was called for (Maccari, Caggiano). With regard to Catholic Action speeches were made which represented the extremes of opinion already

mentioned (Suenens, Barbero). The necessity of a relation of trust between hierarchy and laity was urged (Šeper); a lay advisory board to the bishop was proposed (Leven); clericalism was to be shunned like the plague (Rugambwa, Carter, Ziadé); the rights of the laity individually and in the community must be stressed even more (Tenhumberg). But, on the other hand, one speaker condemned laicism (D'Agostino) and another called for docility and obedience from the laity in the apostolate towards the bishop and the pastor. The complaint was made that the schema spoke too much about a general duty to practise the apostolate (Browne). The absence of the treatment of various themes was noted, e.g. sports; use of leisure time; tourism; patriotism; the problem of youth; public opinion in the Church; secular institutes. All of these themes were at one time to be found in the schema but they were then deleted by the Commission or omitted for the sake of brevity.

In the special debate only 23 fathers spoke, 3 of them on 9 October 1964. At this stage only a few new points of view were expressed: personal help in the missions should be stressed (Soares de Resende); the references to charitable works should pay more attention to concrete and widespread problems (László), without thereby ignoring efforts towards the establishment of a generally just human order; the social question is one that should generally occupy the central place in the apostolate today (Larraín Errázuriz, Civardi, Padin); but in so doing the transformation of the worldly order must not be regarded in a triumphalist or overly optimistic manner. In work undertaken together with non-Catholics one should clearly distinguish between Christians and non-Christians (Höffner). Mention was made of the importance of international Catholic organizations. A warning was issued not to limit the apostolate of the laity simply to the institutionalized apostolate. It was claimed several times that the statements on Catholic Action, "the prototype of the apostolate" (Nicodemo), were too minimalistic and non-committal. One speaker claimed that the phrase Catholic Action carried political connotations with it in some countries (Heenan). As questions of education and formation were playing an increasingly important role, a separate chapter on formation for the apostolate was requested (Pluta), even an international study centre, a type of "university for Catholic Action" (Soares de Resende). With regard to the Secretariat for the Apostolate of the Laity, which was planned by the Holy See, it was stressed that it must not be formed according to the pattern of Roman curial bodies, that both its officials and its members should primarily be laymen (Heenan, Padin). The lay speaker emphasized the necessity of a living dialogue between priests and laity.

With the close of the debate on 13 October 1964, Bishop Hengsbach thanked the fathers for their interventions: several misunderstandings could be cleared up without much difficulty by clearer formulations; other questions, such as those concerning Catholic Action, were purposely left open in order to reach the two-thirds majority which was needed. Many wishes could be readily fulfilled: i.e. a closer correspondence of this schema to that on the Church; a clearer presentation of the nature, the basis, and the goals of the lay apostolate; additional material on the special spirituality of the lay state and on formation for the lay apostolate; clarification of the relations between the apostolate and the Christian witness in the world, with special reference to the social work of the Church; greater unification and co-ordination of the various forms of the apostolate according to its inner nature; a more dynamic plan for future development; and finally a better style. The *relator* requested that more time be granted to the Commission to examine the numerous wishes of the fathers, to wait for the final form of the draft on the Church in the Modern World, and to give more time to the Commission to profit further from the experience of laymen.

The general and specialized *modi* of the fathers were collected by the Secretariat; they were duplicated and distributed to the members of the Commission for their use. Besides the material already collected between the two sessions, the material collected during the debate made up 27 pages;[34] that comprising the general positions read out in the aula filled 108 pages and that on specific topics 167 pages.[35] Even before the beginning of the third session 4 episcopal conferences and 10 fathers had sent in their material to the Commission. During the discussion of the draft in the aula 144 fathers expressed their opinions orally or in writing; 8 of these *modi* were in the name of episcopal conferences.[36]

As early as 9 October 1964 a plenary session was convened for the organization of the five subcommissions on the five chapters of the text in order to treat the recommendations and corrections of the fathers. A letter was sent to the moderators on the same day complaining about the lack of order in the debate, and requesting sufficient time for debate in the aula. On 10 October a second letter followed, which requested that Bishop Hengsbach be allowed to give his report, which, as we have already mentioned, was given on 13 October 1964. Meanwhile the subcommissions began their work on the *modi* of the fathers. A plenary session of the Commission was fixed for 23 October 1964, for the discussion of the new arrangement of the draft. During this session the results of the third subcommission which also dealt with the general recommendations of the fathers were put to the vote, and the spirituality of the laity and formation for the apostolate of the laity were discussed. In the plenary session of the Commission on 5 November 1964 a vote could be taken on the newly-arranged drafts of the five subcommissions.

In the new order for the whole schema proposed on 5 November 1964, there were 26 articles divided into 6 chapters, besides an amended introduction and concluding admonition: the layman's call to the apostolate (4 articles), formerly

---

[34] *Animadversiones a Patribus in Cong. gen. factae super schema de apostolatu laicorum. Supplementum* (mimeogr.).
[35] *Animadversiones a Patribus Conciliaribus in aula factae super schema de apostolatu laicorum* (mimeogr.).
[36] *Sacrosanctum oecumenicum Concilium Vat. sec., Schema decreti de apostolatu laicorum* (Typ. polygl. Vat., 1965), no. 9.

found under the apostolic vocation of laymen; the various aims of the apostolate (4 articles), formerly third in the list; the places and milieus (6 articles), formerly second in the list, as communities and social milieus; the forms of the apostolate (5 articles); significantly enough the earlier titulation was social forms; the preservation of the proper order (4 articles); formation for the apostolate (3 articles). The second and third chapters were thus reversed in order; the organized apostolate does not appear in the title of any of the sections and it was thereby counted as one form among many others; Chapter 6 was a new addition. Besides this arrangement of material the other 15 articles formerly suggested were to be treated either by a schema entitled "Societies of the Faithful in Canon Law" or "The Laity in Canon Law".[37]

Shortly after the end of the third session on 27 November 1964 a new draft prepared by the subcommission with the help of the Secretariat employing the new order of the material as a basis was sent to each of the members of the Commission.[38] The draft, which was also sent to the lay assistants on 1 December 1964 with the request that criticisms and remarks upon it be received by the beginning of January, proposed 30 articles in 6 chapters. As opposed to the order presented on 5 November 1964 there were two new articles added to Chapters 4 and 6. The titles of the sections remained the same, except for Chapter 3 which was now called "On Communities and Environments"[39] and Chapter 4 "The Various Forms of the Apostolate".[40] Chapter 6 again existed only in the titles of the five articles scheduled and still had to be worked out by the subcommission. A text for this which had been prepared in Rome after a conference with several members of the commissions was found to be the object of so many criticisms already that it could not be accepted as the basis for any further work. In spite of this, the text was sent to the members of the Commission together with the critical remarks for their opinion.

The Plenary Commission for the Apostolate of the Laity, which convened from 25 to 30 January 1965 presented the corrections to the first five chapters suggested by 6 bishops, 4 theologians, and 5 laymen; these were printed in a brochure of 45 pages. This also contained a proposed text for the new fourth article on the spirituality of the laity drawn up by Fr. F. Wulf and expanded by the author of this commentary. Another fascicle of 27 pages with 2 texts printed side by side was distributed: a *textus prior,* namely the one printed with the date of 27 April 1964 (only Articles 3 and 15 are missing); and a *textus emendatus,* identical with the one contained in the draft of 27 November 1964, save for a very few corrections. Chapter 6 was here again nothing more than a title. But there

---

[37] *Ordo schematis "De apostolatu laicorum"* (prout in Sessione Plenaria diei 5 Novembris a Subcommissionibus expositus et generatim approbatu atque concordatus est) (mimeogr.).
[38] *Schema decreti de apost. laicorum (Redactio a Subcommissionibus facta,* 27 Nov. 1964), 17 pages (mimeogr.).
[39] "De communitatibus et ambitibus" instead of "de locis et ambitibus" in the draft of 5 Nov. 1964.
[40] "De diversis apostolatus modis" instead of "de formis apostolatus" in the draft of 5 Nov. 1964.

was also separate from this a text-draft of 4 pages for which the Secretariat with Fr. Bogliolo had provided a foundation and which was given its final revision on 23 and 24 January 1965.[41] In nine plenary sessions of 25, 26, 27, 28 and 29 January 1965 after a discussion of the basic elements of the apostolic character of the temporal activities of the Christian, several questions about the nature of the apostolate were resolved which the Dogmatic Constitution on the Church had also left open for discussion. The Commission charged the first subcommission to prepare a *nota* on this subject; this was put in the hands of Bishop Ménager and the *peritus* Klostermann. In the afternoon session of 29 January 1965 the guidelines were laid down according to which the revision committee established on 26 January 1965 (Hirschmann, Papali, Tucci) was to complete the final edition of the revised text. They were concerned especially to avoid repetitions, to review the citations of texts, to improve the stylisitc unity and the organization of the whole. On 30 January 1965 the majority of the members and consultors of the Commission retired to Ariccia for a day of private conferences on the draft of the schema (now Schema XIII) on the Church in the Modern World, where further discussions were also held on the *nota* with regard to the concept of the apostolate.

On 20 March 1965 the revised text of the Decree was distributed to the members and assistants of the Commission.[42] The Secretariat pointed out that in preparing this text the revision committee had in some cases done more than it was supposed to do; the text thus had to be approved first by the Commission before it could be distributed to the Council fathers; this examination was to take place during the session of the mixed commission for Schema XIII from 29 March to 7 April 1965. There was to be further deliberation on the addition of explanatory notes or even amplification of the text with regard to the use of the word "apostolate", which had been discussed at the January session (text-proposals of Ménager, Möhler, Daniélou, and Klostermann).

The new text again consisted of 30 articles, including the complete text for the article on the formation of the laity for the apostolate, and an introduction and concluding admonition. The division of the text into 6 chapters was retained. The title of the third chapter was now "The Various Fields of the Apostolate".[43] The first chapter comprised 3 articles, the second 4, the third 6, the fourth 7, the fifth 5, and the sixth 5 articles. In the first chapter the article on the apostolate to be exercised by all was omitted, and the fifth chapter now began with an introductory article. In comparison with the draft of 27 November 1964, the text was

---

[41] *Animadversiones ad schema de apostolatu laicorum* (redactio 27 Nov. 1964), 45 mimeogr. pages. *Schema decreti de apostolatu laicorum* (25. 1. 1965), 27 mimeogr. pages. *Cap. VI De formatione laicorum ad apostolatum,* 4 mimeogr. pages.

[42] *Schema decreti de apostolatu laicorum* (textus emendatus in sessione plenaria commissionis 25–30 Jan. 1965, revisus a subcommissione redactoria: RR. PP. Papali, Tucci, Hirschmann, et capita 1, 2, 3 denuo revisa ab una manu, R. P. Papali, 20. 3. 1965), 30 mimeogr. pages.

[43] *De variis apostolatu campis.*

considerably revised, especially in the first three chapters. There were, in addition, several changes made in the sequence of the articles.

The Commission met once more for a preparatory session on 30 March 1965 and examined the text in a plenary session on 3 and 6 April 1965. In both sessions the Commission occupied itself with the *nota* on the word and the concept of the "apostolate"; as the Commission did not want to go into any theological detail on the topic, the *nota* themselves were dropped, though their contents were referred to in two additions to Article 2 "on the participation of the laity in the mission of the Church". The text was finally approved, with a few other additions and changes of sequence, especially in Chapter 4; it was presented to the Co-ordinating Commission on 11 May 1965. With the approval of Paul VI it was printed on 28 May 1965 and was then distributed to the fathers.[44]

The new text in its printed form comprised 33 articles divided into 6 chapters, with an introduction and a concluding admonition. The title of Chapter 4 now reads "On The Various Forms of the Apostolate".[45] The additional three articles in this version were due to the fact that the introduction and concluding admonition were counted as articles and because Chapter 4 had 8 instead of 7 articles. The text itself was printed in two adjacent columns, the left being the *textus prior* which was printed on 27 April 1964, the right-hand column being the *textus emendatus*. After the introduction there was a general *relatio* and also a *relatio* for each of the articles as well as one at the end of the text of each chapter. The whole fascicle totalled 70 pages in large format.

With "regard to the teaching" represented by the text the *relatio* pointed out among other things that it was drawn up to correspond to the wish of the fathers that the unity and interrelation of all forms of the apostolate be stressed; with regard to the special character of the apostolate of the laity, care was taken not to limit it to the Christian transformation of the temporal order or to the apostolate which is under the direction of the hierarchy. The wish for a detailed treatment of lay spirituality and for a chapter on the formation for the aposto-late was complied with in the new version. In the face of what were often quite contradictory requirements, the draft sought to preserve a certain equilibrium.

Compared with the printed text of 4 April 1964, the following articles are completely new; Article 3 on the basis of the apostolate of the laity; Article 4 on the spirituality of the laity with reference to the apostolate; Article 12 on youth; Article 14 on national and international spheres; Article 15, which is an intro-duction to Chapter 4; Article 17 on the individual apostolate in various special circumstances; and Article 31 on the adaptation of the formation for each of the various forms of the apostolate. Chapter 6 is new as a separate chapter; parts of Articles 6, 8, 10, 11, 13, 18, 20, 23, 27, 28, 29, 30, 32, and 33 are entirely new. Nevertheless, the remaining articles as well have been largely re-written,

[44] *Sacrosanctum oecumenicum Concilium Vat. sec., Schema decreti de apostolatu laicorum* (Typ. polygl. Vat., 1965).
[45] *De variis apostolatus modis.*

especially in the first three chapters, as was already remarked with reference to the text of 27 November 1964.

The last phase and the final text (14 September 1965 – 18 November 1965)

At the end of August the General Secretary of the Council asked the Commission for its recommendations regarding the type of votes to be taken on the draft and the dates on which they were to be held. On 7 September 1965 the Secretary of the Commission sent the General Secretary a recommendation for the number of votes and requested that the *relator* be given the opportunity to present an explanation of the emendations as was provided for in Article 35 of the conciliar *Ordo*. In the first full session of the Commission on 20 September 1965, this resulted in a modification of the recommendation for the voting prepared by the Secretary which had to be given to the General Secretary that same day. 21 votes were proposed for the following groups of articles: 1–3,4, 5–6,7,8,9–10,11–12, 13–14, 15–17, 18–19, 20–22, 23–25, 26–27, 28–30, 31–33; there were also to be 6 votes for each of the 6 chapters taken as a whole. In these there was to be an opportunity for the fathers to express reservations. In actual fact there were 22 votes taken in the aula since there was a separate vote on the preface. In the session of 20 September 1965, the "Explanation on the Preparation of the Voting" prepared by Bishop Hengsbach was reviewed and approved with minor changes; in addition, the technical procedure for dealing with the reservations yet to be received was determined. To the five subcommissions already functioning, a sixth was added in view of the new chapter on the formation for the apostolate. After the sifting and dividing up of the entire material by the Secretariat and several consultors, the subcommissions were to begin their work; at the conclusion of this they were to prepare a *relatio* for the presentation of their *vota* before the plenary commission. The latter was to vote upon the individual proposals; for approval a two-thirds majority would be necessary. The Plenary Commission was to convene twice weekly from 27 September 1965 and to conclude its work by the end of October. After this, the subcommissions were to prepare the final *relationes*. Everything was to be ready by the beginning of November for the final voting.

In the 134th general congregation on 23 September 1965, the Decree on the Apostolate of the Laity was to be voted upon for the first time. Many feared that a new debate would be required because of the substantial changes in the text. Nevertheless, General Secretary Felici pointed out at the very beginning of the session that the revised draft had been in the hands of the fathers since the beginning of July, so that there had been time enough to study the text and hand in comments. It was thus thought that a new debate was superfluous, and that further proposals for changes could be presented as the sections were voted upon. Bishop Hengsbach then read his "Explanation on the Preparation for the Voting"; he stated that the Commission had endeavoured to treat the schema as a

297

complement to the Constitution on the Church and to make it correspond to "Schema XIII", which was then under discussion. Bishop Hengsbach then referred to several improvements: the article on the spirituality of the laity; on youth; on the greater accentuation of the individual apostolate; and on the chapter on formation for the apostolate. He observed that the text was more dynamic, more unified, and more compact; the old conception nevertheless remained the basis of the work in spite of all the changes which had been undertaken solely according to the wishes of the Council fathers themselves. A separate vote was planned for each important point. In this same session the first 6 votes were taken, the results of which are as follows:

		For	Against	Invalid	Reservations
1st vote	(Art. 1, Introduction)	2218	5	1	
2nd vote	(Art. 2–3: participation of laity in mission of the Church and basis of the apostolate)	2205	18	1	
3rd vote	(Art. 4: lay spirituality)	2185	19	2	
4th vote	(Introduction and Ch. 1 as a whole)	1904	8	5	213
5th vote	(Art. 5–6: the laity in two orders; apostolate of evangelization and sanctification)				
6th vote	(Art. 7: Christian transformation of temporal order)	2068	8	1	

The voting in the 135th general congregation on 24 Sept. 1965 had the following results:

7th vote	(Art. 8: charitable works)	2163	8		
8th vote	(Ch. 2 as a whole)	1975	2		190
9th vote	(Art. 9–10: laity in the communities of the Church)	2161	8	3	
10th vote	(Art. 11–12: family; youth)	2145	14	3	
11th vote	(Art. 13–14: social milieu; national and internat. spheres)	2065	6	2	
12th vote	(Ch. 3 as a whole)	1707	4	1	311
13th vote	(Art. 15–17: apostolate of the individual)	1972	3		

The final votes of the 136th general congregation on 27 Sept. 1965 had the following results:

14th vote	(Art. 18–19: the communal apostolate)	2013	8	1	

		For	Against	Invalid	Reservations
15th vote	(Art. 20–22: Cath. Action; laymen in special service of Church)	2104	35	4	
16th vote	(Ch. 4 as a whole)	1834	7		287
17th vote	(Art. 23–25: relation to hierarchy)	2123	11	5	
18th vote	(Art. 26–27: organizations for co-operation)				
19th vote	(Ch. 5 as a whole)	1894	9	7	230
20th vote	(Art. 28–30: formation for apostolate)	2063	17		
21st vote	(Art. 31–33: adaptation of formation; means of formation, conclusion)	2012	5	3	
22nd vote	(Ch. 6 as a whole and conclusion)	1865	3	5	143

The fewest reservations were expressed for the chapter on the formation for the apostolate (143), then the chapter on the goals of the apostolate (190), the chapter on the call to the apostolate (213), on the proper order (230), on the methods of the apostolate, including the article on Catholic Action (287). The greatest number of reservations were received on the chapter on the fields of the apostolate (311). In all, therefore, there were 1374 reservations to be examined, and because many of these were practically identical they were then reduced to 659 *modi*.

Immediately upon the reception of these reservations by the General Secretary the subcommissions began their work, the results of which were to be examined and then approved in 7 plenary sessions of the Commission on 1,5,7,8,12,14, and 15 October 1965. To facilitate the work of the Commission the Secretariat again issued a double-columned text: on the left-hand side the text which had been approved in the printed draft of 28 May 1965, and on the right-hand side the text which was revised according to the reservations of the fathers which took up 33 pages.[46] In a plenary session of the Commission on 20 October 1965, announced as the last session, the *general relatio* of Bishop Hengsbach, which was to be delivered before the voting on the *modi,* was examined for the last time. Likewise, two more corrections were made, one in Article 4 on the spirituality of the laity and one which concerned women and which was again urgently repeated by the women auditors in Article 9. Then the draft of the decree was sent to press together with the reservations for the vote on the *modi.* The final touches to the draft were made during the "conciliar interval" between 17 and 23 October 1965.

[46] "*De apostolatu laicorum*" (mimeogr.).

The text to be voted upon was already printed when the General Secretary of the Council summoned the Secretary of the Commission, which was due to meet the next morning, to the sacristy of St. Peter's on the afternoon of 6 November 1965, and there gave him a letter from the Under-Secretary of State, Archbishop Dell' Acqua, which contained several *modi* which the Pope urgently recommended for study to the Commission. The Italian text of the letter was in two parts: a) suggested emendations which had already been sent to the Pope in the early summer; b) observations on the treatment of the *modi* in view of these suggested corrections which the Pope handed on to the Commission for study. Together with this letter there was a sheet with a note in the handwriting of Dell' Acqua: *Nota del S. Padre*. Altogether there were 12 corrections involved, of which the 7th, dealing with Article 12, the 10th dealing with Article 19, and the 12th dealing with Article 24, were indicated as being of special importance. Several corrections were concerned with emphasizing the subordination of the apostolate of the laity to hierarchical supervision.

Since voting on the *modi* was scheduled for 9 November 1965, the Commission was convened on the morning of 8 November for a plenary session. Suggestions 1, 2, and 9 were not examined since they were thought to have already been dealt with sufficiently in the treatment of the *modi* previous to this; the rest of the suggestions were considered in detail. On the basis of the 7th proposal 2 changes in the text were suggested with regard to Article 12. Likewise, the 12th suggestion on Article 24 was accepted. These new corrections were sent to the General Secretary of the Council and the Secretary of State on the same day, and a supplementary page was hastily printed with the text of the corrections *(variationes)*. This was distributed to the fathers the next day with the text of the *modi* to be voted upon.[47] This latter text was contained in a volume of 142 pages comprising the draft of the decree in six chapters (9–140), which was preceded by the *general relatio* (5–7), and in the following order: first the text; then the "*relatio* to the individual articles" of the chapter concerned with the results of the September vote; the general reservations *(modi generales)* and the special reservations *(modi particulares);* and finally the question to be voted upon, i.e. whether the treatment of the *modi* by the Commission for each respective chapter could be approved.

In the 155th general congregation on 29 October 1965 General Secretary Felici announced that the voting on the corrections to the draft on the apostolate of the laity was to take place in the next general congregation scheduled for 9 November 1965. Just before the voting Bishop Hengsbach read his report on the work done on the *modi* by the Commission. He pointed out that the Com-

[47] *Sacrosanctum oecumenicum Concilium Vat. sec., Schema decreti de apostolatu laicorum. Variationes in textu schematis decreti a commissione conciliari de fidelium apostolatu propositae* (Typ. polygl. Vat., 1965) *Sacrosanctum oecumenicum Concilium Vat. sec., Schema decreti de apostolatu laicorum. Textus recognitus e. modi a Patribus Conciliaribus propositi a commissione de fidelium apostolatu examinati* (Typ. polygl Vat., 1965).

mission attempted to express some things more clearly without thereby seeking to settle matters which were still subjects of debate among the fathers. He concluded with the remark that this was the first time that any ecumenical council had dealt with the apostolate of the laity in a separate decree and that the experience and co-operation of many laymen and of lay movements had gone into the making of this text. A vote was then taken on the proposed corrections according to chapters, as was scheduled.

The results were as follows:

		For	Against	Invalid
1st vote	(Introduction and Ch. 1 on the call of the laity to the apostolate)	2117	10	
2nd vote	(Ch. 2 on the goals to be achieved)	2099	16	1
3rd vote	(Ch. 3 on the various fields of the apostolate)	2075	12[48]	
4th vote	(Ch. 4 on the various kinds of apostolate)	2061	14	1
5th vote	(Ch. 5 on the order to be observed)	2089	8	
6th vote	(Ch. 6 on the formation for the apostolate)	2100	6	3

On the basis of these positive results in all partial votes, the vote on the entire draft was held during the 157th general congregation on 10 November 1965; the results of this were 2201 affirmative, 2 negative, and 5 invalid votes. With this the Decree on the Apostolate of the Laity was ready for promulgation and was then given to the Pope. He was to decide whether it should be definitively passed in the next public session.

In the following days another further difficulty arose with regard to the formulation of the first *variatio* in Article 12, which had been made at the very last moment. From the text one could receive the impression that youth was somehow considered to be outside the Church; *amore erga Ecclesiam* was substituted by *amore erga Ecclesiae pastores*. Similarly, the Latinist (Abbot Karl Egger) proposed 44 more changes in 15 articles. After these last changes the text upon which the final vote was to be taken was sent to press.[49] The decree was then submitted for a final solemn vote in the 8th public session of Vatican II on 18 November 1965, after the vote on the Dogmatic Constitution on Divine Revelation. The results of this vote were: 2305 affirmative, and 2 negative. After its promulgation the Pope gave a copy each of the Decree to three men and three women lay-auditors. On 19 November 1965 it was discovered that the computing machine had not taken into account 35 affirmative voting-papers as they had not been wholly intact. The corrected official count was therefore

[48] Up to this time the result of the voting was given in the same session. The remaining results were made known only in the 157th general congregation on 10 Nov. 1965.

[49] *Sacrosanctum oecumenicum Concilium Vat. sec., Decretum de apostolatu laicorum de quo agetur in Sessione publica diei 18 nov. 1965* (Typ. polygl. Vat., 1965).

2340 affirmative, and 2 negative votes. Thus, the vote on the apostolate of the laity had the fewest dissenting votes during the whole of the Council:

Decree on the Missionary Activity of the Church: 2394 affirmative, 5 negative;

Decree on the Priests: 2390 affirmative, 4 negative;

Dogmatic Constitution on Divine Revelation: 2344 affirmative, 6 negative;

Decree on the Apostolate of the Laity: 2340 affirmative, 2 negative.

In the following days the official edition of the text was issued by papal authority and was printed after the declaration of approval by the Pope and registration of this by the *vacatio legis*.[50] Several typographical errors had to be corrected for this edition and in paragraph 6 of Article 29 a subject that had been omitted had to be inserted.

---

[50] *Sacrosanctum oecumenicum Concilium Vat. sec., Decretum de apost. laicorum* (Typ. polygl. Vat., 1965).

Commentary

Title and Introduction

As we have already seen in the history of the development of the text, the Commission for the Apostolate of the Laity had to defend the title of its decree before the Secretary of the Council in the very first session. On 22 October 1963, a suggestion was made within the Commission itself by Bishop Guano that the following title be adopted: "De Participatione Laicorum in Ecclesiae Apostolatu", but it did not meet with approval. The following formulation found even less support: "De Laicorum Munere in Apostolatu Ecclesiae". In the plenary session of the Commission on 2 March 1964, Bishop Petit again raised the issue of the title; as well as "Participatio Laicorum in Apostolatu Ecclesiae" "De Laicis in Apostolatu Ecclesiae" was suggested as either title or subtitle. Eventually a separate subcommission was set up to deal with this question (Cardijn, Klostermann, Papali, Tucci, Veronese). But in the end the original title remained. In the voting of September 1965 several German bishops tried in particular to have the title changed by means of *modi*. "De Participatione Laicorum in Missione Ecclesiae" was suggested, either as title or subtitle, prompted by the Constitution on the Church and by the "optical difficulties" in the use of the word "apostolate". The Commission eventually turned down this proposal which was supported by only 5 fathers with the reason that the title had always been the same and that it was clear from the whole context that what was involved was the participation of the laity in the mission of the Church.[51]

Even if the Commission had been more favourably disposed to this suggestion, such a change would have been impossible since it would have had to be made without a discussion, which was no longer possible. But perhaps this was just as well. For this change could have led to further difficulties and misunderstandings, since it might, for example, have seemed that the laity took part in something which existed outside the Church and of which they were not an essential part,

---

[51] *Schema decreti de apost. laicorum. Textus recogn. et modi . . .*, no. 16.

as had already been argued against the proposal of Guano. One could indeed speak of a participation of Christians — laity as well as hierarchy — in the mission of Christ, as is done in Article 2 ("laici, muneris . . . Christi participes effecti"), but not properly of participation in the mission of the Church. Article 2 in fact continues: "suas partes in missione totius populi Dei explent in Ecclesia et in mundo". Similarly, the Constitution on the Church says: "pro parte sua missionem totius populi christiani in Ecclesia et in mundo exercent". Of course the same Constitution defines the apostolate of the laity most definitely as a "participatio ipsius salvificae missionis Ecclesiae",[52] but here there is no possibility of the same sort of misunderstanding from the context, since the same sentence refers to the inner basis of such a "participatio" namely the "deputatio ad apostolatum per baptisma et confirmationem".

It is also of great significance that the Council kept to the use of the word and the concept "apostolate" in connection with the laity, and indeed, as we shall see, for a very well-founded and comprehensive reason, and that it did not simply identify this word with the apostolic office of the New Testament writings (Gal 2:8; Rom 1:5; 1 Cor 9:2; cf. also 2 Cor 12:12; Acts 1:25). The Council considered the laity in terms of that mission which proceeded from the Father, who sent his Son into the world "that the world might be saved through him" (Jn 3:17), that mission for the witness of which and the participation in which Christ determined his Church as a whole. To this mission the Church is bound until the return of Christ at the end of time. Thus, the mission concerns every member of the Church by virtue of the common calling which every Christian has in the basic charism of faith and baptism, but also by virtue of the special states and charisms of each. Thus the laity do not have a share in this mission for some special reason or purpose but quite simply because they are themselves the Church. The first hints of this extended concept of the apostolate are to be found in the New Testament, and even more clearly in the use of the title of apostle in the early Church. Similarly, all Christians have been filled with charisms by the pouring out of the Spirit (Acts 2:17f.; 1 Cor 2:13, 15) and have grown together with Christ the original apostle (Heb 3:1; Rom 6:5) and they have thereby already been empowered and commissioned as a "royal priesthood" which is to "declare his wonderful deeds" (1 Pet 2:9; Acts 4:31) and to form a "council by divine calling", namely the ἐκκλησία.[53] Such a conception was indeed not always obvious. Almost a century earlier Vincent Pallotti, since canonized, was engaged in what was then a fruitless struggle in Rome to have the Christian apostolate extended to the lay world.[54]

---

[52] Const. dogm. de Eccl., nn. 31, 33.
[53] Cf. F. Klostermann, Das christliche Apostolat (1962), pp. 67–215; H. Küng, Strukturen der Kirche (1962), pp. 22–35; 198f., n. 2, E. T.: Structures of the Church (1963); Y. Congar, "Konzil als Versammlung und grundsätzliche Konziliarität der Kirche", Gott in Welt. Festgabe für K. Rahner, II (1964), p. 148 and in general pp. 135–65.
[54] F. Klostermann, Das christliche Apostolat, pp. 198–201.

Likewise, the attempt to exclude the social or temporal activities of the laity from the apostolate, and therefore to change the title accordingly, was rejected already in 1964.[55] The second decisive concept which is contained in the title is likewise in need of an explanation: the concept of the laity. The Decree on the Apostolate of the Laity is unfortunately in need of more precise definition. One would have to approach Article 31 in the light of the whole content of the Decree and from the indication given in note 2 to the introduction of the fourth chapter of the Constitution on the Church: "The term laity is here understood to mean all the faithful except those in holy orders and those in a religious state sanctioned by the Church." This appears at first sight to be the usual negative definition. But the Christian state which is here given as the *genus proximum* is something very positive, though on the other hand there is nothing specifically "lay" about it. Nevertheless, even in this *differentia specifica* which at first appears to be so negative something positive is hidden. For it is precisely the fact that the laity has not been called for a special office or religious state, and that it is free from those special and lasting commitments connected with holy orders and the religious profession, which gives them those special opportunities and tasks which they would not have as clerics or as religious, although these tasks are of the greatest importance for the Church and the world, to mention only the field of political engagement, for example. Even those particular callings in which the laity may be engaged receive from this fact a special significance. Clerics and religious, of course, have duties of the greatest importance, especially within the Church, but because of their special and lasting bond with the Church they must renounce many other tasks and opportunities even when they also do the same professional work as their lay brethren, or even when, as in the Eastern Church, the clerics are also married. This positive aspect hidden in the formulation is something which is only realized through each of the various professions which laymen may also exercise and which then by virtue of their baptism and Christian faith become supernatural professions gifted with different charisms and special graces by God.[56] As we shall see in what follows, the Decree is addressed especially to those laymen who live "in the midst of the world and of secular transactions" (Article 2), though this cannot, as we shall also see, be said to cover all those who are not clerics or religious.

Article 1. This article, which is explicitly titled the introduction, places this Decree within the context of the whole Council. Not only have the Constitutions on the Church and on the Liturgy spoken of the "special participation of the laity in the mission of the Church which in every respect is absolutely necessary", but so also have the Decrees on the Instruments of Social Communication, Ecumenism, the Bishops' Pastoral Office, the Church's Missionary Activity, on the

---

[55] *Schema decreti* (1964), no. 30.
[56] Cf. *Const. dogm. de Eccl.*, nn. 12; 31; notice the *suo modo* and the *pro parte sua* in the first paragraph; cf. also p. 32.

305

Ministry and Life of Priests, and the Declaration on Christian Education.[57] In this Decree, however, the Council addresses itself in a special way to Christian laymen (christifideles laicos) "in order to give more weight to the apostolic activity of the people of God". The Apostolic Constitution for the Convocation of Vatican II cited in the notes explicitly refers to the call, to the apostolate of the Church, of the laity, "who have become more conscious of their significance within the Church and especially of their duty to co-operate with the ecclesiastical hierarchy".[58] Another reason for this special conciliar decree was also given: the apostolate of the laity should never be lacking in the Church and especially not at the present time, because it is something which flows from the Christian vocation as such. Reference is made here to the spontaneous and fruitful apostolate of the laity as it existed in the apostolic period of the early Church.

In the second paragraph it is pointed out that there is no less a need for the apostolate now than in apostolic times; there is indeed an even greater urgency in our day for an apostolate of much greater scope and depth. The greater scope of such an apostolate is due to the "population explosion", to the almost immeasurable broadening of the field of the apostolate through the greater ease of communication and travel brought about by modern science and technology, and similarly to the complexity and interdependence of human relationships brought about by these means; the depth of the new apostolate, on the other hand, may be thought of as the new range of problems provoked by such a development. It is stressed that many of these new fields are accessible only to laymen, and that the solution of these new problems is dependent upon the technical ability of such "laymen". The urgency of this apostolate — for it is only this which is being considered here — is thus increased even more by the growing "autonomy of many areas of human life". The legitimacy of this autonomy is fully recognized,[59] though it is also conceded that it can lead to ethical and religious conflicts and to "difficult crises within the Christian life". From the way in which these things are formulated here, however, it is made clear that there is no necessary connection between these developments and the problems which, in fact, have arisen. Finally, reference is made to those regions in which there is a dearth of priests or in which priests are hindered by force in the performance of their tasks (previous mention was made of hindrances dictated by circumstance); in such cases the Church is "present and active" almost exclusively through laymen.[60]

In the growing consciousness of that particular apostolic responsibility which is proper to the laity the Council sees the work of the Spirit, who responds in this

---

[57] Cf. n. 2 in the introduction. In the text published after the vote the Decrees on the Missions and on the Ministry and Life of Priests were no longer cited.

[58] Const. Apost. of John XXIII, Humanae Salutis of 25 December 1961: AAS 54 (1962), p. 7. Cf. n. 1 in the introduction.

[59] Cf. Const. past. de Eccl. in mundo huius temp., nn. 36; 40; 42; 55; 59; 76; Decl. de educatione christiana, n. 10.

[60] See also Const. dogm. de Eccl., n. 33.

way to the "manifold and pressing need" of the apostolate of the laity. In the note pertaining to this passage reference is made to the familiar words in the address of Pius XII to the new cardinals on 20 February 1946, in which he speaks of the "essential mission" of the Church "to form the whole of mankind so to work ceaselessly for the construction of a sure foundation for society . . . Thus considered, the faithful and the laity stand in the front line of the ecclesiastical life. For them the Church is the living principle of human society. Therefore it is especially their duty above all others to be conscious always that we do not belong to the Church, we are the Church, the community of the faithful."[61] The same note also refers to the address of Pius XII to the participants of the first world congress of JOC on 25 August 1957, which stressed the need of youth in the Church's work: the young "must make Christ the Saviour known, and so work that his law of love may penetrate every region of private and public life...". Therefore, the Pope concludes, "a spirit of co-operation with the Church, the missionary spirit, must grow (in them) ever more".

The concluding sentence indicates the purpose and goal of the decree and also formulates the important task of the Council in describing "the nature, character, and diversity of the lay apostolate" together with its "basic principles" and directives for its more effective exercise" which are to be the norm for the future reform of canon law. In fact, the papal commission set up for this reform on 17 February 1966 had contacted the post-conciliar Commission for the Apostolate of the Laity to learn of its wishes in this matter and the secretary of this Commision was named consultor to the Commission for the Reform of the *CIC*. The passage now under consideration was found for the first time with the same wording in the printed text of the draft of 1965, and not only replaced what were then Articles 14 and 15 in the edition of 1964 (expressly referred to in the 1965 edition) — both of them under the heading "Associationes fidelium in iure condito et condendo" — but it also replaced the decree "De fidelium associationibus" planned originally by the Commission for the Discipline of the Clergy and Faithful, and even the later "Appendix ad Schema Decreti de Apostolatu Laicorum — quaedam elementa pro revisione Codicis Iuris Canonici" desired by the Commission for the Apostolate of the Laity, which we have already mentioned in the history of the text.

---

[61] *AAS* 38 (1946), pp. 149f. The reference given on pp. 101–2 has no bearing on our subject. Cf. also n. 3 in the introduction.

The Layman's Call to the Apostolate

This basic chapter of the decree was intended, at the wish of the fathers, to summarize the most important points of the chapter on the Laity in the Constitution on the Church. Article 3 was inserted into the text only as a result of the debate of October 1964.

Article 2 treats of "the participation of the laity in the mission of the Church".[62] It begins with the general task of the Church which is described as a twofold one: through the spread of Christ's dominion over all the earth "all men are to share in Christ's saving redemption", and, through these men who are partakers of that redemption, the whole world is to be ordered in relation to him. The Church fulfils the first task chiefly in its service of preaching and sanctifying, only in this is the Church as a whole subject; the second is carried out by redeemed men, certainly through their prayers, but above all through their secular activity performed in the spirit of the gospel of Jesus. This passage purposely speaks about the kingdom of Christ and not of the kingdom of God, for what is meant here is "the kingdom in its present aspect"; instead of the static concept evoked by the word kingdom we should consider God's *active dominion* in Christ which is as yet only in a state of incompletion and partial fulfilment.[63]

Every activity is thus to be called apostolic which is directed towards this goal, which before God is but one single goal and one single mission. At the same time the fathers stress the fact that the Church accomplishes this apostolate "through all of its members", though in different ways. This is effected not only in the tasks of evangelization and sanctification, but also in the orientation of all aspects of the world towards Christ. It is thus not possible to attempt to separate these tasks sharply as is sometimes done, giving to the clergy as their proper sphere of

---

[62] The individual articles = *numeri* of authentic Latin text, have no titles; those indicated here with quotation marks originated with the commissions concerned and were also found in the *sub secreto* edition issued previous to the authentic text.
[63] Cf. R. Schnackenburg, *Gottes Herrschaft und Reich* (1965⁴), p. 247 f., E. T.: *God's Rule and Kingdom* (1963).

apostolic activity the Church and to the laity, the world. In proceeding thus one would inevitably arrive at the "two types of Christians" already mentioned in the *Decretum* of Gratian: the ecclesiastical and the worldly, the spiritual and the fleshly, the perfect and the imperfect.[64]

In this connection the Commission was again and again in danger of being forced into extreme positions which were diametrically opposed to each other, and this from two parties: in the attempt to delineate the true character of the apostolate of the laity, the one wished to limit it to the Christian orientation of the temporal order, and the other to the direct support of the hierarchical apostolate and, if possible, only to that apostolate under the direction and authority of the hierarchy; in their efforts to find the right relation between the apostolate of evangelization and sanctification and the apostolate of the Christian orientation of the temporal order, the one side wished to stress unity to such an extent that by the subordination of the whole of the apostolate to the leadership of the hierarchy there was danger of a new "ecclesialization" of the world, while the other side wished to have the difference between the two so strongly marked that the two orders would appear to stand, unconnected, side by side, by which the apostolic character of the secular activity of the laity would appear to be obscured. Even among the interventions we can find evidence of attempts to fetter the entire apostolate of the laity "sub ductu hierarchiae",[65] although the opinion of the Council as a whole in this matter had long since taken a different direction. Bishop McGrath had already stressed in the aula on 22 October 1963 that "the Christian civilization is no ecclesiastical civilization and even less is it a clerical civilization", though one should also add that even the expression "Christian civilization" is an unfortunate one. In the present version of the text, however, the Decree found the right compromise in this matter and excludes the misinterpretation of such an "ecclesialization" of the world.[66]

In this way the concept of the universal apostolate is preserved in complete agreement with Articles 31 and 33 of the Constitution on the Church; this apostolate embraces clerics and laity and the operation of both in the Church and in the world, as well as their activity as citizens of this world. Accordingly, the whole life of a Christian, his worldly life included, also has part in the mission of the Church as the life of one who is baptized, and in that it is taken up in faith it always has at the same time an ecclesial and therefore apostolic character. The inner reason for this lies in the fact that the whole Christian vocation is already by nature "also a vocation to the apostolate" . . . and this refers back to an idea

---

[64] C 7 C XII: *PL* CLXXXVII, 884 f.; see also Cardinal Humbert von Silva Candida in *Monumenta Germaniae Historica, Libelli de lite*, I, p. 208: "The laity should care only for their own things, namely worldly affairs, and clerics for their own things, namely the things of the Church . . . Just as the clerics take upon themselves nothing worldly, so neither should the laity take anything spiritual upon themselves."

[65] *Textus recogn. et modi* . . ., 24 and 26, *modi* 63, 77, 80.

[66] Cf. the *relatio generalis of the Schema decreti*, . . . (1965), pp. 10 f.

expressed already in the introduction. One cannot translate "vocatio christiana" here with "vocation to Christendom", for what is meant is not an act which has occurred once, perhaps far in the past, but the permanent call of Christendom, an appeal which characterizes Christian existence itself. This is then exemplifed in the image of the body taken from the Epistle to the Ephesians: the whole body which "according to the functioning in due measure of each single part, derives its increase".[67] A passive member thereby passes away not only for the body as a whole, for the Church, but also for itself.

The phrase "the functioning in due measure of each single part" provides the motto for the way in which the laity is now called upon specifically to participate in the mission of the Church. The first sentence asserts once again the unity of the mission *(missionis)* — one could also say of the apostolate — above all the differences in ministration *(ministerii);* mention is then immediately made of the office of the apostles and their successors as opposed to the laity's "own role" *(suas partes)* in the priestly, prophetic, and royal office of Christ in the "mission of the whole people of God". What was expressed in a general way in the very first paragraph is here applied concretely to the laity: they share in both tasks of the Church and thus they realize their "own role in the Church and in the world".[68] With regard to their activity in the world, in so far as it is a penetrating *(perfundendum)* and perfecting *(perficiendum)* of the temporal order of things with the spirit of the gospel, it is again stressed that it is a "witness to Christ", therefore an apostolate "which promotes the salvation *(salutem)* of men". Salvation here is to be understood in the supernatural sense. The phrase which is here and elsewhere used in connection with the influence of the Christian in the world, "spiritu evangelico perfundere ac perficere", is meant to stress the apostolic nature of this activity. *Perfundere* means "to pour over completely", "to penetrate and flow over", "to suffuse through and through". If a man — and this is a condition — performs a temporal task and is penetrated and filled with the spirit of the Gospel, then the spirit of the Gospel, the love of Christ, becomes active and present in his action; then his work will be infused with that same love of Christ as well as of the men in partnership with whom that self-same work was perhaps performed, for instance, at the office or the factory.

The last sentence of this paragraph which once again stresses the activity of the lay state which is lived "in the midst of the world and of secular transactions" does not of course detract anything from what has been said above, namely that the laity also have their own tasks within the Church and that their state is to be interpreted accordingly. It is noteworthy that any type of activity in the world is seen as a divine vocation and always described as an activity which is "as a kind of leaven". But one should not force either the meaning of the word "state" *(status)* or of the word "proper" *(proprium)*. The Commission replied to a

[67] Eph 4:15 f. was already quoted in Article 30 of the Constitution *De Ecclesia*.
[68] The note refers to Article 31 of the Constitution *De Ecclesia,* upon which our section has been intentionally modelled.

reservation on Article 7 that the phrase *proprium munus* meant only that the laity have *primas partes* in the temporal order.[69]

This article was most strongly influenced by the debate on the *nota*, which we have already mentioned in the history of the text, which was supposed to explain the nature of the apostolate. Instead of the *nota* for which there were eight different recommendations in the spring of 1965, the fathers finally settled for two insertions in the text, which we now find in this article. There were three different preliminary formulations which were printed for the first time in the edition of 1965. An important passage occurs in the first paragraph, in which it is asserted that the task of the Church is seen to be the orientation of the whole world to Christ: "et per eos mundus universus re vera ad Christum ordinetur" . . . — in all earlier formulations it was given as "gloria Dei fiat". The most significant of the insertions is contained in the second paragraph: "Apostolatum reapse exercent . . . ad salutem hominum inserviat". The penultimate formulation makes the point still more clearly, though it also states what the Council did not wish to say: the sentence "A laici . . . et in mundo" was continued with: "et sic apostolatum vero et proprio sensu exercent, sive sua activitate in evangelizationem et sanctificationem hominum, sive saltem in rerum temporalium usum et ordinem spiritu evangelico perfundendum et perficiendum intendentes, ita vero ut in activitate ipsa illa animatio christiana vel testimonium Christi appareat (cf. Mt 5:16). Aedificatio ordinis temporalis secundum rei naturam posita qua talis apostolatus non est, nisi et intentione forsan mere subiective apostolica, etsi ille ordo sic dispositus valoribus christianis vias pandit. Insuper respiciendum est, quod laici de quibus hic imprimis loquimur in medio mundi negotiorum . . ."

In the discussion which was carried on through the ensuing months the central question was: when could something be called an apostolate, and, especially, to what extent has the activity of the Christian in the world, whose direct goal was of a profane and temporal nature, an apostolic character and hence could be called an apostolate? The question was whether in the latter case an objective justice would be sufficient, i.e. fulfilment of actions according to those laws which have been placed in things by God, or whether this objective justice would be sufficient in connection with a subjective apostolic spirit, or whether the latter was at all necessary. It was debated whether it was enough that the temporal activites under consideration proceeded from faith and love or whether in these activities the inner bond of the agent with Christ must become visible and recognizable and in that sense take on the character of a witness; similarly, it was questioned whether it was sufficient to intend the objective attitude or orientation in the spirit of the gospel, or whether this intention must also somehow be made manifest (cf. Mt 5:16). We are not concerned here with the solution of these problems, but only with the question to what extent the text of the Council solved them or left them open. According to all that has been said, one

---

[69] Cf. "Das Zweite Vat. Konzil", I, pp. 264 ff.; *Textus recogn. et modi* . . ., 56, *modus* 58.

must say that the activity of the Christian in the world considered only in its abstract nature is not yet an apostolate, since the Christian has a duty to exercise this like every other man, and because as an activity which seeks to attain a worldly goal, it lies outside the tasks and the sphere of the Church's mission. This worldly activity can, however, be properly ordered or not by virtue of the inner relation of temporal things to God and to Christ and, based on creation and redemption, thus to the kingdom of God, and also because of the relation of these things to the mission of the Church and to the Christian life which these things can either hinder or promote according to whether they are rightly used, i.e. according to the will of God. Likewise, they can take on a greater or a lesser apostolic character simply according to the intention of the Christian in so ordering them according to the spirit of Christ, so that such activity can also be called an apostolate in the broader sense; it can be a "witness for Christ" and "serve to promote the salvation of men".

In this matter the Council was careful to avoid committing itself to any specialized terms, though pressure was put upon it to do so both in the Commission as well as in the aula; such terms were, for instance, the apostolate in the broader and narrower sense, the direct and indirect apostolate, the apostolate in the literal or figurative sense. These terms were in fact in use in various writings on the subject previous to this, and had widely deviating meaning. It was for this reason that the *vero et proprio sensu* was struck out of the preliminary draft of the second insertion. Similarly, the expression *consecratio mundi,* desired by many, was not used because of the variety of its meaning, although Article 34 of the Constitution on the Church says of the laity that "as worshipers whose every deed is holy, they consecrate the world itself to God" *(Deo consecrant)*. The word *consecrare* here, of course, is not to be taken in its ritual sense as a setting apart or a withdrawing from ordinary use. This was made clear in a German translation commissioned by the German bishops. One must not forget that this expression derives from the *Martyrologium Romanum* where it is used on 25 December to refer to the incarnation: "Jesus Christus . . . mundum volens adventu suo piissimo consecrare". Here precisely the opposite is meant from a consecration which sets things or a person apart: the whole world is consecrated through his coming. Thus, the whole world, by virtue of the sacred and the divine, is no longer something "sacral" outside the world; it can exist in the midst of the profane world. Cardinal Montini, in a pastoral letter to the Church of Milan, and in full agreement with the address of Pius XII on the Second World Congress for the Apostolate of the Laity on 5 October 1957 referred to the duty of Christians in the world to mediate between their religious or sacral sphere and the social and temporal one. In so doing they effect a *consecratio mundi,* i.e. they "penetrate the vast sphere of the profane world with Christian principles and powerful natural and supernatural virtues".[70]

---

[70] Address of Pius XII, 5. 10. 1957: *AAS* 49 (1957), p. 927. Cf. the *relatio* in *Schemata decreti*

The Council, in the face of opposition from many of the fathers, held fast to the conviction that the worldly activities of the Christian, as a penetration of temporal things with the Christian spirit, represent a participation in the mission of the Church and are thus *pars apostolatus,* just like prayer uttered with an apostolic intention or acts of mortification which are performed in such a spirit. But this is in effect an obvious broadening by the Council of the concept of churchliness and hence of the apostolate, so that after the Council one should perhaps distinguish between three different activities of the members of the Church: the official Church activity which the faithful "perform in the name of the Church in co-operation with their pastor"; the unofficial Church activity which the faithful perform as members of the Church and at the same time as "citizens of the world who are nevertheless guided by their Christian consciences",[71] i.e. under their own responsibility but still in conscious union with the Church of Jesus and in the light of the principles of revelation made known by this visible Church; and finally that activity which is performed without any subjective or objective relation to the mission of the visible Church — an activity which is therefore purely worldly and completely neutral with regard to the mission of the visible Church, as, for example, going for a walk purely for the sake of personal recreation. The latter action can, of course, be a supernatural and Christian activity if it is performed in the grace of Christ, and it might even be called an "ecclesiastical" activity in the very broadest sense because of the historical nature of salvation in the Church. But this takes place on a completely different plane from that of the apostolic activity we are speaking of here, where some direct relation can be established between the activity of the Christian and the mission of the Church. In the language of the Council one can, and indeed must, give not only to the first but also to the second of these three activities the name of the Apostolate.[72]

This article reveals yet another basic problem. If, namely, we take seriously what is said about the variety of services and callings in the one mission of the Church, and if we see these callings as divine callings for the proper fulfilment of which God also sends his specific gifts, the charisms, then it is simply not true that within Christendom there are only two special vocations, one of priestly office and one of the religious state; there are many more different states without which the Church could never fulfil its mission. From this point we should perhaps pursue the tendencies of the Council even further and consider its ideas more deeply. But at this point the mere opposition of hierarchy and non-hierarchy,

(1964), no. 26f. and in the *Textus recogn. et modi,* p. 5; M.-D. Chenu, "Die Laien und die 'Consecratio mundi' ", in G. Baraúna, ed., *De Ecclesia,* I (1966), pp. 289–307, in which the pastoral letter of Cardinal Montini is also quoted, pp. 289f.

[71] Cf. *Const. past. de Eccl. in mundo huius temp.,* n. 76.

[72] Cf. K. Rahner, "Grundsätzliches zur Einheit von Schöpfungs- und Erlösungswirklichkeit", and "Vollzugsmomente im konkreten Weltverhältnis" in *Handbuch der Pastoraltheologie,* II/2 (1966), pp. 211ff.; 217–21; 231–39.

clerics and non-clerics, whom one calls laymen, begins to become problematic, and this is still the case if one places the religious on the side of the clergy. There is here at bottom a conception which proceeds only from the hierarchy and which sees, judges and orders everything from this point. In reality, however, one must always proceed from the Lord of the Church, from him in whom we are all "one people destined to be God's own" (1 Pet 2:9). But within this people and in the pursuit of its welfare there are very many callings and ministries, some of which overlap others, and some of which one can group according to fixed categories: thus bishops, presbyters, and deacons can be grouped as *christifideles clerici*[73], the members of different orders and communities similar to orders as *christifideles religiosi* (though one should perhaps find a better designation for them since all Christians are supposed to be *religiosi*); Christians in the married state, who have been consecrated and strengthened by a separate sacrament to this ministry so important for society and the Church, and who are known as *christifideles matrimonio coniuncti;* Christians who have offered themselves for various services in the Church for longer periods of time without receiving any special consecration and who are referred to as *christifideles in speciali servitio ecclesiae;* and finally those Christians, married or unmarried, who in the midst of the world have responsible tasks which in their variety are of the greatest importance to the Church and the world, and who are known as *christifideles saeculares:* teachers, administrators, doctors, workers, though one might include in the latter category "prophets" as well as musicians, poets and painters, if we think of Bruckner, Claudel, or Cézanne.

If this way of considering the various types of Christians were to be adopted, all clericalism or even laicism would no longer have any justification. In addition, one would not be subjected to the painful spectacle of attempts to try to find something "positive" in the lay state. For what is concretely positive is not to be found by contrasting it with the clergy, but in its own specific charisms.

From such a point of view it is understandable that a suggestion was made to abolish the expression "layman" altogether and to speak instead simply of Christians, as the word "lay" is used in an artificial sense which is further distorted by the meaning of "a non-professional".[74] We are, without doubt, still too much influenced by the medieval division of the people of God into two parts. In this connection there is something to be said for the suggestion of several Council fathers that we should speak of a *status communis christifidelium* next to the clerical state and that of the counsellors.[75] Just as it would not have much meaning to divide the citizens of a state arbitrarily into officials and non-officials, doctors and non-doctors, workers and non-workers, it does not appear to be particularly

---

[73] Cf. the expression "christifideles laici" in Article 1.

[74] W. Dirks made this suggestion on the occasion of a press conference in Rome in a discussion with the author, and Prof. E. Weinzierl has recently made similar suggestions, independently of the author.

[75] *Schema decreti* (1964), no . 30.

practical to divide the NT people of God into clerics and non-clerics (laymen). Merely as a group contrasted with the clerics (even if one included the religious as well) there is still no proper *status* or *ordo laicorum* but only very different kinds of "lay" ministries, or perhaps one should rather say ministries which could be practised by laymen as well, since what is typical for them is not their lay character.

Similarly, the special worldly character which the Constitution on the Church as well as our decree ascribe to the laity cannot be taken as the characteristic hallmark for all non-clerics and non-religious, for which reason one cannot simply group these people together as "laymen in the world" — we prefer to pass over here altogether the bizarre expression "secular priest". With perfect right "laymen" who have given their whole life and work for decades in the service of the Church and who, by their calling, stand in the direct ministry of the Church in the world, explain that they feel themselves in no way to be laymen in the world, though they have never considered entering an order or even a secular institute.

Article 3. How justified our previous considerations have been is shown in this article, which treats of "the bases of the apostolate of the laity". This article, as well as the following one on the spirituality of the laity, was added to the document later on the basis of the discussion in October 1964.

Throughout this article the subject is really the basis of the apostolate of the Christian and not specifically of the laity. The duty and the right to exercise the apostolate, and even the Lord's commission to do so, is explained as deriving from the union of the Christian in the Church with Christ the head; the directly ecclesial character of this union derives from baptism and confirmation, as well as from the other sacraments and especially the Eucharist, since it communicates love and constantly nourishes it. Of this love it is said that it is the soul of the entire apostolate: the apostolate exists through love. Its ultimate source lies in the inner-trinitarian bosom of the Father who sent his Son, the apostle Jesus (Heb 3:1) into the world out of love, that the world might be saved through him (Jn 3:16 f.; cf. 1 Jn 4:10). But Jesus' redemptive apostolic life and death is but a work of love by which he loved us to the end (Jn 13:1; cf. 15:9); and therefore "by this we know love, that he laid down his life for us; and we ought to lay down our lives for the brethren" (1 Jn 3:16). This is precisely what we mean by apostolate. This love, however, which is "the love of God", namely the love by which God loved us and by which he sent us his apostle Jesus (cf. Rom 5:6 ff.),[76] is "poured out in our hearts through the Holy Spirit which is given to us" (Rom 5:1). Only in the Spirit, which is both the Spirit of the Son and of the Father, can we also love with the love of the Father and the Son and carry out his mission, his apostolate. Union with Christ which is only an individualistic and private confrontation with Christ, seen only as a union with "the bridegroom of the soul", therefore represents a gross misunderstanding. Even growth with

---

[76] Cf. O. Kuss, *Der Römerbrief* (1957), pp. 205–13.

Christ in his death and his resurrection, as it takes place in baptism (Rom 6:5) is a growing together with the head of the ἐκκλησία; one can only celebrate the Eucharist legitimately within this community and for its growth. A eucharistic celebration which does not have consequences for the concrete life of the fraternal community about Jesus, fails in its proper task; in such a case the whole eucharistic convocation would result not in mutual uplift, but in injury (1 Cor 11:17f.). The Eucharist must "gather the community together from the ends of the earth" as was expressed in the vivid consciousness of the Didaché (Did 9:4; cf. 10:3, 5f.); similarly, Thomas calls the Eucharist the "sacrament of ecclesiastical unity".[77] All this calls for a great change in our interpretation of eucharistic piety.

Baptism and confirmation represent a direct "consecration into a royal priesthood and a holy people" whereby "the Church as a whole is priestly in so far as each of its faithful is in direct relation to God".[78] Even in the treatment of the reservations a final attack against the reality of the priesthood of the faithful had to be warded off, and in so doing an appeal was made to the Constitution on the Church, which clearly sees both the official priesthood as well as the general priesthood as a true participation in the priesthood of Christ.[79] Following after the quotation from 1 Pet 2:4–10, the content of this apostolate which flows from the royal priesthood is shown to consist in the bringing of spiritual sacrifices through the whole work of one's life and in the "witness to Christ over all the earth". Sacrifice and preaching are the duties of the priesthood. "In Christ" (1 Pet 2:5) "who gave himself up for us, a fragrant offering and sacrifice to God" (Eph 5:2), and with whom we are united as Christians, in whom we are made "one" (Gal 3:28), the entire Christian life becomes a "living sacrifice, holy and acceptable to God, which is your spiritual sacrifice" (Rom 12:1), which makes everything else an "irreal and improper worship", since "the Spirit . . . is the most living of all realities".[80] Even at this point it is evident how real that priesthood is, from which all this flows. Not only sacrifice, but the task of preaching as well, is imposed upon all the members of the community of Jesus; the substance of this preaching (according to 1 Pet 2:9f.) is the great deeds of God, and especially the deed of the election of the faithful by God (cf. Acts 2:11; 1 Cor 14:23).

The second paragraph is concerned with the inner driving-force of the apostolate which all Christians have; it is concerned with the great gifts of the Spirit, with those powers to believe, to love, and to hope which are given with sanctifying grace, and also with the great and new command of love (Mt 22:38f.), by which others can know that we are of God (1 Jn 2:5–11). The Church is essentially the community of those who believe, hope, and love. In faith, hope,

---

[77] *Summa Theologica*, III, q. 73, a. 4 r.
[78] K. H. Schelkle, *Die Petrusbriefe und der Judasbrief* (2nd ed., 1964), p. 64, and in general pp. 58,–65.
[79] *Textus recogn. et modi*, 27, *modus* 87.
[80] Schelkle, *op. cit.*, p. 59.

and love the community of Jesus is built up from within and held together; but as a believing, hoping, and loving community it constantly reaches beyond its own confines and becomes a witness to others. It becomes a community which encompasses all others in the love of Jesus (cf. Jn 3:16) and thus it leads to the outward growth of love (Eph 4:16), "that you may have fellowship with us; and our fellowship is with the Father and with his Son Jesus Christ" (1 Jn 1:3). The apostolate is here described as concern "for the glory of God which will be made manifest through the coming of his kingdom" — so must the passage probably be translated, since we can of ourselves do nothing to directly influence this coming (cf. Mk 13:22) — and as concern "for the eternal life of all men" which (according to Jn 17:3) consists in this, that men acknowledge the one true God and him whom he has sent, Jesus Christ. In the next paragraph this is described as a "working together to make the divine message of salvation known and accepted by all men throughout the world". This apostolate, it is once more asserted, is an obligation which is imposed on all as a "splendid burden".

The next paragraph refers then to the "special gifts of the Spirit" which are given to the individual Christian beyond those common Christian gifts "for the exercise of this apostolate" in "mutual service". It was also explicitly requested in the October discussion of 1964 that the significance of the Spirit and his gifts be even more strongly underlined as the foundation of all apostolic activity. The Christian vocation is always realized concretely in the individual Christian, according to his personality, his personal and immediate social situation, and according to his profession, his position in the Church and in society. Everything, in fact, even being a slave can be conceived of in faith as κλῆσις: a supernatural election, a calling in the Lord (1 Cor 7:22), for the task to which the Lord has distributed one (1 Cor 7:17), and in the fulfilment of which God gives to each the particular gifts and charisms one needs: the grace of God is a "varied" grace (1 Pet 4:10). Indeed, the Christian calling is frequently considered in the pages of the NT to be a charism in itself, whether it be in the married or unmarried state (cf. 1 Cor 7:7).[81] According to the passage of the First Epistle of Peter quoted in the text "each has received a gift" (similarly 1 Cor 12:7), for which reason one should doubtless consider these not to be any extraordinary display of the Spirit but rather "those which are less dramatic" *(charismatum etiam simpliciorum)*. Some of these are mentioned: everyday gifts such as ministry, teaching, admonition, comforting, love (Rom 12:6ff.), help rendered to others (1 Cor 12:28), which indeed are counted among the "higher gifts" (1 Cor 12:31).

The reception of charisms brings with it privileges and duties in the Church and in the world. With regard to the use of these gifts there the freedom of the Spirit is given as much emphasis as the contact with the Church-community or

---

[81] Cf. F. Klostermann, "Entmythologisierung des Priestertums und der Priesterberufung", *Der Seelsorger* 36 (1966), pp. 10–21.

with the leaders of the community, though the latter have the right to test the genuineness of such gifts and their ordered application. But they are also admonished not to use their supervisory function as a fire-extinguisher, thus quenching the flames of the Spirit, which seems to be regarded as a danger. Up to the very end attempts to water down or completely eliminate the passages referring to charisms had to be countered.[82] The notes to this article show that the ideas expressed in it had in the main already been voiced in the chapters on the People of God and on the Laity in the Constitution on the Church.

Article 4. This article, "on the spirituality of the laity with regard to the apostolate", was added in its completely new form at the request of the fathers in October 1964, and evidently it was made on the basis of the consideration that the lay apostolate presupposes a transformation in the entire attitude, piety, and spirituality of the Christian laity. In addition, on the occasion of the general debate on the schema on the Church in the 34th general congregation on 5 December 1962, in connection with the treatment of charisms, it was requested that something be prepared on the spirituality proper to the laity, and especially of the married laity. In the text of the Preparatory Commission there was already a chapter "De spiritu apostolico" with 5 articles, which was eventually the basis of the present article. In the light of our considerations up to this point we should, of course, speak less of *one* type of spirituality, since there are as many types as there are single types of laymen. We must in fact recognize very different types of spiritualities based on the internal and external circumstances of life or adapted to the given situation and profession of those concerned, though they are ultimately nothing else, and could be nothing else, but variations on the imitation of the one and only Christ. There could be no one particular type of imitation as, for instance, the monastic form, which for a long time was the only one that really counted. The decree of course is concerned here not with a detailed presentation of the spirituality of the laity as such, but only with an indication of its significance for the apostolate. Nor is this the place to delve into the problems surrounding the topic of "spirituality" itself.[83]

After the remarks contained in the last article it is not to be wondered at if it is now first of all asserted that the fruitfulness of the apostolate depends upon the vitality of our union with Christ. For the strengthening of that union every Christian has essentially "the same spiritual aids common to all", among which "active participation in the sacred liturgy" is especially to be recommended; the liturgy is indeed the "fountain from which all the power of the Church flows", as the Constitution on the Liturgy expressly states in connection with "apostolic work".[84] It should be observed that the apostolate is here consciously placed in the perspective of the apostolic movement which proceeds from the Father

---

[82] Cf. Schelkle, *op. cit.*, p. 119; *Textus recogn. et modi*, 31 f., *modi* 113; 117 f.; 120.

[83] Cf. J. Sudbrack, "Vom Geheimnis christlicher Spiritualität: Einheit und Vielfalt", *Geist und Leben* 39 (1966), pp. 24–44; H. U. v. Balthasar, *Verbum Caro*, I (1960), pp. 226–44.

[84] *Const. de sacra lit.*, n. 10.

and which came to us through the "apostle" Jesus (Heb 3:1). It is the Father, therefore, who is the "fountain and origin of the whole apostolate". On the basis of several *modi* which rightly complained about the "unclear theology of the mission", the phrase *missus a patre* was subsequently added.[85]

What is peculiar to the laity is the relation of their union with Christ to their concrete life in the world and their growth in this union and in holiness, which is achieved by means of their activity in the world. This is their special way to greater holiness, upon which they must travel, in spite of all difficulties, in joyful and confident readiness, in prudence and in patience: these are clearly the virtues which they must practise in the dangers and in the darkness of their life in the world. Thus, the laity sanctify themselves in the very course of their life through the world. Service in the world is of course not yet in itself divine service, but it can become so for those who are bound to God and it can also help to advance them in that sacred bond. Such service in the world is not bound solely to the world, for besides involving an awareness of the immanence of God in the world it also recognizes his transcendence above that world. But the laity suffer the temptations which the world also offers and consequently they also are in need of asceticism; but even such asceticism must still be "determined by one's particular task in the world".[86] Here it becomes clear again that the decree really has in mind but one particular type of lay Christian, namely the Christian in the world.

The notes to this article refer mainly to passages in the Constitution on the Church which speak of the call of all Christians to holiness and to perfection: ". . . all the faithful, whatever their condition or state, are called *(vocantur)* by the Lord, each in his own way, to that perfect holiness whereby the Father himself is perfect".[87] And then after mention has specifically been made in the chapter "On the Call of the Whole Church to Holiness" of bishops, priests, deacons, laymen in the special service of the Church, of married laymen and parents, of widows, widowers, and single laymen, of workers, and of the sick and the infirm, we have the following passage: "All of Christ's faithful, therefore, whatever be the conditions, duties, and circumstances of their lives, will grow in holiness day by day through these very situations, if they accept all of them with faith from the hand of their heavenly Father, and if they co-operate with the divine will by showing every man through their earthly activities the love with which God has loved the world."[88] In this connection the omission of the expression *status perfectionis* to refer to the religious state in many conciliar documents is noteworthy. Even the schema on the Apostolate of the Laity which was printed in 1963 still used this expression in its second article.

This spiritual life as a continual fulfilment of faith, hope and love is then

---

[85] *Textus recogn. et modi,* 33, modi 123 f.
[86] Cf. L. Scheffczyk, *Christliche Weltfrömmigkeit* (1964), pp. 46–62.
[87] *Const. dogm. de Eccl.,* n. 11.
[88] *Const. dogm. de Eccl.,* n. 41.

described in greater detail. The decisive and inexhaustible source of apostolic spirituality is mentioned first of all: the *meditatio verbi Dei,* through which, according to the Constitution on Divine Revelation, "the surpassing worth of knowing Christ Jesus" (Phil 3:8) is gained. But it is also emphasized here that "prayer must be accompanied by the reading of holy Scripture, so that conversation between man and God is made possible; for we address him when we pray; we hear his voice when we read the word of God".[89]

Thus we are vouchsafed the light of faith; in it we are enabled, through the eyes of Christ, to see God in everything — "always and everywhere" — to see his will in what befalls us — in the cautious formulation of the text —, to see Christ in all men, even those who are farthest from us and to place in the right perspective the value that temporal things have in themselves and in their orientation towards human goals. Here a completely new state of the world is opened up for many Christians which is of the greatest significance for Christians in the world, for their spirituality and for their vision of the world and their work in the world. The world is here no longer seen as a means for the accomplishment of our "true" task or as a hindrance on the way to it, but it is taken seriously as a value in itself, as a reality issuing from the creative hand of God. In contrast to this, a mimeographed edition of the draft of the year 1965 referred to the world and the social relations of Christians within it with the expression "tamquam medium ad perfectionem acquirendam".

In this connection we should note well what the Pastoral Constitution on the Church in the Modern World has to say on the subject of the relation between our earthly work and culture with the ultimate kingdom of God in the following careful phrasing: ". . . the (eschatological) expectation of a new earth must not weaken but rather stimulate our concern for cultivating this one. For here grows the body of a new human family, a body which even now is able to give some kind of foreshadowing of the new age. Earthly progress must be carefully distinguished from the growth of Christ's kingdom. Nevertheless, to the extent that the former can contribute to the better ordering of human society, it is of vital concern to the kingdom of God. For after we have obeyed the Lord, and in his spirit nurtured on earth the values of human dignity, brotherhood and freedom, and indeed all the good fruits of our nature and enterprise, we will find them again, but freed of stain, burnished and transfigured . . . when Christ hands over to the Father a kingdom eternal and universal . . ."[90] The Church's teaching authority is, however, explicitly charged with the duty to teach about man and society, about work and leisure, about the significance and place of the arts and technical inventions, the place of earthly goods and human institutions and their significance for the salvation of men, and their place in the building up of the body of Christ.[91]

Faith is intimately related to hope; they are both powers which belong to this

[89] *Const. dogm. de divina revel.,* n. 25.
[90] *Const. past. de Eccl. in mundo huius temp.,* n. 39.
[91] *Decr. de past. episc. munere in Eccl.,* n. 12.

"intermission" of the Church. Only he can hope who believes; but the believer can do no more than hope, for as yet we see nothing (cf. Rom 8:24f.). We are as yet under the law of the cross, though we trust in its resurrection. We should notice the reference to the paschal mystery here, which also plays no small role in the Constitution on the Liturgy.[92] The content of hope is given as "the revelation of the sons and daughters of God", namely their glory. This passage doubtless has Rom 8:18–21 in mind, and in fact this passage was actually quoted in the penultimate version of the text. This glory is such that it includes and transcends all creation in brightness, bringing about the new heaven and the new earth (Rev 21:1). This hearkens back to what was said before about "temporal things" and "the value which they have in themselves". This hope too is only possible for us in union with Christ. Since "we were buried with him by baptism into death" (Rom 6:4), our life is "hidden with Christ in God" until he, our new and true life, becomes manifest and until our glory is manifested in him (Col 3:3f.). Until that hope is fulfilled, we are to live our pilgrims' existence in this world, amid the contradictions of this life, "the sufferings of this present time" (Rom 8:18), as "chosen exiles" (1 Pet 1:1; cf. 17; 2:11; Eph 2:9),[93] and we are to exercise the generosity needed for the apostolate. The latter is here again considered according to its twofold task as spreading the kingdom of God and as penetrating and perfecting the temporal order with the spirit of Christ.

Lastly, it is shown how love fructifies the life of the Christian for the apostolate, whereby that love is meant "which comes from God". This is an echo of 1 Jn 4:7, which asserts that the true Christian is known by his love, just as those who belong to "the world" (in the Johannine sense) are recognized by hate, and that everyone who truly loves, in so far as he loves, is born of God, and that one can recognize rebirth in God from the sign of love.[94] This love must first be shown in one's own circle, in the brotherly community about Jesus, and requires the removal of anything which could disturb that love. The passage quoted from 1 Peter 1 mentions the "unfeigned love of the brethren" (cf. v. 22). Such Christian brotherhood, "the friendship of Christians among themselves", namely the friendship which is possible in the Lord Jesus, which is active in positive assistance "in every need" which is spoken of again at the conclusion of the paragraph, is a preliminary condition for trustworthy witness; only in this way can men lead others to Christ (cf. Acts 2:46; 5:13).[95] This love which stems from God, the love by which he loves us and which he gives to us through his Spirit, enables us "to express the true spirit of the beatitudes" in our own lives: the spirit of poverty manifest in a certain indifference to the value of temporal goods; the spirit of a sober and realistic humility which is fed from the contemplation of God and which "in every circumstance and relation recognizes and fulfils the life one

[92] *Const. de sacra lit.,* nn. 5f.; 61; 104; 106f.; 109.
[93] Cf. F. Klostermann, *Prinzip Gemeinde* (1965), pp. 31–33.
[94] Cf. R. Schnackenburg, *Die Johannesbriefe* (2nd ed., 1962), p. 203f., E. T. in preparation.
[95] Cf. F. Klostermann, *op. cit.,* pp. 53–58; *Textus recogn. et modi,* p. 38, *modus* 165.

has as a gift", in the face of all vain or boastful attempts at self-assertion.[96] In this way also the credibility of a Christian witness is increased; but in this way too the foundations of the apostolic life are laid, as well as a readiness to further it.

Reference is then made to several concrete situations in which Christians in the world may find themselves and from which their whole "spiritual life" must "take its special quality": marriage or celibacy, health or sickness, professional and social position and activity. Here it is also clear that worldly things do not stand outside the spiritual world nor can they be considered as hostile or obstructive, but rather should they be allowed to fructify and give to that life its particular stamp. Those opportunities which Christians in the world have and the possibilities which are open to them in such varied circumstances must be carefully used and cultivated, and those charisms which each of them have — obviously given to them to cope with their peculiar circumstances — should be well employed. A few sentences later a list of such activities and gifts is given, e.g. professional skill, family and civic spirit, honesty, humanity, justice, sincerity, kindness, the courage to see things through to the end — all things which appear very natural but without which there can be no true Christian life, and all of which become spiritual gifts in faith (cf. Rom 12:6ff.; 1 Cor 12:28; 13:1; 14:1; 1 Pet 4:10). But likewise the various associations and institutes which attract the individual Christian according to his own particular interests, each develop their own type of spirituality which such Christians should try to influence and from which they, in turn, should be shaped in their own spiritual life. Similarly, charismatic personalities and movements which arise within the Church at certain times can continue to exert their influence in such institutions.

The concluding paragraph puts before us the image of Mary, "the perfect example of this type of spiritual and apostolic life". In an attempt to find the one basic spirituality in the Church which lies at the bottom of all other spiritualities that are directed towards special tasks and functions and accessible to all, Hans Urs v. Balthasar holds up the spirituality of Mary, the handmaiden of the Lord who allowed herself to be formed by nothing else but the one divine Word.[97] This is even more significant in our connection when one thinks of the Marian character of the non-hierarchical apostolate, the apostolate common to all Christian laymen. Yves Congar thus called Mary the first laywoman.[98]

---

[96] Cf. H. Schlier, *Der Brief an die Galater* (12th ed., 1962), p. 269.

[97] H. U. v. Balthasar, *Verbum Caro,* I, pp. 234–7.

[98] Y. M.-J. Congar, *Priester und Laien* (1965), p. 311; cf. F. Klostermann, *Das christliche Apostolat,* pp. 242–63, p. 792.

CHAPTER II

The Goals to be Achieved

This chapter was called "the pivot of the whole schema" by the *relatio* of 1965.[99] It is unfortunate that the original and not very happy threefold division of the Commission and the special part of the draft of the text was retained here.[100] It becomes especially problematic in one chapter which was to treat of the goals to be achieved by the apostolate. In fact, however, as is immediately made clear by the introductory **Article 5,** we are concerned here with only two goals which correspond to the twofold mission of the Church, or more exactly to those two tasks which are included in the one mission of the Church already referred to, and both of which, as is especially noted, are anchored in the redemptive work of Christ.[101] The laity are here likewise expressly designated as executors of the whole mission of the Church, both in the Church and in the world, "in the spiritual as well as in the temporal order". Thus they have in a certain sense a more universal role in the apostolate than the hierarchy itself, which as such only has very limited possibilities and powers in the worldly order, as we shall see. Though the necessary distinction between the two orders is observed, express mention is made as well of the final unity which embraces both and which they derive from their origin in God and in his plan and its completion in the new creation of the kingdom of God, and which also originates in the person of those Christians in the world who must be guided in both orders by an undivided Christian conscience.

There was great uncertainty within the Commission with regard to the terminology in connection with the Christian formation of the temporal order. Such terms were first used as *christiana aedificatio; instauratio; perfectio; institutio* or *animatio; in Christo restaurare* or *instaurare; spiritu evangelico imbuere; perfundere; perficere; pervadere; informare; lege morali; quam caritas perficit; exstruere et ad Deum per Christum ordinare* — and these in various combinations. In the present text the following formulations are to be found: *mundum ad Christum ordinare* (Article 2);

---

[99] *Schema decreti* (1965), no. 26.
[100] *As in Schema decreti* (1963).
[101] Cf. Article 2.

323

rerum temporalium ordinem spiritu evangelico perfundere ac perficere (Articles 2, 5); *ordinem rerum temporalium spiritu christiano informare et perficere* (Articles 4, 13); *ordinem rerum temporalium christiane instaurare* (title to Article 7, though this is not printed in the official text); *ordinem rerum temporalium instaurare iugiterque perficere* (Article 7, although it here refers to the task common to all men); *ordinem rerum temporalium instituere et ad Deum per Christum ordinare* (Article 7, the "instituere" here also refers to the task all men have in common); *ordinem rerum temporalium in Christo instaurare* (Article 7); *ordinis temporalis instauratio* (Article 7, again as the task of all men); *instaurare ordinem temporalem, ut ulterioribus vitae christianae principiis conformis reddatur* (Article 7); *mundum sanctificare et in Christo animare* (Article 16); *ordinem temporalem aedificare et gerere — rationes agendi altiores in lumine fidei quaerere* (Article 16: the first without doubt refers to the common task); *animatio christiana ordinis temporalis* (Article 19); *instauratio christiana ordinis rerum temporalium* (Article 31). One notices the attempts that were made to avoid expressions which might be misinterpreted as "triumphalist", at least when the text speaks of the contribution of the Christian, in order to avoid the interpretation that the Christians regard themselves the true builders of the temporal order,[102] or that a new "ecclesialization" of the world was being attempted. Thus, from the very start such ambiguous expressions were avoided as "Christianization" or "re-Christianization", the Christian or "spiritual conquest of the world", and even "under the direction of the hierarchy".[103]

All the expressions which were finally adopted refer only to that modest, ministering, and co-operative share of the Christian in the common worldly tasks, whereby he is only to compete with others, apart from the necessary sphere of professional knowledge, in a truer acknowledgment of the light of revelation and the demands of the love of Christ, in order to be better able to form and use the world according to this light and this love. Nothing else is meant by *ordinare ad Christum*, or *ad Deum per Christum; spiritu evangelico* or *christiane* or *in Christo perfundere; informare, animare, perficere, instaurare animatio* or *instauratio christiana*. In the *relatio* of 1964 the *christiane instaurare* is explicitly interpreted as *secundum principia christiana*,[104] just as it is in Article 7: *ulterioribus vitae christianae principiis conformis reddere*. Similar to this is the *rationes agendi altiores in lumine fidei quaerere* of Article 16.

The most vigorous expression which we encounter here is *mundum sanctificare* (Article 16). But here too there can be no question of sanctification in the strict sense of consecration, that is a setting apart of something from its ordinary use. Also it should be noted that the sanctification referred to is a sanctification of the

---

[102] Cf. the remark of the *relatio* in *Schema decreti* (1965), no. 27 f.

[103] Cf. address of Pius XII, 5 Oct. 1957, to the Second World Congress for the Apostolate of the Laity: *AAS* 49 (1957), p. 925: "The acceptance by the layman of a particular mission, a mandate from the hierarchy, if this associates him more closely with the spiritual conquest of the world, which leads the Church under the direction of her pastors . . ."

[104] *Schema decreti* (1964), no. 41.

world and not primarily of men, thus including irrational creation which is unable to respond to the grace of God. And so what is meant here refers to a setting of things in relation to God, which is brought about in such a way that men are present in this world who are bound to God in Christ, that they might save it from the indignities to which men have subjected it and to form it in the spirit of Christ, without thereby wishing to take away its "worldliness". But this is just what all the other expressions are trying to indicate, as we have explained in the reference to the phrase "spiritu evangelico perfundere ac perficere" in Article 2, and even of *consecrare* in the Christian sense.

The word *instauratio* offers some difficulty in translation when it is used here in connection with the temporal order. Where that temporal task is meant which is a duty to all men, then it has something of the sense of "building up", but where it concerns the special task of the Christian it would be better translated by a word like "orientation", in order to avoid any possibility of a triumphalist interpretation. It must be made clear that this "orienting of all things to Christ" refers to what is indicated by the other expressions, namely the task — often a very modest one — of making the Spirit of Christ present and active "as a leaven" in the midst of the world "as it were from within", and thus to help in its sanctification *(ad mundi sanctificationem)*, as Article 31 of the Constitution on the Church has already formulated it. It is not something which is added to things from without and which could only come from Christians, which would be but a new form of ecclesial triumphalism; but what we are dealing with here is more properly the discovery of that which God himself has originally placed in the world, in things, and in men. Such a discovery is not the privilege of Christians alone, for it is possible that in certain circumstances a non-Christian may uncover it sooner and in a more genuine way than many a Christian. Perhaps this point of view, as it is expressed in the Decree on the Apostolate of the Laity as well as in other Council documents, is in fact somewhat inadequate, as some have already complained.[105] The concrete significance of all these things has recently been explained by K. Rahner and J. B. Metz.[106]

Article 6. This article deals with the apostolate of the Christian in the world for the "evangelization and sanctification of men". Instead of evangelization and sanctification, the printed text of 1964 has "conversio et progressus ad Deum".[107] Previous to the new arrangement of the material the subject of the present article was titled "de apostolatu ad regnum Christi directe provehendum".

The mission of the Church primarily and directly concerns the salvation of men, as is indicated in the Lord's commission to his disciples (Mt 28:18). Salvation, however, is imparted to us "in faith and in grace", though one should not separate the two: for "by grace you have been saved through faith" (Eph 2:8),[108] and it is also through faith that "Christ may dwell in your hearts . . .

105 *HK* 20 (1966), p. 303.   106 *Handbuch der Pastoraltheologie,* II/2 (1966), pp. 231–39; 261–67.
107 *Schema decreti* (1964), no. 10; 27 f.; 40.
108 Cf. H. Schlier, *Der Brief an die Epheser* (2nd ed., 1958), pp. 115 f.

being rooted and grounded in love" (Eph 3:17). Faith not only takes its origin in grace, it is grace itself and through it one already possesses salvation.[109] But since "faith comes from what is heard, and what is heard comes by the preaching of Christ" (Rom 10:17), the apostolate of the Church and of all its members is directed towards the spreading of the gospel of Christ and thereby to the mediation of his grace. In spite of the special duty of the ministry of the word and the sacraments entrusted to the clergy, the laity are also given "a very important role to play" in this ministry; we are also referred to the way in which the service of the pastors and the apostolate of the laity mutually complement one another. The *relatio* of 1965 explicitly rejects a suggestion according to which the lay apostolate "is nothing other than co-operation or continuation of the specifically hierarchical apostolate in things religious"; for even in the attainment of these goals of evangelization and sanctification "there can be an apostolate proper to the laity".[110] For the same reasons the Commission also had to reject those *modi* which, apparently issuing from similar misconceptions, did not want to recognize any mutually complementary relation between clergy and laity in this sphere.[111] As will be apparent from what follows, the task of laymen as "fellow-workers for the truth" is much more extensive than one would suppose from the quotation from 3 Jn 8, which really only refers primarily to material assistance, hospitality, and care for pilgrims.[112]

Next it is shown in what this complement to the order of evangelization and sanctification consists, with respect to the apostolate of the laity: first the power of the witness of the Christian life, the community (κοινωνία) of faith (Phm 6) is mentioned, the proclamation of the gospel of Christ in deeds, already referred to in the first sentence, which is able to lead men to faith and to God. There are also many opportunities for proclamation by one's own word: exchanges in a faith between parents and children, friends and comrades, superiors and inferiors; the ministry of the word (Acts 20:24) in normal family-life, in one's profession and society, also to non-believers in order to lead them to faith, as well as to other Christians to strengthen them in the faith and to rouse them to an apostolic life of their own for the furtherance of the gospel. It is noteworthy that the Council does not hesitate to apply to Christians in the world what Paul, who had been called by the Lord as an apostle, has said of his own duty to proclaim. Thus the laity, by virtue of their incorporation into the community of Christ through baptism, are to assist both in the building-up of the community from within and in its mission towards other men.

Nevertheless, in saying all this the basic distinction between the apostolate of evangelization and of sanctification must not be neglected. Our apostolic service of evangelization is more direct than that of sanctification. We can and we must

[109] Cf. O. Kuss, *Der Römerbrief,* pp. 396 f.
[110] *Schema decreti* (1965), no. 27.
[111] *Textus recogn. et modi* (1965), 47, *modus* 2; p. 50, *modus* 18.
[112] R. Schnackenburg, *Die Johannesbriefe,* p. 290 (E. T. in preparation).

proclaim the gospel of Jesus; but only God can sanctify, for to sanctify means to give the very life and love of God himself. Apart from the more instrumental services to be rendered in the dispensing of the sacraments, we can only help to create some of the human conditions within which men may be better disposed to answer and to open themselves to the appeal of the love of God.

How far this co-operative service for the truth, "the ministry of the word and sacrament" by laymen can proceed on the basis of their own ecclesiastical mission in the community of Christ, and to what "official" service they can proceed beyond the qualification through baptism, is described in Article 24.

The note refers us to passages from both of the first encyclicals of Pius XI and Pius XII. Pius XI, referring to 1 Pet 2:9, speaks of the "spread of the knowledge and the love of Christ in private or in public" through "the faithful in the lay state . . . as lay apostles"; Pius XII speaks of the absolute duty to the apostolate as a result of baptism, namely "for the spread of the kingdom of God . . . to work for its growth, and to bring within its fold those who are not yet members of it", as well as of the "participation of the laity in the hierarchical apostolate" as is carried out in the form of Catholic Action.

Here as well the Council goes one step further: it "earnestly exhorts the laity, each according to his natural gifts and learning" to be active in examining the Christian principles in revelation, in defending them in new situations, and in confronting new problems and the respective application of Christian principles to these varied and changing problems of our time. What is involved here is no longer direct assistance in pastoral care, e.g. in proclaiming the word — which was already mentioned — but a contribution to something which must precede preaching, namely the task of advising pastors and in teaching and in theological study.

The Council is clearly of the opinion that Christians in the world here have a specific task arising from their knowledge of their professions, their social milieu, and the world. One should think here of all the contributions made at present by psychology, sociography, sociology, medicine, economics, history, and especially the history of culture and modern times, by philosophy and philology, the history of religions, fundamental theology, moral and pastoral theology, liturgy, homiletics, catechetics, ecumenical studies, the history of dogma, Church history, and biblical studies. Theology is not only constantly being asked new questions but it also receives assistance in finding new answers. "For recent studies and the findings of science, history, and philosophy raise new questions which influence life and demand new theological investigations . . . Through a sharing of resources and points of view, let those who teach in seminaries, colleges, and universities try to collaborate with men well versed in the other sciences. Theological studies should also attempt to gain a profound knowledge of revealed truth, but should not neglect contemporary ties, in order to help men from the many fields of science to achieve a more comprehensive understanding of what faith means. This common effort will very greatly aid in the formation of priests. It will enable them to present to our contemporaries the doctrine of the Church concerning God, man, and the world in a manner better suited to them, with the result that they will receive it more willingly."[113]

Similar assistance can be expected by the pastors, from the highest prelate to the lowest assistant, in the complexity and subtlety of many problems in the field of pastoral care, in all the involvements and complexity of modern life in which the Word of God must ever anew become flesh; and such assistance is to be expected especially from the Christian representatives of these sciences. Neither can the authentic teaching office do without such help today. "In pastoral care, appropriate use must be made not only of theological principles, but also of the findings of the secular sciences, especially of psychology and sociology. Thus the faithful can be brought to live the faith in a more thorough and mature way."[114]

Yet even the ordinary Christian of the world in his own concrete life can help his pastor in a no less important way: his preaching, his advice in the confessional, his priestly counsel, his methods, and the leadership of his community will be sure of a concrete, certain and objective success when he has the experience, the friendly counsel, and the criticism of men who hold a position of responsibility in this life. It is they who must give to the pastors the images, the language, and the vision of the world which the latter are to use. It is they who are to help find suitable forms for praying, singing, self-expression, and the projecting of oneself into the world that are in tune with our time. This is not a question of the representation of pastors in areas which are closed to them, or a kind of auxiliary assistance due to the lack of priests or special emergency situations; here true and necessary co-operation would be possible, true teamwork involving clergy and laity "each according to his own special gifts and formation", a mutual assistance which is ever more in demand. The decree goes on to indicate that the reasons for the present urgency of such a task are not to be found in a lack of men attracted by priestly vocation but in the "new questions of our time" and the errors which at present threaten to corrupt the very foundations of human society.

Even beyond this necessary co-operation of the laity in pastoral care and theology the laity are encouraged to contribute to the formation of Christian principles through the study of theology itself. The Pastoral Constitution on the Church in the Modern World explicitly states: ". . . it is to be hoped that many laymen will receive an appropriate formation in the sacred sciences, and that some will develop and deepen these studies by their own labours." It also expressly says that "all the faithful, clerical and lay, possess a lawful freedom of inquiry and of thought, and the freedom to express their minds humbly and courageously about those matters in which they enjoy competence."[115] If the

---

[113] Const. past. de Eccl. in mundo huius temp., n. 62.
[114] Ibid.   [115] Ibid.

Council is to be taken seriously, then the laity are to be allowed to take degrees and to hold chairs in theology, provided of course that the ordinary conditions of study are fulfilled. Women are not to be excluded, and the laity are also to be given the opportunity for applying these studies. Gifts are charisms which are not to be squandered; and theology both in its research and in its teaching is in great need of those few theological first-class brains which need not be bound to the reception of orders. On this topic as well a *modus* had to be rejected which wanted to limit the participation of the laity.[116]

It is striking that though the exercise of the apostolate of sanctification and the participation of the laity in the "ministry of the sacraments" is mentioned in this article, it is in no way further elaborated. Reference is made to the family in this way in Article 11 of the decree and other groups are mentioned in various other Council documents. Thus, the Constitution on the Church both in the chapter on the "People of God" as well as in that on the "Laity" refers to the consequences of the general priesthood of the faithful, especially when the laity take "over their own part in the celebration of the liturgy" and when in the eucharistic celebration they are themselves co-offerers, co-priests, and co-sacrifice.[117] One of the main concerns of the Constitution on the Liturgy is to once more make possible the active participation of the members of the people of God, each in his own function; it has given them back the eucharistic chalice, it has made them dispensers of the sacramentals, it has once more bound the sacrament of marriage, as all other sacraments, to the eucharistic action itself.[118]

Article 7. This treats of the second apostolic task of the Christian in the world: "the Christian orientation of the temporal order". It is pointed out first of all that even the worldly tasks of the Christian, the formation and perfecting of the temporal order, therefore the goods of life, the family, culture, business, art, the career-world, and political and social institutions are in themselves not a direct apostolic task. They are rather tasks which are given to the Christian in common with all other men according to the plan of God. Explicit reference is once more made to a quotation from Gen 1:31, repeating what Article 4 had already hinted at before, that all these temporal goods are not only the means for the attainment of the final goal of men, those means which one may then dispense with upon attainment of the goal, as though they were meaningless in themselves, but that they have a value implanted in them by God, either considered by themselves or as a part of the whole of the temporal order. This natural goodness of theirs takes on a special dignity as a result of their relation to the human person, for whose service they were created. Thus any form of Manichean dualism is rejected. In the redemptive order, moreover, the whole cosmos has been brought together and united in Christ. This unity of the temporal and spiritual order must not be misunderstood as to its origin and its goal (cf. Col 1:16; 1 Cor 15:24f.).

---

[116] *Textus recogn. et modi,* 52, *modus* 31.

[117] Cf. *Const. dogm. de Eccl.,* nn. 10f.; p. 24.

[118] *Const. de sacra lit.,* nn. 11; 14; 21; 30; 41; 55; 79; 100; 101.

It is neither a reason for rejecting the temporal nor for conceiving of it according to some mistaken ecclesialism. The temporal order and all that belongs to it retains its own significance for the welfare of men; it preserves its own legitimate autonomy, its own proper goals, laws and methods. This point was made even more strongly in the text on the basis of the October discussion of 1964 in order to avoid any misunderstanding with respect to the Church's intention to dominate the temporal sphere.[119] The ultimate determination of the temporal world issuing from God and from Christ is fulfilled in its own innate value and significance for the full vocation of men and not merely for their natural vocation. It is significant that an intervention wishing to add "et ad Deum adducant" to the first sentence of the article, and which appeared again among the suggested changes at the very last minute, was rejected for the reason that "the temporal order has a value in itself".[120] Another intervention suspected this obviously too positive a conception of temporal things of being, "Teilhardism".[121]

After these fundamental considerations on the meaning of temporal order as such, the text describes the corruption of this order by sinful men in the course of history. There is in our time an all too naive trust in purely technical progress and a tendency to make idols out of merely temporal things, which leads to a reversal of the proper relationships and makes men the slaves of things. This is where the task of the Church begins. It must, in as far as it comes within the scope of its mission and competence, enable men so to fulfil their temporal duties that temporal things will be given their full and proper value and will thus be capable of fulfilling once more their service in "the full vocation of men". They must help men to open themselves to the true value of things instead of allowing themselves to be dominated by them, so that the fulfilment of their complete vocation is facilitated instead of endangered.

There are two tasks especially which are involved here, as they were distinguished in the "nota" planned at one time on the nature of the apostolate: one is concerned with the healing of those wounds in the temporal order which come from sin and the other which is concerned with a positive approach opening this order to Christian values. All this is referred to as "constructing the temporal order rightly and orienting it to God through Christ". *Recte instituere* here is of course to be taken as the general task which is common to all men, and *ordinare per Christum ad Deum* as the specific Christian contribution which involves both the healing of wounds and the positive formation of things. Revelation gives us not a few insights into the nature and meaning of man and the world, and instructs us about not a few moral and spiritual aids for acting according to these insights.

Then the tasks of the pastors and laity are distinguished, whereby under pastors *(pastores)* one should primarily understand the legitimate magisterium.

---

[119] *Schema decreti* (1965), no. 29.
[120] *Textus recogn. et modi*, 53, *modus* 37.
[121] *Textus recogn. et modi*, 54, *modus* 44.

These pastors are to proclaim the principles underlying the meaning and the custom of the world and to offer every moral and spiritual aid.[122] Christians in the world — they are the only ones referred to here — must perform their duties in the world directly and definitively in the light of the principles, assisted by the pastors of the Church, and motivated by the love of Christ; but they are to do so using their own particular skills and acting on their own responsibility, in fraternal solidarity with their fellow-men. The full and true adherence to those laws peculiar to the temporal order, and its formation according to the *ulteriora principia* of the Christian life are once more stressed, together with the necessary adaptation to "the shifting circumstances of time, place, and person". Christian social action is especially singled out for mention in "this type of apostolate", an action which it is hoped will be extended to the whole cultural sphere. This passage is almost all that remains of what was once the fourth part of the Decree on the Apostolate of the Laity in Social Action which, in the edition of 1962, filled as many as 48 pages.[143] The rest of it is now to be found in the Pastoral Constitution on the Church in the Modern World. This one sentence in particular was re-inserted in the text as a result of the wish expressed by the fathers in their *vota*.[124]

We have here, as the decree itself says, "a task which belongs especially to the laity", and indeed one which belongs so exclusively to them as Christians in the world that it could not be carried out by any of the religious, clerics, or hierarchy unless at the same they had some profane profession or function in the secular world. The particular nature of this apostolate of the Christian in the world consists primarily of his activity as a citizen of this world and consequently in spheres for which the Church itself has no direct authority. In this apostolate laymen must allow their general attitude and approach to be determined by general Christian principles, namely those which are contained in "the word of God whether written or handed down";[125] but whatever is not covered by those principles but is only to be determined by the actual secular insight to be derived from family-affairs, or from a professional or social situation by those who must often decide in very different ways for a variety of different reasons, the Church cannot impose as a duty by her authority, not, that is, without overstepping her competence. For she does not have these insights herself, not at least as the Church, and she is in no position to acquire them.[126] Similarly, in the concrete application of those principles referred to, the Church as such cannot help, and not even the ecclesiastical office of the Christian in the world can be of much assistance, since from general principles alone one can arrive at many different

---

[122] Cf. Const. past. de Eccl. in mundo huius temp., nn. 41; 43; 76; *Decr. de past. episc. munere in Eccl.*, n. 12.

[123] *Schema const. de apost. laicorum,* Pars IV: "De apost. laicorum in actione sociali" (1962).

[124] *Schema decreti* (1965), no. 29.

[125] *Const. dogm. de divina rev.*, n. 10.

[126] *Const. past. de Eccl. in mundo huius temp.*, n. 43.

solutions to actual problems. Knowledge of the actual situation and a concrete solution to the problems it presents depends upon the objective insight of the people involved. At this point the Christian in the world can no longer appeal to the Church and certainly not to the official representatives of its authority; what is called for is personal responsibility and a personal risk.

The Pastoral Constitution on the Church in the Modern World dealt with this problem at some length.[127] In it these principles are indicated in a more concrete way, not only with regard to the economic and social activity of the Christian but also for the life of the political community as well.[128] In every area of the apostolate it is of the greatest importance that Christians in the world be able to distinguish clearly between "what a Christian conscience leads them to do in their own name as citizens, whether as individuals or in associations, and what they do in the name of the Church and in union with her bishops".[129] They must guard themselves, therefore, from compromising the Church in their worldly activity and from "ecclesialization" of the world in their churchly activity.

The recommendation that the expression *actio catholicorum* be taken up again to refer to the worldly activity of the Christian, was rejected by the Commission already in 1964, because it is used "only in special cases and otherwise only rarely or even not at all"[130] — not to mention the inherent ambiguity of the phrase.

Notes to this section refer to passages in the two great social encyclicals of Leo XIII and Pius XI, as well as to the radio address of Pius XII on the occasion of the 50th anniversary of *Rerum Novarum,* in which the significance and the competence of religion and of the Church in the solution of social questions is upheld, not indeed as regards the "technical side of the social structure" but for that "side of social order which connects the Church with the moral sphere and into which her influence extends".

Article 8. This article is really an appendix and all that is left of what was once part 3 "On the Apostolate of the Laity in Charitable Works", which comprised 18 pages in the first draft of the text.[131] In the September voting of 1965 several fathers attempted to have the chapter divided into two sections to correspond to the two goals of the apostolate described in Articles 6 and 7. This had already been attempted in vain in the Commission itself. The Commission wished to retain the threefold division, as the *relatio* remarked, "on purely practical and conventional grounds".[132] The fathers wished to say something about charitable works and could find no better place for the treatment of this

---

[127] *Ibid.,* nn. 36; 40; 42f.; 55; 59; 75f.; cf. also *Const. dogm. de Eccl.,* n. 36; Decl. de educatione chrst., n. 10.

[128] *Ibid.,* nn. 72; 75f.

[129] *Ibid.,* n. 76; similarly *Const. dogm. de Eccl.,* n. 36.

[130] *Schema decreti* (1964), no. 42.

[131] *Schema const. de apost. laicorum,* Pars III: "De apost. laicorum in actione caritativa" (1962).

[132] *Textus recogn. et modi* 6.

subject. Thus, the last article of this chapter speaks of love as the "origin and power" of all apostolic activity, and it speaks of charitable works as a direct expression of Jesus. The passage which is quoted from St. Matthew is perhaps not very happily chosen as it refers to miracles performed upon the sick and the dead. One might more aptly consider Mt 5:7; Jn 10:14f.; 13:14; 15:9–13; 1 Jn 3:16.

The next two paragraphs deal with Jesus' commandment of love, whereby the enrichment of love which is expressed in the NT is seen to lie in the recognition that Jesus himself is present in those who hunger and thirst, who are alone, naked, sick and captive. The inner reason which is given for this is that the whole human race has been brought together through the incarnation into a super-natural solidarity as one family of brothers, that it has been united with Christ, and that love has been made the sign of discipleship to Jesus. Thus, the community of Jesus must appear "at all times" as a fraternal community and a union of love, just as at the beginning the eucharistic community was embodied as a community of brotherly love *(agape)*. Without this "embodiment of love"[133] the celebration of the Eucharist loses its innermost meaning; without it an essential feature of the community of Jesus is lacking and it is no longer recognizable as his com-munity. And so the activity of love is the duty and the privilege of the Church, which she can never renounce. But she also values whatever contributions others may make here as, for example, public institutions, which are expressly mentioned. Several compromising formulations from earlier textual drafts were eliminated.[134] Readiness to help those who are not able to look after themselves and for those unfortunates who are looked down upon in the community and in society is part of the Church's care for her own, which is the only priority she is allowed to have after the example of the Lord.[135]

The decree then addresses itself to the present situation. The growth of all men into one family, no longer possible only as an ideal but also a technically feasible and tangible goal, forces us also to learn and to experience the universal need of humanity. It gives to the task of our love new, world-wide possibilities and obligations. Every type of need must be ferreted out: material, spiritual, individual, and social; those dependent upon the will of men and those resulting from chance circumstance; and as far as possible these must be overcome either by material, intellectual, or spiritual means, or at least mitigated and made more bearable. This obligation belongs not only to individuals, as is pointed out in the last sentence of the section, but also to societies and nations — and particularly to those who themselves are prosperous.

The article closes by warning against various ignoble motives which might possibly creep into our performance of charitable works and dangers which

[133] Cf. H. U. v. Balthasar, *Herrlichkeit,* I (1962), p. 553.
[134] Cf. *Schema const. de apost. laicorum,* Pars III (1962), 7 (n. 4).
[135] Cf. *CIC,* can. 467 f.; *Const. past. de Ecclesia in mundo huius temp.,* nn. 42; 76, and the fine intro-duction of John XXIII's social encyclical, the model for this article.

might poison our motives and turn them into the opposite of what we had intended. One cannot deny that we have been victims to such temptations repeatedly in the past. One can avoid these most easily by seeing in each of our neighbours, according to the light of revelation (Gn 1:26f.), the image of God and the brother of Christ, indeed Christ himself (Mt 25:40). Assistance, depending upon the spirit in which it is given, the dignity and freedom of the recipient; we can seek by our aid to gain some influence and power over others and abuse it for purposes of proselytizing. Assistance can cover over the legitimate unwillingness of the recipient to be helped. The best type of assistance, it is noted, is the removal of the causes of need and to provide means for self-help. Particularly in connection with the latter, Article 69 of the Pastoral Constitution on the Church in the Modern World refers to the teaching of the early Fathers: "Feed the man dying of hunger, because if you do not feed him you will have killed him."

Note 5 refers to the condemnation, in the encyclical *Mater et Magistra*, of "a new form of colonialism" which consists in the wrong use of economic help to bring pressure to bear upon those who are economically weaker. An earlier version of the text contained a warning against works which were nothing other than "mera instrumenta fidei propagandae"; one father had even proposed the works: "mera instrumenta proselytos indigno modo faciendi".[136] For similar reasons a proposed change in the text was judged to be unacceptable by the 1965 *relatio*, which wanted to stress that all charitable works are expressly directed towards the furtherance of the kingdom of God: "charitable works have an apostolic value in themselves, not only as instruments or opportunities for evangelizing".[137]

The concluding section admonishes us to hold works of charity in high esteem and to aid projects for private or public assistance, "including international programmes"; we are urged to strive towards co-operation "with all men of good will".

---

[136] *Schema const. de apost. laicorum,* Pars III (1962), p. 12 (n. 17); *Schema decreti* (1964), no. 44.
[137] *Schema decreti* (1965), no. 29.

CHAPTER III

The Various Fields of the Apostolate

The title of this chapter was repeatedly changed; the chapter itself did not always occupy its present place in the text and was only to be found in this form since the radical abbreviation of the text in 1964. As the introductory **Article 9** says, we are concerned here with "the more important fields of action" in the apostolate, both in the Church and in the world. A distinction is no longer made between the subject and object of the apostolate, as was done in earlier versions of the text. Mention is now made simply of fields of apostolic activity, whose agents are at the same time both subjects and objects of the apostolate.

The passage mentioning women was first included in the text as a *modus* at the instigation of the laywomen auditors, since a previous article on women, men, and youth in the apostolate had to be eliminated in the process of shortening the text. In the printed edition of 1963 there was at least one article planned for each of these.[138] This passage refers to the growing importance of women in society today, a development from which the Church has undoubtedly been slow to draw all the necessary consequences. It should be recalled that it is only in very recent times that women have been allowed to take degrees in theology and even now it is not possible everywhere; to mention but one point in this regard.[139] In earlier versions of the text many other fields of action were to be included and had been worked out in detail; these are now to be found in part in the Pastoral Constitution on the Church in the Modern World: work; culture; leisure, including tourism; areas influenced by materialism; the sense for morality and public morals; and also public life.

Article 10. This article describes as the first field for apostolic activity the Church communities in the narrower sense: the parish; the diocese; the entire Church; where the laity are to exercise directly their priestly, prophetic, and royal participation in the Church's work of evangelization and sanctification.[140]

---

[138] *Schema decreti de apost. laicorum* (1963), no. 18f.
[139] Cf. H. van der Meer, "Die Stellung der Frau in der Römisch-Katholischen Kirche", *Documentazione Olandese del Concilio* (Doc), n. 194.
[140] Cf. what is said with regard to Article 6.

It is here that the co-operative association of laity and clergy should be most effective and "the power of the laity" should be most intimately joined "to the work of the pastors of the Church".[141] The activity of the laity in this field is described as being absolutely necessary by the decree; the apostolate of the pastors *(pastores)* — what is meant here is undoubtedly the entire hierarchical apostolate from the parish to the whole Church — can only in this way find its full expression. As those who assisted Paul in early times, so now does the laity "supply what is lacking to their brethren and refresh the spirit of pastors and of the rest of the faithful". There must be a mutual exchange of faith between and strengthening of priest and laity. One might even refer to 1 Thess 3:6ff., which tells how the faith of the Thessalonians first assisted Paul in his affliction and distress and how he then longed to see them again, that he in his turn might perfect what was lacking in their faith. Gradually laymen are able to exercise a certain mediating function between pastors and their flocks.

The following are then mentioned in connection with this work: participation in the apostolic works of the community, thus a more community-orientated apostolate; the work of leading back those who are far removed from the Church; proclamation of the word of God especially in catechetical instruction; the offering of the special professional skills of laymen in pastoral care and parish administration. With regard to the latter, we must think of the advisory capacity of the laity as also of the full-time exercise of office at every level of Church organization. This will again be mentioned in Article 24. The decree expects a more efficient pastoral activity and administration of the Church from such co-operation. The inner source of such activity is again described as active participation in the liturgy.[142]

These fundamental remarks are then applied to parish activity, which is seen as the prototype for a common apostolate: it is to bring together the many human differences found within its boundaries and draw them all into the universality of the Church, thus making the parish the "small cell" or nucleus, as it is called in the next paragraph, for the whole Church. Close co-operation and contact of the laity with the priests in the common tasks within the parish should be the rule. A reservation which desired to see this co-operation limited to "those who were specially suited or specially gifted" was rejected.[143] Two tasks affected by such co-operation are then named: the laity are to make known to the Church, represented by the parish, the problems which men face in the present world as well as questions about salvation, which may then be considered and resolved in common by laity and clergy; likewise, they are to support the apostolic and missionary initiative of the parish, whereby under "missionary" we should understand the efforts made in converting and preaching the gospel to others as opposed to the apostolic task of helping others along the way of faith to

---

[141] *Const. dogm. de Eccl.*, n. 37.   [142] Cf. Article 4.
[143] *Textus recogn. et modi,* 74, *modus* 34.

sanctification. With regard to the first task, it is characteristic that even the layman's efforts to transmit his experience and vision of the world today, independent of the problematical nature of salvation are considered to be significant. In fact, this knowledge is the necessary basis for effective preaching and pastoral care; this alone would be a rich enough fruit of this contact and dialogue between laity and pastors, even on the parish level.

It may also be mentioned that in the last paragraph reference is made to the parish as our "Church community". This should not be romantically misinterpreted; what it means is that it is in the parish that those substructures can most readily be created in which the primary, functional and social relationships are still possible and where that brotherhood is still to be experienced, which is the essence of any community of Jesus.[144] This decree, therefore, appears to lay great weight on the place of the parish, the territorial parish, as the point of departure for any apostolic work. Sociology itself stresses more and more today the significance of the domicile, the home and the family, even in the large cities. "Geographical and ecological factors with their particular sociological features exert a much greater influence than professional or commercial factors."[145] Thus, the parish as a unit of limited area takes on a completely new significance today.

But this is not to be interpreted as a refusal to recognize the very real problems confronting the parish in its attempts to adapt itself to contemporary conditions and needs. The parish organization itself must become flexible; it needs a greater variety of subdivisions, and especially the additional formation of nuclei in the various milieus, to be brought about by subdivisions according to category, re-grouping and even through personal parishes which can only in part be restricted within a given territory. It is worth mentioning that the expression *communitas paroecialis,* used in the printed edition of the text of 1963 and which one father condemned as utopian with regard to metropolitan parishes, was finally eliminated from the text. There was a long discussion in the Commission followed by interventions upon the nature of the relation between territorial and personal parishes; both forms appeared side by side in the edition of 1963 and were considered to be equally important: *paroecia, territorialis vel personalis.* But the present text omits the passage altogether and the solution to the question thus remains open.[146] After a long and detailed discussion the Commission also rejected another addition which some fathers tried to have accepted at the last

[144] Cf. L. Vranckx, *Soziologie der Seelsorge* (1965).
[145] A. Weyand, *Formen religiöser Praxis in einem werdenden Industrieraum* (1963), p. 118; cf. K. Rahner, "Betrieb und Pfarre", *Stimmen der Zeit* 153 (1953–54), pp. 401–11; R. Lange, "Die Pfarre im Spannungsfeld der pluralistischen Gesellschaft als soziologisches Strukturproblem", *ibid.* 174 (1963–64), pp. 419–34; Inst. für kirchliche Sozialforschung, *Bevölkerungsstruktur u. religiöse Praxis in Krems,* part III: *Familie und Religionspraxis* (1965); *Bevölkerungsstruktur und religiöse Praxis in der Stadt Salzburg,* parts I and III (1965).
[146] *Schema decreti* (1964), no. 38.

minute, namely to give preference to the parochial apostolate through the *ordo caritatis*.

The parish is essentially the cell of a diocese. For this reason the laity should also have understanding for the needs of the diocese and direct their efforts accordingly. The bishops should invite the faithful to participate in such corporate endeavours, and by this the Council of course did not mean general, empty or only formal invitations which could not possibly produce results. The bishop should win those among the laity "for diocesan projects" who possess the necessary qualifications, and at a stage when there is still something to be decided and changed and not just to gain subsequent approval after decisions have been made. When the matter to be dealt with concerns planning for pastoral care, seminary education, or diocesan cultural committees or advisory boards, then help should be enlisted from scientists and those with practical skills: e. g. sociologists, psychologists, teachers, doctors, musicians, architects, painters, and sculptors.

There are also problems which as such overstep the boundaries of a particular parish, diocese, or even nation, and within which the full dimensions of these problems cannot be seen, let alone be solved. The text speaks of the differences between the needs of cities and those of rural areas, and of the spiritual as well as of the material needs of the people of God dispersed throughout the world (cf. 1 Pet 1:1), and likewise of personal and material assistance in the missions.[147] Problems of this sort are constantly increasing in scope due to the daily increase in population-mobility and even in the mobility of whole peoples, due to greater facilities for contact between men and the exchange of news. For the solution of these problems there is need of an equally great "mobility" in spiritual and intellectual matters, as well as organizational measures through interparochial, interdiocesan, national and international bodies. Work is only beginning in these fields. By and large we do not use to the full those opportunities which we already have for brotherly assistance, for the exchange of those gifts which have been given to us, for the collegial and universal responsibility of all for all, and also for communication between communities. We do not employ these opportunities in the missionary-field proper, or to alleviate the suffering of persecuted communities or to further mutual brotherly help in our own countries, for example, when supra-diocesan matters and questions of diocesan pastoral care are involved or when supra-diocesan study centres have to be set up. To interpret the so-called reevaluation of the episcopal office by Vatican II in the sense of a narrow "diocesanism" would be the worst sort of misunderstanding of the intentions of this Council. It is worth mentioning that the Ignatian admonition contained in the printed text of 1963 (Article 52) "nihil sine episcopo" was found by one of the fathers to be an unfortunate insertion, since "an excessive cult of the parish or diocese" now has something anachronistic about it. The Commission did not

[147] Cf. *Decr. de activitate missionali Eccl.*, nn. 21; 41.

comply with this wish in the edition of 1964 (Article 6), but the passage was finally omitted in the definitive text.[148]

It is precisely for such interparochial and supra-diocesan tasks that the laity are to be especially engaged, and chiefly experts from the various fields concerned. For among those talents which we are supposed to return in part to God, we should not only understand those of a financial nature, but also gifts and charisms; those who are entrusted with the service of administration are also responsible for seeing that these talents are used for the building-up of the community and are not wasted (cf. 1 Cor 14:5).

Article 11. This treats of the "apostolate of married persons and of the family", which is of unique significance not only for the Church, but for the whole human society as well. Earlier versions of the text treated of the family in different chapters as subject and object of the apostolate,[149] and they went into much more detail with respect to the apostolic tasks in connection with relatives, servants, and neighbours. One should also note that the Pastoral Constitution on the Church in the Modern World also treats of the family.

The text now before us speaks first of the apostolate which married persons have "on behalf of each other, their children, and all others in their household". The latter group, according to the meaning of the Latin word *familiares* and on the basis of earlier and more detailed versions of the text, must be taken to mean all those who are in any way connected with the family, such as relatives, servants, guests, apprentices who sleep or at least eat with the family, and student-boarders. Towards all of these the married couple are to be "champions of the faith" and "witnesses of the faith". For their children they should be "the first to proclaim the faith and rear them in it". *Primi fidei praecones et educatores* should be translated with this rendering instead of with "the first to communicate their faith and to educate them". This is very important: it is only because of the faith of its own family that a child can be baptized at all. The child's faith is an offshoot of the faith of the parents, and it is their faith which is to nourish the newborn faith until it grows and reaches maturity.[150] If the family does not fulfil this charge, either because faith is lacking or because of indolence and laxity, then the faith of the child will normally fail to mature into a truly personal faith and will remain instead in an infantile state only to be rejected later or gradually to disappear. Sociological studies of the family show, in fact, how true this is. The religious attitude and practice of young people is influenced by the family far beyond their early school years, far more than by companions or even by one's work-milieu.[151]

The Christian family should not only be a school for the faith but a school for the apostolate as well, and not so much in the form of a theoretical preparation for some future work but rather as an obvious and natural growth into the

---

[148] *Schema decreti* (1964), no. 38.
[149] So also the first printed version of the text, 1962.
[150] Cf. F. Klostermann, *Prinzip Gemeinde,* pp. 100–6.
[151] Cf. the studies mentioned in n. 137.

"Christian and apostolic life", i. e. a life which as such expresses itself in an apostolic manner. The text also indicates that it is not the words of the parents which are decisive but rather their example. "Exemplo" was added at the wish of the fathers because the influence of the Christian family is greater "by what it is rather than by what it does".[152] Then that assistance is mentioned which the parents are able to give to their children in the choice of a vocation, a choice which is becoming increasingly more difficult to make,[153] as well as the help which they can give in nourishing a priestly or religious vocation, should there be signs of it, for such a vocation can nowhere grow better or more genuinely than in the family. No artificially created milieu can replace it. It is notable that in both of these passages and also in those passages where reference is made to the general choice of a state of life, the word *vocatio* is used, indicating that every career is to be considered a vocation if it is carried out in faith.[154]

The third section underlines the special apostolate of married persons, which is particularly threatened today: the living witness to the indissoluble and sacred character of the marriage bond, the right and duty of parents and guardians to educate children, and the defence of the dignity and inner life of the family. Everyone is aware of how much all these are endangered today by the influence of cinema and the press, of public morals generally, and of however many other influences there are which are hostile to family-life. Through co-operation with all men of good will we are to work to ensure the legal preservation of these rights, and the humane organization of emigration and immigration in order to protect the family as a unit.

The apostolate of the family, nevertheless, reaches far beyond the immediate circle of the family; for it has already received from God a decisive function in society. For the fulfilment of its mission it must show itself to be "the domestic sanctuary of the Church through the mutual affection of its members and the common prayer they offer to God". This can only be achieved when "the whole family is involved in the liturgical worship of the Church, and if it provides active hospitality towards guests and those who need justice and other good works; it must be a sanctuary, a holy place for meeting, love and sacrifice, union with God, and a selfless openness towards others. All this, however, means the overcoming of that type of narrow bourgois family so frequently encountered in the 19th century and which might be characterized by the saying "My home is my castle". A family is the "domestic sanctuary of the Church" in that it represents an imitation of the mystery of the relation of Christ to his Church (cf. Eph 5: 32).[155] The entire first part of this paragraph, beautiful as it is, only came to be inserted through an intervention of 279 Council fathers.[156]

[152] *Schema decreti* (1965), no. 37.
[153] Cf. T. Scharmann, *Jugend in Arbeit und Beruf* (1965).
[154] Cf. under Articles 2 and 3.
[155] Cf. H. Schlier, *Der Brief an die Epheser*, pp. 255–63.
[156] *Textus recogn. et modi*, p. 78, *modus* 67.

In the second part of the paragraph several concrete forms of this apostolate of the family are mentioned which is opened towards society at large: schooling and catechetical work, adoption of abandoned infants, assistance to adolescents, support of engaged couples, married couples and families in material or moral need, and care for the aged and infirm. With respect to the aged it is pointed out that they are to be given a fairer share of the benefits of economic progress, to which they have also contributed in the past. In all of these things it is of the utmost importance that people be educated and properly formed for marriage and for family-life. At the Sixth International Conference of the "European Federation for the Formation of Catholic Adults" (FEECA) in 1966 a 5-stage course of formation was recommended: the first stage on life in general should treat of questions affecting daily life, the mode of life and elementary instruction in sexual matters; this should be followed by instruction for the engaged, the married, for parents, and then general instruction in family-life. In the last stage the family should be treated as a unit with its own rhythm of life and its celebrations and feasts in the course of the liturgical year.

The next section deals with the special significance of the family in mission countries, or in "newly established" churches or in areas where the Church is under special duress. It was taken over by the 1965 Commission from the draft printed in 1965. In places where the Church is being persecuted it is the family which provides the one possible nucleus and school for Christian life.

Finally, mention is made of the usefulness of organized family groups and societies. The original *opportunum est*[157] was weakened to *opportunum esse potest,* since the goals of this apostolate can also be realized by other means. *Aliquos coetus* is intentionally given a very wide meaning: it can include groups which pursue largely family-political ends, or groups which have a more directly apostolic aim.

Article 12. This article on youth first appeared in the text in the edition of 1965, and was expressly desired by the fathers. The content as well was almost entirely determined by the discussion which took place in October 1964.

In the first place the great change in the lives of young people is described: their greater importance in social and even political life, which remarkably enough was testified to by a document from the year 1904; the great changes which have taken place in intellectual attitudes; their relationships with their own families; the changes in social and economic relations which have so often been effected too rapidly, and the inadequate preparation of the young for such new burdens.

On the basis of this heightened social significance of young people a correspondingly heightened apostolic activity is required, for which the natural capacity of youth is well fitted: we only need to mention the greater consciousness of their own personalities; their vitality; their zest for life; their superabundant

---

[157] *Ibid.,* 80, *modus* 83.

energy, their eagerness to assume personal responsibilities and to participate in social and cultural life. This natural zeal must be imbued with the spirit of Christ and must be inspired by obedience to and love for the shepherds of the Church if it is to be fruitful. For this, as it is then remarked, the young themselves are to become the apostles of youth, exercising their own responsibility within their own milieu. Both of the references in the notes to this section give the example of the Young Christian Workers (JOC); the first with a quotation from the well-known passage in *Quadragesimo Anno:* "the first and nearest apostle of the workers must of course be a worker. The apostle for tradesmen and business-men must come from those circles".

At the wish of the fathers a separate section was devoted to the dialogue between adults and the present generation, a dialogue which is to further mutual understanding and enrichment.[158] In this way adults can and should attract young people to the apostolate: through example, counsel, and assistance. The original text ended here.[159] In the present text there is yet another sentence added on the attitudes of the young, which by its introductory *Juvenes vero* appears to be a parallel to the previous section beginning with *adulti,* but which as far as the contents are concerned is undoubtedly to be interpreted in a general way rather than in relation to that apostolate of which the *adulti* sentence exclusively speaks. This incongruence is to be explained by the fact that the sentence stems from those *modi* which were given to the Commission from higher authorities "at the last minute" and which among other things wished to stress the duties of the young to authority, especially to the Church, to their elders and to tradi-tion. From these *modi* likewise stems the passage about "obedience to and love for the shepherds of the Church" in the previous section.[160] The sentence stresses the respect and the trust which the young are to have for adults. It goes on to mention the natural inclination which the young have for whatever is new, which is seen as something truly positive. But they are to have as well "proper *(debite)* respect for worthwhile traditions" *(laudabiles traditiones),* whereby one must qualify both the *debite* and the *laudabiles.* For there is also an unreasonable respect for one's elders which refuses to recognize anything positive in what is new, and there are traditions which are anything but worthwhile.

The last sentence touches upon the specific apostolic activity of children. A *modus* which desired to see the title of the article extended to include children as well was not accepted. In itself this is not significant since the titles are all missing in the official edition. Nevertheless, at the end of the article, two lines were added on the "apostolate" of children.[161] Perhaps it was intentional that the somewhat vague expression *apostolica actuositas* was chosen instead of *apostolatus.* But even children can be "true living witnesses to Christ" in their own way and according to their own capacities. The decree only refers to their witness among

[158] *Schema decreti* (1965), no. 38.   [159] *Ibid.,* no. 33.
[160] *Variationes in textu* (1965); cf. n. 47.
[161] *Textus recogn. et modi,* 81 and 83, *modi* 86 and 103.

their comrades through an exemplary life, which we must certainly not regard as a reference to that distorted image of the typical "model child" but rather to full and normal child-life formed according to the faith. As experience teaches us, children can also help to waken in adults or even in parents a faith which has perhaps died or has been lying dormant.

Article 13 treats of the "apostolate of the social milieu" and summarizes what once made up Articles 7 and 8 in the printed edition of 1964, which dealt with "the proper milieu" and of "groups open to all".[162] In the 1963 edition it was stated that this apostolate is to be exercised "primarily among those of the same type *(a simili erga similem)*. Critical voices were soon heard voicing protest, for they found this too narrow a view in no way corroborated by the actual history of the Church. Actually there is a deeper principle at stake here, namely what it is that constitutes true neighbourliness, as the *relatio* of 1964 had already pointed out.[163] The present text therefore is much more cautious and mentions the apostolate "of like toward like" only as one possibility.

First it describes what is involved in this apostolate: the formation of the world and milieu in the spirit of Christ, where milieu can mean the sphere of work or leisure, school, the family or residential district, or one's chosen companions. This apostolate is represented as a duty of the laity upon whom it weighs the heavier since others who are strangers to this milieu, whether they be laymen or clerics, simply could not fulfil it. But here only those laymen are meant who are active in a concrete milieu. Singled out for mention in this field besides the apostolate of like toward like, are the complements to the witness of one's life through the testimony of the word and through brotherly assistance. One would of course think of the apostolate itself as brotherly assistance, but one should also remember that such purely human, selfless, brotherly help already possesses in itself the power of witness and that without this witness the apostolic word loses most of its credibility. The notes refer to the concluding section of *Quadragesimo Anno* which speaks of the specialized apostolate of the laity and the necessary training which the laity are to have for it.

The next paragraph stresses first the fact that Christians in the world fulfil in this way an indispensable mission of the Church, as we have already seen.[164] It continues by describing some of the inner attitudes of those who bear this apostolate, which on the one hand give it its efficacy but on the other hand also have great apostolic significance through the fact that they win men to Christ through their existence alone, or prepare men so to be won, or gradually transform the entire social or working milieu. The virtues which are especially mentioned in this regard are unity of life and faith; righteousness in all activities; brotherly love and solidarity; readiness to fulfil one's commitments in the family, society, or in one's profession. The Jocist slogan contained in the earlier version of the text, "see, judge, act", was eventually omitted. Against various criticisms

---

[162] *Schema decreti* (1964), no. 39.   [163] *Ibid.*, no. 38 f.   [164] Cf. under Article 7.

the Commission argued at that time that the words referred in no way to a definite form of the apostolate but indicated "a general method for any apostolate, and even any human undertaking".[165] In the present version the similar passage is to be found in Article 29 in a very general connection.

Finally, the object of this apostolate is even more precisely defined. Nobody is to be excluded from this milieu, nor anyone from amongst a group of equals or an immediate circle of friends. One must consider all the levels of the milieu concerned, those who are in subordinate positions and also on occasion those who are in positions of authority. Even the refusal by a subordinate to perform morally dubious tasks ordered by his superior may be an apostolic deed. No spiritual or temporal goods should be excluded from the range of apostolic care, for man in the concrete situation is here directly involved. Of course there are forms of the official apostolate of the Church which, because of the incompetence of the Church and the purity of her mission, must avoid any direct type of temporal engagement; but even here for the sake of the credibility and efficacy of the apostolate, and for reasons of humanity one must know the whole "life, work, suffering, and hopes" (cf. Phil 4 : 8) of one's brethren and at the same time share in them oneself. This is related to that solidarity of which we have already spoken above. Similarly, the explicit proclamation of Christ to those laymen "who are near" is again underlined; this is for many the only way to learn who Christ is.

Article 14 treats of the "vast field of the apostolate in the national and international fields". This was also a victim of the move to abbreviate the text in 1964, even though the Preparatory Commission had caused many detailed studies to be made on the subject and although sufficient texts were available. The reinsertion of this article, with partly new passages of text was a result of the debate in the aula in October 1964. This is all the more gratifying in the face of the strong diocesanism existing and the great need for recruitment in the international field.

In this field too "laymen are stewards of Christian wisdom". What is involved is in part the Christian penetration of the temporal order. Although there are tasks of evangelization and sanctification for the laity, here too, this article refers almost exclusively to the first task, that of Christian penetration. The task of evangelization and sanctification has already been touched on in Article 10. The first two sections treat more the national field and the last two the international.

Those obligations which devolve upon all Catholics are mentioned first: love for one's own country; the loyal fulfilment of civic obligations — especially the various obligations of benefactory (including social) and legal justice; the promotion of the true common weal; a personal contribution towards the formation of a healthy and vigorous public opinion; a corresponding influence

---

[165] *Schema decreti* (1964), no. 9, 39.

on legislature affecting public welfare and morality. Then those Catholics are mentioned who are specially qualified to play a part in public affairs, who have confirmed faith and a corresponding knowledge of Christian doctrine; they should not refuse to accept either public responsibilities or office. This does not mean that there are not good reasons for refusing such office, whether for family reasons, one's profession, or any other reason which may even concern the public welfare. But if such offices are open to the laity and they are able to accept them, they should do so, and they should realize that in the proper fulfilment of such tasks they not only serve the common welfare but because of the inter-relation of the temporal and spiritual orders they are also preparing a way for the gospel. They will accomplish the latter, however, when only these two conditions are fulfilled: a special professional knowledge and awareness of the light of revelation.[166]

Of special importance in this sphere, likewise, is co-operation with all men of good will: a dialogue in which Catholics should endeavour to acquire greater "prudence and courtesy" (*prudentia* here is not used in the sense of sagacity but means the special professional knowledge already referred to). There is need as well to contribute to the perfection of public and social institutions in the spirit of the gospel. An overly cautious reservation which wanted to have the phrase *sub prudenti vigilantis hierarchiae* added here, was rejected.[167]

In the international sector it is the function of the lay apostolate to promote and when necessary to clarify the increasing sense of solidarity among all peoples. And on the basis of this solidarity too the laity should be well informed about international affairs, about the questions and solutions, theoretical as well as practical, which arise in this field, especially with regard to developing nations. The note refers us to the conclusion of Part 3 of *Mater et Magistra,* which speaks of the world-wide extent of social problems and the co-operation on the inter-national level which is necessary to cope with them.

The last section treats of the activity of Christians in their growing contacts with those of other lands, how they must offer their contributions in work, developing and travel among foreign peoples. A brotherly readiness to give and to receive, together with the consciousness of being "journeying messengers of Christ", should characterize the fundamental attitude of the Christian in such situations.

---

[166] Cf. under Articles 2 and 7. [167] *Textus recogn. et modi,* p. 87, *modus* 129.

CHAPTER IV

The Various Methods of the Apostolate

On the basis of the discussion in October 1964 the title of the following section was changed from "On the Social Forms of the Apostolate" to its present more comprehensive one to emphasize sufficiently the significance of the purely personal apostolate of the individual. For this reason considerable changes were made in the text, with the result that the chapter now really comprises two parts, the first of which treats of the personal apostolate and the second the social apostolate, as indicated by the introductory **Article 15.** Thus every direction has been treated in the text, and it can no longer be criticized for representing as an ideal only "the man who is organized in every respect" or for being concerned solely with the problems of Catholic associations. The earlier article on the "Associations of the Faithful in Present and Future Church Law" was, as we have already noted, added to the introduction in an abbreviated form.

Article 16, "On the Significance and the Variety of the Personal Apostolate", once followed what was Article 2, "On the Apostolate to be Exercised by One and All", though it then had a very different form.[168] The expression *apostolatus individualis* (previously used) was eliminated by a *modus* which pointed out that "strictly speaking there can be no individual apostolate".[169]

The article treats first of the origin and the significance of the apostolate exercised by the individual Christian. Its undying source is a genuine Christian life, fed by the everlasting well of water given to us by Jesus and mentioned in Jn 4:14. The apostolate which is meant here is also in its turn the source for every other form of the apostolate — as it were, their prototype, fruitful always and everywhere, at times the only form that is either suitable or possible. In this connection one should remember the situations described in Article 17. To this type of apostolate the laity are always and everywhere called — through their very baptism — and they are obliged to take it up, even where there is no opportunity or possibility of practising a community-form of the apostolate.

---

[168] *Schema decreti* (1964), no. 6.
[169] *Ibid.* (1965), no. 40 (line 17); *Textus recognitus et modi*, p. 96, *modus* 6.

The wide range of this personal apostolate embraces every sort of apostolic goal and task: evangelization and sanctification as well as the Christian orientation of the temporal order. These are probably the two spheres of activity intended in the mention of that building-up of the community of Christ that is effected by evangelization and sanctification, and of the animation of the world in Christ. We should also relate the sanctification of the world to this latter *(mundum sanctificant)*, which is already indicated by the grammatical coupling. In the same sense, Pius XII, in his address to the Second World Congress for the Apostolate of the Laity, spoke of the "sanctification of the world", though he used a word that the present text is careful to avoid, namely *consecratio:* "The sanctification of the world is essentially the task of men who share most fully in the economic and social life and who are members of governmental and juridical organizations."[170] Certainly there is also a fundamental *consecratio* and *sanctificatio mundi* if we consider the incarnation or even the sacraments and sacramentals. But this is not what is referred to here, even though laymen may also participate in this sacramental sanctification of the world.

At the wish of the fathers[171] several concrete forms of the personal apostolate are enumerated, following first of all the order given in Articles 6–8. That witness of lay-life in the world, founded on faith, hope and love is considered to be the highest form of the apostolate appropriate at the present time. For in this way Christ himself abides in those who believe in him (cf. Jn 15:3–8). Next is mentioned the apostolate of the word "which is absolutely necessary under certain circumstances", and here again referred to the proclamation of Christ *(Christum annuntiant),* by which is meant that witness to Christ which is on occasion required of everybody in his family, his profession, and society. We are also referred to the other tasks of research and teaching, "according to situation and ability", as well as to public avowal of this teaching.

In the sector of the temporal order the following tasks are named: the search for "loftier motives of action *(principia)* in the family, in professional, cultural, and social life and for the lives of others in the light of faith. Thus the laity co-operate in the work of God and for his praise. For in that they shape the world according to the light of faith; their co-operation in the work of God is already in itself objective praise of God, which can naturally also become subjective praise if such work is done with the conscious intention of thus praising God by this work. Nothing else is meant when Article 34 of the Constitution on the Church speaks of the "sanctification" *(consecrare)* of the world through the laity who are "as worshipers whose every deed is holy" *(qua adoratores ubique sancte agentes).*

An admonition is then given, corresponding to Article 8, which bids the laity to make love the inner power and expression of their whole life.

Another section is added which states that one "can have an impact on all men

---

[170] Address of Pius XII, 5. 10. 1957: *AAS* 49 (1957), p. 927. Cf. n. 70, what is said under Article 2, as well as the commentary to Article 34 of the Constitution on the Church.
[171] *Schema decreti* (1965), no. 47.

and contribute to the salvation of the whole world" through the liturgy, prayer, penance, and the acceptance of the labours and the hardships of life. It is especially in the bearing of our various burdens in life, our distress, our helplessness, our prostration and our persecuted state, that we "carry in our body the death of Jesus" (2 Cor 4:8 ff.) and complete in our earthly flesh "what remains of Christ's afflictions for the sake of his body, that is, the Church" (Col 1:24). The remarkable passage to which the text refers us is only understandable if we look upon it as the intercommunication between the individual members and the member-communities which make up the whole community of Jesus (cf. 1 Cor 12:26; Eph 4:16; Col 2:19). The *relatio* to the text of the year 1965 notes that the Commission did not wish to settle the question as to whether prayer and penance were an apostolate, which some fathers wished to see affirmed and others wished to see denied. The Commission therefore limited itself to mentioning prayer and penance as means by which the laity can lead men to salvation.[172] The Council did not adopt the opinion of Pius XII, according to which "it is preferable to consider the apostolate of prayer and personal example as an apostolate in the broader or analogous sense of the word".[173] But it does not attempt such distinctions in this matter, as we have already remarked.[174]

Article 17 treats of the personal apostolate in situations in which this is the only possible form or where it is the one that is most appropriate, for example when the freedom of the Church is seriously restricted and when the laity must, wherever possible, take the place of priests (often under heroic circumstances) — here the Synod expressly wished to thank the laity for such activity — or when Catholics are living as a minority or in a diaspora situation. In these circumstances, or in similar ones determined by the milieu, it is noted that small informal discussion groups or nuclei can be of great use since individual members can keep one another from isolation through friendship and the sharing of experience, and since they can thus be a visible sign to others of the community of Jesus as a true bond of love. Thus the strength of the community is also able to assist those in such difficult situations through the personal apostolate and to make that apostolate fruitful. One should not only think here of the strength which is gained by the mutual help and encouragement which such members can give to each other, but also of the strength to be drawn from the presence of the Lord which is promised to all those who gather together in his name. The following article refers explicitly to this. One can also apply these things to the situation of the Church in a state of persecution. An earlier version pointed out, with reference to 1 Pet 2:11, that the Christian situation is already (by its very nature) a diaspora-situation.[175] On the basis of Mt 10 one could indeed say that the Church's state has always been one of persecution.

---

[172] *Ibid.,* no. 47.
[173] Address of Pius XII, 5 Oct. 1957: *AAS* 49 (1957), p. 928.
[174] Cf. n. 70.
[175] *Schema decreti* (25 Jan. 1965), 27 pages (mimeogr.), no. 16.

This article appeared in its revised form in the 1965 version; it had already appeared in the text of 1963, at least as far as its contents were concerned,[176] though it was subsequently omitted from the text of 1964.

With **Article 18,** treating of the importance of the apostolate practised in community, we proceed to the second part of this chapter. The fathers insisted on this form of the apostolate,[177] not only because of its greater efficiency, but also because the Church is a community Church, especially as is revealed in such expressions for the Church as *People of God*[178] and *Body of Christ.* In addition we have the promise of the special presence of Christ in the common activity of Christians.[179] This common activity must reveal itself in the apostolate within the family, the parish, the diocese, and also within freely chosen groups — *coetus* was chosen on purpose to indicate the widest possible term for such associations. In all these forms of common endeavour the Church should appear as the community that she really is.

It is only then that mention is made of the greater effectiveness of the common apostolate in the ecclesiastical communities proper, as well as in the various milieus: it gives the individual support, facilitates the formation for the apostolate as well as its planning and direction.

Finally, the necessity of the common apostolate in the present circumstances is held before our eyes. Not only does the text stress the "closer involvement" of all the groups in the Church, but the fathers also wished to stress the fact that care must be taken to adapt all these organizational forms to the mentality and social structure of those concerned.[180] Without this adaptation to the cultural and social situation the apostolate would remain ineffectual today; it would have no lasting fruit or would even fail altogether, if it were applied with no regard for the social pressure of public opinion or institutions in the area concerned. This applies to the town and city milieus of our own European society as well as those of other continents.[181]

Article 19 deals in general with "the great range of the apostolate carried out in community". In an address to the Assembly of the International Federation of Catholic Men, *Unum Omnes,* on 8 December 1956, with a reference to 1 Cor 12:4ff., Pope Pius XII mentioned all the various types of groups, and Catholic Action as well, "whose pivot is a parish, a milieu, a profession, or a work. Each has its own methods and this necessary difference must be respected. Uniformity is neither possible nor desirable, for it corresponds neither to the different practical circumstances nor the materials and human capabilities actually involved. It is, nevertheless, good if the distribution of the work and

---

[176] Cf. *Schema decreti* (1965), no. 41; and *Schema decreti* (1963), no. 20f.

[177] *Ibid.* (1965), no. 48.

[178] Cf. F. Klostermann, *Prinzip Gemeinde; Const. dogm. de Eccl.,* Cap. II.

[179] Cf. *Const. de sacra lit.,* n. 7.   [180] *Schema decreti* (1965), no. 48.

[181] Cf. *Const. de sacra lit.,* nn. 37–40: "normae ad aptationem ingenio et traditionibus populorum perficiendam."

material is well organized, and this presupposes the Christian virtues of humility and abnegation so that the blind zeal of some may not be an obstacle to the efforts of others."

After this a grouping of the many forms of apostolic associations is given according to the goals of each, and according to whether they attempt to carry out the general apostolic goal of the Church or only of a partial goal in the sense of the twofold division of these goals which was at one time undertaken in the second chapter.[182]

Those associations are especially singled out for mention which promote that inner unity between the life and the faith of their members as was described in Article 4. As the *relatio* of 1965 said, this is a kind of criterium by which we can order all the various types.[183] Associations of the apostolate must never become ends in themselves, but should always "serve to fulfil the Church's mission to the world"; they are justified only to the extent to which they are true to this goal. The "mission to the world" *(missio circa mundum)* naturally embraces the tasks of evangelization and sanctification and not only the Christian animation of the world; *circa Deum* would thus have to be interpreted as "praise of God". The "apostolic power" of these associations depends upon the correspondence of their goals with the goals of the Church, as well as on the power of the Christian witness and the spirit of the gospel, which animates the individual members as well as the association as a whole. Also there are evidently gradations in the apostolic efficacy of such associations and the criteria are given by which we may distinguish them. This is also to be of service to the associations in their own self-examination. The fathers insisted on the insertion "to try to ward the danger of professionalism in the apostolate".[184]

Among those changes which were proposed at the last minute by "higher authority" an additional phrase was to be added to the second sentence here: "et communione cum sacra hierarchia". The Commission, which had already rejected a similar suggestion,[185] could not be persuaded to accept this since Chapter 5 dealt at length with the relation of the apostolate to the hierarchy and also because in the last section of this article "the preservation of the necessary connection with the authority of the Church" was stressed.

The next section explains the consequences in Article 14 for the life of international Catholic organizations. Their forms must correspond to the progressive institutionalization and development of modern society in order that they may be fit instruments for the world-wide tasks of the Church of today. But such effectiveness is only possible if the Church has organizations which have been adapted to the needs of present society, and an international and world-wide orientation of the separate groups and individual members. This again presupposes considerable efforts in the education of Christians for such an end.

---

[182] Cf. Articles 6 ff.   [183] *Schema decreti* (1965), no. 48.   [184] *Ibid.*
[185] *Textus recogn. et modi,* 101, *modus* 46.

The last section establishes the basic right of the lay Christian to found apostolic associations and to be active in them, even to direct them. Certain restrictions to this right are enumerated: first of all the preservation of the necessary connection with the authority of the Church; then the avoidance of a wastage in energy by struggles over the competence of either the laity or the supervising hierarchy — this not only applies to new foundations but also when decisions have to be made about those existing associations that are to be retained; finally consideration of the special features of a land or a people when apostolic forms are transferred from one land to another. The mission encyclical of John XXIII, *Princeps Pastorum,* also referred to this latter aspect; in it he commended on the one hand a vigorous Catholic Action, but also on the other "an adaptation of the forms of the apostolate to local conditions and requirements", so that "the various types of apostolate are not overly taxed, thus hindering or dissipating precious energies resulting in the attainment of only part of the goals whereby the particular type of activity remains incomplete, imperfect, and too specialized. Where some types of activity might be successful in one place, they can in another be less successful due to the difference of environment and need".

The right which is spoken of here is but one application of the natural and inborn right of men to band together for any honourable purpose be it social, economic, cultural, or educational in character. It is the application of the general right of freedom in forming groups and associations. It is a right which is grounded in the social nature of man "who is placed together with other men so that what his nature requires but cannot of itself achieve, he may achieve in community with others".[186] This right can only be restricted by superior authorities for reasons of the common good. It is valid also in the ecclesiastical sphere and even in the sphere of evangelization and sanctification; it is bound up with the existence of the person in the Church (*CIC,* can. 87) and may not be infringed upon either by the ecclesiastical authorities or the civil authorities, except again for reasons of the common good. Indeed, these two authorities are obliged to guard this right. The laity have the right "to work together for all of those ends which are not opposed to the Catholic faith and moral teachings, including those ends which lie directly within the competence of the Church and which serve the fulfilment of her mission in the world". This "freedom to form associations, which each of us has by natural right as a human person, is also ours as legal persons in the Church according to Church law".[187] The Church long ago recognized this right, as was pointed out in the detailed reply of the conciliar congregation in response to a query from the Bishop of Carrientes in the Argentine, quoted in note 6. This is precisely the attitude of the decree, which again assumes in this matter a sound middle position between two opposing factions, one of which wished to stress only freedom from the hierarchy, but the

---

[186] Encyclical *Libertas praestantissimum* of Leo XIII, 20 June 1888: *ASS* 20 (1888), p. 604.

[187] H. Keller and O. v. Nell-Breuning, *Das Recht der Laien in der Kirche* (1950), pp. 49 f.; for the whole section cf. F. Klostermann, *Das christliche Apostolat,* pp. 820–4.

other dependence upon the hierarchy and uniformity "under the guise of unity and strength".[188] Those restrictions in this right referred to in this section do all apply to the common good of the Church.

A number of interventions were made even in the last phase of the formation of the decree, attempting to brand this teaching on the freedom to form associations as *valde periculosa* for all associations indiscriminately, and thus also for those established for the penetration of the Christian influence into the temporal order. They wished to have such associations founded and directed *sub ductu hierarchiae catholicae* or at least to require the hierarchy's express consent and approbation. Some attempted to make out of this *ius* a *facultas;* to make the right appear as a gift which may or may not be given. Even among the "last-minute" recommendations for correction there was one which thought it best to replace *ius* with *facultas*. But the Commission defended the text, since what is at stake here is in fact a right, as is quite clear from the detailed *modus* of the conciliar congregation from the year 1920 which was quoted. In addition to this, it was noted that the text dealt in general terms and thus had to be valid for those associations too for the founding of which neither the approval nor the consent of the hierarchy was necessary.[189]

Article 20 is concerned with a specific category of the common apostolate of the laity, whose significance was also pointed out in Article 33 of the Constitution on the Church: "Besides this apostolate" — which issues from baptism and confirmation — "the laity can also be called on in various ways to practise a more direct form of co-operation in the apostolate of the hierarchy." In a *relatio* on this subject explicit reference was made to Catholic Action.[190] As is clear from this description and from the text of the decree itself, what is meant is not so much a special organization as a special type of organization. Only in this way would such a treatment be justified in our connection, since the Commission had decided not to mention any organization by name, in spite of many attempts to the contrary. Catholic Action does not represent only one definite organization, especially if we consider the present world-situation, but rather a certain species of the common apostolate which embraces very many and very different organizations, even those which are not specifically called Catholic Action, as, for example the *Jeunesse Ouvrière Chrétienne*.[191] It was, nevertheless, necessary to say something about this category of organization since many bishops had requested that Catholic Action be treated expressly in the course of the Council.[192]

[188] Cf. *Schema decreti* (1964), no. 45f.; *Schema decreti* (1965), no. 48f.

[189] *Textus recogn. et modi,* 101f., *modi* 47–54.

[190] *Sacrosanctum oecumenicum Concilium Vat. sec., Schema constitutionis de ecclesia* (Typ. polygl. Vat., 1964), p. 136.

[191] Cf. *Commissio permanens conventum internationalium apostolatui laicorum provehendo, De laicorum apostolatu organizato hodie toto in orbe terrarum diffuso. Documenta collecta et systematice exposita pro Patribus Concilii Oecumenici Vaticani II.* (Typ. polygl. Vat., 1963).

[192] 416 bishops handed in *vota* in this connection already before the Council: *Acta et documenta Concilio oecumenico Vaticano II. apparando.* Series I (Antepraeparatoria), Appendix voluminis II.

The text which we have before us is the result of long discussions which began as far back as the preparatory phase of the Council. In most of the sections scarcely a sentence, and in many sentences scarcely a word, has been retained of the original formulation. We have already noted in the history of the development of the text that the Commission vigorously defended the text already prepared against all attacks in the Central Commission, in the aula, and against extra-conciliar forces as well, and was able to retain its basic structure and formulation save for several insignificant changes. This text represents a compromise between two diametrically-opposed conceptions or models of Catholic Action. The extreme representatives of these positions attempted again and again in the Preparatory Commission, in the Conciliar Commission, and in the aula as well, to make a world-concept out of their own interpretation. In a somewhat simplified way one might say that the concept of the Mediterranean countries, especially Italy and Spain, was directly opposed to that of the Anglo-Saxon countries, especially England and the United States, in which countries the name "Action" has something of a political undertone. Likewise, the various *relationes* which were given with the printed editions of the text reflect this struggle and they stress the fact that the Council text cannot go into detail, as was often requested, and that it must take account of the historical, geographical, cultural, and social differences between the various nations. Likewise, the meanings of words are not the same everywhere and there is much that cannot be given general application; one must indeed preserve unity where necessary but one must also be anxious to preserve freedom where this is more important.[193] The reservations expressed were often found to contradict one another: the one side feared a narrow favouring or even monopoly of the apostolate by the hierarchical mandate, and for the other the indecisiveness of the text with respect to Catholic Action was a matter of concern. The latter group thus wished to have a fuller representation of the teaching of the Popes on this matter, i. e. the mandate. The Commission could only state again and again that it had taken the only possible "middle road" which was expressly acknowledged by not a few of the fathers.[194] Both of these fronts were apparent in the various *modi* as well.[195]

The text begins with a historical introduction, as in the very first printed edition of 1962.[196] It is stressed that in the last decades, in many nations and at the initiative of the laity themselves, various forms of apostolic activity for the

Analyticus conspectus consiliorum et votorum quae ab episcopis et praelatis data sunt. Pars I et II (Typ. polygl. Vat., 1962). Similarly in the proposals of the Roman Dicasteries: *Acta et documenta,* Series I, Volumen III: *Proposita et monita SS. Congregationum Curiae Romanae* (Typ. polygl. Vat., 1960), and in the reports of Church and Catholic faculties and universities: *Acta et documenta,* Series I, Vol. IV, Pars I et II (Typ. polygl. Vat., 1961), our theme appears repeatedly. During the discussion of this text in the Council itself several fathers requested a more detailed presentation.
[193] *Schema decreti* (1964), no. 28; 47 ff.
[194] *Schema decreti* (1965), no. 49.
[195] *Textus recogn. et modi,* 103–8.
[196] *Schema constitutionis* (1962), Pars II, 10.

laity and associations had been developing, which were and are still characterized by a close union with the hierarchy and a pursual of goals which were and still are properly apostolic *(proprie apostolicos)*. This, moreover, is the one place where the historical presentation is interrupted by an insertion included as a result of the discussion in October 1964: *persecutae sunt et persequuntur*.[197] With respect to the goals, another *modus* was rejected which wanted to replace *fines proprie apostolicos* with *fines apostolicos evangelisationis*. As the reason for this reservation it was asserted that one should not exclude the "animation of the temporal order" from the object of the mission of the Church.[198] Historically it was never excluded from Catholic Action, as the formulation of Pius X shows.[199] How far the associations referred to here are, or should be, responsible for the animation of the temporal order can be seen from what follows. It is noted that associations of this sort, namely those with similar characteristics, do not represent something absolutely new in our time, as Pius XI always stressed with respect to Catholic Action,[200] and as the Constitution on the Church also remarked.[201]

To these associations belong also those recommended and promoted by the "Popes and many bishops", such as Catholic Action. It is stated that they can make use of different methods of approach, that they have "produced excellent results for Christ's kingdom" and that they were thus "deservedly recommended and promoted" by the supreme ecclesiastical authorities. In the end, the well-known definition of Catholic Action formulated by Pius XI and Pius XII was added as a result of the discussion held in October 1964, though the expression used by Pius XI, *participatio,* was avoided and the word *cooperatio* was adopted instead from Pius XII.[202] He, however, used it in connection with the phrase *in* (!) *apostolatu hierarchico* while Article 33 of the Constitution on the Church has *cooperatio ... cum* (!) *apostolatu hierarchiae* (!). One *modus* said that *cooperatio* represented too close a coupling of the apostolate proper to the laity with that of the hierarchy, but it was rejected. Even the suggested change of the *"in"* *apostolatu hierarchico* to *cum* was not accepted, though it improved the text.[203] Moreover, even Pius XII's mode of expression was not consistent. Among other things he spoke only of an assistance which the laity might render to the hierarchical apostolate or the apostolate of the hierarchy, though he also spoke at times of a co-operation.[204] It was supposed, in vain, that there was a distinction

---

[197] *Schema decreti* (1965), no. 42.

[198] *Textus recogn. et modi,* no. 104, *modus* 65.

[199] F. Klostermann "Katholische Aktion nach dem II. Vatikanum", *Der Seelsorger* 36 (1966), pp. 310f.

[200] Examples in F. Klostermann, *Das christliche Apostolat,* p. 430.

[201] *Const. dogm. de Eccl.,* n. 33.

[202] *Schema decreti* (1965), no. 42. Cf. also the history of the text in this commentary, as well as F. Klostermann, *Das christliche Apostolat,* pp. 647–50.

[203] *Textus recogn. et modi,* 104, *modi* 67 and 68.

[204] Cf. Y. Congar, *Der Laie* (1956), pp. 599f., E. T.: *Lay People in the Church* (1964).

between the "hierarchical apostolate" and the "apostolate of the hierarchy". Our text speaks in the same way of *cooperatio laicorum in apostolatu hierarchico* and *laica cooperantes . . . cum Hierarchia*. It is also worth mentioning that our text uses the "in" with the ablative and not with the accusative, which would only indicate a certain direction, although Pius XI in the same connection uses the "in" with the accusative: "Actio Catholica definitur laicorum hominum in apostolatum hierarchicum collaboratio."[205]

The note refers us to two papal documents in support of the definition used in the text. In the well-known letter of Pius XI to Cardinal Bertram on 13 November 1928 on the subject of Catholic Action, he wrote: "Apparet Actionem Catholicam alio non spectare, nisi ut laici apostolatum hierarchicum (!) quodammodo participent"; and Pius XII in his address to the leaders of the Italian Catholic Action on 4 September 1940 spoke of "la collaborazione (!) dei laici all'apostolato gerarchico (!)".

What our text actually understands by these definitions, which are obviously capable of varying interpretations, will be made clear from what follows. It is significant that the definition was incorporated into the text only as a result of the efforts of one group of fathers — not without opposition from another group — and that it was intentionally used by the Commission only in the historical section and only in the formulation "the collaboration of the laity in the apostolate of the hierarchy" instead of "participation in . . .". In fact the definition, especially if understood in the sense of a "participation", would no longer appear to correspond to our present-day conceptions of the function of the laity in the Church and of the nature of Catholic Action and would thus appear to be outdated by the course of development. The laity is here still conceived of too much in the sense of a body which exists for the execution of tasks, as an "extended arm of the hierarchy", instead of being seen within its own proper function and responsibility in the Church. At any rate, only a small sector of the many tasks within Catholic Action can be properly designated as collaboration or co-operation or even as participation in the hierarchical apostolate of the Church. Such a definition does not do justice to that specifically "lay" quality, which is so characteristic of the Christian in the world, nor the genuine co-responsibility of the laity within the Church. Catholic Action does not cease to be an apostolate of the Church because it is partially co-operation or even participation in the hierarchical apostolate, and in it the laity too are co-responsible members of the Church and not only by reason of the mediation of the hierarchy. Thus the word "co-operation" is more general — and perhaps even vaguer than the word "participation"; however, when it is used in relation to the hierarchical apostolate to describe the entire sphere of the tasks of Catholic Action, it is less likely to lead to misunderstanding. Similarly, co-operation in the hierarchical apostolate must not be understood as though the apostolate of the Christian in the world in

[205] Letter of Pius XI to Cardinal Schuster, 28 Aug. 1934: *A A S* 26 (1934), p. 586.

Catholic Action were determined only by the hierarchical apostolate. All those who are engaged in the apostolate of the Christians in the world can and indeed under certain circumstances must make certain observations and pass these on to the hierarchy, who had no way of discovering these for themselves. Thus, according to the present conception of the Church and of Catholic Action, one could perhaps speak of Catholic Action with less chance of being misunderstood as "an official or public and institutional participation or share of the laity in the apostolate of the Church".

It is also made clear in this section that Catholic Action is a genuine apostolate of the laity. For this reason a *modus* supported by 48 fathers which wanted to see Catholic Action established as an apostolate between that of the hierarchy and the laity was rejected on the grounds that it was "not in the sense of the accepted text".[206] For similar reasons it was necessary to assert that this form of the apostolate came into being through the initiative of the laity themselves. One *modus* wished to substitute *congregati sunt* for *sese congregarunt? quia a hierarchia congregari debent.*[207] It is a fact that the organizations of the Catholic Action developed gradually out of the spontaneous Catholic Movement of the eighteenth and nineteenth centuries, as can be clearly proved for the Italian Catholic Action.[208]

Now an attempt is made to characterize this particular category of apostolates — they are considered to form a particular category. These forms of the apostolate are not necessarily those founded in the last decades; similar older institutions must also be considered if they are characterized by the features enumerated in the following paragraph. This indicates that not only the associations to which the hierarchy "has given the name of Catholic Action" in recent decades are meant here: in certain circumstances this could have organizational consequences, particularly with regard to closer co-operation. An insertion was made at the express wish of the fathers after the debate in 1964 that these forms of the apostolate must be particularly modern in their approach, whether they are part of Catholic Action or not.[209] Nine fathers presented *modi* asking for the deletion of this insertion, but all were rejected.[210] From the first printed version on it has been stressed that a genuine Catholic Action must be "concentrated and affirmed" in the features enumerated.[211] A *modus* contradicting this was rejected.[212]

The first feature is the goal. The direct aim of the organizations meant here is "the apostolic goal of the Church". The first version of the text reads:

---

[206] *Textus recogn. et modi,* 103, *modus* 58.
[207] *Ibid.,* 104, *modus* 62.
[208] Cf. F. Klostermann, "Katholische Aktion nach dem II. Vatikanum", *Der Seelsorger* 36 (1966), pp. 309–19.
[209] *Schema decreti* (1965), no. 44.
[210] *Textus recogn. et modi,* 105, *modi* 69 and 70.
[211] *Schema constitutionis* (1962), Pars II; 11.
[212] *Textus recogn. et modi,* 105, *modus* 71.

"generalis finis apostolicus ipsius Ecclesiae". The alteration was made after the debate in October 1964 to eliminate misunderstanding. Mention is now made of the penetration of different communities, not only of different milieus, in order not to foster the impression that the organizations of the general Catholic Action (*Actio Catholica generalis*) had been excluded, and that only those specialized for certain milieus (*Actio Catholica specialis*) had been included.[213] The goal is described in more detail as being "the orientation towards the evangelization and sanctification of men as well as of the Christian formation of their conscience, "so that they may — on their own responsibility — penetrate and animate the various communities and milieus in which they live with the spirit of the gospel. The latter indicates the contribution of Catholic Action to world-service to humanity; this task is by no means restricted to members of Catholic Action, nor even to the Church. Milieus are those of the family or profession; a *modus* that requested the insertion of *vitae* was rejected as superfluous.[214] The *in ordine ad* is significant here; the earlier version had the wording: "quod ad homines evangelisandos et sanctificandos attinet".[215] The present text has thus been extended and comprehends as its goal not only evangelization and sanctification, but whatever tends towards this by virtue of its nature; "the apostolic goal of the Church is more than evangelization and sanctification", it was said while rejecting another restrictive *modus*.[216]

It is clear from the whole formulation of the text that this statement of the aims of the associations of Catholic Action excludes everything which is not directed toward evangelization and sanctification or towards the formation of the Christian conscience but only towards purely temporal, and strictly worldly goals. The Christian formation of the temporal order itself cannot thus be the task of Catholic Action, since it is not as such the immediate task of the Church (*finis immediatus*). The "penetration and perfecting of the order of temporal things" indeed belongs to the mission of the Church,[217] but she can only exercise this mission through those who are entrusted with the building up of the temporal order, i. e. only through Christians in the world, for such a Christian inspiration and penetration of the temporal order cannot take place at all except in and through the structures of this order, for which the Church herself has neither a mission nor competence. In this respect the Church can only put forward the general principles of revelation in whose light — and in the light of their own professional skill — Christians in the world must seek to find concrete solutions on their own responsibility.[218] Here the faithful must "learn how to distinguish carefully between those rights and duties which are theirs as members of the Church and those which they have as members of human society".[219] They

---

[213] *Schema decreti* (1965), no. 50; cf. *Schema constitutionis* (1962), Pars II, 11.
[214] *Textus recogn. et modi,* 105, *modus* 74.
[215] *Schema decreti* (1965), no. 44.
[216] *Textus recogn. et modi,* no. 105, *modus* 73.   [217] Cf. Article 5.
[218] Cf. under Articles 5 and 7.   [219] *Const. dogm. de Eccl.,* n. 36.

must distinguish between what a Christian conscience leads them to do in their own names as citizens, either as individuals or as associations, and what they do in the name of the Church and in union with her shepherds", as, for example, in Catholic Action.[220]

And so Catholic Action cannot in principle go further than the Church, or even the hierarchical apostolate itself, and with respect to its effectiveness in the temporal order it can proceed only as far as its activity is motivated by general Christian principles. Differences can only arise for tactical reasons but not because of different basic standpoints. In everything which goes beyond the aim and task of the Church Catholic Action will have to exercise the greatest restraint and its opinions here can only have the character of suggestions. Certainly, like the Church herself, it has been commissioned with the service of love. Therefore from the attitude which true love demands, it should offer its help and counsel with due deference in all situations of human need; more is not required of it. This is why many of the statutes of Catholic Action impose upon its leaders a certain reserve in the acceptance of party-political office and they even designate some functions as incompatible with certain leading positions so that the holders of such office do not appear to compromise the Church in their worldly activity, and the world in their ecclesiastic activity — i. e. in Catholic Action.[221] Not even Catholic Action can become a means to "conquer the world" by some devious route in the sense of a new ecclesialization.

On the other hand there can be no question of limiting Catholic Action only to pastoral assistance within the Church, as was actually maintained by some. From the very beginning it was never conceived of in this manner. On the contrary, in Italy under Pius X it even included works of cultural, social, economic, and civic-political significance. Similarly, after the reform of Benedict XV, when those organizations which served mainly temporal aims and broke away from Catholic Action, leaving it to concentrate upon its proper tasks, it still emphasized its duty to study individual, family, professional, social and cultural problems in the light of Christian principles and to promote the corresponding education of the Christian conscience of Catholics.[222] It was Pius XI in particular who repeatedly stressed the social tasks of Catholic Action: the renewal of the individual, of the family, and of public life; the realization, consolidation, defence, propagation, and restoration of the kingdom of Christ in public and private life.[223] The Church was for him, above all else, "active within society".[224] And this is what Catholic Action also becomes, through its formation of conscience

---

[220] Const. past. de Eccl. in mundo huius temp., n. 76.
[221] Cf. Katholische Aktion Österreichs und Politik, a declaration of principle approbated by the bishops of Austria and binding for Catholic Action, published by the Working Committee of the Catholic Action of Austria (1963).
[222] F. Klostermann, "Katholische Aktion nach dem II. Vatikanum", loc. cit., pp. 309–19.
[223] Cf. examples in F. Klostermann, Das christliche Apostolat, pp. 540, 996.
[224] Osservatore Romano, 19 June 1926.

in the service of the world, and through its service as a good Samaritan in the alleviation of misery, which has already been mentioned before.

The second feature is that of the genuine lay-character of these organizations. Those ways "peculiar" to the laity and the contribution of their own particular experience must be protected in the co-operation with the hierarchy. One *modus* even wanted to see the phrase *iuxta modum proprium* omitted from the text.[225] In addition the special type of relation which the laity should have to the hierarchy should not hinder the laity from exercising responsibility in the administration of these organizations, nor hamper their "judgment of the conditions in which the pastoral activity of the Church has to be conducted" or the "planning and execution of a programme of action". This means a very decisive limitation of the activity of the hierarchy in that it must respect this personal responsibility and the experience which the laity alone have. Even in Catholic Action it is certainly not true that everything is to be done only *ad nutum hierarchiae* as many unenlightened people seem to think. Many of the practices adopted in order to humiliate the laity and quash their proposals should undergo substantial correction. Of course what has been said about judgment of the conditions in which the pastoral activity of the Church is to be conducted, is to be seen primarily in connection with Catholic Action; but such "judgment of conditions" by the laity should also be respected by the hierarchy in its own pastoral activity, since it is dependent upon the special experience and professional skill of laymen.[226] In any case we shall see whether the ecclesiastical office-bearers will preserve this atmosphere of trust at all levels of their activity so that mature Christians can develop their own initiative and skill even at the parish-level. We shall see whether the true task of the laity is being carried out in the proper sphere of the Church and in the closest co-operative partnership with the hierarchy, or whether Catholic Action is becoming merely the action of a group of subordinates, yes-men and poster-stickers, thus losing one of its essential characteristics and thus really ceasing to be Catholic Action at all. In reaction to this, the virulent layman may well turn to those organizations which are least dependent upon the Church or the hierarchy.

But one cannot say, on the other hand, that the special bond which is formed with the hierarchy through Catholic Action is from the very start a hindrance to a genuine, creative, and personal responsibility or to the true leadership of the Christian in the Church. That would be tantamount to claiming that leadership would only be possible in totalitarian systems ruled by absolute dictators, and there only by one person. For in every other type of system there are, even in the profane sphere, only shared responsibilities with gradations of importance ranging from top to bottom. This is especially true in the community of Jesus in which "all share a true equality with regard to the dignity and the activity

---

[225] *Textus recogn. et modi,* 105, *modus* 75.
[226] *Const. dogm. de Eccl.,* n. 37.

common to all the faithful for the building up of the Body of Christ",[227] and in which a basic, universal, and collegial responsibility of all for all rules the whole community.[228] Moreover, Pius XII had already addressed himself to those who wanted to deny the truly lay character of those Christians in the world who had held such positions, especially by mandate, in Catholic Action. He defended this very lay-character: "This apostolate will always remain an apostolate of the laity and does not become a 'hierarchical apostolate' even when it is exercised with an ecclesiastical mandate."[229]

The third characteristic feature of genuine Catholic Action concerns its specific organizational character. We must consider here a category of the common apostolate in which the laity, namely Christians in the world, are joined together *ad instar organici corporis. Ad instar* or *ad modum organici corporis,* i. e. in an organic or corporate structure, is a juridical expression (cf. *CIC,* can. 686 § 3; 693 §3; 707). Associations formed in this way, i. e. corporately, have a head and members and a higher and lower order defined by statute; in the Church law of that time these bodies established by law were termed *sodalitia* (can. 707 § 1). Associations, on the other hand, have no statutory head and no possibility for its members to appear as a body; these are only bound together by the exigencies of certain tasks, as is the case with eucharistic associations or apostolates of prayer.[230] The special advantages of such a corporate body are considered to lie in the fact that the communal responsibility and community-nature of the Church is best expressed through collegial co-operation, and also in the grater efficacy of such apostolic work.[231] The request of one reservation to eliminate the phrase "aptius Ecclesiae communitas significetur" was rejected.[232]

The last of these characteristic features defines the specific relation of this organization to the hierarchy. First of all mention is again made of the initiative of the laity — and this is especially significant. Such organizations cannot namely be initiated or founded only from above. This was not even the normal way in the past,[233] although it has always been possible. They originate through the initiative of the laity as well, through a spontaneous movement of stouthearted laymen.[234] After the discussion in October 1964, in the passage which speaks of the initiative of the hierarchy *vocati* was replaced by the weaker *in-*

[227] *Ibid.,* n. 32; cf. n. 10f.
[228] Cf. F. Klostermann, *Prinzip Gemeinde,* pp. 36–40; also *Das christliche Apostolat,* pp. 714–26; 745–54.
[229] Address of Pius XII to the Second World Congress for the Apostolate of the Laity, 5. 10. 1957: *AAS* 49 (1957), p. 928.
[230] Cf. J. Beil, *Das kirchliche Vereinsrecht nach dem CIC* (1932), pp. 43–49; E. Eichmann and K. Mörsdorf, *Lehrbuch des Kirchenrechtes,* I (9th ed., 1959), p. 559.
[231] Cf. Article 18, paragraphs 3 and 4.
[232] A *modus* which wanted to see this passage eliminated was rejected: *Textus recogn. et modi,* 106, *modus* 78.
[233] F. Klostermann, "Katholische Aktion nach dem II. Vatikanum", *loc. cit.,* pp. 309–19.
[234] Cf. F. Klostermann, *Das christliche Apostolat,* pp. 637f.

vitati, in order to stress precisely this free character of the layman's co-operation. For not all laymen have the opportunity to follow such a call, and they can only decide themselves whether under the circumstances they are able to do so.[235] The Church can only be served in this field by men who offer themselves to her by their own free choice, at least in so far as adults are concerned. The text again refers back to the definition of Catholic Action as "collaboration in the apostolate of the hierarchy", but in order to stress the particular nature of the collaboration it adds to *cooperatio* the word *directa,* in the sense of "without mediation". Thus, the word *in* was replaced by *cum,* which means that the phrase can be interpreted in the sense of a collaboration distinct from the hierarchy, or also the partnership between both in this work.

The special relation of Catholic Action to the hierarchy lies in the fact that as all other organizations of this nature, it functions "under the higher direction of the hierarchy itself". By hierarchy primarily those are meant whom the Holy Spirit has made overseers "to feed the Church of the Lord" (Acts 20:28). Thus they are those to whom the service of leadership is entrusted: the bishops for their dioceses, and the Pope for the entire Church. Certainly the bishop, in the exercise of his office, can make use of the organs which are designed for his assistance, that is, the priests and deacons,[236] making them his "spiritual assistants" and giving to them a certain delegated function. In this capacity they are also to be the pastoral counsellors of the laity and help them in the formation of a true Christian conscience. However, they may never exceed their competence and for the rest should "limit themselves in their activity to their priestly duties", as Pius XII recommends.[237] The final responsibility itself must be borne by the bishop, and this is indicated by the word *ipsius.*

The phrase *superius moderamen* needs some words of explanation. It must be taken together with the second characteristic feature and must not be interpreted as a negation of what was said in that section. There is a certain tension between the two, but they are not contradictory. The *moderamen* of course goes far beyond vigilance in teaching and order, both of which are the prerogative of hierarchy in any apostolate. *Moderamen* means responsibility as well, for which reason the first edition of the text expressly speaks of a *corresponsibilitas* of the hierarchy.[238] But the accentuation lies upon the *superius;* it means the final responsibility, the approval of the statutes, of the organs of leadership, and the most important resolutions which are made; but for the rest it means restriction to the marking-out of a wide area, within which there must be scope for freedom, initiative and action. This also means extension to the laity of a relation of partner-

---

[235] Cf. *ibid.,* pp. 66–713 on the duty to perform this type of apostolate; address of Pius XII to the First World Congress for the Apostolate of the Laity, 14 Oct. 1951: *AAS* 43 (1951), p. 787.

[236] *Const. dogm. de Eccl.,* nn. 28f.

[237] Address of Pius XII to the members of Italian Catholic Action, 3 May 1951: *AAS* 43 (1951), p. 376.

[238] *Schema constitutionis* (1962), Pars II, 11.

ship, especially to those who occupy leading positions; it means the employment of their experience in every field and in the formation of every significant decision. It means as well constant dialogue with the laity and the willingness to seek information from those among the laity who are competent to give it. There is no longer any place here for the isolated decisions of a monologistic and absolute ruler. Rather must the words of Cyprian to his deacons and priests be remembered: "It has been a rule of mine ever since the beginning of my episcopate never to decide anything without their counsel or without the consensus of the people or solely according to my own personal opinion."[239] After this one can hardly think of the bishop as the proper head of Catholic Action, as has often been the case.

This *superius moderamen* is also related to the official character of Catholic Action, as has been repeatedly stressed in ecclesiastical documents. "Dependence (upon the hierarchy) is to be closest in Catholic Action, for it represents in a concrete way the official apostolate of the laity. It is a tool in the hand of the hierarchy and should at the same time be looked upon as an extension of its arm. It is thus according to its nature subordinated to the direction of the Church authorities."[240] "Catholic Action always has the character of an official apostolate of the laity."[241] The image which is used here by Pius as elsewhere in ecclesiastical documents, "instrument in the hand of the hierarchy", or "extension of the arm of the hierarchy", should of course not be misunderstood in the sense of a "blind tool", without a mind of its own or self-responsibility: an inert mechanism. This would indeed lead to an undermining or even a complete cessation of true Catholic Action. This official character of Catholic Action naturally does not imply any sort of total domination by the hierarchy, which our decree expressly excludes.[242]

Finally, it is pointed out — still under the fourth characteristic — that the hierarchy can also confirm this collaboration by an explicit mandate. In the first edition of the text this sentence was connected with the fourth characteristic, though still as a separate sentence;[243] in a later edition the idea appeared as a separate paragraph,[244] then it was again inserted into this paragraph on the fourth characteristic by means of the word *quae*.[245] The first edition also put it somewhat more sharply: *hierarchiae est;*[246] but in the present version it appears only as a possibility. These

---

[239] *Ep.* XIV, 4: *PL,* IV, 240. For the whole section cf. F. Klostermann, *Das christliche Apostolat,* pp. 713–59.

[240] Address of Pius XII to the First World Congress for the Apostolate of the Laity, *loc. cit.,* p. 789.

[241] Address of Pius XII to the Second World Congress for the Apostolate of the Laity, 5 Oct. 1957: *AAS* 49 (1957), p. 929.

[242] Cf. the conclusion of Article 20, as well as Articles 21 and 24. Other examples: F. Klostermann, *Das christliche Apostolat,* pp. 641–6.

[243] *Schema constitutionis* (1962), Pars II, 11.

[244] *Schema decreti* (1964), no. 15.

[245] As already in the *Schema decreti* (1965), no. 44.

[246] *Schema constitutionis* (1962), Pars II, 11.

vacillations show what difficulties the teaching on the mandate encountered in the Commission and in the Council itself. It had already been pointed out in the Commission that even Popes and bishops did not always use this expression, and above all not with the same meaning when they did use it. Similarly it was shown that bishops in certain situations, especially under persecution, preferred not to speak in public pronouncements of a mandate.[247] Thus, in spite of contrary voices, circumspect formulations were generally preferred in the text. But even in the aula there were extreme differences of opinion. Many fathers considered the explicit mandate to be precisely the distinguishing feature of Catholic Action, even the foundation of its co-operation with the apostolate of the hierarchy; one *modus* even requested that *potest* here be replaced by *debet*. Others, however, suggested that the whole of the teaching on the mandate should be eliminated.[248] Thus the text again represents a middle course, refraining from essentially theological controversy, and leaves it to the proper authorities whether to decide on an explicit mandate or not. A more precise description of this mandate is indicated only later in Article 24.[249] For the rest, the text seems to presuppose that an implicit mandate is already given in the very admittance of an organization in the *superius moderamen;* it can then be made explicit or not. A suggestion to include the implicit mandate in the sentence referring to the possibility of an explicit mandate was discussed by the Commission as early as 1963 and was expressly rejected by the *relatio* to the printed text of 1965.[250]

The next paragraph asserts the competence of the hierarchy, i. e. the individual bishop or episcopal conference for the diocese and nation and the Pope for the whole Church, to decide which organization possesses simultaneously *(simul)* all four of these characteristic features just named. In fact, for the greatest efficiency in the apostolate it is desirable that the bishops should proceed in a unified fashion within their own nations in this matter at least. One *modus* even wanted to see responsibility in this matter put in the hands of an episcopal conference, a suggestion which had also been made previously in the Commission.[251] Only such organizations would then be considered as Catholic Action, and as regards these four features, this would have certain consequences for the individual organizations themselves as well as for the hierarchy.

Apart from these considerations, the name and forms of such organizations can be adapted to "local and national needs". The unpresuming nature of the name is especially important in the case of organizations in the Anglo-Saxon world. With regard to the form, Pius XI, who had made Catholic Action into a world-wide movement, asserted that it implied no fixed method or structure but was to adapt itself to the circumstances of time and place as far as such adapta-

---

[247] *Acta commissionis conciliaris* (1966), p. 17.

[248] *Textus recogn. et modi,* 106, *modi* 81 ff.

[249] Cf. F. Klostermann, *Das christliche Apostolat,* pp. 641–6.

[250] *Schema decreti* (1965), no. 50; *Acta commissionis conciliaris* (1966), p. 17.

[251] *Textus recogn. et modi,* 107, *modus* 85; *Acta commissionis conciliaris* (1966), p. 177.

tion did not contradict the nature and task of the movement.[252] This has been exemplified in the further development of the movement in Italy and in other countries, though occasionally the Italian model has been too slavishly followed. New and longstanding organizations were integrated into Catholic Action: the *Jeunesse Ouvrière Chrétienne* of Joseph Cardijn on a world-wide basis; or on the national basis the *Legio Mariae*. Thus, in the course of time very different models of Catholic Action were developed: some federated, some unitarian; some general and some specialized; some on the parish level and some on the supra-parochial level; some directed towards universal goals and some towards limited ones, and some, to a greater or lesser degree, with the character of an élite.[253] The Council wished to approve of them all, though there were attempts, as we have already seen, to promote one certain model or one certain method superior to all the others. No dogmatism or monism concerning method will be able to appeal to the Council as its authority.

The Council attempted to present with unusual clarity those elements which (independent of methods, forms, and names, bound to a given time or place) are essential for any genuine Catholic Action. And so the end of a certain stage of development has been reached and the foundation for further stages is laid; and with this the organizational problem has receded into the background.

The decree does not go into any detail with respect to the different types of possible Catholic Action. Earlier versions of the text at least referred to them in notes, especially to the distinction between *Actio Catholica generalis* and *Actio Catholica specializata*, since this was repeatedly requested.[254] In the edition of 1963 there are two notes of one printed page each,[255] the first of which gives a sketch of the historical development of the apostolate of the laity up to the beginning of Catholic Action modelled on Italian lines, the second of which goes into more detail on the subject of the various forms of Catholic Action. In the latter mention is made of the unitarian concept with the four pillars of the natural states; the general and specialized Catholic Action; the federated idea; organizations which do not bear the name of Catholic Action, although they have an explicit mandate; and other similar organizations. In the edition of 1964 the historical notes were omitted and the others were radically abbreviated.[256] In the final text even these abbreviated notes disappeared. The text refuses to commit itself to particular formulations, though many fathers repeatedly desired them. The *relatio* to the text of 1964 explicitly stated that they "did not want to fix what was still in flux nor close any doors for future development".[257]

---

[252] Similarly in the letter of Pius XI to Cardinal Bertram, 13 Nov. 1928: *AAS* 20 (1928), pp. 384–7; similarly, Nuncio Pacelli in an address to the Magdeburg Catholic Conference on 5 Sept. 1928: E. Pacelli, *Erster deutscher Nuntius beim Deutschen Reich, gesammelte Reden ausgewählt und eingeleitet von L. Kaas* (1930), pp. 137–40.

[253] Cf. F. Klostermann, "Katholische Aktion nach dem II. Vatikanum", *loc. cit.*, pp. 309–19.

[254] Thus already in *Schema constitutionis* (1962), Pars II; 10.   [255] *Schema decreti* (1963), no. 35 f.

[256] *Ibid.* (1964), no. 19; similarly *ibid.* (1965), no. 46.   [257] *Ibid.* (1964), no. 28.

How much importance the Council accords to the four characteristic features of Catholic Action, is to be seen from the fact that the last section particularly recommends co-operation between priests and laity in order to increase the further efficacy of such work. This is a public invitation to the Catholic Action groups in various countries to examine their interpretation of their own function and, if need be, to correct it accordingly. If the four characteristics mentioned before were taken seriously as criteria, it would lead to the solution of many problems which have arisen in many countries inside and outside the Catholic Action in connection with the relation between the kingdom of God and the building up of the temporal world, on the evangelization and sanctification of the temporal sphere and the Christian penetration of the temporal order, that is, problems concerning a Church structure in which the Christian can fully integrate all references, including his earthly ones; this involves a new comprehensive and integral Christian concept, the temporal and even the political engagement of Catholic Action in which the laity will have enough freedom of movement with regard to the reform of the Church from within. This also involves a new orientation of Catholic Action in connection with atheism, as well as new criteria for the best way in which to build up the world in general. According to the teaching of Vatican II the worldly activity of the Christian is undoubtedly to be seen in the mission of the Church and therefore to be interpreted as an apostolate, provided that it is carried out in the spirit of the gospel. But he must do this on his own responsibility and not in the name of the Church. On the other hand Catholic Action is a genuine lay apostolate and not merely a form of pastoral assistance in the narrower sense, as a substitute for a hierarchy which is for some reason prevented from carrying out its duties, is restricted in its activity or is even non-existent. Nor can it be an instrument of a new form of integration, which seeks once more to subject the world to clerical rule.

The entire last section was already contained in the first editions of the text,[258] but became a victim of the need to abbreviate.[259] In the discussion of October 1964 it was requested that it be re-incorporated into the text.[260] Apart from the emphasis on the four characteristic features of Catholic Action mentioned above, the section contained an "emphatic" recommendation of the institutions in this category of the common apostolate which "surely answer the needs of the apostolate of the Church among many peoples". Already in the introduction to the four characteristic features it was pointed out that these forms of apostolic activity "exercise an apostolate of great value for our time". One *modus* wished once more the repression of the entire section, while another wished to have Catholic Action expressly mentioned; both were rejected as not corresponding to the intentions of the majority of the fathers. Another *modus* wanted to have a warning added against an improper entanglement in politics. But this *modus*

---

[258] *Schema constitutionis* (1962), Pars II, 12; *Schema decreti* (1963), no. 34.

[259] *Schema decreti* (1964), no. 14f.

[260] *Ibid.* (1965), no. 50, 44f.

was thought to be unnecessary in this connection, and although in itself justified, it was pointed out that its particular concern had been considered in the text on the first characteristic.[261]

The text concludes with an invitation for brotherly co-operation with other forms of the apostolate, which in itself shows that the recommendations made were not intended to favour one particular form of the apostolate and certainly not to lead to a monopoly in this field. The text seems rather to be of the opinion that this type of apostolate has a special place today because of its mediating function and that both laity and the hierarchy should therefore consider whether it might not be introduced in places where it does not yet exist, although a certain receptiveness should at least be visible. Because of its nature as lay activity in the world, Catholic Action can convey directly to the Church the vision and the contribution of the world and can share in the discovery and the proclamation of religious and moral principles. Conversely, by means of its official and ecclesiastical character it can give to the world a vision of the Church and can give to Christians in the world the assistance of the Church by theoretical and methodical formation in the apostolate. Thus it combines both the laymen's ability and knowledge of the world with the work of the shepherd[262] and provides the Church with the possibility of a world-wide strategy that is more urgent than ever in the present social situation.

Article 21. Opposed to any sort of uniformist ideas, this article speaks once again of the proper evaluation of all forms of apostolic associations. In this, however, we can notice a certain order. Those groups which are considered by the hierarchy to be especially modern or appropriate for a given locality or whose work is considered to be especially urgent in given circumstances are especially to be valued and favoured. In an earlier version mention was made of associations "within the diocese and the parish", but the present text keeps to very general remarks and speaks only of interdiocesan and international associations.[263] The latter were expressly included among those groups thought to be most needed today, as is stated in Article 14. This last sentence was only introduced into the text as a result of the discussion in October 1964.[264] One *modus,* representing an extreme "diocesan" point of view, wished to see it omitted, so that nothing "be founded which is outside the jurisdiction of the local hierarchy". Another *modus* wished to replace *hierarchia* with *conferentia episcopalis;* but here as well it was decided to retain the more general expression which can be applied to any sort of association. Some other restrictive proposals were rejected, such as those dealing with associations for the Christianization of the communities of the world or for the advancement of Catholicism and the unity of the Church. What is important for an association to be recommended

[261] *Textus recogn. et modi,* 107 f., *modi* 66–88 and 91.
[262] *Const. dogm. de Ecclesia,* n. 37.
[263] *Schema decreti* (1965), no. 50.
[264] *Ibid.,* no. 51.

by the hierarchy is not so much the evaluation of the explicit goals or theological reasons, but rather its understanding of the present time, as is pointed out in the rejection of such a *modus*.[265] Thus circumstances dictated by time and locality alone can stress the apostolic urgency of any particular type of association.

Article 22, which is the last of this chapter, treats of "those laymen who are especially devoted to the service of the Church". Entirely new categories of ecclesiastical vocation have arisen in the last decades in which the laity, married or single, can place "themselves and their professional skill" at the service of the Church "either permanently or temporarily", that is, at the service of the Church's associations, institutions, or activities either within their own nation or in the international sector, in the missions as well as in regions where the Church has only just been established. This refers primarily to laymen who work in a full-time official capacity in the Church's service within their own country: teachers of religion, teachers in schools of every type, assistants in pastoral care, full-time officials in lay apostolic associations or in the Church administration. But we should also think here of native catechists and helpers, as well as of all kinds of missionary assistants: mission doctors, sisters, and social and development helpers in other lands. The missionary encyclicals of the last Popes testify to the growing importance of these new vocations.[266] A completely new "state" of Christians in the Church is developing, in which they can offer their own special type of service to the Church. We have already remarked that, strictly speaking, we are no longer concerned here with Christians in the world, but with a new category of Christians.

This category of lay Christians in the direct service of the Church brings with it new problems, especially with regard to the hierarchy. The text speaks of "pastors" which we must first of all interpret as meaning the bishops who have the final responsibility for such activity, then the priests under whose immediate authority such work is carried out. What is important here is on the one hand a proper acceptance of such laymen and co-operation in brotherly partnership; the necessary instruction, the spiritual support and encouragement and on the other the corresponding external circumstances. The text speaks not only of the requirements of charity and expediency, but also of justice and of the necessity to provide the appropriate standard of living for lay-workers and their families: often enough they are married and must therefore receive adequate remuneration. Not only the cultural conditions and standard of living in the country to which such laymen are sent, but also that of their homeland should be taken into consideration. As a minimum requirement one must observe the social legislation of the country concerned. Problems will undoubtedly arise from this, but these must be confronted and solved. The words *quam maxime* indicate that due attention

---

[265] *Textus recogn. et modi,* 108 f., *modi* 93–96.
[266] Cf. the encyclical of Pius XII *Evangelii praecones,* of 2 June 1951: *AAS* 43 (1951), pp. 510–17; but especially the encyclical of John XXIII, *Princeps Pastorum,* of 28 Nov. 1959: *AAS* 51 (1959), pp. 848–62.

must be paid to such possibilities. At any rate good will must not be abused; what is owed in all fairness is not to be replaced by charitable gifts. Renunciation of what is justly owed can only proceed from the free choice of him to whom these things are due, and even he is free to do this only in so far as he alone is affected. As the number of laymen engaged in the service of the Church grows, it becomes more and more urgent that these problems be solved. How important these things are for the Church may be seen from the fact that Pius XII referred to them at the Second World Congress for the Apostolate of the Laity: "One should consider that the words of the Lord, 'the worker is worthy of his hire', must apply to the laity as well. We are often amazed to see that people must be reminded at the Mission Congresses for the Lay Apostolate of their duty to give to these assistants the remuneration which is their due. The catechist is often fully occupied with his missionary tasks and consequently he and his family are totally dependent upon the Church for his support. On the other hand the lay apostle must not take it amiss if he is asked not to make any excessive demands upon the mission which supports him."[267]

This article too naturally had a long history. The theme was already to be found among the wishes of the bishops for topics to be dealt with at the Council.[268] In the text two chapters have been compressed together from the first version: Chapter 5 of the first part on "the laity in the special service of the Church" and Chapter 8 of the second part on "the apostolate of the laity in the foreign missions".[269] The two topics were treated together in the edition of 1963,[270] but this text was then abbreviated and included in the chapter on "the preservation of good order"[271] and was then transferred later to the present chapter, as the topic is important for the personal as well as for the common apostolate. A suggested "correction", which wanted to have the laymen involved here referred to as *laici auxiliares,* was rejected.[272] It is worth noting that among the *modi* to this section all those were rejected which wished to tone down the accentuation given to just requirements and adequate payment for families.[273]

---

[267] Address of Pius XII to the Second World Congress for the Apostolate of the Laity, 5 Oct. 1957: *AAS* 49 (1957), p. 927.
[268] *Acta et documenta Concilio oecumenico Vat. II apparando,* Series I, Appendix vol. II, Pars I, p. 569.
[269] *Schemata constitutionum,* Series quarta (1963), pp. 66, 113–17.
[270] *Schema decreti* (1963), no. 20.
[271] See the *Schema decreti* (1964), no. 16.
[272] This was already so in the *Schema decreti* (1965), no. 45, 51.
[273] *Textus recogn. et modi,* 109 f., *modi* 97 and 102.

The Preservation of Good Order

This chapter summarizes everything which concerns the "order of the apostolate" of the laity. In the first version of the decree these references were scattered throughout the text, especially in the general section in separate chapters on "the relation to the hierarchy" (Chapter 2), and on "the task of priests in the apostolate of the laity" (Chapter 3), on "mutual co-ordination" (Chapter 8), as well as in various other places in the special section.[274] The 1963 edition fused the chapters on "the relation to the hierarchy" and on "mutual co-ordination" under the second title of the general section on "the order to be observed in the apostolate", though it also had pertinent articles in other places.[275] It was only the 1964 edition, in which the entire material of the decree was re-ordered, which first attempted to bring everything together in one chapter "de ordine servando", which was to become the fifth. Chapter 6 was only added in the edition of 1965.[276]

The introductory **Article 23** was first added to the text in the edition of 1965, although use was made of material formerly found in other places.[277] The theme which it introduces is the necessary incorporation of all personal and community apostolates of the laity into the one apostolate of the entire Church, to preserve the bond which it already has with the officials of the Church which is called an "essential element of the Christian apostolate", and for the sake of the equally necessary co-operation among the various projects of the apostolate, for the suitable order of which *(congrue ordinanda)* the hierarchy is responsible. When mention is made of the incorporation of the lay apostolate (or better, the organic ingrafting — *insertus esse debet*) into the apostolate of the whole Church, the apostolate of the laity is of course not considered as being distinct from this. On the contrary, it is thought of as being an organic part of it, as the *relatio* explicitly states.[278]

---

[274] Cf. *Schema constitutionis,* 4 Partes (1962).

[275] *Schema decreti* (1963), no. 13–17.

[276] *Ibid.* (1964), no. 15–18.

[277] *Ibid.* (1965), no. 52.

[278] *Textus recogn. et modi,* 115 f., *modus* 3.

The second section more or less gives the reason for this chapter. After the *relatio* of 1964 an episcopal conference wished the text to show that the necessity of such co-ordination was founded especially in the building-up of the one Church.[279] According to the text, the spirit of unity which is called for by our one baptism in the one spirit for the formation of one body (1 Cor 12:13; cf. Eph 4:4f.) requires not only "the community of the spirit" (Col 2:1), brotherly love, attainment of common goals, the avoidance of destructive rivalries between the various forms of the apostolate through due respect for all forms (also mentioned in Article 21), but also "proper co-ordination" between them. Finally, the particular urgency of such co-operation between the apostolic forms is again stressed. As the *relatio* remarked, this second section was added as an answer to those who wished a theological rather than a juridical approach to be adopted.[280] It gives us an indication of the spirit in which the following section and remarks are to be understood, for they are in part of a necessarily juridical cast. The spirit which breathes life into us must be the spirit of unity, of love, and of brotherhood. This brotherhood must above all else "be resplendent in the whole apostolate of the Church". This will keep us from fanaticism, blind or loveless zeal, or want of consideration in the apostolate. It will make us better able to listen to others, to wait, to have patience, to be a true partner in dialogue, to be able to learn from others, and it will teach us as well to have a more human approach in our religious and apostolic communities.

By the hierarchy, to which responsibility for the order of the whole aspostolate is ascribed, we are undoubtedly supposed to understand in the first place the high office-bearers themselves, i. e. the bishops. Their authority will naturally express itself in very different ways, according to the manner of apostolic activity which is concerned, i. e. according to the concrete relationships to the hierarchy which the particular activity demands; for "the lay apostolate admits of different types of relationships with the hierarchy", as the next article asserts. The present article, which does not go into detail in referring to the various grades of relationships, for this reason expresses itself deliberately in a very cautious and general way. First it speaks of only one bond *(coniunctio)* with the hierarchy, then of a co-operation *(cooperatio)* in the various activities which is to be determined by the hierarchy, where the *congrue* already indicates that there are various methods of procedure. And finally it explicitly mentions a co-ordination *(coordinatio)* to which there is again attached not only a qualifying *apta* but also a mention of the particular character of the activity of the work concerned which is to be preserved. The connection of many forms of the personal apostolate with the hierarchy is naturally a very loose one, as is mentioned at the beginning of the article; but as a matter of principle one should not isolate even this apostolate from the one mission of the Church as is revealed in the Lord, as the text rightly asserts. With respect to the task of co-ordination, the hierarchy is to cultivate a

---

[279] *Schema decreti* (1964), no. 55.   [280] *Schema decreti* (1965), no. 57.

special reserve, since they are to have only a supervisory function, which again is restricted to the Church's teaching and its common welfare. Only within the strict requirements of this common welfare, therefore, can the hierarchy exercise an authoritative co-ordinating function; in everything which goes beyond this it can but offer its services, stimulate, and invite. This will determine the future tone, and this is the sense of the *servata uniuscuiusque propria indole*. The treatment of the different *modi* also lay in this direction. Not only were those rejected which wanted to put the stress too narrowly upon "authority", and which wanted to speak only of "the obedience due" instead of the "due respect for the particular character of each organization", but also those which wanted to have freedom and autonomy overstressed too much.[281]

The note refers us to the letter of Pius XI, of 27 October 1935, to the Cardinal Archbishop of Rio de Janeiro and the bishops of Brazil, where he speaks of the greater demands made upon Catholic Action. Errors in this reference had even slipped into the official printed text which appeared after the promulgation (*AAS* 58 [1956], p. 856) referring to the letter as an encyclical though there is no verification of this in the *AAS*, and also dated erroneously with 30 April 1936. The reference is intended to testify to the mutual respect which should be had for all forms of the apostolate in the Church and the efficient co-ordination of all, with the preservation of the special character of each. What is most striking in the letter is an almost military conception of unity and alliance of all the forces involved, the co-ordinating and directing function of Catholic Action as the *acies bene ordinata*. Pius XI could not imagine any association "which had neither any connection nor any association with Catholic Action or, what is even worse, would engage in disputes with those organizations", and he therefore warns against a "dissipation and weakening of Catholic energies". "All energies and all activities are to be so distributed and at the same time so harmoniously organized that each group can fully achieve what it desires without prejudice to the other groups." But whatever is not directly involved in Catholic Action but serves to promote, for example, piety or the social apostolate, should be of service to it in the form of auxiliary assistance. Only within such a unity will the particular nature of the individual members and "army-groups" become fully apparent; within it "there should be no forcing together of the freely budding and blossoming life of the individual parts, but the progressive growth of the members and capacities so that the value and dignity and the proper place of each member may shine forth in the life of the whole". We have intentionally gone into more detail in connection with this note for it points very well not only to the parallelism which was intended, but also to the change in accentuation from a more outward unity conceived in a military sense — this image occurs repeatedly — to one that is more organic, inwardly oriented, differentiated, brotherly, and suffused by one single spirit.

---

[281] *Textus recogn. et modi,* 116 f., *modi* 4 f.; 9; 11 f.

The last paragraph indicates that the incorporation of the apostolate of the laity into the apostolate of the entire Church must result not only in the "unanimity and apostolic co-operation" of the laity among themselves but also in their relations to the secular and religious clergy, and with the religious in general (as was suggested by one *modus*).[282] As there is at bottom only one single apostolate, the mission of the Church which is to be accomplished through all these various different services, this unity is always to be found among all these activities and groups; nevertheless, such unity and co-operation can be particularly expressed in special types of activity.

Article 24 speaks of the various relationships which exist between apostolic activities of different categories and the hierarchy. First those tasks are briefly indicated which concern the hierarchy in general, with respect to the personal and common forms of the lay apostolate. The text first mentions the way in which such activities are to be promoted according to their aims and greatly varying circumstances: recognition and praise for the work which is being achieved; encouragement to carry on in spite of difficulties; the invitation for co-operation in apostolic activities and for their spiritual and material support; personal and financial assistance; the opening of houses, clubrooms, recreation-centres and playgrounds with Church funds. The Church provides the principles *(principia)* for the work of the apostolate of the laity especially by its preaching;[283] this is the light which the laity have the right to expect from their shepherds[284] and which is given to the Church in "the word of God, whether written or handed down".[285] In the light of these principles — the Council repeatedly stresses this — the laity must themselves then proceed in their tasks on their own responsibility, whenever these tasks have to do with things of the world.[286] Even the intellectual and "spiritual helps" *(subsidia spiritualia)* are very different: the proclamation of Christian principles is one such help. It is aided by the co-operation of suitable pastors, presbyters, and deacons acting as general and spiritual counsellors, as theologians, formers of conscience and spiritual companions, as spiritual assistants in apostolic works; for the laity "have the right to expect from their priests light and spiritual strength for their activity".[287] But that formation for the apostolate of which the last chapter in our decree treats, including the foundation for the specific apostolic spirituality, is one of those aids which is mainly a priestly service. Direction of the apostolic activity towards the common good of the Church and supervision with respect to teaching and order are named as being tasks of the hierarchy. Both belong together:

---

[282] *Ibid.,* 117, *modus* 16.
[283] *Const. past. de Eccl. in mundo huius temp.,* n. 41; 43; 76; *Decr. de pastorali episc. munere in eccl.,* n. 12.
[284] *Const. past. de Eccl. in mundo huius temp.,* n. 43; cf. *Decr. de apost. laicorum,* n. 7.
[285] *Const. dogm. de divina revel.,* n. 10; *Const. past. de Eccl. in mundo huius temp.,* n. 33.
[286] *Const. past. de Eccl. in mundo huius temp.,* n. 43.
[287] *Ibid.,* n. 43.

the care for the common good is always the task of authority, and the preservation of "teaching *(doctrina)* and order" is an essential part of the common welfare of the Church. The word *doctrina* was first introduced into the text as the result of a *modus*.[288]

After ascertaining these abiding fundamental relationships of any type of apostolic work to the hierarchy, the text goes on to mention those different relationships which are possible in concrete cases. This variation depends primarily upon the form but also upon the formal and legal type of the apostolic activity concerned, whether it has come into being "by the free choice of the laity" and been maintained as such, as is described in the next paragraph; or whether it is an activity undertaken under the direction of the hierarchy and under its responsibility, regardless of content. It depends therefore on whether an activity is meant to serve some immediate spiritual end or not. But the nature and objects of the activity too as they are enumerated, for instance, at the beginning of Article 19, have a certain influence upon the manner of the relation to the hierarchy, at least in so far as these are not undertaken as activities with directly temporal aims, apart from certain historically conditioned situations. For "Christ, to be sure, gave his Church no proper mission in the political, economic, or social order. The purpose which he set before her is a religious one";[289] indeed, "she must in no way be confused with the political community, nor be bound to any political system".[290]

Next the various types of apostolate are enumerated, according to the extent of their dependency upon the hierarchy. The lowest level is formed by the "many" activities which the laity have created in virtue of that freedom to form associations which was proclaimed in Article 19, and which they also are free to direct since they have never subjected them to the ecclesiastical authority. Laymen have this freedom also with regard to works with directly apostolic goals, as we have already stated and as is clear from the decision of the Conciliar Congregation of 13 November 1920. A *modus* which tried to limit this freedom to works promoting the Christian infusion of the temporal order was explicitly rejected.[291] The decree is careful to state that this independence in no way signifies a lessening of value. The value of such activities will be apparent from their aims and objects, where activities with direct temporal ends are concerned, e. g., cultural, economic, social, or political aims which need be of no lesser apostolic importance since a world ordered in justice and love is also "better prepared for the seed of the word of God", and since the laity in this way "will open wider the Church's doors, through which the message of peace can enter the world".[292] This independence can also be dictated by the external situation, for example,

---

[288] *Textus recogn. et modi,* 118, *modus* 20; cf. F. Klostermann, *Das christliche Apostolat,* pp. 588–624.

[289] *Const. past. de Eccl. in mundo huius temp.,* n. 42.

[290] *Ibid.,* n. 76; cf. n. 40.

[291] *Textus recogn. et modi,* 118, *modus* 23.

[292] *Const. dogm. de Eccl.,* n. 36.

as when the ecclesiastical authority is hindered in its effectiveness and only laymen are able to exercise initiative in certain fields. In such circumstances the mission of the Church can be better fulfilled through completely spontaneous activities and initiative, and indeed it may be that it can be fulfilled only in this way.

Because of the apostolic importance of such spontaneous works, whether they pursue immediate apostolic goals or are only directed towards the Christian infusion or penetration of the temporal order,[293] they are "frequently praised and recommended by the hierarchy". One can easily detect the language of the *CIC* in this "associationes . . . saltem commendatae" (can. 684). Such praise or recommendation, however, has no consequences in Church law; nor does it normally follow that each bishop in his diocese or each pastor in his parish must establish or promote such works and associations, nor is every good Christian obliged to become a member to offer his services to such works. What it means is only that the faithful may join such groups with a good conscience, knowing that they are serving a good cause.

The nomenclature gives rise to certain difficulties here. The decision of the conciliar congregation quoted and other documents as well give this type of association the expression *societates laicae* which is immediately defined further as *id est non ecclesiasticae*. But this name no longer corresponds to Vatican II's concept of the Church, since it might easily be thought to imply that the laity do not fully belong to the Church or that these associations have nothing at all to do with the Church and her authority. It might also be thought that the opposite of such groups, *associationes ecclesiasticae*, were exclusively composed of clerics or directed solely by them (as is presupposed by can. 698, for instance). In view of the broad concept of the apostolate used by Vatican II, according to which the Christian influence upon the temporal order is considered to be an apostolate and part of the mission of the Church in the world,[294] one must be able to designate such groups and works as being in a certain sense "ecclesiastical", though in an unofficial manner, if one wishes to go beyond such a general manner of speaking as is "recommended by the Church".[295] The words "in ecclesia" at the beginning of this section indicate the "ecclesiastical" character of such works; indeed, when one *modus* wished to have the phrase "in the Church" eliminated because "it has no juridical status in the Church", the Commission answered that they can be "in the Church without special juridical status".[296] The expression used occasionally by canonists,[297] "private associations" goes in the same direction, for "private" is used in the sense of being distinct from official rather than from public groups. All other expressions such as "free associations", "Catholic

[293] Article 19.
[294] Cf. Articles 2; 5; 7; 19.
[295] Cf. F. Klostermann, *Das christliche Apostolat*, pp. 829–42.
[296] *Textus recogn. et modi*, 118, *modus* 22.
[297] Thus E. Eichmann and K. Mörsdorf, *Lehrbuch des Kirchenrechtes*, I (9th ed., 1959), p. 557.

associations", etc., are thus not to be recommended because of their ambiguity in this connection.

The above-mentioned minimal requirements of a supervision of teaching and order for the common good of the Church must be demanded for this whole group of apostolic works and associations because of their relationship to the hierarchy. But beyond this they are to be considered as *autonomae,* even after the decision of the conciliar congregation quoted in the letter to the Bishop of Corrientes in the Argentine. Strictly speaking, one cannot refer here to a dependency upon the hierarchy but only to a relationship with the hierarchy. Even in the suggested corrections,[298] as well as in the *modi* handed in at the discussion in October 1964,[299] there were the most contradictory opinions: one group thought that the laity were given too much freedom and wanted more stress on the leading authority of the hierarchy and texts that would emphasize the directives *(praecepta)* of the hierarchy; the other group thought that the freedom of the laity was threatened even in this text. Nevertheless, because of these discussions the text was actually toned down even more.[300] The Commission refused to accept those *modi* which represented either extreme, but it was especially vigorous in rejecting those wishing to limit lay freedom, since they were contrary to the wishes of the majority of the fathers.[301]

The concluding sentence is significant in that it demands the approval of the appropriate ecclesiastical authority for the inclusion of the word "Catholic" in such nomenclature. In all versions of the text, including the one which was presented for the vote and the presentation of *modi,* mention was made of "inclusive or explicit approval". Suggestions, and even *modi,* which wished to have the "inclusive" or even both adjectives omitted were not accepted.[302] In the text which was voted on, however, both additions were left out as was requested in the 12 changes proposed "at the last minute": *per non dar ansa a possibili interpretazioni abusive.* The printed text with both *variationes* in Articles 12 and 24 gives as the reason for this what was already given as the reason for the rejection of the elimination of: *ne ansa detur interpretationibus non desideratis — mutatio interpretationibus non desideratis faveret.* The elimination of the passage was undoubtedly meant to stress the competence of the hierarchy; but the situation had hardly been changed because of this. For even now the hierarchy could hardly be prevented from satisfying themselves with an implicit approval.

Likewise the question as to what manner of works this approval refers to can hardly give rise to serious difficulties. The whole section, to be sure, concerns itself with "apostolic works" *(incepta apostolica).* Nevertheless, one cannot limit the *nullum inceptum* to apostolic works. The very use of the word *autem*

---

[298] *Schema decreti* (1965), no. 57.
[299] *Textus recogn. et modi,* 117 f.
[300] *Schema decreti* (1965), no. 52.
[301] *Textus recogn. et modi,* 117 f., *modi* 17 f.
[302] *Ibid.,* 119, *modus* 26; cf. *Schema decreti* (1964), no. 1; *Schema decreti* (1965), no. 57.

in this sentence facilitates such an interpretation, but even more the sense and the inner justification of the whole definition. This justification is derived from the fact that a work that calls itself publicly "Catholic" lays claim to a certain "churchliness" and thus in a way involves the Church at the same time. The danger of such involvement is in general much greater with non-apostolic works with purely temporal aims than it is with works which are by nature apostolic. Thus, it would be better for organizations which represent the interests of special groups, e. g. political parties or business groups, not to use the name Catholic in order to avoid identifying the Church with these particular interests. The same arguments would apply for not using the word "Christian" in similar connections.

The definition is itself not entirely new. The Secretary of State had already in 1955 requested the approval of the Apostolic See for international Catholic organizations and had forbidden Catholics and Catholic groups to enter those organizations which were not given this approval.[303] Similar decisions were made by the Austrian Bishops' Conference in 1958 and 1959 for Austria,[304] which were at least provisionally covered by the Apostolic Nuncio in Vienna in 1955 — without prejudicing later decisions from Rome; the competence of the Church is expressly stated.[305]

Another level in these different types of relationship between laity and hierarchy is represented by those apostolic forms recognized "expressly by the hierarchy *(explicite agnoscuntur)* even though it be in different ways". The formulation here had changed very greatly in the course of the history of the text, and it is necessary to know something of this history in order to realize fully what is meant here. In the first version of the text there was a single article which spoke of "apostolic undertakings" which "are established by the hierarchy *(eriguntur),* or those which have been given only its approbation or praise *(simplici probatione vel etiam laude donantur)*".[306] In the 1963 version of the text in one single article having the title "Approbatio vel Laus", it was asserted that "certain forms of the apostolate have been established or approved *(instituuntur vel agnoscuntur)* by the hierarchy up to the present" — evidently forming one category — "or recommended by the hierarchy *(aut commendantur)*" — obviously another category.[307] In the 1964 version the passage on the works which have been praised or recommended had been joined to the section on the works which have come into being through the free initiative of the laity; the section with which we are now concerned only mentioned certain forms of the apostolate which "were recognized by Church law *(a iure ecclesiae recognoscuntur)*".[308] As the result of a recommendation made

---

[303] Letter of the Secretary of State to Ordinaries, 27. 6. 1955, n. 232707; Nuntiatura Apostolica Vienna, 28. 8. 1955, n. 12355.

[304] Records of the Austrian Bishops' Conference, 18/19 Feb. 1958 and 16/17 March 1959.

[305] Nuntiatura Apostolica, Vienna 7 Feb. 1955, n. 11579.

[306] *Schema Constitutionis* (1962), Pars I, n. 13.

[307] *Schema decreti* (1963), p. 13.   [308] *Schema decreti* (1964), no. 16.

during the discussion in October 1964 the *a iure* was eliminated as being superfluous, though the phrase "in different ways" was added in its place.[309] A *modus* then recommended that instead of the undoubtedly ambiguous verb *agnoscuntur* the phrase *approbantur vel eriguntur* again be used. But the *modus* was rejected since "it was the intention to avoid an overly juridical manner of speaking".[310] A different *modus* which applied the text to Catholic Action thought that it was superfluous since this point had already been treated; but this too was rejected, not because the text did not refer to Catholic Action, but because it was not thought to be a mere repetition but rather a further clarification.[311]

Because of all this and also because of the treatment of the *modi,* it is clear that this passage refers to works and associations which up to now have been called "ecclesiastical" *(ecclesiasticae)* associations, or, as the *relatio* of the conciliar congregation said when quoting the decision of that Congregation, "those of strictly ecclesiastical character", among which are also to be included the organizations and works of Catholic Action. Moreover, the whole passage would be superfluous if it were taken to refer only to inofficial works and associations. Thus, in so far as we are treating of associations we are in fact dealing with that group of associations which are meant in can. 696, who owe their existence to establishment by the hierarchy. According to can. 686 § 1 this can be done in two ways: "by institution *(erecta)* or at least by approbation *(saltem approbata)*"; only these groups can be counted among the ones "recognized in the Church", though greater clarity would have been gained by using the "recognized by Church law" from the 1964 version.[312] This is the sense which must be given to the expression used in can. 479 § 2, *legitimae associationes.* As opposed to private or unofficial organizations of the Church, one could also speak here of official ecclesiastical organizations. This expression is also to be found in ecclesiastical documents. Thus Pius XII says: "Catholic Action always has the character of an official apostolate of the laity";[313] and Cardinal Gracias, at the First World Congress for the Apostolate of the Laity, speaks of an "official or institutional apostolate".[314]

The text wishes to stress the fact that official recognition can come about in "various ways". This refers primarily to the *erectio* and *approbatio* of can. 686 § 1 already mentioned, depending upon whether it was brought about through the initiative of the hierarchy or not. For there can be associations which have first come into being through private initiative, and which might at first have been unofficial associations which were then given official recognition subsequently, i. e. were formally established or approved. Their statutes must then be examined

---

[309] *Schema decreti* (1965), no. 57.

[310] *Textus recognitus et modi,* 119, *modus* 29.

[311] *Ibid.,* 119, *modus* 28. [312] *Schema decreti* (1964), no. 16.

[313] Address of Pius XII to the Second World Congress for the Apostolate of the Laity, 5. 10. 1957: *AAS* 49 (1959), p. 929; cf. nn. 240f.

[314] *Actes du Congrès Mondial pour l' Apostolat des laïques,* I (1952), p. 178.

according to canon law by the Holy See or by a competent diocesan authority in charge of such matters and they can only be changed thereafter with the approval of the ecclesiastical authorities (can. 689). They are then exclusively under the authority of the Church's jurisdiction and visitation (can. 250 § 2; pp. 686–725)[315] with respect to statutes, direction, and administration. Among those differences mentioned one should also include the differences in the types of association which fall under the category referred to in this place. Pius XII has stated, as we have already mentioned, that Catholic Action always belongs to the official apostolate of the laity; indeed, on the same occasion he speaks of "the apostolate of the laity in the proper sense", which "for the most part is organized in Catholic Action groups and in other institutions of apostolic aims approved by the Church (approuvées; cf. can. 686 § 1)."[316] As opposed to the inofficial ecclesiastical organizations, the works and associations spoken of here are limited also by their goals to those which correspond to the nature and the direct mission of the Church herself, and thus to those which do not follow purely temporal aims (charitable works are included here),[317] although this qualification is only made explicit in the following section: "associations and projects which have an immediately spiritual purpose".[318]

Among these associations and works with immediate spiritual purposes which are explicitly recognized by Church law, another class is singled out, which has an even closer bond to the hierarchy and its "apostolic function". Among the notes to the 1963 printed text there is, by the way, an explicit reference to a mandate only in connection with the apostolic works which have an immediate spiritual goal, since the hierarchy has no authority in the purely temporal order nor responsibility for the activity of laymen in this order.[319]

In the very choice of these works the hierarchy has the exclusive initiative, and in this the common welfare of the Church is to be the deciding factor, since this alone can justify such a close relation to the hierarchy, though at the same time it means a greater limitation of the freedom of the laity concerned and especially of those engaged in the direction of such works, of course without prejudice to the original free choice of those involved. It is immediately noted, however, that in spite of the close connection of these forms of the apostolate with the apostolic office the proper nature and individuality of these apostolates should be respected. One should think in this connection of those characteristics enumerated in Article 20, among which the activity of the layman "on his own responsibility" is especially singled out. Therefore whoever understands these forms of the apostolate only as the carrying out of the directives of the hierarchy has misunder-

---

[315] Cf. F. Klostermann, *Das christliche Apostolat,* pp. 843–53.
[316] Address of Pius XII, 14 Oct. 1951: *AAS* 43 (1951), pp. 787, 789; similar the address of Pius XII, 5 Oct. 1957: *AAS* 49 (1957), pp. 925, 929.
[317] Cf. Article 8.
[318] The same reservation in E. Eichmann and K. Mörsdorf, *Lehrbuch des Kirchenrechtes,* I, p. 558.
[319] *Schema decreti* (1963), no. 17.

stood them from the very start. "This act of the hierarchy" brings with it the acceptance of a special responsibility for such works and their particular promotion through the hierarchy, which is understandable from the fact that every act can only be undertaken for reasons of the common good of the Church.

Finally, it is pointed out as a fact that "in various ecclesiastical documents" this act is called a mandate, though the decree goes no further into the nature of such a mandate nor into its juridical consequences, and certainly not into any theories upon the subject. The *relatio* of 1965 even states explicitly that the text does not want to settle controversies.[320] After all this one can safely say that the mandate for apostolic works and associations referred to here in no way confers participation in the prerogatives of the hierarchy with regard to ordination and spiritual guidance. Nor does it give members a *missio canonica,* as the text goes on to say. But it does preserve their full lay character.[321] One would not do justice to the nature of the mandate if one interpreted it in an overly strict juridical sense as being similar to a mandate contracted by civil law or an ecclesiastical legal delegation (can. 197; p. 203 § 1). The mandate does not directly concern individuals but only associations and works; it confers that special relation to the hierarchical office and the special responsibility on the part of the hierarchy already mentioned. This can come about in an explicit way; but in certain circumstances it might be more prudent not to speak of a mandate at all but instead to create facts which show that such a mandate is concretely in force.[322]

Since the hierarchy can confer such an explicit mandate without further ado upon Catholic Action groups, according to Article 20, it is clear that the conditions required by such a mandate must have been fulfilled, which a comparison with the section on the four characteristics of such action will confirm. The *specialis responsabilitas* which is not directly referred to in Article 20, is undoubtedly included in the *actio et directa cooperatio cum apostolatu hierarchico* and in the *superius moderamen.* There is thus no contradiction between this text and the sentence referring to the mandate in Article 20, as was feared in one *modus.*[323] The present text only asserts what in fact is to be found in ecclesiastical documents; Article 20 speaks about the possibility of the ecclesiastical hierarchy conferring an explicit mandate.

This section also has its history. In the texts of the years 1963 and 1964 there is a detailed explanatory note which speaks of a *specialis directio et responsabilitas* of the hierarchy and of a conferral of its mission *(suam missionem ei impertit), sic integrans apostolatum laicorum apostolatui Hierarchiae velut unum continuum cum eo.* In the 1964 text the *directio* had already been struck out. In the same note to the 1963 text this integration of the apostolate of the laity into that of the hierarchy

---

[320] *Ibid.* (1965), no. 57.
[321] Cf. ref. to mandate in address of Pius XII, 5 Oct. 1957: *AAS* 49 (1957), pp. 925, 928, and F. Klostermann, *Das christliche Apostolat,* pp. 641–6.
[322] Ibid., p. 643 (n. 3); 646 (n. 9).
[323] *Textus recognitus et modi,* 106f., *modus* 83.

"exercises by necessity that minimum of direction without which it could not take upon itself the responsibility for the activity of the laymen though for the rest it leaves the laity the greatest freedom in their apostolate. The laity again are to strive so to make their activities which they have freely chosen correspond to the spirit of the hierarchy in order that its apostolate might itself be a true complement *(complementum)* to the apostolate of the hierarchy."[324] The text of 1965 offers several explanatory corrections; the notes on the mandate were eliminated altogether because of various ambiguities.[325] The *relatio* of the 1964 text reported on the divergent *vota* of the fathers. While some wished to have all the passages referring to the mandate eliminated because they were completely vague both terminologically and theologically, since "every baptized person already has a mandate for the apostolate in dependence upon his bishop", others wished to see this teaching dilated upon even more.[326] In view of this situation the Commission held to the text except for very few minor changes. Even individual *modi* tried to have the text changed in the most varied directions: one thought the limitation to works with immediate spiritual goals to be an unacceptable limitation of the field of the apostolate and of Catholic Action; two fathers wanted the whole section struck out as an encroachment upon the freedom and equality of the laity and one desired that the sentence concerning the mandate be dropped. Other reservations, on the other hand, thought that "the possibility of the laity acting on their own responsibility" was extremely dangerous and wanted the passage eliminated or the *sua sponte* replaced by the colourless *per seipsos* or *directe*. The Commission was obliged to reject all of these reservations because they were not desired by the majority of the fathers and because they were contradictory to the teaching given in the chapter on the laity in the Constitution on the Church.[327]

Finally, the text speaks again of another form of the apostolate with an even closer connection of the laity with pastoral offices *(officiis)* — earlier it was "of the hierarchy"; "pastoral" here refers not only to the office of the bishop, but also of the priests and in certain circumstances of the deacons. In this work "certain tasks" *(munia quaedam)* are entrusted to the laity on the basis of a mission on the part of the hierarchy; at the end of this section the somewhat stronger word *munus* is used, which can also mean "service" or even "office". Examples of such tasks include religious instruction, the liturgy, and pastoral care. Evidently in contrast to the category named above, mention is made here only of laity "fully subject to higher ecclesiastical direction in the performance of such work" *(plene subduntur superiori ecclesiasticae moderationi)*.

We must again consider the history behind the present version of the text to understand it fully. In the first version of the text there was mention only of a

---

[324] *Schema decreti* (1963), no. 17; cf. *Schema decreti* (1964), no. 20.
[325] *Ibid.* (1965), no. 53, 57.
[326] *Ibid.* (1964), no. 51 f.
[327] *Textus recognitus et modi,* 119, *modi* pp. 30 ff. Cf. *Const. dogm. de Eccl.,* no. 33.

missio canonica, by virtue of which the laity partake in the hierarchical apostolate *(hierarchicum apostolatum quodammodo participant).* After mentioning the complete subjection to the ecclesiastical direction the text again stated that the apostolate of the laity in the Church was thereby made official *(officialis in ecclesia evadit).*[328]

The edition of 1963 used basically the same text *(ipsius Hierarchiae apostolatum suo modo participant);* the concrete fields of this mission are enumerated in a note, where they are more fully described. As liturgical acts such duties are mentioned as are to be carried out by those in lower orders, such as the sacristans or acolytes; further concessions are made in the mission-field as well as for the celebration of the Eucharist in times of persecution. With respect to the proclamation of the word, reference is made to can. 1333 § 1 and to catechists in the missions. Also in connection with pastoral care reference is made to the catechists in the missions who must take over practically all of the pastoral functions for which ordination is not required. There are also emergency-situations in Catholic countries. In conclusion, the text mentions the administration of temporal ecclesiastical goods, where lay administrators are to be preferred to the clergy because of their greater competence, whereby they can free the clergy for directly spiritual tasks. As to the nature of this *missio canonica,* it is said to confer offices *(munera)* upon the laity which usually belong to the clergy, but that it does not confer either the power of ordination or spiritual guidance; the laity would have to be engaged because of a lack of priests or because of their greater competence in such matters. They are thus conceived of as instruments of ecclesiastical authority. This is truly a participation *(participatio)* in the hierarchical apostolate and is therefore wholly dependent upon the delegating authority. This activity is hence called an apostolate of the laity, not *ratione obiecti,* but only *ratione subiecti,* since it is exercised by the laity. Therein lies the difference, as the same note points out, between this type of relation and the mandate spoken of in the previous section: by a mandate the hierarchy binds the apostolic activity of the laity to itself so that the laity do not only act in their own name (which they could always do), but also in the name of the ecclesiastical authority and in conjunction with it. By the *missio canonica* clerical actions *(actus clericales)* are entrusted to the laity for which they have no special competence.[329]

Similarly, the 1964 text speaks still of a *missio canonica* and again even names some of the tasks which are included in it. The notes are somewhat abbreviated; strangely enough nothing is mentioned about administration in the notes or in the text,[330] and the reason given was that "the Commission did not think it opportune" to speak of "the administration of the temporal goods of the Church".[331] The passage "munia . . . quae proprie ad ipsam Hierarchiam pertinent" was changed to "quae propius cum officiis Hierarchiae cohaerent". The rec-

---

[328] *Schema constitutionis* (1962), Pars I, n. 11.
[329] *Schema decreti* (1963), no. 16f.
[330] *Ibid.* (1964), no. 16, 20.
[331] *Ibid.,* no. 52.

ommendation "quae membris ecclesiae ex se non competunt" was rejected. Another recommendation from an episcopal conference was rejected, which wished to replace "participatio laicorum apostolatus hierarchici" with "co-operatio specialis et officialis", since "the *missio cononica* does in fact confer a *participatio*". A sentence from the 1963 edition already contradicted this: "eorum apostolatus officialis in ecclesia fit" — through the *missio canonica* — since "every apostolate on the basis of the mandate contained in the sacrament of confirmation can in a certain sense already be called 'official'".[332] But there can, indeed, be differing opinions as to the validity of this reasoning.

The 1965 text speaks only of a *missio*, "in order not to enter into canonistic controversies"; also the passage about a "participation *suo modo* in the apostolate of the hierarchy itself" was deleted. Instead of the expression "the proclamation of the word" the much wider expression "the requirements of Christian teaching" is used, which can be applied to the teaching office in secondary schools and universities, i. e. to the theological teaching-office. Both the note on the *missio canonica* and the one on the mandate were omitted.[333]

From the entire history of the text it is perfectly clear that what is meant here is not only the official conferral of certain tasks, but also proper offices which are mainly held by members of the hierarchy and fall within their sphere of competence, but for the carrying out of which no ecclesiastical ordination or divine commission to administer spiritual guidance is necessary. They may thus be conferred upon laymen too without changing their lay status. While normally the mandate only concerns tasks which the laity can carry out anyway, but which they now perform in conjunction with the ecclesiastical authority, on the basis of their mandate, they may also perform tasks on the basis of this mission which they would not be justified to perform without such a mission. We are dealing here with a *missio specialis,* therefore, or it could also be called a special mandate bound to a special mission of this type.

To this belongs not only the official teaching authority, which one ordinarily calls the *missio canonica,* but also the conferment of ecclesiastical "offices in the broader sense" or any other special tasks — all those things for the exercise of which neither ordination to law nor an official pastoral mandate is necessary and which according to the present canon law, can already be conferred upon the laity.[334] The tasks involved here are not only catechetical instruction for children but also preaching to adults, preaching in the course of those non-liturgical divine services which do not require the presence of a priest and sometimes the function of preaching in other types of divine service. To offices in the broader sense there also belong managerial positions in ecclesiastical action-groups and associations, e. g. in Catholic Action, in Church administration, pastoral tasks, etc. It should be considered whether in revising can. 118

---

[332] *Ibid.,* pp. 52 f.

[333] *Schema decreti* (1965), no. 53, 58.

[334] Cf. F. Klostermann, *Das christliche Apostolat,* pp. 655–8.

the exercise of genuine jurisdictional powers might not on occasion be delegated to laymen, e. g. in legal cases. It should be a general rule in the Church that ecclesiastical offices which can be carried out by laymen equally well or even better than by the clergy should in fact be conferred upon them. The Council has undoubtedly given many impulses in this direction. The employment of laymen in post-conciliar commissions, the announced intention of summoning lay-consultors to the Roman dicasteries are promising beginnings. Mention was also made of the employment of laymen in the diplomatic service of the Vatican, and as representatives of the Church at important international meetings.

From all that has been said we can understand what is meant by the perhaps unfortunate expression "wholly subject *(plene subduntur)* to higher ecclesiastical direction". *Superius moderatio* means nothing more than the *superius moderamen* of Article 20.[335] And so the hierarchy should restrict itself here as well to the very highest positions, corresponding to the nature of the *missio* concerned. The word "fully" is intended to stress the difference from the usual sort of mandate: not only are the relations of lay activities to the apostolate in themselves here described but also the right to organize such activities, which proceeds from the hierarchy. For the rest, it very much depends upon the nature of the *missio* how these relationships will appear in concrete cases. A diplomat, for instance, will most often be much more closely bound to his mission than will a leader of youth groups, the president of a Catholic Action group, or a teacher of theology. A professional knowledge will often be required for the exercise of such offices which is not necessarily to be expected of the hierarchy. It would be a great misunderstanding if, for example, a lay catechist under the authority of the Church were given less freedom in his classes and methods of instruction than any other sort of teacher. It is significant that the Pastoral Constitution on the Church in the Modern World mentions precisely in connection with the need of giving laymen the opportunity to take up theological studies and research, the "adhering to the methods and requirements proper to theology" and the "application of scientific aims" as well as to the "lawful freedom of inquiry and of thought and the freedom to express their opinion in all those matters in which laymen enjoy competence".[336] Up to now the different forms of the apostolate have been treated simply according to the extent of their relationship to the hierarchy, i. e. according to the degree of their dependence upon it. In the main activities were considered which, for the most part, pursued immediate spiritual aims, apart from unofficial associations. The last section treats of the tasks of the hierarchy in relation to organizations which have direct spiritual aims for which the ecclesiastical authority has no direct responsibility. This text was included in this article only in the 1964 version at the express wish of the fathers. The *relatio* of 1965 explicitly states that the passage which was originally at the beginning of the article was put to the end,

---

[335] Cf. Article 20.
[336] *Const. past. de Ecclesia in mundo huius temporis,* n. 62.

in order to point out more effectively the different types of competence which the hierarchy has in the religious and temporal order.

This section gives in greater detail what was already briefly sketched by Article 7: the hierarchy is responsible for preaching the authentic interpretation of the moral principles necessary for right actions, they are to judge whether such activities and institutions conform to these moral principles, — i. e. in the temporal order and with reference to temporal goods — and they are also to decide what is necessary for the protection and the promotion of supernatural values since the Church cannot live as a Church in the midst of the world without a certain degree of worldliness and the use of worldly means (cf. can. 1495 f.; 1499).

To this also belongs an account of the scope necessary for the activities of the Church. The Church today no longer places her hope in state privileges: she is, as the Pastoral Constitution on the Church in the Modern World says, ready to renounce these in order to prove the purity of her mission.[337] The one thing which she demands is "the freedom to believe and to proclaim her faith; the freedom to love her God; the freedom to live and to proclaim the gospel of life to other men".[338] In connection with the duty of judging whether temporal institutions conform to moral principles and the extent to which the Church must use temporal aid, we are to exercise "careful consideration" and "consultation with experts", since in these matters she has special need of worldly knowledge and experience. From this alone it is clear that laymen are meant to be included in such work. The laity themselves can also help in the formation of Christian principles, as was stated already in Article 6. Just as in Article 7, so also here, the hierarchy are to restrict themselves to their "main" spiritual tasks; in the temporal sphere itself they enjoy no competence. The present formulation was the result of a reservation which feared a misunderstanding that the hierarchy is to have such competence in worldly affairs as well (e. g. in politics); the text previously read "ad ea (principia) applicanda".[339]

Article 25 was originally a separate chapter with 9 articles, titled "On the Duties of Priests in the Apostolate of the Laity".[340] The present text speaks only in general terms of the assistance of the clergy in this apostolate. Strictly speaking, it does not fit at all into a chapter on the order to be preserved in the apostolate of the laity. First of all two things are recommended to the consideration of bishops, pastors, and even the entire secular and religious clergy: the fact that the right and duty to exercise the apostolate is something common to all the faithful and the special role which the laity are to have in the building up of the Church, which is here to be equated simply with the apostolate. For the Church is built up by evangelization and sanctification, but indirectly it is substantially promoted as well by the Christian transformation of the temporal order. The address of Pius XII at the Second World Congress for the Apostolate of the

---

[337] *Ibid.,* n. 76.   [338] Conciliar message to heads of government: *AAS* 58 (1966), pp. 10 f.

[339] *Textus recognitus et modi,* 120, *modus* 36.

[340] Schema constitutionis (1962), Pars I, Cap. III.

Laity referred to in the notes, stresses the proper share which the laity are to exercise in this building-up and the freedom and self-responsibility which they are to enjoy in the *consecratio mundi*. In general terms he says: "The laity should be entrusted with those tasks which they could execute as equally well as or even better than the priest." Because of this common nature of the whole apostolate and its unity, bishops and pastors and the whole clergy are to work together with the laity in brotherly (!) co-operation. From the consideration of the specific nature of the apostolic task of the laity we should go on to consider the special concern *(specialis cura)* which the laity should have for it. The notes refer to Article 37 of the Constitution on the Church where it speaks of the mutual relationships between laity and pastors through which they are able to assist each other and which they owe to each other. A large part of this article stems from the 1963 draft of the Decree on the Laity, as is noted in the textual draft of 1964.[341]

The second section deals with priests who are to help in promoting special forms of the apostolate of the laity and who are to be at the disposal of such apostolic groups either as their main task or as an auxiliary task. Article 17 of the first textual edition particularly mentions the "local, especially diocesan, and national as well as international undertakings".[342] The priests are to be formed for this work with care and they should be well suited for their particular task. General qualities, both natural and spiritual, should play a large role in determining appointments for this work. The note refers us to the apostolic exhortation of Pius XII to the clergy on the holiness which is required of the priestly life. The prerequisites for such tasks will of course be very different, according to whether the particular form of the apostolate deals with children, youth, adults, men, women, workers, intellectuals, or artists. They must nevertheless all "adhere faithfully to the spirit and the teaching of the Church", which will be referred to again. This duty to choose and properly educate priests in the early years of their formation is the duty especially of the ecclesiastical authority. And in this formation they must make use of the "brotherly" counsel of responsible laymen who occupy leading positions in the form of the apostolate concerned, as is said in Article 37 of the Constitution on the Church. As the *relatio* of 1965 recounted, the *episcopi seligant* was changed at the wish of several fathers to the more general *seligantur* in order to leave open the possibility of allowing clerical assistants to be elected, as is already the practice in several associations.[343] With respect to this formation, a *modus* from 9 fathers wanted to see special institutes immediately recommended; but it was rejected on the grounds that it went too much into detail. The suggestion was, nevertheless, referred to the episcopal conferences.[344] Only under such conditions can priestly helpers fulfil their functions as will now be described.

---

[341] Cf. commentary on Article 37 of the Dogmatic Constitution on the Church in vol. I of this work.

[342] *Schema constitutionis* (1962), Pars I, n. 17.

[343] *Schema decreti* (1965), no. 58.   [344] *Textus recognitus et modi*, 122, *modus* 48.

These functions are summarized first in a general way as a service *(ministerium)* and as pastoral activity *(actio pastoralis)*, and this already indicates how these are to be carried out (cf. Lk 22:25 ff.; Jn 13:13–16), though the boundaries of such a ministry are also indicated. The pastoral ministry is then more precisely described: on the basis of their mission these priests represent the hierarchy and thus they must learn to see things in the perspective of this mission and not to substitute their own private opinions under the cloak of hierarchical authority. Within the framework of this "representation" the priests are the interpreters of the directions of the bishops, they are to preach the Church's doctrine, form consciences, and be spiritual leaders *(adsint)*. They should also strive to further good relations between the laity and the hierarchy, "always adhering faithfully to the spirit and teaching of the Church". They should cultivate the spiritual life and the apostolic mentality of the associations entrusted to them; but they should also act as brotherly counsellors in promoting the apostolic initiative and activities of such groups. Finally, they are to search for those ways which can make the apostolic work more fruitful through "continuous dialogue with the laity" and promote the spirit of unity both inside and outside these associations. Here again we can see that the priests are limited to their proper duty as spiritual helpers and counsellors in the pastoral ministry.[345]

While religious clergy are already explicitly included in the first sentence of the article referring to the clergy in general, religious (including nuns) are again mentioned especially in the last section. The decree expects from them at least appreciation of apostolic works and, where possible, also assistance in such activity, naturally according to the spirit and norms of their particular communities. It is significant that "the spirit" is here given first place. The note refers to Article 8 of the Decree on the Religious which treats of the apostolic character of the more "active" communities and of the necessary agreement of their "observances and customs with the demands of the apostolate" and with its specific character.[346] The tasks recommended as being proper to them are the support, furtherance, and complementing of priestly functions, all of which are to be expected by virtue of the essential unity of the Christian apostolate. Concretely one must consider the types of personal and material assistance which can be given according to the possibilities available: the use of materials and men, assistance in children's and youth-groups, in work with adults, in the work of formation, in spiritual consolation. The orders which are entrusted with education are to be concerned especially with making their schools schools for the apostolate. It is remarkable into how much concrete detail the various ecclesiastical documents go here.[347]

[345] Cf. address of Pius XII to members of the Italian Catholic Action, 3 May 1951: *AAS* 32 (1951), p. 37.

[346] *Decretum de accommodata renovatione vitae religiosae,* n. 8. Reference could also have been made to n. 2c.

[347] Cf. F. Klostermann, *Das christliche Apostolat,* pp. 691–4.

The text was greatly improved by the discussions of October 1964: its previous paternalistic tone disappeared with the addition of the element of brotherliness and dialogue. Many wishes with regard to the formation of priests had to be referred to the schema on the Ministry and Life of Priests and the schema on Priestly Formation.[348] Several *modi* attempted in vain to have the old paternalistic, hierarchical tone restored, even to the extent of wishing to replace the word *fraterne* with *paterne*.[349]

Article 26 corresponds to an earlier chapter "on mutual co-ordination", which comprised 4 articles.[350] The only part which was retained in the 1964 edition was Article 20, which dealt only with "mutual co-operation" as its title indicated, thus taking into account more the freedom and the autonomy of individual apostolic works.[351] In the 1965 text Article 26 was already headed "various means for achieving mutual co-operation *(cooperatione inservientibus)*".[352]

Since the first two sections of what was once Article 20 in the 1964 text have been incorporated into the introductory Article 23 of the present text, the first section of this article treats of the diocesan councils which are to be established. The qualifying phrase *in quantum fieri potest* was added only as the result of a *modus,* and is meant to indicate the various levels which exist in diocesan work.[353] The goal of these councils is to assist in the apostolic work of the Church in every direct and indirect apostolic sphere. The expression *concilia* also indicates an advisory capacity towards the bishop as is expressly stated in the last sentence of the section. We should consider first of all the mere advisory function of this council in relation to the various works which are carried out within the diocese. This is indicated in the next sentence, which stresses not only the protection of the proper character and autonomy of each organization but which also expresses, somewhat cautiously, a hope that these councils will eventually "be able to promote" the mutual co-ordination of apostolic groups, i.e. that they will be able to provide a helpful basis for voluntary co-ordination, though they will also offer a good opportunity for the ecclesiastical authority to form a plan or a model for the possibly necessary authoritative co-ordination for the common welfare of the Church. It will also give the Church authority the chance to stimulate and, if absolutely necessary, also to issue directives to such groups.

The chief members of these councils according to the last formulations[354] would appear to be laymen, with whom clerics and religious are to co-operate as need arises or as the task requires *(convenienter)*. Some of these members would be commissioned directly by the episcopal authority, especially the clerics involved, since this would be an official diocesan council commissioned mainly

---

[348] *Schema decreti* (1965), no. 58; cf. also *Textus recognitus et modi,* 123, *modus* 60.

[349] *Textus recognitus et modi,* 120f., *modi* 39–42, 46.

[350] *Schema constitutionis* (1962), Pars I, Cap. VIII: cf. also *Schema decreti* (1963), no. 15.

[351] *Ibid.* (1964), no. 17.   [352] *Ibid.* (1965), no. 54.

[353] *Textus recognitus et modi,* 123, *modus* 61.

[354] Already in *Schema decreti* (1965), no. 54.

for the "various apostolic works", to function according to the recommendations given in Article 23.

Such councils are naturally not to be identified with the desired pastoral commissions referred to in the Decree on the Bishops' Pastoral Office, which are to be recommended for assistance in the pastoral work of each diocese, for the study of conditions in the diocese, and to which clerics, religious and laity should be elected under the presidency of the bishop.[355] Both decrees are silent on the question of the eventual co-ordination of the functions and personnel of both councils; they leave such matters to the discretion of the bishops, or the bishops' conferences, respectively, as is expressly recommended in the motu proprio of Paul VI, *Ecclesiae Sanctae,* of 6 August 1966, I, n. 17 (*AAS* 58 [1966], p. 767).

The import of note 7 is not entirely clear; it refers to a passage in the works of Benedict XIV, the former Cardinal Prosper Lambertini, where he speaks of diocesan synods and the eventual participation of laymen in such synods.

Similar councils are recommended for inner-diocesan affairs, in the parish, the deanery, as well as for supradiocesan matters, such as those on a provincial, national, continental, and even world level, in so far as they do not already exist. Of course the text adds the phrase "where possible" in this connection. The *relatio* of 1964 stressed particularly that "according to local and diocesan needs several or only one commission may be established". The earlier editions spoke of one or more national commissions.[356] *Modi* wishing to limit the conditions even more were turned down.[357] Note 8 refers again to the letter of Pius XI to the episcopacy of Brazil in which parochial, diocesan, and national co-ordinating councils were mentioned, which were to "knit the various associations into a unity". The co-ordinating body at that time was certainly thought to be Catholic Action.

The last section recommends the establishment of a "special secretariat . . . at the Holy See". Its task would be primarily "the service and encouragement of the lay apostolate"; it would serve as a communication centre for all of the various apostolic programmes, a study centre where research could be made into modern problems arising in these fields, and it could assist the hierarchy and the laity with advice in their apostolic works. As is expressly stated here, the different movements and action groups of the apostolate of the laity should be represented in this secretariat, "and here clergy and religious also are to co-operate with the laity". This latter formulation was chosen as the result of a *modus.* In the text of 1964, both in this passage and the one referring to the diocesan council, clerics, religious, and laity were simply together.[358] The text does not go into

---

[355] *Decr. de pastorali episcoporum munere in Ecclesia,* n. 27.
[356] *Schema decreti* (1964), no. 55; cf. *Schema constitutionis* (1962), Pars I, n. 54; *Schema decreti* (1963), no. 15.
[357] *Textus recognitus et modi,* 124, *modi* 64 f.
[358] *Ibid.,* 125, *modus* 70; cf. *Schema decreti* (1964), no. 17 f.; (1965), no. 54 f.

any detail with regard to such representation. A system of delegation or rotation will have to be found, or some combination of both, since the simultaneous representation of all activities could hamper the effectiveness of the council, and since not only international but also national organizations must be represented together with the experts in various fields. This secretariat has already been set up in the meantime through the motu proprio *Catholicam Christi Ecclesiam* of Paul VI on 6 January 1967 (*AAS* 59 [1967], pp. 25–28).

This body was already mentioned in the first edition of the text, though in the following formulation: "The fathers recommend to the wise judgment of the Pope whether it be profitable to comply with the requests of several bishops who desire that a type of Roman Congregation *(aliqua Sacra Romana Congregatio)* be established for the counselling of the apostolate of the laity, especially for larger associations and other international Catholic groups." A note to this effect referred to the wishes of the fathers as expressed in pre-Conciliar suggestions.[359] The text of 1963 had already contained a much broader and more definite request for *quoddam particularis et sui iuris officium seu secretariatus* from the Holy See.[360] This formulation was preceded by a detailed discussion in the Commission, in the course of which Cardinal Civardi mentioned that Pius XI had planned a "Congregatio pro Actione Catholica", but that the plans were publicized prematurely and caused bishops and directors of associations to fear that their own freedom would be endangered. Mention was also made of a *speciale organum* or a *congregatio novi generis;* at any rate what was wanted was the most general formulation possible for a body with a capacity different from the advisory capacity exercised by the normal Roman Congregation.[361] The text of 1964 spoke only of a *quidam particularis secretariatus* at the Holy See. [362] From the *relatio* it was clear that the opinions of the fathers were for the most part at variance; while many feared a strengthening of centralism and so wanted at the most only national secretariats or at least a secretariat with precisely defined areas of competence, others desired a Roman Congregation in the proper sense. The general tendency was clearly towards the loosest form possible.[363] The discussion of October 1964 also moved in this direction, as the *relatio* to the text of 1965 noted: the secretariat was to have a pastoral character and should in no way be conceived of after the fashion of a Roman dicastery. Further details were requested, such as the determination of the competence of such a secretariat in a manner broad enough to include the recognition of the new international organizations, the determining of the type of co-operation to be practised, constant dialogue between the hierarchy and the laity, a preponderance of the lay element, and the possibility of allowing the laity to consult public opinion.[364]

---

[359] *Schema constitutionis* (1962), Pars I, n. 54.

[360] *Schema decreti* (1963), no. 15.

[361] *Acta commissionis conciliaris "de fidelium apostolatu"*, pp. 12f., 35.

[362] *Schema decreti* (1964), no. 18.

[363] *Ibid.,* no. 56ff.   [364] *Ibid.* (1965), no. 58f.

The *modi* show a fear of a new type of centralism and in part desired sharper and more explicit statements to the effect that the organ should not be an *organismus directionis,* but only *consilii;* similarly they wished to have the lay character more strongly emphasized.[365] Apart from minor modifications, the Commission thought that the basic demands were already sufficiently fulfilled in the text.

Article 27 deals with the co-operation of the laity with other Christians and with non-Christians as well. In the first two printed versions there was an article in the section "on the apostolate of the laity in social action" entitled "on the co-operation of Catholics with others" and "on the type of assistance to be given in work with non-Catholics".[366] In the 1963 text, in the section "on the lay apostolate in charitable works", there is an article entitled "co-operation with non-Catholics in charitable works".[367] From these texts and especially from Articles 82 and 74 of the printed version of 1963, Article 21 of the 1964 edition was formed. As is pointed out in the *relatio* to this text, the opinions of the fathers diverged very greatly: some thought the principle of co-operation as it was there presented to be extremely dangerous, while others considered the text to be merely permissive and not sufficiently positive. The text was finally improved on the lines of the latter.[368] The discussion of October 1964 also increased its positive tone. From this point onwards co-operation between Christians and with non-Catholics was treated in two separate sections. References were made to similar stimuli given in the draft of the Constitution on the Church in the Modern World as well as to the furtherance of dialogue with atheists. The remark that this co-operation was of special importance in temporal activities was a novelty; originally there was mention of this matter only in connection with the co-operation to be practised in social and charitable works.[369] Several modi which were fearful of the opinions expressed in the voting and which wanted to weaken the passage again, and even to delete the entire article, were rejected and even refuted by reference to the material already contained in the Decree on Ecumenism.[370]

The first section of the present text treats of the co-operation of Catholics with other Christians. The recommendation for, and indeed, as it is sometimes called, the necessity for such co-operation has its deepest root in the common evangelical heritage of the Church Fathers, from which derives our common duty to witness to the Christian way of life. This requirement concerns not only individual Catholics but also the various communities of the Church. The groups directly concerned are dioceses, parishes, religious communities, and communities similar to religious groups, ecclesiastical societies and institutes;

---

365 *Textus recognitus et modi,* 124 f., *modi* 68–77.
366 *Schema constitutionis* (1962), Pars IV, nn. 10 and 19; cf. also *Schema decreti* (1963), no. 82, 89.
367 *Schema decreti* (1963), no. 74.
368 *Ibid.* (1964), no. 18, 58.
369 *Ibid.* (1965), no. 55, 59.
370 *Textus recognitus et modi, modi* 79–82, 127.

in the broader sense it also includes every community which calls itself Catholic, or even the gathering of two or three in Christ's name (cf. Mt 18:20). All are summoned to ecumenical responsibilities; the ecumenical attitude is practically made the characteristic or measure of Christendom. Co-operation is to be practised at every level, national as well as international, and it can involve the actions of individuals and communities.

The note to this section refers us first to a passage in *Mater et Magistra* which speaks of the co-operation of Catholics "in their business relationships and in social work with men of other beliefs". The passage would be more apt in the next section. There is also a fitting reference to Article 12 of the Decree on Ecumenism according to which all Christians should acknowledge their faith in the one triune God and in the incarnate Son and should witness to this faith in common endeavour. Next mention is made of the co-operation of Christians in the social sphere: in the safeguarding of human dignity; in the furtherance of peace; the application of the gospel to social problems; the cultivation of scholarship and the arts in a Christian spirit; aid against hunger; catastrophes, illiteracy, poverty, homelessness and unjust distribution of prosperity. The article concludes: "by this dynamic and prudent co-operation, which is of special importance in temporal activities, the laity bear witness to Christ, the Saviour of the world, as well as to the unity of the human family".

This section is ecumenically of the greatest importance. The question arises, nevertheless, as to what manner of co-operation is meant here: only that in the temporal sphere or that which is involved in directly apostolic spheres as well? Certainly any sort of co-operation is ecumenically significant. One can scarcely learn more about others or understand them better than in common work and in the solution of common problems. The activity of love has always been the sign and the expression, that is, the testimony of the disciples of Jesus, which is finally to be the deciding factor between salvation and damnation (cf. Mt 25:34–45).[371] Nevertheless, one must reflect upon whether or not something more is meant here; whether it is sufficient to co-operate in social or charitable works, to pray in common for unity,[372] and to engage in theological dialogue on a "level of equality",[373] but then for the rest to allow everyone to make an individual profession of his faith in the triune God and his Son made flesh — separately from the others and in the end to have everyone give separate witness. We must inquire whether "common efforts for the witness of our hope" and "the common duty of the Christian witness" reaches further than this; whether or not we are obliged to do more by the *commune patrimonium evangelicum,* the common faith in the Father and his Son, our Lord, and in the common Spirit, by taking seriously the one baptism and the dominion of the one Spirit in us all, namely to adhere to a common profession and to a common witness. The

[371] Cf. Article 8.
[372] *Decr. de oecumenismo,* n. 8.
[373] *Ibid.,* n. 9.

Decree on the Missions speaks in fact of a "common profession of faith in God and in Jesus Christ before non-Christians, in so far as there is a common foundations for it". The true basis of this co-operation should be "Christ their common Lord"; his name should bring us together not only as private persons but also as Churches and ecclesiastical communities.[374] We must all seriously consider what the present situation demands of us.

The second section deals with the co-operation of Catholics and even of all Christians with non-Christians. That which binds everyone to "similar co-operation" is here said to be "the common human values". Partners in this co-operation are, on the one hand "Christians who pursue apostolic goals", and on the other hand non-Christians who acknowledge these common values. But in what does this co-operation consist? Since we are here considering co-operation with non-Christians, in contrast to the first section, it could hardly mean works of direct evangelization and sanctification, but rather works of the Christian penetration of the temporal order. The original text mentioned a participation of Catholics in "action or even organizations for the attainment of honourable temporal aims".[375] Even such temporal works can and should attain apostolic significance and even have an apostolic character for Christians, as we have already seen.[376] The Commission thus rejected a *modus* with an appeal to the concept of the apostolate in the second chapter, which wanted to have the passage about the pursuit of apostolic goals omitted.[377] Basing themselves upon this concept, the members of the Commission were also able to defend the similarity of co-operation *(similem quoque cooperationem)*.[378] In the same way a *modus* was rejected which wanted to have the entire section deleted, since it thought one could not recommend co-operation with unbelievers, e.g. atheistic materialists.[379] But even this is possible if the co-operation is concerned with things in the temporal order, and also if unbelievers recognize "the common human values". Those values are referred to which the Council repeatedly recommended to the Christians as well, e. g. proficiency in work, a good family and civic spirit; and those virtues which are concerned with social situations, e.g. honesty, justice, sincerity, kindness, courage; [380] certain "moral values and principles", as a *modus* expressed it;[381] and the recognition of the natural moral laws which are treated in the 1963 version.[382]

The concluding section summarizes the whole by saying that the laity are to bear witness to Christ through this co-operation and for the unity of the

---

[374] *Decr. de activitate missionali Ecclesiae,* n. 15.
[375] *Schema decreti* (1963), no. 82.
[376] Cf. under Articles 2 and 7.
[377] *Textus recognitus et modi,* 127, *modus* 88.
[378] *Ibid.,* 126, *modus* 87.
[379] *Ibid.,* 126, *modus* 85.
[380] Cf. Article 4.
[381] *Textus recogn. et modi,* 126, *modus* 84.
[382] *Schema decreti* (1963), no. 82.

human family as well. The first of these would be taken as referring more to co-operation with other Christians, which already has a direct character of Christian witness even when it occurs only in the sphere of social or charitable works; the second refers more to co-operation with non-Christians. One *modus* wished to have the remark omitted which stated that this co-operation is of special importance in temporal matters, as it thought that while such co-operation is more difficult in the spiritual areas, it is not of lesser importance there. The present text speaks thus only of a "great importance", without using the comparative.[383] We have also tried to point out particularly how co-operation between Christians should not limit itself to co-operation in temporal matters. The "great importance" of the co-operation of Catholics with all men of good will in the temporal sphere nevertheless remains, for the simple reason that it is the will of God "that all men should constitute one family and treat one another in the spirit of brotherhood",[384] that man "through his dealings with others, through reciprocal duties, and through brotherly dialogue, develops all his gifts and is thus able to rise to his destiny",[385] and that all men might help to form an awareness of "genuine universal solidarity and responsibility",[386] that we might work together "in order to build up the world in genuine peace",[387] because this co-operation, on the other hand, also gives Christians the possibility "to penetrate the world with the Christian spirit" and "to be witnesses to Christ in all things and in the midst of human society".[388] The note refers again to Article 12 of the Decree on Ecumenism and to Article 15 of the Constitution on the Church which speaks of the many bonds which unite us to those "who, being baptized, are honoured with the name of Christian".[389]

[383] *Textus recognitus et modi,* 127, *modus* 90.
[384] *Const. past. de Ecclesia in mundo huius temporis,* n. 24.
[385] *Ibid.,* n. 25.
[386] *Ibid.,* n. 90.
[387] *Ibid.,* n. 92.
[388] *Ibid.,* n. 43.
[389] *Const. dogm. de Ecclesia,* n. 15.

Formation for the Apostolate

The chapter "on the formation for the apostolate" was first to be found in the present form in the version of 1965.[390] But one should not forget that the very first printed text had a chapter in its main section "on education and preparation of the laity for the apostolate", and also that in the section "on the apostolate in charitable works" as well as in the section "on the apostolate in social works" there was a chapter on the formation for the apostolate, not to mention of course the references scattered throughout the text.[391] The 1963 version, in its first general part, summarized everything which was to be said upon "the formation of the laity for the apostolate", concentrating in 9 articles the fourth and last titles.[392] On the day that the 1963 version was accepted by the Co-ordinating Commission, i.e. at the beginning of April 1963, the same Commission gave to the Commission for the Apostolate of the Laity the task of preparing an *Instructio de formatione ad apostolatum* which was considered within the Commission itself to be a part of a directory then planned, and which was to be published as a *documentum Concilii,* if not *auctoritati Concilii* or published only after the Council itself. Actually in the course of 1963 the draft of such an instruction was prepared on the basis of the text already at hand, and was distributed on 3 December 1963. In the sketch for a *Directorium generale* dated 20 January 1964 two appendices were planned: the first "De formatione laicorum ad apostolatum", and the second "De munere sacerdotum in apostolatu laicorum". As it became clear in March 1964 that there would be no *Instructio de formatione,* a single article "de formatione apostolica" was prepared for the very abbreviated text of 1964 which was to be the third of the first chapter "on the apostolic vocation of the laity".[393] In the discussion of October 1964 not a few fathers desired a more detailed and

---

[390] *Schema decreti* (1965), no. 60–66.
[391] *Schema constitutionis* (1962), Pars I, Cap. X; Pars III, Cap. VII; Pars IV, Tit. I, Cap. IV; cf. also Pars II, n. 23.
[392] *Schema decreti* (1963), no. 27 ff.
[393] *Ibid.* (1964), no. 7 f.; pp. 33 ff.; cf. *Acta commissionis conciliaris "de fidelium apostolatu",* p. 40; pp. 74 ff.; 93, 96 f.; 141 f., 160, 182–87.

more substantial treatment of the formation for the apostolate, and even a separate chapter upon it.[394] Thus the present text was formed from parts of the previous text.

Article 28 treats first of all — at the express desire of the fathers[395] — of the absolute necessity of formation for the apostolate, without which its full effect would not be attainable. Such formation must be diversified and thorough. It must on the one hand not only keep pace with the continuous spiritual and doctrinal progress of laymen themselves, but must be adapted to circumstances, which vary according to the affairs, persons, and the duties involved in such apostolic activity. But in spite of this more dynamic side of such diversified and progressive training, there is another side dealing with unification and completeness. For it must not only do justice to the personalities of those to be formed but also to the fundamentals which are common to all Christian teaching. As far as the fundamentals of this formation are concerned, the decree refers in a note to other conciliar documents, especially to the Constitution on the Church in the chapters on the people of God, on the laity, and on the general vocation to sanctity in the Church. It refers as well, on the basis of a reservation,[396] to Articles 4, 6, 7, and 12 of the Decree on Ecumenism which deal with ecumenism as such, the renewal of the Church, inner conversion, and co-operation with the separated brethren; it refers also to Article 4 of the Decree on the Apostolate of the Laity and even to the spirituality of the laity.[397] Finally, the formation which is common to all Christians is distinguished from the special formation which is to be given for special forms of the apostolate. Thus, this article, besides stressing the necessity of an apostolic formation, gives us a certain insight into the special nature of such a formation, which is treated in part in the following article.

Article 29 gives several "principles in the formation of the laity for the apostolate". The ideas behind this section stem in the main from the discussion of October 1964. First, a general principle is put forward: the apostolic formation of the laity treated of in the document, i. e. Christians in the world, receives its special character from the worldly character of the vocation of these laymen and their spirituality.[398] This is understandably based upon the fact that the laity share in the mission of the Church, though in their own manner.

Formation for the apostolate should be based as well upon a certain type of formation of the whole human person, which again cannot be the same for all but which must be adapted to suit the gifts and the circumstances of each and must accord with his inner and outer needs. One should include here under gifts the natural and supernatural virtues, talents, and special charisms, and possibly those which relate to the family, the profession, and the general life-environ-

---

[394] *Schema decreti* (1965), no. 67.
[395] *Ibid.,* no. 67.
[396] *Textus recognitus et modi,* 135, *modus* 3.
[397] Cf. *Schema decreti* (1965), no. 67.
[398] Cf. under Articles 2 and 4.

ment in a given city or country, as well as to the social class and the general cultural level of a land or a continent. All these things are not simply to be juxtaposed or regarded merely as an outward veneer: they must also be an integrated possession from within. In support of this it is said that the lay apostle must be well-informed about the world around him and the general situation of the present time which he can only achieve if he is an "active member of his own society" and allows its culture, its knowledge, technology, and art to influence him.

The foundation of this universally human formation of the person must be a spiritual formation which is to be the fundament of all forms of the apostolate. The apostolate is essentially, as we have seen, the fulfilling of the mission of Christ and of the Church. One only learns how to fulfil this mission and the apostolate best by penetrating into the mystery of Christ and of his Church, or rather allowing oneself to be penetrated by them. This happens in faith when one lives in the divine mystery of creation and redemption, allowing oneself to be moved by the Spirit of the Father and the Son from which the whole Church lives and which is the principle of all love upon earth: the love of the Father, of the world, and of men. Accordingly spiritual formation is formation in faith, formation according to which one is able to see God, men, the world, sin, and salvation with the eyes of Christ. It means formation in hope together with the Church, who is the bridge awaiting her Lord and the new earth; it means formation in love, in the loving embrace of God who is given to men and to the world "through the Holy Spirit who is given to us" (Rom 5:5). Without this spiritual formation there can be no apostolate. Yet we should not forget that even this spiritual formation cannot remain isolated from human or natural formation; it must be integrated into a unified and comprehensive whole, as was already mentioned in Article 28.

Thorough theoretical instruction must be added to this, graded according to the age, the capacity and the position of the one concerned both in the world and in the Church. Greater apostolic responsibility requires more intensive apostolic formation, also in the theoretical aspects. All of this indicates the dynamic character of the formative process which has an even greater importance in an educative society such as that in which we live. The particular topics of study which are mentioned are theology, ethics, and philosophy. There are certainly forms of the apostolate which require a full academic training in theology and philosophy from laymen as well, as required for teaching-posts in secondary schools and universities. But even apart from that, the normal service in the world requires from laymen holding positions of responsibility in the apostolate an above-average knowledge of theology, ethics, and philosophy, for pastors are not always well versed enough to be able to give a concrete solution to all the questions, often very difficult ones, which arise, nor are they always competent to do so, as the text says elsewhere. In such cases it is for the laity to take on their proper roles "enlightened by Christian wisdom and giving close attention to the teaching authority of the Church".[399] The light of revelation must be joined to the knowledge of concrete skills in order to effect the Christian ordering of temporal things which is the task of laymen in the world. Thus we can understand why Vatican II calls it "very desirable" that "many laymen will receive an appropriate formation in the sacred sciences and that some will develop and deepen these studies by their own labours".[400] That ethical and philosophical problems have no small role to play in this is obvious, if one thinks only of the social problems involved. In an earlier version there was express mention of the social teaching of the Church[401] and even in the penultimate version of an *institutio ethica-socialis*.[402] Article 31 returns to this theme in connection with the Christian ordering of the temporal sphere.

Even these more intellectual and theoretical instructions must be part of a general formation, as is added immediately, as part of a universal human culture which is to include practical as well as technical training. The passage on general formation was first inserted into the text as the result of a *modus*.[403] Moreover, the Pastoral Constitution on the Church in the Modern World devotes one article to this education *de educatione ad hominis integrum cultum*.[404] This integration involves all the cultural values of the whole human person, an *integra formatio* such as was recommended at the beginning of this chapter. By practical formation one must consider, using the text of 1964 as a basis for interpretation,[405] formation by exercise and practice; and by technical formation the learning of suitable methods which change and improve according to circumstance, whether it be in the organization of dialogue with others or leading a discussion or an assembly.

The next section again returns to the fostering of natural human values which must precede the apostolate, though it is connected with the general formation. The apostolate is chiefly a matter of love, humanity, and contact with others; but there is need as well for a life in brotherhood, teamwork, conversation with others — all those things which are called "art" in the text and which must be learned as such. The previous text also referred to the art of listening, of following others, and also, on occasion, of obeying others.[406]

Lastly, the text speaks of the continual progress to be made in apostolic formation, how it begins in the smallest things and gradually grows. This refers not only to theoretical formation but even more to the spiritual formation, which is here described as learning how to "view, judge, and do all things in the light of faith" — a clear reflection of the well-known principle of Cardijn. It also refers

---

[399] *Const. past. de Ecclesia in mundo huius temporis,* n. 43.

[400] *Ibid.,* n. 62.

[401] *Schema constitutionis* (1962), Pars I, n. 69.

[402] *Schema decreti* (1965), no. 61.

[403] *Textus recognitus et modi,* 136, *modus 6.*

[404] *Const. past. de Ecclesia in mundo huius temporis,* n. 61.

[405] *Schema decreti* (1964), p. 7.

[406] *Schema decreti* (1965), no. 61.

to the practical formation by which one develops oneself further in joint action with others. The note refers to the passage in the social encyclical of John XXIII, which also mentions the three stages of seeing, judging, and acting and then stresses the fact that "youth should not only learn these steps theoretically, but also, where possible, in a practical way". Similarly the address of Pius XII to the First International Boy Scouts' Congress is quoted: "If you form yourselves personally and in community you will find yourselves already in the service of the Church and you will work at the tools of your future apostolate. The broader and deeper the foundations laid, the more solid and imposing will be the structure of your Christian lives . . . but this formation must be open from the very earliest years to suitable concrete methods of observation and consideration of the social, natural, and supernatural realities." Men who are daily growing in maturity and also meeting ever more complex problems need a formation which day by day deepens their theoretical and practical knowledge.

In conclusion, there is a recommendation of the unity and the integrity, the harmony and the balance necessary for the full development of the human person. It is striking how strongly the bond and the unity between the natural human formation and the supernatural formation of the whole human person is stressed in this article.

The last section indicates the importance of this formation in the apostolate for the worldly activity of the Christian, i. e. the Christian penetration of the world, not as though this formation was of less importance for evangelization and sanctification but only because it is of greater importance in the worldly sphere. And so, on the basis of such an apostolic formation, the laity can fulfil their function in the world, presupposing that they have necessary knowledge of their worldly tasks, and at the same time make the Church present and operative in the world, as Article 33 of the Constitution on the Church says.

Article 30 treats of those who have the obligation to provide for apostolic formation. And they are precisely those who have the obligation to provide ordinary Christian education, since Christian education is essentially education for the apostolate, just as being a Christian means being an apostle. As soon as the child is capable of genuine formation, its apostolic formation begins. This is especially important with adolescents and young adults and when they assume responsibilities, then the formation must progress in order to keep up with the demands of these new circumstances.

The first educators in the apostolate are thus the parents. Under their leadership and especially through their example the whole family and all those connected with it should "become a sort of apprenticeship for the apostolate". What is important here is not so much verbal instruction as learning by doing and living. One has to learn how to live for others, how to assist others in material and spiritual need, both the younger members of the family as well as the older and perhaps infirm members of the household. The driving-force behind this must be the love of God, a love which must go beyond the small circle of the family and relations to embrace all men. The narrow limits of the family are transcended in order to care for the needs of society and the whole Christian community. This was perhaps easier to accomplish in the large families of past times, as the children lived together with aging relatives and grandparents, but this means that an even greater responsibility devolves upon the parents of today.

The children then grow naturally out of this elementary school for the apostolate into the different ecclesiastical and worldly communities which must be experienced as necessary complements to the family and not merely as responsibilities to be borne concurrently with it. The children must gradually learn to accept responsibilities in these other communities. The decree states that children should be active in the parish and should not feel themselves to be merely passive members, looked after by others. For this participation there should not only be childrens' groups and communities but also pastoral care for children and even liturgical services especially for them. Thus priests already have a place in such apostolic formation. In the discussion of October 1964 it was expressly recommended that the laity (parents) and the hierarchy should co-operate in the apostolic education of children.[407] Only in this way can a narrow-minded "family egoism" be avoided.

The decree considers it to be natural that Catholic schools as well as other Catholic institutes for formation and education should be schools for the apostolate, in which one can learn to think and to act in a "catholic" and apostolic way. If the results of schooling contradict this, then the reasons must be found and measures must be taken to correct the situation, for otherwise the very purpose of such institutions is dubious.[408] Where such formation or facilities are lacking, a greater responsibility devolves upon the parents, the pastor, and the various apostolic associations. As the result of a *modus* proposed by 34 fathers, the greater stress put upon the Catholic school as a precondition for the apostolate in the previous text was significantly toned down.[409] Besides parents, pastors, and associations, teachers and educators also need to be equipped for such apostolic training according to their vocation and office, whether they have positions in Catholic schools or elsewhere. Their vocation is already an exceptional form of the lay apostolate. But this vocation can only be carried out in a truly Christian spirit when it is at the same time concerned with formation and education for the apostolate. In order to carry out the spiritual, theoretical, technical and practical education which is necessary, such teachers need a corresponding training in spiritual and ascetical matters, in philosophy and in pedagogical methods.[410]

Finally, apostolic formation is the obligation of all lay-groups and associations, even if they do not pursue apostolic goals in themselves but only other super-

[407] *Ibid.,* no. 68.
[408] Cf. *Textus recognitus et modi,* 138, *modi* 21 f.
[409] *Ibid.,* 138, *modi* 19 f.
[410] *Ibid.,* 138, *modi* 21 f.

natural goals, e. g. personal sanctification. One *modus* wanted to have the Third Order mentioned here.[411] Such apostolic formation must naturally be orientated to the goals of the groups concerned: if they have only personal sanctification as their aim, then they must at least communicate the spiritual foundations of the apostolate, since there can be no personal sanctification without the apostolate; if they have directly apostolic aims, then they must undergo a comprehensive, theoretical, spiritual and practical apostolic formation. Another quotation from *Mater et Magistra* stresses the important role of the lay apostolate movement in the work of formation: "This is the special task of those whose goal it is to fulfil all the duties of the present in the Christian spirit. Here many members can in fact educate themselves in daily action and then be in a better position to lead the young in the performance of such duties."

Associations of this sort are for many the normal way to a broader apostolic formation; they must often take on the tasks of the school and other educative bodies, even of the family, or at least complement these. The decree refers to yet another important way of forming people in apostolic works: by formation given in small groups for controlling and examining methods and one's daily life by measuring them against the success achieved and the example set by the gospel. In the discussion of October 1964 reference was made to the importance of associations for the understanding of the law of solidarity.[412] References to individual associations were omitted in this connection, and for this reason a *modus* which wanted to have secular institutes named was rejected.[413]

The concluding section makes the important general observation that such apostolic formation must be "designed to take into account the whole lay apostolate". Especially when this formation is carried on by associations, there is a danger that the apostolate will only be considered according to the particular aims of those associations. But the real task of such formation is to educate the members of these groups to a complete apostolic life as it is realized in the family, in one's profession, and in society as a whole. Likewise, the work of such groups does not absolve the individual, especially the adult, from his personal responsibilities, from forming himself for the apostolate, from developing his talents and employing his charisms, which are given that he might help others: "for the equipment of the saints, for the work of ministry, for building up the body of Christ" (Eph 4:12).

Article 31 was introduced into the text as a new article in the edition of 1965.[414] It offers several suggestions for the formation needed by special forms of the apostolate. The article is divided according to the three main groupings given in the second chapter. The text was abbreviated and revised in tone as a result of the *modi* put forward by 60 of the fathers, who wanted to have all traces of triumphalism, paternalism and pharisaism removed.[415]

---

[411] *Ibid.*, 138, *modus* 24.   [412] *Schema decreti* (1965), no. 68.
[413] *Textus recogn. et modi*, 138, *modus* 25.   [414] *Schema decreti* (1965), no. 63.
[415] *Textus recognitus et modi*, 131, *modus* 29.

A special type of formation is proposed for the apostolate of evangelization and sanctification in which the laity are to engage in conversation with others, whether they be believers or non-believers, "in order to manifest Christ's message to all men". The note refers to an encyclical of Pius XII to the hierarchy of the United States of America of 1 November 1939, in which the Pope recommended to the laity a thorough knowledge of religion "to be gained through libraries, discussions, and study-centres", especially "for those who share in the hierarchical apostolate", in order that they might "instruct the ignorant, overcome adversaries, and give profit to those who are of good will". It also refers to an address of Pius XII to graduates of Italian Catholic Action at Whitsuntide in 1953, in which he develops much the same thought: "There is a true need for educated Catholic leaders today to get well-acquainted with this world of lasting and eternal truths and to make it their own ever more deeply, as well as all the riches of our faith. The religious instruction which they have received in their youth, be it ever so thorough, is not sufficient either for their maturity or for the new questions which have arisen since then and which assume primary importance. Therefore, strive for a deep penetration into the foundations of the faith, its structure and the individual truths which form it." Both passages are concerned with that deeper knowledge of the faith which is of special importance for any form of the apostolate since their real task is to make known the message of Christ.

The various types of modern materialism call for a special sort of evangelization. For this work laymen are not only to engage in theoretical discussions, for which they need a good knowledge of the Catholic truths in dispute, but they are to witness to such truths even more by an evangelical life. The passage, which is somewhat surprising in this place, is what has remained of the former chapter "On the apostolate of the laity in areas influenced by materialism, and particularly by Marxism".[416] This chapter once had a long preamble with a detailed note and 8 articles. It was hotly debated in the preparatory period of the Council, and the fathers then wanted to treat not only of Marxist or Communistic Eastern European materialism but also of the practical Western form of materialism. The phrase *praesertim marxistico* was still to be found in the first printed version of 1962. In the edition of 1963 the chapter was already reduced to one single article, which then only mentioned materialism *sive practicus sive theoreticus*.[417] The tone was also substantially moderated. In the abbreviated version of 1964 the article did not even appear; in the text of 1965 it occupied the same place as in the present text. Due to various *modi* the text was again abbreviated and reduced to merely mentioning those tasks which are to be carried out by Catholics in this respect. It should be recalled that atheism is only treated in the Pastoral Constitution on the Church in the Modern World, and there no longer in a polemical or apologetic manner.[418]

---

[416] *Schema constitutionis,* Pars II, Tit. II, Cap. VII.

[417] *Schema decreti* (1963), no. 35.

[418] *Const. past. de Ecclesia in mundo huius temporis,* nn. 20 f.

With regard to the Christian ordering of the temporal sphere, laymen are to be instructed in the true meaning and value of temporal things, both in themselves and in their relation to the total fulfilment of the human person; they are to be taught to use things with consideration for the common welfare and to organize suitable groups. The fathers also wished that reference be made to Christian moral and social teachings and their application.[419] The laity are not only to contribute their share in the application of such teaching to concrete cases, but also to further the development of such teaching itself. The latter was included in the text as a result of the recommendations of various *modi*. All this helped to diminish the paternalistic tone which was once so painfully evident, especially in this section. The only trace of this still to be found is in the first sentence: *laici edoceantur* — as though the laity here could only be at the receiving end of instruction which others, presumably the clergy (non-laity), are to give. In fact, the laity themselves can engage in this instruction just as well. The notes refer to two addresses of Pius XII, one to the participants of the Universal Congress of the World Federation of Young Catholic Women dealing with so-called situation-ethics and the problem of the formation of conscience, and the other to members of the Christian Association of Italian Workers on the significance of the work of religious and moral instruction in Christian worker-organizations, especially with regard to "the rights and duties of the worker in the light of the divine order of the world". The Pope makes special mention of the priests and laity who are to act as teachers in this work.

In connection with works of love and mercy, apostolic formation should be concerned to instil the virtues of compassion and generosity in their charges from childhood onwards. One *modus* recommended the *quoque* here to avoid the impression that this type of formation is needed only in connection with works of charity.[420] The note refers to an address of Pius XII to the delegates of the Assembly of Charity Associations, which treats of the apostolate of love.

Apart from a short passage on certain centres of formation, **Article 32** was also to be found for the first time in the edition of 1965. It deals with the various aids to be used in the work of formation. The express desires of the fathers were important in determining the form of this section as well.[421]

Various traditional types of aid in spiritual, theoretical, and methodical formation are mentioned first. In agreement with the Dogmatic Constitution on Revelation, aids which promote a deeper understanding of Scripture are also named.[422] There is also a striking emphasis on the means of acquiring a better understanding of the current social situation, without which there can be no effective type of apostolate. What is important here is a knowledge of the particular needs and advantages of the times, to be gained from familiarity with the

---

[419] *Schema decreti* (1965), no. 68.

[420] *Textus recognitus et modi,* 139, *modus* 31.

[421] *Schema decreti* (1965), no. 64, 68.

[422] *Cf. Const. dogm. de divina revelatione,* nn. 22 f.

results of modern cosmology, anthropology, psychology, sociology, history, philosophy, art, and literature. The note refers to the social encyclical of John XXIII, which urges the spread of Catholic social teaching "in Catholic schools at every level" and its "incorporation into the formative work of parishes and apostolic lay movements". The encyclical mentions "newspapers and periodicals, scholarly publications and popular journals, radio and television" as possible instruments for achieving this.

All of these aids should certainly be adapted to the form of the apostolate concerned, i.e. they should be orientated to the milieus, age, sex, standard of education, and profession of those concerned. The text mentions the success which centres of study and advanced institutes have had and they are recommended for those localities where they do not yet exist. Likewise, the text urges the establishment of "centres of documentation and study" for every field of the apostolate. *Studia* means doctrine and research. Besides theological study, mention is also made of those other sciences which are especially concerned with the analysis of situations, e.g. methodology. In this way, it is stated, the natural capacities of the laity can be better developed for the apostolate. The Church cannot afford to ignore those rare above-average talents which do exist. In such centres not only can many laymen who serve the Church only temporarily or for longer periods of time receive formation and engage in detailed research, but also those who are experts in various relevant fields of secular studies can be associated with these centres. Perhaps this form of the apostolate, so well suited to our times, can more effectively achieve the task which it was once thought could be carried out by Catholic universities. It is obvious that such well-equipped centres are only feasible for large areas, for if they are not of the highest quality, they would have no justification.

Modi which wanted to have the phrase *sub episcopi auctoritate* or *per Pastorem* added in this article, as well as in the following one, were rejected with a reference to Chapter 5.[423]

Article 33 concludes the text with an earnest entreaty from the Council to all of the laity that they should follow the call of the apostolate. The special appeal which is made to the younger generation corresponds to a *votum* from the discussion of October 1964.[424] Mention is again made of the foundation of every apostolate,[425] of the inner bond they all have with Christ and his mission, and of the total submersion into the attitude of Christ which is required: his readiness to serve even to the last form of abnegation, the taking on of the form of another (a reference to Phil 2:5). Just as the Lord once sent not only the Twelve (Lk 9:1–6) but also the seventy-two to be his heralds in every place to which he himself wanted to go (Lk 10:1) — "the missionary sermon was here as little a prerogative of the Twelve as later after Easter"[426] — so today he sends

---

[423] *Textus recognitus et modi,* 140, *modi* 30 and 40.
[424] *Schema decreti* (1965), no. 68.
[425] Cf. Articles 3 f.   [426] J. Schmid, *Das Evangelium nach Lukas* (1960), p. 184.

laymen to be his helpers in the one apostolate which is to be carried out in such diverse ways according to the ever new "time of his coming". Thus will they spend themselves completely, as Paul did for the whole community at Corinth, in the work of the Lord, namely in their apostolic tasks. Even when they do not see the fruit of their labours they should realize that their labours have not been fruitless in the Lord, in the risen Lord through whom God gives victory to us as well, for "death is swallowed up in victory; O death, where is thy victory? O death, where is thy sting?" (1 Cor 15:55–58.)

SUBJECT INDEX

Prepared by Lalit Adolphus

INDEX OF NAMES

411

303